Major Problems in
American Environmental History

MAJOR PROBLEMS IN AMERICAN HISTORY SERIES

GENERAL EDITOR

THOMAS G. PATERSON

Major Problems in
American Environmental History

DOCUMENTS AND ESSAYS

EDITED BY
CAROLYN MERCHANT
UNIVERSITY OF CALIFORNIA, BERKELEY

D.C. HEATH AND COMPANY
Lexington, Massachusetts   Toronto

Address editorial correspondence to:

D. C. Heath
125 Spring Street
Lexington, MA 02173

Acquisitions Editor: James Miller
Developmental Editor: Sylvia Mallory
Production Editor: Carolyn Ingalls
Designer: Jan Shapiro
Photo Researcher: Sharon Donahue
Photography Coordinator: Martha Shethar
Production Coordinator: Michael O'Dea
Permissions Editor: Margaret Roll

Cover: "The Big Wetland I" by Gabor Peterdi. The
       Metropolitan Museum of Art, Gift of Mr. and
       Mrs. Warren Brandt, 1983. (1983.39)

Published simultaneously in Canada.

Printed in the United States of America.

International Standard Book Number: 0-669-24993-9

Library of Congress Catalog Number: 92-81866

10   9   8   7   6   5   4   3   2   1

To my students

Preface

Recalling the spring of 1970, historian Roderick Nash of the University of California at Santa Barbara wrote, "It was very satisfying to list a new course entitled 'American Environmental History' with the registrar of my university. . . . I was responding to cries for environmental responsibility which reached a crescendo in the first months of that year. . . . But on the way back to my office, misgivings began. They grew into anxieties . . . as 450 students enrolled in the inchoate course. What was I going to do with them?"*

That same spring, tens of thousands of people, responding to environmental and social problems made visible by the protest movements and political activism of the 1960s, participated in the first Earth Day. Earlier in the decade, Rachel Carson's *Silent Spring* (1962) had challenged Americans to confront the "deadly elixirs" of pesticides and nuclear radiation that threatened wildlife and human life alike. Paul Ehrlich's *The Population Bomb* (1968) had alerted many to the potential effects of exponentially growing populations on scarce resources, and Garrett Hardin's essay "Tragedy of the Commons" (1968) had sounded an alarm about the depletion and pollution of the world's oceans, air, and soils. Whether the consequence of the Judeo-Christian mandate to subdue and replenish the earth, or of the damaging effects of world capitalism and state socialism on diminishing resources, or of governments' failure to regulate polluting industries and avaricious consumers, an urgent new awareness of the environmental crisis galvanized people to action. The United States Congress passed a series of environmental laws. Environmental organizations and action groups sprang up around the nation and the world. And as never before, scholars began researching environmental issues and writing works that analyzed the causes and consequences of environmental problems.

During the 1970s, out of this widespread interest in the fate of the earth, environmental history emerged as a new field of scholarship. Courses at colleges and universities soon built upon Nash's own highly influential *Wilderness and the American Mind* (first published in 1967), as well as on various histories of conservation and of the American West, the works of nature writers such as Henry David Thoreau and Aldo Leopold, and Native American stories and traditions. Across the country, students were suddenly seeking courses probing humans' relationships with nature, the different ways in which women and men have interacted with nature, the evolution of conservation policies, and the history of resource depletion. Environmental pollution, environmental engineering, and energy conservation also arose as new fields of inquiry.

---

*Roderick Nash, "American Environmental History: A New Teaching Frontier," *Pacific Historical Review* 363 (1974), 362–372.

Then in 1976, following spirited discussions on the need for new vehicles for communicating these ideas, historian John Opie, currently of the New Jersey Institute of Technology, founded the American Society for Environmental History and the journal *Environmental Review* (now *Environmental History Review*). Since then, environmental history has matured as a field and has established links with national and regional history societies, environmental and professional organizations, and related fields such as ecology, the history of science, forest history, agricultural history, legal history, and Native American history. Papers on environmental history have regularly appeared on the programs and in the journals of major historical associations; "A Round Table: Environmental History" was the centerpiece of the March 1990 issue of *The Journal of American History*. A new generation of books and articles is appearing as more students and teachers identify themselves as environmental historians, not only in the United States but elsewhere in the world. The field is lively and expansive, presenting new frameworks for interpretation and new ideas for debate.

Why do people study environmental history? Today, interest in the earth — its past, present, and future — commands worldwide attention. The unprecedented Earth Summit (1992) in Rio de Janeiro brought together government leaders and environmental organizations from around the globe to address the issue of environmentally responsible development. As concern mounts over the quality of environments and human life in the future, the study of past environments — how they were used and how they changed — provides guidance for the formation of governmental policy. Leaders can learn from environmental history. For example, pioneers' settlement of and subsequent hardships in the arid American West, where droughts were all too frequent, prompted governmental funding of reclamation and dam projects, a theme explored in chapters 9 and 10 of this volume. Moreover, environmental history instills an appreciation of the complexity of human interactions with nature and in this way contributes to a fuller understanding of history. Thus knowledge of Pueblo Indian environments and spiritual traditions in what became the southwestern United States, and of the difficulties encountered by Spanish troops and missionaries in introducing European cattle, crops and religion to America, casts new light on the conflicts that arose between these two cultures, as Chapter 2 examines. Further, environmental history illuminates the ways in which natural resources fulfill people's day-to-day needs for food, clothing, shelter, and energy, and shows how quickly precious resources can be depleted when treated as commodities. Farming, for example, has different effects on local ecology, depending on whether land is used to raise subsistence crops or to grow produce for the market, as Chapter 5 reveals.

And there are still other reasons to study environmental history. Historical writings about nature offer aesthetic or spiritual perceptions of humans' place in the natural world that continue to inspire respect and reverence for nature and to foster positive change. Poets who wrote about the natural world; the Hudson River school of painters; New England transcendentalists, among them Ralph Waldo Emerson and Henry David Thoreau; and nature writers John Muir and Mary Austin initiated an appreciation of wilderness that influenced the creation of the national parks, a subject treated in chapters 6 and 11. Finally, environmental history reveals class, race, and gender differences among people as they settle in new areas and play a part in those environments' use and abuse. White, black, Chinese, and Mexican miners contributed in different ways to the extraction of gold and to the environmental deterioration of California (see Chapter 8); women and men perceived the Great Plains grasslands differently and contributed different technologies to the region's settlement and exploitation (see Chapter 9). Such histories and case studies offer invaluable perspectives to a world whose very survival depends on shifting from exploitative to environmentally responsible development, and from inequality to social justice.

Major Problems in American Environmental History is the result of more than a decade of teaching environmental history. This volume, like its companions in the *Major Problems* series, draws on both documents and essays. It is intended as a primary text in a one- or two-term environmental history or environmental studies course, but it also may be assigned to provide an environmental dimension to introductory classes in United States history. Chapter introductions discuss the place, period, and particular focus of each case history. The documents for each chapter provide a variety of perspectives written or spoken by those who lived in and helped to create the history of a specific environment. These primary sources stimulate students to form their own opinions on environmental history and, through discussion with others, to develop confidence in their own interpretations. The essays offer a range of views, demonstrating that scholars often draw conflicting conclusions from the same primary sources. This format encourages students to evaluate each interpretation, as well as to gain an understanding of the ways in which different underlying assumptions and positions influence the writing of history.

No single anthology or text can do justice to all places, periods, and peoples. Some works on environmental history offer a regional, period, or ethnic focus, and some a policy or legal focus, whereas others center on human responses to nature or incorporate international perspectives. The materials in this volume trace the transformation of the North American environment from colonial times to the present. *Major Problems in American Environmental History* focuses on diverse natural resources — such as furs, timber, soils, grasses, water, and minerals — that drew people of different genders, races, and national origins to different environments. The documents and essays explore the ways in which these environments were perceived, used, managed, and conserved, and they look at both the history of ecological deterioration and the history of conservation and preservation. Throughout, I have made a special effort to include the voices of women and minorities. And readers may be surprised to discover that several chapters even offer points of view other than those of human beings — those of a beaver, a female fox, a boll weevil, a buffalo, and a white-pine forest, for example. These challenge us to think in nonhomocentric, more truly ecological ways.

In approaching environmental history, it may be helpful for students first to construct their own personal environmental histories. Some students are descended from people long native to the Americas, but most are the descendants of more recent newcomers, either free or enslaved. These past generations have used and shaped their environments, often with very different goals and values from generations living today. In inquiring about the environments in which they, their parents, and their grandparents grew up, students might ask what natural resources sustained their families' livelihoods and how their families participated in environmental change. To what extent were their environments "natural" as distinct from human-made; to what degree were they native as distinct from exotic (that is, transformed by nonnative species)? Students might also explore the roles that race, ethnicity, class, and gender have played in the way their ancestors have interacted with their environments. And they might ponder how their forebears' personal values with regard to the world around them differed from their own values. Finally, readers might reflect on what kind of environment they want for the future. Then, after reading and discussing the documents and essays in this book, students might consider how these investigations, and the new insights gained from them, might have altered their original interpretations of their families' past. Instructors and students also might decide to collaborate on a supplementary chapter of documents and essays highlighting their own particular region or unique experiences.

In compiling this volume, I am grateful for contributions, suggestions, and evaluations from my students and teaching assistants over the past several years, in particular Michael Allen, Yaakov Garb, Debora Hammond, Michael Heiman, Barbara Leibhardt, Sandra Marburg, Marian Stevens, Thomas Wellock, Robert Weyeneth, and Tamara Whited. Colleagues who shared their ideas and syllabi helped broaden the scope of the book, as did reviewers who provided formal written comments on the table of contents: William Cronon, University of Wisconsin, Madison; Matthew Dennis, University of Oregon; Wesley A. Dick, Albion College; Gordon B. Dodds, Portland State University; Arthur F. McEvoy, Northwestern University; Martin V. Melosi, University of Houston; Donald J. Pisani, University of Oklahoma; William F. Steirer, Clemson University; Richard White, University of Washington; and Donald Worster, University of Kansas. Thomas Paterson, general editor of the *Major Problems in American History* series, and Sylvia Mallory, senior developmental editor at D. C. Heath, encouraged me to focus the chapters, sharpen the questions, and consider additional viewpoints. I am much obliged to Margaret Roll, who spent many hours requesting permissions, and to Carolyn Ingalls for overseeing countless details of copyediting and production. Finally, I am deeply indebted to Charles Sellers, who over the years has profoundly influenced my interpretation of American history and helped me to conceptualize my course in environmental history.

I welcome readers' feedback on and suggestions for improving this anthology. I also would be interested in receiving copies of supplementary chapters that students create or other projects that grow out of the study of this volume.

C.M.

Contents

C H A P T E R   4
Soil Exhaustion in the Early Tobacco South
Page 94

C H A P T E R   5
Farm Ecology in the Early Republic
Page 133

CHAPTER 6
Nature Versus Civilization in the Nineteenth Century
Page 170

CHAPTER 7
The Cotton South Before and After the Civil War
Page 209

C H A P T E R   8
Mining California's Earth in the Nineteenth Century
Page 247

C H A P T E R   9
Great Plains Grasslands Exploited
Page 286

C H A P T E R 10
Resource Conservation in an Industrializing Society
Page 338

C H A P T E R 11
Wilderness Preservation at the Turn of the Century
Page 383

C H A P T E R 12
Urban Pollution and Reform in the Twentieth Century
Page 414

C H A P T E R 13
The Emergence of Ecology in the Twentieth Century
Page 444

C H A P T E R 14

From Conservation to Environment in the Mid-Twentieth Century

Page 484

C H A P T E R 15

The Contemporary Environmental Movement

Page 523

A P P E N D I X
Page i

D O C U M E N T   S O U R C E S
Page xiii

CHAPTER
1

What Is Environmental
History?

ψ

*Environmental history offers an earth's-eye view of the past. It addresses the
many ways in which humans have interacted with the natural environment over
time. As one of the newest perspectives within the discipline of history, it is a
field still in the process of self-definition. It affords the exciting challenge of
engaging in a dialogue with the documents of the past to create new
interpretations of history.*

For environmental historians, the term environment *relates to the natural
and human-created surroundings that affect a living organism or a group of
organisms' ability to maintain themselves and develop over time. The word*
ecology *refers to the* relationships *between these organisms and their
surroundings. In the case of humans, ecology also includes social and cultural
patterns. Ecological history is therefore somewhat broader than environmental
history, but the two terms often are used interchangeably.*

*Environmental history's pictures of the past derive from a colorful palette of
sources. From the natural history side come data on climatic fluctuations,
geological changes, plant and animal ecology, and microbial life. From the
human past, environmental history draws on artifacts such as tools for extracting
resources; account books of traders; journals of explorers; court records of births
and deaths; laws; diaries of farmers; interviews with slaves; Indian myths and
legends; paintings, poetry, and essays about nature; scientific investigations; and
the musings of philosophers.*

*Environmental historians ask a number of questions of these sources. How
and why did people living in a particular place at a particular time use and
transform their environment? How did people of different cultural backgrounds
and of both genders perceive, manage, exploit, and conserve their environments?
What differing economic forms, or modes of production (such as gathering,
hunting, fishing, farming, ranching, mining, and forestry), evolved in particular
habitats? What problems of pollution and depletion arose under industrialization
and urbanization? What political and legal conflicts, struggles, and compromises
emerged over resource use and conservation? How did people's attitudes toward
nature and their mental constructions of nature change over time? And how do*

1

changing concepts of ecology influence the interpretations of environmental historians? In attempting to answer these kinds of questions, environmental historians have developed a variety of conceptual approaches, four of which are considered in this chapter.

❧ E S S A Y S

The essays that follow offer contrasting frameworks for interpreting environmental history. In the first selection, Donald Worster, Hall Distinguished Professor of American history at the University of Kansas, discusses three of the environmental historian's most important sources—ecology, modes of production, and ideas—and then analyzes subsistence and capitalist agriculture as examples of modes of production. The second essay, a critique of Worster's discussion of modes of production, is by William Cronon, professor of history at the University of Wisconsin, Madison. Cronon emphasizes the need for social environmental histories that take into account race, class, gender, and the modes by which societies reproduce themselves over time. Worster's framework also contrasts with that of Alfred W. Crosby, professor of American studies at the University of Texas at Austin, the author of the third essay. Crosby offers a more narrowly focused framework of biological causation for understanding why Europeans historically have been so successful in expanding into temperate regions throughout the world. Europeans and their "portmanteau biota"—the associated livestock, diseases, varmints, and weeds brought to the New World on the colonists' ships—disrupted native peoples' lands and lives, giving Europeans an ecological advantage in colonizing the globe. The fourth essay, by Carolyn Merchant, professor of environmental history at the University of California at Berkeley, draws on Worster's interacting levels of ecology, production, and consciousness and on Crosby's idea of "ecological imperialism" but adds a new level: that of biological and social reproduction. Merchant emphasizes the possibility of rapid revolutionary transformations of local ecosystems from both within and without.

Ecological History

DONALD WORSTER

Forty years ago a wise, visionary man, the Wisconsin wildlife biologist and conservationist Aldo Leopold, called for "an ecological interpretation of history," by which he meant using the ideas and research of the emerging field of ecology to help explain why the past developed the way it did. At that time ecology was still in its scientific infancy, but its promise was bright and the need for its insights was beginning to be apparent to a growing number of leaders in science, politics, and society. It has taken a while for historians to heed Leopold's advice, but at last the field of environmental history has begun to take shape and its practitioners are trying to build on his initiative.

From Donald Worster, "Transformations of the Earth: Toward an Agroecological Perspective in History," A Roundtable: Environmental History, *Journal of American History*, 76, no. 4, March 1990, pp. 1087–1106, excerpts. Copyright Organization of American Historians, 1990.

Leopold's own suggestion of how an ecologically informed history might proceed had to do with the frontier lands of Kentucky, pivotal in the westward movement of the nation. In the period of the revolutionary war it was uncertain who would possess and control those lands: the native Indians, the French or English empires, or the colonial settlers. And then rather quickly the struggle was resolved in favor of the Americans, who brought along their plows and livestock to take possession. It was more than their prowess as fighters, their determination as conquerors, or their virtue in the eyes of God that allowed those agricultural settlers to win the competition; the land itself had something to contribute to their success. Leopold pointed out that growing along the Kentucky bottomlands, the places most accessible to newcomers, were formidable canebrakes, where the canes rose as high as fifteen feet and posed an insuperable barrier to the plow. But fortunately for the Americans, when the cane was burned or grazed out, the magic of bluegrass sprouted in its place. Grass replaced cane in what ecologists call the pattern of secondary ecological succession, which occurs when vegetation is disturbed but the soil is not destroyed, as when a fire sweeps across a prairie or a hurricane levels a forest; succession refers to the fact that a new assortment of species enters and replaces what was there before. In Kentucky, the foremost of those new species was bluegrass, and a wide expanse of bluegrass was all that any rural pioneer, looking for a homestead and a pasture for his livestock, could want. Discovering that fact, Americans entered Kentucky by the thousands, and the struggle for possession was soon over. "What if," Leopold wondered, "the plant succession inherent in this dark and bloody ground had, under the impact of these forces, given us some worthless sedge, shrub, or weed?" Would Kentucky have become American territory as, and when, it did?

Actually, the facts in the case are more complicated than Leopold could explore in the confines of his essay, and they argue for something more than a simple form of environmental determinism, which is what a casual reader might see in his example. Kentucky bluegrass was not a native species, but a European import. Brought by immigrants to the country in the holds of ships, its seed spread through the travels and droppings of their cattle, sprouting first around salt licks, where the animals congregated, then spreading into newly disturbed land like the canebrakes, where it gained ascendancy over its indigenous competitors, much as the colonists were doing over the Indians. The winning of Kentucky was, in other words, helped immensely by the fact that the human invaders inadvertently brought along their plant allies. So, on continent after continent, went the triumph of what Alfred Crosby, Jr., has called "ecological imperialism."

It is with such matters that the new field of ecological or environmental history (most practitioners prefer to use the latter label as more inclusive in method and material) deals. This new history rejects the common assumption that human experience has been exempt from natural constraints, that people are a separate and uniquely special species, that the ecological consequences of our past deeds can be ignored. The older history could hardly deny that people have been living for a long while on this planet, but its general disregard of that fact suggested that they were not and are not truly part of the planet.

Environmental historians, on the other hand, realize that scholarship can no longer afford to be so naïve.

The field of environmental history began to take shape in the 1970s, as conferences on the global predicament were assembling and popular environmentalist movements were gathering momentum. It was a response to questions that people in many nations were beginning to ask: How many humans can the biosphere support without collapsing under the impact of their pollution and consumption? Will man-made changes in the atmosphere lead to more cancer or poorer grain harvests or the melting of the polar ice caps? Is technology making people's lives more dangerous, rather than more secure? Does *Homo sapiens* have any moral obligations to the earth and its circle of life, or does that life exist merely to satisfy the infinitely expanding wants of our own species? History was not alone in being touched by the rising concern; scholars in law, philosophy, economics, sociology, and other areas were likewise responsive. It is surely a permanent response, gaining significance as the questions prompting it increase in urgency, frequency, and scope. Environmental history was born out of a strong moral concern and may still have some political reform commitments behind it, but as it has matured, it has become an intellectual enterprise that has neither any simple, nor any single, moral or political agenda to promote. Its goal is to deepen our understanding of how humans have been affected by their natural environment through time, and conversely and perhaps more importantly in view of the present global predicament, how they have affected that environment and with what results.

Much of the material for environmental history, coming as it does from the accumulated work of geographers, natural scientists, anthropologists, and others, has been around for generations and is merely being absorbed into historical thinking in the light of recent experience. It includes data on tides and winds, ocean currents, the position of continents in relation to each other, and the geological and hydrological forces creating the planet's land and water base. It includes the history of climate and weather, as these have made for good or bad harvests, sent prices up or down, promoted or ended epidemics, or led to population increase or decline. All these have been powerful influences on the course of history, and they continue to be so. In a somewhat different category from these physical factors are the living resources of the earth, or the biota, which the ecologist George Woodwell calls the most important of all to human well-being: the plants and animals that, in his phrase, "maintain the biosphere as a habitat suitable for life." Those living resources have also been more susceptible to human manipulation than nonbiological factors, and at no point more so than today. We must include the phenomenon of human reproduction as a natural force giving form to history, and by no means a negligible force, as the last few decades of explosive global fertility have amply demonstrated.

Defined in the vernacular then, environmental history deals with the role and place of nature in human life. It studies all the interactions that societies in the past have had with the nonhuman world, the world we have not in any primary sense created. The technological environment, the cluster of things that people have made, which can be so pervasive as to constitute a kind of "second nature" around them, is also part of this study, but in the very specific sense that technology is a product of human culture as conditioned by the nonhuman environment. But with such phenomena as the desert and the water cycle, we encounter autonomous, independent energies that do not derive from the drives and inventions of any culture. It might be argued that as the human will increasingly makes its imprint on forests, gene pools, and even oceans, there is no practical way to distinguish between the natural and the cultural. However, most environmental historians would argue that the distinction is worth keeping, for it reminds us that not all the forces at work in the world emanate from humans. Wherever the two spheres, the natural and the cultural, confront or interact with one another, environmental history finds its essential themes.

There are three levels on which the new history proceeds, each drawing on a range of other disciplines and requiring special methods of analysis. The first involves the discovery of the structure and distribution of natural environments of the past. Before one can write environmental history one must first understand nature itself—specifically, nature as it was organized and functioning in past times. The task is more difficult than might first appear, for although nature, like society, has a story of change to tell, there are few written records to reveal most of that story. To make such a reconstruction, consequently, the environmental historian must turn for help to a wide array of the natural sciences and must rely on their methodologies, sources, and evidence, though now and then the documentary materials with which historians work can be a valuable aid to the scientists' labors.

The second level of environmental history is more fully the responsibility of the historian and other students of society, for it focuses on productive technology as it interacts with the environment. For help on understanding this complicated level, in which tools, work, and social relations are intermixed, historians in the new field have begun to turn to the extensive literature dealing with the concept of "modes of production," emphasizing (as most of those who use the phrase have not) that those modes have been engaged not merely in organizing human labor and machinery but also in transforming nature. Here the focus is on understanding how technology has restructured human ecological relations, that is, with analyzing the various ways people have tried to make nature over into a system that produces resources for their consumption. In that process of transforming the earth, people have also restructured themselves and their social relations. A community organized to catch fish at sea may have had very different institutions, gender roles, or seasonal rhythms from those of one raising sheep in high mountain pastures. A hunting society may have had a very different configuration from that of a peasant agricultural one. On this level of inquiry, one of the most interesting questions is who has gained and who has lost power as modes of production have changed.

Finally, forming a third level for the environmental historian is that more intangible, purely mental type of encounter in which perceptions, ideologies, ethics, laws, and myths have become part of an individual's or group's dialogue with nature. People are continually constructing cognitive maps of the world around them, defining what a resource is, determining which sorts of behavior may be environmentally degrading and ought to be prohibited, and generally choosing the ends to which nature is put. Such patterns of human perception, ideology, and value have often been highly consequential, moving with all the power of great sheets of glacial ice, grinding and pushing, reorganizing and recreating the surface of the planet.

The great challenge in the new history does not lie in merely identifying such levels of inquiry, but in deciding how and where to make connections among them. Do the lines of historical causality run from the first, the level of nature, through technology and on to ideology, as a strict environmental determinist would insist? Or do the lines run in precisely the opposite direction, so that nature itself is finally nothing more than the product of human contrivance or desire? This is, of course, an age-old debate over explanation, one that the new history has only inherited, not invented; the debate is too large and complex to reproduce, let alone pretend to resolve, here. Suffice it to observe that most environmental historians seem to have settled philosophically on a position that is at once materialist and idealist; they commonly maintain that the historian cannot rigidly adhere a priori to any single theory of causality but must be open to context and time. In some cases the shifting patterns of the natural order — a sustained condition of severe aridity, for instance, or an abrupt shift from a wet to a dry cycle — have been powerful, forcing people to adapt on both the productive and the cognitive levels. In other cases, however, and increasingly in modern times, when the balance of power has shifted more and more away from nature and in favor of humans, the third level, the sum of people's perceptions and ideas about nature, has clearly become the decisive one in promoting change. . . .

Humans have extracted an extraordinarily diverse array of resources from the natural world, and the number and magnitude of them is growing all the time. But the most basic and revealing of them in the study of human ecology have been the resources we call food. Every group of people in history has had to identify such resources and create a mode of production to get them from the earth and into their bellies. Moreover, it is through that process that they have been connected in the most vital, constant, and concrete way to the natural world. Few of those modes of producing food, however, have been approached by historians from an ecological perspective. If we are to make further progress in understanding the linkages human beings make to nature, developing that perspective and applying it to food production must be one of the major activities of the new field. . . .

But historians wanting to undertake an ecological analysis should be aware that lately the conventional ecosystem model sketched above has been coming under considerable criticism from some scientists, and there is no longer any consensus on how it functions or how resilient it is. Are ecosystems as stable as scientists have assumed, the critics ask, or are they all susceptible to easy upset? Is it accurate to describe them as firmly balanced and orderly until humans arrive on the scene, as some of the older textbooks suggested, or is human disturbance only one of the many sources of instability in nature? Even more disputed are these questions: How and when do people begin to produce changes in ecosystems that might be called damaging, and when does that damage become irreversible? No one really disputes that the death of all its trees, birds, and insects would mean the death of a rain forest, or that the draining of a pond would spell the end of that ecosystem; but most changes, induced by humans or otherwise, are not so catastrophic, and the concept of damage has no clear definition or easy method of measurement. Dependent as it is on ecological theory for assistance in analysis and explanation, the new field of environmental history finds itself in a very awkward position — caught in the middle of a revisionist swing that has left in some disarray the notion of what an ecosystem is and how it works, that has even cast doubt on such old intuitive notions as "the balance of nature" and the role of diversity in promoting ecological stability. Historians have long had to deal with such revisionism in their own field and are only too familiar with the resulting confusion. Learning from that experience, they should not rush to assume that the latest scientific paper on the ecosystem is the true gospel or that yesterday's notions are now completely wrong; on the other hand, if they want to work collaboratively with scientists, they must be careful not to borrow their ideas of nature unthinkingly or innocently from outmoded textbooks or discarded models.

Those theoretical disputes should not obscure the fact that ecological science continues to describe a natural world that is marvelously organized and vital to human existence. Nature, in the eyes of most ecologists, is not an inert or formless or incoherent world that awaits the hand of people. It is a world of living things that are constantly at work, in discernible patterns, producing goods and services that are essential for the survival of one another. Microorganisms, for example, are endlessly busy breaking down organic matter to form the constituents of soil, and other organisms in turn make use of that soil for their own nutrition and growth. The science of ecology still reveals a realm beyond our human economies, and beyond the work we do in them, a realm that has been described as a vast, elaborate, complex "economy of nature," an organized realm that is working energetically and skillfully to satisfy the needs of all living things, creating what might be called the indispensable "values" of existence. Without the smooth functioning of that greater economy, without those values that are brought into being by a hardworking nature, no group of people could survive for an hour, and the making of history would come to an abrupt end.

An ecosystem then is a subset of the global economy of nature — a local or regional system of plants and animals working together to create the means of survival. Starting from this understanding, the historian ought to ask how we can best proceed from the ecosystem concept to understand the human past more completely. Taking that next step requires us to adopt still another concept — what some have begun to call an *agroecosystem*, which, as the name suggests, is an ecosystem reorganized for agricultural purposes — a domesticated ecosystem. It is a restructuring of the trophic processes in nature, that is, the processes of food and energy flow in the economy of living organisms. Everywhere such a restructuring involves forcing the productive energies in some ecosystem to serve more exclusively a set of conscious purposes often located outside it — namely, the feeding and prospering of a group of humans. . . .

Unquestionably, all agriculture has brought revolutionary changes to the planet's ecosystems; and, most agroecologists would agree, those changes have often been destructive to the natural order and imperfect in design and execution. Yet as they have gained understanding of how agricultural systems have interacted with nature, scientists have discovered plenty of reasons to respect the long historical achievement of billions of anonymous traditional farmers. As Miguel A. Altieri writes, "Many farming practices once regarded as primitive or misguided are being recognized as sophisticated and appropriate. Confronted with specific problems of slope, flooding, droughts, pests, diseases and low soil fertility, small farmers throughout the world have developed unique management systems to overcome these constraints." . . .

The landscapes that resulted from such traditional practices were carefully integrated, functional mosaics that retained much of the wisdom of nature; they were based on close observation and imitation of the natural order. Here a field was selected and cleared for intensive crop production; there a forest was preserved as supply of fuel and mast; over there a patch of marginal land was used for pasturing livestock. What may have appeared scattered and happenstance in the premodern agricultural landscape always had a structure behind it — a structure that was at once the product of nonhuman factors and of human intelligence, working toward a mutual accommodation. In many parts of the world that agroecosystem took thousands of years to achieve, and even then it never reached any perfect resting point. Rises and falls in human numbers, vagaries of weather and disease, external pressures of wars and taxes, tragedies of depletion and collapse, all kept the world's food systems in a constant state of change. Yet, examined over the long duration, they had two remarkably persistent, widely shared characteristics, whether they were in medieval Sweden or ancient Sumer, in the Ohio River valley or the Valley of Mexico, whether the systems were based on maize or wheat or cassava. First, traditional agroecosystems were based on a predominately subsistence strategy in which most people raised what they themselves consumed, though now and then they may have sent some of their surplus off to cities for the sake of trade or tribute. Second, subsistence-oriented agroecosystems, despite making major changes in nature, nonetheless preserved much of its diversity and complexity, and that achievement was a source of social stability, generation following generation.

So it was, that is, until the modern era and the rise of the capitalist mode of production. Beginning in the fifteenth century and accelerating in the eighteenth and nineteenth centuries, the structure and dynamics of agroecosystems began to change radically. I believe the capitalist reorganization carried out in those years and beyond into our own time brought as sweeping and revolutionary a set of land-use changes as did the Neolithic revolution. Despite its importance, we have not yet fully understood why this second revolution occurred nor asked what its effect has been on the natural environment. I submit that the single most important task for scholars in the history of modern agroecology is to trace what Karl Polanyi has called "the great transformation," both in general planetary terms and in all its permutations from place to place.

When I speak of the capitalist mode of production in agriculture I mean something broader than Marxists do when they use the phrase. For them, the crucial distinguishing feature of the new mode has been the restructuring of *human* relations: the buying of labor as a commodity in the marketplace and the organizing of it to produce more commodities for sale. In my view, the buying of labor is too narrow a feature to cover so broad, multifaceted, and changing a mode as capitalism, even considered in merely human terms. It would leave out the slave-owning cotton planters of the American South, who bought people, not merely their labor; it would not include the agribusiness wheat farmers of the Great Plains, who have seldom had access to hired hands and have invested in technology instead; and today it would have to omit from the realm of capitalism the California grower who has just bought a mechanical tomato harvester to replace all his migrant workers. In order to define capitalism more adequately, some have extended it to any organization of labor, technology, or technique for producing commodities for sale in the marketplace. If few agricultural producers have been capitalists in the strict Marxist sense, it is said, more and more of them have become "capitalistic" over the past four centuries, and nowhere more so than in the United States. . . .

Capitalism introduced still another innovation, one that would change profoundly the way people related to nature in general: It created for the first time in history a general market in land. All the complex forces and interactions, beings and processes, that we term "nature" (sometimes even elevate to the honorific status of a capitalized "Nature") were compressed into the simplified abstraction, "land." Though not truly a commodity in the ordinary sense, that is, something produced by human labor for sale on the market, land became "commodified"; it came to be regarded as though it were a commodity and by that manner of thinking was made available to be traded without restraint. Whatever emotional meanings that land had held for the self and its identity, whatever moral regard it had engendered, now was suppressed so that the market economy could function freely. The environmental implications in such a mental change are beyond easy reckoning.

What actually happened to the world of nature, once it had been reduced to the abstraction "land," is one of the most interesting historical problems presented by the capitalist transformation and will require a great deal more research by environmental historians. . . . Environmental history aims to bring back into our awareness that significance of nature and, with the aid of modern science, to discover some fresh truths about ourselves and our past.

Ecological Prophecies

WILLIAM CRONON

Donald Worster is surely right when he asserts that environmental history, at its most basic level, "deals with the role and place of nature in human life." And yet even so seemingly straightforward a definition suggests the difficult challenge this new field poses for scholars. Environmental historians perform a delicate interdisciplinary balancing act in trying to reconcile the insights of their colleagues in history, ecology, geography, anthropology, and several other fields. Like ecologists, they are more committed than most historians to the proposition that the natural world has an autonomous place in history. For

From William Cronon, "Modes of Prophecy and Production: Placing Nature in History," A Roundtable: Environmental History, *Journal of American History* 76, no. 4 March 1990, pp. 1122–31, excerpts. Copyright Organization of American Historians, 1990.

them, the story of the prairie bluestem, for instance, or the smallpox virus, or the common barnyard pig, may be no less important than the story of a presidential administration or a war. And yet unlike most ecologists, they share with other historians the belief that nature can only exist in time, that the particulars of historical environmental change are no less important than the timeless abstractions of ecological processes. To make matters worse, they understand that the very term they use to describe the environment — *nature* — is itself an astonishingly complex human construction: as Raymond Williams once remarked, "the idea of nature contains, though often unnoticed, an extraordinary amount of human history." . . .

One of my chief reservations about Worster's proposed research agenda . . . is its potentially excessive materialism. He calls for an approach that would begin with food and the ways people "create a mode of production" to get food "from the earth and into their bellies." Insofar as looking at food will encourage historians to reconstruct the intricate web of linkages between human beings and other organisms, I can only applaud such a strategy. But it is essential to remember that *food*, like *nature*, is not simply a system of bundled calories and nutrients that sustains the life of a human community by concentrating the trophic energy flows of an ecosystem; it is also an elaborate cultural construct. How and why people choose to eat what they do depends as much on what they *think* — about themselves, their relations to each other, their work, their plants and animals, their gods — as on the organisms they actually eat.

Partly because our own work has broken free from the theoretical context for which mode of production was invented, no environmental historian has yet offered a finite taxonomy of modes. Environmental historians have most commonly relied on the anthropologists' distinction between hunter-gatherer and agricultural societies, with capitalism usually added as a rather awkward third term to the set. Worster himself has offered two other modes of production as being particularly germane to the history of the twentieth-century North American West: a pastoral mode that characterizes the arid rural West and a hydraulic mode based on the centralized authority of a bureaucratic state that characterizes the arid urban West. And yet he does not try to reconcile those terms either with the capitalist mode of production (which presumably overlaps both) or with all the other possible modes that one could conjure up on the basis of a particular technology, work process, or resource. Why not a salmon-fishing mode of production? A plow-agricultural mode of production? A petroleum-burning mode of production? . . .

More useful, I believe, would be a tool kit of analytical approaches that would help us locate in a given historical situation the critical linkages between people and the ecosystems they inhabit. Rather than start with the system as a whole, as mode of production would have us do, we should start (like modern ecologists) with *relationships*. Having identified the most important of these for the subject we are studying, we could then seek a deeper and more precise understanding of cultural and ecological change.

I would therefore begin at a very general level of inquiry: What are the most fruitful places to start as we set about the task of understanding cultures and ecosystems in history? What conceptual tools should we use at the outset of our work, and what questions do they suggest we should ask? Worster's . . . essay offers some such tools — the extent to which a given agriculture simplifies its ecosystem, exports its output, defines its crops as commodities, and sustains the fertility of its soil — but there are many more. Some we can borrow directly from other disciplines: for instance, the seasonal fluctuations of climate, the cycling of nutrients in ecosystems, or the association of species in regular patterns. They teach us to ask questions such as: How much seasonal variation in environmental productivity does a particular human community face during an ordinary year? How do its members explain such variation to themselves? How much of the output of their biological system do people store to provide food during the least productive seasons? How reliable is the system from year to year, and how do people try to protect themselves from its least reliable aspects? On what other organisms do they most rely for their own subsistence? How do they conceive of their relationships to those organisms? And so on. By pursuing questions such as these we can begin to construct a systematic picture of how people relate to the world around them and ultimately create a portrait of what Worster might wish to call their "mode of production." I care little about the label; for me, the more important issue is how we arrived at the portrait, how well-defined our questions are, how rigorously we have answered them, and how carefully we have worked out their implications.

Not all of the approaches in our methodological tool kit can be borrowed directly from other disciplines; some will have to be modified before we can readily use them. These include the much-contested concepts of *equilibrium* and *community*, which together underlie the old idea of the "balance of nature" that so often supplies the analytical (and moral) scale against which we measure the environmental effects of human societies. As Worster notes, the ecologists have been busy complicating (if not undermining) all three concepts. Ironically, their efforts to understand ecosystems in more historical terms have made them suspicious of the very models of ecological "community" — stable, self-equilibrated, organic, functionalist — on which our own balance-of-nature arguments rely. We need to grapple with their arguments, since so many of our analyses conclude that human communities (especially capitalist ones) have often radically destabilized the ecosystems on which they depend.

Our interest in *destabilized* ecosystems suggests that we need to develop a more precise definition of "stability" and "sustainability" as we evaluate the ability of human societies to maintain their resource bases without encountering ecological limits. Most environmental historians share with modern environmentalism a political and moral critique of societies that destroy their resource base. We are fuzzy, however, about the time horizon we have in mind when we speak of stability, and we rarely explore very carefully just how static or dynamic we expect the equilibrium between human groups and nature to be. Too often we romanticize nature (and "traditional" societies) as unchanging, when neither ecologists nor anthropologists will permit us such a description any longer. We cannot simply label as capitalist or modern all forces for ecosystemic change, and as traditional or natural all forces for stability. The tautology of such an approach is too self-evident.

We can no longer assume the existence of a static and benign climax community in nature that contrasts with dynamic, but destructive, human change. Rather than benign natural stasis and disruptive human change, we need to explore differential *rates* and *types* of change. Under what circumstances, for instance, do domesticated grazing animals reduce ground cover and increase erosion of topsoil? In a farming community, how do we measure and evaluate declines in soil fertility (a term that itself requires better definition than we ordinarily give it)? Are such changes primarily a function of population density, political-economic context, or some more idealist belief system? Put another way: Are capitalist pigs intrinsically more destructive than noncapitalist pigs? Do the people we study idealize the stability of their place in nature, or do they seek a more dynamic (perhaps "progressive"?) relationship with the ecosystems they inhabit? When we critique "capitalist" peoples for the destructive consequences of their faith in progress, what is the counterfactual alternative against which we implicitly measure them? And so on. Questions such as these may make it harder for us to speak in simple terms about ecological damage, but *damage* is another conceptual tool in need of refinement. Tools of this sort would seem to me more useful than mode of production as starting points, for we can in fact only hope to construct mode of production with their help.

Two additional problems with ecological modes of production point to further difficulties for environmental history as a field. One is holism, which is a common tendency of many disciplines that study the environment. On the one hand, holistic analysis has the great attraction of encouraging historians to see nature and humanity whole, to trace the manifold connections among people and other organisms until finally an integrated understanding of their relations emerges. On the other hand, holism discourages us from looking as much as we should at conflict and difference *within* groups of people. It can bias us toward functionalist models of social and ecological community, in which all members of a society or ecosystem agree on its ends and are equally responsible for its activities. When Worster asserts that "every group of people in history . . . had to . . . create a mode of production," he follows the practice of most environmental historians in speaking about human beings in group terms, as collective actors reshaping the landscape around them according to their seemingly monolithic interests. (The most extreme example of that practice is the environmentalists' habit of attributing monolithic agency—and gender—to the human species as a whole with such singular constructions as "Man exploits the earth and fouls his nest.") Since people's manipulation of nature is almost always a collective activity, some such formulation is linguistically unavoidable—as this sentence itself demonstrates. But one must proceed very carefully to avoid missing the individuals and subgroups whose roles in that activity differ. To say that "peasants" or "farmers" or "Indians" or "colonists" collectively modified their ecosystems in a particular way can lend force and clarity to one's analysis, but often at the expense of subtlety and complexity.

If I were to point to the greatest weakness of environmental history as it has developed thus far, I would criticize its failure to probe below the level of the group to explore the implications of social divisions for environmental change. We lack, for instance, an environmental history of southern agriculture that adequately explores the different roles of slaves and masters and poor whites in reshaping the regional landscape (to say nothing of the different roles of men and women in the same process). Southern historiography is certainly rich with the materials for such an analysis, but a hypothetical environmental historian might too readily be tempted to ascribe environmental change to "southern society" or "tobacco and cotton agriculture" or "the slave mode of production." None of those formulations helps much in teasing apart the diverse material roles and perceptual experiences of different people in the holistic "system." Our work on the environmental experiences of many other groups of people remains sadly undeveloped: in the face of social history's classic categories of gender, race, class, and ethnicity, environmental history stands much more silent than it should. An oversimplified holism is a chief reason for this failure of the field, and little in Worster's essay helps guard against its dangers.

The final warning I might make about modes of production has to do with the mode that dominates Worster's argument: capitalism. It would be foolish to argue against Worster's claim that the growth of capitalism over the past half millennium has been one of the greatest forces for environmental change in human history. His critique of capitalist agriculture — its commodification of land, its drastic ecological simplification, its affection for dangerously vulnerable monocultures, its promotion of divisions of labor that in the long run can do great damage to nature and human community — is one that for the most part I share. The narrative Worster offers of a transition out of a traditional subsistence agriculture into a market-oriented capitalist agriculture has great force, and environmental historians would be foolish to ignore that great transformation. His emphasis on capitalism is crucial, and so too is his effort to remind historians that even the most urban industrial societies are ultimately agricultural at their base: environmental history without agricultural history is inconceivable.

And yet there may be danger even in so compelling an argument. The greatest attraction of Marx's modes of production was their ability to fit a complex series of historical changes to a single narrative trajectory that organized both past history and future prophecy — from past feudalism to present capitalism to future communism. The modes were so encompassing that virtually any social change could be accommodated within them, giving what might otherwise have appeared incomprehensibly complex the familiar Aristotelian shape of beginning, middle, and end. The same attraction holds for environmental historians. Even though most of us agree about only one mode of production — the capitalist one — that mode allows us to narrate our stories as an endless series of transitions, out of some "traditional" predecessor and into the world we know. The ecological contradictions of capitalism, which we both discover in history and borrow from modern environmentalism, supply the basis for a powerful prophecy about the future environmental disasters that capitalism could (will?) all too easily spawn. If we follow Worster's lead by framing environmental history as a transition into and out of capitalism, we energize our historical argument with all the power of prophecy. . . .

If we pursue modes of production, we must give equal attention to the broader cultural systems in which they are embedded, and the modes of *reproduction* that transmit them from generation to generation. We should be wary of excessive holism. Although there is great analytical value in being able to describe the broad connections between people and the other organisms with which they share the world, we should never lose sight of the fact that different people experience those connections in quite different ways. As Worster argues, "one of the most interesting questions . . . is who has gained and who has lost power as . . . modes of production have changed." The exploration of social and environmental *difference* — and of its relation to *power* — needs to find a more prominent place in our work. So too do all landscapes in which power and difference express themselves, even those that seem on their face least natural: cities, highways, slums, factories, hospitals, corporations, military installations, all the many places that give shape to the modern world. Cities in particular deserve much more work than they have received. Environmental history continues to have too strong a bias toward the wild and the rural, when in fact the field's intellectual commitment to discovering environmental connections ought to leave no corner of the planet untouched by its scholarship.

Ecological Imperialism

ALFRED W. CROSBY

None of the major genetic groupings of humankind is as oddly distributed about the world as European, especially Western European, whites. Almost all the peoples we call Mongoloids live in the single contiguous land mass of Asia. Black Africans are divided between three continents — their homeland and North and South America — but most of them are concentrated in their original latitudes, the tropics, facing each other across one ocean. European whites were all recently concentrated in Europe, but in the last few centuries have burst out, as energetically as if from a burning building, and have created vast settlements of their kind in the South Temperate Zone and North Temperate Zone (excepting Asia, a continent already thoroughly and irreversibly tenanted). In Canada and the United States together they amount to nearly ninety percent of the population; in Argentina and Uruguay together to over ninety-five percent; in Australia to ninety-eight percent; and in New Zealand to ninety percent. The only nations in the Temperate Zones outside of Asia which do not have enormous majorities of European whites are Chile, with a population of two-thirds mixed Spanish and Indian stock, and South Africa, where blacks outnumber whites six to one. How odd that these two, so many thousands of miles from Europe, should be exceptions in *not* being predominantly pure European.

Europeans have conquered Canada, the United States, Argentina, Uruguay, Australia, and New Zealand not just militarily and economically and technologically — as they did India, Nigeria, Mexico, Peru, and other tropical

Excerpts from *The Texas Quarterly* 21, Spring 1978, pp. 10–22. Reprinted with the permission of the author, Alfred Crosby.

lands, whose native peoples have long since expelled or interbred with and even absorbed the invaders. In the Temperate Zone lands listed above Europeans conquered and triumphed demographically. These, for the sake of convenience, we will call the Lands of the Demographic Takeover. . . .

Any respectable theory which attempts to explain the Europeans' demographic triumphs has to provide explanations for at least two phenomena. The first is the decimation and demoralization of the aboriginal populations of Canada, the United States, Argentina, and others. . . . Why did so few of the natives of the Lands of the Demographic Takeover survive?

Second, we must explain the stunning, even awesome success of European agriculture, that is, the European way of manipulating the environment in the Lands of the Demographic Takeover. . . .

In attempting to explain these two phenomena, let us examine four categories of organisms deeply involved in European expansion: (1) human beings; (2) animals closely associated with human beings — both the desirable animals like horses and cattle and undesirable varmints like rats and mice; (3) pathogens or microorganisms that cause disease in humans; and (4) weeds. Is there a pattern in the histories of these groups which suggests an overall explanation for the phenomenon of the Demographic Takeover or which at least suggests fresh paths of inquiry?

Europe has exported something in excess of sixty million people in the past few hundred years. Great Britain alone exported over twenty million. The great mass of these white emigrants went to the United States, Argentina, Canada, Australia, Uruguay, and New Zealand. (Other areas to absorb comparable quantities of Europeans were Brazil and Russia east of the Urals. These would qualify as Lands of the Demographic Takeover except that very large fractions of their populations are non-European.)

In stark contrast, very few aborigines of the Americas, Australia, or New Zealand ever went to Europe. Those who did often died not long after arrival. The fact that the flow of human migration was almost entirely from Europe to her colonies and not vice versa is not startling — or very enlightening. Europeans controlled overseas migration, and Europe needed to export, not import, labor. But this pattern of one-way migration is significant in that it reappears in other connections.

The vast expanses of forests, savannahs, and steppes in the Lands of the Demographic Takeover were inundated by animals from the Old World, chiefly from Europe. Horses, cattle, sheep, goats, and pigs have for hundreds of years been among the most numerous of the quadrupeds of these lands, which were completely lacking in these species at the time of first contact with the Europeans. By 1600 enormous feral herds of horses and cattle surged over the pampas of the Río de la Plata (today's Argentina and Uruguay) and over the plains of northern Mexico. By the beginning of the seventeenth century packs of Old World dogs gone wild were among the predators of these herds.

In the forested country of British North America population explosions among imported animals were also spectacular, but only by European standards, not by those of Spanish America. In 1700 in Virginia feral hogs, said one witness, "swarm like vermaine upon the Earth," and young gentlemen were entertaining themselves by hunting wild horses of the inland counties. In Carolina the herds of cattle were "incredible, being from one to two thousand head in one Man's Possession." In the eighteenth and early nineteenth centuries the advancing European frontier from New England to the Gulf of Mexico was preceded into Indian territory by an *avant-garde* of semi-wild herds of hogs and cattle tended, now and again, by semi-wild herdsmen, white and black.

The first English settlers landed in Botany Bay, Australia, in January of 1788 with livestock, most of it from the Cape of Good Hope. The pigs and poultry thrived; the cattle did well enough; the sheep, the future source of the colony's good fortune, died fast. Within a few months two bulls and four cows strayed away. By 1804 the wild herds they founded numbered from three to five thousand head and were in possession of much of the best land between the settlements and the Blue Mountains. If they had ever found their way through the mountains to the grasslands beyond, the history of Australia in the first decades of the nineteenth century might have been one dominated by cattle rather than sheep. As it is, the colonial government wanted the land the wild bulls so ferociously defended, and considered the growing practice of convicts running away to live off the herds as a threat to the whole colony; so the adult cattle were shot and salted down and the calves captured and tamed. The English settlers imported woolly sheep from Europe and sought out the interior pastures for them. The animals multiplied rapidly, and when Darwin made his visit to New South Wales in 1836, there were about a million sheep there for him to see.

The arrival of Old World livestock probably affected New Zealand more radically than any other of the Lands of the Demographic Takeover. Cattle, horses, goats, pigs and—in this land of few or no large predators—even the usually timid sheep went wild. In New Zealand herds of feral farm animals were practicing the ways of their remote ancestors as late as the 1940s and no doubt still run free. Most of the sheep, though, stayed under human control, and within a decade of Great Britain's annexation of New Zealand in 1840, her new acquisition was home to a quarter million sheep. In 1974 New Zealand had over fifty-five million sheep, about twenty times more sheep than people.

In the Lands of the Demographic Takeover the European pioneers were accompanied and often preceded by their domesticated animals, walking sources of food, leather, fiber, power, and wealth, and these animals often adapted more rapidly to the new surroundings and reproduced much more rapidly than their masters. To a certain extent, the success of Europeans as colonists was automatic as soon as they put their tough, fast, fertile, and intelligent animals ashore. The latter were sources of capital that sought out their own sustenance, improvised their own protection against the weather, fought their own battles against predators and, if their masters were smart enough to allow calves, colts, and lambs to accumulate, could and often did show the world the amazing possibilities of compound interest.

The honey bee is the one insect of worldwide importance which human beings have domesticated, if we may use the word in a broad sense. Many species of bees and other insects produce honey, but the one which does so in greatest quantity and which is easiest to control is a native of the Mediterranean area and the Middle East, the honey bee (*Apis mellifera*). The European has probably taken this sweet and short-tempered servant to every colony he ever established, from Arctic to Antarctic Circle, and the honey bee has always been one of the first immigrants to set off on its own. Sometimes the advance of the bee frontier could be very rapid: the first hive in Tasmania swarmed sixteen times in the summer of 1832.

Thomas Jefferson tells us that the Indians of North America called the honey bees "English flies," and St. John de Crèvecoeur, his contemporary, wrote that "the Indians look upon them with an evil eye, and consider their progress into the interior of the continent as an omen of the white man's approach: thus, as they discover the bees, the news of the event, passing from mouth to mouth, spreads sadness and consternation on all sides."

Domesticated creatures that traveled from the Lands of the Demographic Takeover to Europe are few. Australian aborigines and New Zealand Maoris had a few tame dogs, unimpressive by Old World standards and unwanted by the whites. Europe happily accepted the American Indians' turkeys and guinea pigs, but had no need for their dogs, llamas, and alpacas. Again the explanation is simple: Europeans, who controlled the passage of large animals across the oceans, had no need to reverse the process.

It is interesting and perhaps significant, though, that the exchange was just as one sided for varmints, the small mammals whose migrations Europeans often tried to stop. None of the American or Australian or New Zealand equivalents of rats have become established in Europe, but Old World varmints, especially rats, have colonized right alongside the Europeans in the Temperate Zones. Rats of assorted sizes, some of them almost surely European immigrants, were tormenting Spanish Americans by at least the end of the sixteenth century. European rats established a beachhead in Jamestown, Virginia, as early as 1609, when they almost starved out the colonists by eating their food stores. In Buenos Aires the increase in rats kept pace with that of cattle, according to an early nineteenth century witness. European rats proved as aggressive as the Europeans in New Zealand, where they completely replaced the local rats in the North Islands as early as the 1840s. Those poor creatures are probably completely extinct today or exist only in tiny relict populations.

The European rabbits are not usually thought of as varmints, but where there are neither diseases nor predators to hold down their numbers they can become the worst of pests. In 1859 a few members of the species *Orytolagus cuniculus* (the scientific name for the protagonists of all the Peter Rabbits of literature) were released in southeast Australia. Despite massive efforts to stop them, they reproduced — true to their reputation — and spread rapidly all the way across Australia's southern half to the Indian Ocean. In 1950 the rabbit population of Australia was estimated at 500 million, and they were outcompeting the nation's most important domesticated animals, sheep, for the grasses and herbs. They have been brought under control, but only by means of artificially fomenting an epidemic of myxomatosis, a lethal American rabbit disease. The story of rabbits and myxomatosis in New Zealand is similar.

Europe, in return for her varmints, has received muskrats and gray squirrels and little else from America, and nothing at all of significance from Australia or New Zealand, and we might well wonder if muskrats and squirrels really qualify as varmints. As with other classes of organisms, the exchange has been a one-way street.

None of Europe's emigrants were as immediately and colossally successful as its pathogens, the microorganisms that make human beings ill, cripple them, and kill them. Whenever and wherever Europeans crossed the oceans and settled, the pathogens they carried created prodigious epidemics of smallpox, measles, tuberculosis, influenza, and a number of other diseases. It was this factor, more than any other, that Darwin had in mind as he wrote of the Europeans' deadly tread.

The pathogens transmitted by the Europeans, unlike the Europeans themselves or most of their domesticated animals, did at least as well in the tropics as in the temperate Lands of the Demographic Takeover. Epidemics devastated Mexico, Peru, Brazil, Hawaii, and Tahiti soon after the Europeans made the first contact with aboriginal populations. Some of these populations were able to escape demographic defeat because their initial numbers were so large that a small fraction was still sufficient to maintain occupation of, if not title to, the land, and also because the mass of Europeans were never attracted to the tropical lands, not even if they were partially vacated. In the Lands of the Demographic Takeover the aboriginal populations were too sparse to rebound from the onslaught of disease or were inundated by European immigrants before they could recover.

The First Strike Force of the white immigrants to the Lands of the Demographic Takeover were epidemics. A few examples from scores of possible examples follow. Smallpox first arrived in the Río de la Plata region in 1558 or 1560 and killed, according to one chronicler possibly more interested in effect than accuracy, "more than a hundred thousand Indians" of the heavy riverine population there. An epidemic of plague or typhus decimated the Indians of the New England coast immediately before the founding of Plymouth. Smallpox or something similar struck the aborigines of Australia's Botany Bay in 1789, killed half, and rolled on into the interior. Some unidentified disease or diseases spread through the Maori tribes of the North Island of New Zealand in the 1790s, killing so many in a number of villages that the survivors were not able to bury the dead. After a series of such lethal and rapidly moving epidemics, then came the slow, unspectacular but thorough cripplers and killers like venereal disease and tuberculosis. In conjunction with the large numbers of white settlers these diseases were enough to smother aboriginal chances of recovery. First the blitzkrieg, then the mopping up.

The greatest of the killers in these lands was probably smallpox. The exception is New Zealand, the last of these lands to attract permanent European settlers. They came to New Zealand after the spread of vaccination in Europe, and so were poor carriers. As of the 1850s smallpox still had not come ashore, and by that time two-thirds of the Maori had been vaccinated. The tardy arrival of smallpox in these islands may have much to do with the fact that the Maori today comprise a larger percentage (nine percent) of their country's population than that of any other aboriginal people in any European colony or former European colony in either Temperate Zone, save only South Africa.

American Indians bore the full brunt of smallpox, and its mark is on their history and folklore. The Kiowa of the southern plains of the United States have a legend in which a Kiowa man meets Smallpox on the plain, riding a horse. The man asks, "Where do you come from and what do you do and why are you here?" Smallpox answers, "I am one with the white men — they are my people as the Kiowas are yours. Sometimes I travel ahead of them and sometimes behind. But I am always their companion and you will find me in their camps and their houses." "What can you do?" the Kiowa asks. "I bring death," Smallpox replies. "My breath causes children to wither like young plants in spring snow. I bring destruction. No matter how beautiful a woman is, once she has looked at me she becomes as ugly as death. And to men I bring not death alone, but the destruction of their children and the blighting of their wives. The strongest of warriors go down before me. No people who have looked on me will ever be the same."

In return for the barrage of diseases that Europeans directed overseas, they received little in return. Australia and New Zealand provided no new strains of pathogens to Europe — or none that attracted attention. And of America's native diseases none had any real influence on the Old World — with the likely exception of venereal syphilis, which almost certainly existed in the New World before 1492 and probably did not occur in its present form in the Old World.

Weeds are rarely history makers, for they are not as spectacular in their effects as pathogens. But they, too, influence our lives and migrate over the world despite human wishes. As such, like varmints and germs, they are better indicators of certain realities than human beings or domesticated animals.

The term *weed* in modern botanical usage refers to any type of plant which — because of especially large numbers of seeds produced per plant, or especially effective means of distributing those seeds, or especially tough roots and rhizomes from which new plants can grow, or especially tough seeds that survive the alimentary canals of animals to be planted with their droppings — spread rapidly and outcompete others on disturbed, bare soil. Weeds are plants that tempt the botanist to use such anthropomorphic words as aggressive and opportunistic.

Many of the most successful weeds in the well-watered regions of the Lands of the Demographic Takeover are of European or Eurasian origin. French and Dutch and English farmers brought with them to North America their worst enemies, weeds, "to exhaust the land, hinder and damnify the Crop." By the last third of the seventeenth century at least twenty different types were widespread enough in New England to attract the attention of the English visitor, John Josselyn, who identified couch grass, dandelion, nettles, mallowes, knot grass, shepherd's purse, sow thistle, and clot burr and others. One of the most aggressive was plantain, which the Indians called "English-Man's Foot."

European weeds rolled west with the pioneers, in some cases spreading almost explosively. As of 1823 corn chamomile and maywood had spread up to but not across the Muskingum River in Ohio. Eight years later they were over the river. The most prodigiously imperialistic of the weeds in the eastern half of the United States and Canada were probably Kentucky bluegrass and white clover. They spread so fast after the entrance of Europeans into a given area that there is some suspicion that they may have been present in pre-Columbian America, although the earliest European accounts do not mention them. Probably brought to the Appalachian area by the French, these two kinds of weeds preceded the English settlers there and kept up with the movement westward until reaching the plains across the Mississippi.

Old World plants set up business on their own on the Pacific coast of North America just as soon as the Spaniards and Russians did. The climate of coastal southern California is much the same as that of the Mediterranean, and the Spaniards who came to California in the eighteenth century brought their own Mediterranean weeds with them via Mexico: wild oats, fennel, wild radishes. These plants, plus those brought in later by the Forty-niners, muscled their way to dominance in the coastal grasslands. These immigrant weeds followed Old World horses, cattle, and sheep into California's interior prairies and took over there as well.

They did not push so swiftly into the coastal Northwest because the Spanish, their reluctant patrons, were slow to do so, and because those shores are cool and damp. Most of the present-day weeds in that region had to come with the Russians or Anglo-Americans from similar areas on other coasts. The Northwest has a semi-arid interior, however, into which some European plants like redstem filaree spread quite early, presumably from the prairies of California.

The region of Argentina and Uruguay was almost as radically altered in its flora as in its fauna by the coming of the Europeans. The ancient Indian practice, taken up immediately by the whites, of burning off the old grass of the pampa every year, as well as the trampling and cropping to the ground of indigenous grasses and forbs by the thousands of imported quadrupeds who also changed the nature of the soil with their droppings, opened the whole countryside to European plants. In the 1780s Félix de Azara observed that the pampa, already radically altered, was changing as he watched. European weeds sprang up around every cabin, grew up along roads, and pressed into the open steppe. Today only a quarter of the plants growing wild in the pampa are native, and in the well-watered eastern portions, the "natural" ground cover consists almost entirely of Old World grasses and clovers.

The invaders were not, of course, always desirable. When Darwin visited Uruguay in 1832, he found large expanses, perhaps as much as hundreds of square miles, monopolized by the immigrant wild artichoke and transformed into a prickly wilderness fit neither for man nor his animals.

The onslaught of foreign and specifically European plants on Australia began abruptly in 1778 because the first expedition that sailed from Britain to Botany Bay carried some livestock and considerable quantities of seed. By May of 1803 over two hundred foreign plants, most of them European, had been purposely introduced and planted in New South Wales, undoubtedly along with a number of weeds. Even today so-called clean seed characteristically contains some weed seeds, and this was much more so two hundred years ago. By and large, Australia's north has been too tropical and her interior too hot and dry for European weeds and grasses, but much of her southern coasts and Tasmania have been hospitable indeed to Europe's willful flora.

Thus, many — often a majority — of the most aggressive plants in the temperate humid regions of North America, South America, Australia, and New Zealand are of European origin. It may be true that in every broad expanse of the world today where there are dense populations, with whites in the majority, there are also dense populations of European weeds. Thirty-five of eighty-nine weeds listed in 1953 as common in the state of New York are European. Approximately sixty percent of Canada's worst weeds are introductions from Europe. Most of New Zealand's weeds are from the same source, as are many, perhaps most, of the weeds of Australia's well-watered coasts. Most of the European plants that Josselyn listed as naturalized in New England in the seventeenth century are growing wild today in Argentina and Uruguay, and are among the most widespread and troublesome of all weeds in those countries.

In return for this largesse of pestiferous plants, the Lands of the Demographic Takeover have provided Europe with only a few equivalents. The Canadian water weed jammed Britain's nineteenth century waterways, and North America's horseweed and burnweed have spread in Europe's empty lots, and South America's flowered galinsoga has thrived in her gardens. But the migratory flow of a whole group of organisms between Europe and the Lands of the Demographic Takeover has been almost entirely in one direction. Englishman's foot still marches in seven league jackboots across every European colony of settlement, but very few American or Australian or New Zealand invaders stride the waste lands and unkempt backyards of Europe.

European and Old World human beings, domesticated animals, varmints, pathogens, and weeds all accomplished demographic takeovers of their own in the temperate, well-watered regions of North and South America, Australia, and New Zealand. They crossed oceans and Europeanized vast territories, often in informal cooperation with each other — the farmer and his animals destroying native plant cover, making way for imported grasses and forbs, many of which proved more nourishing to domesticated animals than the native equivalents; Old World pathogens, sometimes carried by Old World varmints, wiping out vast numbers of aborigines, opening the way for the advance of the European frontier, exposing more and more native peoples to more and more pathogens. The classic example of symbiosis between European colonists, their animals, and plants comes from New Zealand. Red clover, a good forage for sheep, could not seed itself and did not spread without being annually sown until the Europeans imported the bumblebee. Then the plant and insect spread widely, the first providing the second with food, the second carrying pollen from blossom to blossom for the first, and the sheep eating the clover and compensating the human beings for their effort with mutton and wool.

There have been few such stories of the success in Europe of organisms from the Lands of the Demographic Takeover, despite the obvious fact that for every ship that went from Europe to those lands, another traveled in the opposite direction.

The demographic triumph of Europeans in the temperate colonies is one part of a biological and ecological takeover which could not have been accomplished by human beings alone, gunpowder notwithstanding. We must at least try to analyze the impact and success of all the immigrant organisms together — the European portmanteau of often mutually supportive plants, animals, and microlife which in its entirety can be accurately described as aggressive and opportunistic, an ecosystem simplified by ocean crossings and honed by thousands of years of competition in the unique environment created by the Old World Neolithic Revolution.

The human invaders and their descendants have consulted their egos, rather than ecologists, for explanations of their triumphs. But the human victims, the aborigines of the Lands of the Demographic Takeover, knew better, knew they were only one of many species being displaced and replaced; knew they were victims of something more irresistible and awesome than the spread of capitalism or Christianity. One Maori, at the nadir of the history of his race, knew these things when he said, "As the clover killed off the fern, and the European dog the Maori dog — as the Maori rat was destroyed by the Pakeha [European] rat — so our people, also, will be gradually supplanted and exterminated by the Europeans." The future was not quite so grim as he prophesied, but we must admire his grasp of the complexity and magnitude of the threat looming over his people and over the ecosystem of which they were part.

Ecological Revolutions

CAROLYN MERCHANT

Environmental history has reached a point in its evolution in which explicit attention to the theories that underlie its various interpretations is called for. . . . Theories about the social construction of science and nature that have emerged over the past decade in the wake of Thomas Kuhn's *Structure of Scientific Revolutions* [1962] constitute one approach. They accept the relativist stance toward science set forth in the first edition of Kuhn's book. (He backed away from that position toward a view of the progress of knowledge in a second edition [1970].) Marxist theories that attempt to understand history as constructions of the material-social world existing in particular times and places provide a second influence. The theory of ecological revolutions that follows draws on the above social construction approaches and uses New England as a case study.

Two major transformations in New England land and life took place between 1600 and 1860. The first, a colonial ecological revolution, occurred during the seventeenth century and was externally generated. It resulted in the

Text by Carolyn Merchant from "The Theoretical Structure of Ecological Revolutions," *Environmental Review*, 11 no. 4, Winter, 1987, pp. 265–74. Reprinted with permission from *Environmental History Review*, © 1987, the American Society for Environmental History.

collapse of indigenous Indian ecologies and the incorporation of a European ecological complex of animals, plants, pathogens, and people. It was legitimated by a set of symbols that placed cultured Europeans above wild nature, other animals, and "beastlike savages." It substituted a visual for an oral consciousness and an image of nature as female and subservient to a transcendent male God for an animistic fabric of symbolic exchanges between people and nature.

The second transformation, a capitalist ecological revolution, took place roughly between the American Revolution and about 1860. That second revolution was internally generated and resulted in the reintroduction of soil nutrients and native species. It demanded an economy of increased human labor, land management, and a legitimating mechanistic science. It split human consciousness into a disembodied analytic mind and a romantic emotional sensibility.

My thesis is that ecological revolutions are major transformations in human relations with non-human nature. They arise from changes, tensions, and contradictions that develop between a society's mode of production and its ecology, and between its modes of production and reproduction. Those dynamics in turn support the acceptance of new forms of consciousness, ideas, images, and world views. The course of the colonial and capitalist ecological revolutions in New England may be understood through a description of each society's production, reproduction, and forms of consciousness, the processes by which they broke down, and an analysis of the new relations between the emergent colonial or capitalist society and non-human nature.

Two frameworks of analysis offer springboards for discussing the structure of such ecological revolutions. In *The Structure of Scientific Revolutions* (first edition), Thomas Kuhn approached major transformations in scientific consciousness from a perspective internal to the workings of science and the community of scientists.

One of the strengths of Kuhn's provocative account is its recognition of stable world views in science that exist for relatively long periods but are rapidly transformed during times of crisis and stress. One of its limitations is its failure to incorporate an interpretation of social forces external to the daily activities of science practitioners in their laboratories and field stations. Social and economic circumstances affect internal developments in scientific theories, at least indirectly. A viewpoint that incorporates social, economic, and ecological changes is required for a more complete understanding of scientific change.

A second approach to revolutionary transformations is that of Karl Marx and Friedrich Engels. According to their base/superstructure theory of history, social revolutions begin in the economic base of a particular social formation and result in a fairly rapid transformation of the legal, political, and ideological superstructure. In the most succinct statement of his theory of history, Marx wrote:

> At a certain stage of their development, the material productive forces of society come in conflict with the existing relations of production. . . . Then begins an epoch of social revolution. With the change of the economic foundation the entire immense superstructure is more or less rapidly transformed.

One weakness of that approach is the determinism Marx assigns to the economic base and the sharp demarcation between base and superstructure. But its strength lies in its view of society and change. If a society at a given time can be understood as a mutually supportive structure of dynamically interacting parts, then the process of its breakdown and transformation to a new whole can be described. Both Kuhn's theory of scientific revolution and Marx's theory of social revolution are starting points for a theory of ecology and history.

Science and history are both social constructions. Science is an ongoing negotiation with non-human nature for what counts as reality. Scientists socially construct nature, representing it differently in different historical epochs. Those social constructions change during scientific revolutions. Historians also socially construct the past in accordance with concepts relevant to the historian's present. History is thus a continuing negotiation between the historian and historical sources. Ecology is a particular twentieth-century construction of nature relevant to the concerns of environmental historians.

A scientific world view answers three key questions:

(1) What is the world made of? (the ontological question)
(2) How does change occur? (the historical question)
(3) How do we know? (the epistomological question)

World views such as animism, Aristotelianism, mechanism, and quantum field theory construct answers to these fundamental questions differently.

Environmental history poses similar questions:

(1) What concepts describe the world?
(2) What is the process by which change occurs?
(3) How does a society know the natural world?

The concepts most useful for this approach to environmental history are ecology, production, reproduction, and consciousness. Because of the differences in the immediacy of impact of production, reproduction, and consciousness on non-human nature, a structured, leveled framework of analysis is needed. This framework provides the basis for an understanding of stability as well as evolutionary change and transformation. Although change may occur at any level, ecological revolutions are characterized by major alterations at all three levels. Widening tensions between the requirements of ecology and production in a given habitat and between production and reproduction initiate those changes. Those dynamics in turn lead to transformations in consciousness and legitimating world views. (See Figure 1.)

Since the Scientific Revolution of the seventeenth century, the West has seen nature primarily through the spectacles of mechanistic science. Matter is dead and inert, remaining at rest or moving with uniform velocity in a straight line unless acted on by external forces. Change comes from outside as in the operation of a machine. The world is a clock, adjustable by human clock makers; nature is passive and manipulable.

An ecological approach to history asserts the idea of nature as a historical actor. It challenges the mechanistic tradition by focusing on the interchange of energy, materials, and information among living and non-living beings in the natural environment. Non-human nature is not passive, but an active complex that participates in change over time and responds to human-induced change. Nature is a whole of which humans are only one part. We interact with plants, animals, and soils in ways that sustain or deplete local habitats, but through science and technology, we have greater power to alter the whole in a short period of time.

But like the mechanistic paradigm, the ecological paradigm is a socially constructed theory. Although it differs from mechanism by taking relations, context, and networks into consideration, it has no greater or lesser claim to ultimate truth than do earlier paradigms. Both mechanism and ecology construct their theories through a socially sanctioned process of problem identification, selection and deselection of particular "facts," inscription of the selected facts into texts, and the acceptance of a constructed order of nature by the scientific community. But laboratory and field ecology merge through the replication of laboratory conditions in the field. Farm, field, and forest are

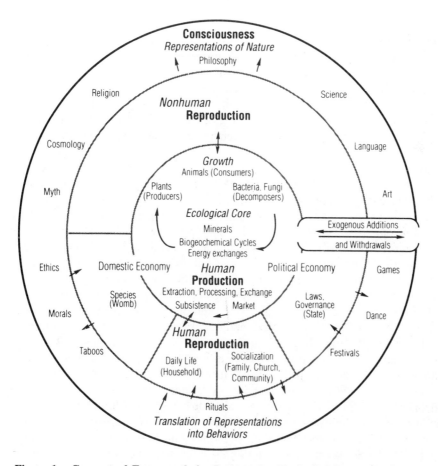

Figure 1.   Conceptual Framework for Interpreting Ecological Revolutions

viewed as an ecological whole that includes both non-human nature and the human designer. The ecological approach of the twentieth century, like the earlier mechanistic one, has resulted from a socially constructed set of experiences sanctioned by scientific authority and a set of social practices and policies.

Production is the human counterpart of "nature's" activity. The need to produce subsistence to reproduce human energy on a daily basis connects human communities with their local environments. Production for subsistence (or use) from the elements (or resources) of nature and the production of surpluses for market exchange are the primary ways in which humans interact directly with the local habitat. An ecological perspective unites the laws of nature with the processes of production through exchanges of energy. All animals, plants, and minerals are energy niches involved in the actual exchange of energy, materials, and information. The relation between human beings and the non-human world is reciprocal; when humans alter their surroundings, "nature" responds to those changes through ecological laws.

Production is the extraction, processing, and exchange of nature's parts as resources. In traditional cultures exchanges are often gifts or symbolic alliances while in market societies they are exchanged as commodities. For much of Western history, humans have produced and bartered food, clothing, and shelter primarily within the local community to reproduce daily life. But when commodities are marketed for profit, as in capitalist societies, they are often removed from the local habitat to distant places and exchanged for money. Marx and Engels distinguished between use-value production, or production for subsistence, and production for profit. When people "exploit" non-human nature, they do so in one of two ways: they either make immediate or personal use of it for subsistence, or they exchange its products as commodities for personal profit or gain.

New England is a significant historical example because several types of production evolved within the bounds of its present geographical area. Native Americans engaged primarily in gathering and hunting in the north and in horticulture in the south. Colonial Americans combined mercantile trade in natural resources with subsistence-oriented agriculture. The market and transportation revolutions of the nineteenth century initiated the transition to capitalist production. Historical bifurcation points within the evolutionary process can be identified *roughly* between 1600 and 1675 (the colonial ecological revolution) and between 1775 and 1860 (the capitalist ecological revolution).

To continue over time, life must be reproduced from generation to generation. The habitat is populated and repopulated with living organisms of all kinds. Biologically, all species must reproduce themselves intergenerationally. For humans, reproduction is both biological and social. Each adult generation must maintain itself, its parents, and its offspring so that human life may continue. And each individual must reproduce its own energy and that of its offspring (intragenerationally) on a daily basis through gathering, growing, or preparing food. Socially, humans must reproduce future laborers by passing on family and community norms. And they must reproduce and maintain the larger social order through the structures of governance and laws (such as property inheritance) and the ethical codes that reinforce behavior.

Thus, although production is twofold—oriented toward subsistence use or market exchange—reproduction is fourfold, having both biological and social articulations.

Reproduction is the biological and social process through which humans are born, nurtured, socialized, and governed. Through reproduction sexual relations are legitimated, population sizes and family relationships are maintained, and property and inheritance practices are reinforced. In subsistence-oriented economies, production and reproduction are united in the maintenance of the local community. Under capitalism production and reproduction separate into two different spheres.

Claude Meillassoux's *Maidens, Meal, and Money* (1981) best explains the necessary connections between biological and social reproduction in subsistence economies. Production, he argues, exists for the sake of reproduction; the production and exchange of human energy are the keys to the reproduction of human life. Food must be extracted or produced to maintain the daily energy of producing adults, to maintain the energy of the children who will be the future producers, and to maintain that of the elders, the past producers. In this way reproducing life on a daily (intragenerational) basis through energy is linked directly to the intergenerational reproduction of the human species.

Although the biological reproduction of life is possible only through the necessary connections between inter- and intragenerational reproduction, the community as a self-perpetuating unit is maintained by social reproduction. In addition, the political, legal, or governmental structures that maintain the mode of production will play the role of reproducing the social whole.

Whereas Meillassoux was interested primarily in the concept of reproduction in subsistence societies, sociologist Abby Peterson examined the gender-sex dimension in politics to formulate an analysis of reproduction in capitalist societies. Under capitalism, the division of labor between the sexes has meant that men bear the responsibility for and dominate the production of exchange commodities, while women bear responsibility for reproducing the work force and social relations. Peterson argues:

> Women's responsibility for reproduction includes both the biological reproduction of the species (intergenerational reproduction) and the intragenerational reproduction of the work force through unpaid labor in the home. Here too is included the reproduction of social relations—socialization.

Under capitalist patriarchy, reproduction is subordinate to production.

Meillassoux's and Peterson's work offers an approach by which the analysis of reproduction can be advanced beyond demography to include daily life and the community itself. The sphere of reproduction is fourfold, having two biological and two social manifestations: (1) the intergenerational reproduction of the species (both human and non-human), (2) the intragenerational reproduction of daily life, (3) the reproduction of social norms within the family and community, and (4) the reproduction of the legal-political structures that maintain social order within the community and the state. The fourfold sphere of reproduction exists in a dynamic relationship with the twofold (subsistence or market-oriented) sphere of production.

Production and reproduction are in dynamic tension. When reproductive patterns are altered, as in population growth or changes in property inheritance, production is affected. Conversely, when production changes, as in the addition or depletion of resources or in technological innovation, reproductive structures are altered. A dramatic change at the level of either reproduction or production can alter the dynamic between them, resulting in a major transformation of the social whole.

Socialist-feminists have further elaborated the interaction between production and reproduction. In a 1976 article, "The Dialectics of Production and Reproduction in History," Renaté Bridenthal argues that changes in production give rise to changes in reproduction, creating tensions between them. For example, the change from an agrarian to an industrial capitalist economy — one that characterized the capitalist ecological revolution — can be described in terms of tensions, contradictions, and synthesis within the gender roles associated with production and reproduction. In the agrarian economy of colonial America, production and reproduction were symbiotic. Women participated in both spheres because the production and reproduction of daily life were centered in the household and domestic communities. Likewise, men working in barns and fields and women working in farmyards and farmhouses socialized children into production. But with industrialization, the production of items such as textiles and shoes moved out of the home into the factory, while farms became specialized and mechanized. Production became more public, reproduction more private, leading to their social and structural separation. For working-class women, the split between production and reproduction imposed a double burden of wage labor and housework; for middle-class women, it led to enforced idleness as "ladies of leisure."

In New England the additional tensions between the requirements of intergenerational reproduction and those of subsistence production in rural areas also stimulated the capitalist ecological revolution. A partible system of patriarchal inheritance meant that farm sizes decreased after three or four generations to the point that not all sons inherited enough land to reproduce the subsistence system. The tensions between the requirements of subsistence-oriented production (a large family labor force) and social reproduction through partible inheritance (all sons must inherit farms) helped create a supply of landless sons, wage laborers for the transition to capitalist agriculture. The requirements of reproduction in its fourfold sense, therefore, came into conflict with the requirements of subsistence-oriented (use-value) production, stimulating a movement toward capital-intensive market production.

Consciousness is the totality of one's thoughts, feelings, and impressions, the awareness of one's acts and volitions. Group consciousness is a collective awareness by an aggregate of individuals. Both environments and culture shape individual and group consciousness. In different historical epochs, particular characteristics dominate a society's consciousness. Those forms of consciousness, through which the world is perceived, understood, and interpreted, are socially constructed and subject to change.

A society's symbols and images of nature express its collective consciousness. They appear in mythology, cosmology, science, religion, philosophy, language, and art. Scientific, philosophical, and literary texts are sources of the ideas and images used by controlling elites, whereas rituals, festivals, songs, and myths provide clues to the consciousness of ordinary people. Ideas, images, and metaphors legitimate human behavior toward nature and are translated into action through ethics, morals, and taboos. According to Charles Taylor, particular intellectual frameworks give rise to a certain range of normative variations and not others, because their related values are not accidental. When sufficiently powerful, world views and their associated values can override social changes. But if they are weak, they can be undermined. A tribe of New England Indians or a community of colonial Americans may have a religious world view that holds it together for many decades while its economy is gradually changing. But eventually with the acceleration of commercial change, ideas that had formerly existed on the periphery, or among selected elites, may become dominant if they support and legitimate the new economic directions.

For Native American cultures, consciousness was an integration of all the bodily senses in sustaining life. In that mimetic consciousness, culture was transmitted intergenerationally through imitation in song, myth, dance, sport, gathering, hunting, and planting. Aural/oral transmission of tribal knowledge through myth and transactions between animals, Indians, and neighboring tribes produced sustainable relations between the human and the non-human worlds. The primal gaze of locking eyes between hunter and hunted initiated the moment of ordained killing when the animal gave itself up so that the Indian could survive. (The very meaning of the gaze stems from the intent look of expectancy when a deer first sees a fire, becomes aware of a scent, or looks into the eyes of a pursuing hunter.) For Indians engaged in an intimate survival relationship with nature, sight, smell, sound, taste, and touch were all of equal importance, integrated in a total participatory consciousness.

When Europeans took over Native American habitats during the colonial ecological revolution, vision became dominant within the mimetic fabric. Although imitative, oral, face-to-face transactions still guided daily life for most colonial settlers and Indians, Puritan eyes turned upward toward a transcendent God who sent down his word in written form in the Bible. Individual Protestants learned to read so that they could interpret God's word for themselves. The biblical word in turn legitimated the imposition of agriculture and artifact in the new land. The objectifying scrutiny of fur trader, lumber merchant, and banker who viewed nature as resource and commodity submerged the primal gaze of the Indians. Treaties and property relations that extracted land from the Indians were codified in writing. Alphanumeric literacy became central to religious expression, social survival, and upward mobility.

The Puritan imposition of a visually oriented consciousness was shattering to the continuation of Indian animism and ways of life. With the commercializing of the fur trade and the missionary efforts of Jesuits and Puritans, a society in which humans, animals, plants, and rocks were equal subjects was changed to one dominated by transcendent vision in which human subjects were separate from resource objects. That change in consciousness characterized the colonial ecological revolution.

Table 1.1   Ecological Revolutions

| | REVOLUTION 1 COLONIAL → | | REVOLUTION 2 CAPITALIST → |
	NATIVE AMERICAN SOCIETY	PREINDUSTRIAL SOCIETY	INDUSTRIAL SOCIETY
Nonhuman nature	Nature as self-active: Corn Mother, active spirits; Active subjects: animals, trees, rocks; Named places	Nature as active vice-regent of God: virgin, mother; Passive objects, commodities; Mapping of space as private property	Nature as passive female: teacher of mechanical laws, moral model; Scientific objects, natural resources; Cartesian grid system to map land and planet
Human production (economy)	Gathering-Hunting-Fishing; Female farming: long-fallow/polycultures	"Extensive," subsistence agriculture, use-value economy in local communities; mercantile trade; Male-Female production spaces	Intensive market agriculture, exchange value economy, market system permeates U.S. interior; Male-dominated machine production
Human reproduction —Biological	Steady state: equilibrium of populations	Growth of population: reproduction of labor force	Demographic transition, sublimation of sexuality into economic production ("spermatic economy")
—Social	Tribal villages: reproduction of daily subsistence	Family farm: farmer as midwife to nature; wife as midwife to humans	Nuclear households: home as sphere of female and mother; emotive, romantic
—Political	Tribal councils	Jeffersonian, agrarian politics	Hamiltonian, market politics
Forms of consciousness	Mimetic consciousness: imitation, equality of all senses	Visual consciousness: domination of visual signs, signatures, written symbols	Analytic consciousness: domination of mental, disembodied intellect, numbering
Symbols of nature	Animism, reciprocity between humans and nature	Organicism, religious retribution, fatalistic acceptance of nature	Mechanism, domination and mastery of nature
Knowledge	Monistic thinking: identification, face-to-face, subject-to-subject relationships	Analogical thinking: sympathy/antipathy, similarities/differences	Dualistic thinking: subject/object, mind/body, male/female

The rise of an analytical, quantitative consciousness was a feature of the capitalist ecological revolution. Capitalist ecological relations emphasized efficient management and control of nature. With the development of mechanistic science and its use of perspective diagrams, visualization was integrated with numbering. The superposition of scientific, quantitative approaches to nature and its resources characterized the capitalist ecological revolution. Through education, analytic consciousness expanded beyond that of dominant elites to include most ordinary New Englanders.

Viewed as a social construction, "nature" (as it was conceptualized in each social epoch—Indian, colonial, and capitalist) is not some ultimate truth that was gradually discovered through the scientific processes of observation, experimentation, and mathematics. Rather, it was a relative, changing structure of human representations of "reality." Ecological revolutions are processes through which different societies change their relationship to nature. They arise from tensions between production and ecology, and between production and reproduction. The results are new constructions of nature, both materially and in human consciousness.

ᵜ *F U R T H E R* *R E A D I N G*

Kendall E. Bailes, ed., *Environmental History: Critical Issues in Comparative Perspective* (1985)

Alfred W. Crosby, *Ecological Imperialism: The Biological Expansion of Europe* (1986)

Roderick Nash, "American Environmental History: A New Teaching Frontier," *Pacific Historical Review* 41 (1972), 362–372

John Opie, "Environmental History: Pitfalls and Opportunities," *Environmental Review* 7 (1938), 8–16

Joseph M. Petulla, *American Environmental History: The Exploitation and Conservation of Natural Resources* (1977)

Lawrence Rakestraw, "Conservation History: An Assessment," *Pacific Historical Review* 43 (1972), 271–288

"Theories of Environmental History," *Environmental Review* 11 (special issue, Winter 1987), 251–305

Richard White, "Historiographical Essay, American Environmental History: The Development of a New Field," *Pacific Historical Review* 54 (1985), 297–335

Donald Worster, "History as Natural History: An Essay on Theory and Method," *Pacific Historical Review* 53 (1984), 1–19

——————, ed., *The Ends of the Earth* (1989)

—————— et al., "A Roundtable: Environmental History," *Journal of American History* 76, 4 (March 1990), 1087–1147

CHAPTER 2

Native American Ecology
and European Contact

☘

Some 30,000 years ago, peoples of Asian origin migrated across the Bering land bridge and then, about 14,000 years ago, down the North American corridor as glaciers melted. They expanded southward and southeastward into North and South America and subsequently eastward as the ice melted, reaching northeastern Canada about 7,500 years ago. As they moved into different environments, they developed ecologically adapted means of subsistence and unique cultures, including technologies for capturing fish, waterfowl, and small and large mammals and for harvesting native plants and cultivating crops. We find two examples of different ecological adaptations in the histories of the Pueblo Indians of the arid American Southwest and the Micmac Indians of the wetter, colder Northeast.

At the time these Native Americans encountered Europeans in the fifteenth century, the Pueblos were living in walled, multistoried pueblos and practicing settled, irrigated agriculture. Their incipient "hydraulic" societies were growing maize, beans, and squash, hunting antelope, and gathering wild desert fruits. In contrast, the Micmac Indians in the region that is now the Gaspé Peninsula of Canada (just below the mouth of the St. Lawrence River) lived above the latitude at which maize could reliably be harvested and were a nomadic gathering-hunting-fishing people.

Encounters between Pueblos and Spanish in the Southwest and between Micmacs and French in the Northeast altered the ecological habitats and the cultures of these Native Americans. Although the transformation processes in the two cases shared similarities, they were also different. Spanish explorers moving north from Mexico into Pueblo territory sought gold, silver, and copper in the mesa lands of the Southwest; European fishers and fur traders extracted living organisms from the Gaspé region for the European trade. Both groups brought with them devastating components of what Alfred Crosby called their portmanteau biota—European diseases such as smallpox, measles, diphtheria, and bubonic plague—to which Native Americans had no immunity, the Bering ice fields having long ago filtered out those disease-bearing microbes. A smallpox pandemic in 1520–1524 probably reached the Pueblos, causing a mortality rate above 50 percent, followed by measles in 1531–1533 and bubonic plague in 1545–1548. The Micmacs probably were affected by smallpox epidemics that occurred in the Northeast in 1639, 1649–1650, 1669–1670, 1677–1679 and 1687–1691 and by measles in 1633–1634 and 1658–1659. These diseases undercut the Indians' ability to reproduce themselves and their cultures, increasing their vulnerability and receptivity to missionary teachings. Jesuit and Franciscan missionaries undermined the Indians' earth-based orally transmitted religions as "superstitious" and converted them to a belief in a transcendent male god who sent down his written word in the Bible.

The Spanish and French introduced other ecological components of the portmanteau biota to the regions as well. These included livestock such as horses, cattle, goats, and sheep; crops such as Old World grains, peas, and vegetables; and weeds and varmints. These imports altered the native ecology but added to the Indians' subsistence. In the Northeast, the fur trade changed the local ecology, transformed Indians' traditional relationships with the animals they hunted, and created a market for European manufactured goods such as metal hunting and fishing implements, kettles, and blankets. These examples of the Pueblos and the Micmacs illustrate possible interactions among ecology, production, reproduction, and ideas about nature.

≬ D O C U M E N T S

Because Native American cultures were transmitted orally and visually through stories, dance, pottery, baskets, costumes, and masks, the earliest written records of Indian beliefs and ways of life come mainly from European explorers, missionaries, artists, and other observers. The documents in this section reflect the viewpoints and cultural biases of the Europeans who explored and colonized the New World. The first document, a report by Hernán Gallegos of an expedition in 1580 to what is now New Mexico, describes the roles of Pueblo Indian men and women in producing their subsistence — foods, clothing, and shelter. The second selection, a narrative by Spanish explorer Antonio de Espejo, a member of the Chamuscado–Rodríguez expedition of 1582, reveals the extent to which Pueblo villages successfully developed and relied on irrigation to create large surpluses of stored foods.

The third document presents the 1601 testimony of Ginés de Herrera Horta, a twenty-five-year-old legal assessor and auditor who was sent to work for colonizer Don Juan de Oñate. Horta was appearing at an investigation, ordered by the Spanish viceroy, into Oñate's activities in New Mexico. He reports on Oñate's brutality toward the Pueblos and reveals changes in Indian attitudes toward the Spanish since colonization in 1598.

The fourth and fifth documents were written by missionaries who lived with the Micmac Indians of the Gaspé Peninsula. They record not only the Indians' methods and ethics of hunting and food preparation but also their transformation under the fur trade. In the fourth selection, dating from 1672, the Jesuit Nicolas Denys discusses Micmac life before and after the fur trade; the final document, from 1691, features the recollections of Father Chrestien Le Clercq on the ways in which hunters imitated the habits of their prey, adhered to rituals for disposing of their remains, and respected the power of menstruating women.

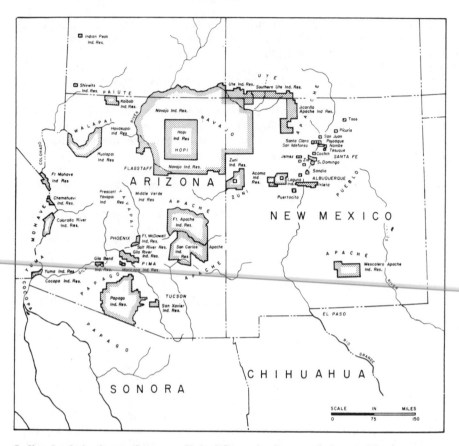

Indian lands in the southwestern United States in the twentieth century

Map from *The Pueblo Indians of North America* by Edward P. Dozier, copyright © 1970 by Holt, Rinehart and Winston, Inc., reprinted by permission of the publisher.

A Spanish Explorer Views the Pueblos, 1580

The people sustain themselves on corn, beans, and calabashes. They make tortillas and corn-flour gruel (*atole*), have buffalo meat and turkeys — they have large numbers of the latter. There is not an Indian who does not have a corral for his turkeys, each of which holds a flock of one hundred birds. The natives wear Campeche-type cotton blankets, for they have large cotton fields. They raise many small shaggy dogs — which, however, are not like those owned by the Spaniards — and build underground huts in which they keep these animals. . . .

Excerpts from "[Hernán Lamero] Gallegos' Relation of the Chamuscado-Rodríguez Expedition," Trans. and ed. by George P. Hammond and Agapito Rey. *The Rediscovery of New Mexico, 1580–1594*, The University of New Mexico Press, 1966, vol. 3, excerpts from pp. 83–6; originally published in Sante Fe, NM, 1927; translation from original in Archivo General de Indias at Seville. Reprinted by permission of University of New Mexico Press.

After we took our leave of this people, the Indians led us to a large pueblo of another nation, where the inhabitants received us by making the sign of the cross with their hands in token of peace, as the others had done before. As the news spread, the procedure in this pueblo was followed in the others.

We entered the settlement, where the inhabitants gave us much corn. They showed us many ollas and other earthenware containers, richly painted, and brought quantities of calabashes and beans for us to eat. We took a little, so that they should not think we were greedy nor yet receive the impression that we did not want it; among themselves they consider it disparaging if one does not accept what is offered. One must take what they give, but after taking it may throw it away wherever he wishes. Should one throw it to the ground, they will not pick it up, though it may be something they can utilize. On the contrary, they will sooner let the thing rot where it is discarded. This is their practice. Thus, since we understood their custom, we took something of what they gave us. Moreover, we did this to get them into the habit of giving freely without being asked. Accordingly, they all brought what they could. The supply of corn tortillas, corn-flour gruel, calabashes, and beans which they brought was such that enough was left over every day to feed five hundred men. Part of this the natives carried for us. The women make tortillas similar to those of New Spain, and tortillas of ground beans, too. In these pueblos there are also houses of three and four stories, similar to the ones we had seen before; but the farther one goes into the interior the larger are the pueblos and the houses, and the more numerous the people.

The way they build their houses, which are in blocks, is as follows: they burn the clay, build narrow walls, and make adobes for the doorways. The lumber used is pine or willow; and many rounded beams, ten and twelve feet long, are built into the houses. The natives have ladders by means of which they climb to their quarters. These are movable wooden ladders, for when the Indians retire at night, they pull them up to protect themselves against enemies since they are at war with one another.

These people are handsome and fair-skinned. They are very industrious. Only the men attend to the work in the cornfields. The day hardly breaks before they go about with hoes in their hands. The women busy themselves only in the preparation of food, and in making and painting their pottery and *chicubites*, in which they prepare their bread. These vessels are so excellent and delicate that the process of manufacture is worth watching; for they equal, and even surpass, the pottery made in Portugal. The women also make earthen jars for carrying and storing water. These are very large, and are covered with lids of the same material. There are millstones on which the natives grind their corn and other foods. These are similar to the millstones in New Spain, except that they are stationary; and the women, if they have daughters, make them do the grinding.

These Indians are very clean people. The men bear burdens, but not the women. The manner of carrying loads, sleeping, eating, and sitting is the same as that of the Mexicans, for both men and women, except that they carry water in a different way. For this the Indians make and place on their heads a cushion of palm leaves, similar to those used in Old Castile, on top of which they place and carry the water jar. It is all very interesting.

The women part their hair in Spanish style. Some have light hair, which is surprising. The girls do not leave their rooms except when permitted by their parents. They are very obedient. They marry early; judging by what we saw, the women are given husbands when seventeen years of age. A man has one wife and no more. The women are the ones who spin, sew, weave and paint. Some of the women, like the men, bathe frequently. Their baths are as good as those of New Spain.

In all their valleys and other lands I have seen, there are one hundred pueblos. We named the region the province of San Felipe and took possession of it in the name of his Majesty by commission of his Excellency, Don Lorenzo Suárez de Mendoza, Count of Coruña, viceroy, governor and captain-general of New Spain.

Spanish Explorers Observe Pueblo Irrigation, 1582

They have fields planted with corn, beans, calabashes, and tobacco (*piciete*) in abundance. These crops are seasonal, dependent on rainfall, or they are irrigated by means of good ditches. They are cultivated in Mexican fashion, and in each planted field the worker has a shelter, supported by four pillars, where food is carried to him at noon and he spends the siesta; for usually the workers stay in their fields from morning until night just as do the people of Castile. . . .

We left the province of the Emexes, and after going west for three days, some fifteen leagues, came to a pueblo named Acoma, which we thought had more than six thousand souls. Acoma is built on top of a lofty rock, more than fifty estados high, and out of the rock itself the natives have hewn stairs by which they ascend and descend to and from the pueblo. It is a veritable stronghold, with water cisterns at the top and quantities of provisions stored in the pueblo. Here the Indians gave us many blankets and chamois skins, belts made from strips of buffalo hide that had been dressed like Flanders leather, and abundant supplies of corn and turkeys.

These people have their fields two leagues distant from the pueblo, near a medium-sized river, and irrigate their farms by little streams of water diverted from a marsh near the river. Close to the sown plots we found many Castile rosebushes in bloom; and we also found Castile onions, which grow wild in this land without being planted or cultivated. In the adjacent mountains there are indications of mines and other riches, but we did not go to inspect them because the natives there were numerous and warlike.

The mountain dwellers, who are called Querechos, came down to serve the people in the towns, mingling and trading with them, bringing them salt, game (such as deer, rabbits, and hares), dressed chamois skins, and other goods in exchange for cotton blankets and various articles accepted in payment. Their form of government and other characteristics were the same as in the rest of the provinces. They held a solemn ceremonial dance for us, in which the people dressed very gaily and performed juggling tricks, including some with live snakes that were quite elaborate, all of which was most interesting to watch.

These Indians presented us with ample provisions of everything they had, and then, after three days, we left their province.

A Spaniard Testifies on the Effects
of Pueblo Colonization, 1601

In Mexico, July 30, 1601, Factor Don Francisco de Valverde called as witness the bachiller, Ginés de Herrera Horta, a resident of this city, who took his oath in due legal manner and promised to tell the truth. On being questioned the witness stated that he went to the provinces of New Mexico about a year and a half ago, more or less, as chief auditor and legal assessor to Don Juan de Oñate, governor of the said provinces. . . . They reached the pueblo of San Gabriel, New Mexico, which is the place where Don Juan de Oñate has established his headquarters. The whole region is pacified and the natives of that district have rendered obedience to his majesty, all by the efforts of Don Juan de Oñate. . . .

Asked how long he stayed in New Mexico, the witness said that he remained there three or four months, more or less. The reason that he remained only such a short time was that the governor refused to recognize the commission which he brought as auditor and legal assessor. In view of this, the witness asked his permission to return. . . .

Asked what good and bad experiences the Spaniards had encountered, what opposition, what modes of offense or defense the Indians had offered from the time the governor arrived in the province until March 23 of the present year, . . . the witness declared that two days before he started out from the camp, the commissary of the friars, Fray Juan de Escalona, of the seraphic order of Saint Francis, . . . took him to the secrecy of his cell, and told him . . . in detail what had happened to the Indians of a pueblo named Acoma, which is situated on a high rock.

. . . Don Juan de Zaldívar, nephew of the governor, . . . had gone with twelve or fourteen men to explore and seek new things not yet known. . . . They came to the pueblo of Acoma, where they asked the Indians for provisions. The natives furnished them some, and the Spaniards proceeded on their journey about two leagues beyond the pueblo.

Then the maese de campo, Captain Escalante, Diego Núñez, and other men turned back to ask again for provisions, fowl, and blankets, and even to take them by force. When the Indians saw this, they began to resist and to defend themselves. This witness was told that the Spaniards had killed one or two Indians. Then the Indians killed the maese de campo and Diego Núñez and the others with rocks and slabs of stone. When the governor learned of this, he declared war by fire and sword against the Indians of the pueblo. . . . He set out with seventy soldiers to punish the aforesaid Indians. Afraid of what the Spaniards might do, the natives refused to surrender, but defended themselves.

Thus the punishment began, lasting almost two days, during which many Indians were killed. Finally, overcome and exhausted from the struggle, the

Excerpts from George P. Hammond and Agapito Rey. *Don Juan de Oñate, Colonizer of New Mexico, 1595–1628*, University of New Mexico Press, 1953, pp. 643–56, excerpts. Reprinted by permission of University of New Mexico Press.

Indians gave up, offering blankets and fowl to the sargento mayor and his soldiers, who refused to accept them. Instead, the sargento mayor had the Indians arrested and placed in an estufa [hole]. Then he ordered them taken out one by one, and an Indian he had along stabbed them to death and hurled them down the rock. When other Indian men and women, who had taken shelter in other estufas, saw what was going on, they fortified themselves and refused to come out. In view of this, the sargento mayor ordered that wood be brought and fires started and from the smoke many Indian men, women, and children suffocated. This witness was told that some were even burned alive. All of the men, women, and children who survived were brought to the camp as prisoners. The governor ordered the children placed in the care of individuals. The men and women from eighteen to nineteen years of age were declared slaves for twenty years. Others were maimed by having their feet cut off; this witness saw some of them at the said camp. He was told that most of the slaves had run away, that they had tried to reestablish the pueblo, and that the governor neither authorized nor prevented this, but dissimulated, although this witness heard that he wanted to send someone or go himself to see the said pueblo. . . . The reason why the commissary charged this witness on his conscience to tell this story was because he considered the punishment and enslavement of the Indians unjust and that the viceroy should order the prisoners liberated. . . .

The Indians of [Jumanes pueblo] are all orderly, peaceful, and timid, and live in great fear of the Spaniards.

Asked how many Spaniards there were in the said provinces at the time he left, the witness said that there were about one hundred and fifty soldiers, forty-two to fifty of them married.

Asked what cattle there were in those provinces and that Don Juan had at his camp for the service and provisioning of his people, the witness said he thought that there might be one thousand head of sheep and goats, more or less. He saw most of this livestock at a pueblo named Santa Clara, and at San Miguel, in the care of a certain Naranjo. The rest of the animals were at the camp. This witness did not see any mares, but he heard that there were some, though he did not learn how many. He heard that they had taken fifteen hundred horses on the first expedition, of which many were lost; some died and others were found shot with arrows. He heard that altogether, including those taken at first as well as those sent with the reinforcements, there might be five hundred left. As for the cattle, when this witness arrived at the said camp, he noticed that they were not slaughtering or eating beef because the cattle had been consumed. Some told him that they had slaughtered the oxen they had used to pull their carts, and that they were plowing with horses. So he thinks that there may be four hundred head of cattle left, which are those that were taken with the reinforcements. Of these, they have been killing seven animals each week. This provides a very limited supply of meat for each soldier, so they do not eat it throughout the week. This witness understands that the said stock will soon be exhausted, because he heard it said that they do not reproduce very well in that land. On the contrary, the stock will give out, as he has stated. As for oxen, there are no more left than those taken with the carts when the reinforcement was sent, and these number perhaps one hundred and fifty. As to mules, there must be two hundred and fifty or three hundred, including those which came with the carts taken by the friars. . . .

Asked whether the governor had levied any tribute or personal service on the friendly and peaceful Indians under his jurisdiction to work the fields, harvest the crops, or do other necessary labors in his camp, the witness said that all he knows is that every month the soldiers go out by order of the governor to all the pueblos to procure maize. The soldiers go in groups of two or three and come back with the maize for their own sustenance. The Indians part with it with much feeling and weeping and give it of necessity rather than of their own accord, as the soldiers themselves told this witness. If any kernels fall on the ground, the Indians follow and pick them up, one by one. This witness has seen this happen many times. Some of the Indians, men and women, who formerly lived at this pueblo where the camp now is, remained there and bring wood and water for the Spaniards, so that the latter would give them some maize. This witness has seen it himself. He was told that the Indians store their maize for three and four years to provide against the sterility of the land, for it rains very seldom, although there is much snow, which helps to moisten the ground so that they may harvest what they plant.

The tribute which the governor has levied on the Indians requires that each resident give a cotton blanket per year. Those who have no blankets give tanned deerskins and buffalo hides, dressed in their usual manner. The lack of blankets is due to the scarcity of cotton grown there. This witness has seen the cotton next to the maize fields of the Indians. He was assured that, in the pueblos where the soldiers went, if the natives said that they had no blankets to give, the soldiers took them from the backs of the Indian women and left them naked. . . .

As for personal services, this witness does not know that they have been imposed on the natives, except that when there is need to repair a house the Spaniards ask the governor's permission to bring some Indian women to repair it, for, as he has stated, the women are the ones who do this. The Spaniards also employ Indians to help plant the vegetables and cultivate the soil. This witness has seen Spaniards plowing all by themselves, without the assistance of Indians. He has heard that wheat does very well, and that this is because at the camp there is water for irrigation, which is not found elsewhere, and so wheat is grown only there. He does not know nor has he heard that it is planted anywhere else. . . .

The people are also troubled by the sterility of the land, so they will lack provisions for some time to come, and also because the Indians are few and the pueblos more than eighty leagues apart, including those that are said to have more people, as they are at that distance from the camp. For these reasons, this witness does not think that the people could be maintained without great cost to his majesty in provisions, clothing, and other things. Even if his majesty should incur much expense to help them, this witness believes that if the people were free to choose they would prefer to abandon the land and seek their livelihood around here. He never heard a single one say that he was there of his own will, but through force and compulsion. What his excellency, the viceroy of New Spain, should know and remedy is that the orders he transmits to those regions are neither obeyed nor carried out. . . .

So this witness considers the preservation of those provinces very difficult, for the reasons stated. All of this is the truth, under his oath; and he ratified his testimony. He said that he was twenty-five years old, more or less, and that the general questions of the law did not concern him. Signed, DON FRANCISCO DE VALVERDE MERCADO. LICENTIATE GINÉS HERRERA HORTA. Before me, MARCOS LEANDRO, royal notary.

Nicholas Denys on the Micmac Fur Trade, 1672

The hunting by the Indians in old times was easy for them. They killed animals only in proportion as they had need of them. When they were tired of eating one sort, they killed some of another. If they did not wish longer to eat meat, they caught some fish. They never made an accumulation of skins of Moose, Beaver, Otter, or others, but only so far as they needed them for personal use. They left the remainder where the animals had been killed, not taking the trouble to bring them to their camps. . . .

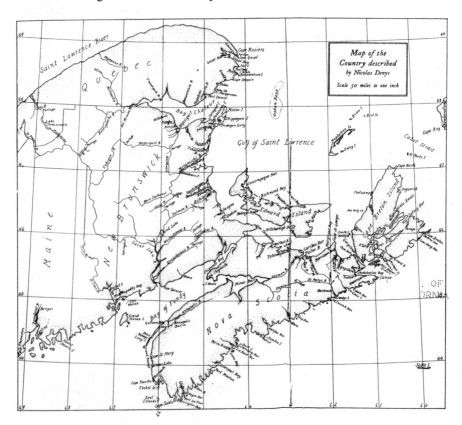

Map of the Country described by Nicolas Denys
Scale 50 miles to one inch

The Indians to-day practise still their ancient form of burial in every respect, except that they no longer place anything in their graves, for of this they are entirely disabused. They have abandoned also those offerings, so frequent and usual, which they made as homage to their *manitou* [spirit] in passing by places in which there was some risk to be taken or where indeed there had happened some misfortune [or other].

Since they cannot now obtain the things which come from us with such ease as they had in obtaining robes of Marten, of Otter, or of Beaver, [or] bows and arrows, and since they have realised that guns and other things were not found in their woods or in their rivers, they have become less devout. Or, it would be better to say, [they have become] less superstitious since the time when their offerings have cost them so much. But they practise still all the same methods of hunting, with this difference, however, that in place of arming their arrows and spears with the bones of animals, pointed and sharpened, they arm them to-day with iron, which is made expressly for sale to them. Their spears now are made of a sword fixed at the end of a shaft of seven to eight feet in length. These they use in winter, when there is snow, to spear the Moose, or for fishing Salmon, Trout, and Beaver. They are also furnished with iron harpoons, of the use of which we have spoken before.

The musket is used by them more than all other weapons, in their hunting in spring, summer, and autumn, both for animals and birds. With an arrow they killed only one Wild Goose; but with the shot of a gun they kill five or six of them. With the arrow it was necessary to approach an animal closely: with the gun they kill the animal from a distance with a bullet or two. The axes, the kettles, the knives, and everything that is supplied them, is much more convenient and portable than those which they had in former times, when they were obliged to go to camp near their grotesque kettles, in place of which to-day they are free to go camp where they wish. One can say that in those times the immovable kettles were the chief regulators of their lives, since they were able to live only in places where these were.

With respect to the hunting of the Beaver in winter, they do that the same as they did formerly, though they have nevertheless nowadays a greater advantage with their arrows and harpoons armed with iron than [they had] with the others which they used in old times, and of which they have totally abandoned the use.

But at present, and since they have frequented the fishing vessels, they drink in quite another fashion. They no longer have any regard for wine, and wish nothing but brandy. They do not call it drinking unless they become drunk, and do not think they have been drinking unless they fight and are hurt. However, when they set about drinking, their wives remove from their wigwams the guns, axes, the mounted swords [spears], the bows, the arrows, and [every weapon] even their knives, which the Indians carry hung from the neck. . . .

At the present time, so soon as the Indians come out of the woods in spring, they hide all their best skins, bringing a few to the establishments in order to obtain their right to something to drink, eat, and smoke. They pay a part of that which was lent them in the autumn to support them, without which they would perish of hunger. They insist that this is all their hunting for the winter has produced. As soon as they have departed, they go to recover the skins which they have hidden in the woods, and go to the routes of the fishing ships and keep watch. If they see any vessels, they make great smokes to let it be known that they are there. . . .

A peschipoty is anything which is closed by a string or secured like a purse, provided that the whole does not surpass in size a bag for holding prayer-books. They are made of Marten, of Squirrel, of Muskrat, or other little animals; others are of Moose skin, or of Sealskin. . . . Those made of skins have strings like the purses, and all those peschipotys serve to hold tobacco or lead for hunting. The Indian women fix the price to the fishermen according to the kind of skin and its fantastic ornamentation, which they call *matachiez*; it is made from Porcupine quills, white, red, and violet, and sometimes with their wampum, of which I have already spoken. With these they obtain many things from the sailors.

The women and the older girls also drink much but by stealth, and they go to hide themselves in the woods for that purpose. The sailors know well the rendezvous. It is those who furnish the brandy, and they bring them into so favourable a condition that they can do with them everything they will. All these frequentations of the ships have entirely ruined them, and they care no longer for Religion. . . . Such is the great difference between their present customs and those of the past. . . .

A Jesuit Missionary Recalls
Micmac Hunting Rituals, 1691

The most ingenious method which our Gaspesians have for taking the Moose is this. The hunters, knowing the place on the river where it is accustomed to resort when in heat, embark at night in a canoe, and, approaching the meadow where it has its retreat, browses, and usually sleeps, one of them imitates the cry of the female, while the other at the same time takes up water in a bark dish, and lets it fall drop by drop, as if it were the female relieving herself of her water. The male approaches, and the Indians who are on the watch kill him with shots from their guns. The same cunning and dexterity they also use with respect to the female, by counterfeiting the cry of the male.

The hunting of the Beaver is as easy in summer as it is laborious in winter, although it is equally pleasing and entertaining in both of these two seasons, because of the pleasure it is to see this animal's natural industry, which transcends the imagination of those who have never seen the surprising evidences thereof. Consequently the Indians say that the Beavers have sense, and form a separate nation; and they say they would cease to make war upon these animals if these would speak, howsoever little, in order that they might learn whether the Beavers are among their friends or their enemies.

The Beaver is of the bigness of a water-spaniel. Its fur is chestnut, black, and rarely white, but always very soft and suitable for the making of hats. It is the great trade of New France. The Gaspesians say that the Beaver is the beloved of the French and of the other Europeans, who seek it greedily; and I have been unable to keep from laughing on overhearing an Indian, who said to me in banter, *Tahoé messet kogoüar pajo ne daoüi dogoüil mkobit.* "In truth, my brother, the Beaver does everything to perfection. He makes for us kettles, axes, swords, knives, and gives us drink and food without the trouble of cultivating the ground." . . .

[The beaver] cuts trees into pieces of different lengths, according to the use it wishes to make of them. It rolls them on the ground or pushes them through the water with its forepaws, in order to build its house and to construct a dam which checks the current of a stream and forms a considerable pond, on the shore of which it usually dwells. There is always a master Beaver, which oversees this work, and which even beats those that do their duty badly. They all cart earth upon their tails, marching upon their hind feet and carrying in their fore-paws the wood which they need to accomplish their work. They mix the earth with the wood, and make a kind of masonry with their tails, very much as do the masons with their trowels. They build causeways and dams of a breadth of two or three feet, a height of twelve or fifteen feet, and a length of twenty or thirty; these are so·inconvenient and difficult to break that this is in fact the hardest task in the hunting of the Beaver, which, by means of these dams, makes from a little stream a pond so considerable that they flood very often a large extent of country. They even obstruct the rivers so much that it is often necessary to get into the water in order to lift the canoes over the dams, as has happened several times to myself. . . .

The Beaver does not feed in the water, as some have imagined. It takes its food on land, eating certain barks of trees, which it cuts into fragments and transports to its house for use as provision during the winter. Its flesh is delicate, and very much like that of mutton. The kidneys are sought by apothecaries, and are used with effect in easing women in childbirth, and in mitigating hysterics.

Whenever the Beaver is hunted, whether this be in winter or in summer, it is always needful to break and tear down the house, all the approaches to which our Indians note exactly, in order, with greater assurance of success, to besiege and attack this animal which is entrenched in his little fort.

In Spring and Summer they are taken in traps; when one of these is sprung a large piece of wood falls across their backs and kills them. But there is nothing so interesting as the hunting in the winter, which is, nevertheless, very wearisome and laborious. For the following is necessary; one must break the ice in more than forty or fifty places: must cut the dams: must shatter the houses: and must cause the waters to run off, in order to see and more easily discover the Beavers. These animals make sport of the hunter, scorn him, and very often escape his pursuit by slipping from their pond through a secret outlet, which they have the instinct to leave in their dam in communication with another neighbouring pond. . . .

The bones of the beaver are not given to the dogs, since these would lose, according to the opinion of the Indians, the senses needed for the hunting of the beaver. No more are they thrown into the rivers, because the Indians fear lest the spirit of the bones of this animal would promptly carry the news to the other beavers, which would desert the country in order to escape the same misfortune.

They never burned, further, the bones of the fawn of the moose, nor the carcass of martens; and they also take much precaution against giving the same to the dogs; for they would not be able any longer to capture any of these animals in hunting if the spirits of the martens and of the fawns of the moose were to inform their own kind of the bad treatment they had received among the Indians.

. . . The women and girls, when they suffer the inconveniences usual to their sex, are accounted unclean. At that time they are not permitted to eat with the others, but they must have their separate kettle, and live by themselves. The girls are not allowed, during that time, to eat any beaver, and those who eat of it are reputed bad; for the Indians are convinced, they say, that the beaver, which has sense, would no longer allow itself to be taken by the Indians if it had been eaten by their unclean daughters. Widows never eat of that which has been killed by the young men; it is necessary that a married man, an old man, or a prominent person of the nation shall be the one who hunts or fishes for their support. So scrupulously do they observe this superstitious custom that they still at this day relate with admiration how a Gaspesian widow allowed herself to die of hunger rather than eat moose or beaver which was left in her wigwam even in abundance, because it was killed by young men, and widows were not permitted to eat it. . . .

❦ E S S A Y S

In the first selection, Ramón Gutiérrez, a professor of history at the University of California at San Diego, argues that when Jesus came to the society of the Pueblos, their "corn mothers" went away. He relates how the Pueblos' creation stories explain these Indian peoples' emergence from the earth, their belief in the gifts of the corn mothers, and their rituals of corn planting and animal hunting. He discusses how sixteenth-century explorations of the Southwest led ultimately to the breakdown of the Pueblo way of life under Spanish colonizers and Franciscan missionaries, who forcibly took over the Pueblos and installed Catholic churches and belief systems. The Franciscans' domesticated animal herds, crops, and plows offered Indian men and boys new roles, and their "Virgin Mary" rituals accommodated and transformed the native corn-mother rituals. By contrast, Calvin Martin of Rutgers University theorizes in the second selection that the Micmac Indians, devastated by diseases that undermined their morale, abandoned their belief in the spiritual power of animals and that, in response to the fur trade, they overharvested their moose herds and beaver colonies. Both writers stress the role of beliefs in the maintenance of cultural ecology but offer different views on the process of transformation of Indian cultures by Europeans.

Pueblos and Spanish in the Southwest

RAMÓN GUTIÉRREZ

In the beginning two females were born underneath the earth at a place called Shipapu. In total darkness Tsichtinako (Thought Woman) nursed the sisters, taught them language and gave them each a basket that their father Uchtsiti had sent them containing the seeds and fetishes of all the plants and animals that were to exist in the world. Tsichtinako told the sisters to plant the four pine tree seeds they had in their basket and then to use the trees to ascend to the light. One grew so tall that it pushed a hole through the earth. Before the sisters climbed up the tree from the underworld, Thought Woman taught them how to praise the Sun with prayer and song. Every morning as the Sun rose, they would thank him for bringing them to the light by offering with outstretched hands sacred cornmeal and pollen. To the tones of the creation song, they would blow the offering to the sky, asking for long life, happiness, and success in all their endeavors.

When the sisters reached the earth's surface it was soft, spongy, and not yet ripe. So they waited for the Sun to appear. When it rose, the six directions of the cosmos were revealed to them: the four cardinal points, the earth below, and the four skies above. The sisters prayed to the Sun, and as they did, Thought Woman named one of the girls Iatiku and made her Mother of the Corn clan; the other she named Nautsiti, Mother of the Sun clan.

"Why were we created?" they asked. Thought Woman answered, "Your father Uchtsiti made the world by throwing a clot of his blood into space, which by his power grew into the earth. He planted you within it so that you would bring to life all the things in your baskets in order that the world be complete for you to rule over it." . . .

After Thought Woman departed, Iatiku took earth from her basket and made the season spirits: Shakako, the ferocious spirit of winter, Morityema, the surly spirit of spring, Maiyochina, the warm spirit of summer, and Shruisthia, the grumpy spirit of fall. Iatiku told the people that if they prayed properly to these spirits they would bring moisture, warmth, ripening, and frost, respectively.

Next Iatiku, their Corn Mother, took dirt from her basket and created the katsina, the Cloud-Spirits or ancestor dead who were to live beneath a lake in the West at Wenimats. Tsitsanits (Big Teeth) was brought to life first as ruler of the katsina, then many other katsina were brought to life. Some looked like birds with long beaks and bulging eyes, others had large animal snouts, and still others were moon creatures with horns sticking out of their heads like lunar crescents. "Your people and my people will be combined," Iatiku told the katsina. "You will give us food from your world and we will give you food from our world. Your people are to represent clouds; you are to bring rain." Iatiku then took cornmeal and opened a road four lengths long so that the

Excerpts reprinted from *When Jesus Came, The Corn Mothers Went Away: Marriage, Sexuality, and Power in New Mexico* by Ramón A. Gutiérrez with the permission of the publishers, Stanford University Press. © 1991 by the Board of Trustees of the Leland Stanford Junior University.

katsina could travel to Wenimats and along which they would return when called.

"Now we are going to make houses," said Corn Mother. Suddenly a house made of dirt and trees grew out of the earth resembling in shape the mesa and mountain homes of the season deities. Each of Iatiku's daughters constructed a house for their children and when they were all ready, Iatiku laid them out into a town. "All is well but . . . we have no sacred place, we have no *kaach* [kiva]," Iatiku said. She taught the oldest man of the Oak clan how to build religious houses underneath the earth's surface to resemble Shipapu, the place of emergence.

The people did not have a father of the game animals, so Iatiku appointed a Shaiyaik (Hunt Chief), taught him the songs and prayers of the hunt, gave him an altar, and showed him how to make stone fetishes and prayer sticks to secure the power of the prey animals. . . .

The origin myth of the Acoma Indians just presented likened human life to plant life. Seeds held the potential to generate life. When planted deep within Mother Earth and fertilized by the sky's vivifying rain, seeds germinated, grew into plants, and eventually bore seeds that repeated the cycle of life. Like a sprouting maize shoot rooted in the earth or a child coming forth from its mother's womb, so the Pueblo Indians described their emergence from the underworld.

All of the Pueblos have origin myths that dramatically depict the ideological structure of their world. Myths express the values and ideals that organize and make people's lives meaningful. They explain how the universe was created, its various components, and the tensions and balances that kept it intact. . . . Like the life contained within a seed that sprouts, bears fruit, and dies, only to be reborn again from a seed, so the Pueblo Indians conceived of time and of their historical past.

Gift exchange in Pueblo society created dyadic status relationships between givers and receivers. A gift properly reciprocated with a countergift established the exchanging parties as equals, there being no further claim one could make of the other. If a gift giver initiated an exchange with a highly respected or knowledgeable person to obtain blessings, religious endowments, or ritual knowledge, such as when a parent offered a medicine man gifts so that he would present their child to the rising sun, the obligation created was fulfilled through a proper countergift. But if only one side gave and the other side could not reciprocate, the receiver out of gratitude had to give the presenter unending obedience and respect. . . .

From the moment of their creation the Corn Mothers were indebted to their father for the baskets he had given them. Since they had nothing to give him in return, they did as Tsichtinako instructed, daily singing his praises and offering him food. Humans and animals, just like their mythic ancestors, were bound by these rules of reciprocity in gifting, noted Fray Alonso de Benavides in 1634:

> If they went hunting, they would offer meal to the heads of deer, rabbits, hares, and other dead animals that they had in their houses, believing that this

would enable them to catch much game. When they wanted to go fishing, they first offered meal into the river, hoping by this means to obtain a big catch. . . . Whenever they went to war they offered meal and other things to the scalps of the enemy nation which they had brought back as trophies of those they had slain. . . .

The Pueblo Indians viewed the relations between the sexes as relatively balanced. Women and men each had their own forms of wealth and power, which created independent but mutually interdependent spheres of action. The corn fetish every child was given at birth and the flint arrowhead with which boys were endowed symbolized these relations and expressed the basic preoccupations of a people living in a semi-arid environment. Corn and flint were food and water, but they were also the cosmic principles of femininity and masculinity. Female and male combined as corn seeds and rain combined to perpetuate life. Corn plants without rain would shrivel and die; water without corn was no life at all. The ear of corn infants received represented the Corn Mothers that had given life to all humans, plants, and animals. At Acoma Pueblo this corn fetish is still called Iatiku, because it contains her heart and breath. For this reason too the Hopi called this corn fetish "mother." "Corn is my heart, it will be to [you] . . . as milk from my breasts," Zia's Corn Mother told her people. Individuals kept this corn fetish throughout their entire lives, for if crops failed its perfect seeds held the promise of a new crop cycle.

If the corn ear represented the feminine generative powers latent in seeds, the earth, and women, the flint arrowhead represented the masculine germinative forces of the sky. Father Sun gave men flint arrowheads to bring forth rain, to harness heat, and to use as a weapon in the hunt. The noise emitted by striking together two pieces of flint resembled the thunder and lightning that accompanied rain. Rain fertilized seeds as men fertilized their women. Without rain or semen life could not continue. The flint arrowhead was the sign of the hunter and warrior. Sun gave his sons, the Twin War Gods, arrowheads with which to give and take away life. From flint too came fire. When men struck flint and created that gift Sun gave them at the beginning of time, they transformed that which was raw into that which was cooked. To the Pueblo Indians flint, rain, semen, and hunting were to male as corn, earth, and childbearing were to female. . . .

Large portions of a woman's day were spent preparing meals for her household. Corn, beans, and squash were the main staples of the diet. Corn was the most important and symbolic of these. It was boiled whole, toasted on the cob, or dried and ground into a fine powder easily cooked as bread or gruel. Every day a woman and her daughters knelt before metates, grinding corn to feed their gods, their fetishes, and their kin. The women worked joyfully at this task, observed Castañeda in 1540. "One crushes the maize, the next grinds it, and the third grinds it finer. While they are grinding, a man sits at the door playing a flageolet, and the women move their stones, keeping time with the music, and all three sing together." . . .

Men's spatial location in village life correlated closely with their roles in the sexual division of labor. Three distinct but overlapping spaces were defined as masculine. The first zone was created through kinship and marriage obligations to women. Sons had to work their mothers' corn plots, brothers those of their sisters, husbands those of their mothers-in-law. "The men attend to the work in the cornfields," observed Gallegos in 1582. "The day hardly breaks before they go about with hoes in their hands." He continued: "The men bear burdens, but not the women." When wood was needed for the construction of a house or to stoke the cooking fires, the household's matriarch dispatched the men to "bring the firewood . . . and stack it up," noted Castañeda in 1540. . . .

The men of every pueblo considered their town to be the center of the universe and placed their main kiva at the vortex of a spatial scheme that extended outward to the four cardinal points, upward to the four skies above, and downward to the underworld. Kivas were usually round (sometimes square) subterranean structures that conjoined space and time to reproduce the sacred time of emergence. Located at the center of the kiva's floor was the *shipapu*, the earth's navel, through which the people emerged from the underworld and through which they would return.

The kiva was circular to resemble the sky. A hole in the center of the roof, the only entrance and source of light, symbolized the opening through which the Corn Mothers climbed onto the earth's surface. The profane space outside and the sacred space within the kiva were connected by a ladder called "rainbow" made of the same pine tree the sisters had used to emerge. The kiva floor had a fire altar that commemorated the gift of fire, and a hollow, dug-out place that represented the door to the house of the Sun, the Moon, and the mountains of the four cardinal points. The walls had altars on which were placed stone fetishes representing all the animals and deities of the world.

Rain was the Pueblo Indians' central preoccupation and the essential ingredient for fecundity. Men recognized that Mother Earth and women had immense capacities to bring forth life, but to realize this potential the sky had to fructify the earth with rain and men their wives with semen. Thus what the people worshipped most, said Hernando de Alarcón in 1540, was "the sun and water." Why did they worship water? According to Coronado it was "because it makes the maize grow and sustains their life, and that the only other reason they know is that their ancestors did so."

The rain chief was one of the most powerful men in every village because he knew how to conjure rain both by calling Horned Water Snake and the katsina. The Pueblos equated serpentine deities with rain. The Horned Water Serpent of the Pueblos united the vertical levels of the cosmos. He lived both upon the earth and below it and so combined the masculine germinative forces of the sky (rain) with the feminine generative power of the earth (seeds). The phallic representations of Horned Water Snake were cloaked in feathers as a god of lightning and rain. The earliest Pueblo rock drawings depict him as a zigzag line with a horned triangular head and as a lightning snake attached to a cloud burst.

Horned Water Serpent was also feminine and lunar. "Sun is male, Moon is female," maintain the Acoma Indians. The serpent's ability to shed its skin and to be born anew undoubtedly resembled the moon's birth and death every 28 days. In decorative motifs the measured zigzags of the lightning snake and the coiled spiral of the rattlesnake evoked those rhythms governed by the moon: the rains, the agricultural calendar, and a woman's menstrual flow. Water Serpent's horns, too, were lunar. Each horn represented the moon's crescent; with two, the lunar cycle was complete.

Horned Water Serpent, then, provided the Pueblo Indians with fecundity and abundance by joining together the levels of the cosmos (sky/earth, earth/underworld) and social existence (male/female, life/death).

The Pueblo Dead — the katsina — were also potent rain spirits tied to the living in bonds of reciprocity. It was the rain chief who knew how to call the katsina and did so by offering them prayer sticks and gifts, asking them to visit with rain, food, and fertility. Katsina lived at the place of emergence underneath lakes and on mountain tops. Missives to the katsina were dispatched as puffs of smoke, which as mimetic magic beckoned the cloud spirits to visit. At death Puebloans became clouds. That is why to this day the Hopi harangue their dead saying: "You are no longer a Hopi, you are a Cloud. When you get yonder you will tell the chief to hasten the rain clouds hither." . . .

Hunting practices for rabbit, antelope, deer, and buffalo were all very similar. We focus here on deer hunting because deer meat was the most abundant and highly prized, and because men thought of women as two-legged deer. A deer hunt was organized whenever food reserves were low, when a ceremonial was to be staged, or when the katsina were going to visit.

For four days the hunt chief led the hunt society's members in song, prayer, prayer-stick making, and smokes. . . . During these four days, and for four days after the hunt, men were sexually continent. Hunters believed that animals disliked the smell of women and would not allow themselves to be captured by a man so contaminated. To rid himself of such odor, a hunter purified his body with emetic drinks and smokes. If a man was to accomplish his goal, neither his mind nor his heart could be dissipated by the thought of women.

The hunt began on the fourth day. Transformed into the animals they hunted, the hunters donned deerskins with the head and antlers still attached. The hunt chief selected the hunting ground and dispersed the men around its edges, forming a large circle. Slowly the circumference of the circle tightened and the deer became exhausted. Finally the deer were wrestled to the ground and choked. A deer was suffocated so that its breath and spirit would be reborn as more game, and because only the skins of suffocated animals could be used as hunt costumes. . . . The carcass was then carried back to the pueblo, where it was adopted into the hunter's maternal household through ritual intercourse and ritual feeding. "We are glad you have come to our home and have not been ashamed of our people," Acoma's women would tell the deer as they offered it cornmeal. The hunter's relatives rubbed their hands over the deer's body and then across their own faces to obtain its beauty and strength. Finally, the hunter purified himself with juniper smoke so that the deer spirit would not haunt him. The meat was divided between the hunt chief who had taught the boy how to hunt and the hunter's household of affiliation. . . .

In a largely horticultural society women asserted and could prove that they had enormous control and power over seed production, child-rearing, household construction, and the earth's fertility. Men admitted this. But they made a counterclaim that men's ability to communicate with the gods and to control life and death protected the precarious balance in the universe by forestalling village factionalism and dissent. . . .

These, then, were the contours of Pueblo Indian society in the sixteenth century. Each pueblo was an aggregation of sedentary horticulturists living in extended matrilineal households, supplementing their existence through hunting and warfare. Elders controlled the organization of production and, through the distribution of its fruits as gifts and ritual blessings, perpetuated the main inequalities of life; the inequality between juniors and seniors and between successful and unsuccessful seniors. The household and all the activities symbolically related to it belonged to women; the kivas and the pueblo's relationships with its gods was the province of men. That said, we turn . . . to discuss the arrival of the Spanish conquistadores. . . .

From the conquistadores' perspective, the Pueblo Indians were an inferior breed close to savages: "a people without capacity," "stupid," and "of poor intelligence." Marveling at the houses he saw at the Zuñi pueblos in 1540, Coronado's comments are telling: "I do not think that they have the judgment and intelligence needed to be able to build these houses in the way in which they are built, for most of them are entirely naked."

Coronado's troops . . . reconnoitered the Tusayan (Hopi) pueblos of eastern Arizona, the Grand Canyon, and Quivira, a land east of New Mexico, which the Indians said was rich in gold, silver, and silks. The infantry that had been slowly marching north . . . arrived . . . in late November 1540 . . . proceeded to Alcanfor Pueblo in Tiguex province (near Bernalillo) for the winter because it had abundant food.

The intensity of that winter brought exploration temporarily to a halt. The troops huddled at Alcanfor rapidly succumbed to hunger and cold. Coronado's troops extracted blankets and corn from the Tiguex pueblos by force, and when the soldiers satisfied their lust with Indian women but gave nothing in return, the Indian men declared war. The Spaniards retaliated with their own war of blood and fire, ordering "200 stakes be driven into the ground to burn them alive." One hundred warriors were burned at the stake and hundreds more were massacred as they fled the Spaniards.

When the spring thaw arrived, Coronado renewed his search for Quivira (villages of the Wichita Indians, in Kansas), which he beheld in August 1541. But there was no gold!

Throughout the autumn and winter of 1541, Coronado's troops shivered in the cold, hungry and constantly engaged in Indian skirmishes. And so, when news reached Coronado in April 1542 that the Indians of Sonora were in rebellion, he and his forces abandoned New Mexico, bringing to a close the first period of Spanish interest in the area.

From 1581 to 1680, Franciscans provided the impetus for colonization in New Mexico. For most of this period the friars were virtual lords of the land. They organized the Indians into a theocracy that lasted until the Pueblo Revolt in 1680. . . . The Franciscans organized two expeditions to reconnoiter New Mexico: one, in 1581, was led by Fray Agustín Rodríguez, under the command of Francisco Sánchez Chamuscado; the other, in 1582, was led by Antonio de Espejo, and was ostensibly to rescue two friars who had remained in the Pueblos after the 1581 expedition.

Glowing reports from the Franciscans about New Mexico reached King Philip II, and as a result, license was issued in 1595 to one of New Spain's most illustrious sons, Don Juan de Oñate, for the conquest and colonization of the Kingdom of New Mexico. . . . The mightier, well-fortified towns received the conquistadores as they did other visiting tribes, gifting and hosting them as a sign of goodwill. At "the great pueblo of the Emes [Jémez]," wrote Oñate in his itinerary, "the natives came out to meet us, bringing water and bread." At Acoma "the Indians furnished us liberally with maize, water, and fowls." And at the Hopi Pueblos "the natives came out to welcome us with tortillas, scattering powdered flour over us and our horses as a sign of peace and friendship . . . and gave us a fine reception." . . .

What the Puebloans thought they gave as gifts, the *españoles* thought had been surrendered as tribute. Indeed, the surface calm that had greeted the colonizers erupted violently in December 1598, precisely over the meaning of Indian gifts and how cheerfully they should be surrendered. . . . When a soldier named Vivero stole two turkeys, a bird sacred to the Indians, and violated an Indian maiden, Acoma's warriors attacked, killing Zaldívar and twelve men. A few soldiers survived the fracas by jumping off the edge of Acoma's mesa to the sand dunes below. With the sentinels that had been left watching the horses they retreated to San Juan. Oñate encountered the survivors of Acoma's battle on December 13 as he was returning from Zuñi to San Juan. Immediately, plans were made to punish Acoma. If the colony was to survive, stern and swift action would have to be taken. Oñate reasoned that any hesitation might be interpreted by the Indians as a sign of weakness and might encourage other pueblos to similar rebellions. . . . When the fighting ended, 800 Indian men, women, and children lay dead. Eighty men and 500 women and children were taken as prisoners to Santo Domingo to stand trial. . . .

Acoma's residents were found guilty of murder and failing to surrender willingly the provisions the Spaniards demanded. . . . Oñate informed the viceroy that if the colony was to survive, reinforcements were necessary. On Christmas eve, 1600, 73 men arrived. . . .

[But] many of the kingdom's settlers . . . returned to New Spain, complaining that the province contained no precious metals, that the climate was harsh, that the natives were ferocious, that a drought in 1600 had caused widespread starvation, and that Oñate was a selfish, power hungry, and elusive manager of colonial affairs. The Franciscans, eager to limit the number of civilians in New Mexico, supported the settlers' grievances and chimed in with a few of their own. Oñate lived "dishonorably and scandalously with women . . . married and unmarried." He had been excessively harsh with the Indians, extracting food and clothing through torture, allowing his soldiers to abuse women, thereby severely hampering conversions. According to the friars the Indians understandably asked, "if [you] who are Christians cause so much harm and violence, why should [we] become Christians?" Unable to answer the question, the friars thought it best if the settlers left and the province remained a mission field. . . .

. . . The Franciscans established . . . charismatic domination over the Pueblo Indians. . . . They attempted to portray themselves to the Indians as supermen who controlled the forces of nature. . . . One of the first functions the friars assumed was that of potent rain chiefs. Because the Pueblo cosmology was not very different from that of the Indians of central Mexico, the friars were well aware of the symbolic power of rain in the Pueblo belief system. . . . When the[y] . . . entered San Juan Pueblo, they found the earth parched and the crops wilted for lack of rain. The friars constructed a cross, prayed for rain, and ordered the Indians to do likewise. Then, "while the sky was as clear as a diamond, exactly twenty-four hours after the outcry had gone up, it rained . . . so abundantly that the crops recovered." San Juan's inhabitants rejoiced and presented many feathers, corn meal, and other gifts to the crucifix and to the friars. . . .

The friars' animal magic . . . far exceeded anything hunt chiefs could conjure. The only animals the Pueblos had domesticated were the turkey, for its feathers rather than for its meat, and the dog, as a beast of burden. The appearance of friars shepherding enormous flocks of docile animals, their escorts riding atop horses that were stronger, faster, and more obedient than any animal they had ever seen before, was quite astounding. The rapid reproduction of the European herds, which, according to a 1634 account by Fray Alonso de Benavides, nearly doubled every fifteen months, and the introduction of beef, pork, and mutton into the native diet marginalized the role of the hunt chiefs. Here was a permanent, year-round meat supply that, at least for the moment, was not the object of intense competition between neighboring villages and Athapaskan bands, or subject to the vicissitudes of the hunt chiefs' magic.

. . . The padres won female allies by protecting women's rights, by respecting some of the spatial loci of their power, by instructing them that men and women were equal before God, and by allowing them to continue their worship of the Corn Mother, albeit transmogrified as the Blessed Virgin Mary. Throughout the colonial period, when men—Indian or Spanish—engaged in extramarital sex with native women and failed to reciprocate with gifts, it was the friars who protected women's rights, demanding redress from the culprits. Pueblo women, much like their European counterparts, retained control of the household and over the rearing of children, particularly of the girls who were of little import to the friars. Pueblo women were barred from active participation in male rites. So it was also under Christian rule: women served the priests as auxiliaries, cleaned the church and its altar linens, baked the communion bread, prepared food for feasting, and witnessed men's power to communicate with the gods.

The friars posed not only as fathers to their Indian parishioners, but also as mothers, offering them all the religious, social, and economic benefits of maternity. Among the matrilineal Puebloans, the mother provided one's clan name, totemically named household fetishes, care and sustenance through adolescence, and the use of seeds and land on which to cultivate them. The friar as *mater* offered the young very similar gifts, thereby indebting the children to him. At baptism they were given Christian names by the priest. He was the keeper of the Christian fetishes (religious statuary, devotional pictures, relics, and so on). Daily he called them for instruction in the Gospel and the mores of civilization. At the mission boys received wheat and vegetable seeds, fruit trees, plows and hoes to work the land more efficiently, beasts of burden to expand their cultivation, and most important of all, the recognition of land rights vested in men. Pueblo boys had little contact with their fathers before their adolescent katsina initiation into a kiva. The missions presented the children a radically different model of adult male behavior. Here were grown men caring for children. In church the youths saw images of St. Anthony of Padua fondling the infant Christ, of St. Christopher carrying the Christ child on his shoulders, and of St. Joseph holding his foster son in his arms. That the Franciscans poured so much energy into the care and rearing of juveniles must have reinforced the perception that the friars were also mothers, much as Pueblo town chiefs were regarded as the father and mother of all people.

The gifts Indian children obtained from their Franciscan "mothers" were experienced as losses by their natal mothers. Assessing the erosion of power Pueblo women experienced as a result of the Spanish conquest, we see the contours of what Friedrich Engels described in *The Origins of Family, Private Property and the State*, as the "historic overthrow of Mother Right." Conquest by a patriarchal society meant that Pueblo women lost to men their exclusive rights to land, to child labor, to seeds, and even to children. A thorough discussion of this process is beyond our scope. Here, suffice it to say that all of the Puebloans were matrilineal at the time of the conquest, and that those Puebloans who were in closest contact with Spanish towns became patrilineal or bilateral. Those Puebloans who most resisted Christianization — the Hopi, the Zuñi, and the Keres at Acoma — remained matrilineal. Among these people we still find a vibrant array of women's fertility societies, spirited ceremonials to vivify the earth, and a host of descendant earth-bound symbols that celebrate femininity. Among the Puebloans who became most acculturated to European ways — the Tewa and the Keres (except Acoma) — women's fertility societies were suppressed, their dances to awaken men's germinative powers were outlawed as too sinful, and, given the explicit phallic symbolism of the Snake Dance and the "demonic" character of the katsina dances, these elements of Pueblo ceremonialism largely disappeared. The native symbolism that remained was almost totally ascendant and masculine (sun, fire, arrows, and eagles) — symbols that meshed well with those of European patriarchal religion.

. . . The summer solstice celebrated Mother Earth's fecundity and the secret of life the Corn Mothers had given humanity. The prominence of the Mater Dolorosa in the passion plays and the Way of the Cross was certainly one attempt to gloss this seasonal gender disparity, for throughout the Old World and the New, the Blessed Virgin Mary was frequently presented to neophytes as a metamorphosed grain goddess. To accommodate the Indians' summer fertility rituals, Holy Week was followed closely by a time dedicated to Mary, the month of May. By the eighteenth century, Mary and the Corn Mothers had been merged in religious iconography and myth. The Virgin now appeared cloaked in garb decorated with corn ears and stalks with the moon at her feet, surrounded by flowers and butterflies, Indian symbols of fertility. . . .

For Indian residents of small New Mexican pueblos constantly under attack, despoiled of their food, and forced to abandon well-watered spots, the mission fathers offered the semblance of protection. In numbers there was strength, and behind the massive wall of the mission compound there was security. Christianization to these persons meant a reliable meat supply, iron implements of various sorts, and European foods: wheat, legumes, green vegetables, melons, grapes, and a variety of orchard fruits. It does not strain the imagination to envision why such persons, understandably nervous and ambivalent at the arrival of the "Children of the Sun," might have allied themselves as Christians with the new social order.

Micmacs and French in the Northeast

CALVIN MARTIN

Among the first North American Indians to be encountered by Europeans were the Micmacs who occupied present-day Nova Scotia, northern New Brunswick and the Gaspé Peninsula, Prince Edward Island, and Cape Breton Island. According to the Sieur de Dièreville, they also lived along the lower St. John River with the Malecites, who outnumbered them. For our present purposes, the Micmac territory will be considered an ecosystem, and the Micmac occupying it will be regarded as a local population. These designations are not entirely arbitrary, for the Micmac occupied and exploited the area in a systematic way; they had a certain psychological unity or similarity in their ideas about the cosmos; they spoke a language distinct from those of their neighbors; and they generally married within their own population. There were, as might be expected, many external factors impinging on the ecosystem which should also be evaluated, although space permits them only to be mentioned here. Some of these "supralocal" relations involved trade and hostilities with other tribes; the exchange of genetic material and personnel with neighboring tribes through intermarriage and adoption; the exchange of folklore and customs; and the movements of such migratory game as moose and woodland caribou. The Micmac ecosystem thus participated in a regional system, and the Micmac population was part of a regional population.

The hunting, gathering, and fishing Micmac who lived within this Acadian forest, especially along its rivers and by the sea, were omnivores (so to speak) in the trophic system of the community. At the first trophic level, the plants eaten were wild potato tubers, wild fruits and berries, acorns and nuts, and the like. Trees and shrubs provided a wealth of materials used in the fashioning of tools, utensils, and other equipment. At the time of contact, none of the Indians living north of the Saco River cultivated food crops. Although legend credits

Abridged from "The European Impact on the Culture of a Northeastern Algonquin Tribe: An Ecological Interpretation," by Calvin Martin from *William and Mary Quarterly*, 31, Jan. 1974, pp. 7–26. Reprinted by permission of the author.

the Micmac with having grown maize and tobacco "for the space of several years," these cultigens, as well as beans, pumpkins, and wampum (which they greatly prized), were obtained from the New England Algonquians of the Saco River area (Abnakis) and perhaps from other tribes to the south.

Herbivores and carnivores occupy the second and third trophic levels respectively, with top carnivores in the fourth level. The Micmac hunter tapped all three levels in his seasonal hunting and fishing activities, and these sources of food were "to them like fixed rations assigned to every moon." In January, seals were hunted when they bred on islands off the coast; the fat was reduced to oil for food and body grease, and the women made clothing from the fur. The principal hunting season lasted from February till mid-March, since there were enough marine resources, especially fish and mollusks, available during the other three seasons to satisfy most of the Micmacs' dietary needs. For a month and a half, then, the Indians withdrew from the seashore to the banks of rivers and lakes and into the woods to hunt the caribou, moose, black bear, and small furbearers. At no other time of the year were they so dependent on the caprice of the weather: a feast was as likely as a famine. A heavy rain could ruin the beaver and caribou hunt, and a deep, crustless snow would doom the moose hunt.

Since beaver were easier to hunt on the ice than in the water, and since their fur was better during the winter, this was the chief season for taking them. Hunters would work in teams or groups, demolishing the lodge or cutting the dam with stone axes. Dogs were sometimes used to track the beaver which took refuge in air pockets along the edge of the pond, or the beaver might be harpooned at air holes. In the summer hunt, beaver were shot with the bow or trapped in deadfalls using poplar as bait, but the commonest way to take them was to cut the dam in the middle and drain the pond, killing the animals with bows and spears.

Next to fish, moose was the most important item in the Micmac diet, and it was their staple during the winter months when these large mammals were hunted with dogs on the hard-crusted snow. In the summer and spring, moose were tracked, stalked, and shot with the bow; in the fall, during the rutting season, the bull was enticed by a clever imitation of the sound of a female urinating. Another technique was to ensnare the animal with a noose.

Moose was the Micmacs' favorite meat. The entrails, which were considered a great delicacy, and the "most delicious fat" were carried by the triumphant hunter to the campsite, and the women were sent after the carcass. The mistress of the wigwam decided what was to be done with each portion of the body, every part of which was used. Grease was boiled out of the bones and either drunk pure (with "much gusto") or stored as loaves of moose-butter; the leg and thigh bones were crushed and the marrow eaten; the hides were used for robes, leggings, moccasins, and tent coverings; tools, ornaments, and game pieces were made from antlers, teeth, and toe bones, respectively. According to contemporary French observers, the Micmac usually consumed the moose meat immediately, without storing any, although the fact that some of the meat was preserved rather effectively by smoking it on racks, so that it would even last the year, demonstrates that Micmac existence was not as hand-to-mouth as is commonly believed of the northeastern Algonquian. Black bear were also taken during the season from February till mid-March, but such hunting was merely coincidental. If a hunter stumbled upon a hibernating bear, he could count himself lucky.

As the lean months of winter passed into the abundance of spring, the fish began to spawn, swimming up rivers and streams in such numbers that "everything swarms with them." In mid-March came the smelt, and at the end of April the herring. Soon there were sturgeon and salmon, and numerous waterfowl made nests out on the islands — which meant there were eggs to be gathered. Mute evidence from seashore middens and early written testimony reveal that these Indians also relied heavily on various mollusks, which they harvested in great quantity. Fish was a staple for the Micmac, who knew the spawning habits of each type of fish and where it was to be found. Weirs were erected across streams to trap the fish on their way downstream on a falling tide, while larger fish, such as sturgeon and salmon, might be speared or trapped.

The salmon run marked the beginning of summer, when the wild geese shed their plumage. Most wildfowl were hunted at their island rookeries; waterfowl were often hunted by canoe and struck down as they took to flight; others, such as the Canadian geese which grazed in the meadows, were shot with the bow.

In autumn, when the waterfowl migrated southward, the eels spawned up the many small rivers along the coast. From mid-September to October the Micmac left the ocean and followed the eels, "of which they lay in a supply; they are good and fat." Caribou and beaver were hunted during October and November, and with December came the "tom cod" (which were said to have spawned under the ice) and turtles bearing their young. In January the subsistence cycle began again with the seal hunt.

As he surveyed the seasonal cycle of these Indians, Father Pierre Biard was impressed by nature's bounty and Micmac resourcefulness: "These then, but in a still greater number, are the revenues and incomes of our Savages; such, their table and living, all prepared and assigned, everything to its proper place and quarter." Although we have omitted mention of many other types of forest, marine, and aquatic life which were also exploited by the Micmac, those listed above were certainly the most significant in the Micmacs' food quest and ecosystem.

Frank G. Speck, perhaps the foremost student of northeastern Algonquian culture, has emphasized that hunting to the Micmacs was not a "war upon the animals, not a slaughter for food or profit." Denys's observations confirm Speck's point: "Their greatest task was to feed well and to go a hunting. They did not lack animals, which they killed only in proportion as they had need of them." From this, and the above description of their effective hunting techniques, it would appear that the Micmac were not limited by their hunting technology in the taking of game. As Denys pointed out, "the hunting by the Indians in old times was easy for them. . . . When they were tired of eating one sort, they killed some of another. If they did not wish longer to eat meat, they caught some fish. They never made an accumulation of skins of Moose, Beaver, Otter, or others, but only so far as they needed them for personal use. They left the remainder [of the carcass] where the animals had been killed, not taking the trouble to bring them to their camps." Need, not technology, was the ruling factor, and need was determined by the great primal necessities of life and regulated by spiritual considerations. Hunting, as Speck remarks, was "a *holy occupation*"; it was conducted and controlled by spiritual rules.

The bond which united these physical and biological components of the Micmac ecosystem, and indeed gave them definition and comprehensibility, was the world view of the Indian. The foregoing discussion has dealt mainly with the empirical, objective, physical ("operational") environmental model of the observer; what it lacks is the "cognized" model of the Micmac.

Anthropologists regard the pre-Columbian North American Indian as a sensitive member of his environment, who merged sympathetically with its living and nonliving components. The Indian's world was filled with superhuman and magical powers which controlled man's destiny and nature's course of events. Murray Wax explains:

To those who inhabit it, the magical world is a "society," not a "mechanism," that is, it is composed of "beings" rather than "objects." Whether human or nonhuman, these beings are associated with and related to one another socially and sociably, that is, in the same ways as human beings to one another. These patterns of association and relationship may be structured in terms of kinship, empathy, sympathy, reciprocity, sexuality, dependency, or any other of the ways that human beings interact with and affect or afflict one another. Plants, animals, rocks, and stars are thus seen not as "objects" governed by laws of nature, but as "fellows" with whom the individual or band may have a more or less advantageous relationship.

For the Micmac, together with all the other eastern subarctic Algonquians, the power of these mysterious forces was apprehended as "manitou" — translated "magic power" — much in the same way that we might use the slang word "vibrations" to register the emotional feelings emanating (so we say) from an object, person, or situation.

The world of the Micmac was thus filled with superhuman forces and beings (such as dwarfs, giants, and magicians), and animals that could talk to man and had spirits akin to his own, and the magic of mystical and medicinal herbs — a world where even inanimate objects possessed spirits. Micmac subsistence activities were inextricably bound up within this spiritual matrix, which, we are suggesting, acted as a kind of control mechanism on Micmac land-use, maintaining the environment within an optimum range of conditions.

In order to understand the role of the Micmac in the fur trading enterprise of the colonial period, it is useful to investigate the role of the Micmac hunter in the spiritual world of precontact times. Hunting was governed by spiritual rules and considerations which were manifest to the early French observers in the form of seemingly innumerable taboos. These taboos connoted a sense of cautious reverence for a conscious fellow-member of the same ecosystem who, in the view of the Indian, allowed itself to be taken for food and clothing. The Indian felt that "both he and his victim understood the roles which they played in the hunt; the animal was resigned to its fate."

That such a resignation on the part of the game was not to be interpreted as an unlimited license to kill should be evident from an examination of some of the more prominent taboos. Beaver, for example, were greatly admired by the Micmac for their industry and "abounding genius"; for them, the beaver had "sense" and formed a "separate nation." Hence there were various regulations associated with the disposal of their remains: trapped beaver were drawn in public and made into soup, extreme care being taken to prevent the soup from spilling into the fire; beaver bones were carefully preserved, never being given to the dogs — lest they lose their sense of smell for the animal — or thrown into the fire — lest misfortune come upon "all the nation" — or thrown into rivers — "because the Indians fear lest the spirit of the bones . . . would promptly carry the news to the other beavers, which would desert the country in order to escape the same misfortune." Likewise, menstruating women were forbidden to eat beaver, "for the Indians are convinced, they say, that the beaver, which has sense, would no longer allow itself to be taken by the Indians if it had been eaten by their unclean daughters." The fetus of the beaver, as well as that of the bear, moose, otter, and porcupine, was reserved for the old men, since it was believed that a youth who ate such food would experience intense foot pains while hunting.

Taboos similarly governed the disposal of the remains of the moose — what few there were. The bones of a moose fawn (and of the marten) were never given to the dogs nor were they burned, "for they [the Micmac] would not be able any longer to capture any of these animals in hunting if the spirits of the martens and of the fawns of the moose were to inform their own kind of the bad treatment they had received among the Indians." Fear of such reprisal also prohibited menstruating women from drinking out of the common kettles or bark dishes. Such regulations imply cautious respect for the animal hunted. The moose not only provided food and clothing, but was firmly tied up with the Micmac spirit-world — as were the other game animals.

Bear ceremonialism was also practiced by the Micmac. Esteem for the bear is in fact common among boreal hunting peoples of northern Eurasia and North America, and has the following characteristics: the beast is typically hunted in the early spring, while still in hibernation. It is addressed, when either dead or alive, with honorific names; a conciliatory speech is made to the animal, either before or after killing it, by which the hunter apologizes for his act and perhaps explains why it is necessary; and the carcass is respectfully treated, those parts not used (especially the skull) being ceremonially disposed of and the flesh consumed in accordance with taboos. Such rituals are intended to propitiate the spiritual controller of the bears so that he will continue to furnish game to the hunter. Among the Micmac the bear's heart was not eaten by young men lest they get out of breath while traveling and lose courage in danger. The bear carcass could be brought into the wigwam only through a special door made specifically for that purpose, either in the left or right side of the structure. This ritual was based on the Micmac belief that their women did not "deserve" to enter the wigwam through the same door as the animal. In fact, we are told that childless women actually left the wigwam at the approach of the body and did not return until it had been entirely consumed. By means of such rituals the hunter satisfied the soul-spirit of the slain animal. Of the present-day Mistassini (Montagnais) hunter, Speck writes that "should he fail to observe these formalities an unfavorable reaction would also ensue with his own soul-spirit, his 'great man' . . . as it is called. In such a case the 'great man' would fail to advise him when and where he would find his game. Incidentally the hunter resorts to drinking bear's grease to nourish his 'great man.' " Perhaps it was for a similar reason that the Micmac customarily forced newborn infants to swallow bear or seal oil before eating anything else.

If taboo was associated with fishing, we have little record of it; the only explicit evidence is a prohibition against the roasting of eels, which, if violated, would prevent the Indians from catching others. From this and from the fact that the Restigouche division of the Micmac wore the figure of a salmon as a totem around their neck, we may surmise that fish, too, shared in the sacred and symbolic world of the Indian.

Control over these supernatural forces and communication with them were the principal functions of the shaman, who served in Micmac society as an intermediary between the spirit realm and the physical. The lives and destinies of the natives were profoundly affected by the ability of the shaman to supplicate, cajole, and otherwise manipulate the magical beings and powers. The seventeenth-century French, who typically labeled the shamans (or *buowin*) frauds and jugglers in league with the devil, were repeatedly amazed at the respect accorded them by the natives. By working himself into a dreamlike state, the shaman would invoke the manitou of his animal helper and so predict future events. He also healed by means of conjuring. The Micmac availed themselves of a rather large pharmacopia of roots and herbs and other plant parts, but when these failed they would summon the healing arts of the most noted shaman in the district. The illness was often diagnosed by the *buowin* as a failure on the patient's part to perform a prescribed ritual; hence an offended supernatural power had visited the offender with sickness. At such times the shaman functioned as a psychotherapist, diagnosing the illness and symbolically (at least) removing its immediate cause from the patient's body.

It is important to understand that an ecosystem is holocoenotic in nature: there are no "walls" between the components of the system, for "the ecosystem reacts as a whole." Such was the case in the Micmac ecosystem of precontact times, where the spiritual served as a link connecting man with all the various subsystems of the environment. Largely through the mediation of the shaman, these spiritual obligations and restrictions acted as a kind of control device to maintain the ecosystem in a well-balanced condition. Under these circumstances the exploitation of game for subsistence appears to have been regulated by the hunter's respect for the continued welfare of his prey — both living and dead — as is evident from the numerous taboos associated with the proper disposal of animal remains. Violation of taboo desecrated the remains of the slain animal and offended its soul-spirit. The offended spirit would then retaliate in either of several ways, depending on the nature of the broken taboo: it could render the guilty hunter's (or the entire band's) means of hunting ineffective, or it could encourage its living fellows to remove themselves from the vicinity. In both cases the end result was the same — the hunt was rendered unsuccessful — and in both it was mediated by the same power — the spirit of the slain animal. Either of these catastrophes could usually be reversed through the magical arts of the shaman. In the Micmac cosmology, the overkill of wildlife would have been resented by the animal kingdom as an act comparable to genocide, and would have been resisted by means of the sanctions outlined above. The threat of retaliation thus had the effect of placing an upper limit on the number of animals slain, while the practical result was the conservation of wildlife.

The injection of European civilization into this balanced system initiated a series of chain reactions which, within a little over a century, resulted in the replacement of the aboriginal ecosystem by another. From at least the beginning of the sixteenth century, and perhaps well before that date, fishing fleets from England, France, and Portugal visited the Grand Banks off Newfoundland every spring for the cod, and hunted whale and walrus in the Gulf of St. Lawrence. Year after year, while other, more flamboyant men were advancing the geopolitical ambitions of their emerging dynastic states as they searched for precious minerals or a passage to the Orient, these unassuming fishermen visited Canada's east coast and made the first effective European contact with the Indians there. For the natives' furs they bartered knives, beads, brass kettles, assorted ship fittings, and the like, thus initiating the subversion and replacement of Micmac material culture by European technology. Far more important, the fishermen unwittingly infected the Indians with European diseases, against which the natives had no immunity. Commenting on what may be called the microbial phase of European conquest, John Witthoft has written:

> All of the microscopic parasites of humans, which had been collected together from all parts of the known world into Europe, were brought to these [American] shores, and new diseases stalked faster than man could walk into the interior of the continent. Typhoid, diphtheria, colds, influenza, measles, chicken pox, whooping cough, tuberculosis, yellow fever, scarlet fever, and other strep infections, gonorrhea, pox (syphilis), and smallpox were diseases that had never been in the New World before. They were new among populations which had no immunity to them. . . . Great epidemics and pandemics of these diseases are believed to have destroyed whole communities, depopulated whole regions, and vastly decreased the native population everywhere in the yet unexplored interior of the continent. The early pandemics are believed to have run their course prior to 1600 A.D.

Disease did more than decimate the native population; it effectively prepared the way for subsequent phases of European contact by breaking native morale and, perhaps even more significantly, by cracking their spiritual edifice. It is reasonable to suggest that European disease rendered the Indian's (particularly the shaman's) ability to control and otherwise influence the supernatural realm dysfunctional — because his magic and other traditional cures were now ineffective — thereby causing the Indian to apostatize (in effect), which in turn subverted the "retaliation" principle of taboo and opened the way to a corruption of the Indian-land relationship under the influence of the fur trade.

Much of this microbial phase was of course protohistoric, although it continued well into and no doubt beyond the seventeenth century—the time period covered by the earliest French sources. Recognizing the limitations of tradition as it conveys historical fact, it may nevertheless be instructive to examine a myth concerning the Cross-bearing Micmac of the Miramichi River which, as recorded by Father Chrestien Le Clercq, seems to illustrate the demoralizing effect of disease. According to tradition, there was once a time when these Indians were gravely threatened by a severe sickness; as was their custom, they looked to the sun for help. In their extreme need a "beautiful" man, holding a cross, appeared before several of them in a dream. He instructed them to make similar crosses, for, as he told them, in this symbol lay their protection. For a time thereafter these Indians, who believed in dreams "even to the extent of superstition," were very religious and devoted in their veneration of this symbol. Later, however, they apostatized:

> Since the Gaspesian [Micmac] nation of the Cross-bearers has been almost wholly destroyed, as much by the war which they have waged with the Iroquois as by the maladies which have infected this land, and which, in three or four visitations, have caused the deaths of a very great number, these Indians have gradually relapsed from this first devotion of their ancestors. So true is it, that even the holiest and most religious practices, by a certain fatality attending human affairs, suffer always much alteration if they are not animated and conserved by the same spirit which gave them birth. In brief, when I went into their country to commence my mission, I found some persons who had preserved only the shadow of the customs of their ancestors.

Their rituals had failed to save these Indians when threatened by European diseases and intergroup hostilities; hence their old religious practices were abandoned, no doubt because of their ineffectiveness.

Several other observers also commented on the new diseases that afflicted the Micmac. In precontact times, declared Denys, "they were not subject to diseases, and knew nothing of fevers." By about 1700, however, Dièreville noted that the Micmac population was in sharp decline. The Indians themselves frequently complained to Father Biard and other Frenchmen that, since contact with the French, they had been dying off in great numbers. "For they assert that, before this association and intercourse [with the French], all their countries were very populous, and they tell how one by one the different coasts, according as they have begun to traffic with us, have been more reduced by disease." The Indians accused the French of trying to poison them or charged that the food supplied by the French was somehow adulterated. Whatever the reasons for the catastrophe, warned Biard, the Indians were very angry about it and "upon the point of breaking with us, and making war upon us."

To the Jesuit fathers, the solution to this sorry state of affairs lay in the civilizing power of the Gospel. To Biard, his mission was clear:

> For, if our Souriquois [Micmac] are few, they may become numerous; if they are savages, it is to domesticate and civilize them that we have come here. . . . We hope in time to make them susceptible of receiving the doctrines

of the faith and of the christian and catholic religion, and later, to penetrate further into the regions beyond.

The message was simple and straightforward: the black-robes would enlighten the Indians by ridiculing their animism and related taboos, discrediting their shamans, and urging them to accept the Christian gospel. . . . The priests attacked the Micmac culture with a marvelous fervor and some success. . . .

The result of this Christian onslaught on a decaying Micmac cosmology was, of course, the despiritualization of the material world. Commenting on the process of despiritualization, Denys (who was a spectator to this transformation in the mid-seventeenth century) remarked that it was accomplished with "much difficulty"; for some of the Indians it was achieved by religious means, while others were influenced by the French customs, but nearly all were affected "by the need for the things which come from us, the use of which has become to them an indispensable necessity. They have abandoned all their own utensils, whether because of the trouble they had as well to make as to use them, or because of the facility of obtaining from us, in exchange for skins which cost them almost nothing, the things which seemed to them invaluable, not so much for their novelty as for the convenience they derived therefrom."

In the early years of the fur trade, before the establishment of permanent posts among the natives, trading was done with the coastwise fishermen from May to early fall. In return for skins of beaver, otter, marten, moose, and other furbearers, the Indians received a variety of fairly cheap commodities, principally tobacco, liquor, powder and shot (in later years), biscuit, peas, beans, flour, assorted clothing, wampum, kettles, and hunting tools. The success of this trade in economic terms must be attributed to pressure exerted on a relatively simple society by a complex civilization and, perhaps even more importantly, by the tremendous pull of this simple social organization on the resources of Europe. To the Micmac, who like other Indians measured the worth of a tool or object by the ease of its construction and use, the technology of Europe became indispensable. But as has already been shown, this was not simply an economic issue for the Indian; the Indian was more than just "economically seduced" by the European's trading goods. One must also consider the metaphysical implications of Indian acceptance of the European material culture.

European technology of the sixteenth and seventeenth centuries was largely incompatible with the spiritual beliefs of the eastern woodland Indians, despite the observation made above that the Micmacs readily invested trading goods with spiritual power akin to that possessed by their own implements. As Denys pointed out, the trade goods which the Micmac so eagerly accepted were accompanied by Christian religious teachings and French custom, both of which gave definition to these alien objects. In accepting the European material culture, the natives were impelled to accept the European abstract culture, especially religion, and so, in effect, their own spiritual beliefs were subverted as they abandoned their implements for those of the white man. Native religion lost not only its practical effectiveness, in part owing to the replacement of the traditional magical and animistic view of nature by the exploitive European view, but it was no longer necessary as a source of definition and theoretical support for the new Europe-derived material culture. Western technology made more "sense" if it was accompanied by Western religion.

Under these circumstances in the early contact period, the Micmac's role within his ecosystem changed radically. No longer was he the sensitive fellow-member of a symbolic world; under pressure from disease, European trade, and Christianity, he had apostatized — he had repudiated his role within the ecosystem. Former attitudes were replaced by a kind of mongrel outlook which combined some native traditions and beliefs with a European rationale and motivation. . . .

European contact should thus be viewed as a trigger factor, that is, something which was not present in the Micmac ecosystem before and which initiated a concatenation of reactions leading to the replacement of the aboriginal ecosystem by another. European disease, Christianity, and the fur trade with its accompanying technology — the three often intermeshed — were responsible for the corruption of the Indian-land relationship, in which the native had merged sympathetically with his environment. By a lockstep process European disease rendered the Indian's control over the supernatural and spiritual realm inoperative, and the disillusioned Micmac apostatized, debilitating taboo and preparing the way for the destruction of wildlife which was soon to occur under the stimulation of the fur trade. For those who believed in it Christianity furnished a new, dualistic world view, which placed man above nature, as well as spiritual support for the fur trade, and as a result the Micmac became dependent on the European marketplace both spiritually and economically. Within his ecosystem the Indian changed from conservator to exploiter. All of this resulted in the intense exploitation of some game animals and the virtual extermination of others. Unfortunately for the Indian and the land, this grim tale was to be repeated many times along the moving Indian-white frontier. Life for the Micmac had indeed become more convenient, but convenience cost dearly in much material and abstract culture loss or modification.

The historiography of Indian-white relations is rendered more comprehensible when the Indian and the land are considered together: "So intimately is all of Indian life tied up with the land and its utilization that to think of Indians is to think of land. The two are inseparable." American Indian history can be seen, then, as a type of environmental history, and perhaps it is from this perspective that the early period of Indian-white relations can best be understood.

❦ F U R T H E R   R E A D I N G

Paula Gunn Allen, *The Sacred Hoop: Recovering the Feminine in American Indian Traditions* (1986)

———, *Spider Woman's Granddaughters: Traditional Tales and Contemporary Writing by Native American Women* (1989)

James Axtell, *The European and the Indian: Essays in the Ethnohistory of Colonial North America* (1981)

Gretchen M. Bataille and Kathleen Mullen Sands, *American Indian Women* (1984)

J. Baird Callicott and Thomas W. Overholt, *Clothed-in-Fur and Other Tales: An Introduction to an Ojibwa World View* (1982)

Maria Chona (Papago), *Papago Woman*, ed. Ruth Underhill (1936)

Harold Courlander, *The Fourth World of the Hopis* (1971)

Richard Erdoes and Alfonso Ortiz, eds., *American Indian Myths and Legends* (1984)

Mona Etienne and Eleanor Leacock, eds., *Women and Colonization* (1980)

Jack Forbes, *Apache, Navaho, and Spaniard* (1963)

Geronimo (Apache), *Geronimo: His Own Story,* ed. S. M. Barrett (1966)

Ramon A. Gutiérrez, *When Jesus Came the Corn Mothers Went Away: Marriage, Sexuality, and Power in New Mexico* (1990)

J. Donald Hughes, *American Indian Ecology* (1983)

Harry C. James, *Pages from Hopi History* (1974)

Shepard Kreech III, ed., *Indians, Animals, and the Fur Trade: A Critique of Keepers of the Game* (1981)

Left Handed (Navajo), *Left Handed, Son of Old Man Hatt: A Navaho Autobiography,* ed. Walter Dyk (1938)

Calvin Martin, *Keepers of the Game: Indian-Animal Relationships and the Fur Trade* (1978)

————, ed., *The American Indian and the Problem of History* (1987)

Carolyn Niethammer, *Daughters of the Earth: The Lives and Legends of American Indian Women* (1977)

Alfonso Ortiz, *The Tewa World: Space, Time, Being and Becoming in a Pueblo Society* (1969)

Polingaysi Qoyawayma, *No Turning Back: A Hopi Indian Woman's Struggle to Live in Two Worlds* (1964)

Helen Sekaquaptewa (Hopi), *Me and Mine: The Life Story of Helen Sekaquaptewa as Told to Louise Udall* (1969)

Leslie Marmon Silko (Laguna), *Storyteller* (1981)

Edward Holland Spicer, *Cycles of Conquest: The Impact of Spain, Mexico, and the United States on the Indians of the Southwest, 1533–1960 (1962)*

Don C. Talayesva (Hopi), *Sunchief: The Autobiography of a Hopi Indian* (1974)

John Upton Terrel, *Pueblos, Gods, and Spaniards* (1973)

Christopher Vecsey and Robert W. Venables, eds., *American Indian Environments: Ecological Issues in Native American History* (1980)

Frank Waters, *Book of the Hopi* (1963)

Richard White, "Native Americans and the Environment," in W. R. Swagerty, ed., *Scholars and the Indian Experience* (1984), 179–204

————, *The Roots of Dependency: Subsistence, Environment, and Social Change Among the Choctaws, Pawnees, and Navajos* (1983)

Alber Yava (Tewa-Hopi), *Big Falling Snow: A Tewa-Hopi Indian's Life and Times and the History and Traditions of His People*, ed. Harold Courlander (1978)

CHAPTER 3

The New England Forest
in the Seventeenth Century

❦

*After several abortive attempts, English settlers established the Plymouth colony
in New England in 1620 and the Massachusetts Bay Colony at Boston in 1629.
Seventeenth-century New England had a resource-extractive economy based on
the four Fs: forests, furs, fish, and farms. England provided investors and
manufactures; the colonies, a rich reserve of natural resources.*

*The southern New England Indians whom the English settlers encountered
used cleared patches in the lowland forests to plant corn, beans, and squash and
depended on the upland forests for hunting the animals they needed for meat
and clothing. They "managed" the forests by burning them to accommodate
hunting and travel and to create grassy pastures for deer. The colonists, in
contrast, established settled agriculture, extracting forest resources for subsistence
and trading them for much needed manufactured goods and staples — iron tools,
kettles, nails, guns, ammunition, clothing, windows, paper, coffee, tea, and
sugar.*

*From the perspectives of the beaver and the white pine tree, each extraction
transformed a forest home. Beaver created complex pond ecosystems in the forests
that left tree stumps and brush for grouse, rabbits, and cavity-nesting birds;
watering spots for deer and moose; and foraging sites for foxes, raccoons, bears,
and wildcats. The spruce-hemlock forests of northern New England and the
white pine–oak forests of the region's southern reaches sustained a variety of tree
and bush species, wildflowers, mammals, insects, and birds. The colonists
simplified these ecosystems by trapping beaver for the fur trade and breaking
down their dams for tillage and pasture sites. They converted the forests into
farms and extracted pines for masts, oak for barrel staves, and ash for farm
implements.*

*The colonists added to the complexity of this ecosystem by introducing
European crops (wheat, barley, oats, and rye), livestock (cows, oxen, sheep,
pigs, goats, and chickens), herbs, weeds, varmints, and diseases. These all
affected the composition of the forest. Colonial settled agriculture, moreover,
competed with the Indians' use of forest clearings for horticulture and with the
native peoples' meat and clothing reserves. The arrival of Europeans*

dramatically changed New England's ecology, in turn undercutting the resources that Indians required for subsistence. By the late seventeenth century, the region's Indians, colonists, beaver, and forests all had participated in an ecological revolution that transformed ecology and human production, reproduction, and consciousness.

☙ D O C U M E N T S

The following documents relate the environmental history of the New England forest from several points of view. In the first selection, William Bradford, governor and historian of Plymouth colony, captures the Pilgrims' concept of the forest as a vast wilderness and describes its transformation through trade and farming. Bradford also provides graphic evidence of the devastating effects of smallpox on the Indians of the Connecticut River Valley in 1634. The next two documents illuminate the Puritans' use of biblical ideas to justify transforming the forest environment. John Winthrop, governor of the Massachusetts Bay Colony, in the second selection cites Genesis 1:28 as a mandate for subduing the new lands, replenishing them with English people, and improving them through agriculture and trade. Thomas Morton, in his 1632 *New English Canaan*, excerpted in the third document, employs the biblical view of Canaan as a promised land, along with the image of nature as female—a virgin whose fruits could be enjoyed when Puritan industry and art transformed the resources of the New World forests. He also describes Indian burning of the forests for better hunting and traveling.

The fourth and fifth documents depict the ways in which Indian women and men used the forest for subsistence. Colonist William Wood's *New England's Prospect*, published in 1634, portrays Indian women's construction of houses and tending of forest garden patches as successful subsistence techniques. Roger Williams, the founder of the Rhode Island colony and an astute observer of the Narragansett Indians, discusses Native Americans' uses of the forest for hunting, their myths concerning trees, and their hypotheses concerning colonial needs for firewood as a motive for settlement.

The sixth and seventh documents look at the New England forest from the perspectives of a wealthy colonial timber merchant and of England's need for white pines for ship masts. Nicholas Shapleigh's 1682 estate, the subject of the sixth document, reveals large profits obtained from lumbering, fur trading, and farming. In the final excerpt, New Hampshire governor Jonathan Belcher, responding to the timber crisis in England, summarizes the British Broad Arrow policy, reserving white pines for the king's use, and warns the colonists not to exploit New England's timber for their private gain.

The New England Landscape

William Bradford Faces
a "Hideous and Desolate Wilderness," 1620–1635

After long beating at sea they fell with that land which is called Cape Cod; the which being made & certainly known to be it, they were not a litle joyful. After some deliberation had amongst themselves & with the master of the ship, they tacked about and resolved to stand for the southward (the wind & weather being fair) to find some place about Hudsons river for their habitation. But after they had sailed that course about half the day, they fell amongst dangerous shoals and roaring breakers, and they were so far intangled there with as they conceived themselves in greater danger; & the wind shrinking upon them withall, they resolved to bear up again for the Cape, and thought themselves happy to get out of those dangers before night overtook them, as by Gods providence they did. And the next day they got into the Cape-harbor where they rode in safety. . . .

Being thus arived in a good harbor and brought saf to land, they fell upon their knees & blessed the God of heaven, who had brought them over the vast & furious ocean, and delivered them from all the perils & miseries thereof, again to set their feet on the firm and stable earth, their proper element. . . . Being thus past the vast ocean, and a sea of troubles before in their preparation (as may be remembered by that which went before), they had now no friends to welcome them, nor inns to entertain or refresh their weatherbeaten bodies, no houses or much less towns to repair to, to seek for succor. It is recorded in scripture as a mercy to the apostle & his shipwrecked company, that the barbarians showed them no small kindness in refreshing them, but these savage barbarians, when they met with them (as after will appear) were readier to fill their sides full of arrows then otherwise. And for the season it was winter, and they that know the winters of that country know them to be sharp & violent, & subject to cruel & fierce storms, dangerous to travel to known places, much more to search an unknown coast. Besides, what could they see but a hideous & desolate wilderness, full of wild beasts & wild men? and what multitudes there might be of them they knew not. Neither could they, as it were, go up to the top of Pisgah, to view from this wilderness a more goodly country to feed their hopes; for which way soever they turned their eyes (save upward to the heavens) they could have litle solace or content in respect of any outward objects. For summer being done, all things stand upon them with a weather-beaten face; and the whole country, full of woods & thickets, represented a wild & savage hue. If they looked behind them, there was the mighty ocean which they had passed, and was now as a main bar & gulf to separate them from all the civil parts of the world. . . . What could now sustain them but the spirit of God & his grace? May not & ought not the children of these fathers, rightly say: *Our fathers were Englishmen which came over this great ocean, and were ready to perish in this wilderness.* . . .

But that which was most sad & lamentable was, that in 2. or 3. months' time half of their company died, especially in Jan: & February, being the depth of winter, and wanting houses & other comforts; being infected with the scurvy & other diseases, which this long voyage & their inaccommodate condition had brought upon them; so as there died some times 2. or 3. of a day, in the foresaid time; that of 100. & odd persons, scarce 50. remained. And of these in the time of most distress, there was but 6. or 7. sound persons, who, to their great commendations be it spoken, spared no pains, night nor day, but with abundance of toil and hazard of their own health, fetched them wood, made them fires, dressed them meat, made their beds, washed their loathsome clothes, clothed & unclothed them; in a word, did all the homely and necessary offices for them which dainty and queasy stomachs cannot endure to hear named; and all this willingly and cheerfully, without any grudging in the least, showing herein their true love unto their friends and brethren.

* * * *

All this while the Indians came skulking about them, and would sometimes show themselves aloof of, but when any approached near them, they would run away. And once they stole away their tools where they had been at work, & were gone to dinner. But about the 16. *of March* a certain Indian came boldly amongst them, and spoke to them in broken English, which they could well understand, but marvelled at it. . . . His name was *Samaset*; he told them also of another Indian whose name was *Squanto*, a native of this place, who had been in England & could speak better English then himself. Being, after some time of entertainment & gifts, dismissed, a while after he came again, & 5. more with him, & they brought again all the tools that were stolen away before, and made way for the coming of their great Sachem, called *Massasoyt*; who, about 4. *or* 5. *days after*, came with the chief of his friends & other attendants, with the aforesaid *Squanto*. With whom, after friendly entertainment, & some gifts given him, they made a peace with him (which hath now continued this 24. years). . . . *Squanto* continued with them, and was their interpreter, and was a special instrument sent of God for their good beyond their expectation. He directed them how to set their corn, where to take fish, and to procure other commodities, and was also their pilot to bring them to unknown places for their profit, and never left them till he died. He was a *native of this place*, & scarce any left alive besids himself. He was caried away with divers others by one *Hunt*, a master of a ship, who thought to sell them for slaves in Spain; but he got away for England, and was entertained by a merchant in London, & employed to New-foundland & other parts, & lastly brought hither into these parts by one Mr. *Dermer*, a gentle-man employed by Sr. Ferdinando Gorges & others, for discovery, & other designs in these parts.

* * * *

Anno: 1621

[April] Afterwards they (as many as were able) began to plant ther corn, in which service Squanto stood them in great stead, showing them both the manner how to set it, and after how to dress & tend it. Also he told them except they got fish & set with it (in these old grounds) it would come to nothing, and he showed them that in the middle of April they should have store enough come up the brook, by which they began to build, and taught them how to take it, and where to get other provisions necessary for them; all which they found true by trial & experience. Some English seed they sew, as wheat & peas, but it came not to good, either by the badness of the seed, or lateness of the season, or both, or some other defect.

* * * *

[September] They began now to gather in the small harvest they had, and to fit up their houses and dwellings against winter, being all well recovered in health & strength, and had all things in good plenty; for as some were thus employed in affairs abroad, others were exercised in fishing, about cod, & bass, & other fish, of which they took good store, of which every family had their portion. All the summer there was no want. And now began to come in store of fowl, as winter approached, of which this place did abound when they came first (but afterward decreased by degrees). And besides water fowl, there was great store of wild Turkeys, of which they took many, besides venison, &c. Besides they had about a peck a meal a week to a person, or now since harvest, Indian corn to that proportion. Which made many afterwards write so largely of their plenty here to their friends in England, which were not feigned, but true reports.

In November, about that time twelfth month that themselves came, there came in a small ship to them unexpected or looked for, in which came Mr. Cushman (so much spoken of before) and with him 35. persons to remain & live in the plantation; which did not a little rejoice them. And they when they came a shore and found all well, and saw plenty of victuals in every house, were no less glad. . . . So they were all landed; but there was not so much as biscuit-cake or any other victuals for them, neither had they any bedding, but some sorry things they had in their cabins, not pot, nor pan, to dress any meat in; nor overmany clothes, for many of them had brushed away their coats & cloaks at Plymouth as they came. But there was sent over some burching-lane suits in the ship, out of which they were supplied. The plantation was glad of this addition of strength, but could have wished that many of them had been of better condition, and all of them better furnished with provisions; but that could not now be helped. . . .

This ship (called the Fortune) was speedily dispatched away, being laden with good clapbord as full as she could stow, and 2. hogsheads of beaver and otter skins, which they got with a few trifling commodities brought with them at first, being altogether unprovided for trade; neither was there any amongst them that ever saw a beaver skin till they came here, and were informed by Squanto. The freight was estimated to be worth near 500. pounds. . . .

Anno Dom: 1634

I am now to relate some strange and remarkable passages. There was a company of people lived in the country, up above in the river of Connecticut, a great way from their trading house there, and were enemies to those Indians which lived about them, and of whom they stood in some fear (being a stout people). About a thousand of them had inclosed them selves in a fort, which they had strongly palisaded about. 3. or 4. Dutch men went up in the beginning of winter to live with them, to get their trade, and prevent them for bringing it to the English, or to fall into amity with them; but at spring to bring all down to their place. But their enterprise failed, for it pleased God to visit these Indians with a great sicknes, and such a mortality that of a 1000. above 900. and a half of them died, and many of them did rot above ground for want of burial, and the Dutch men almost starved before they could get away, for ice and snow. But about Feb: they got with much difficulty to their trading house; whom they kindly relieved, being almost spent with hunger and cold. Being thus refreshed by them divers days, they got to their own place, and the Dutch were very thankful for this kindness.

This spring, also, those Indians that lived about their trading house there fell sick of the small pox, and died most miserably; for a sorer disease cannot befall them; they fear it more than the plague; for usually they that have this disease have them in abundance, and for want of bedding & lining and other helps, they fall into a lamentable condition, as they live on their hard mats, the pox breaking and mattering, and running one into another, their skin cleaving (by reason thereof) to the mats they lie on; when they turn them, a whole side will fly of at once, (as it were,) and they will be all of a gore blood, most fearful to behold; and then begin very sore, what with cold and other distempers, they die like rotten sheep. The condition of this people was so lamentable, and they fell down so generally of this disease, as they were (in the end) not able to help one another; no, not to make a fire, nor to fetch a little water to drink, nor any to bury the dead; but would strive as long as they could, and when they could procure no other means to make fire, they would burn the wooden trays & dishes they ate their meat in, and their very bows & arrows; & some would crawl out on all four to get a little water, and some times die by the way, & not be able to get in again. But those of the English house, (though at first they were afraid of the infection,) yet seeing their woeful and sad condition, and hearing their pitifull cries and lamentations, they had compassion of them, and daily fetched them wood & water, and made them fires, got them victuals whilst they lived, and buried them when they died. For very few of them escaped, notwithstanding they did what they could for them, to the hazard of themselves. The chief Sachem him self now died, & almost all his friends & kindred. But by the marvelous goodness & providence of God not one of the English was so much as sick, or in the least measure tainted with this disease, though they daily did these offices for them for many weeks together. And this mercy which they showed them was kindly taken, and thankfully acknowledged of all the Indians that knew or heard of the same; and their masters here did much commend & reward them for the same. . . .

John Winthrop Quotes Genesis
on Subduing the Earth, 1629

First, it will be a service of great consequence to the Church to carry the Gospel into that part of the world, to encourage the conversion of the heathens and to raise a bulwark against the kingdom of Anti-Christ that the Jesuits are laboring to establish in those countries.

2. All the other true churches of Europe are *brought to desolation*; . . . and it may be that God has provided this place as a refuge for many people whom he means to save from the general calamity. . . .

3. *This land [England] growes weary of her Inhabitants*, so much so that man, the most precious of all creatures, is here treated as viler and baser than the earth we walk upon. Masters have to be forced by the authorities to support their servants and parents to maintain their own children. All towns complain of the burden of their poor. . . .

4. The whole earth is the Lord's garden, and he has given it to the sons of man upon a condition (Genesis 1:28): Increase and multiply, replenish the earth and subdue it. . . . Why, then, should we stay here striving for places to live (many men sometimes spending as much labor and money to recover or keep an acre or two of land as would secure them many hundred acres of equally good or better land in another country), and meanwhile allow a whole continent . . . to lie empty and unimproved?

5. We have risen to such a height of intemperance and such an excess of extravagance that hardly any man's property is sufficient to enable him to keep up with his equals, and he who falls behind must live in scorn and contempt. . . .

6. The fountains of learning and religion are so corrupted (in addition to the impossible cost of education) that most children . . . are perverted, corrupted, and utterly demoralized by the multitude of evil examples and the wicked government in those schools and universities.

Thomas Morton Praises the New English Canaan, 1632

The Authors Prologue.

If art & industry should doe as much
As Nature hath for Canaan, not such
Another place, for benefit and rest,
In all the universe can be possest,
The more we proove it by discovery,
The more delight each object to the eye
Procures, as if the elements had here
Bin reconcil'd, and pleas'd it should appeare,
Like a faire virgin, longing to be sped,
And meete her lover in a Nuptiall bed,
Deck'd in rich ornaments t' advance her state
And excellence, being most fortunate,
When most enjoy'd, so would our Canaan be
If well employ'd by art and industry
Whose offspring, now shewes that her fruitfull wombe
Not being enjoy'd, is like a glorious tombe,
Admired things producing which there dye,

And ly fast bound in darck obscurity,
The worth of which in each particuler,
Who list to know, this abstract will declare.

In the Moneth of June, Anno Salutis: 1622. It was my chaunce to arrive in the parts of New England with 30. Servants, and provision of all sorts fit for a plantation: And whiles our howses were building, I did endeavour to take a survey of the Country: The more I looked, the more I liked it.

And when I had more seriously considered of the bewty of the place, with all her faire indowments, I did not thinke that in all the knowne world it could be paralel'd. For so many goodly groues of trees; dainty fine round rising hillucks: delicate faire large plaines, sweete cristall fountaines, and cleare running streames, that twine in fine meanders through the meads, making so sweete a murmering noise to heare, as would even lull the sences with delight a sleepe, so pleasantly doe, they glide upon the pebble stones, jetting most jocundly where they doe meete; and hand in hand runne downe to Neptunes Court, to pay the yearely tribute, which they owe to him as soveraigne Lord of all the springs. Contained within the volume of the Land, Fowles in abundance, Fish in multitude, and discovered besides; Millions of Turtledoves one the greene boughes: which sate pecking, of the full ripe pleasant grapes, that were supported by the lusty trees, whose fruitfull loade did cause the armes to bend, which here and there dispersed (you might see) Lillies and of the Daphnean-tree, which made the Land to mee seeme paradice, for in mine eie, t'was Natures Master-peece: Her cheifest Magazine of, all where lives her store: if this Land be not rich, then is the whole world poore.

* * * *

The Salvages are accustomed, to set fire of the Country in all places where they come; and to burne it, twize a yeare, vixe at the Spring, and the fall of the leafe. The reason that mooves them to doe so, is because it would other wise be so overgrowne with underweedes, that it would be all a copice wood, and the people would not be able in any wise to passe through the Country out of a beaten path. . . .

And least their firing of the Country in this manner; should be an occasion of damnifying us, and indaingering our habitations; wee our selves have used carefully about the same times; to observe the winds and fire the grounds about our owne habitations, to prevent the Dammage that might happen by any neglect thereof, if the fire should come neere those howses in our absence.

For when the fire is once kindled, it dilates and spreads it selfe as well against, as with the winde; burning continually night and day, untill a shower of raine falls to quench it.

And this custome of firing the Country is the meanes to make it passable, and by that meanes the trees growe here, and there as in our parks: and makes the Country very beautifull, and commodious.

William Wood on Indian Women's Housing and Horticulture, 1634

Of their women, their dispositions, employments, usage by their husbands, their apparel, and modesty.

[Women's] employments be many: First their building of houses, whose frames are formed like our garden-arbors, something more round, very strong and handsome, covered with close-wrought mats of their own weaving, which deny entrance to any drop of rain, though it come both fierce and long, neither can the piercing North wind find a cranny, through which he can convey his cooling breath, they be warmer than our English houses; at the top is a square hole for the smoke's evacuation, which in rainy weather is covered with a pluver; these be such smoky dwellings, that when there is good fires, they are not able to stand upright, but lie all along under the smoke, never using any stools or chairs, it being as rare to see an Indian sit on a stool at home, as it is strange to see an English man sit on his heeles abroad. Their houses are smaller in the Summer, when their families be dispersed, by reason of heat and occasions. In Winter they make some fifty or threescore foot long, forty or fifty men being inmates under one roof; and as is their husbands' occasion these poor tectonists are often troubled like snails, to carry their houses on their backs sometime to fishing-places, other times to hunting-places, after that to a planting place, where it abides the longest: an other work is their planting of corn, wherein they exceed our English husband-men, keeping it so clear with their Clam shell-hoes, as if it were a garden rather than a corn-field, not suffering a choking weed to advance his audacious head above their infant corn, or an undermining worm to spoil his spurns. Their corn being ripe, they gather it, and drying it hard in the Sun, convey it to their barns, which be great holes digged in the ground in form of a brass pot, sealed with rinds of trees, wherein they put their corn, covering it from the inquisitive search of their gourmandizing husbands, who would eat up both their allowed portion, and reserved seed, if they knew where to find it. But our hogs having found a way to unhinge their barn doors, and rob their garners, they are glad to implore their husbands' help to roll the bodies of trees over their holes, to prevent those pioneers, whose thievery they as much hate as their flesh.

Roger Williams on Indian Uses of the Forest, 1643

Obs. This question they oft put to me: Why come the *Englishmen* hither? and measuring others by themselves; they say, It is because you want *firing*: for they, having burnt up the *wood* in one place, (wanting draughts to bring *wood* to them) they are faine to follow the *wood*; and so to remove to a fresh new place for the *woods* sake. . . .

They are so exquisitely skilled in all the body and bowels of the Countrey (by reason of their huntings) that I have often been guided twentie, thirtie, sometimes fortie miles through the woods, a streight course, out of any path. . . .

With friendly joyning they breake up their fields, build their Forts, hunt the Woods, stop and kill fish in the Rivers, it being true with them as in all the World in the Affaires of Earth or Heaven: By concord little things grow great, by discord the greatest come to nothing. . . .

. . . They have it from their Fathers, that *Kautántowwit* made one man and woman of a stone, which disliking, he broke them in pieces, and made another man and woman of a Tree, which were the Fountaines of all mankind. . . .

The Natives hunt two wayes:

First, when they pursue their game (especially Deere, which is the generall and wonderfull plenteous hunting in the Countrey:) I say, they pursue in twentie, fortie, fiftie, yea, two or three hundred in a company, (as I have seene) when they drive the woods before them.

Secondly, They hunt by Traps of severall sorts, to which purpose, after they have observed in Spring-time and Summer the haunt of the Deere, then about Harvest, they goe ten or twentie together, and sometimes more, and withall (if it be not too farre) wives and children also, where they build up little hunting houses of Barks and Rushes (not comparable to their dwelling houses) and so each man takes his bounds of two, three, or foure miles, where hee sets thirty, forty, or fiftie Traps, and baits his Traps with that food the Deere loves, and once in two dayes he walks his round to view his Traps.

A Timber Merchant's Estate, 1682

A true Inventory of the Moneys goods Cattle & Chattels belonging & appertaining to the Estate of Major Nicho. Shapleigh, of Kittery in the Province of Maine In New England deceased, taken and apprized by us whose names are here subscribed, this 9th day of May 1682: which are as follows.*

	£	S	D
Inprs† to so much In Cash or ready money	055	17	00
It‡to 70 ounces of plate at 6s p§ oz	021	00	00
It to his wearing apparel thirteen pounds 13s	013	13	00
It to a Parcel of worn Pewter, at 6 pounds 7s	006	07	00
It to a Parcel of New Pewter apprized at	009	03	00
It 68lb of beaver at 5s p lb at Otter skin 5s, a Moose skin 8s	017	00	00
It two hats & a Case 20s, his riding horse & furniture 5: 10: 00	006	10	0
It The home stall, dwelling house out houses orchards grandings pastures fields with all appurtenances hereunto belonging with all other out-lands hereto adjoining, the Timber of the saw Mills only, excepted	500	00	00
It the saw Mill & Grist Mill, and their accommodations at Kittery valued	300	00	00
It William Ellinghams Interest purchased by Major Shapleigh in his life time lying on the North side of the Creek	050	00	00
It about thirty Acres of Marsh lying at Sturgeon Creek	090	00	00
It Ten thousand foot of boards or thereabouts at the Saw Mills	010	00	00
It Three horses apprized at 50s p horse	007	00	00
It eleven oxen 38£: eleven Cows: 27: 10: 00, 3 3 year old Cattle: 7: 10: 00, four two years old at six pounds	079	00	00
It four yearlings 4: 00: 00: 11 sheep & five lambs 4 pounds	008	00	00
It a Parcel of swine at 10£: 4 Negroes 3 men one woman & one little Negro all at ninety pounds	100	00	00
	1273	10	0
It Two Irish boys, one to serve about two years, & one 3 years	010	00	0
It Great Guns & Carriages seven pounds, a great fowling piece that Samson Whitte borrowed 30s, four New Muskets four pounds 4 small guns 40s: a blunderbuss 15s	015	05	0
Two Timber Chains 40s six draft Chains 48s, 6 yokes ready fitted with rings & staples 24s, two plows 16s, two Clevises 5s			
It a Cart & wheels 35s one pair logging Wheels & drags 4: 10: 0	012	18	0
It Two pair of Mast Wheels decayed with Iron work 3 pounds ⎫	008	00	0
It Two Mast Chains & 1/3 of another Chain at 5 £ ⎭			
It 12 old axes, two spades, 1 pair of hand screws, too scythes two drawing knives, Carpenters tools & Turning tools five pounds	005	00	0
It one pair of large steelyards at Mr Richd Waldens	003	00	0
It In the smiths shop one pair of bellows, small Tools & old Iron	002	10	0
It one old lighter, one shallop with old Rigging & furniture at	010	00	0
It 3 great hay Canoes & a Coasting Canoe	005	00	0
It one old Cloak at 35s	001	15	0
	73	08	0

*In the columns, 1 pound (£) equals 20 shillings (s), and 1 shilling (s) equals 12 pence (d).
†**Inprs**: Probably abbreviation for *in principio*, meaning "in the beginning."
‡**It**: Abbreviation for *item*, meaning "also," to introduce each article in a list.
§**p**: Abbreviation for *per*.

A Governor Enforces the King's Forest Policy, 1730

By His Excellency Jonathan Belcher Esqr Captain General &
Governour in Chief in and over His Maj'ties Province of
New Hampshire in New England —

A Proclamation to prevent the Destruction or Spoil of
His Majesties Woods. —

Forasmuch as the Preservation of His Majesties Woods within this and the neighbouring Provinces is highly necessary for furnishing the Royal Navy, and divers Acts of Parliament have been accordingly from time to time made & pass'd for that end; notwithstanding which and the care of this Governmt to prevent & punish the Destruction and spoil of His Majesties Woods, many evil minded Persons have broke thro' the restraints of the Law in that behalf; and have for their own private gain made great wast of such trees as might be fit for His Majesties service. . . . It is enacted "That from and after the Twenty first day of September one thousand seven hundred & twenty two, no Person or Persons within the Colonys or plantations of Nova Scotia, New Hampshire, the Massachusetts Bay & Province of Mayne, Rhode Island, & Providence Plantations, the Narraganset Countrey, or Kings province, and Connecticut in New England & New York & New Jersey in America, or within any of them do or shall presume to cut, fell or destroy any white pine trees, not growing within any Township or the bounds, lines, or limits thereof in any of the said Colonies or plantations without His Majesties Royal Lycense. . . . And whereas their late Majestys King William & Queen Mary for the better providing & furnishing Masts for the Royal Navy. . . . did reserve to themselves their heirs & successors all Trees of the Diameter of twenty four inches & upwards at twelve inches from the ground growing upon any soil or Tract of Land within the said Province or Territory, not then before granted to any private Person: In order therefore to make the said Reservation more effectual, Be it further Enacted by the Authority aforesaid That no Person or Persons whatsoever within the said Province of the Massachusetts Bay or New England do or shall presume to cut or destroy any white pine trees of the Diameter of twenty four inches, or upwards at twelve inches from the ground, not growing within some soil or Tract of Land within the said Province granted to some private person or Persons before the seventh day of October which was in the year 1690 without His Majesties Lycense first had and obtained. . . .

Dated this thirtieth day of October 1730. . . . GOD SAVE THE KING —

⚘ *E S S A Y S*

The essays feature environmental histories written from three different viewpoints. In the first selection, Jim O'Brien, an American historian who has written on the history of the New Left and contributed to the journal *Radical America*, offers a history of North America from the vantage point of the beaver. In considering how the fur trade affected the beaver, O'Brien turns history upside down, suggesting that capitalism transforms everything from fur hats to the enjoyment of nature into commodities. Samuel F. Manning, in the second essay, focuses on the environment from the perspective of the colonists. Manning explores the importance of the natural resources around them to the colonists' livelihood and examines the beginnings of forest legislation in America, as enacted in the Broad Arrow policy reserving pine trees of specified dimensions for government use rather than entrepreneurial profit. The third essay, by historian Charles F. Carroll of the University of Lowell, re-creates the New England environment at the time of English settlement and shows how it was transformed ecologically by colonial farming and trade.

A Beaver's Perspective on North American History

JIM O'BRIEN

Robert Benchley was talked out of a diplomatic career after he turned in a college thesis on a certain fishing treaty, written from the point of view of the fish. At the risk of some comparable punishment, it may be interesting to describe the sweep of events on our continent from the vantage point of what beavers have done and what has happened to them. As I hope will be clear, such as exercise when applied to this particular animal gives us a way, not only to gnaw at the limits of our species-centrism, but to comprehend our own history in North America as well.

There are two reasons for thus calling the beavers front and center from the vast ranks of our fellow mammals. One is that they manipulate the physical landscape more than any other animal besides the human. In the course of blocking streams and accumulating a food supply they cut down certain trees, drown others at their roots, raise the water table, check soil erosion and flooding, create a new home for a host of aquatic animals, and (over time, as the pond fills in with silt and organic material) leave rich meadow lands. There is a sense in which it would be fully legitimate to say that North America was "empty" until the first beavers waddled along and began applying their industry to it.

The second reason for singling out the beaver has nothing whatever to do with the first. By the simple accident of their fur—which has tiny barbs that facilitate a type of hat manufacturing practiced in Europe, and which in the late winter has a rich, smooth texture—the beaver became an irresistible magnet that guided European penetration of the North American interior for nearly three centuries. The "fur trade," it was called. Other animals such as marten, otter, muskrat, bear, wolverine, mink, you name it, were sought, but above all other lures was the beaver. It is Canada's national symbol to this day. In the onrush of the "fur trade," not only was the beaver threatened with extinction but the Indians (who supplied the animals in exchange for the products of European technology) had their traditional cultures severely jarred and their own numbers drastically reduced. Elsewhere, Spaniards sought gold and silver and slaves, but the more advanced capitalist cultures of northern Europe made an even

Excerpts from Jim O'Brien, "The History of North America From the Standpoint of the Beaver," *Free Spirits* 1, *Annals of the Insurgent Imagination*, 1982, pp. 45–54. Reprinted by permission of the author.

greater impact on the New World by simply setting a high price for the skin of a dead animal. . . .

The beaver has been significant for other species, including our own, and the following outline history will indicate how.

1. *Beginnings*. Unlike humans, who came here fully evolved over the "Siberian land bridge," beavers were here for millions of years, experimenting with different sizes and shapes. The prehistoric giant beaver (*Castoroides ohioensis*) cut a striking figure in the northern lakes, reaching eight feet in length and weighing as much as a black bear. It coexisted with the earliest humans in North America, then became extinct along with other Ice Age behemoths as the climate warmed. Less spectacular but more of a survivor was the dam-building *Castor canadensis*, a close cousin to the European *Castor fiber*. The differences between these two species, which are apparently due to the geographical isolation of North America from the Eurasian land mass after the last Ice Age, are too subtle for the average predator to notice. For the historian, the only difference is that *Castor canadensis* was far more numerous.

. . . [Beavers] live on vegetation, and above all on the bark and young shoots of trees. (That's why they never made it to South America, you see: the dry treeless deserts of northern Mexico stood in their way.) Armed with four big incisors, which stay sharp because they keep growing through a lifetime and wear out faster on one side of the tooth than the other, they collect their delicacies by cutting down the whole tree. And the less edible parts of the tree, along with rocks, mud, old boots, and whatever else is available, go into making dams and lodges. These are necessary because the beaver on land is slow, conspicuous, and a potential meal for the nearest hungry wolf, bear, wolverine, bobcat, or coyote. (Only a potential meal, let us add. Beavers have sharp teeth and hind claws and are built compactly. There are even instances where they've dragged the would-be diner to the water and administered a quick drowning.) It is in the water that the beaver becomes fast and elusive, vulnerable only to the relatively scarce river otter. Hence the dam, which uses a small stream to create a pond. Even the winter freeze can be finessed: with the water level raised, the beaver colony can build a lodge big enough to house an underwater food supply plus above-water compartments with a thick roof; the builders need never leave the lodge except to swim under the ice, and thus they are fully protected from land predators during the winter months.

In a continent filled with trees for millions of square miles, the beaver had free rein. As a beaver colony expands and begins putting pressure on the surrounding food supply — beavers have to stay as close to the water as possible for protection — an instinct is triggered by which parents will expel their older offspring from the colony on pain of injury and even death. The outcasts may be able to set up another dam slightly downstream, or they may have to make the perilous overland trek for a suitable site. On the way, or after finding the stream, each will try to attract a beaver of the opposite sex and thereby found a new colony. Life expectancy is around twelve years, and an offspring may be exiled at age two, so it is easy to guess that a beaver during its lifetime may have descendants who live dozens of miles away. By the time the Europeans came, beavers had long since expanded throughout the area where the lay of the land made it possible.

2. *A human presence.* Of course the Europeans weren't the first people here, though you would never know it from reading the average history book. Anthropologists are now tossing around figures like nine million for the pre-Columbian population of the New World north of Mexico — an extraordinary figure which was not reattained by European immigrants for *more than three centuries.* While any species is important first of all to itself, the advent of humans was important to the beaver as well. Here was that wonder of wonders, horror of horrors, a land animal that could chase the beaver out of the water and kill it when it chose. The technique was crude — it typically involved breaking the ice with axes and setting dogs after the fleeing prey — but adequate. (It was to prevail for well over two centuries after the beginnings of the fur trade in the 1500s.) The human beings could kill the beaver at will.

Here we come to an interesting question of values. Let us make clear at the outset that the Indians did not threaten the beaver as a species. The great naturalist Ernest Thompson Seton estimated toward the end of his career that there were 60 million beaver in North America when the Europeans came. It is hard to imagine how there could have been more even in the absence of the Indians. Now the question is: How do we look on the relationship of two species, one of which hunts, traps, and tries to kill the other? Each individual encounter may be marked by violence and cruelty on the one side, helpless terror on the other. In a stable relationship, though, the predation is often an alternative to starvation and disease.

As Calvin Martin reminds us in *Keepers of the Game: Indian–Animal Relations and the Fur Trade* the primal world view includes a belief that people appropriated animals for their use only, and with, in some sense, the permission of the spirits of those animals. The killing of animals was part of an elaborate and complex culture, full of beliefs which worked to insure that particular kinds of animals would not be overkilled. Woodland Indians enjoyed a stable relationship with nature that an ecologist of today can only look at in envy.

3. *The Europeans.* In the Donald Duck comic book *Tralla La* (May–June 1954), Donald and the three nephews parachute into a remote valley whose inhabitants are blissfully unaware of the outside "civilized" world. By mistake one of the nephews lets a bottle cap fall to the ground; on finding it the natives suddenly go berserk and begin fighting each other for the privilege of offering their most valued possessions for more bottle caps. The whole society has been instantly disrupted. David Wagner ("An Interview with Donald Duck," *Radical America*, January–February, 1973) calls this a brilliant critique of Western imperialism.

In fact, the comic book is backwards history, as we can see from the experience of North America. In that historical instance it was the Europeans who went berserk. They came here first for gold and silver, then for fur for decorative hats, then for drugs (tobacco, sugar, and coffee). Was any of these an intrinsically useful product? The use-value of the products the Indians got in the "fur trade" — cloth, guns, steel axes, metal cooking utensils, the one exception being alcohol — was far higher than the use-value of what the Europeans came here for. At the point of contact it is the European mentality that needs explaining, not that of the Indians.

Of course the Europeans weren't really crazy. They just had a very different social system. As soon as the beaver pelts on the one hand, and the European trade goods on the other hand, are stripped of their practical uses and distilled into European currencies, we see that the disproportion is all the other way. One nineteenth-century student of the trade concluded that the profits had gone as high as 2,000 percent. In England and France — the Dutch were squeezed out fairly early — the buying and selling of beaver fur became an important source of what is disarmingly called an "economic surplus." We can define an economic surplus as a concentration of wealth within a society such that the people who control that wealth have the power to direct the labor of other people in the society — and thereby gain further wealth and further power. A society may have an abundance of everything it needs — for example, a hunting and gathering society in which people have to do only four or five hours a day of what we would call work, and are quite comfortable — but unless the wealth is unequally distributed there is no economic surplus because nobody has power to harness the labor of others for his own purposes. One important effect of the fur trade, as of the production of crops like sugar and tobacco, was to help make northern European society more unequal, and thus further the cause of economic development, alias "progress." . . .

But, to keep the beaver at the center of our concerns, the specific relationship that matters here is that the French, Dutch, and British quickly discovered that *Castor canadensis* had fur very much like that of its almost-extinct cousin *Castor fiber*, and that the Indians knew how to trap it if they were of a mind to do so. The Europeans offered trade goods. More to the point, they offered diseases. Such ills as smallpox, measles, whooping cough, and chicken pox, which had become childhood diseases in Eurasia over the course of centuries, were entirely new to the Americas. Everywhere they had a catastrophic effect. Indian medicine, even though it was at least as good as the European medicine of that age, had no cure; and Indian cultures had no explanation that was not acutely demoralizing. It was this awesome loss of cultural cohesion — not to say loss of life — that led many woodland Indians to abandon their traditional practices and collaborate in the European animal trade.

The results for the beaver were catastrophic. There was a wave of destruction fanning out from the St. Lawrence River, from the Dutch and English colonies on the Atlantic seaboard, later from Hudson's Bay, and still later from John Jacob Astor's fistful of the Oregon coast. In the final stages of expansion, in the Rockies, legendary white "mountain men" like Jim Bridger dispensed with the Indian trade altogether and wrought enormous destruction on their own. And after the trappers came the white settlers, appropriating for their own exclusive use a landscape that had once been home for both humans and an immense array of "wild" animals.

Even as European fashions changed, with less demand for beaver hats, the trapping of the diminished beaver population continued, especially in Canada. Between 1853 and 1877 the Hudson's Bay Company sold almost three million beaver skins on the London market. By 1891 the author of a book on the beaver could write that "progress is no respecter of persons or animals, so we must face the matter squarely and prepare to pay tribute to the loss of the great beaver host which will soon leave us forever." Of the beaver's ultimate extinction, "no possible question can exist."

4. *Back from the Brink.* As any resident of a wooded, hilly countryside today knows, the North American beaver did not disappear as a species. It is hard to sort out the historical causation here, but the fact is that around the turn of the century American states and Canadian provinces began to pass laws strictly controlling the killing of beaver. . . .

In effect, human governmental agencies assumed a managerial role in relation to the beaver. The traditional four-legged predators such as the wolverine ("the beaver eater," it was sometimes called), wolf, bear, bobcat, and fox had been reduced to negligible numbers. The partial check they had once exerted on the beaver's proliferation had been removed, but at the same time vast areas of woodland were destroyed to make way for farms, towns, and cities. Therefore, public agencies have stepped in, and the situations they deal with are complicated. The naturalists Lorus and Margery Milne tell the story of a beaver colony on a remote tributary of the Arkansas River in Colorado which built a series of dams between 1949 and 1955, then outstripped the food supply and migrated *en masse.* In 1957 the untended dams gave way to the spring thaw, and "a wall of muddy water rushed across roads and fields, engulfing human establishments without warning." Having broken into the pre-existing web of life, modern society has had to take control of this particular strand. And it is not easy.

Perhaps it is too bad that Robert Beverley [see Chapter 4] was wrong, that the beaver did not have a king or a superintendent who "walks in State by them all the while, and sees that every one bear his equal share of the burden; while he bites with his Teeth, and lashes with his Tail, those that lag behind, and do not lend all their strength." If they had, the names of these dignitaries might somehow have come down to us today, for our historical records. As it is, you have to be a scientist or a beaver even to tell the males from the females, let alone pick out individuals. All we know about the 4,000-foot-long beaver dam found near Berlin, New Hampshire — that's pretty close to a mile — is that "some beavers" built it. "Some beavers" also built the 750-foot canal that was found near Longs Peak, Colorado, in 1911; canals, often built with locks, are in some ways the beaver's most impressive feat, providing a way to bring distant vegetation to the pond without risking too long a sojourn on dry land. "Some beavers" built a giant lodge housing at least thirty-seven of their number, as described by a Hudson's Bay trader, and felled a tree measuring more than three feet in diameter and 100 feet high in British Columbia. If beavers were like modern human beings, we would not know who actually carried out these exploits but we would at least have a name to attach to them — the name of whoever commissioned the work.

There may be a sense in which the ubiquitous "Warning — I Brake for Animals" bumper stickers are the most encouraging mass phenomenon of recent years. In part they represent a simple concern for highway safety, a plea against tailgating, but they also express a revulsion against the power that modern society holds over the natural world (in this case the power to crush an animal between a heavy machine and a strip of concrete). They are a forceful reminder that, for all we have done to destroy parts of nature and undertake the "management" of what is left, we are after all a *part* of nature. We have, in some profound sense, more in common with the helpless skunk or chicken on the highway than we do with the inanimate object at whose wheel we sit. In an age that tells us otherwise, it is an important insight. . . .

With the elaboration of capitalist civilization, happiness becomes more and more a commodity to be purchased on the one side and profited from on the other. Even the enjoyment of nature becomes a commodity (witness the vital role of the railroads in lobbying for creation of the National Parks system in the early twentieth century). Work is rigidly separated from "leisure," and the latter is defined by "consumption." . . .

The same cultural logic that converted beavers into capital by abstracting the animal and attaching value only to the fur has a similarly limited use for ordinary human beings. In the face of capital accumulation, the fact that we are all human gives us no claim on the mercy of the accumulators. When, as a culture, we lost our kinship with the animals, we lost something profound that has not been replaced.

And this gets us back to the relationship between the beaver and history. It is the *commerce* in beaver that is endlessly documented in the records that are the acceptable grist for historians. The thousands of years in which beavers and humans lived side by side as elements of nature are virtually opaque to us. History, even when it focuses directly on an animal, can treat the animal only as a historical object, not as a subject.

So the world in which the beaver had a spirit is hidden from history. Unless history is augmented with enlightened anthropology, and poetry too, there is no way to understand that world—no way even to glimpse it. And this is not a trivial matter. What is at stake is not simply a way of looking at the past, but the urgent need to find our way out of the cultural logic of capitalism. Human potentiality is much more varied than anyone could realize who knew only the history of the modern age; and this is important for us to grasp. Fighting to understand the past is, after all, part of a bigger struggle to survive the future.

A Colonist's Perspective
on the New England Environment

SAMUEL F. MANNING

Settlement, and the Beginnings of New England Trade

New England of 1620 was a wilderness territory offering little incentive for commercial settlement. The fish were already being taken by home vessels without need of any but temporary shore facilities. Furs, obtained by trade with Indians, were slipping into the hands of the Dutch at New Amsterdam as well as to the French by way of the Acadian settlements and the St. Lawrence. Standing timber was too bulky to cut and assemble for shipment without

Excerpts from *New England Masts and the King's Broad Arrow*, by S. F. Manning (Kennebunk, Me: Thomas Murphy, 1979) pp. 23–32, 45–49.

extensive shore establishment, and timber was too expensive to ship transatlantic without preferential duties in the home market. English colonies to the south of New England had commercial advantage due to their gentler climates and longer growing seasons. Virginia and the Carolinas produced foodstuffs, tobacco, rice and indigo in exportable quantities. Further south, the island colonies of Barbados, Nevis, St. Kitts and (later) Jamaica would give up general cropping for a sure-sell specialty in sugar products. For the London merchants a New England venture meant shiploads of colonist supplies and Indian-trade goods risked against return cargoes of whatever raw products could be mustered by settlers taken to that region. Settlement was tried at the mouth of Maine's Kennebec River in 1607 by the Plymouth Company with colonists led by George Popham. Although some furs were returned by trade with the local Indians, winter hardship and the death of its leader doomed the Popham colony to failure. Foothold on Massachusetts Bay was gained thirteen years later by Pilgrim zealots underwritten (for settlement in Virginia) by an association of English merchants headed by Thomas Weston.

Between the Pilgrim arrival in 1620 and the arrival of Admiralty mast ships in 1652 lay three decades of land clearing, hardscrabble farming, and grubbing for return cargoes to pay for supplies sent from England. The 1620's saw returns of furs gained by Pilgrim shrewdness in trading with Indians at truck houses established at the head of navigation on the Kennebec and the Connecticut rivers, and closer to home at the headwaters of Buzzards Bay. Neither the Pilgrims of the 1620's nor the Puritans of the 1630's were versed in seamanship or fishing. A colonial fishing industry got going very slowly due to inexperience and lack of boats. Skilled shipwrights arriving with the flood of Puritan settlers in the 1630's built some shallops for fishing, notably at Salem, but were hampered by lack of capital, nails, cordage, and sailcloth. Lack of money to pay their accustomed wages turned many incoming tradesmen to clearing land for farms. There was some production of hand sawn boards, hand split barrel staves ("clapboards," in older parlance) etc. to send back with the returning immigrant ships, but most incoming trade of the 1630's was the exchange of immigrant possessions for land, cattle, and the materials for new homes. Shipbuilding, to 120 tons, had begun with a few vessels built at Medford, Salem, and on Richmond Island near Casco Bay in Maine. A water-powered sawmill had been established at Berwick, and a tide-powered sawmill at Agamenticus. Pine boards, hand split shingles, and clapboards were added to whatever outbound cargoes of dried codfish or farm produce could be accumulated in surplus. English demand for masts and naval stores was well known to the settlers. Although there was some attempt to grow hemp, flax, and to reduce wood to its naval oils, these products never really took hold as a New England product. There is no doubt that some of the mast cargoes returned to England during this period went back with the discharged immigrant ships. However, loading of masts aboard a regular carrier assumes that the tallest trees of the forest have been cut, moved, hewn and assembled for shipment in a hostile, unpopulated region much further east.

The stream of Puritan immigrants which provided New England settlers with trade goods for nearly a decade closed down in the late years of the 1630's.

England was in revolution. Religious and civil reforms begun by the Long Parliament gave English Puritans incentive to stay at home. Economic depression was felt in New England as incoming ships continued to land needed goods without offering immigrant demand for homesteading essentials. However, Boston merchants probing the hemisphere for colonist markets had discovered that oak staves and heading for wet storage containers — pipes, hogsheads, casks, barrels — could be sold to wine producers in the Canary and the Azores islands. In fact there was considerable demand for American white oak which made excellent cooperage for the aging and transport of wine. Staves and heading sent to the wine islands returned wine cargoes to the English market where credits could be offset against goods delivered to New England. This first independent New England export was soon extended to the winemakers of Spain and Portugal who welcomed American dried codfish surplus along with the barrel shooks. Colonial fishing effort had increased and was seeking markets. Shipbuilding industry came to life at Boston and Charlestown, and the first vessels constructed were for carrying shaken casks and dried codfish to the wine islands. Docks everywhere were piled high with staves and heading which departed in large shipments along the wine route. Private speculation in masts and trunnels began with a shipment from Boston to England in 1645. Similar shipments were made during the three years following. In 1650 a new and broader market opened for New England merchants striving to get on their feet: staves and heading of porous red oak, for sugar and molasses casks. The island of Barbados had dropped all other crops and stripped the land of timber in favor of sugar production. Oak for cooperage was needed along with structural timber for rolling machinery, mill buildings, slave quarters, wharves, etc. Dried fish was in demand for feeding slaves and mill hands. The opportunity extended to other Caribbean islands which had also converted to sugar production. Returned sugar, molasses and rum cargoes were saleable just about anywhere. By 1652 New England lumbering, shipbuilding, fishing and overseas trading had made a solid start from primitive beginnings just 30 years before. One can only speculate that if the restrictions and incentives of the oncoming Broad Arrow Policy had been applied to New England when the 1630's Puritan immigration slumped, American appetite for competitive enterprise might have died at birth.

The Broad Arrow Policy

With arrival of mast ships dispatched by the Admiralty in 1652, annual shipment of New England masts to English dockyards began. The mast logging effort was well paid. It sought the best trees in the New England pine forest and required undamaged delivery of the whole tree trunk at specified coastal shipping locations. The work took tremendous skill in the felling and in the overland or water delivery of the logs. Hard money was paid for the labor by the London timber contractors. But gold paid for mast logs could not buy food where planting had been neglected, and many a new settlement of farmer/loggers was to experience winter starvation before the lesson was learned.

New England masts were free enterprise in 1652. The Admiralty's move to get mast logs out of the forest produced the labor force, the woods technology, and the holding facilities to make a business of masts along the growing routes of New England trade. Sawmills followed the loggers and took a growing share of the felled pines for conversion to now-merchantable boards, joists and other structural lumber. Since the Admiralty contracts called for supplying Navy dockyards at Antigua and Jamaica as well as England, an extended mast trade with the French colonies in the sugar islands as well as the needs of Spanish shipbuilders along the wine cask route were not ignored by New England merchants. A sound, dressed log for a great mast was frequently worth more than £100 throughout the whole period discussed. If reduced to wide boards, its delivered lumber was saleable for wooden construction at a figure more easily collected by the woodland entrepreneur. With British pressure for dependable delivery of New England pine masts, a wholesale colonial lumber industry began to flourish. By 1685 colonial merchandising of New England white pines had reached a point where the Admiralty felt that strong measures were needed to protect the remaining mast trees in the settled locations as well as further to the east where lumbering was bound to occur. Accordingly a Surveyor of Pines and Timber in Maine was appointed by the Crown to oversee the Admiralty's mast interests in New England. His commission called for a survey of the Maine woods within 10 miles of any navigable waterway as well as the blazing of all suitable mast pines with the King's mark. Appointment of a Surveyor was the first step in the formation of a colonial forest policy.

England had restored the monarchy under two successive Stuart kings. A war with Spain was concluded in 1660, a second war with the Dutch in 1667, and a third war with the Dutch in 1674. There was continuing need for ships' masts as well as a sudden demand for American lumber of any kind following the great London fire of 1666. As William and Mary ascended the throne in 1689, naval construction was stepped up to meet an oncoming struggle with the French. A new timber crisis developed in the dockyards as the growing hostility of Sweden threatened to close passage to the Baltic. To insure a continuing and dependable supply of masts and naval stores from the American colonies, Parliament moved to commandeer the American pines and to control their destruction by mast entrepreneurs, shingle splitters, and sawmill operators. It was basically a mercantilist move to shift timber emphasis from the Baltic where trade was one-sided, and to force the colonials to focus on export of raw materials rather than develop their own competing finished products. Laws designed to protect the American pines for exclusive use of the Royal Navy became collectively known as the Broad Arrow Policy. Its symbol, the so-called "broad arrow" (a 3-legged letter A without the horizontal bar), was the ancient mark emblazoned on all property of the Royal Navy including prisoners. The Broad Arrow would be cut into every American pine adjudged suitable for a King's mast by the Surveyor of Pines and Timber. Its shadow hung over all pines in most of the American colonies.

Enacted piecemeal between 1691 and 1729, the Broad Arrow Policy governed New England land rights and woodland activity until outbreak of the American Revolution broke its grip in 1775. Carried to Canada with American loyalists, the Broad Arrow Policy continued to supply masts from the Canadian woods until wooden spars were replaced by iron.

Mast Agents and Surveyors

English masts had always come from abroad. Mast timber had been purchased throughout the years from London contractors who retained agents in the Baltic ports where suitable sticks were assembled for export. When North America was turned to for a fresh supply of bigger wood, it was these same mast contractors who obtained license to cut American pines reserved for the King.

Mast agents for the London contractors took up residence in New England. Some of their names became linked with the future of the region: Samuel Waldo, mast agent at Boston; Mark Hunking Wentworth, mast agent at Portsmouth; Thomas Westbrook, to be succeeded by George Tate, mast agent at Falmouth (now Portland); and Edward Parry, at Georgetown (now Bath). Nothing prevented these mast agents from setting up as lumber merchants on their own accounts. Most of them became rich and powerful men in their respective colonies. The mast agents were, in a sense, New England managers of commercial enterprises based in London. They were not King's officers, but licensees of licensees permitted to harvest the Crown timber.

The King's man in New England was the Surveyor of Pines and Timber in Maine. He was given four deputies. Appointments to this post began in 1685. At first the surveys extended ten miles inland from any navigable waterway. Then as the trees disappeared and the need for them continued, the Surveyor and his deputies sought to range the whole of the pine belt from Nova Scotia westward to the St. Lawrence. . . .

The King's Surveyor was hardly popular with the New England colonists. The office was badly paid to begin with, and the area to be covered by this officer and his four deputies was tremendous. It was work enough just to find and mark the trees which tended to disappear when the incisors of the Broad Arrow had passed through. Swamp law governed the future of informers. The colonial courts increasingly sided with the violators as conditions slid toward the Revolution.

* * * *

Outbreak of the Revolution ended the Broad Arrow Policy in New England. In April, 1775, news of Bunker Hill and Lexington stopped all shipments of masts to the King. Waiting mast cargoes were seized by the colonists at Portsmouth, Falmouth and Georgetown. The load of mast baulks seized by the colonists from the mast ship *Minerva* was reported to be rotting in Portland harbor fifty years later.

Mast logging as a marine trade did not end in New England with eclipse of the Broad Arrow Policy. Pine masts continued to be cut and shipped by Yankee traders to whomever would buy them at the highest price. France was a good customer for New England masts during the Revolution. England continued to import them, although on a commercial basis, after the war had ended. But the King had other trees in North America. Until about 1825, great pines marked with the broad arrow continued to move out of the valleys of the Saint John and the Mirmichi to the King's depot at Halifax.

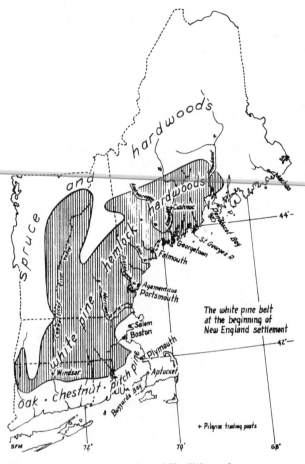

New England forest types at the beginning of English settlement

Source: Samuel F. Manning, *New England Masts and the King's Broad Arrow* (Kennebunk, ME: Thomas Murphy, 1979), p. 20.

A Forest's Perspective on Ecological Transformation

CHARLES F. CARROLL

Dense and Open Woodlands

In New England at the time of the first English settlements there were vast junglelike thickets interrupted only infrequently by narrow, meandering Indian paths or an occasional cornfield, river meadow, or sand plain. John Winthrop, the governor of the Massachusetts Bay Company, wrote of almost impenetrable tangles of trees and underbrush growing close to the seashore north and south of Boston, and the Pilgrims found similar thickets even on outer Cape Cod. One visitor to northern New England said that even many swamps were "infinitely thick set with Trees and Bushes of all sorts," and in 1694 the commanders of a British expedition against Canada described the vegetation on both sides of Lake Champlain as "a mere morase cumbered with underwood where men cannot go upright, but must creep through bushes for whole days' marches, and impossible for horse to go at any time of the year." During the summer, many sections of the New England woodlands were often obstructed by a snarl of such woody vines as climbing ferns, ivy, and ampelopsis.

Even after the leaves had fallen and portions of the undergrowth had withered and died, many New England woodland tracts remained almost impassable. In the nineteenth century, Thoreau noted that in the virgin forests of Maine the ground was everywhere spongy and saturated with moisture; in the early twentieth century, a layer of humus almost a foot deep was found in the primeval forest in Litchfield County, Connecticut. The older trees, rotting within, continually creaked, even when the air was calm. With little warning, massive trunks snapped and tons of timber crashed onto the forest floor. Many travelers in the North American forest mentioned the countless fallen and decaying trees that blocked their paths. When the great trees fell, their roots, together with the soil that had nourished them, shot forth from the ground, leaving large holes. Mosses soon gathered on the fallen and decaying trunks and limbs, and insects began their work beneath the pale green halo. Before long the mightiest forest giant was transformed into a pile of humus that nourished its successors.

Although there were dense and impassable woodlands in many sections of New England, a number of the early explorers and settlers emphasized the open, parklike quality of the countryside. Verrazzano, entering the woodlands near Newport Harbor, observed that they were so free of underbrush that they "could be penetrated even by a large army." Champlain noted that the forests in the interior of the Saco region were open, and another observer mentioned swamps farther north in Maine composed of spruce trees, "under the shades whereof you may freely walk two or three mile together."

Reprinted from Charles F. Carroll in *The Timber Economy of Puritan New England*, Brown University Press, pp. 33–6, 37, 123–4, 124–6, 127, © 1973 by Brown University. By permission of University Press of New England.

Although it is probable that where large trees were common their shade alone prevented the growth of underbrush and vines, Thomas Morton believed that the Indians had kept the forest open: "The savages are accustomed, to set fire of the country in all places where they come; and to burn it, twice a year, viz., at the spring and the fall of the leafe." The Indians' purpose in burning the woods is not entirely clear. Morton says that they did it to make the forest passable, Roger Williams that they did it to destroy vermin and keep down weeds and thickets.

At least in southern New England, the Indians significantly altered parts of the primeval forest long before the arrival of the European settlers. But the burned-over areas probably were not very extensive; forest dwellers would surely realize that a great woodland fire could easily rage out of control. A fire set by Indians to drive out one of the early English exploration parties was limited to a one-mile area, and during the first years of Plymouth Colony, two Pilgrims were surprised to discover a burned-over region five miles in length.

Nature may have had a greater influence than the Indians on the development of dense and open forest tracts in New England. Fires can be started by lightning and internal combustion as well as by men. The rise and fall of the water table, snow and ice storms, and winds, hurricanes, and tornadoes exert a strong influence over all botanical communities. Mighty trees can withstand fire and weather for centuries and then succumb to disease. The destruction of the underbrush and the lower branches of the trees by deer and other browsing animals can significantly alter the relation of trees, plants, and animals. And insects can disturb what appears to be a peaceful, verdant world, as in 1668, when John Winthrop, Jr., reported that caterpillars had destroyed great numbers of oaks and other species in the forests of southern New England. When trees were stripped of leaves by insects, plants that had been shaded for many years by the larger trees might regain their vigor, compete for dominance, and eventually alter the composition of the forest.

Sylvan Giants

The several vegetation regions of New England contained trees that varied greatly in age and size. Where the trees were young, the forest may have been quite dense. Along the Kenduskeag Stream near Bangor, Champlain saw thick woods that extended far into the interior. John Winthrop, Jr., observed that in many parts of New England, especially in the south, there were stands containing only a "few large old timber trees of oak."

Sometimes the young trees mingled with ancient ones, but where soil, moisture, and wind provided optimum conditions for the growth of a particular species, large trees prevailed. These were the sylvan giants before which the first explorers and settlers stood in awe, the trees that produced an environment much different from the vapid woodlands of the present day.

The white pine was by far the tallest of the New England forest giants, dominating the landscape wherever it was numerous. The bark of a huge white pine was as rough as that of an oak or elm, and the lower portion of the tree was often bare of limbs up to 100 feet from the ground. Today the scrawny, youthful descendants of this once-majestic species, with smooth bark and branches almost touching the ground, give only an inkling of the dark and mysterious forest created by their ancestors.

The Wilderness Transformed

By the late seventeenth century, much of New England was still covered by a vast forest, and thousands of settlers were clearing the woodlands, killing rattlesnakes, and building traps to catch the wolves that were destroying cattle. Even where the dangerous animals had been driven out, there were still "vast numbers of Frogs, toads, owls, batts, and other Vermin" at the edge of the uncleared land. But a short distance from the frontier—and especially in Boston—there were streets "full of Girles and Boys sporting up and downe, with a continued concourse of people," and crafts that depended on timber products were thriving.

The shipbuilders of Boston were producing over half the shipping tonnage launched in New England, and shipbuilding had created a prosperous local trade in white and black oak, chestnut, larch, and red cedar framing timbers, in spruce and white pine trees for masts, and in pitch and tar. (Unlike their English counterparts, who were often forced to purchase timber abroad, Boston ship-wrights could easily obtain even specially shaped trees for stems, sterns, and ribs.) Shipbuilding encouraged the development of a number of specialized woodworking industries as well—to build superstructures, install fittings, and decorate the vessels.

Cooperage also thrived in Boston and other seacoast towns. Because vast amounts of staves were collected at Boston for shipment overseas, it was never a problem to procure supplies there, and coopers made thousands of casks each year for shipbuilders, brewers, distillers, fishermen, and merchants. They also made wooden pails, churns, tubs, and other utensils for foreign markets and for the settlers.

As a meat-packing center and the major port of entry for hides from the West Indies, Boston was the tanning center of New England. The bark of young white oak trees was preferred for tanning cowhides, and although large numbers of such oaks could not be found everywhere in New England, enough tanbark was available in the coastal regions, especially south of Boston.

. . . By the end of the century, over half a million acres of woodland had been cleared for farming. In some regions sheep grazed on peaceful meadows reminiscent of the gentle English countryside, and English fruits, grains, and vegetables grew where dank, murky forests or swamps had been. In the open areas, such English plants as the daisy, buttercup, clover, chickory, hawkweed, and dandelion had replaced the native wild flowers, which, no longer protected by the trees, died from exposure to the sun.

The forest was the greatest obstacle to the expansion of agriculture, but it was also the source of timbers for houses, outbuildings, and fences—and of firewood, the ashes of which served as a fertilizer. And in many settlements farmers supplemented their meager incomes by producing timbers, staves, hoops, and shingles for the artisans and merchants of the port towns. They also made feeding troughs from elm logs, and plows, harrows, shovels, flails, and pitchforks of ash and oak. Ink was made from oak galls, and dyes from many species, among them the sumac, hickory, butternut, hemlock, ash, sassafras, dogwood, alder, birch, oak, and maple. Maple sugar and honey were also taken from the forest, for West Indian sugar was expensive. Wild cherries, wild plums, blueberries, and currants added variety to the settlers' diet. From the forest, too, came the bark and wood of the walnut, spruce, birch, and sassafras for making beer; nut oils for purgatives; the bark of the willow, oak, alder, and birch for suppuratives; cherry bark for cough remedies; and the sap of the white pine and hemlock for astringents.

On the edge of the forest there was good hunting, and game was part of the New England diet. The passenger pigeons and blackbirds that often attacked the cornfields were killed and eaten in large numbers, and in Connecticut so many deer were killed by 1698 that the General Court limited the hunting season. Whereas in England most people were forbidden to hunt with a gun, marksmanship was essential for survival in the New England forest. . . .

Pollution of the environment and waste of natural resources are often considered consequences of the Judeo-Christian belief that man should have dominion over all nature. And indeed, before John Winthrop set out for the American colonies, he wrote: "The whole earth is the Lords garden, and he hath given it to the sonnes of men, and with a gen[eral] Commission: Gen: 1:28: increace and multiplie, and replenish the earth and subdue it." But the seventeenth-century colonists' attitude toward nature was not as simple as that. Town records show that south of the Merrimack, where settlers were not wholly dependent on the sale of timber products they themselves could make, the cutting of timber trees was restricted by various laws. The system of land ownership in the early New England towns encouraged preservation of timber, for townships were granted to groups of men known as proprietors, who distributed land among themselves and other settlers but had the sole right to large tracts of common, or undivided, land held in reserve. Although the proprietors of a town allowed all of its inhabitants to take some building timber, fuel, and other essential wood from the common land, much of the valuable timber was reserved for the proprietors.

. . . Late in the seventeenth century, and even in the eighteenth century, after hundreds of thousands of acres of timberland had been destroyed, New Englanders seem to have noticed only a few of the many significant changes that resulted from the clear-cutting of the forests: drier air, stronger winds, the disappearance of small streams, and a decline in the number of wolves, bears, and other wild animals. They considered most of these changes beneficial.

ψ *F U R T H E R   R E A D I N G*

Bernard Bailyn, *The New England Merchants in the Seventeenth Century* (1955)
————, *The Ordeal of Thomas Hutchinson* (1974)
Paul Boyer and Stephen Nissenbaum, *Salem Possessed* (1974)
Richard L. Bushman, *From Puritan to Yankee* (1967)

Charles F. Carroll, *The Timber Economy of Puritan New England* (1973)

Peter N. Carroll, *Puritanism and the Wilderness* (1969)

William Cronon, *Changes in the Land: Indians, Colonists, and the Ecology of New England* (1983)

William A. Haviland and Marjory W. Power, *The Original Vermonters: Native Inhabitants Past and Present* (1981)

Stephen Innes, *Labor in a New Land* (1983)

Lloyd C. Irland, *Wildlands and Woodlots: The Story of New England's Forests* (1982)

Kenneth Lockridge, *A New England Town: The First Hundred Years* (1970)

Calvin Martin, "Fire and Forest Structure in the Aboriginal Eastern Forest," *Indian Historian* 6 (1973)

Carolyn Merchant, *Ecological Revolutions: Nature, Gender, and Science in New England* (1989)

Perry Miller, ed., *The American Puritans: Their Prose and Poetry* (1956)

————, *The New England Mind: The Seventeenth Century* (1939)

Edmund S. Morgan, *The Puritan Dilemma: The Story of John Winthrop* (1958)

Roderick Nash, *Wilderness and the American Mind*, 3d ed. (1982)

Sumner Chilton Powell, *Puritan Village* (1963)

Howard Russell, *Indian New England Before the Mayflower* (1980)

Neal Salisbury, *Manitou and Providence: Indians, Europeans, and the Making of New England* (1982)

William Simmons, *Spirit of the New England Tribes (1986)*

Frank Speck, *Penobscot Man*, (1940)

John Stilgoe, *Common Landscape of America, 1580–1845* (1982)

Henry David Thoreau, *The Maine Woods* (1877)

Laurel T. Ulrich, *Good Wives: Image and Reality in the Lives of Women in Northern New England, 1650–1750* (1982)

Michael Williams, *Americans and Their Forests: A Historical Geography* (1989)

Harold F. Wilson, *The Hill Country of Northern New England: Its Social and Economic History, 1790–1830* (1936)

Richard G. Wood, *A History of Lumbering in Maine, 1820–1861* (1935)

Alden T. Vaughan and Francis J. Bremer, eds., *Puritan New England* (1977)

CHAPTER 4

Soil Exhaustion in

the Early Tobacco South

 ❦

---

*If a particle of soil in Virginia could write its own environmental history, it
might describe its journey from the Appalachian Mountains down rushing
streams to the tidewater lowlands along Chesapeake Bay. It would relate meeting
and mixing with particles of sand and clay to form a rich, reddish mold as
spring river waters receded; its nourishing of oaks and pines, cypress and
sweetgums, blueberries and huckleberries; and its continual replenishment by
squirrel and bird droppings, leaf litter, earthworms, and fungi. For thousands of
years, the soil particle existed in this state of flux. Then one day, it was scorched
by burning branches and planted with a crop of Indian corn and beans for a
few short years, before suddenly being hoed up and planted with tobacco. Soon,
weakened and deprived of its nitrogen, phosphorus, and calcium, it momentarily
supported wheat before succumbing — in utter exhaustion — to nurturing the roots
of sedge, sorrel, and pine seedlings. In this sour and acidic state, surrounded by
gullies and hillocks overgrown with weeds, it lay recuperating until one day it
was plowed, manured, and limed by an energetic farmer who finally returned
its lost nutrients.*

*This chapter focuses on the use, depletion, and restoration of Chesapeake
Bay soils under tobacco cultivation in the colonial and post-revolutionary periods.*

❦ D O C U M E N T S

Our study of the environmental history of the Tobacco South begins with pictures
and descriptions that reveal the cultural assumptions and lenses through which
Europeans saw the New World. Artist John White did numerous sketches and
paintings of plants, mammals, and Indian life as a member of a failed 1585–1586
effort to settle Roanoke Island off the coast of North Carolina and subsequently as
leader of the 1587 Roanoke "Lost Colony." Realizing that the colony could not
subsist on its own, he returned to England on an expedition for supplies; by the
time he reached Roanoke again in 1590, it was deserted. The colonists, including

his daughter, her husband, and their newly born child Virginia Dare, had left word that they had gone to "Croatoan." White's Indian drawings were engraved by Theodore de Bry and published in 1590 as illustrations to Thomas Harriot's *Briefe and True Report of the New Found Land of Virginia.*

The second document relates the discovery by Jamestown settlers Raphe Hamor (1614) and John Rolfe (1616–1617) that tobacco could answer their need for a staple crop to be traded with England for manufactured items. So successful was "the weed" in producing profits, however, that Sir Thomas Dale, who followed John Smith as governor of the colony, ruled that each colonist must also plant sufficient food to feed his family and servants. In the third document, William Fitzhugh, a wealthy Virginia planter, describes his holdings in a 1686 letter to Dr. Ralph Smith of Bristol, England, for the purpose of arranging an exchange of some of his Virginia properties for rural or urban income-producing properties in England. In the early eighteenth century the Tobacco South was considered such an agreeable place to live that Virginia planter Robert Beverley could, in the fourth document dating from 1705, describe the land as a garden affording such pleasures as to make the colonists grow lazy and sink, like the Indians, into a childlike harmony with nature.

Tobacco cultivation and its social culture, as the fifth and sixth documents reveal, was supported by two deeply interconnected forms of degradation — of the land and of African slaves. In 1775 an anonymous traveler wrote about tobacco management and mismanagement in Virginia and Maryland in a critique entitled *American Husbandry*. Twelve years later, in 1787, Thomas Jefferson described American slavery as the product of such deeply rooted prejudices that it would be impossible to assimilate black people wholly and equally into American culture. Although one of the more enlightened planters and statesmen of his time, Jefferson was a slaveholder and nevertheless believed that "nature" had created real differences that made blacks inferior in reasoning power to whites.

The final two documents spotlight blacks' own responses to the charge of "natural" differences and to the human degradation this assumption entails. Olaudah Equiano, born in West Africa in 1745, was enslaved at the age of eleven in his native land. Subsequently brought on a slave ship to Barbados and then Virginia, Equiano was sold to a planter. Sold next to a British naval officer and then a Philadelphia merchant, he finally bought his freedom and wrote his autobiography (1791), from which the seventh document is taken. Benjamin Banneker, born in Maryland in 1731, became a farmer, mechanic, surveyor, and astronomer who predicted a solar eclipse, prepared almanacs, and served on the commission that surveyed the new capital city of Washington. His letter to Thomas Jefferson in 1792, excerpted in the final selection, prompted the then secretary of state to revise his opinions about the reasoning capacity and mathematical abilities of African-Americans.

As a group the documents reveal the many levels of symbolic and political meaning used by humans to describe and depict "nature" as the physical world, to define the "natural" conditions necessary for human life, to assert the "nature" of human beings, and to construct a dualism between nature and culture.

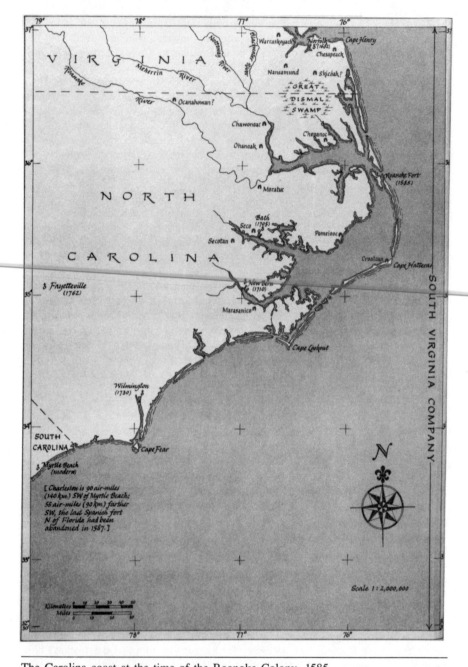

The Carolina coast at the time of the Roanoke Colony, 1585

Source: From *The Complete Works of Captain John Smith, 1580–1631*, edited by Philip L. Barbour. Published for the Institute of Early American History and Culture, Williamsburg, Virginia. Copyright © 1986 by The University of North Carolina Press. Reprinted by permission.

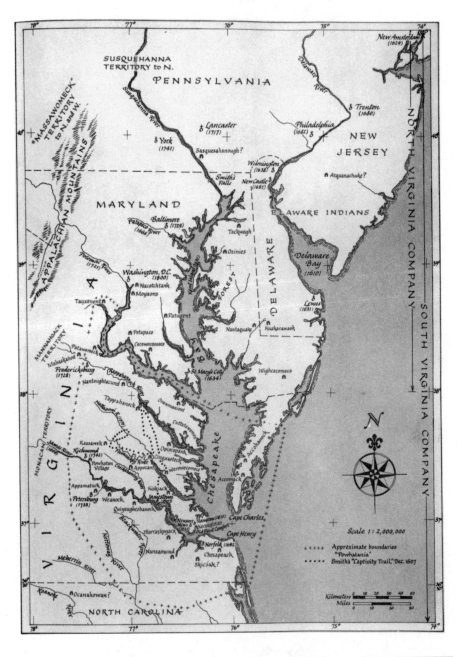

The Chesapeake Bay region during the period of European colonization

Source: From *The Complete Works of Captain John Smith, 1580–1631*, edited by Philip L. Barbour. Published for the Institute of Early American History and Culture, Williamsburg, Virginia. Copyright © 1986 by The University of North Carolina Press. Reprinted by permission.

Diagram of the town of Secota

Source: Rare Book Division, The New York Public Library, Astor, Lenox and Tilden
Foundations.

John White Depicts Indian Planting and Fishing in Virginia, 1590

The Town of Secota

Their towns that are not enclosed with poles are commonly fairer. Then such as are enclosed, as appeareth in this figure which lively expresseth the town of Secota. For the houses are scattered here and there, and they have gardens expressed by the letter E. wherein grows tobacco, which the inhabitants call Uppowoc. They have also groves wherein they take deer, and fields wherein they sow their corn. In their corn fields they build as it were a scaffolde where on they set a cottage like to a round chair, signified by F. wherein they place one to watch for there are such number of fowls, and beasts, that unless they keep the better watch, they would soon devour all their corn. For which cause the watchman maketh continual cries and noise. They sow their corn with a certain distance noted by H. otherwise one stalk would choke the growth of another and the corn would not come into its ripening G. For the leaves thereof are large, like unto the leaves of great reeds. They have also several broad plots C. where they meet with their neighbours, to celebrate their chief solemn feasts . . . and a place D. where after they have ended their feast they make merry together. Over against this place they have a round plot B. where they assemble themselves to make their solemn prayers. Not far from which place there is a large building A. wherein are the tombs of their kings and princes . . . . Likewise they have garden noted by the letter I. wherein they use to sow pumpkins. Also a place marked with K. wherein they make a fire at their solemn feasts, and hard without the town a river L. from whence they fetch their water. This people therefore void of all covetousness live cheerfully and at their hearts ease. But they solemnize their feasts in the night, and therefore they keep very great fires to avoid darkeness, and to testify their Joy.

The Manner of Making Their Boats

The manner of making their boats in Virginia is very wonderful. For whereas they want instrument of iron, or other like unto ours, yet they know how to make them as handsomely, to sail with where they like in their rivers, and to fish with all, as ours. First, they choose some long, and thick tree, according to the bigness of the boat which they would frame, and make a fire on the ground above the root thereof, kindling the same by little, and little with dry moss of trees, and chips of wood that the flame should not mount up too high, and burn too much of the length of the tree. When it is almost burned through, and ready to fall they make a new fire, which they suffer to burn until the tree falls of its own accord. Then burning of the top, and boughs of the tree in such wise that the body of the same may retain its just length, they raise it upon posts laid over crosswise upon forked posts, at such a reasonable height as they may handsomely work up to it. Then they take off the bark with certain shells; they reserve the innermost part of the length, for the nethermost part of the boat. On the other side they make a fire according to the length of the body of the tree, saving at both the ends. That which they think is sufficiently burned, they quench and scrape away with shells, and making a new fire they burn it again, and so they continue sometimes burning and sometimes scraping, until the boat have sufficient bottoms. This god induces this savage people with sufficient reason to make things necessary to serve their turns.

Making boats
Source: William L. Clements Library, University of Michigan.

Their Manner of Fishing in Virginia

They have likewise a notable way to catch fish in their rivers, for whereas they lack both iron and steel, they fasten to their reeds or long rods, the hollow tail of a certain fish like to a sea crab instead of a point, wherewith by night or day they strike fish and take them up into their boats. They also know how to use the prickles and pricks of other fish. They also make wares, with setting up reeds or twigs in the water, which they so plant one within another, that they grow still narrower, and narrower, as appeareth by this figure. There was never seen among us so cunning a way to take fish withal, whereof sundry sorts as they found in the rivers unlike unto ours, which are also of a very good taste. Doubtless it is a pleasant sight to see the people, sometimes wading, and going sometimes sailing in those rivers, which are shallow and not deep, free from all care of heaping up riches for their posterity, content with their state, and living friendly together of those things which god of his bounty hath given unto them, yet without giving him and thanks according to his desert [deserving]. So savage is this people, and deprived of the true knowledge of god. For they have none other than is mentioned before in this work.

Virginia Settlers Discover Tobacco,
1614–1617

Raphe Hamor Extols
the Valuable Commodity Tobacco, 1614

The valuable commodity tobacco, so much prized in England, which every man may plant and tend with a small part of his labor, will earn him both clothing and other necessities. . . . Though none has yet been shipped to England, let no man doubt that it is as good as West Indies Trinidado or Caracus. Having taken up the subject, I must not forget the gentleman, worthy of much commendation, who first took the trouble to try it in 1612, Mr. John Rolfe, partly from the love he has long had for it and partly to develop a profitable commodity to benefit the colonists. . . . My own experience and trial of its goodness persuades me that no country under the sun can or does produce more pleasant, sweet, and strong tobacco than I have tasted there from my own planting. However that was the first year we tried it, and we did not know much about how to cure it and pack it. But there are people there now who learned enough from last year's well observed experience that I have no doubt they will produce and ship this year such tobacco that even England will acknowledge its goodness.

John Rolfe on the Ease
of Growing Tobacco, 1616–1617

Tobacco . . . thrives so well that no doubt, after a bit more experiment and experience in curing it, it will compare with the best in the West Indies. . . . To prevent the people—who are generally inclined to covet profit, especially after they have tasted the sweet results of their labors—from spending too much of their time and labor planting tobacco, which they know can be sold easily in England, and so neglecting their cultivation of grain and not having enough to eat, it is provided by the foresight and care of Sir Thomas Dale that no tenant or other person who must support himself shall plant any tobacco unless he cultivates, plants, and maintains every year for himself and every man servant ten acres of land in grain. . . . Thus they will be supplied with more than enough for their families and can harvest enough tobacco to buy clothing and the other necessities needed by themselves and their households. For an easy-going laborer can maintain and tend two acres of grain and cure a good quantity of tobacco, that being still the principal commodity that the colony produces. . . .

A Virginia Planter Describes His Holdings, 1686
To Doctor Ralph Smith

April 22nd. 1686

Doctr. Ralph Smith

In order to the Exchange you promised to make for me, & I desired you to proceed therein, to say to Exchange an Estate of Inheritance in land there of two or three hundred pound a year, or in houses in any Town of three or four hundred pound a year, I shall be something particular in the relation of my concerns here, that is to go in return thereof. As first the Plantation where I now live contains a thousand Acres, at least 700 Acres of it being rich thicket, the remainder good hearty plantable land, without any waste either by Marshes or great Swamps the Commodiousness, conveniency, & pleasantness yourself well knows, upon it there is three Quarters well furnished, with all necessary houses, ground & fencing, together with a choice crew of Negros at each plantation, most of them this Country born, the remainder as likely as most in Virginia, there being twenty nine in all, with Stocks of cattle & hogs at each Quarter. Upon the same land is my own Dwelling house, furnished with all accommodations for a comfortable & gentle living, as a very good dwelling house, with 13 Rooms in it, four of the best of them hung, nine of them plentifully furnished with all things necessary & convenient, & all houses for use well furnished with brick Chimneys, four good Cellars, a Dairy, Dovecoat, Stable, Barn, Hen house Kitchen & all other conveniences, & all in a manner new, a large Orchard of about 2500 Apple trees most grafted, well fenced with a Locust fence, which is as durable as most brick walls, a Garden a hundred foot square, well pailed in, a Yard wherein is most of the foresaid necessary houses, pallizado'd in with locust Punchens, which is as good as if it were walled in, & more lasting than any of our bricks, together with a good Stock of Cattle hogs horses, Mares, sheep &c, & necessary servants belonging to it, for the supply and support thereof. About a mile & half distance a good water Grist mill, whose tole I find sufficient to find my own family with wheat & Indian corn for our necessitys & occasions. Up the River in this Country three tracts of land more, one of them contains 21996 Acres another 500 acres, & one other 1000 Acres, all good convenient & commodious Seats, & which in a few years will yield a considerable annual Income. A Stock of tobacco with the Crops & good debts lying out of about 250000 lb. besides sufficient of almost all sorts of goods, to supply the families & the Quarter's occasions for two if not three years. Thus I have given you some particulars, which I thus deduce, the yearly Crops of corn & tobacco together with the surplus of meat more than will serve the family's use, will amount annually to 60000 lb. Tobo. which at 10 shillings per Ct. [hundred weight] is 300£ annum, & the Negroes increase being all young, & a considerable parcel of breeders, will keep that Stock good forever.

Excerpts from *William Fitzhugh and His Chesapeake World, 1676–1701*, edited by Richard Beale Davis. Copyright © 1963 by The University of North Carolina Press. Used by permission.

The stock of Tobo. managed with an inland trade, will yearly yield 60000 lb. tobacco without hazard or risk, which will be both clear without charge of housekeeping, or Disbursements for Servants' cloathing. The Orchard in a very few years will yield a large supply to plentiful housekeeping, or if better husbanded, yield at least 15000 lb. tobacco annual Income. What I have not particularly mentioned, your own knowledge in my affairs is able to supply, if any are so desirous to deal for the Estate without the stock of tobacco I shall be ready & willing, but I will make no fractions of that; either all or none at all shall go. I have so fully discoursed you in the affair, that I shall add no farther instructions, but leave it to your prudent & careful management, & would advise that if any Overtures of such a nature should happen, immediately give an account thereof to Mr. Nicholas Hayward Notary public near the Exchange London, both of the person treating, & the place situation, Quantity & quality of the Estate, who will take speedy & effectual care, to give me a full & ready account thereof, which I hope you will . . . [take] all opportunitie do to

Sir Your W. ff. [William Fitzhugh]

Robert Beverley on Indians and Nature in Virginia, 1705

"The Indians of Virginia Are Almost Wasted"

The Indians of Virginia are almost wasted, but such Towns, or People as retain their Names, and live in Bodies, are hereunder set down; All which together can't raise five hundred fighting men. They live poorly, and much in fear of the Neighbouring Indians. Each Town, by the Articles of Peace in 1677. pays 3 Indian Arrows for their Land, and 20 Beaver Skins for protection every year.

In Accomac are 8 Towns, viz.

Matomkin is much decreased of late by the Small Pox, that was carried thither.

Gingoteque. The few remains of this Town are joined with a Nation of the Maryland Indians.

Kiequotank, is reduced to very few Men.

Matchopungo, has a small number yet living.

Occahanock, has a small number yet living.

Pungoteque. Governed by a Queen, but a small Nation.

Oanancock, has but four or five Families.

Chiconessex, has very few, who just keep the name.

Nanduye. A Seat of the Empress. Not above 20 Families, but she hath all the Nations of this Shore under Tribute.

In Northampton. Gangascoe, which is almost as numerous as all the foregoing Nations put together.

In Prince George. Wyanoke, is almost wasted, and now gone to live among other Indians.

In Charles City. Appamattox. These Live in Colonel Byrd's Pasture, not being above seven Families.

In Surry. Nottawayes, which are about a hundred Bow men, of late a thriving and increasing People.

By Nansamond. Meheering, has about thirty Bowmen, who keep at a stand.

Nansamond. About thirty Bow-men: They have increased much of late.

In King Williams County, 2. Pamunkie, has about forty Bow-men, who decrease.

Chickahomonie, which had about sixteen Bow-men, but lately increased.

In Essex. Rappahannock, is reduced to a few Families, and live scattered upon the English Seats.

In Richmond. Port-Tabago, has [a]bout five Bow-men, but Wasting.

In Northumberland. Wiccocomoco, has but three men living, which yet keep up their Kingdom, and retain their Fashion; they live by themselves, separate from all other Indians, and from the English.

. . . I have given a succinct account of the Indians; happy, I think, in their simple State of Nature, and in their enjoyment of Plenty, without the Curse of Labour. They have on several accounts reason to lament the arrival of the Europeans, by whose means they seem to have lost their Felicity, as well as their Innocence. The English have taken away great part of their Country, and consequently made every thing less plenty amongst them. They have introduced Drunkenness and Luxury amongst them, which have multiplied their Wants, and put them upon desiring a thousand things, they never dreamed of before. I have been the more concise in my account of this harmless people, because I have inserted several Figures, which I hope have both supplied the defect of Words, and rendered the Descriptions more clear. I shall in the next place proceed to treat of Virginia, as it is now improved, (I should rather say altered,) by the English; and of its present Constitution and Settlement.

"Have You Pleasure in a Garden?"

Of the Temperature of the Climate, and the Inconveniences Attending It

The Natural Temperature of the Inha[bit]ed part of the Country, is hot and moist: though this Moisture I take to be occasioned by the abundance of low Grounds, Marshes, Creeks, and Rivers, which are everywhere among their lower Settlements; but more backward in the Woods, where they are now Seating, and making new Plantations, they have abundance of high and dry Land, where there are only Crystal Streams of Water, which flow gently from their Springs, and divide themselves into innumerable Branches, to moisten and enrich the adjacent Lands.

The Country is in a very happy Situation, between the extremes of Heat and Cold, but inclining rather to the first. Certainly it must be a happy Climate, since it is very near of the same Latitude with the Land of Promise. Besides, As *Judaa* was full of Rivers, and Branches of Rivers; So is *Virginia*: As that was seated upon a great Bay and Sea, wherein were all the conveniences for Shipping and Trade; So is *Virginia*. Had that fertility of Soil? So has *Virginia*, equal to any Land in the known World. In fine, if any one impartially considers all the Advantages of this Country, as Nature made it; he must allow it to be as fine a Place, as any in the Universe; but I confess I am ashamed to say anything of its Improvements, because I must at the same time reproach my Countrymen with a Laziness that is unpardonable. If there be any excuse for them in this Matter, 'tis the exceeding plenty of good things, with which Nature has blest them; for where God Almighty is so Merciful as to work for People, they never work for themselves.

All the Countries in the World, seated in or near the Latitude of *Virginia*, are esteemed the Fruitfulest, and Pleasantest of all Climates. As for Example, *Canaan, Syria, Persia*, great part of *India, China* and *Japan*, the *Morea, Spain, Portugal*, and the coast of *Barbary*, none of which differ many Degrees of Latitude from *Virginia*. These are reckoned the Gardens of the World, while *Virginia* is unjustly neglected by its own Inhabitants, and abused by other People. . . .

. . . If People will be persuaded to be Temperate, and take due care of themselves, I believe it is as healthy a Country, as any under Heaven: but the extraordinary pleasantness of the Weather, and the goodness of the Fruit, lead People into many Temptations. The clearness and brightness of the Sky, add new vigour to their Spirits, and perfectly remove all Splenetic and sullen Thoughts. Here they enjoy all the benefits of a warm Sun, and by their shady Groves, are protected from its Inconvenience. Here all their Senses are entertained with an endless Succession of Native Pleasures. Their Eyes are ravished with the Beauties of naked Nature. Their Ears are Serenaded with the perpetual murmur of Brooks, and the thorow-base [continuo] which the Wind plays, when it wantons through the Trees; the merry Birds too, join their pleasing Notes to this rural Consort, especially the Mock-birds, who love Society so well, that whenever they see Mankind, they will perch upon a Twig very near them, and sing the sweetest wild Airs in the World: But what is most remarkable in these Melodious Animals, they will frequently fly at small distances before a Traveller, warbling out their Notes several Miles an end, and by their Music, make a Man forget the Fatigues of his Journey. Their Taste is regaled with the most delicious Fruits, which without Art, they have in great Variety and Perfection. And then their smell is refreshed with an eternal fragrance of Flowers and Sweets, with which Nature perfumes and adorns the Woods almost the whole year round.

Have you pleasure in a Garden? All things thrive in it, most surprisingly; you can't walk by a Bed of Flowers, but besides the entertainment of their Beauty, your Eyes will be saluted with the charming colours of the Humming Bird, which revels among the Flowers, and licks off the Dew and Honey from their tender Leaves, on which it only feeds. It's size is not half so large as an

English Wren, and its colour is a glorious shining mixture of Scarlet, Green, and Gold. Colonel *Byrd*, in his Garden, which is the finest in that Country, has a Summer-House set round with the *Indian* Honeysuckle, which all the Summer is continually full of sweet Flowers, in which these Birds delight exceedingly. Upon these Flowers, I have seen ten or a dozen of these Beautiful Creatures together, which sported about me so familiarly, that with their little Wings they often fanned my Face.

A Traveler Describes Tobacco Cultivation, 1775

This plant [tobacco] is cultivated in all parts of North America, from Quebec to Carolina, and even the West Indies; but, except in Maryland, Virginia, and North Carolina, they plant no more than for private use, making it an object of exportation only in these provinces, where it is of such immense consequence.

It was planted in large quantities by the Indians, when we first came to America, and its use from them brought into Europe; but what their method of culture was is now no longer known, as they plant none, but buy what they want of the English. Tobacco is raised from the seed, which is sown in spring upon a bed of rich mould; when about the height of four or five inches, the planter takes the opportunity of rainy weather to transplant them. The ground which is prepared to receive it, is, if it can be got, a rich black mould; fresh woodlands are best: sometimes it is so badly cleared from the stumps of trees, that they cannot give it any ploughings; but in old cultivated lands they plough it several times, and spread on it what manure they can raise. The negroes then hill it; that is, with hoes and shovels they form hillocks, which lie in the manner of Indian corn, only they are larger, and more carefully raked up: the hills are made in squares, from six to nine feet distance, according to the land; the richer it is the further they are put asunder, as the plants grow higher and spread proportionally. The plants in about a month are a foot high, when they prune and top them; operations, in which they seem to be very wild, and to execute them upon no rational principles; experiments are much wanting on these points, for the planters never go out of the beaten road, but do just as their fathers did, resembling therein the British farmers their brethren. They prune off all the bottom leaves, leaving only seven or eight on a stalk, thinking that such as they leave will be the larger, which is contrary to nature in every instance throughout all vegetation. In six weeks more the tobacco is at its full growth, being then from four and a half to seven feet high: during all this time, the negroes are employed twice a week in pruning off the suckers, clearing the hillocks from weeds, and attending to the worms, which are a great enemy to the plant; when the tobacco changes its colour, turning brown, it is ripe and they then cut it down, and lay it close in heaps in the field to sweat one night: the next day they are carried in bunches by the negroes to a building called the tobacco house, where every plant is hung up separate to dry, which takes a month or five weeks; this house excludes the rain, but is designed for the admission of as much air as possible. They are then laid close in heaps in the tobacco houses for a week or a fortnight to sweat again, after which it is sorted and packed up in hogsheads; all the operations after the plants are dried must be done in moist or wet weather, which prevents its crumbling to dust. . . .

One of the greatest advantages attending the culture of tobacco is the quick, easy, and certain method of sale. This was effected by the inspection law, which took place in Virginia in the year 1730, but not in Maryland till 1748. The planter, by virtue of this, may go to any place and sell his tobacco, without carrying a sample of it along with him, and the merchant may buy it, though lying a hundred miles, or at any distance from his store, and yet be morally sure both with respect to quantity and quality. For this purpose, upon all the rivers and bays of both provinces, at the distance of about twelve or fourteen miles from each other, are erected warehouses, to which all the tobacco in the country must be brought and there lodged, before the planters can offer it to sale; and inspectors are appointed to examine all the tobacco brought in, receive such as is good and merchantable, condemn and burn what appears damnified or insufficient. The greatest part of the tobacco is prized, or put up into hogsheads by the planters themselves, before it is carried to the warehouses. Each hogshead, by an act of assembly, must be 950 lb. neat [net] or upwards; some of them weigh 14 cwt. and even 18 cwt. and the heavier they are the merchants like them the better; because four hogsheads, whatsoever their weight be, are esteemed a tun, and pay the same freight. The inspectors give notes of receipt for the tobacco, and the merchants take them in payment for their goods, passing current indeed over the whole colonies; a most admirable invention, which operates so greatly that in Virginia they have no paper currency.

The merchants generally purchase the tobacco in the country, by sending persons to open *stores* for them; that is, warehouses in which they lay in a great assortment of British commodities and manufactures; to these, as to shops, the planters resort, and supply themselves with what they want, paying, in inspection receipts, or taking on credit according to what will be given them; and as they are in general a very luxurious set of people, they buy too much upon credit; the consequence of which is, their getting in debt to the London merchants, who take mortgages on their plantations, ruinous enough, with the usury of eight per cent. But this is apparently the effect of their imprudence in living upon trust.

Respecting the product of tobacco, they know very little of it themselves by the acre, as they never calculate in that manner, and not many tobacco grounds were ever measured: all their ideas run in the proportion per working hand. Some are hired labourers, but in general they are negroe slaves; and the product, from the best information I have gained, varies from an hogshead and a half to three and an half per head. The hogshead used to be of the value of 5£. but of late years it is 8£. per head, according to the goodness of the lands and other circumstances. But [as for] the planters, none of them depend on tobacco alone, and this is more and more the case since corn has yielded a high price, and since their grounds have begun to be worn out. They all raise corn and provisions enough to support the family and plantation, besides exporting considerable quantities; no wheat in the world exceeds in quality that of Virginia and Maryland. Lumber they also send largely to the West Indies. The whole culture of tobacco is over in the summer months; in the winter the negroes are employed in sawing and butting timber, threshing corn, clearing new land, and preparing for tobacco; so that it is plain, they make a product per head, besides that of tobacco.

Suppose each negroe makes two hogsheads of tobacco, or 16£. and 4£. in corn, provisions, and lumber, besides supporting the plantation, this is a moderate supposition; and if true, the planter's profit may be easily calculated: the negroe costs him 50£. his cloathing, tools, and sundries, 3£.; in this case, the expence of the slave is only the interest of his cost, 2£. 10s. and the total only makes 5£. 10s. a year. To this we must add the interest of the planter's capital, province taxes, &c. which will make some addition, perhaps thirty or forty shillings per head more, there will then remain 12£. 10s. a head profit to the planter. . . .

There is no plant in the world that requires richer land, or more manure than tobacco; it will grow on poorer fields, but not to yield crops that are sufficiently profitable to pay the expences of negroes, &c. The land they found to answer best is fresh woodlands, where many ages have formed a stratum of rich black mould. Such land will, after clearing, bear tobacco many years, without any change, prove more profitable to the planter than the power of dung can do on worse lands: this makes the tobacco planters more solicitous for new land than any other people in America, they wanting it much more. Many of them have very handsome houses, gardens, and improvements about them, which fixes them to one spot; but others, when they have exhausted their grounds, will sell them to new settlers for corn-fields, and move backwards with their negroes, cattle, and tools, to take up fresh land for tobacco; this is common, and will continue so as long as good land is to be had upon navigable rivers: this is the system of business which made some, so long ago as 1750, move over the Alleg[h]any mountains, and settle not far from the Ohio, where their tobacco was to be carried by land some distance, which is a heavy burthen on so bulky a commodity, but answered by the superior crops they gained. . . .

A very considerable tract of land is necessary for a tobacco plantation; first, that the planter may have a sure prospect of increasing his culture on fresh land; secondly, that the lumber may be a winter employment for his slaves and afford casks for his crops. Thirdly, that he may be able to keep vast stocks of cattle for raising provisions in plenty, by ranging in the woods; and where the lands are not fresh, the necessity is yet greater, as they must yield much manure for replenishing the worn-out fields. This want of land is such, that they reckon a planter should have 50 acres of land for every working hand; with less than this they will find themselves distressed for want of room.

But I must observe that great improvements might be made in the culture of this crop; the attention of the planters is to keep their negroes employed on the plants and the small space that the hillocks occupy, being very apt to neglect the intervals; the expence of hoeing them is considerable, and consequently they are apt to be remiss in this work. Here they ought to substitute the horse-hoeing management, which would cost much less, and be an hundred times more effectual.

The tobacco planters live more like country gentlemen of fortune than any other settlers in America; all of them are spread about the country, their labour being mostly by slaves, who are left to overseers; and the masters live in a state of emulation with one another in buildings (many of their houses would make no slight figure in the English counties), furniture, wines, dress, diversions, &c. and this to such a degree, that it is rather amazing they should be able to go on with their plantations at all, than they should not make additions to them: such a country life as they lead, in the midst of a profusion of rural sports and diversions, with little to do themselves, and in a climate that seems to create rather than check pleasure, must almost naturally have a strong effect in bringing them to be just such planters as foxhunters in England make farmers. . . .

Before I quit these observations on this part of the husbandry of Virginia and Maryland, I should remark that to make a due profit on tobacco, a man should be able to begin with twenty slaves at least, because so many will pay for an overseer: none, or at least very few, can be kept without an overseer, and if fewer than twenty be the number, the expence of the overseer will be too high; for they are seldom to be gained under 25£. a year, and generally from 30 to 50£. But it does not follow from hence, that settlers are precluded from these colonies who cannot buy twenty negroes; every day's experience tells us the contrary of this; the only difference is, that they begin in small; and either have no slaves at all, or no more than what they will submit to take care of themselves; in this case, they may begin with only one or two, and make a profit proportioned to that of the greater number, without the expence of an overseer. . . . Settlers of all kinds fix in these colonies, with advantages as great, if not greater, than any others. The culture of corn and other provisions is as profitable here as any where else; and plantations are every day left by tobacco planters, who quit and sell them at low prices, in order to retire backwards for fresh land, to cultivate tobacco to advantage; besides which, the new country is to be had here, equally with any other province, and upon terms as advantageous.

It is no slight benefit to be able to mix tobacco planting with common husbandry; this is as easily done as can be wished, and is indeed the practice of the greatest planters. A man may be a farmer for corn and provisions, and yet employ a few hands on tobacco, according as his land or manure will allow him. This makes a small business very profitable, and at the same time easy to be attained, nor is any thing more common throughout both Maryland and Virginia.

Thomas Jefferson on the "Nature" of Blacks and Worn-Out Tobacco Lands, 1787

"Deep Rooted Prejudices"

It will probably be asked, Why not retain and incorporate the blacks into the state, and thus save the expence of supplying, by importation of white settlers, the vacancies they will leave? Deep rooted prejudices entertained by the whites; ten thousand recollections, by the blacks, of the injuries they have sustained; new provocations; the real distinctions which nature has made; and many other circumstances, will divide us into parties, and produce convulsions which will probably never end but in the extermination of the one or the other race. — To these objections, which are political, may be added others, which are physical and moral. The first difference which strikes us is that of colour. Whether the black of the negro resides in the reticular membrane between the skin and scarf-skin [epidermis], or in the scarf-skin itself; whether it proceeds from the colour of the blood, the colour of the bile, or from that of some other secretion, the difference is fixed in nature, and is as real as if its seat and cause were better known to us. And is this difference of no importance? Is it not the foundation of a greater or less share of beauty in the two races? Are not the fine mixtures of red and white, the expressions of every passion by greater or less suffusions of colour in the one, preferable to that eternal monotony, which reigns in the countenances, that immoveable veil of black which covers all the emotions of the other race? Add to these, flowing hair, a more elegant symmetry of form, their own judgment in favour of the whites, declared by their preference of them, as uniformly as is the preference of the Oran-ootan for the black women over those of his own species. The circumstance of superior beauty, is thought worthy attention in the propagation of our horses, dogs, and other domestic animals; why not in that of man? Besides those of colour, figure, and hair, there are other physical distinctions proving a difference of race. They have less hair on the face and body. They secrete less by the kidnies, and more by the glands of the skin, which gives them a very strong and disagreeable odour. This greater degree of transpiration renders them more tolerant of heat, and less so of cold, than the whites. Perhaps too a difference of structure in the pulmonary apparatus, which a late ingenious experimentalist has discovered to be the principal regulator of animal heat, may have disabled them from extricating, in the act of inspiration, so much of that fluid from the outer air, or obliged them in expiration, to part with more of it. They seem to require less sleep. A black, after hard labour through the day, will be induced by the slightest amusements to sit up till midnight, or later, though knowing he must be out with the first dawn of the morning. They are at least as brave, and more adventuresome. But this may perhaps proceed from a want of forethought, which prevents their seeing a danger till it be present. When present, they do not go through it with more coolness or steadiness than the whites. They are more ardent after their female: but love seems with them to be more an eager desire, than a tender delicate mixture of sentiment and sensation. Their griefs are transient. Those numberless afflictions, which render it doubtful whether heaven has given life to us in mercy or in wrath, are less felt, and sooner forgotten with them. In general, their existence appears to participate more of sensation than reflection. To this must be ascribed their disposition to sleep when abstracted from their diversions, and unemployed in labour. An animal whose body is at rest, and who does not reflect, must be disposed to sleep of course. Comparing them by their faculties of memory, reason, and imagination, it appears to me, that in memory they are equal to the whites; in reason much inferior, as I think one could scarcely be found capable of tracing and comprehending the investigations of Euclid; and that in imagination they are dull, tasteless, and anomalous. It would be unfair to follow them to Africa for this investigation. We will consider them here, on the same stage with the whites, and where the facts are not apocryphal on which a judgment is to be formed. It will be right to make great allowances for the difference of condition, of education, of conversation, of the sphere in which they move. Many millions of them have been brought to, and born in America. Most of them indeed have been confined to tillage, to their own homes, and their own society: yet many have been so situated, that they might have availed themselves of the conversation of their masters; many have been brought up to the handicraft arts, and from that circumstance have always been associated with the whites. Some have been liberally educated, and all have lived in countries where the arts and sciences are cultivated to a considerable degree, and have had before their eyes samples of the best works from abroad. The Indians, with no advantages of this kind, will often carve figures on their pipes not destitute of design and merit. They will crayon out an animal, a plant, or a country, so as to prove the existence of a germ in their minds which only wants cultivation. They astonish you with strokes of the most sublime oratory; such as prove their reason and sentiment strong, their imagination glowing and elevated. But never yet could I find that a black had uttered a thought above the level of plain narration; never see even an elementary trait of painting or sculpture. In music they are more generally gifted than the whites with accurate ears for tune and time, and they have been found capable of imagining a small catch. Whether they will be equal to the composition of a more extensive run of melody, or of complicated harmony, is yet to be proved. Misery is often the parent of the most affecting touches in poetry. — Among the blacks is misery enough, God knows, but no poetry. Love is the peculiar œstrum of the poet. Their love is ardent, but it kindles the senses only, not the imagination. Religion indeed has produced a Phyllis Whately [Wheatley, see Chapter 6]; but it could not produce a poet. The compositions published under her name are below the dignity of criticism. The heroes of the Dunciad are to her, as Hercules to the author of that poem. . . .

Notwithstanding these considerations which must weaken their respect for the laws of property, we find among them numerous instances of the most rigid integrity, and as many as among their better instructed masters, of benevolence, gratitude, and unshaken fidelity. — The opinion, that they are inferior in the faculties of reason and imagination, must be hazarded with great diffidence. To justify a general conclusion, requires many observations, even where the subject may be submitted to the Anatomical knife, to Optical glasses, to analysis by fire, or by solvents. How much more then where it is a faculty, not a substance, we are examining; where it eludes the research of all the senses; where the conditions of its existence are various and variously combined; where the effects of those which are present or absent bid defiance to calculation; let me add too, as a circumstance of great tenderness, where our conclusion would degrade a whole race of men from the rank in the scale of beings which their Creator may perhaps have given them. To our reproach it must be said, that though for a century and a half we have had under our eyes the races of black and of red men, they have never yet been viewed by us as subjects of natural history. I advance it therefore as a suspicion only, that the blacks, whether originally a distinct race, or made distinct by time and circumstances, are inferior to the whites in the endowments both of body and mind. It is not against experience to suppose, that different species of the same genus, or varieties of the same species, may possess different qualifications. Will not a lover of natural history then, one who views the gradations in all the races of animals with the eye of philosophy, excuse an effort to keep those in the department of man as distinct as nature has formed them? This unfortunate difference of colour, and perhaps of faculty, is a powerful obstacle to the emancipation of these people. Many of their advocates, while they wish to vindicate the liberty of human nature, are anxious also to preserve its dignity and beauty. Some of these, embarrassed by the question "What further is to be done with them?" join themselves in opposition with those who are actuated by sordid avarice only. Among the Romans emancipation required but one effort. The slave, when made free, might mix with, without staining the blood of his master. But with us a second is necessary, unknown to history. When freed, he is to be removed beyond the reach of mixture.

"Tobacco Culture Is Fast Declining"

Before the present war we exported . . . according to the best information I can get, nearly as follows:*

In the year 1758 we exported seventy thousand hogsheads of tobacco, which was the greatest quantity ever produced in this country in one year. But its culture was fast declining at the commencement of this war and that of wheat taking its place: and it must continue to decline on the return of peace. I suspect that the change in the temperature of our climate has become sensible to that plant, which, to be good, requires an extraordinary degree of heat. But it requires still more indispensably an uncommon fertility of soil: and the price which it commands at market will not enable the planter to produce this by manure. Was the supply still to depend on Virginia and Maryland alone, as its culture becomes more difficult, the price would rise, so as to enable the planter to surmount those difficulties and to live. But the western country on the Missisipi, and the midlands of Georgia, having fresh and fertile lands in abundance, and a hotter sun, will be able to undersell these two states, and will oblige them to abandon the raising tobacco altogether. And a happy obligation for them it will be. It is a culture productive of infinite wretchedness. Those employed in it are in a continued state of exertion beyond the powers of nature to support. Little food of any kind is raised by them; so that the men and animals on these farms are badly fed, and the earth is rapidly impoverished. The cultivation of wheat is the reverse in every circumstance. Besides cloathing the earth with herbage, and preserving its fertility, it feeds the labourers harvest, raises great numbers of animals for food and service, and diffuses plenty and happiness among the whole. We find it easier to make an hundred

---

*Jefferson included a table of exports from Virginia listed in order of dollar amounts of revenue as follows: Tobacco; Wheat; Indian corn; Shipping; Masts, planks, skantling, shingles, staves; Tar, pitch, turpentine; Peltry, viz. skins of deer, beavers, otters, muskrats, racoons, foxes; Pork; Flaxseed, hemp, cotton; Pit-coal, pig-iron; Peas; Beef; Sturgeon, whiteshad, herring; Brandy from peaches and apples, and whiskey; Horses.

bushels of wheat than a thousand weight of tobacco, and they are worth more when made.

Olaudah Equiano Describes His Enslavement, 1791

The first object which saluted my eyes when I arrived on the coast was the sea, and a slave ship, which was then riding at anchor, and waiting for its cargo. These filled me with astonishment, which was soon connected with terror, when I was carried on board. I was immediately handled, and tossed up to see if I were sound, by some of the crew; and I was now persuaded that I had gotten into a world of bad spirits, and that they were going to kill me. Their complexions too differing so much from ours, their long hair, and the language they spoke (which was very different from any I had ever heard), united to confirm me in this belief.

Indeed, such were the horrors of my views and fears at the moment, that, if ten thousand worlds had been my own, I would have freely parted with them all to have exchanged my condition with that of the meanest slave in my own country. When I looked round the ship too and saw a large furnace or copper boiling, and a multitude of black people of every description chained together, every one of their countenances expressing dejection and sorrow, I no longer doubted of my fate; and, quite overpowered with horror and anguish, I fell motionless on the deck and fainted.

When I recovered a little, I found some black people about me, who I believed were some of those who had brought me on board, and had been receiving their pay; they talked to me in order to cheer me, but all in vain. I asked them if I were not to be eaten by those white men with horrible looks, red faces, and long hair. They told me I was not: and one of the crew brought me a small portion of spirituous liquor in a wine glass; but being afraid of him, I would not take it out of his hand. One of the blacks therefore took it from him and gave it to me, and I took a little down my palate, which, instead of reviving me, as they thought it would, threw me into the greatest consternation at the strange feeling it produced, having never tasted any such liquor before.

Soon after this, the blacks who brought me on board went off, and left me abandoned to despair. I now saw myself deprived of all chance of returning to my native country, or even the least glimpse of hope of gaining the shore, which I now considered as friendly; and I even wished for my former slavery in preference to my present situation, which was filled with horrors of every kind, still heightened by my ignorance of what I was to undergo.

I was not long suffered to indulge my grief; I was soon put down under the decks, and there I received such a salutation in my nostrils as I had never experienced in my life: so that with the loathsomeness of the stench and crying together, I became so sick and low that I was not able to eat, nor had I the least desire to taste anything.

I now wished for the last friend, death, to relieve me; but soon, to my grief, two of the white men offered me eatables; and, on my refusing to eat, one of them held me fast by the hands, and laid me across, I think, the windlass, and tied my feet, while the other flogged me severely.

I had never experienced anything of this kind before; and although, not being used to the water, I naturally feared that element the first time I saw it, yet nevertheless, could I have got over the nettings, I would have jumped over the side, but I could not; and, besides, the crew used to watch us very closely who were not chained down to the decks, lest we should leap into the water: and I have seen some of these poor African prisoners most severely cut for attempting to do so, and hourly whipped for not eating. This indeed was often the case with myself.

In a little time after, amongst the poor chained men, I found some of my own nation, which in a small degree gave ease to my mind. I inquired of these what was to be done with us? They gave me to understand we were to be carried to these white people's country to work for them. I then was a little revived, and thought, if it were no worse than working, my situation was not so desperate.

But still I feared I should be put to death, the white people looked and acted, as I thought, in so savage a manner; for I had never seen among any people such instances of brutal cruelty; and this not only shewn towards us blacks, but also to some of the whites themselves.

One white man in particular I saw, when we were permitted to be on deck, flogged so unmercifully with a large rope near the foremast, that he died in consequence of it; and they tossed him over the side as they would have done a brute. This made me fear these people the more; and I expected nothing less than to be treated in the same manner.

I could not help expressing my fears and apprehensions to some of my countrymen: I asked them if these people had no country, but lived in this hollow place (the ship)? They told me they did not, but came from a distant one.

"Then," said I, "how comes it in all our country we 'never heard of them!' " They told me because they lived so very far off. I then asked where were their women? Had they any like themselves? I was told they had: "And why," said I, "do we not see them?" They answered, because they were left behind.

I asked how the vessel could go? They told me they could not tell; but that there were cloth put upon the masts by the help of the ropes I saw, and then the vessel went on; and the white men had some spell or magic they put in the water when they liked in order to stop the vessel. I was exceedingly amazed at this account, and really thought they were spirits. I therefore wished much to be from amongst them, for I expected they would sacrifice me: but my wishes were vain; for we were so quartered that it was impossible for any of us to make our escape.

While we stayed on the coast I was mostly on deck; and one day, to my great astonishment, I saw one of these vessels coming in with the sails up. As soon as the whites saw it, they gave a great shout, at which we were amazed; and the more so as the vessel appeared larger by approaching nearer. At last she came to an anchor in my sight, and when the anchor was let go I and my countrymen who saw it were lost in astonishment to observe the vessel stop; and were now convinced it was done by magic.

Soon after this the other ship got her boats out, and they came on board of us, and the people of both ships seemed very glad to see each other. Several of the strangers also shook hands with us, black people, and made motions with their hands, signifying I suppose, we were to go to their country; but we did not understand them.

At last, when the ship we were in had got in all her cargo, they made ready with many fearful noises, and we were all put under deck, so that we could not see how they managed the vessel.

But this disappointment was the least of my sorrow. The stench of the hold while we were on the coast was so intolerably loathsome that it was dangerous to remain there for any time, and some of us had been permitted to stay on the deck for the fresh air; but now that the whole ship's cargo were confined together, it became absolutely pestilential.

The closeness of the place, and the heat of the climate, added to the number in the ship, which was so crowded that each had scarcely room to turn himself, almost suffocated us. This produced copious perspirations, so that the air soon became unfit for respiration, from a variety of loathsome smells, and brought on a sickness among the slaves, of which many died, thus falling victims to the improvident avarice, as I may call it, of their purchasers.

This wretched situation was again aggravated by the galling of the chains, now become insupportable; and the filth of the necessary tubs, into which the children often fell, and were almost suffocated. The shrieks of the women, and the groans of the dying, rendered the whole a scene of horror almost inconceivable.

Happily perhaps for myself I was soon reduced so low here that it was thought necessary to keep me almost always on deck; and from my extreme youth I was not put in fetters. In this situation I expected every hour to share the fate of my companions, some of whom were almost daily brought upon deck at the point of death, which I began to hope would soon put an end to my miseries. Often did I think many of the inhabitants of the deep much more happy than myself. I envied them the freedom they enjoyed, and as often wished I could change my condition for theirs. . . .

During our passage I first saw flying fishes, which surprised me very much: they used frequently to fly across the ship, and many of them fell on the deck. I also now first saw the use of the quadrant; I had often with astonishment seen the mariners make observations with it, and I could not think what it meant. They at last took notice of my surprise: and one of them, willing to increase it, as well as to gratify my curiosity, made me one day look through it. The clouds appeared to me to be land, which disappeared as they passed along. This heightened my wonder; and I was now more persuaded than ever that I was in another world, and that every thing about me was magic.

At last we came in sight of the island of Barbadoes, at which the whites on board gave a great shout, and made many signs of joy to us. We did not know what to think of this; but as the vessel drew nearer we plainly saw the harbour, and other ships of different kinds and sizes; and we soon anchored amongst them off Bridge-Town.

Many merchants and planters now came on board, though it was in the evening. They put us in separate parcels, and examined us attentively. They also made us jump, and pointed to the land, signifying we were to go there. We thought by this we should be eaten by these ugly men, as they appeared to us; and, when soon after we were all put down under the deck again, there was much dread and trembling.

Benjamin Banneker Responds to Thomas Jefferson, 1792

I suppose it is a truth too well attested to you, to need a proof here, that we are a race of beings, who have long labored under the abuse and censure of the world; that we have long been looked upon with an eye of contempt; and that we have long been considered rather as brutish than human, and scarcely capable of mental endowments.

Sir, I hope I may safely admit, in consequence of that report which hath reached me, that you are a man less inflexible in sentiments of this nature, than many others; that you are measurably friendly, and well disposed towards us; and that you are willing and ready to lend your aid and assistance to our relief, from those many distresses, and numerous calamities, to which we are reduced.

Now Sir, if this is founded in truth, I apprehend you will embrace every opportunity to eradicate that train of absurd and false ideas and opinions, which so generally prevails with respect to us; and that your sentiments are concurrent with mine, which are, that one universal Father hath given being to us all; and that he hath not only made us all of one flesh, but that he hath also, without partiality, afforded us all the same sensations and endowed us all with the same faculties; and that however variable we may be in society or religion, however diversified in situation or color, we are all in the same family and stand in the same relation to him. . . .

Sir, I freely and cheerfully acknowledge, that I am of the African race, and in that color which is natural to them of the deepest dye; and it is under a sense of the most profound gratitude to the Supreme Ruler of the Universe, that I now confess to you, that I am not under that state of tyrannical thraldom, and inhuman captivity, to which too many of my brethren are doomed, but that I have abundantly tasted of the fruition of those blessings, which proceed from that free and unequalled liberty with which you are favored. . . .

Sir, suffer me to recall to your mind that time, in which the arms and tyranny of the British crown were exerted, with every powerful effort, in order to reduce you to a state of servitude. . . .

This, Sir, was a time when you clearly saw into the injustice of a state of slavery, and in which you had just apprehensions of the horror of its condition. It was now that your abhorrence thereof was so excited, that you publicly held forth this true and invaluable doctrine, which is worthy to be recorded and remembered in all succeeding ages: "We hold these truths to be self-evident, that all men are created equal; that they are endowed by their Creator with certain unalienable rights, and that among these are, life, liberty, and the pursuit of happiness."

Here was a time, in which your tender feelings for yourselves had engaged you thus to declare, you were then impressed with proper ideas of the great violation of liberty, and the free possession of those blessings, to which you were entitled by nature; but Sir, how pitiable is it to reflect, that although you were so fully convinced of the benevolence of the Father of Mankind, and of his equal and impartial distribution of these rights and privileges, which he hath conferred upon them, that you should at the same time counteract his mercies, in detaining by fraud and violence so numerous a part of my brethren, under groaning captivity, and cruel oppression that you should at the same time be found guilty of that most criminal act, which you professedly detested in others with respect to yourselves.

I suppose that your knowledge of the situation of my brethren is too extensive to need a recital here; neither shall I presume to prescribe methods by which they may be relieved, otherwise than by recommending to you and all others, to wean yourselves from those narrow prejudices which you have imbibed with respect to them, and as Job proposed to his friends, "put your soul in their souls' stead"; thus shall your hearts be enlarged with kindness and benevolence towards them; and thus shall you need neither the direction of myself or others, in what manner to proceed herein.

And now, Sir, although my sympathy and affection for my brethren hath caused my enlargement thus far, I ardently hope that your candor and generosity will plead with you in my behalf, when I make known to you, that it was not originally my design; but having taken up my pen in order to direct to you, as a present, a copy of my Almanac, which I have calculated for the succeeding year, I was unexpectedly and unavoidably led thereto.

This calculation is the product of my arduous study, in this most advanced stage of life; for having long had unbounded desires to become acquainted with the secrets of nature, I have had to gratify my curiosity herein through my own assiduous application to Astronomical Study, in which I need not recount to you the many difficulties and disadvantages which I have had to encounter.

❦ *E S S A Y S*

The essays look at conflicting versions of the history of the Tobacco South. The first selection, by Ronald Takaki, professor of ethnic studies at the University of California at Berkeley, focuses on how perceptions of differences in black, red, and white bodies resulted in discrimination and enslavement under capitalist agriculture. The English projected onto blacks and Indians the animal-like, instinctual forces from which they sought to distinguish themselves as "civilized" peoples. In the second essay, historian Timothy H. Breen of Northwestern University considers the mind of the planter. Breen argues that tobacco agriculture created a tobacco culture — a symbolic world that permeated every aspect of mental life. In the third essay, historian Avery O. Craven, formerly of the University of Chicago, describes the environmental conditions that make tobacco cultivation successful and graphically depicts the environmental degradation that follows. Analyzing soil exhaustion in the Tobacco South as the product of both a profit-oriented labor-intensive system of agriculture and a nutrient-devouring crop, he outlines the beginnings of an agricultural-improvement movement to reverse soil degradation. Whether the rise and fall of the Tobacco South was caused by the slave system of production, the mind set of the planter class, the environmental conditions of soils and climate, or some interaction among these factors is the central question posed by this chapter in environmental history.

Slaves' Bodies

RONALD TAKAKI

The Revolution successfully expelled the "Savage" king, but it did not remove "savages" from America. Blacks and Indians remained. Long before whites had declared their independence from England and sought to become republicans, English culture-makers and political leaders had associated both groups with the instinctual life; and in the very way they identified peoples of color, they were defining themselves as men of "civilization." This psychological process, while it reflected some general fears of English culture, evolved in relation to the development of capitalist production in America. English definitions of Indians and blacks served as more than "aids to navigation" for Englishmen in their venture into America. They also encouraged English immigrants to appropriate Indian land and black labor as they settled and set up production in the New World, and enabled white colonists to justify the actions they had committed against both peoples. This process of interaction among psychological needs, ideology, and economic interests functioned dynamically in the English settlement of America.

Even before the English migration to America was fully under way and even before the arrival of those "twenty Negars" on the coast of Virginia in 1619, Englishmen had felt a need to separate themselves from both the instinctual part of the self and from blacks and Indians. This separation may be seen in William Shakespeare's *The Tempest*, written and performed in 1611. In it, Prospero is a man of intellect, a scholar, and the antithesis of Caliban, "a savage and deformed slave." The ex-duke of Milan images Caliban as everything he believes he is not: a "bastard," a "thing of darkness," "filth," sexuality, a threat to his fair daughter's virginity. Racially, Caliban is not white: He has a dark complexion, his mother is from Africa, he lives in the "Bermoothes" or possibly the "Indes." Thus he could be African, American Indian, or even Asian; he belongs to a "vile race" and Prospero calls him a "devil, a devil, on whose nature Nurture can never stick!" Exiled from civilization, Prospero has taken the island from Caliban and forced the native to live in its rocky and desolate regions. While he segregates Caliban physically and socially, however, Prospero uses him as a slave, a worker who "serves in offices that profit" the white master. Viewing Caliban as a creature of passions, Prospero angrily condemns him for seeking to "violate the honor of my child." The master, assigning all the passions to the native, must enslave and brutalize him before Prospero realizes the "thing of darkness" is himself.

In an uncanny way, America became a larger theater for *The Tempest*. As it turned out, the play was the thing: English fantasies of the stage were acted out in reality in the New World. As Englishmen made their "errand into the wilderness" of America, they took lands from red Calibans and made black Calibans work for them. Far from English civilization, they had to remind themselves constantly what it meant to be civilized—Christian, rational, sexually controlled, and white. And they tried to impute to peoples they called "savages" the instinctual forces they had within themselves. They feared, to use Lawrence's language, the "dark forest" within and the "strange gods" who came forth from the forest into the "little clearing" of their known selves and then went back. As civilized men, they believed they had to have the courage to dominate their passional impulses, and make certain those "dark gods" remained hidden. Thus, as Winthrop Jordan has pointed out, Englishmen in America

> were attempting to destroy the living image of primitive aggressions which they said was the Negro but was really their own. Their very lives as social beings were at stake. Intermixture and insurrection, violent sex and sexual violence, creation and destruction, life and death—the stuff of animal existence was rumbling at the gates of rational and moral judgment. If the gates fell, so did humanness; they could not fall; indeed there could be no possibility of their falling, else man was not man and his civilization not civilized. We, therefore, we do not lust and destroy; it is someone else. We are not great black bucks of the fields. But a buck *is* loose, his great horns menacing to gore into us with life and destruction. Chain him, either chain him or expel his black shape from our midst, before we realize that he is ourselves.

This fear of the instinctual life was aggravated during the era of the American Revolution. As patriot leaders and culture-makers urged white Americans to be self-governing, they cast onto blacks and Indians those qualities they felt republicans should not have, and they denied the "black bucks" contained within themselves. On the eve of the Revolution, Arthur Lee of Virginia sharply separated blacks from republican society in his *Essay in Vindication of the Continental Colonies of America*. Negroes were cruel and cunning, he wrote; they ate like "absolute brutes" and believed in "the most gross idolatry." "Aristotle . . . declared that slaves could not have virtue, but he knew not any who were so utterly devoid of any semblance of virtue as are the Africans; whose understandings are generally shallow, and their hearts cruel, vindictive, stubborn, base, and wicked." Here, then, were a people, devoid of virtue in a society which required virtue if it were to be independent and republican. Indians, too, were viewed as creatures of passion: They were wild and primitive, and lacked the control and inclination to labor which whites believed were necessary if men were to be civilized. In an extreme view of Indians, writer Hugh Henry Brackenridge of Pennsylvania referred to them as "animals, vulgarly called Indians." Even Benjamin Franklin, a self-proclaimed "friend" of the Indian, expressed mild scorn for the original Americans. "The proneness of human Nature to a life of ease, of freedom from care and labour," he remarked "appears strongly in the little success that has hitherto attended every attempt to civilize our American Indians. . . ." Unlike whites, they did not work but depended instead on the spontaneous productions of nature to supply almost all their wants; even their hunting and fishing could not be regarded as labor when game was so plentiful.

What both blacks and Indians, as they were viewed by white society, shared was clear: Like Caliban, they were not masters over their natural life. In terms of the American Revolution, they were not republicans. The rational part of the self, republican leaders insisted, must be in command. Identifying whites with rationality or mind, they associated peoples of color with the body. Thus mind was raised to authority over the other parts of the self, and whites were raised above blacks and Indians. As republicans in the new American nation, white men felt they had to guard themselves against the needs of the instinctual life which they claimed were ascendant in peoples of color.

While the Revolution contained tendencies which reinforced existing caste lines, it also provided a basis for a criticism of slavery. As they rebelled against the "slavery" of British tyranny, some patriot leaders also recognized the contradiction present within their society, and found it difficult to demand their freedom while denying it to blacks. In his pamphlet on *The Rights of the British Colonies Asserted and Proved*, James Otis bluntly asked: "The colonists are by law of nature freeborn, as indeed all men are, white or black. . . . Does it follow that 'tis right to enslave a man because he is black? Will short curl'd hair like wool . . . help the argument? Can any logical inference in favour of slavery, be drawn from a flat nose, a long or a short face?" Similarly [Thomas] Paine believed blacks were human beings, entitled to freedom and dignity, and condemned both the African slave trade and slavery. In 1775, even before he wrote *Common Sense*, Paine had raised the moral issue of slavery in America: "The great Question may be — what should be done with those who are en-slaved already?" The states in the North which had small numbers of slaves responded positively to the question and abolished slavery. In 1780, for exam-ple, the Pennsylvania Assembly declared its wish to extend a portion of the freedom they had won to the blacks and release them from thralldom. "It is not for us to enquire why, in the creation of mankind, the inhabitants of the several parts of the earth were distinguished by a difference in feature or complexion. It is sufficient to know that all are the work of the Almighty Hand." Still, another question remained: Could all, regardless of complexion, be republicans and Americans?

Twenty-five years before the Declaration of Independence, Benjamin Franklin had already offered his thoughts on the complexion of society in America in his essay *Observations Concerning the Increase of Mankind*. He noted that the number of "purely white People" in the world was propor-tionately very small. All Africa was black or tawny, Asia chiefly tawny, and "America (exclusive of the new comers) wholly so." The English were the "principle Body of white People," and Franklin wished there were more of them in America. "And while we are . . . *Scouring* our Planet, by clearing

America of Woods, and so making this Side of our globe reflect a brighter Light to the Eyes of Inhabitants in Mars or Venus," he declared, "why should we in the Sight of Superior Beings, darken its People? why increase the Sons of Africa, by Planting them in America, where we have so fair an opportunity, by excluding all Blacks and Tawneys, of increasing the lovely White . . . ?" The question was not so simple for the men of the Revolution. It was not a matter of "excluding" "Blacks" and "Tawneys": They were already in America and in large numbers.

The American Revolution made the issue immensely complicated and vexing, and compelled whites to define the relationship between race and the republic. Indeed, if the Revolutionary experiment were to succeed, many republican leaders were convinced, American society — the "lovely White" — must not be stained. Afraid of the diversity within themselves, they feared cultural and racial diversity in the society around them.

No wonder the men of the Revolution, meeting in the First Congress of the United States, enacted the Naturalization Law of 1790. In the debates, Congress affirmed its commitment to the "pure principles of Republicanism" and its determination to develop a citizenry of good and "useful" men, a homogeneous society. Only the "worthy part of mankind" should be encouraged to settle in the new republic and be eligible for citizenship. Every prospective citizen would have to go through a probationary period which would give him time to understand republican principles, acquire a taste for republican government, and demonstrate "proper and decent behavior." In this careful screening process, the nation would be able to exclude "vagrants," "paupers," and "bad men." It would admit only the virtuous, only the individual "fit" for the society into which he was to be "blended." Thus the naturalization law required him to reside in the United States for two years, and make "proof" in a common law court that he was a person of good character. But first he had to be "white."

The Naturalization Law of 1790 explicitly linked race to republican nationality. It not only defined the norms of conduct and thought for Americans in the new nation: Citizenship was reserved for republicans, and citizens were expected to have republican manners and morals. It also specified a complexion for the members of the new nation as it gave expression to the hopes and fears of a republican society determined to cage the "black buck" still loose in the fields, increase the "lovely White," and carry forward the Revolution, which required virtue as the foundation of liberty and which had created a world without a king where men had to govern themselves.

Planters' Minds

T. H. BREEN

Late in the 1760s, Richard Henry Lee composed an essay entitled "The State of the Constitution of Virginea." Considering Lee's modern reputation as an outspoken defender of American liberties, one might assume that the manuscript dealt primarily with British corruption and parliamentary oppression. In point of fact, however, Lee focused upon another topic. After briefly describing the colony's political structure, he turned to "our staple" and explained how Virginians cultivated tobacco. Lee analyzed each step in the long agricultural routine — sowing, transplanting, weeding, topping, cutting, curing, and packing — for, in his opinion, it was important for people unfamiliar with this culture (perhaps the ministers of George III who were busy devising new ways to tax the colonists?) to understand exactly "how much labour is required on a Virginean estate & how poor the produce."

Lee's preoccupation with the production of tobacco would not have surprised his neighbors on Virginia's Northern Neck (the northern peninsula of Virginia located between the Potomac and Rappahannock Rivers), men like Landon Carter, John Taylor, and George Washington. After all, it is twentieth-century historians who insist on treating these people as lawyers, as statesmen, and as theorists, as almost anything in fact, except as planters. This essentially political perspective distorts our understanding of the world of the eighteenth-century Virginians. Tobacco touched nearly every aspect of their existence. It was a source of the colony's prosperity, a medium for commercial transactions and payment of local taxes, and a theme of decorative art. Indeed, the majority of the planters' waking hours were spent, as they would have said, in "making a crop." Almost every surviving letterbook from this period contains a detailed description of tobacco production, and even Thomas Jefferson, who never distinguished himself as a successful plantation manager, instructed a European correspondent in the mysteries of cultivating the Virginia staple.

Though Virginians acknowledged the profound impact that tobacco had had upon the colony's social and economic development, they regarded the staple with a critical eye. Many planters readily admitted that the crop's effect upon their lives and the lives of their fathers had not been entirely beneficial. A case in point was the Chesapeake settlement pattern, a use of space that distinguished the people of this region from most other colonial Americans. The earliest Virginians had carved out riverfront estates often located miles from the nearest neighbor. As time passed, colonists spread west and north along the waterways in search of fresh lands on which to establish their sons and daughters. Each generation faced the same problem; each behaved much as its predecessor had done. Crown officials complained that dispersed living invited military disaster and discouraged urban development, but even those Virginians who recognized the desirability of prosperous commercial centers refused to abandon their isolated plantations.

By the middle of the eighteenth century, most planters accepted that dispersed settlement was an inevitable product of a particular type of agriculture. Tobacco may not in fact have caused dispersion — the early planters might have done more to maintain the fertility of their original tracts — but contemporary Virginians nevertheless blamed their staple for scattering men and women across the countryside. In 1775, for example, the anonymous author of *American Husbandry* informed his readers of what every Virginian knew from firsthand experience: "A very considerable tract of land is necessary for a tobacco plantation." The writer estimated that planters required at least fifty acres for each field laborer, for if they possessed less land, "they will find themselves distressed for want of room."

Virginia's dispersed settlement pattern had obvious cultural implications. Social relations among the colony's great planters were less frequent, less spontaneous than were those enjoyed by wealthy town-dwellers in other parts of America. Religious services, no doubt, brought people together, but churches were often inconveniently located. Inclement weather frequently kept planters at home. Militia practice occasionally broke the work routine, and it was not unusual for planters to use these gatherings as an excuse to get roaring drunk. Meetings of the county courts served a social as well as legal function. But however important these events may have been, the great majority of the planter's life was spent on his plantation in the company of family, servants, and slaves. Schooling, for those who could afford it, usually occurred at home, the responsibility of private tutors.

Some Virginians found this "solitary and unsociable" existence boring. Like William Fitzhugh, Virginia's most affluent seventeenth-century planter, they relied on libraries to compensate for the absence of "society that is good and ingenious." Sometimes even books must have seemed poor substitutes for regular contact with outsiders. In 1756 Edmund Pendleton, a young and promising lawyer, protested that he had failed to hear an important piece of news because he lived isolated in "a forest."

In this society the cultivation of tobacco in large measure determined the planters' sense of time, their perception of appropriate behavior at particular moments throughout the year. A comparison with the production of other staples helps make the point. Each crop, be it coffee, sugar, or tobacco, possesses a distinct character — almost a personality — and thus places different demands on the people who grow it. Some staples, for example, require a great expenditure of labor over a relatively short period of time, perhaps a month or two of drudgery associated with the harvest; in sugar-making regions especially, this exhausting season can be followed by months of unemployment or underemployment. Other staples generate more balanced work rhythms. Under these conditions the tasks necessary to transform seeds into a marketable commodity are spread over the entire year, and there is no extraordinary crisis period, such as when the sugar cane is cut, which alone determines whether the enterprise will be a success.

Work schedules, of course, influence the timing of other, seemingly unrelated activities. In many countries, the personality of the major crop determines when festivals are held — in other words, when the cultivators and their families have the leisure to organize such events. In the coffee-growing sections of early twentieth-century Puerto Rico, "traditional ceremonies . . . marked a sharp transition from work to nonwork."

In the cultivation of other staples such as tobacco, there is no clear break between labor and leisure. As grown in eighteenth-century Virginia, the crop placed major demands upon the planter and his laborers throughout the year. From the moment they put out the seed to the time that they loaded hogsheads on British vessels, the workers were fully occupied in making a crop. Tobacco was not like wheat, a plant that colonial farmers sowed and simply waited to harvest. The Virginia staple could never be taken for granted. It dictated a series of tasks, any one of which, if improperly performed, could jeopardize many months of hard work. Each step in the annual process required skill, judgment, and luck. No wonder that a French traveler reported that "the culture of tobacco is difficult, troublesome, and uncertain."

By the time this man visited Virginia, the Tidewater planters had established a familiar work routine. Indeed, it did not change significantly over the entire colonial period. It became a piece of customary knowledge, passed from fathers to sons, masters to slaves, American-born blacks to newly imported Africans. As one eighteenth-century observer noted, "This process varies more or less in the different plantations, but the variations are not by any means considerable." This production schedule, repeated annually throughout a planter's lifetime, on plantations scattered throughout Virginia, was a powerful element in the development and persistence of the tobacco mentality. The cultivation of this staple provided planters with a stock of common experiences; indeed, it sustained a "silent" language, a vocabulary of work imprinted so deeply upon the minds of people who grew it that they were barely conscious of how many assumptions and ideas they actually shared. Richard Henry Lee was probably correct: unless one understands exactly what was at stake at every point—the dangers, the requirements, and the critical, often subtle decisions made by planters throughout the year—one cannot fully comprehend the relation of culture to agriculture or why the later switch from tobacco to wheat so upset the symbolic world of the Tidewater gentry.

Exhausted Soils

AVERY O. CRAVEN

The agricultural life of Virginia and Maryland, from earliest colonial days well down to the eve of the Civil War, was carried on under conditions which gave wide play to the destructive forces of [soil] depletion. Physical surroundings were unusually favorable to the direct forces of "exhaustion"; their economic life was begun under frontier conditions; . . . and a whole life was erected upon an exploitive agriculture, that had to be greatly changed before the economic effort which supported it could be altered. "Soil exhaustion" and tobacco cultivation went hand in hand.

The Colonial Period, 1606–1783

Agriculture is fundamentally conditioned by geographic and climatic conditions. Soils, topography, rainfall, etc., not only influence crops but methods as well. . . .

Text by Avery Odelle Craven, Ph. D., *Soil Exhaustion as a Factor in the Agricultural History of Virginia and Maryland, 1606–1860,* 1965 [originally published 1926], pp. 24, 25–35, 82–94, 97, 98, 163. Reprinted by permission of Peter Smith, Publishers, Inc.: Gloucester, MA.

Virginia and Maryland are part of a geographic unit that may be roughly divided into three distinct physical sections: — the Coastal Plain, the Piedmont Plateau, and the Appalachian mountainous region.

The Coastal Plain stretches from the water's edge back to the head of navigation where the older crystalline rocks of the Piedmont break sharply to form a fall line in the rivers, and the flat plains give way to the rolling uplands. It seldom rises over a hundred feet above the sea level and is cut everywhere with bays and inlets, and intersected by broad parallel rivers. The soils have been transported largely from the regions above the fall line and vary greatly in their composition and texture, ranging from pure sand to a sandy loam with occasional areas of silt and clay. . . . Here and there throughout the plain, beds of fossil remains . . . are to be found in the shape of the so called "marl beds," giving a generous supply of calcium carbonate, while near the coast stretches of swamp lands invite drainage and offer large quantities of rich mucks.

The Piedmont Plateau reaches from the fall line on the east to the uncertain border of the Appalachian Mountains on the west. Not more than 30 to 60 miles in width in Maryland, it spreads out across Virginia to a width of some 175 miles at the point where it crosses the North Carolina border. It is a region of variable topography and presents a broad plain-like surface with rolling uplands everywhere cut by narrow river valleys. . . .

The soils of the region are residual, . . . on the whole supplying an abundance of plant food materials. The rocks of the region as a rule are high in potash-bearing minerals and a large amount of iron oxide gives a characteristic reddish hue to the soils in many parts. The fertility is of good average, lower than that of the coastal valleys, but well suited under proper cultivation to the requirements of general farming.

The Appalachian region consists of a line of parallel mountain ridges rising in height to the westward and interspersed with great valleys that open far up into Pennsylvania. In Virginia the region might be further divided into the Blue Ridge, the Great Valley, and the Alleghany Mountains proper, with no sharp division on the east where the Piedmont ridges rise gradually into foothills.

The soils of the Blue Ridge and the Maryland region just north of it, are clay-loams and sandy-loams and closely resemble those of the Piedmont into which they blend. The Valley soils are of all types and a great belt of limestone cuts through it, giving to the loam and clay-loam soils an abundant addition of calcium carbonate debris. It forms a region of high fertility and one well adapted to general farming and grazing. . . .

Originally the larger part of both states was heavily forested and had to be cleared before cultivation could take place — a task so slow and difficult that much of the region was always in timber. Trees grew rapidly and when cultivated lands were abandoned, the forest returned again in a period of a few years. Travelers passing through what appeared to be virgin forest were often surprised to discover the scars of former cultivation and to learn that they were crossing what some twenty years earlier was a tobacco field. Such conditions added much to the problem of labor but afforded some compensation in the form of protection to neglected soils against washing and in the addition of organic materials in the form of falling leaves.

Both Virginia and Maryland are subject to heavy rainfall. The annual precipitation, varying somewhat in different parts, ranges from forty to seventy inches, a third of which comes in concentrated showers during the summer months when cultivation is in progress. This concentrated character of the summer rainfall . . . gives a heavy run-off from the lands. . . .

It is thus apparent that a goodly part of the problem of exhaustion in this region is produced by erosion. . . . Varying in its intensity with the type of agriculture, it nevertheless presented a vital problem in every period and under every system employed. . . .

As frontier regions, the problem of the American Colonies was to find some product for exchange with the old world that would enable them to secure those necessities which a primitive region did not offer. . . . A supply of fish, furs, or timber gave some temporary relief, but the development of a permanent and satisfactory exchange, in the end, depended upon the soil.

Virginia and Maryland early solved this problem with the abundant yields of tobacco which their "lusty soyle" gave forth and by the eagerness with which a ready market absorbed the increasing crops. Within a short period of time a type of life, based on this exchange, was possible that rivaled that of the English gentry and the plantation hospitality and style of living found in the region, filled the less fortunate with envy and the traveller with wonder. "It was merry England transported across the Atlantic, and more merry, light, and joyous than England had ever thought of being." Colonial life came to rest almost completely upon tobacco, and in spite of all efforts at restricting and diversifying production, tobacco became the one object of endeavor. And the very conditions which made it the dominant crop, determined that its production should be at the expense of the soil. The story of colonial tobacco production, therefore, became one of uninterrupted soil depletion.

To begin with, tobacco by its great advantages in exchange excluded all other major crops from the fields and forced an exhausting single-crop type of agriculture upon the soils. Tobacco alone seemed capable of lifting the colonists quickly from the severe conditions of frontier life into the comforts of former days. The European demand for this plant was rapidly increasing and the Spanish supply was far from keeping pace with the growing demands. Prices were so high that in the early days a man's labor in tobacco production yielded him six times as large a return as might be secured from any other crop.

But there were other advantages. The yield of tobacco per acre was high, its keeping qualities good, and its weight, when ready for shipping, comparatively low — advantages great indeed where every acre of land had to be painfully won from the virgin forest, and where markets lay far across a stormy sea. Tobacco alone could stand the long journey, pay the high costs of transportation, and still return a profit to its producer. Furthermore, labor, always scarce, could be concentrated upon a smaller acreage with greater returns from each laborer, and thus also afford a sufficient supply of hands in the winter to clear the new lands needed for future crops. Tobacco growing and land clearing went hand in hand, as we shall see, and so closely did the double task become united that in later years, when tobacco profits had failed, many refused to give it up because they would then have no winter work for their slaves.

Such a course meant soil depletion. The tobacco plant is a heavy consumer of both nitrogen and potash and the removal of the entire growth from the field, as was customary, caused a rapid decline in the available plant food materials at the same time that continued replanting in the soils encouraged toxicity, harmful soil fungi, root rots, and micro-organisms. A superior tobacco could be produced only on fresh land, and after the second crop — usually the best — the quality and quantity began to decline. The planter seldom counted on more than three or four crops from his land before it was abandoned to corn and wheat and then to the pine, sedge, and sorrell growths which usually characterize "sour lands." . . . A constant clearing of the forest was carried on and a constant abandonment of "old fields" followed at the other end. The encroachment upon the forest was so steady that one observer was led to remark that the colonists seemed "to have but one object" — "the plowing up of fresh lands." "He was the cleverest fellow who could show the largest new ground."

As tobacco employed all the labor force and monopolized the best lands, so it also excluded the production of a supply of animal manure by which fertility might have been restored and maintained. This was not a serious matter as long as an abundance of fresh land was available for all, but it produced destructive habits. . . . The building of barns and yards for stock, the laying down of meadows for pasture, and the securing of a supply of winter's food, were out of the question as long as tobacco ruled. . . .

Tobacco from the earliest period was cultivated with the hand and the hoe, the fields being kept clean and the surface soils loose by a continual but shallow stirring at the roots of the plant. Heavy wooden plows were introduced into the colonies around the year 1609, but they were not used in tobacco cultivation because of the constant use of new lands filled with stumps, roots, and other impediments incident to freshly cleared ground. In fact, the plow did not become a factor in the tobacco fields until late in the colonial period, when a check had come to expansion and "old lands" were again brought into use. And even here the cultivation was shallow and the use of the hoe still predominated. The lower reaches of the soil were not touched and turned up to the surface to give new supplies of food materials nor the depth given to the surface soils that would enable them to absorb the rainfall and prevent washing. The whole cultivation thus invited erosion. The clean surface and the constant stirring without piercing the hardpan formed just below, gave added force to the already natural conditions which tended in that direction.

The Post-Revolutionary Period, 1783–1820

The statements of both planters and travelers for the period from 1785 to 1820 bear witness of the continuance of exhausting cultivation, of wasted lands, abandoned fields, neglected stock, and shifting crops. . . . In 1791 George Washington at the request of Arthur Young the noted English agriculturist, made a survey of conditions in northern Virginia and Maryland. . . . His report indicates the widespread continuation of old methods. Summarized, it reveals (1) a steady cropping of lands in tobacco followed by Indian corn with ever lowering yields; (2) the general absence of meadows and stock with only here and there an exceptional farmer making use of manure to prolong the fertility of his lands; (3) and everywhere a tendency to abandon tobacco under the pressure of necessity in favor of wheat. It is of interest to notice that the average yield of wheat is given at little more than ten bushels to the acre, and that in many cases the returns were as low as seven bushels. . . .

The Duc de la Rochefoucauld-Laincourt crossed both Virginia and Maryland in 1795–96 and recorded rather minutely his observations on agricultural methods. Passing along the tidewater he found the farms too large for good cultivation, the cattle "poor and ill favored" and always in the woods; the fields generally planted in corn [and] never manured. . . . In western Maryland where tobacco was "reduced to almost nothing," . . . the ground was never plowed more than two or three inches deep and never manured. As he moved eastward again, conditions became poorer and the old practice existed of planting land in corn the first year, "then wheat for six or seven years without interruption, or as long as the soil will bear any," then fallow while another piece of ground was cleared and "also exhausted in its turn." . . .

Four years after Laincourt had visited Albemarle County, Virginia, a new settler described the country as a "scene of desolation that baffles description — farm after farm . . . worn out, washed and gullied, so that scarcely an acre could be found in a place fit for cultivation." The lands had been "butchered" by the growth of tobacco and even in 1799 there was not a good plough in the entire county. Conditions were so bad that the inhabitants had to make the choice between emigration at once or improvement without delay. . . .

In 1819 both sides of the Chesapeake in Maryland are described as "dreary and miserable in aspect" — "dreary and uncultivated wastes, a barren and exhausted soil, half clothed negroes, lean and hungry stock, a puny race of horses, a scarcity of provender, houses falling to decay, and fences wind shaken and dilapidating," are the terms used by the traveler. A few better farms and farmers were now and then to be found in the region but they stood out against a general background of ruin. . . .

When one turns to the counties in western Maryland, such as Washington, Frederick, and Montgomery, or to certain valleys in the northern portion of the state, he finds decided contrasts. There enough prosperity had come with the foreign demand for wheat and flour to enable leading farmers to begin improvement. . . .

The earliest agencies of the new agricultural life were the owners of great estates. Well back in colonial times a few exceptional planters had carried on experiments and attained some success. The great shift from tobacco to wheat had come about largely from such beginnings. But the great period of effort belongs to the Post-Revolutionary times and was the work of a group already well known in the public life of the new states. Their efforts consisted not only in changes of method and crops but also in the organization of Agricultural Societies and the production of an agricultural literature. Working individually but constantly exchanging ideas by letter or through the press, such men as Washington, Jefferson, Madison, John Taylor, J. M. Garnett, etc., formed what might well be called a school of gentleman farmers who had run counter to the general backward drift. . . .

Washington early established his reputation as a progressive agriculturist. In him the transformation of the planter into the farmer is well exemplified and his efforts at improvement include nearly all of the things attempted in this period. . . . [He] was among the first to understand the importance of good plowing as a means of preserving fertility. In 1769 he tested the value of plowing the earth into ridges as compared with harrowing it out flat as a method of checking the harmful effects of erosion, and during the remainder of his life never ceased his fight against this ever threatening danger. He filled his gullies with old rails, trash and straw, covered them with dirt and manure before planting them with crops. . . .

As early as 1760 at least, he was experimenting with marl as a fertilizer and in that year tested its comparative value with manure and different kinds of mud secured from the river beds on his plantation. He tried out Plaster of Paris (gypsum) and in 1785 sowed his grass seed with carefully measured quantities to ascertain the effects of different amounts upon the yield. The laying down of meadows and the increasing of his manure supply were fundamental in all his efforts at improvement. He planted grasses of different kinds — clover, lucerne, sainfoin, chicory, succory, etc.; he searched out and planted different kinds of cow peas and sowed buckwheat to be turned in as a green manure for the next crop of grain; he constructed sheds for his cattle so that he might "raise manure" and he sought in every way to return to his lands the offal of his barns and pens.

Along with his interest in manure went the effort to increase and improve his stock. "Indifferent" sheep and cattle were culled out from his flocks and better breeds introduced as larger numbers were added. . . .

The work of Washington suggests the threefold lines along which the new movement developed among the great owners: first, the use of better plows and methods in the preparation of the soil for the crops or in the prevention of soil erosion; second, an increased interest in the production of animal manure and the use of artificial fertilizers; and third, the introduction of grass crops for feeding and green dressings as a part of different systems of crop rotation. All were more or less part of a single system of soil improvement but did not always go together and can therefore best be treated separately. . . .

Deep plowing was an essential part of the famous agricultural system now developing in Loudoun County, Virginia, and Montgomery County, Maryland. "The improvement of this valuable machine," (the plow) writes Robert Russell from Loudoun County in 1818, "was the first step we took to improve our lands; we formerly adopted the absurd plan of shallow ploughing leaving the under stratum unbroken which should have been torn up and mixed with the surface; we have constructed our ploughs much larger and stronger, the mould boards are all of cast iron. We seldom break our land with less than three horses to a plough, which enables us to plough our ground deep. . . ."

The addition of animal and vegetable manures to the soil together with the use of artificial fertilizers constitute the second part of the improvement program. . . . It was the first step taken by Jefferson in the recovery of his lands which had been so widely cleared and impoverished during his absence abroad and in the cabinet; Madison considered it absolutely necessary for improvement; it was fundamental in John Taylor's system; Landon Carter, Fielding Lewis, Col. Bosley, Hill Carter, etc., made it a first object and so on down the list from the highest to the lowest who faced the future with a determination to improve their wasted lands.

The value of the liquids from the stable was early realized and drains from each stall were constructed by some farmers so that not a particle would be lost. . . . A few learned the necessity of protecting the manure pile from the rain and weather and more than one man proclaimed the doctrine "that the size of the manure pile is the measure of success in agriculture."

Marl, which was to become so important in the next period through the work of Edmund Ruffin, was tried in various parts of the two states in this period. . . . The early trials are of interest largely because of the later importance of this fertilizer rather than because of any immediate consequences.

The credit for the introduction of Plaster of Paris or gypsum seems to belong to John Alexander Binns of Loudoun County, Virginia, though something can be said for the claims of his neighbor Israel Janney. Binns combined with deep plowing the use of gypsum. . . . The results were marked especially on wheat and he continued his experiments in the following years with other plants. He found gypsum to greatly benefit grass plots and by its use on clover he raised a worn and exhausted farm, on which his neighbors thought he must starve, to a high degree of fertility. So marked were the effects on white clover that many thought he had collected all the manure in the countryside and applied it to the field.

It is hardly necessary to list the different grasses tested by the various improvers. Jefferson, like Washington, tried out lucerne, chicory, succory, sainfoin, and various kinds of clover, and what these leaders did, other men in different parts of the states were doing also. But clover was generally the grass finally selected in all regions where it would grow and clover became the legume in most rotations.

Nor can a list of the different rotations be given. They differed with almost every individual — and most individuals shifted from time to time — and ranged from the simplest three and four field shifts to the more elaborate systems that required from eight to nine years to complete their course.

The system advocated by John Beale Bordley was based upon the Norfolk system of England. It included three crops of clover, and one each of wheat, potatoes, maize, peas, and barley. He advocated a heavy use of manure, rich earth, marl, and ashes and contended that his system would restore exhausted fields to a new degree of fertility. "Grass," wrote Bordley, "is the great basis of Farming products; it gives dung; dung gives vigor to the earth that gives all things."

* * * *

If capitalistic agriculture wrought greatest ruin it showed an equal capacity for the work of improvement. It was upon the larger plantations, where capital and a careful division of labor could be practiced, that the most rapid recovery took place and the greatest advances were made.

The destructive practices of the Old South were, in fact, in the beginning merely the normal product of frontier conditions. The dependence upon a single crop produced by whatever methods gave largest immediate returns regardless of the waste entailed; the thrusting of the burdens of abnormal production upon land because it was more plentiful than either capital or labor; the placing of an exaggerated value upon the crop which first furnished the surplus by which exchange with the outside world was established — all these were typical frontier practices which have characterized all frontiers.

♥ *F U R T H E R   R E A D I N G*

Hugh H. Bennett, *The Soils and Agriculture of the Southern States* (1921)
T. H. Breen, *Tobacco Culture: The Mentality of the Great Tidewater Planters on the Eve of Revolution* (1985)
Paul G. E. Clemens, *The Atlantic Economy and Colonial Maryland's Eastern Shore: From Tobacco to Grain* (1980)
Albert E. Cowdrey, *This Land, This South: An Environmental History* (1983)
Avery O. Craven, *Soil Exhaustion as a Factor in the Agricultural History of Virginia and Maryland, 1606–1860* (1925)
Carville Earle, "The Myth of the Southern Soil Miner: Macrohistory, Agricultural Innovation, and Environmental Change," in *The Ends of the Earth*, ed. Donald Worster (1988)
Jack D. Forbes, *Black Africans and Native Americans: Color, Race, and Caste in the Evolution of Red-Black Peoples* (1988)
John Hope Franklin, *The Free Negro in North Carolina, 1790–1860* (1943)
Eugene D. Genovese, *The Political Economy of Slavery: Studies in the Economy and Society of the Old South* (1967)
Lewis C. Gray, *History of Agriculture in the Southern United States to 1860* (1958)
Charles Hudson, *The Southeastern Indians* (1976)
Luther P. Jackson, *Free Negro Labor and Property Holding in Virginia, 1830–1860* (1942)
Winthrop Jordan, *White over Black: American Attitudes Toward the Negro, 1550–1812* (1968)
William Katz, *Black Indians: A Hidden Heritage* (1987)
Fanny Kemble, *Journal of a Residence on a Georgian Plantation in 1838–1839* (1863, 1961)
Allan Kulikoff, *Tobacco and Slaves: The Development of Southern Cultures in the Chesapeake, 1680–1800* (1986)
Karen Kupperman, *Roanoke: The Abandoned Colony* (1984)
————, *Settling with the Indians: The Meeting of English and Indian Cultures in America, 1580–1640* (1980)
Daniel Littlefield, *Rice and Slaves: Ethnicity and the Slave Trade in Colonial South Carolina* (1981)
————, *Africans and Creeks: From the Colonial Period to the Civil War* (1979)
————, *Africans and Seminoles: From Removal to Emancipation* (1977)
————, *The Chickasaw Freedmen: A People Without a Country* (1980)
William M. Matthew, *Edmund Ruffin and the Crisis of Slavery in the Old South* (1988)
Russell R. Menard, "The Tobacco Industry in the Chesapeake Colonies, 1617–1730: An Interpretation," *Research in Economic History* 5 (1980), 109–177

James Merrell, *The Indians' New World: Catawbas and Their Neighbors from European Contact Through the Era of Removal* (1989)

Edmund S. Morgan, *American Slavery, American Freedom: The Ordeal of Colonial Virginia* (1975)

Michael Mullin, *American Negro Slavery: A Documentary History* (1976)

Theda Perdue, *Slavery and the Evolution of Cherokee Society, 1540–1866* (1979)

———, *Native Carolinians: The Indians of North Carolina* (1985)

David B. Quinn and Alison M. Quinn, eds., *The First Colonists: Documents on the Planting of the First English Settlements in North America, 1584–1590* (1982)

Helen Rountree, *The Powhatan Indians of Virginia: Their Traditional Culture* (1989)

Parke Rouse, Jr., *Planters and Pioneers: Life in Colonial Virginia* (1968)

Timothy Silver, *A New Face on the Countryside: Indians, Colonists, and Slaves in South Atlantic Forests, 1500–1800* (1990)

Peter Wood, *Black Majority: Negroes in Colonial South Carolina* (1974)

CHAPTER
5

Farm Ecology
in the Early Republic

❦

In the eighteenth century, an expanding population moved inland from the coastal plain and settled in hilly regions above the first falls of the rivers, beyond easy access to navigable waterways. In New England people founded towns in the hills on either side of the Connecticut River; in Pennsylvania they moved westward from Philadelphia into Chester and Lancaster counties and then southwestward into the Great Valley of the Appalachians; in Virginia and Maryland they migrated upcountry into the piedmont; and in the Carolinas they established communities inland, along the Roanoke, Cape Fear, Peedee and Santee rivers. Many of the new settlers were members of religious groups immigrating to America. English Congregationalists continued to expand into central New England; Scots-Irish Presbyterians from northern Ireland migrated to the Delaware River Valley and then southwestward into the Appalachians; and Quakers, Lutherans, Amish, and Calvinists from Germany settled in Pennsylvania and the Appalachians, bringing their agricultural traditions with them.

Most of the new settlers lived in small towns oriented toward agricultural production for subsistence. They bartered food, clothing, tools, and labor with their neighbors. Their farms were ecological units that circulated nutrients within the farm boundaries through crop production, livestock grazing, and forest burning. The farmers interacted with the outside world by marketing and purchasing goods. Manufactured items such as guns, ammunition, and kettles, as well as staples not produced in the village, such as sugar, tea, and spices, could be bartered at the local store, whereas the farmers' potash and livestock, more readily transportable, were traded in more distant markets. In areas surrounding the major cities — Philadelphia, New York, Boston, Newport, and Charleston — trade in agricultural produce was more dynamic than in the interior, because it intersected with and supported the staple-exporting economy of the coastal plain. Although historians disagree about the extent of market trade, eighteenth-century America was primarily agrarian, combining an inland subsistence-oriented economy with a coastal mercantile-exporting economy. This chapter examines the ecological impacts of this agrarian-minded society.

❦ D O C U M E N T S

The following documents set out differences in the values and farming practices of a subsistence-oriented farm family, whose life focuses on hard work, adequate yields, and satisfaction from farm ownership, and a market-oriented farm family, whose values revolve around hard work, marketable surpluses, and satisfaction from profits. Documents one through three and five represent the lives and values of ordinary farmers at the subsistence end of the spectrum; the others, those at the market-oriented end. Gradations between these two poles existed in accordance with environmental conditions, accessibility to transport, race, gender, and social status.

In the first document, the anonymous author of *American Husbandry* (1775) describes New England farmers as obtaining good harvests by continually bringing fresh soils into cultivation but lacking incentives to increase yields and profits through agricultural improvement. The second and third documents present the idealized subsistence farmer as the backbone of the American economy, although both writers were propertied elites. J. Hector St. John de Crèvecoeur was a French nobleman who traveled in Pennsylvania, New York, and the Carolinas from 1759 to 1769, after which he married and settled on a farm in New York until 1780. His *Letters from an American Farmer* (1782) contrast the free, hard working American "tillers of the earth" with rich European aristocrats and propertiless poor, suggesting that cultivating the soil fosters an American purity and contentment unknown in the Old World. Similarly, Thomas Jefferson, a Virginia planter with a large estate at Monticello, in 1787 characterizes ordinary farmers "who labor in the earth" as the "chosen people of God" and recommends that manufacturing, which fosters economic differences, remain in Europe.

In the fourth document, Benjamin Rush, doctor, abolitionist, and educator, describes the German farmers of Pennsylvania in 1789 as frugal and industrious people who grew wheat and vegetables for the Philadelphia market. Document five is from the account book of an Acworth, New Hampshire, farmer showing how he bartered of goods and services with a neighbor between 1807 and 1812. The sixth document is excerpted from an almanac diary for 1820 of a farm widow, Anna Howell (1769–1855), of Gloucester County, New Jersey, who at the age of fifty inherited a farm and fisheries on the Delaware River from her husband, Joshua. She kept her diaries from 1819 to 1839 in interleaved almanacs so that her farm management each year might benefit from the errors of previous years. John James Audubon, author of the next document, shows how the expansion of the United States to the Mississippi River after 1815 offered opportunities for settlers from worn-out lands in Virginia to take up fresh lands in Mississippi. Here the seductive power of the market is graphically portrayed as the husbands and sons of family after family raft down the river to New Orleans with produce, returning with profits and commodities for their wives and daughters. In the last document, Calvin Colton, a political essayist and member of the Whig party, in 1844 characterizes America as a "country of self-made men" and the American environment as a source of "inexhaustible wealth." In reality, this worldview applied to white Euramerican males only, not to women, blacks, Indians, or Mexicans. As in the previous chapter, the documents pose probing questions about human nature. Are people "naturally" competitive and entrepreneurial or altruistic and sharing, or are these attributes historically constructed and dependent on environments, economic systems, and cultural characteristics?

A Traveler Views the Mistakes
of New England Farmers, 1775

Concerning the country management of America, . . . it is . . . of consequence to understand the defects of their agriculture as well as the advantages of it. . . .

The cultivated parts of New England are . . . in such condition that in Great Britain they would be thought in a state of devastation; yet here it all arises from carelessness. Live hedges are common, yet the plenty of timber in many parts of the province is such that they neglect planting these durable, useful, and excellent fences, for the more easy way of posts and rails, or boards, which last but a few years and are always out of repair. . . . In many plantations, there are only a few inclosures about the houses, and the rest lie like common fields in England, the consequence of which is much useless labour in guarding crops from cattle.

Respecting their system, a distinction is to be made between the parts which have been many years in culture, and which, from the neighbouring population, are grown valuable; in these, lands are much better managed than in the frontier parts of the province, where land is of little value and where all the new settlers fix. In the former, the farmers lay down a system which they seem tolerably to adhere to, though with variations. They sow large quantities of maize, some wheat, barley, oats, buckwheat, pease, and beans, turneps, and clover: hemp and flax in small parcels. And these they throw after one another with variations, so as to keep the land, as well as their ideas permit, from being quite exhausted; which they effect by the intervention of a ploughed summer fallow sometimes. When the land has borne corn for several years, till it threatens to yield no more, then they so[w] clover among the last crop and leave it as a meadow for some years to recover itself. . . .

Instead of such management, I shall venture to recommend the following system:

1. Summer fallow.
2. Maize.
3. Pease or beans.
4. Barley or oats.
5. Turneps.
6. Wheat.
7. Clover for three, four, or five years.
8. Wheat.

I think such a system is well adapted to their climate and soil. . . . In this system I consider maize, barley, oats, and wheat, as crops that exhaust the land; but pease, beans, turneps, and clover, as such as rather improve. . . it. . . . .

Maize is reckoned a great exhauster in New England. . . . The culture is something similar to that of hops; being planted in squares of about five feet, and when up, the plant is earthed into little hillocks: . . . The misfortune is [that] they do not always keep the plantations of maize clean, or the earth so loose in the intervals as it ought to be, in which case one may easily conceive that the land may be left totally exhausted; but this effect would be vastly lessened by being more assiduous in the culture, while the crop was growing, [and] absolutely to destroy all weeds, and keep the vacant spaces in garden order. . . .

Turneps, and other articles of winter food for cattle, they are extremely inattentive to; the great want of the country . . . is the want of dung, and yet they will not take the only method of gaining it, which is the keeping great stocks of cattle, not ranging through the woods, but confined to houses or warm yards. This can only be done by providing plenty of winter food: at present, they keep no more than their hay will feed, and some they let into the woods to provide for themselves, not a few of which perish by the severity of the cold. Great stores of turneps, or other roots, and perhaps cabbages better still, would make their hay and straw go much further, and by means of plenty of litter, for which this country is in many respects very well provided, they might raise such quantities of manure as would double the fertility of all their lands. . . . A more general culture of the various sorts of clovers would also increase the means of keeping cattle, and consequently raising more dung, which is in all parts of the world, whatever may be the climate, the only means of getting good arable crops. Besides, turneps or other roots, cabbages, clover, &c. in their growth and the culture which such receive as stand single, much improve the land, as all good farmers in England have well known these hundred years. Nor have the New Englanders any reason to fear the having too much cattle for the constant export of beef, pork, and live stock of all kinds, to the West Indies, which is a market that will never fail them, let their quantity be almost what it may. And this mention of cattle leads me to observe that most of the farmers in this country are, in whatever concerns cattle, the most negligent ignorant set of men in the world. Nor do I know any country in which animals are worse treated. Horses are in general, even valuable ones, worked hard and starved: they plough, cart, and ride them to death, at the same time that they give very little heed to their food; after the hardest day's works, all the nourishment they are like to have is to be turned into a wood, where the shoots and weeds form the chief of the pasture; unless it be after the hay is in, when they get a share of the after-grass. . . . This bad treatment extends to draft oxen; to their cows, sheep, and swine; only in a different manner, as may be supposed. There is scarce any branch of rural economy which more demands attention and judgment than the management of cattle; or one which, under a judicious treatment, is attended with more profit to the farmer in all countries; but the New England farmers have in all this matter the worst notions imaginable.

I must, in the next place, take notice of their tillage, as being weakly and insufficiently given: worse ploughing is no where to be seen, yet the farmers get tolerable crops; this is owing, particularly in the new settlements, to the looseness and fertility of old woodlands, which, with very bad tillage, will yield excellent crops: a circumstance the rest of the province is too apt to be guided by, for seeing the effects, they are apt to suppose the same treatment will do on land long since broken up, which is far enough from being the case. Thus, in most parts of the province, is found shallow and unlevel furrows, which rather scratch than turn the land; and of this bad tillage the farmers are very sparing, rarely giving two ploughings if they think the crop will do with one; the consequence of which is their products being seldom near so great as they would be under a different management. Nor are their implements well made, or even well calculated for the work they are designed to perform; of this among other instances I may take the plough. The beam is too long; the supporters ought to be moveable, as they are in ploughs in England and in Scotland; the plough share is too narrow, which is a common fault; and the wheels are much too low. . . .

The harrows are also of a weak and poor construction; for I have more than once seen them with only wooden teeth, which however it may do for mere sand in tilth, must be very inefficacious on other soils. . . . The carts and waggons are also in some parts of the province very awkward ill made things, in which the principles of mechanics are not at all considered. There are however some gentlemen near Boston, who, having caught the taste of agriculture, which has for some years been remarkable in England, have introduced from thence better tools of most sorts and at the same time a much better practice of husbandry. . . .

Another article, which I shall here mention, is that of timber, which already grows so scarce upon the south coasts, that even fire-wood in some parts is not cheap. . . . They not only cut down timber to raise their buildings and fences, but in clearing the grounds for cultivation they destroy all that comes in their way, as if they had nothing to do but to get rid of it at all events, as fast as possible. Instead of acting in so absurd a manner, which utterly destroys woods of trees which require an hundred years to come to perfection, they ought, in the first settling and cultivating their tracts of land, to inclose and reserve portions of the best woods for the future use of themselves, and the general good of the country. . . . If the legislature does not interfere in this point, the whole country will be deprived of timber, as fast as it is settled. For nothing is of more importance to this country, though a colony, than timber: the plenty which has hitherto abounded makes the planters so regardless of their essential interests as to think it a commodity of little or no value. . . .

Let me . . . observe further that the New Englanders are also deficient in introducing . . . carrots, parsnips, potatoes, Jerusalem artichokes, beets, lucerne, sainfoine, and particularly cabbages. . . . In these colonies . . . land costs nothing; they have enough of various soils to try every thing. . . . But this circumstance, which is such an undoubted advantage, in fact turns out the contrary; and for this reason, they depend on this plenty of land as a substitute for all industry and good management; neglecting the efforts of good husbandry, which in England does more than the cheapness of the soil does in America.

J. Hector St. John de Crèvecoeur Asks, "What Is an American?" 1782

I wish I could be acquainted with the feelings and thoughts which must agitate the heart and present themselves to the mind of an enlightened Englishman, when he first lands on this continent. He must greatly rejoice that he lived at a time to see this fair country discovered and settled; he must necessarily feel a share of national pride, when he views the chain of settlements which embellishes these extended shores. . . . Here he beholds fair cities, substantial villages, extensive fields, an immense country filled with decent houses, good roads, orchards, meadows, and bridges, where an hundred years ago all was wild, woody, and uncultivated! . . . He is arrived on a new continent; a modern society offers itself to his contemplation, different from what he had hitherto seen. It is not composed, as in Europe, of great lords who possess everything, and of a herd of people who have nothing. Here are no aristocratical families, no courts, no kings, no bishops, no ecclesiastical dominion, no invisible power giving to a few a very visible one; no great manufacturers employing thousands, no great refinements of luxury. The rich and the poor are not so far removed from each other as they are in Europe. Some few towns excepted, we are all tillers of the earth, from Nova Scotia to West Florida. We are a people of cultivators, scattered over an immense territory, communicating with each other by means of good roads and navigable rivers, united by the silken bands of mild government, all respecting the laws, without dreading their power, because they are equitable. We are all animated with the spirit of an industry which is unfettered and unrestrained, because each person works for himself. If he travels through our rural districts he views not the hostile castle, and the haughty mansion, contrasted with the clay-built hut and miserable cabin, where cattle and men help to keep each other warm, and dwell in meanness, smoke, and indigence. A pleasing uniformity of decent competence appears throughout our habitations. The meanest of our log-houses is a dry and comfortable habitation. Lawyer or merchant are the fairest titles our towns afford; that of a farmer is the only appellation of the rural inhabitants of our country. It must take some time ere he can reconcile himself to our dictionary, which is but short in words of dignity, and names of honour. There, on a Sunday, he sees a congregation of respectable farmers and their wives, all clad in neat homespun, well mounted, or riding in their own humble waggons. There is not among them an esquire, saving the unlettered magistrate. There he sees a parson as simple as his flock, a farmer who does not riot on the labour of others. We have no princes, for whom we toil, starve, and bleed: we are the most perfect society now existing in the world. Here man is free as he ought to be. . . .

The next wish of this traveller will be to know whence came all these people? They are a mixture of English, Scotch, Irish, French, Dutch, Germans, and Swedes. From this promiscuous breed, that race now called Americans have arisen. . . .

What then is the American, this new man? He is either an European, or the descendant of an European, hence that strange mixture of blood, which you will find in no other country. I could point out to you a family whose grandfather was an Englishman, whose wife was Dutch, whose son married a French woman, and whose present four sons have now four wives of different nations. *He* is an American, who leaving behind him all his ancient prejudices and manners, receives new ones from the new mode of life he has embraced, the new government he obeys, and the new rank he holds. He becomes an American by being received in the broad lap of our great *Alma Mater*. Here individuals of all nations are melted into a new race of men, whose labours and posterity will one day cause great changes in the world. Americans are the western pilgrims, who are carrying along with them that great mass of arts, sciences, vigour, and industry which began long since in the east; they will finish the great circle. . . . The American is a new man, who acts upon new principles; he must therefore entertain new ideas, and form new opinions. From involuntary idleness, servile dependence, penury, and useless labour, he has passed to toils of a very different nature, rewarded by ample subsistence — This is an American.

British America is divided into many provinces, forming a large association, scattered along a coast 1500 miles extent and about 200 wide. This society I would fain examine, at least such as it appears in the middle provinces; if it does not afford that variety of tinges and gradations which may be observed in Europe, we have colours peculiar to ourselves. For instance, it is natural to conceive that those who live near the sea, must be very different from those who live in the woods; the intermediate space will afford a separate and distinct class.

Men are like plants; the goodness and flavour of the fruit proceeds from the peculiar soil and exposition in which they grow. We are nothing but what we derive from the air we breathe, the climate we inhabit, the government we obey, the system of religion we profess, and the nature of our employment. . . .

Those who live near the sea, feed more on fish than on flesh, and often encounter that boisterous element. This renders them more bold and enterprising; this leads them to neglect the confined occupations of the land. They see and converse with a variety of people, their intercourse with mankind becomes extensive. The sea inspires them with a love of traffic, a desire of transporting produce from one place to another; and leads them to a variety of resources which supply the place of labour. Those who inhabit the middle settlements, by far the most numerous, must be very different; the simple cultivation of the earth purifies them, but the indulgences of the government, the soft remonstrances of religion, the rank of independent freeholders, must necessarily inspire them with sentiments, very little known in Europe among people of the same class. . . . As citizens it is easy to imagine, that they will carefully read the newspapers, enter into every political disquisition, freely blame or censure governors and others. As farmers they will be careful and anxious to get as much as they can, because what they get is their own. . . . Industry, good living, selfishness, litigiousness, country politics, the pride of freemen, religious indifference, are their characteristics. If you recede still farther from the sea, you will come into more modern settlements; they exhibit the same strong lineaments, in a ruder appearance. Religion seems to have still less influence, and their manners are less improved.

Now we arrive near the great woods, near the last inhabited districts; there men seem to be placed still farther beyond the reach of government, which in some measure leaves them to themselves. How can it pervade every corner; as they were driven there by misfortunes, necessity of beginnings, desire of acquiring large tracts of land, idleness, frequent want of economy, ancient debts; the re-union of such people does not afford a very pleasing spectacle. When discord, want of unity and friendship; when either drunkenness or idleness prevail in such remote districts; contention, inactivity, and wretchedness must ensue. There are not the same remedies to these evils as in a long established community. The few magistrates they have, are in general little better than the rest; they are often in a perfect state of war; that of man against man, sometimes decided by blows, sometimes by means of the law; that of man against every wild inhabitant of these venerable woods, of which they are come to dispossess them. There men appear to be no better than carnivorous animals of a superior rank, living on the flesh of wild animals when they can catch them, and when they are not able, they subsist on grain. He who would wish to see America in its proper light, and have a true idea of its feeble beginnings and barbarous rudiments, must visit our extended line of frontiers where the last settlers dwell, and where he may see the first labours of settlement, the mode of clearing the earth, in all their different appearances; where men are wholly left dependent on their native tempers, and on the spur of uncertain industry, which often fails when not sanctified by the efficacy of a few moral rules. There, remote from the power of example and check of shame, many families exhibit the most hideous parts of our society. They are a kind of forlorn hope, preceding by ten or twelve years the most respectable army of veterans which come after them. In that space, prosperity will polish some, vice and the law will drive off the rest, who uniting again with others like themselves will recede still farther; making room for more industrious people, who will finish their improvements, convert the loghouse into a convenient habitation, and rejoicing that the first heavy labours are finished, will change in a few years that hitherto barbarous country into a fine fertile, well regulated district. Such is our progress, such is the march of the Europeans toward the interior parts of this continent. In all societies there are off-casts; this impure part serves as our precursors or pioneers; my father himself was one of that class, but he came upon honest principles, and was therefore one of the few who held fast; by good conduct and temperance, he transmitted to me his fair inheritance, when not above one in fourteen of his contemporaries had the same good fortune.

Forty years ago this smiling country was thus inhabited; it is now purged, a general decency of manners prevails throughout, and such has been the fate of our best countries.

* * * *

To examine how the world is gradually settled, how the howling swamp is converted into a pleasing meadow, the rough ridge into a fine field; and to hear the cheerful whistling, the rural song, where there was no sound heard before, save the yell of the savage, the screech of the owl or the hissing of the snake? Here an European, fatigued with luxury, riches, and pleasures, may find a sweet relaxation in a series of interesting scenes, as affecting as they are new. England, which now contains so many domes, so many castles, was once like this; a place woody and marshy; its inhabitants, now the favourite nation for arts and commerce, were once painted like our neighbours. The country will flourish in its turn, and the same observations will be made which I have just delineated. Posterity will look back with avidity and pleasure, to trace, if possible, the era of this or that particular settlement.

Thomas Jefferson on the Agrarian Ideal, 1787

We never had an interior trade of any importance. Our exterior commerce has suffered very much from the beginning of the present contest. During this time we have manufactured within our families the most necessary articles of cloathing. Those of cotton will bear some comparison with the same kinds of manufacture in Europe; but those of wool, flax and hemp are very coarse, unsightly, and unpleasant: and such is our attachment to agriculture, and such our preference for foreign manufactures, that be it wise or unwise, our people will certainly return as soon as they can, to the raising raw materials, and exchanging them for finer manufactures than they are able to execute themselves.

The political œconomists of Europe have established it as a principle that every state should endeavour to manufacture for itself: and this principle, like many others, we transfer to America, without calculating the difference of circumstance which should often produce a difference of result. In Europe the lands are either cultivated, or locked up against the cultivator. Manufacture must therefore be resorted to of necessity not of choice, to support the surplus of their people. But we have an immensity of land courting the industry of the husbandman. Is it best then that all our citizens should be employed in its improvement, or that one half should be called off from that to exercise manufactures and handicraft arts for the other? Those who labour in the earth are the chosen people of God, if ever he had a chosen people, whose breasts he has made his peculiar deposit for substantial and genuine virtue. It is the focus in which he keeps alive that sacred fire, which otherwise might escape from the face of the earth. Corruption of morals in the mass of cultivators is a phenomenon of which no age nor nation has furnished an example. It is the mark set on those, who not looking up to heaven, to their own soil and industry, as does the husbandman, for their subsistance, depend for it on the casualties and caprice of customers. Dependance begets subservience and venality, suffocates the germ of virtue, and prepares fit tools for the designs of ambition. This, the natural progress and consequence of the arts, has sometimes perhaps been retarded by accidental circumstances: but, generally speaking, the proportion which the aggregate of the other classes of citizens bears in any state to that of its husbandmen, is the proportion of its unsound to its healthy parts, and is a good-enough barometer whereby to measure its degree of corruption. While we have land to labour then, let us never wish to see our citizens occupied at a work-bench, or twirling a distaff. Carpenters, masons, smiths, are wanting in husbandry: but, for the general operations of manufacture, let our work-shops remain in Europe. It is better to carry provisions and materials to workmen there, than bring them to the provisions and materials, and with them their manners and principles. The loss by the transportation of commodities across the Atlantic will be made up in happiness and permanence of government. The mobs of great cities add just so much to the support of pure government, as sores do to the strength of the human body. It is the manners and spirit of a people which preserve a republic in vigour. A degeneracy in these is a canker which soon eats to the heart of its laws and constitution.

Benjamin Rush Praises the Market Farmers of Pennsylvania, 1789

1st. In settling a tract of land, . . . [the German Inhabitants of Pennsylvania] always provide large and suitable accommodations for their horses and cattle, before they lay out much money in building a house for themselves. The barn and stables are generally under one roof, and contrived in such manner as to enable them to feed their horses and cattle, and to remove their dung, with as little trouble as possible. The first dwelling house upon this farm is small, and built of logs. It generally lasts the life time of the first settler of a tract of land; and hence they have a saying, that "a son should always begin his improvements where his father left off," — that is, by building a large and convenient stone house.

2d. They always prefer good land or that land on which there is a large quantity of meadow ground. From an attention to the cultivation of grass, they often double the value of an old farm in a few years, and grow rich on farms, on which their predecessors of whom they purchased them, have nearly starved. They prefer purchasing farms with some improvements to settling a new tract of land.

3d. In clearing new land, they do not girdle the trees simply, and leave them to perish in the ground, as is the custom of their English or Irish neighbors; but they generally cut them down and burn them. In destroying under-wood and bushes, they generally grub them out of the ground; by which means a field is as fit for cultivation the second year after it is cleared, as it is in twenty years afterwards. The advantages of this mode of clearing, consist in the immediate product of the field, and in the greater facility with which it is ploughed, harrowed and reaped. The expense of repairing a plough, which is often broken two or three times in a year by small stumps concealed in the ground, is often greater than the extraordinary expense of grubbing the same field completely, in clearing it.

4th. They feed their horses and cows, of which they keep only a small number, in such a manner, that the former perform twice the labor of those horses, and the latter yield twice the quantity of milk of those cows, that are less plentifully fed. There is great economy in this practice, especially in a country where so much of the labour of a farmer is necessary to support his domestic animals. A German horse is known in every part of the state: indeed he seems to "feel with his lord, the pleasure and the pride" of his extraordinary size or fat.

5th. The fences of a German farm are generally high, and well built; so that his fields seldom suffer from the inroads of his own or his neighbours, horses, cattle, hogs, or sheep.

6th. The German farmers are great economists of their wood. Hence they burn it only in stoves, in which they consume but a 4th or 5th part of what is commonly burnt in ordinary open fire places: besides, their horses are saved by means of this economy, from that immense labour, in hauling wood in the middle of winter, which frequently unfits the horses of their neighbours for the toils of the ensuing spring. Their houses are, moreover, rendered so comfortable, at all times, by large close stoves, that twice the business is done by every branch of the family, in knitting, spinning, and mending farming utensils, that is done in houses where every member of the family crowds near to a common fire-place, or shivers at a distance from it, — with hands and fingers that move, by reason of the cold, with only half their usual quickness.

They discover economy in the preservation and increase of their wood in several other ways. They sometimes defend it, by high fences, from their cattle; by which means the young forest trees are suffered to grow, to replace those that are cut down for the necessary use of the farm. But where this cannot be conveniently done, they surround the stump of that tree which is most useful for fences, viz., the chestnut, with a small triangular fence. From this stump a number of suckers shoot out in a few years, two or three of which in the course of five and twenty years, grow into trees of the same size as the tree from whose roots they derived their origin.

7th. They keep their horses and cattle as warm as possible in winter, by which means they save a great deal of their hay and grain; for those animals when cold, eat much more than when they are in a more comfortable situation.

8th. The German farmers live frugally in their families, with respect to diet, furniture and apparel. They sell their most profitable grain, which is wheat; and eat that which is less profitable, but more nourishing, that is, rye or Indian corn. The profit to a farmer, from this single article of economy, is equal, in the course of a life time, to the price of a farm for one of his children. They eat sparingly of boiled animal food, with large quantities of vegetable, particularly sallad, turnips, onions, and cabbage, the last of which they make into sour crout. They likewise use a large quantity of milk and cheese in their diet. . . .

9th. The German farmers have larger or profitable gardens near their houses. They contain little else but useful vegetables. Pennsylvania is indebted to the Germans for the principal part of her knowledge in horticulture. There was a time when turnips and cabbage were the principal vegetables that were used in diet by the citizens of Philadelphia. . . . Since the settlement of a number of German gardeners in the neighborhood of Philadelphia, the tables of all classes of citizens have been covered with a variety of vegetables, in every season of the year; and to the use of these vegetables, in diet, may be ascribed the general exemption of the citizens of Philadelphia from diseases of the skin.

10th. The Germans seldom hire men to work upon their farms . . . except in harvest. . . . The wives and daughters of the German farmers frequently forsake, for a while, their dairy and spinning-wheel, and join their husbands and brothers in the labour of cutting down, collecting and bringing home the fruits of their fields and orchards. The work of the gardens is generally done by the women of the family.

11th. A large and strong waggon covered with linen cloth, is an essential part of the furniture of a German farm. In this waggon, drawn by four or five large horses of a peculiar breed; they convey to market over the roughest roads, between 2 or 3 thousand pounds weight of the produce of their farms. In the months of September and October, it is no uncommon thing, on the Lancaster and Reading roads, to meet in one day from fifty to an hundred of these waggons, on their way to Philadelphia, most of which belong to German farmers.

12th. The favourable influence of agriculture, as conducted by the Germans in extending human happiness, is manifested by the joy they express upon the birth of a child. No dread of poverty, nor distrust of Providence from an increasing family, depress the spirits of these industrious and frugal people. Upon the birth of a son, they exult in the gift of a ploughman or a waggoner; and upon the birth of a daughter, they rejoice in the addition of another spinster, or milkmaid to their family. . . .

13th. The Germans take great pains to produce, in their children, not only habits of labour, but a love of it. . . . They prefer industrious habits to money itself. . . .

14th. The Germans set a great value upon patrimonial property. This useful principle in human nature prevents much folly and vice in young people. It moreover leads to lasting and extensive advantages, in the improvement of a farm; for what inducement can be stronger in a parent to plant an orchard, to preserve forest trees or to build a commodious and durable house, than the idea, that they will all be possessed by a succession of generations, who shall inherit his blood and name.

15th. The German farmers are very much influenced in planting and pruning trees, also in sowing and reaping, by the age and appearances of the moon. This attention to the state of the moon has been ascribed to superstition; but if the facts related by Mr. Wilson in his observations upon climates are true, part of their success in agriculture must be ascribed to their being so much influenced by it.

16th. From the history that has been given of the German agriculture, it will hardly be necessary to add that a German farm may be distinguished from the farms of the other citizens of the state, by the superior size of their barns; the plain, but compact form of their houses; the height of their inclosures; the extent of their orchards; the fertility of their fields; the luxuriance of their meadows, and a general appearance of plenty and neatness in everything that belongs to them.

Edward Slader's Account Book, 1807–1812

Nathaniel Sawyer Debtor to Edward Slader [What Slader Is Owed]			*Contra Credit [What Slader Is Paid]*		

1807

			1807		
			Nov.	—Credit by one pound 1/4 putty	$ .15
Oct. 9	—To pasturing two heiffers 16 weeks at /10 per week—13/4	$2.22		—By 12 bricks	.07
	—To pasturing one pair of four-year-old steers 11 weeks at 1/8	3.05	*Dec. 24*	—By one dollar and seventy cents	1.07
	—Dr. to six quarts of salt for said cattle	.31	*1808*		
	—To 1/4 pound white lard	.07	*Jan. 11*	—By part of a day killing hogs	$ .33
		$5.65	*Aug. 25*	—By one days work yourself	.58
		−5.44	*Dec. 20*	—By part of a day killing hogs	.33
		$ .21			

1812

			1809		
Dec. 29	—Dr. to two bushels of oats at 2/6 per bushel	$ .83	*Jan. 19*	—By making Sled by agreement	$1.00
		$6.48	*Nov. 28*	—By one day yourself butchering hogs	.58
			Dec. 18	—By dressing calf	.20
					$4.94

1810

Jan. 17	—By butchering hogs	$ .50
		$5.44

1812

Dec. 29	—Cr. by butchering	$1.04
		$6.48

From Old Sturbridge Village, Sturbridge, Ma, manuscript OSV 451.1/1978.

Anna Howell's Farm Diary, 1820

May

May 1st. Planted cucumbers. The ground as dry as ashes.

3rd. A considerable frost killed the beans in my garden.

6th Planted Water Melons.

16 The wind blowing violently from the N. E. accompanied with a drizzling rain. The weather very cold.

17th Still cold and stormy.

20th There has been one continued storm for the last week. Replanted Nutmeg Melons and cucumbers.

From Anna Blackwood Howell Diary, 1820 Manuscript from American Antiquarian Society, Worcester, Mass. Reprinted with permission.

1st Raining nearly all day. The sun has not shone one hour at a time for the last eight days.

22nd Planted sweet potatoes.

24th Replanted Nutmeg Melons. Those that were up being generally kill'd by the wet and cold weather.

26th Began to plant field corn. Replanted water melons.

Manuscript page from Anna Howell's farm diary, May 1820. This diary page faced the almanac page shown on page 147. The transcription appears on page 145. Courtesy, American Antiquarian Society.

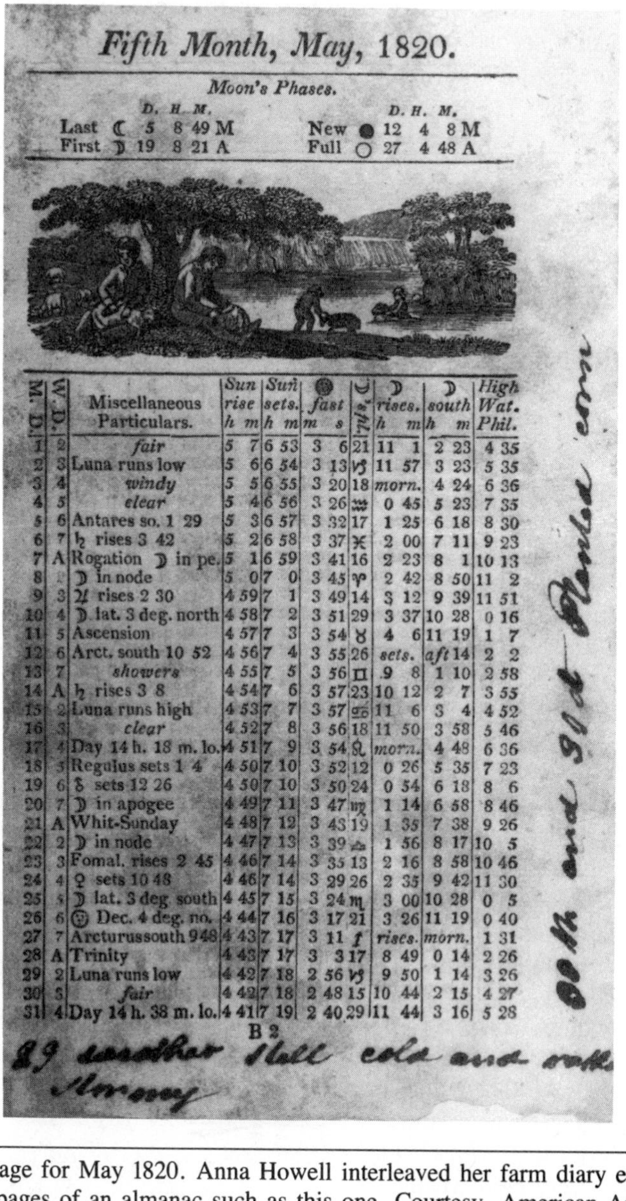

Fifth Month, May, 1820.

Moon's Phases.

	D. H. M.		D. H. M.
Last ☾	5 8 49 M	New ●	12 4 8 M
First ☽	19 8 21 A	Full ○	27 4 48 A

M. D.	W. D.	Miscellaneous Particulars.	Sun rise h m	Sun sets h m	☉ fast m s	☽	☽ rises h m	☽ south h m	High Wat. Phil.
1	2	fair	5 7	6 53	3 6	21	11 1	2 23	4 35
2	3	Luna runs low	5 6	6 54	3 13	♑	11 57	3 23	5 35
3	4	windy	5 5	6 55	3 20	18	morn.	4 24	6 36
4	5	clear	5 4	6 56	3 26	♒	0 45	5 23	7 35
5	6	Antares so. 1 29	5 3	6 57	3 32	17	1 25	6 18	8 30
6	7	♄ rises 3 42	5 2	6 58	3 37	♓	2 00	7 11	9 23
7	A	Rogation ☽ in pe.	5 1	6 59	3 41	16	2 23	8 1	10 13
8	2	☽ in node	5 0	7 0	3 45	♈	2 42	8 50	11 2
9	3	♃ rises 2 30	4 59	7 1	3 49	14	3 12	9 39	11 51
10	4	☽ lat. 3 deg. north	4 58	7 2	3 51	29	3 37	10 28	0 16
11	5	Ascension	4 57	7 3	3 54	♉	4 6	11 19	1 7
12	6	Arct. south 10 52	4 56	7 4	3 55	26	sets.	aft 14	2 2
13	7	showers	4 55	7 5	3 56	♊	9 8	1 10	2 58
14	A	♄ rises 3 8	4 54	7 6	3 57	23	10 12	2 7	3 55
15	2	Luna runs high	4 53	7 7	3 57	♋	11 6	3 4	4 52
16	3	clear	4 52	7 8	3 56	18	11 50	3 58	5 46
17	4	Day 14 h. 18 m. lo.	4 51	7 9	3 54	♌	morn.	4 48	6 36
18	5	Regulus sets 1 4	4 50	7 10	3 52	12	0 26	5 35	7 23
19	6	☿ sets 12 26	4 50	7 10	3 50	24	0 54	6 18	8 6
20	7	☽ in apogee	4 49	7 11	3 47	♍	1 14	6 58	8 46
21	A	Whit-Sunday	4 48	7 12	3 43	19	1 35	7 38	9 26
22	2	☽ in node	4 47	7 13	3 39	♎	1 56	8 17	10 5
23	3	Fomal. rises 2 45	4 46	7 14	3 35	13	2 16	8 58	10 46
24	4	♀ sets 10 48	4 46	7 14	3 29	26	2 35	9 42	11 30
25	5	☽ lat. 3 deg. south	4 45	7 15	3 24	♏	3 00	10 28	0 5
26	6	☉ Dec. 4 deg. no.	4 44	7 16	3 17	21	3 26	11 19	0 40
27	7	Arcturus south 9 48	4 43	7 17	3 11	♐	rises.	morn.	2 26
28	A	Trinity	4 43	7 17	3 3	17	8 49	0 14	2 26
29	2	Luna runs low	4 42	7 18	2 56	♑	9 50	1 14	3 26
30	3	fair	4 42	7 18	2 48	15	10 44	2 15	4 27
31	4	Day 14 h. 38 m. lo.	4 41	7 19	2 40	29	11 44	3 16	5 28

B 2

Almanac page for May 1820. Anna Howell interleaved her farm diary entries between the pages of an almanac such as this one. Courtesy, American Antiquarian Society.

June

June 1st The weather almost cold enough for frost.
6th Planted a second patch of water and nutmeg melons
12th Planted pumpkins
20th Sent a few beans to market
27th of June. Arthur Powel picked cucumbers for market

July

7th The weather distressingly dry. Picked a small basket of cucumbers for market. Finished reaping and hawled my rye into the barn. I had 87 dozen
8th Hawled the rye from the field that D. Ward has 10. the shares 72 dozen
We had a refreshing shower to day, after a drought of two weeks

August

5th Sent 6 watermelons to market
11th Sent a basket of Nutmeg melons to market
15th Sowed flat turnips in the new ground
22nd Sowed turnips in the barnyard
24th Picked my geese

November

Produce of Fancy Hill farm of 1820
In the field next to D Ward I had 175 baskets of corn
The very dry weather ruined my buckwheat. I had but 6 bushels
Nov 3rd In the barn field I had 215 baskets of corn. 30 bushels flat turnips in the new ground
I had 100 baskets of corn to my share of the ground tilled by D. Ward. I had 99 bushels of rootabaga turnips
Nov. 11th John Fowler to 2 and half days work To cash paid John Fowler $ 1
12th A violent storm accompanied with hail rain and snow
13th I returned from Tuckahoe the wind blowing a gale from the N W the weather severely cold
15th Still very cold weather
18th John Fowler to cash 1 12
Nov 30th very cold weather

John James Audubon Depicts the Squatters of the Mississippi, 1808–1834

Although every European traveller who has glided down the Mississippi, at the rate of ten miles an hour, has told his tale of the Squatters, yet none has given any other account of them than that they are "a sallow, sickly-looking sort of miserable beings," living in swamps, and subsisting on pig-nuts, Indian corn and bear's flesh. It is obvious, however, that none but a person acquainted with their history, manners, and condition, can give any real information respecting them.

The individuals who become squatters choose that sort of life of their own free will. They mostly remove from other parts of the United States, after finding that land has become too high in price; and they are persons who, having a family of strong and hardy children, are anxious to enable them to provide for themselves. They have heard from good authorities, that the country extending along the great streams of the West, is of all parts of the Union the richest in its soil, the growth of its timber, and the abundance of its game; that, besides, the Mississippi is the great road to and from all the markets in the world; and that every vessel borne by its waters, affords to settlers some chance of selling their commodities, or of exchanging them for others. To these recommendations is added another, of ever greater weight with persons of the above denomination, namely, the prospect of being able to settle on land, and perhaps to hold it for a number of years, without purchase, rent or tax of any kind. . . .

I shall introduce to you the members of a family from Virginia, first giving you an idea of their condition in that country, previous to their migration to the west. The land which they and their ancestors have possessed for a hundred years, having been constantly forced to produce crops of one kind or other, is now completely worn out. It exhibits only a superficial layer of red clay, cut up by deep ravines, through which much of the soil has been conveyed to some more fortunate neighbour, residing in a yet rich and beautiful valley. Their strenuous efforts to render it productive have failed. They dispose of every thing too cumbrous or expensive for them to remove, retaining only a few horses, a servant or two, and such implements of husbandry and other articles as may be necessary on their journey, or useful when they arrive at the spot of their choice.

I think I see them at this moment harnessing their horses, and attaching them to their waggons, which are already filled with bedding, provisions, and the younger children; while on their outside are fastened spinning-wheels and looms; and a bucket, filled with tar and tallow, swings between the hind wheels. Several axes are secured to the bolster, and the feeding trough of the horses contains pots, kettles, and pans. The servant, now become a driver, rides the near saddled horse, the wife is mounted on another, the worthy husband shoulders his gun, and his sons, clad in plain substantial homespun, drive the cattle ahead, and lead the procession, followed by the hounds and other dogs. Their day's journey is short and not agreeable: — the cattle, stubborn or wild, frequently leave the road for the woods, giving the travellers much trouble; the harness of the horses here and there gives away, and needs immediate repair; a basket, which has accidentally dropped, must be gone after, for nothing that they have can be spared; the roads are bad, and now and then all hands are called to push on the waggon, or prevent it from upsetting.

Yet by sunset they have proceeded perhaps twenty miles. Rather fatigued, all assemble round the fire, which has been lighted, supper is prepared, and a camp being erected, there they pass the night.

Days and weeks, nay months, of unremitting toil, pass before they gain the end of their journey. They have crossed both the Carolinas, Georgia, and Alabama. They have been travelling from the beginning of May to that of September, and with heavy hearts they traverse the State of Mississippi. But now, arrived on the banks of the broad stream, they gaze in amazement on the dark deep woods around them. Boats of various kinds they see gliding downwards with the current, while others slowly ascend against it. A few inquiries are made at the nearest dwelling, and, assisted by the inhabitants with their boats and canoes, they at once cross the Mississippi, and select their place of habitation.

The exhalations arising from the swamps and morasses around them, have a powerful effect on these new settlers, but all are intent on preparing for the winter. A small patch of ground is cleared by the axe and the fire, a temporary cabin is erected, to each of the cattle is attached a jingling-bell before it is let loose into the neighbouring canebrake, and the horses remain about the house, where they find sufficient food at that season. The first trading boat that stops at their landing, enables them to provide themselves with some flour, fish-hooks, and ammunition, as well as other commodities. The looms are mounted, the spinning-wheels soon furnish some yarn, and in a few weeks the family throw off their ragged clothes, and array themselves in suits adapted to the climate. The father and sons meanwhile have sown turnips and other vegetables; and from some Kentucky flat boat a supply of live poultry has been procured.

October tinges the leaves of the forest, the morning dews are heavy, the days hot, the nights chill, and the unacclimated family in a few days are attacked with ague. The lingering disease almost prostrates their whole faculties, and one seeing them at such a period might well call them sallow and sickly. Fortunately the unhealthy season soon passes over, and the hoar-frosts make their appearance. Gradually each individual recovers strength. The largest ash trees are felled; their trunks are cut, split, and corded in front of the building; a large fire is lighted under night on the edge of the water, and soon a steamer calls to purchase the wood, and thus add to their comforts during the winter.

This first fruit of their industry imparts new courage to them; their exertions multiply, and when spring returns, the place has a cheerful look. Venison, bear's flesh, wild turkeys, ducks, and geese, with now and then some fish, have served to keep up their strength, and now their enlarged field is planted with corn, potatoes, and pumpkins. Their stock of cattle, too, has augmented; the steamer, which now stops there as if by preference, buys a calf or a pig, together with the whole of their wood. Their store of provisions is renewed, and brighter rays of hope enliven their spirits.

Who is he of the settlers on the Mississippi that cannot realize some profit? Truly none who is industrious. When the autumnal months return, all are better prepared to encounter the ague, which then prevails. Substantial food, suitable clothing, and abundant firing, repel its attacks; and before another twelvemonth has elapsed, the family is naturalized.

The sons by this time have discovered a swamp covered with excellent timber, and as they have seen many great rafts of saw logs, bound for the mills of New Orleans, floating past their dwelling, they resolve to try the success of a little enterprise. Their industry and prudence have already enhanced their credit. A few cross-saws are purchased, and some broad-wheeled "carry-logs" are made by themselves. Log after log is hauled to the bank of the river, and in a short time their first raft is made on the shore, and loaded with cord-wood. When the next freshet sets it afloat, it is secured by long grape-vines or cables, until the proper time being arrived, the husband and sons embark on it, and float down the mighty stream.

After encountering many difficulties, they arrive in safety at New Orleans where they dispose of their stock, the money obtained for which may be said to be all profit; supply themselves with such articles as may add to their convenience or comfort, and with light hearts, procure a passage on the upper deck of a steamer, at a very cheap rate, on account of the benefit of their labour in taking in wood or otherwise.

And now the vessel approaches their home. See the joyous mother and daughters as they stand on the bank! A store of vegetables lies around them, a large tub of fresh milk is at their feet, and in their hands are plates filled with rolls of butter. As the steamer stops, three broad strawhats are waved from its upper deck; and soon, husband and wife, brothers and sisters, are in each other's embrace. The boat carries off the provisions, for which value has been left, and as the captain issues his orders for putting on the steam, the happy family enter their humble dwelling. The husband gives his bag of dollars to the wife, while the sons present some token of affection to their sisters. Surely, at such a moment, the Squatters are richly repaid for all their labours.

Every successive year has increased their savings. They now possess a large stock of horses, cows, and hogs, with abundance of provisions, and domestic comfort of every kind. The daughters have been married to the sons of neighbouring Squatters, and have gained sisters to themselves by the marriage of their brothers. The government secures to the family the lands, on which, twenty years before, they settled in poverty and sickness. Larger buildings are erected on piles, secure from the inundations; where a single cabin once stood, a neat village is now to be seen; warehouses, stores, and work-shops, increase the importance of the place. The Squatters live respected and in due time die regretted, by all who knew them.

Thus are the vast frontiers of our country peopled, and thus does cultivation, year after year, extend over the western wilds. Time will no doubt be, when the great valley of the Mississippi, still covered with primeval forests, interspersed with swamps, will smile with corn-fields and orchards, while crowded cities will rise at intervals along its banks, and enlightened nations will rejoice in the bounties of Providence.

Calvin Colton on Self-Made Men, 1844

Providence has us a rich, productive, and glorious heritage. . . . The wealth of the country is inexhaustible, and the enterprise of the people is unsubdued. . . . Give them a good government, and they can not help going ahead, and outstripping every nation on the globe.

Ours is a country, where men start from an humble origin, and from small beginnings rise gradually in the world, as the reward of merit and industry, and where they can attain to the most elevated positions, or acquire a large amount of wealth, according to the pursuits they elect for themselves. No exclusive privileges of birth, no entailment of estates, no civil or political disqualifications, stand in their path; but one has as good a chance as another, according to his talents, prudence, and personal exertions. This is a country of self-made men, than which nothing better could be said of any state of society.

ψ *E S S A Y S*

The following essays explore whether eighteenth-century farming was primarily market driven or subsistence oriented. Using the case of New England, historian William Cronon of the University of Wisconsin, Madison argues in the first selection that, in contrast to Indians, the colonists viewed land as a form of capital to be used for creating wealth. The land provided resources that integrated the colonists into a worldwide capitalist economy. The second essay, by environmental historian Carolyn Merchant of the University of California at Berkeley, argues that although the majority of eighteenth-century New Englanders were subsistence minded, a capitalist orientation marked settlers along the Atlantic and Pacific coasts and the Connecticut River. The ecological impacts of the subsistence sector were significantly less than those of the capitalist-oriented sector. The third essay, by historian John Boles of Rice University, argues that slaves practiced subsistence farming within the South's capitalist-oriented plantation system. Not only did some slaves keep gardens, hunt, and fish, but they often owned pigs and cows, as well as farm equipment and utensils.

These three essays reveal the ways in which ordinary people in the eighteenth and early nineteenth centuries interacted directly with the land through production. The authors pose thought-provoking questions about the driving forces of environmental and cultural transformation.

Land for Markets

WILLIAM CRONON

New England in 1800 was far different from the land the earliest European visitors had described. By 1800, the Indians who had been its first human inhabitants were reduced to a small fraction of their former numbers, and had been forced onto less and less desirable agricultural lands. Their ability to move

Excerpts from *Changes in the Land* by William Cronon. Copyright © 1983 by William Cronon, pp. 159–70. Reprinted by permission of Hill and Wang, a division of Farrar, Straus & Giroux, Inc.

about the landscape in search of ecological abundance had become severely constrained, so that their earlier ways of interacting with the environment were no longer feasible and their earlier sources of food were less easy to find. Disease and malnutrition had become facts of life for them.

Large areas particularly of southern New England were now devoid of animals which had once been common: beaver, deer, bear, turkey, wolf, and others had vanished. In their place were hordes of European grazing animals which constituted a heavier burden on New England plants and soils. Their presence had brought hundreds of miles of fences. With fences had come the weeds: dandelion and rat alike joined alien grasses as they made their way across the landscape. New England's forests still exceeded its cleared land in 1800, but, especially near settled areas, the remaining forest had been significantly altered by grazing, burning, and cutting. The greatest of the oaks and white pines were gone, and cedar had become scarce. Hickory had been reduced because of its attractiveness as a fuel. Clear-cutting had shifted forest composition in favor of those trees that were capable of sprouting from stumps, with the result that the forests of 1800 were physically smaller than they had been at the time of European settlement. The cutting of upland species such as beech and maple, which were accustomed to moist sites, produced drying that encouraged species such as the oaks, which preferred drier soils.

Deforestation had in general affected the region by making local temperatures more erratic, soils drier, and drainage patterns less constant. A number of smaller streams and springs no longer flowed year-round, and some larger rivers were dammed and no longer accessible to the fish which had once spawned in them. Water and wind erosion were taking place with varying severity, and flooding had become more common. Soil exhaustion was occurring in many areas as a result of poor husbandry, and the first of many European pests and crop diseases had already begun to appear. These changes had taken place primarily in the settled areas, and it was still possible to find extensive regions in the north where they did not apply. Nevertheless, they heralded the future. . . .

One of the most perceptive analyses of ecological change in early New England was delivered in a speech by the Narragansett sachem Miantonomo in 1642, just a few years after English colonists began to settle in the vicinity of his people's villages. "You know," he said, speaking of a time just recently past,

> our fathers had plenty of deer and skins, our plains were full of deer, as also our woods, and of turkies, and our coves full of fish and fowl. But these English having gotten our land, they with scythes cut down the grass, and with axes fell the trees; their cows and horses eat the grass, and their hogs spoil our clam banks, and we shall be starved. . . .

All communities exercise choice in their labeling of resources, but they do so in radically different ways. Perhaps the central contrast between Indians and Europeans at the moment they first encountered each other in New England had to do with what they saw as resources and how they thought those resources should be utilized. Indians had a far greater knowledge of what could be eaten or otherwise made useful in the New England environment; their economy defined a correspondingly greater range of resources. But most of those resources were simply used or consumed by the household which acquired them, or, if exchanged, were traded for similar items. Very few resources were accumulated for the explicit purpose of indicating a person's status in the community: wampum, furs, certain minerals, and ornaments of the hunt generally served these purposes. Class authority was maintained more by kin networks and personal alliances than by stores of wealth, and the latter were in any event limited by the community's commitment to geographical mobility. There was thus little social incentive to accumulate large quantities of material goods. A wide range of resources furnished economic subsistence, while a narrow range of resources conferred economic status. The community's social definition of "need" was inherently limited, and made economic abundance a relatively easy attainment for its members. It was for this reason that Roger Williams could write of the Narragansetts: "Many of them naturally Princes, or else industrious persons, are rich; and the poore amongst them will say, they want nothing." Rich and poor alike were relatively easily satiated, and so made relatively slender demands on the ecosystems which furnished their economy its resources.

The same could hardly be said of the European colonists. For them, perceptions of "resources" were filtered through the language of "commodities," goods which could be exchanged in markets where the very act of buying and selling conferred profits on their owners. Because European economies measured many more commodities in terms of money values — abstract equivalencies which could be accumulated, no matter what the resource involved, to become indicators of wealth and social status — they had few of the limitations which constrained the growth of their Indian counterparts. As a result, European markets, as the anthropologist Marshall Sahlins has suggested, at least in theory "erected a shrine to the Unattainable: *Infinite Needs.*" Those needs were determined not only by the local communities which became established in colonial New England but by all the distant places to which those communities sold their goods. The landscape of New England thus increasingly met not only the needs of its inhabitants for food and shelter but the demands of faraway markets for cattle, corn, fur, timber, and other goods whose "values" became expressions of the colonists' socially determined "needs." Ironically, though colonists perceived fewer *resources* in New England ecosystems than did the Indians, they perceived many more *commodities*, and so committed much wider portions of those ecosystems to the marketplace. "Nor could it be imagined," wrote the colonial historian Edward Johnson in 1653, "that this Wilderness should turn a mart for Merchants in so short a space, Holland, France, Spain, and Portugal coming hither for trade."

The process whereby colonists (as well as Indians) linked New England ecosystems to market relationships was neither instantaneous nor continuous. Just because the earliest English explorers perceived the New England coast in terms of its commodities does not mean that their perceptions had immediate ecological consequences. Colonial economies underwent nearly as profound an evolution in New England as those of the Indians. Many English colonists, for example, initially supplemented their agriculture with subsistence activities — hunting and gathering — which looked distinctly Indian; colonists were eventually forced to limit these for the same ecological reasons that Indians did. Colonial systems for fixing property boundaries were not fully articulated until late in the seventeenth century. The degree to which land was committed to commercial production depended upon a host of changing factors: population growth, imperial regulations, ease of transportation to urban markets, and so on. Most early farmers directed only a small margin of their production to market sale. Perhaps their most important attachment to the market was not even related to immediate production — their expectation that the size of that margin would increase, and with it the value of their land. The inhabitants of some New England towns speculated in land almost from the beginning, but others awaited market developments of the late seventeenth and the eighteenth centuries before real estate was treated as so abstract a commodity. Markets, in other words, like commodities, were socially defined institutions which as a result of the transition to capitalism operated very differently at the end of the colonial period than they had at its beginning.

However true this may be, it must nevertheless be repeated that the abstract concept of the commodity informed colonial decision-making about the New England environment right from the start. The colonists brought with them concepts of value and scarcity which had been shaped by the social and ecological circumstances of northern Europe, and so perceived New England as a landscape of great natural wealth. Searching for commodities which would allow them to obtain European goods, they applied European definitions of scarcity — that is to say, European prices — to New England conditions of abundance. Operating in an economy where labor was scarce and difficult to hire, where accumulated capital was smaller than it had been in Europe, colonists turned to the factor of production which could compensate for the ones they lacked: they turned to the land and all it contained. Fish, fur, and lumber were assigned high values because of their scarcities in Europe, but were more or less free goods in New England. They had only to be taken and transported to market to yield a substantial return on invested labor; because of this, they were treated as wasting assets capable of rapid conversion to more liquid capital. Labor costs alone operated as a constraint on their exploitation, since colonists could consume natural wealth as a substitute for capital.

The result was an economy which used natural resources in a way which often appeared to European visitors as terribly wasteful. "In a word," wrote the Swedish traveler Peter Kalm of American farming practices, "the grain fields, the meadows, the forests, the cattle, etc. are treated with equal carelessness." A number of Americans agreed. In 1787, the physician Joseph Warren wrote a critique of American agriculture in which he argued:

> There is, perhaps, no country in the world, where the situations, nature, and circumstances of things, seem to point out husbandry as the most essential and proper business, more than our own; and yet, there is scarcely one where it is less attended to.

More, more for less, less {

Warren attributed this apparent paradox to several factors: the Americans' tendency to farm overlarge tracts of land, their "rage for commerce," their investment of little capital in their farmlands, and their wasteful practices in feeding livestock. At the most basic level, however, what distinguished European and American farms was their production of nearly identical commodities with very different proportions of labor and land. As Warren noted, "Nothing will give a clearer idea of the different management, than the following facts: in England, rents are high and labour low; in America, it is just the reverse, rents are low and the rate of labour high." Here there was no paradox: American relations of production were premised upon ecological abundance, and so attached a higher value to labor than had been the case in Europe. Returns to labor were so high in America precisely *because* returns to land were so low.

Land in New England became for the colonists a form of capital, a thing consumed for the express purpose of creating augmented wealth. It was the land-capital equation that created the two central ecological contradictions of the colonial economy. One of these was the inherent conflict between the land uses of the colonists and those of the Indians. The ecological relationships which European markets created in New England were inherently antithetical to earlier Indian economies, and so those economies were transformed — as much through the agency of the Indians as the Europeans — in ways that need not be repeated here. By 1800, Indians could no longer live the same seasons of want and plenty that their ancestors had, for the simple reason that crucial aspects of those seasons had changed beyond recognition.

But there was a second ecological contradiction in the colonial economy as well. Quite simply, the colonists' economic relations of production were ecologically self-destructive. They assumed the limitless availability of more land to exploit, and in the long run that was impossible. Peter Kalm described the process whereby colonial farmers used new land until it was exhausted, then turned it to pasture and cut down another tract of forest. "This kind of agriculture will do for a time," he wrote, "but it will afterwards have bad consequences, as every one may clearly see." Not only colonial agriculture, but lumbering and the fur trade as well, were able to ignore the problem of continuous yield because of the temporary gift of nature which fueled their continuous expansion. When that gift was finally exhausted, ecosystems and economies alike were forced into new relationships: expansion could not continue indefinitely.

The implications of this second ecological contradiction stretched well beyond the colonial period. Although we often tend to associate ecological changes primarily with the cities and factories of the nineteenth and twentieth centuries, it should by now be clear that changes with similar roots took place just as profoundly in the farms and countrysides of the colonial period. The transition to capitalism alienated the products of the land as much as the products of human labor, and so transformed natural communities as profoundly as it did human ones. By integrating New England ecosystems into an ultimately global capitalist economy, colonists and Indians together began a dynamic and unstable process of ecological change which had in no way ended by 1800. We live with their legacy today. When the geographer Carl Sauer wrote in the twentieth century that Americans had "not yet learned the difference between yield and loot," he was describing one of the most longstanding tendencies of their way of life. Ecological abundance and economic prodigality went hand in hand: the people of plenty were a people of waste.

Land for Subsistence

CAROLYN MERCHANT

As settlers [in eighteenth-century New England] moved inland to found towns without easy access to coastal harbors and navigable rivers, subsistence-oriented farms were generated. Ideas about nature that permeated rural culture formed a continuity with the popular consciousness of seventeenth-century settlers and their English forebears in Renaissance England. Like the cosmos of the precolonial Indian, the eighteenth-century cosmos was alive and animate. But unlike Indian animism with its many deities within animals, plants, and rocks, the English God was transcendent, Nature acting as his vice-regent in the mundane world. Like the consciousness of the Indians, the consciousness of most rural farmers was participatory and mimetic. But unlike that of Indians, it was a participatory consciousness dominated by vision. The oral culture of folk traditions was reinforced by a mix of astrological and alchemic symbols conveyed by elites through the world of print. . . .

Along with the Bible, the almanac was the most prevalent book in colonial households. For either the meagerly or well-educated farming family, the almanac served as a set of mediating symbols that connected the individual to the larger cosmos through diagrams, woodcuts, verses, tables, and advice columns. On the inside cover was the zodiacal "Man of the Signs," along with a table of symbols of the signs of the zodiac and the seven planets. This information was critical to maintaining health. The user was instructed to find the day of the month and note the sign of the zodiac in which the moon was located. By comparing the sign with the man in the woodcut, the part of the body affected on that day could be determined. If the moon was in Leo, the heart was vulnerable, if in Aquarius the legs could develop problems. Each month was heralded with a proverb or verses often accompanied by an illustration embedded with symbolic meaning. Finally, the endpapers reported the latest agricultural discoveries and planting tips. Since almanacs were among the few books a family possessed, these verses and articles received intensive use, conveying guidelines for agricultural decisions and daily behavior. The almanac was, in effect, the colonist's "weekday Bible." . . .

Farmers organized many of their activities according to the astrological theory conveyed by the almanacs. Because of the pull of the moon on water, a full moon would encourage the upward movement of plant fluids. They therefore planted seeds of upward-growing plants, such as corn, rye, and wheat, in

Reprinted, by permission of the author and publisher, from *Ecological Revolutions: Nature, Gender, and Science in New England*, by Carolyn Merchant. © 1989 The University of North Carolina Press.

The Anatomy of Man's body, 1782. Even into the late eighteenth century, almanac makers, although expressing skepticism over the mechanism by which the moon—merely by passing through certain zodiacal signs—could influence one part of the human body more than another, included the Man of the Signs in their publications because their clientele demanded it.

the moon's waxing phase and root crops such as carrots and beets in the wane. Similarly, grafting or transplanting trees under a waning moon helped them set their roots downward. Tanners testified that oak bark peeled off readily in the new of the moon, but stuck closely to the trunk after the moon was full. Animal breeders followed the rule that horses should be gelded in the wane of the moon, while sows should be bred during its increase. . . .

Nathaniel Whittmore's *Almanack* for 1713 advised farmers that "the best time to cut timber . . . is in the old of the moon; in December, January, and February, especially when the moon is in Pisces." [According to] Daniel Staples, a Maine farmer who was born in 1750, . . . fruit trees should be pruned under a waning moon, since the cuts would heal more rapidly. He advised farmers to prune their orchards in May at the end of the waning phase, one to two days before the new moon. . . .

Between 1700, when the inland towns were being settled, and 1790, when ecological crisis and European markets stimulated agricultural intensification, an economy oriented to subsistence and family preservation flourished in inland-upland New England. This form of production differed from traditional European agriculture in that farmers held fee simple titles to their own land, rather than ancestral grazing, tilling, and woodcutting privileges on the commons. And it differed from nineteenth-century capitalist agriculture in that most males owned (or would soon inherit) their own farms, rather than supporting themselves wholly through wage labor. . . .

The New England agroecological unit comprised a farm homestead (with space and technology for both agricultural and nonagricultural production); fields, orchards, and gardens for plant production; pastures, meadows, barns, and dairy for animal production; and a woodlot for fuel. Farm and household products moved off the farm to neighboring farms or more distant markets; purchased or bartered goods entered from outside. Within the farm boundaries, energy (food and fuel) and nutrients moved from one space to another. Forest and pasture provided feed for grazing animals and in turn received animal manure, while meadows supplied fodder to the barnyard for animals during snowy winters. Woodlots transmitted fuel to the homestead and ashes to the soil. Tillage, orchards, and gardens supplied grain, fruits, and vegetables while receiving manure from cattle, pigs, and poultry. Fields and gardens provided flowers for bees and other beneficial insects and birds, but also harbored pests. Whether the farm was a self-sustaining ecological unit depended on the extent to which energy and nutrients were circulated within or moved off the farm.

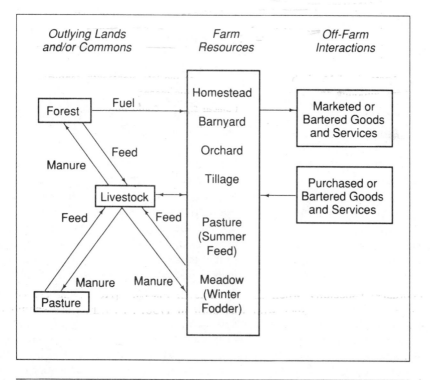

Agricultural Ecology of a New England Farm. Nutrients and energy (food and fuel) are transferred within a farm's boundaries among woodlots, pastures, meadows, tilled fields, orchards, barnyards, and homesteads. Purchased goods are brought in from outside, while farm and home products may be used by the family, marketed, or bartered.

The smaller the farms became and the more their market orientation increased, the greater were the ecological repercussions.

The availability of male and female labor as well as farm sizes and layouts governed the way time and space were used. Whether markets, credit, and outside information were readily available helped to determine a farm's orientation toward production for community subsistence or for commercial markets. A family's needs, goals, and values might tip the balance if choices were available. . . .

Farmers in the inland areas of New England used an "extensive system" of land use that synthesized native American and European methods of agriculture. It consisted of (1) a long-fallow system of clearing woodlands using the Indian method of girdling trees or cutting and burning; (2) adoption of Indian corn, bean, and squash polycultures; (3) the medieval three-field crop rotation system; and (4) upland pasturing. These were successful elements of subsistence agriculture until the late eighteenth century. . . .

The first element of the extensive system of agriculture was a long-fallow method of land clearing. In areas beyond ready access to markets, where agriculture was oriented toward subsistence, the clearing of woodlots proceeded more slowly than along the coasts and northern logging rivers. For example, settlers who in 1733 went to Petersham, Massachusetts (officially founded in 1754), about twenty-five miles northwest of Worcester and about thirty-five miles east of the Connecticut River (above the fall line), lived primarily by subsistence farming for some sixty years before improvements in its few winding, hilly wagon roads began to make market journeys practicable. Here cash was always in limited supply, and the first bank was not established until 1854. But Petersham, a town that doubled its inhabitants from 707 in 1765 to 1,560 in 1790, had cleared only about 10 percent of its forest by 1771 and only 15 percent by 1791. . . .

The second element in the settlers' subsistence system involved the planting of polycultures. Until the European tetrad of wheat, rye, barley, and oats was successfully established, colonists were dependent on the Indians' corn, bean, and squash complex. But in appropriating this form of agriculture, they substituted the ox and plow for the hoe and the male for the female in the field. Rather than planting corn on old hills with stone hoes and corn planters, as had the Indian women, they reduced the labor requirements by plowing, laying out furrows six feet apart to form squares, and planting the corn seed at the intersections. Plows were scarce in new villages but many neighbors shared them, while those without used hoes. Like Indians, colonists planted corn in April after the leaves of the white oak had formed and planted vegetables between the rows. According to John Winthrop, Indians and English both "will plant a kind of beans with the corn . . . and in the vacant places and between the hills, they will plant squashes and pumpkins, loading the ground with as much as it will bear; the stalks of the corn serving instead of poles for the beans to climb up. . . . Many English also after the last weeding their ground sprinkle turnip-seed between the hills, so have after harvest a good crop of turnips in the same field." . . .

The same ecological advantages that enhanced the corn, bean, and squash harvest of the New England Indians aided the farmer's subsistence. These included higher yields from polycultures of mixed crops than from monocultures, genetic adaptations of the three crops to each other, nitrogen fixation from beans, the addition of humus from two weedings per season, insect control by microclimates created through companion planting, and the harboring of insect-eating birds and insect enemies on field borders.

The third element in the agroecological system was crop rotation. Along with European grains, colonial farmers introduced the three-field rotation system of the Middle Ages, a subsistence system that had successfully sustained life for centuries until markets and population increases encouraged more intensive methods of cropping. In New England, the three fields were planted in a sequence that started in the first field with corn in the first year, rye the second, and weed fallow the third year to recover fertility. This combination produced the common staple bread, made from Indian corn and European rye. The second field often contained oats for fodder or barley for beer, instead of rye, with spring wheat being a primary crop after 1640. Wheat blast (black stem rust), after its advent in about 1660, made the wheat crop problematical, however, for the next two centuries. . . . The third field was sometimes sown with buckwheat which cleaned it of weeds and provided flowers for honey bees. Other crops included peas, which, like beans, were a nitrogen-restoring legume, and were used in the staple meals pease porridge and pork and peas; flax for linen; and tobacco for home use.

The fourth element was the pasturing of livestock. The introduced livestock complex consisted of oxen (neat cattle) and horses for draft; cows and goats for milk, butter, and cheese; sheep for mutton and wool; and pigs and beef cattle for salt meat stores. But raising them on American grasses — wild rye (*Elymus* sp.) and broom straw (*Andropogon* sp.) — proved difficult, owing to the large ratio of bulk to food value. Carex, the native meadow grass, provided good hay until livestock herds increased too much. Consequently, English hay — bluegrass and white clover introduced in the seventeenth century, and red clover and timothy (Herd's grass) in the eighteenth — was seeded in upland pastures. After 1750 English hay was planted more widely, helping to restore soil nutrients. Cornstalks and husks, along with wheat and rye straw, supplied additional fodder during the winter. In late summer pigs and beef cattle were fattened on grain for slaughter. . . .

Between 1750 and 1790, upland villages devoted to grazing were founded in central and western New England on hillsides too steep or stony for tillage. Either immediately after the removal of the forest cover, or after one or two years of planting corn or rye among girdled trees, lands were seeded with English grasses and turned to pasture. Drovers gathered up cattle and pigs from local farms and herded them to market towns on hoof. Because the grass was seeded before the soil was exhausted, its natural fertility was retained far longer than in crop-producing areas. The English grasses were efficient conservers, extending the soil's natural fertility in these areas until well into the nineteenth century.

After 1790, pasture expansion resulted primarily from converted worn-out croplands in older market settlements. In the Connecticut Valley and coastal areas such pastures were used principally to raise livestock for manure in order to fertilize grainfields. These pastures showed more rapid deterioration than upland pastures because the lack of manure gradually depleted the soil. Livestock then had to be reduced, in turn lowering crop yields.

In the life cycle of a piece of soil under the four elements of the extensive system, several uses might follow in succession. "Unimproved" woodland would be cut for fuel and placed in tillage. For a few years the "fresh" acreage would produce crops, be rotated through fallow, and perhaps be manured as yields began to fall. Soil, "worn out" for tillage, could then be seeded to hay for a few more years until yields fell below about half a ton per acre, when it might be abandoned to pasture. As pasture in turn wore down, the plot would begin to "keep" fewer and fewer animals. Brush and woods would begin to creep in, and the land would revert back to the category "unimproved" or "unimprovable."

Like Indian subsistence, colonial agriculture depended on the division of labor by gender. Women and men each had separate tasks and separate genderized production spaces. Male and female were equals in subsistence production, each sex being essential to the family's economic survival. The reproduction of social roles took place in these separate spaces. Girls participated in their mothers' space-time zones, boys in those of their fathers.

Men's space extended outward from the barn and had a wider circumference than women's. Heavy square-timbered beams with notched ends, laid out in squares and raised by practiced neighbors who knew the rules, produced the farmer's first barn, center of his world and symbol of his husbandhood. Wood house, smokehouse, corncrib, wagon shed, and springhouse followed, intersecting with women's domain and circumscribing the farmyard. The field layout reflected walking time, with crops nearby, meadows and hayfields beyond, and woodlots and uplands on the periphery. From the farmstead's eye, radii of varying lengths led down dusty roads to the nearby village and the distant town.

Women's domain radiated outward from the farmhouse kitchen. Farmhouses were divided into sleeping rooms, parlor, and kitchen, all expandable as the family grew larger, with a root cellar below. Kitchens could be enlarged by adding ells or sheds with lean-to roofs. Just outside the kitchen door was the essential herb garden and beyond it, as time and labor allowed, the vegetable garden. Outbuildings provided space for butter, cheese making, poultry, and privy; at the orchard's edge, overlapping men's space, trees offered their branches for clothes drying. Beyond lay a friendly neighbor's kitchen, the village store, and the meetinghouse. . . .

Woman's role in production and reproduction was . . . intensely demanding. From tending and slaughtering chickens, cutting and cooking meat, carrying wood, milking cows and goats, to making cheese, butter, candles, and bread, growing and weeding vegetables, spinning and carding wool, often while pregnant or tending young children, she worked hard even into old age, when the farm and its management may have passed entirely into her hands. Like her husband, she engaged in trade and transactions with neighbors and townspeople (both male and female), kept notes (sometimes on the kitchen wall), and sometimes recorded her work life in her diary.

Cheese and butter making were also important contributions to family subsistence and added protein in the diet. The techniques had been handed down from woman to woman since ancient times. . . . The prime cheese season was May to September. About a gallon of milk was needed to produce a pound of cheese for the family each week, two for a pound of butter. The thin cows of the period produced two to four gallons of milk a week. Almost all rural families had at least one milk cow for milk and cheese, with additional cows adding butter to the diet. Those without dairy equipment probably shared or traded products with neighbors. . . .

Butter making required great care and cleanliness. According to the *New England Farmer*, for best quality, the dairy house was to be as close to the springhouse or icehouse as possible since carrying the milk agitated it too much. The tin pails had to be scalded and then sun or fire dried. . . . In the morning, churning began. After the butter was "well come," the buttermilk was released through a plug in the bottom of the churn, cold water was poured in, and the milk was separated out by additional churning. With a wooden ladle, the woman lifted out the butter and worked it with salt three times at one-hour intervals until it was ready to be molded in stone pots or oak kegs.

. . . With nineteenth-century specialization, men began to take over women's traditional areas of dairying, poultry raising, and vegetable production. The traditional dairy areas of western Massachusetts expanded as more farmers took up dairy farming and poultry raising. Agricultural specialization and farm management became significant components of the capitalist ecological revolution.

Slave Subsistence

JOHN BOLES

For white Americans 1776 is the birth of political freedom from Great Britain. Less appreciated is how the ideals so eloquently expressed in Jefferson's Declaration found their way into the hearts and minds of many slaveholders and helped open their eyes to the evil of slavery. In the northern states, where there were far fewer slaves, no large-scale plantation slave economy, and previous sentiment for emancipation, the ideology of liberty pushed hesitant conservatives over the brink. Slowly, beginning with Pennsylvania in 1780 and culminating with New Jersey in 1804, every northern state provided for gradual emancipation of its slaves. (Massachusetts by court decision declared slavery illegal in 1783, becoming the first state actually to end slavery, although the slave trade had been ended almost a decade earlier in some New England colonies.) Hundreds of southern slave owners, smitten with the revolutionary ideology — and on many occasions their hearts warmed by waves of

From John Boles, *Black Southerners, 1619–1866*, 1983, reprinted by permission of the University of Kentucky Press.

evangelical egalitarianism just beginning to take root in the South—provided for the manumission of their slaves. As a result, thousands of former slaves received their freedom from patriot Americans in the generation following 1776. The number of free blacks in the United States increased several fold between then and 1790. The first federal census of that year showed 59,446 free blacks in the nation, 32,357 in the South. Ten years later that number had almost doubled again, with 108,395 in the U.S. and 61,241 in the South. Together with their black brothers who had departed with the British, these Revolutionary freedmen represented the first great gains in liberty achieved by Afro-Americans. Eighty years later, in another great war, hundreds of thousands of slaves would flee to liberating forces and eventually all would win their freedom. But between the Revolution and the Civil War the plantation system came to maturity.

The postwar South faced many problems. Physical property had been destroyed, particularly in South Carolina and Georgia. New trade agreements, including certain markets for agricultural products, had to be negotiated. Tens of thousands of slaves had fled or been taken by retreating British ships. In the confusion and turmoil of the 1780s, tobacco, rice, and indigo production fell far below prewar levels. A decade and a half passed before such staple crops regained their old standing, and their production stagnated thereafter, in part because of soil exhaustion and the region's inadequate transportation network. Farmers in the Chesapeake region increasingly turned to wheat as a money crop, a grain whose smaller labor needs combined with liberalized ideas to produce a willingness to end the African slave trade. In the rice and indigo growing areas of the South, however, the desire to replace wartime slave losses and rebuild destroyed levees and rice irrigation canals soon produced a clamor to keep the African trade open. Out of such compelling needs came the constitutional compromise delaying the federal prohibition of slave imports until 1808.

Most southern whites did not own slaves, and most of those who did possessed only a few. Slaveholding was concentrated in the hands of a significant minority of the population, and plantation-sized slaveholding was confined to a tiny minority. In 1860 approximately 1,918,175 southern whites (or 24 percent) were members of slaveholding families, and 6,120,825 (76 percent) were not. Of the 385,000 heads of households who owned slaves, almost 49 percent possessed fewer than five. If the ownership of a total of twenty slaves is taken as the minimum for running a plantation as opposed to a farm, then only 12 percent of all slaveholders qualified as planters in 1860. Substantially less than 1 percent, or about 2,300 families, owned 100 or more slaves and constituted the planter aristocracy—out of a white population of 8 million. . . .

Both necessity and choice determined that corn and pork would be the foundation of the southern diet for blacks and whites, although rice was the staple in portions of South Carolina and Georgia. Corn grew fairly well in the South, accommodated itself easily to cotton cultivation, was plentiful and easy to preserve, and could be cooked in a great variety of ways. It also was widely used as a food for pigs, which easily adapted to the southern climate. Hogs could run wild in the forests of the South, surviving on acorns, other nuts, and roots until they were penned up and fattened on corn. Southerners of both races preferred pork to beef. . . . The South produced prodigious amounts of corn and pork, and it was quite natural that southern tastes adopted the two as the staple foods of the region. Had they not existed in abundance in the South, the slave diet would have been inestimably worse.

Existing plantation records indicate that there was for all practical purposes a standard minimum slave ration provided by masters. With some variation depending upon the work season and the age and sex of the slaves, this standard was a peck of cornmeal and three to four pounds of bacon (i.e., pork) per slave per week. This represented the food measured out and distributed by the plantation owner; it seldom if ever amounted to the total diet of the slaves. On an almost regular basis molasses was distributed, and when possible coffee, sweet potatoes, peas and beans, squash, various greens, poultry and eggs, and beef were provided. The corn-pork basic element was normally given out every week, and other foods were available on a more seasonal basis. When, as was usual, these were grown on the plantation, they were plentiful enough not to be subject to detailed record-keeping, were sufficiently available not to be kept under lock and key, and were provided according to need. Some large, rationalized plantations gave a certain acreage over to truck crops cultivated and harvested by the slave hands under close planter supervision. This produce would then eventually be prepared in a common kitchen by cooking specialists and fed armylike to the black work force. Occasional large planters who ran this type [of] operation believed there was less theft and waste, better prepared food, and more rest time for their bondsmen as a result. A variant of this system was for the planter to allow the slaves to grow vegetables in their own individual garden plots and even raise chickens and pigs, and then to buy produce from them both for their common kitchen and for his own family's food. With their hard-earned money slaves would then buy extra clothes, presents for spouses and children, whiskey, and perhaps save up in hopes of eventually buying their freedom. However, the huge majority of farmers and planters ran much less organized plantations, leaving a larger proportion of both food production and preparation to the initiative and energy of individual slave families.

Most slaves, whether they lived on small farms or plantations of broad acres, were allowed to cultivate garden plots. They tended their own crops either at the twilight end of the day or on Saturday afternoon or Sundays — practically every owner gave his hands time off for at least part of the weekend. Often the planter would buy fresh vegetables and eggs from his slaves in order to provide them additional incentive, to make available to them some money so they could afford simple luxuries, and because by so doing he avoided the problem of theft commonly associated with a large plantation garden worked by slaves but for the table of the owner. Many slaves on Saturday would carry their surplus produce to crossroads stores or trading communities and sell or barter their items for money or other goods. Slave marketing of their own agricultural produce in southern towns never reached the level it did in some Caribbean islands, but neither was it negligible. Occasionally urban areas would pass ordinances against slaves coming in from the countryside to peddle truck crops and poultry products because the authorities feared such trade stimulated thievery, and they understood and feared that the practice provided slaves with a potentially dangerous pinch of freedom. But ultimately every town was too dependent on such sources of food to prohibit completely this quite literal black market. It was not uncommon for slaves to own pigs, cows, even horses, wagons, boats, and household utensils beyond those provided by the master. Slaves who were sold or moved to different regions were typically reimbursed for their property that the planter deemed inexpedient to move.

The bulk of vegetables grown by slaves in their own garden plots was consumed by the individual families who grew them. Much more common than the communal gardening and preparation of food was the practice of letting each slave family (or cabin group, which sometimes included the extended family along with an occasional single adult) grow and prepare its own food. Although some planters required this because they believed it lessened the spread of disease, most slave owners permitted it because slaves seemed greatly to prefer to manage this important portion of their lives. For bondsmen whose work hours and movement were regimented, the ability to control their garden plot, exercise their gardening skills, and choose their supplementary food crops was an important way of holding on to a portion of their self-identity. Especially significant was the slaves' commitment to cultivating garden vegetables and cooking them as a family activity.

By legal definition the black family was nonexistent, and forces as broad-ranging as the fear of slave sales and the emasculating authority of the owner threatened to destroy it, so slaves utilized every substantive and symbolic way to strengthen their families. Perhaps more important than any other activity cementing the family unit was the production and consumption of food. No other task has been as central to the survival of the family in human history, and here was a realizable and tangible way for fathers to be providers and for creative wives and mothers to show their affection. The family meal, shared by all around the domestic hearth, served to bind together those whose relationship was fragile for reasons beyond their control. Preparing a meal at the end of a long day must have been an onerous task for the tired slave women, but their preference for control over their home life speaks eloquently of their determination to preserve their own humanity. Often a stew begun at the lunch break cooked all afternoon in a heavy iron "spider" set amidst glowing coals on the hearth, where the slow-burning fire never went out.

Discussions of slave food supply have been controversial because it is difficult to quantify the supplemental portion of the black diet. The produce grown in slave garden plots seldom left a trace of evidence in plantation account books, but it made a world of difference to the diet of the bondsmen. Similarly, southern rivers and streams were teeming with fish, particularly the nutritious and tasty catfish, and southern forests offered bountiful game. Forests also provided nuts, herbs, grapes, berries, persimmons, sassafras roots for tea, pokeweed for salad. Rural slaves in their "leisure" time hunted, trapped, fished, and gathered, and the result of these activities added nutritional value and much-wanted variety to their meals. If slaves had had more free time, such delights offered by the fields and streams would no doubt have played an even greater role in their diet. Slaves also took quite liberally from their master's larder, especially on larger plantations. Taking food from another slave was considered stealing by the bondsmen, but helping themselves to their master's supply was not. When they were hungry, or craved some diversity in their diet, it wasn't even necessary to justify redistributing a portion of the plantation's goods. Many a mother risked punishment to provide a treat for her babies; many a male, through such sly augmenting of his family's or girlfriend's diet, felt his manhood enhanced. In a conspiracy of silence slaves helped one another steal from the master.

One rather obvious omission from the slaves' diet was fresh milk, for masters very seldom supplied it as part of the dispensed rations, and slaves — who sometimes had their own hogs and poultry — very rarely had milk cows. Cattle were considered by owners primarily a source of beef (there were surprisingly few "milch" [milk] cows in the antebellum South), and when slaves were given milk, it was mostly sour or buttermilk. For years this was considered by historians to be mistreatment, but biochemically it was appropriate because blacks were deficient in the enzyme lactase, which must be present for the body to break down lactose (milk sugar, a major food component of milk) into digestible form.

Ironically, clabber (sour milk), buttermilk, and several varieties of cream cheese could be digested by lactase-deficient slaves, giving a biological basis to blacks' noted preference for buttermilk. Whether owners realized that milk did not agree with slaves, or did not often distribute it because availability was severely limited by the adverse effect of hot southern temperatures on cows' milk production, or were foiled in providing milk by the absence of refrigeration, or whether, more likely, it was a combination of these factors, the result is clear. Slaves in the Old South drank very little fresh milk for reasons having less to do with mistreatment than with genetics and climate.

The perishability of milk suggests a problem that plagued efforts to maintain balanced diets for everyone in the Old South. Ice houses insulated with soil and sawdust in the Upper South, and spring houses there and in the Deep South, provided only an imperfect means of storing dairy products. The warm climate complicated efforts to preserve meats; pork could be salted and smoked, but such methods were better suited to regions where winters were hard. Generally beef had to be eaten within days, which meant that only large plantations could afford to butcher a yearling although sometimes several farmers would butcher a calf together. Fresh vegetables were simply unavailable throughout much of the winter, but potatoes, turnips, yams, apples, and other fruits could be preserved with sufficient preparation. Dried peas and beans could be kept, but mice and weevils were a severe challenge even to the most careful farm managers. The diet of bondsmen doubtlessly suffered in midwinter when fruits and vegetables were scarce, and malnutrition posed more of a threat to slave health in January, February, and March than in any other season. Nutritional diseases like pellagra (characterized by skin eruptions, digestive and nervous disturbances, and eventual mental deterioration) probably afflicted some slaves in those months. Had the period of least sufficient food not also been the period of least physical labor, there might have been more widespread suffering from dietary deficiencies.

Much nonsense has been written about southern food and southern cooking. Contemporary travelers noted again and again the monotonous sameness of the cuisine, with corn and pork, always too greasy, served in the absence of vegetables (and southerners particularly disliked salads) and washed down with dreary substitutes for coffee. Black cooks were often as bad as white, giving lie to the romanticized belief that every slave woman was a secret gourmet. The largest plantations in the right season could mount mouthwatering feasts with menus as varied as the servings were generous. But most white farmers ate plainly, with an occasional serving of venison or catfish or wild turkey or squirrel to break the routine. The diet of slaves was less varied than that of their owners, and had not their own gardening, hunting, fishing, and gathering added to their rations, their food supply would have been even more limited. Blacks and poor whites who cooked their vegetables and meats together and then poured the extremely nutritious "pot likker" on cornbread, probably received more vitamins than those who ate in higher style.

Controversy has raged over the precise English and African origins of southern cooking, but the American Indians may have contributed more than either Old World cultures. Certainly the English wheat-mutton diet and the various African diets shifted to one based largely upon foods native to America and long utilized by the Indians. A great many of the foods associated with southern cooking — corn, peas, beans, squash, pumpkins, sweet potatoes (all of which can be preserved for long periods) — were adapted from the American Indians. Moreover, Indian ways of preparing food became the southern way: corn transformed into hominy and hominy ground into grits, cornmeal cooked as hoecake, johnny-cake, cornbread, and hush puppies; beans and corn mixed together to form succotash; green ears of corn roasted or boiled whole as corn on the cob; meat cured and smoked on a spit over coals or hickory logs and termed barbecue. Even the practice of growing peas intermixed with the corn (the peas sowed when the corn was laid by), and the planting technique of mounding the dirt around the corn or squash into "hills," were borrowed from Indian agriculturists. Since both Africans and Englishmen were unfamiliar with the flora and fauna of America, they had much to learn from the Indians, who were very visible in all the southern states through the 1830s. In ways historians are only beginning to understand, the first Americans left a permanent imprint on the American soil and not just in place names.

❦ F U R T H E R   R E A D I N G

Joyce Appleby, "Commercial Farming and the 'Agrarian Myth' in the Early Republic," *Journal of American History* 68 (1982), 831–848

Peter Benes, ed., *The Farm* (1988)

Percy Wells Bidwell and John I. Falconer, *History of Agriculture in the Northern United States, 1620–1860* (1941)

Christopher Clark, *The Roots of Rural Capitalism: Western Massachusetts, 1780–1860* (1990)

Steven Hahn and Jonathan Prude, eds., *The Countryside in the Age of Capitalist Transformation* (1985)

James A. Henretta, "Families and Farms in Pre-Industrial America," *William and Mary Quarterly*, 3d ser. 25 (1978), 3-31

Richard Hofstadter, "The Myth of the Happy Yeoman," *American Heritage* 7 (1956), 43–53

Kevin D. Kelly, "The Independent Mode of Production," *Review of Radical Political Economics* 11 (1979), 38–48

Alan Kulikoff, "The Transition to Capitalism in Rural America," *William and Mary Quarterly*, 3d ser. 46, no. 1 (1989), 120–144

James Lemon, *The Best Poor Man's Country: A Geographical Study of Early Southeastern Pennsylvania* (1972)

Rodney C. Loehr, "Self-Sufficiency on the Farm," *Agricultural History* 26 (1952), 37–41

Carolyn Merchant, *Ecological Revolutions: Nature, Gender, and Science in New England* (1989)

Michael Merrill, "Cash Is Good to Eat: Self-Sufficiency and Exchange in the Rural Economy of the United States," *Radical History Review* 3 (1977), 42–71

Robert E. Mutch, "Yeoman and Merchant in Pre-Industrial America: Eighteenth-Century Massachusetts as a Case Study," *Societas* 7 (1977), 279–302

John Solomon Otto, *The Southern Frontiers, 1607–1860: The Agricultural Evolution of the Colonial and Antebellum South* (1990)

Bettye Hobbs Pruitt, "Self-Sufficiency and the Agricultural Economy of 18th-Century Massachusetts," *William and Mary Quarterly*, 3d ser. 41 (1984), 333–364

Winifred B. Rothenberg, "The Market and Massachusetts Farmers, 1750–1855," *Journal of Economic History* 41 (1981), 283–314

Howard S. Russell, *A Long Deep Furrow: Three Centuries of Farming in New England* (1976)

John T. Schlebecker, *Whereby We Thrive: A History of American Farming, 1607–1972* (1975)

Carol Shammas, "How Self-Sufficient Was Early America?" *Journal of Interdisciplinary History* 13 (1982), 247–272

Fred A. Shannon, *The Farmers' Last Frontier: Agriculture, 1860–1897* (1945)

Glenn Trewartha, "Types of Rural Settlement in Colonial America," *Geographical Review* 36 (1946)

CHAPTER 6

Nature Versus Civilization
in the Nineteenth Century

☙

Between the time of Crèvecoeur's Letters from an American Farmer *(1782) and Henry David Thoreau's* Walden *(1854), the concurrent and mutually stimulated transportation and market revolutions brought about a dynamic capitalist economy in the interior of the United States. Military campaigns of the War of 1812 opened up for settlement lands to the Mississippi River, and settlers flocked west during the post-1815 economic boom. Turnpikes, canals, and railroads linked textile and shoe factories in the Northeast, wheat farms in the upper Midwest, coal and iron production sites in Pennsylvania and Ohio, and rice, sugar, and cotton plantations in the South. Steamboats on the Mississippi, Ohio, Erie Canal, and Hudson river systems reduced waterway travel times and costs, and railroads provided land links joining ports, cities, and the hinterland. The market economy increasingly touched the lives of ordinary people, fostering an ethos of competition, personal advancement, and accumulation of wealth. Concurrently, the cumulative effects of environmental deterioration, vanishing wildlife, and forest clearing began to be apparent to eastern elites. Artists, poets, novelists, essayists, travelers, and explorers recorded the results of human settlement and development on nonhuman nature and on non-European humans. Their responses reveal ambivalent feelings about the benefits of "civilization" and those of "nature."*

☙ D O C U M E N T S

In 1772 Phillis Wheatley, an eighteen-year-old African native who had been purchased in 1761 in Boston by Susannah Wheatley, was orally examined and certified by eighteen elite Bostonian citizens as an authentic poet who had studied classical and biblical literature. Published the following year in London, her *Poems on Various Subjects* remained until 1829 (when George Moses Horton published a book of poems) the first book of poetry by a black American and until 1841 (when Ann Plato published a book of essays) the first book of literature by a black woman. The two Wheatley poems of 1773 that are reprinted in the first document concern nature. Using classical references to the nine muses, Aurora, goddess of dawn, Calliope, muse of poetry, and gentle zephyr, or wind, she reveals an appreciation for nature's beauty and for its power as God's agent in the giving and taking of life.

In the second document, taken from a selection of essays written between 1808 and 1834 by John James Audubon, the famous artist reveals himself not only as a painter whose artwork later awakened a nation to the necessity of preserving bird life from hunters but as a participant in that very act of hunting, maiming, and killing beautiful birds that preservationists later deplored. In the third document, excerpted from *The Pioneers* (1823), James Fenimore Cooper similarly writes about shooting birds — specifically, the famous, now extinct passenger pigeons — for sport. Through his spokesperson Natty Bumppo, or Leather-stocking, Cooper powerfully criticizes pioneer wastefulness in response to the apparent abundance of nature.

The fourth document features paintings of the Hudson River school, a group of nineteenth-century artists who appreciated and painted nature for its own sake. Their work captured the beauty of the Hudson River and Catskill areas of New York State, the rivers and mountains of New England, and even the Rocky Mountains and Sierras. Their canvases portray nature as wild, dark, mysterious, and sublime, contrasting it with civilization as light, calm, peaceful, and picturesque. Nature is presented positively, as benign and morally elevating, not as polluted or devastated by industry. Artist George Catlin, the author of the fifth document, dating from 1844, revealed an appreciation of the American Indians of the Great Plains through his paintings and writings. These Euramerican artists value nature and human nature in their "precivilized" forms for their positive qualities.

The sixth and seventh documents are by essayists of the New England Transcendentalist school. Ralph Waldo Emerson, writing in 1844, emphasizes true nature as an ideal, whole, and universal Oversoul — a reality in which the human soul participates as a mind, seeing each natural thing as a mere part of an overarching unity. Applying the mind to nature produces wealth — nature as commodity — and it is the English, Emerson believes, who have produced the science, machines, and economic methods to turn nature into capital. Henry David Thoreau, on the other hand, in excerpts from *Walden* (1854), expresses great skepticism over the disruption of pristine nature by the machine (symbolized by the railroad) and instead infuses subsistence farming (symbolized by his beanfield) with an ethic of preservation.

The final document, by novelist Rebecca Harding Davis, alerted Americans to the degrading effects of industrialization on both nature and human nature. Her "Life in the Iron Mills," published in the *Atlantic Monthly* in 1861, portrayed the animal-like existence of Cornish ironworkers in Wheeling, West Virginia, revealing the costs borne by both humans and nature in the American search for "civilization."

Phillis Wheatley Eulogizes Nature, 1773

An Hymn to the Morning

Attend my lays, ye ever honour'd nine,
Assist my labours, and my strains refine;
In smoothest numbers pour the notes along,

For bright Aurora now demands my song.
 Aurora, hail, and all the thousand dyes,
Which deck thy progress through the vaulted skies;
The morn awakes, and wide extends her rays,
On ev'ry leaf the gentle zephyr plays;
Harmonious lays the feather'd race resume,
Dart the bright eye, and shake the painted plume.
 Ye shady groves, your verdant gloom display
To shield your poet from the burning day:
Calliope, awake the sacred lyre,
While thy fair sisters fan the pleasing fire:
The bow'rs, the gales, the variegated skies
In all their pleasures in my bosom rise.
 See in the east th' illustrious king of day!
His rising radiance drives the shades away —
But oh! I feel his fervid leaves too strong,
And scarce begun, concludes th' abortive song.

An Hymn to the Evening

Soon as the sun forsook the eastern main
The pealing thunder shook the heav'nly plain;
Majestic grandeur! From the zephyr's wing,
Exhales the incense of the blooming spring,
Soft purl the streams, the birds renew their notes,
And through the air their mingled music floats.
 Through all the heav'ns what beauteous dyes are spread!
But the west glories in the deepest red:
So may our breasts with every virtue glow,
The living temples of our God below!
 Fill'd with the praise of him who gives the light,
And draws the sable curtains of the night,
Let placid slumbers soothe each weary mind,
At morn to wake more heav'nly, more refin'd;
So shall the labors of the day begin
More pure, more guarded from the snares of sin.
 Night's leaden sceptre seals my drowsy eyes,
Then cease, my song, till fair Aurora rise.

John James Audubon on Shooting Birds, 1808–1834

As the "Marion" approached the inlet called "Indian Key," which is situated on the eastern coast of the peninsula of Florida, my heart swelled with uncontrollable delight. Our vessel once over the coral reef that every where stretches along the shore like a great wall reared by an army of giants, we found ourselves in safe anchorage, within a few furlongs of the land. The next moment saw the oars of a boat propelling us towards the shore, and in brief time, we stood on the desired beach. With what delightful feelings did we gaze on the objects around us! — the gorgeous flowers, the singular and beautiful plants, the luxuriant trees. The balmy air which we breathed filled us with animation, so pure and salubrious did it seem to be. The birds which we saw were almost all new to us; their lovely forms appeared to be arrayed in more brilliant apparel than I had ever before seen, and as they gambolled in happy playfulness among the bushes, or glided over the light green waters, we longed to form a more intimate acquaintance with them.

Students of nature spend little time in introduction, especially when they present themselves to persons who feel an interest in their pursuits. This was the case with Mr. Thruston, the Deputy Collector of the island, who shook us all heartily by the hand, and in a trice had a boat manned at our service. Accompanied by him, his pilot and fishermen, off we went, and after a short pull landed on a large key. Few minutes had elapsed, when shot after shot might be heard, and down came whirling through the air the objects of our desire. . . .

The pilot, besides being a first-rate shooter, possessed a most intimate acquaintance with the country. . . .

While the young gentlemen who accompanied us were engaged in procuring plants, shells, and small birds, he tapped me on the shoulder, and with a smile said to me, "Come along, I'll shew you something better worth your while." To the boat we betook ourselves, with the Captain and only a pair of tars, for more he said would not answer. The yawl for a while was urged at a great rate, but as we approached a point, the oars were taken in, and the pilot alone "sculling," desired us to make ready, for in a few minutes we should have "rare sport." As we advanced, the more slowly did we move, and the most profound silence was maintained, until suddenly coming almost in contact with a thick shrubbery of mangroves, we beheld, right before us, a multitude of pelicans. A discharge of artillery seldom produced more effect; — the dead, the dying, and the wounded, fell from the trees upon the water, while those unscathed flew screaming through the air in terror and dismay. "There," said he, "did not I tell you so? Is it not rare sport?" The birds, one after another, were lodged under the gunwales, when the pilot desired the captain to order the lads to pull away. Within about half a mile we reached the extremity of the key. "Pull away," cried the pilot, "never mind them on the wing, for those black rascals don't mind a little firing — now, boys, lay her close under the nests." And there we were, with four hundred cormorants' nests over our heads. The birds were sitting, and when we fired, the number that dropped as if dead, and plunged into the water was such, that I thought by some unaccountable means or other we had killed the whole colony. You would have smiled at the loud laugh and curious gestures of the pilot. "Gentlemen," said he, "almost a blank shot!" And so it was, for, on following the birds as one after another peeped up from the water, we found only a few unable to take to wing. "Now," said the pilot, "had you waited until *I had spoken* to the black villains, you might have killed a score or more of them." On inspection, we found that our shots had lodged in the tough dry twigs of which these birds form their nests, and that we had lost the more favourable opportunity of hitting them, by not waiting until they rose. "Never mind," said the pilot, "if you wish it, you may load the *Lady of the Green Mantle* with them in less than a week. Stand still, my lads; and now, gentlemen, in ten minutes you and I will bring down a score of them." And so we did. As we rounded the island, a beautiful bird of the species called Peale's Egret, came up and was shot. We now landed, took in the rest of our party, and returned to Indian Key, where we arrived three hours before sunset.

The sailors and other individuals to whom my name and pursuits had become known, carried our birds to the pilot's house. His good wife had a room ready for me to draw in, and my assistant might have been seen busily engaged in skinning, while George Lehman was making a sketch of the lovely isle.

Time is ever precious to the student of nature. I placed several birds in their natural attitudes, and began to delineate them. A dance had been prepared also, and no sooner was the sun lost to our eye, than males and females, including our captain and others from the vessel, were seen advancing gaily towards the house in full apparel. The birds were skinned, the sketch was on paper, and I told my young men to amuse themselves. As to myself, I could not join in the merriment, for, full of the remembrance of you, reader, and of the patrons of my work both in America and in Europe, I went on "grinding" — not on an organ, like the Lady of Bras d'Or, but on paper, to the finishing, not merely of my outlines, but of my notes respecting the objects seen this day. . . .

It was the end of April, when the nights were short and the days therefore long. Anxious to turn every moment to account, we were on board Mr. Thruston's boat at three next morning. Pursuing our way through the deep and tortuous channels that every where traverse the immense muddy soap-like flats that stretch from the outward Keys to the Main, we proceeded on our voyage of discovery. . . .

Coming under a Key on which multitudes of Frigate Pelicans had begun to form their nests, we shot a good number of them, and observed their habits. The boastings of our pilot were here confirmed by the exploits which he performed with his long gun, and on several occasions he brought down a bird from a height of fully a hundred yards. The poor birds, unaware of the range of our artillery, sailed calmly along, so that it was not difficult for "Long Tom," or rather for his owner, to furnish us with as many as we required. The day was spent in this manner, and towards night we returned, laden with booty, to the hospitable home of the pilot.

The next morning was delightful. The gentle sea-breeze glided over the flowery isle, the horizon was clear, and all was silent save the long breakers that rushed over the distant reefs. As we were proceeding towards some Keys, seldom visited by men, the sun rose from the bosom of the waters with a burst of glory that impressed on my soul the idea of that Power which called into existence so magnificent an object. The moon, thin and pale, as if ashamed to show her feeble light, concealed herself in the dim west. The surface of the waters shone in its tremulous smoothness, and the deep blue of the clear heavens was pure as the world that lies beyond them. The Heron heavily flew towards the land, like the glutton retiring at daybreak, with well-lined paunch, from the house of some wealthy patron of good cheer. The Night Heron and the Owl, fearful of day, with hurried flight sought safety in the recesses of the deepest swamps; while the Gulls and Terns, ever cheerful, gambolled over the water, exulting in the prospect of abundance. I also exulted in hope, my whole frame seemed to expand; and our sturdy crew shewed, by their merry faces, that nature had charms for them too. How much of beauty and joy is lost to them who never view the rising sun, and of whose wakeful existence the best half is nocturnal!

Twenty miles our men had to row before we reached "Sandy Island," and as on its level shores we all leaped, we plainly saw the southernmost cape of the Floridas. The flocks of birds that covered the shelly beaches, and those hovering over head, so astonished us that we could for a while scarcely believe our eyes. The first volley procured a supply of food sufficient for two days' consumption. Such tales, you have already been told, are well enough at a distance from the place to which they refer; but you will doubtless be still more surprised when I tell you that our first fire among the crowd of the Great Godwits laid prostrate sixty-five of these birds. Rose-coloured Curlews stalked gracefully beneath the mangroves; Purple Herons rose at almost every step we took, and each cactus supported the nest of a White Ibis. The air was darkened by whistling wings, while, on the waters, floated Gallinules and other interesting birds. We formed a kind of shed with sticks and grass, the sailor cook commenced his labours, and ere long we supplied the deficiencies of our fatigued frames. The business of the day over, we secured ourself from insects by means of musquito-nets, and were lulled to rest by the cackles of the beautiful Purple Gallinules!

James Fenimore Cooper Laments the "Wasty Ways" of Pioneers, 1823

Elizabeth was awakened by the exhilarating sounds of the martins, who were quarreling and chattering around the little boxes that were suspended above her windows, and the cries of Richard, who was calling, in tones as animating as the signs of the season itself—

"Awake! awake! my lady fair! the gulls are hovering over the lake already, and the heavens are alive with the pigeons. You may look an hour before you can find a hole, through which to get a peep at the sun. Awake! awake! lazy ones! Benjamin is overhauling the ammunition, and we only wait for our breakfasts, and away for the mountains and pigeon shooting." . . .

If the heavens were alive with pigeons, the whole village seemed equally in motion, with men, women, and children. Every species of fire-arms, from the French ducking-gun, with its barrel of near six-feet in length, to the common horseman's pistol, was to be seen in the hands of the men and boys; while bows and arrows, some made of the simple stick of a walnut sapling, and others in a rude imitation of the ancient crossbows, were carried by many of the latter. . . .

Among the sportsmen was to be seen the tall, gaunt form of Leatherstocking [Natty Bumppo], who was walking over the field, with his rifle hanging on his arm, his dogs following at his heels, now scenting the dead or wounded birds, that were beginning to tumble from the flocks, and then crouching under the legs of their master, as if they participated in his feelings at this wasteful and unsportsmanlike execution.

The reports of the fire-arms became rapid, whole volleys rising from the plain, as flocks of more than ordinary numbers darted over the opening, covering the field with darkness, like an interposing cloud; and then the light smoke of a single piece would issue from among the leafless bushes on the mountain, as death was hurled on the retreat of the affrighted birds, who were rising from a volley, for many feet into the air, in a vain effort to escape the attacks of man. Arrows, and missiles of every kind, were seen in the midst of the flocks; and so numerous were the birds, and so low did they take their flight, that even long poles, in the hands of those on the sides of the mountain, were used to strike them to earth. . . .

So prodigious was the number of the birds, that the scattering fire of the guns, with the hurling of missiles, and the cries of the boys, had no other effect than to break off small flocks from the immense masses that continued to dart along the valley, as if the whole creation of the feathered tribe were pouring through that one pass. None pretended to collect the game, which lay scattered over the fields in such profusion as to cover the very ground with the fluttering victims.

Leather-stocking was a silent, but uneasy spectator of all these proceedings, but was able to keep his sentiments to himself until he saw the introduction of the swivel into the sports.

"This comes of settling a country!" he said—"here have I known the pigeons to fly for forty long years, and, till you made your clearings, there was nobody to skear or to hurt them. I loved to see them come into the woods, for they were company to a body; hurting nothing; being, as it was, as harmless as a garter-snake. But now it gives me sore thoughts when I hear the frighty things whizzing through the air, for I know its only a motion to bring out all the brats in the village at them. . . ."

Among the sportsmen was Billy Kirby, who, armed with an old musket, was leading, and without even looking into the air, was firing and shouting as his victims fell even on his own person. He heard the speech of Natty, and took upon himself to reply—

"What's that, old Leather-stocking!" he cried, "grumbling at the loss of a few pigeons! If you had to sow your wheat twice, and three times, as I have done, you wouldn't be so massyfully feeling'd to'ards the divils.—Hurrah, boys! Scatter the feathers. This is better than shooting at a turkey's head and neck, old fellow."

"It's better for you, maybe, Billy Kirby," replied the indignant old hunter, "and all them as don't know how to put a ball down a rifle barrel, or how to bring it up ag'n with a true aim; but it's wicked to be shooting into flocks in this wasty manner; and none do it, who know how to knock over a single bird. If a body has a craving for pigeon's flesh, why! it's made the same as all other creater's, for man's eating, but not to kill twenty and eat one. When I want such a thing I go into the woods till I find one to my liking, and then I shoot him off the branches without touching a feather of another, though there might be a hundred on the same tree. But you couldn't do such a thing, Billy Kirby — you couldn't do it if you tried."

"What's that you say, you old dried cornstalk! you sapless stub!" cried the wood-chopper. "You've grown mighty boasting, sin' you killed the turkey; but if you're for a single shot, here goes at that bird which comes on by himself."

. . . A single pigeon . . . was approaching the spot where the disputants stood, darting first from one side, and then to the other, cutting the air with the swiftness of lightning, and making a noise with its wings, not unlike the rushing of a bullet. Unfortunately for the woodchopper, notwithstanding his vaunt, he did not see his bird until it was too late for him to fire as it approached, and he pulled his trigger at the unlucky moment when it was darting immediately over his head. The bird continued its course with incredible velocity.

Natty lowered the rifle from his arm, when the challenge was made, and, waiting a moment, until the terrified victim had got in a line with his eyes, and had dropped near the bank of the lake, he raised it again with uncommon rapidity, and fired. It might have been chance, or it might have been skill, that produced the result; it was probably a union of both; but the pigeon whirled over in the air, and fell into the lake with a broken wing. At the sound of his rifle, both his dogs started from his feet, and in a few minutes the "slut" brought out the bird, still alive.

The wonderful exploit of Leather-stocking was noised through the field with great rapidity, and the sportsmen gathered in to learn the truth of the report.

"What," said young Edwards, "have you really killed a pigeon on the wing, Natty, with a single ball?"

"Haven't I killed loons before now, lad, that dive at the flash?" returned the hunter. "It's much better to kill only such as you want, without wasting your powder and lead, than to be firing into God's creaters in such a wicked manner. But I come out for a bird, and you know the reason why I like small game, Mr. Oliver, and now I have got one I will go home, for I don't relish to see these wasty ways that you are all practysing, as if the least thing wasn't made for use, and not to destroy."

"Thou sayest well, Leather-stocking," cried Marmaduke, "and I begin to think it time to put an end to this work of destruction."

"Put an ind, Judge, to your clearings. An't the woods His work as well as the pigeons? Use, but don't waste. Wasn't the woods made for the beasts and birds to harbour in? And when man wanted their flesh, their skins, or their feathers, there's the place to seek them. But I'll go to the hut with my own game, for I wouldn't touch one of the harmless things that kiver the ground here, looking up with their eyes on me, as if they only wanted tongues to say their thoughts."

With this sentiment in his mouth, Leather-stocking threw his rifle over his arm, and followed by his dogs, stepping across the clearing with great caution, taking care not to tread on one of the wounded birds that lay in his path, he soon entered the bushes on the margin and was hid from view.

Hudson River Painters Depict Nature, 1836–1849

Kindred Spirits, 1849, by Asher Durand. Performing Arts Research Center, New York Public Library. This painting by the well-known painter of the Hudson River school shows nature poet William Cullen Bryant and nature painter Thomas Cole engaged in conversation in the Catskill Mountains. It commemorates Cole's death in 1848.

View from Mount Holyoke, Northampton, Massachusetts, after a Thunderstorm (The Oxbow), 1836, by Thomas Cole. The Metropolitan Museum of Art, Gift of Mrs. Russell Sage, 1908 (0.228). This painting, considered one of Cole's finest achievements, contrasts rugged cliffs, tree trunks, dark clouds, and wilderness on the left, with light, sunshine, pastoral utopia, and civilization on the right. Humans inhabit a middle ground between nature and civilization.

View on the Hudson, by Albert Bierstadt. Private Collection, Photo: Malcolm Varon, New York City © 1985. Bierstadt, another famous painter of the Hudson River school, not only painted numerous scenes of the Hudson River and the Palisades from his nearby home but also made several trips to the Rocky and Sierra Nevada mountain ranges, where he painted Western scenery.

George Catlin on Indians, Nature, and Civilization, 1844

I . . . closely applied my hand to the labours of the art [of painting] for several years; during which time my mind was continually reaching for some branch or enterprise of the art, on which to devote a whole life-time of enthusiasm; when a delegation of some ten or fifteen noble and dignified-looking Indians, from the wilds of the "Far West," suddenly arrived in the city, arrayed and equipped in all their classic beauty, — with shield and helmet, — with tunic and manteau, — tinted and tasselled off, exactly for the painter's palette!

In silent and stoic dignity, these lords of the forest strutted about the city for a few days, wrapped in their pictured robes, with their brows plumed with the quills of the war-eagle, attracting the gaze and admiration of all who beheld them. After this, they took their leave for Washington City, and I was left to reflect and regret, which I did long and deeply, until I came to the following deductions and conclusions.

Black and blue cloth and civilization are destined, not only to veil, but to obliterate the grace and beauty of Nature. Man, in the simplicity and loftiness of his nature, unrestrained and unfettered by the disguises of art, is surely the most beautiful model for the painter, — and the country from which he hails is unquestionably the best study or school of the arts in the world: such I am sure, from the models I have seen, is the wilderness of North America. And the history and customs of such a people, preserved by pictorial illustrations, are themes worthy the life-time of one man, and nothing short of the loss of my life, shall prevent me from visiting their country, and of becoming their historian.

With these views firmly fixed — armed, equipped, and supplied, I started out in the year 1832, and penetrated the vast and pathless wilds which are familiarly denominated the great "Far West" of the North American Continent, with a light heart, inspired with an enthusiastic hope and reliance that I could meet and overcome all the hazards and privations of a life devoted to the production of a literal and graphic delineation of the living manners, customs, and character of an interesting race of people, who are rapidly passing away from the face of the earth — lending a hand to a dying nation, who have no historians or biographers of their own to portray with fidelity their native looks and history; thus snatching from a hasty oblivion what could be saved for the benefit of posterity, and perpetuating it, as a fair and just monument, to the memory of a truly lofty and noble race. . . .

The Indians (as I shall call them), the savages or red men of the forests and prairies of North America, are at this time a subject of great interest and some importance to the civilized world; rendered more particularly so in this age, from their relative position to, and their rapid declension from, the civilized nations of the earth. A numerous nation of human beings, whose origin is beyond the reach of human investigation, — whose early history is lost — whose term of national existence is nearly expired — three-fourths of whose country has fallen into the possession of civilized man within the short space of 250 years — twelve millions of whose bodies have fattened the soil in the mean time; who have fallen victims to whiskey, the small-pox, and the bayonet; leaving at this time but a meagre proportion to live a short time longer, in the certain apprehension of soon sharing a similar fate. . . .

I am fully convinced, from a long familiarity with these people, that the Indian's misfortune has consisted chiefly in our ignorance of their true native character and disposition, which has always held us at a distrustful distance from them; inducing us to look upon them in no other light than that of a hostile foe, and worthy only of that system of continued warfare and abuse that has been for ever waged against them. . . .

The very use of the word savage, as it is applied in its general sense, I am inclined to believe is an abuse of the word, and the people to whom it is applied. The word, in its true definition, means no more than *wild*, or *wild man*; and a wild man may have been endowed by his Maker with all the humane and noble traits that inhabit the heart of a tame man. Our ignorance and dread or fear of these people, therefore, have given a new definition to the adjective; and nearly the whole civilized world apply the word *savage*, as expressive of the most ferocious, cruel, and murderous character that can be described. . . .

I have roamed about from time to time during seven or eight years, visiting and associating with, some three or four hundred thousand of these people, under an almost infinite variety of circumstances; and from the very many and decided voluntary acts of their hospitality and kindness, I feel bound to pronounce them, by nature, a kind and hospitable people. I have been welcomed generally in their country, and treated to the best that they could give me, without any charges made for my board; they have often escorted me through their enemies' country at some hazard to their own lives, and aided me in passing mountains and rivers with my awkward baggage; and under all of these circumstances of exposure, no Indian ever betrayed me, struck me a blow, or stole from me a shilling's worth of my property that I am aware of.

This is saying a great deal, (and proving it too, if the reader will believe me) in favour of the virtues of these people; when it is borne in mind, as it should be, that there is no law in their land to punish a man for theft — that locks and keys are not known in their country — that the commandments have never been divulged amongst them; nor can any human retribution fall upon the head of a thief, save the disgrace which attaches as a stigma to his character, in the eyes of his people about him. . . .

I cannot help but repeat . . . that the tribes of the red men of North America, as a nation of human beings, are on their wane; that (to use their own very beautiful figure) "they are fast travelling to the shades of their fathers, towards the setting sun;" and that the traveler who would see these people in their native simplicity and beauty, must needs be hastily on his way to the prairies and Rocky Mountains, or he will see them only as they are now seen on the frontiers, as a basket of *dead game*, — harassed, chased, bleeding and dead; with their plumage and colours despoiled; to be gazed amongst in vain for some system or moral, or for some scale by which to estimate their true native character, other than that which has too often recorded them but a dark and unintelligible mass of cruelty and barbarity.

Ralph Waldo Emerson Expounds on Nature and Wealth, 1844

The Over-Soul

Man is a stream whose source is hidden. Our being is descending into us from we know not whence. The most exact calculator has no prescience that somewhat incalculable may not balk the very next moment. I am constrained every moment to acknowledge a higher origin for events than the will I call mine.

As with events, so is it with thoughts. When I watch that flowing river, which, out of regions I see not, pours for a season its streams into me, I see that I am a pensioner; not a cause but a surprised spectator of this ethereal water; that I desire and look up and put myself in the attitude of reception, but from some alien energy the visions come.

The Supreme Critic on the errors of the past and the present, and the only prophet of that which must be, is that great nature in which we rest as the earth lies in the soft arms of the atmosphere; that Unity, that Over-Soul, within which every man's particular being is contained and made one with all other; that common heart of which all sincere conversation is the worship, to which all right action is submission; that overpowering reality which confutes our tricks and talents, and constrains every one to pass for what he is, and to speak from his character and not from his tongue, and which evermore tends to pass into our thought and hand and become wisdom and virtue and power and beauty. We live in succession, in division, in parts, in particles. Meantime within man is the soul of the whole; the wise silence; the universal beauty, to which every part and particle is equally related; the eternal ONE. And this deep power in which we exist and whose beatitude is all accessible to us, is not only self-sufficing and perfect in every hour, but the act of seeing and the thing seen, the seer and the spectacle, the subject and the object, are one. We see the world piece by piece, as the sun, the moon, the animal, the tree; but the whole, of which these are the shining parts, is the soul. . . . The soul gives itself, alone, original and pure, to the Lonely, Original and Pure, who, on that condition, gladly inhabits, leads and speaks through it. Then is it glad, young and nimble. It is not wise, but it sees through all things. It is not called religious, but it is innocent. It calls the light its own, and feels that the grass grows and the stone falls by a law inferior to, and dependent on, its nature. Behold, it saith, I am born into the great, the universal mind. I, the imperfect, adore my own Perfect. I am somehow receptive of the great soul, and thereby I do overlook the sun and the stars and feel them to be the fair accidents and effects which change and pass. More and more the surges of everlasting nature enter into me, and I become public and human in my regards and actions. So come I to live in thoughts and act with energies which are immortal.

Wealth

Every man is a consumer, and ought to be a producer. He fails to make his place good in the world unless he not only pays his debt but also adds something to the common wealth. Nor can he do justice to his genius without making some larger demand on the world than a bare subsistence. He is by constitution expensive, and needs to be rich.

Wealth has its source in applications of the mind to nature, from the rudest strokes of spade and axe up to the last secrets of art. Intimate ties subsist between thought and all production; because a better order is equivalent to vast amounts of brute labor. The forces and the resistances are nature's, but the mind acts in bringing things from where they abound to where they are wanted; in wise combining; in directing the practice of the useful arts, and in the creation of finer values by fine art, by eloquence, by song, or the reproductions of memory. Wealth is in applications of mind to nature; and the art of getting rich consists not in industry, much less in saving, but in a better order, in timeliness, in being at the right spot. One man has stronger arms or longer legs; another sees by the course of streams and growth of markets where land will be wanted, makes a clearing to the river, goes to sleep and wakes up rich. Steam is no stronger now than it was a hundred years ago; but is put to better use. A clever fellow was acquainted with the expansive force of steam; he also saw the wealth of wheat and grass rotting in Michigan. Then he cunningly screws on the steam-pipe to the wheat-crop. Puff now, O Steam! The steam puffs and expands as before, but this time it is dragging all Michigan at its back to hungry New York and hungry England. Coal lay in ledges under the ground since the Flood, until a laborer with pick and windlass brings it to the surface. We may well call it black diamonds. Every basket is power and civilization. For coal is a portable climate. It carries the heat of the tropics to Labrador and the polar circle; and it is the means of transporting itself whithersoever it is wanted. Watt and Stephenson whispered . . . their secret, that *a half-ounce of coal will draw two tons a mile*, and coal carries coal, by rail and by boat, to make Canada as warm as Calcutta; and with its comfort brings its industrial power. . . .

When the farmer's peaches are taken from under the tree and carried into town, they have a new look and a hundredfold value over the fruit which grew on the same bough and lies fulsomely on the ground. The craft of the merchant is this bringing a thing from where it abounds to where it is costly.

Wealth begins in a tight roof that keeps the rain and wind out; in a good pump that yields you plenty of sweet water; in two suits of clothes, so to change your dress when you are wet; in dry sticks to burn, in a good double-wick lamp, and three meals; in a horse or a locomotive to cross the land, in a boat to cross the sea; in tools to work with, in books to read; and so in giving on all sides by tools and auxiliaries the greatest possible extension to our powers; as if it added feet and hands and eyes and blood, length to the day, and knowledge and good will. . . .

Fire, steam, lightning, gravity, ledges of rock, mines of iron, lead, quicksilver, tin and gold; forests of all woods; fruits of all climates; animals of all habits; the powers of tillage; the fabrics of his chemic laboratory; the webs of his loom; the masculine draught of his locomotive; the talismans of the machine-shop; all grand and subtile things, minerals, gases, ethers, passions, war, trade, government — are his natural playmates, and according to the excellence of the machinery in each human being is his attraction for the instruments he is to employ. The world is his tool-chest, and he is successful, or his education is carried on just so far, as is the marriage of his faculties with nature, or the degree in which he takes up things into himself.

The strong race is strong on these terms. The Saxons are the merchants of the world; now, for a thousand years, the leading race, and by nothing more than their quality of personal independence, and in its special modification, pecuniary independence. No reliance for bread and games on the government; no clanship, no patriarchal style of living by the revenues of a chief, no marrying-on, no system of clientship suits them; but every man must pay his scot. The English are prosperous and peaceable, with their habit of considering that every man must take care of himself and has himself to thank if he do not maintain and improve his position in society. . . .

The counting-room maxims liberally expounded are laws of the universe. The merchant's economy is a coarse symbol of the soul's economy. It is to spend for power and not for pleasure. It is to invest income; that is to say, to take up particulars into generals; days into integral eras — literary, emotive, practical — of its life, and still to ascend in its investment. The merchant has but one rule, *absorb and invest*; he is to be capitalist; the scraps and filings must be gathered back into the crucible; the gas and smoke must be burned, and earnings must not go to increase expense, but to capital again. Well, the man must be capitalist. Will he spend his income, or will he invest? His body and every organ is under the same law. His body is a jar in which the liquor of life is stored. Will he spend for pleasure? The way to ruin is short and facile. Will he not spend but hoard for power? It passes through the sacred fermentations, by that law of nature whereby everything climbs to higher platforms, and bodily vigor becomes mental and moral vigor. The bread he eats is first strength and animal spirits; it becomes, in higher laboratories, imagery and thought; and in still higher results, courage and endurance. This is the right compound interest; this is capital doubled, quadrupled, centupled; man raised to his highest power.

The true thrift is always to spend on the higher plane; to invest and invest, with keener avarice, that he may spend in spiritual creation and not in augmenting animal existence. Nor is the man enriched, in repeating the old experiments of animal sensation; nor unless through new powers and ascending pleasures he knows himself by the actual experience of higher good to be already on the way to the highest.

Henry David Thoreau on Nature Versus Civilization, 1854

Sounds

My house was on the side of a hill, immediately on the edge of the larger wood, in the midst of a young forest of pitch pines and hickories, and half a dozen rods from the pond, to which a narrow footpath led down the hill. In my front yard grew the strawberry, blackberry, and life-everlasting, johnswort and gold-enrod, shrub oaks and sand cherry, blueberry and groundnut. Near the end of May, the sand cherry (*Cerasus pumila*) adorned the sides of the path with its delicate flowers arranged in umbels cylindrically about its short stems, which last, in the fall, weighed down with good-sized and handsome cherries, fell over in wreaths like rays on every side. I tasted them out of compliment to Nature, though they were scarcely palatable. The sumach (*Rhus glabra*) grew luxuriantly about the house, pushing up through the embankment which I had made, and growing five or six feet the first season. Its broad pinnate tropical leaf was pleasant though strange to look on. The large buds, suddenly pushing out late in the spring from dry sticks which had seemed to be dead, developed themselves as by magic into graceful green and tender boughs, an inch in diameter; and sometimes, as I sat at my window, so heedlessly did they grow and tax their weak joints, I heard a fresh and tender bough suddenly fall like a fan to the ground, when there was not a breath of air stirring, broken off by its own weight. In August, the large masses of berries, which, when in flower, had attracted many wild bees, gradually assumed their bright velvety crimson hue, and by their weight again bent down and broke the tender limbs.

As I sit at my window this summer afternoon, hawks are circling about my clearing; the tantivy of wild pigeons, flying by twos and threes athwart my view, or perching restless on the white pine boughs behind my house, gives a voice to the air; a fish hawk dimples the glassy surface of the pond and brings up a fish; a mink steals out of the marsh before my door and seizes a frog by the shore; the sedge is bending under the weight of the reed-birds flitting hither and thither; and for the last half-hour I have heard the rattle of railroad cars, now dying away and then reviving like the beat of a partridge, conveying travellers from Boston to the country. For I did not live so out of the world as that boy who, as I hear, was put out to a farmer in the east part of the town, but ere long ran away and came home again, quite down at the heel and homesick. He had never seen such a dull and out-of-the-way place, the folks were all gone off; why, you couldn't even hear the whistle! I doubt if there is such a place in Massachusetts now:—

> In truth, our village has become a butt
> For one of those fleet railroad shafts, and o'er
> Our peaceful plain its soothing sound is—Concord.

The Fitchburg Railroad touches the pond about a hundred rods south of where I dwell. I usually go the village along its causeway, and am, as it were, related to society by this link. The men on the freight trains, who go over the whole length of the road, bow to me as to an old acquaintance, they pass me so often, and apparently they take me for an employee; and so I am. I too would fain be a track-repairer somewhere in the orbit of the earth.

The whistle of the locomotive penetrates my woods summer and winter, sounding like a scream of a hawk sailing over some farmer's yard, informing me that many restless city merchants are arriving within the circle of the town, or adventurous country traders from the other side. As they come under one horizon, they shout their warning to get off the track to the other, heard sometimes through the circles of two towns. Here come your groceries, country; your rations, countrymen! Nor is there any man so independent on his farm that he can say them nay. And here's your pay for them! screams the countryman's whistle; timber like long battering-rams going twenty miles an hour against the city's walls, and chairs enough to seat all the weary and heavy-laden that dwell within them. With such huge and lumbering civility the country hands a chair to the city. All the Indian huckleberry hills are stripped, all the cranberry meadows are raked into the city. Up comes the cotton, down goes the woven cloth; up comes the silk, down goes the woollen; up come the books, but down goes the wit that writes them.

The Beanfield

Meanwhile my beans, the length of whose rows, added together, was seven miles already planted, were impatient to be hoed, for the earliest had grown considerably before the latest were in the ground; indeed they were not easily to be put off. What was the meaning of this so steady and self-respecting, this small Herculean labor, I knew not. I came to love my rows, my beans, though so many more than I wanted. They attached me to the earth, and so I got strength like Antæus. But why should I raise them? Only Heaven knows. This was my curious labor all summer, — to make this portion of the earth's surface, which had yielded only cinquefoil, blackberries, johnswort, and the like, before, sweet wild fruits and pleasant flowers, produce instead this pulse. What shall I learn of beans or beans of me? I cherish them, I hoe them, early and late I have an eye to them; and this is my day's work. It is a fine broad leaf to look on. My auxiliaries are the dews and rains which water this dry soil, and what fertility is in the soil itself, which for the most part is lean and effete. My enemies are worms, cool days, and most of all woodchucks. The last have nibbled for me a quarter of an acre clean. But what right had I to oust johnswort and the rest, and break up their ancient herb garden? Soon, however, the remaining beans will be too tough for them, and go forward to meet new foes.

When I was four years old as I well remember, I was brought from Boston to this my native town, through these very woods and this field, to the pond. It is one of the oldest scenes stamped on my memory. And now to-night my flute has waked the echoes over that very water. The pines still stand here older than I; or, if some have fallen, I have cooked my supper with their stumps, and a new growth is rising all around, preparing another aspect for new infant eyes. Almost the same johnswort springs from the same perennial root in this pasture, and even I have at length helped to clothe that fabulous landscape of my infant dreams, and one of the results of my presence and influence is seen in these bean leaves, corn blades, and potato vines.

I planted about two acres and a half of upland; and as it was only about fifteen years since the land was cleared, and I myself had got out two or three cords of stumps, I did not give it any manure; but in the course of the summer it appeared by the arrowheads which I turned up in hoeing, that an extinct nation had anciently dwelt here and planted corn and beans ere white men came to clear the land, and so, to some extent, had exhausted the soil for this very crop.

Before yet any woodchuck or squirrel had run across the road, or the sun had got above the shrub oaks, while all the dew was on, though the farmers warned me against it, — I would advise you to do all your work if possible while the dew is on, — I began to level the ranks of haughty weeds in my bean-field and throw dust upon their heads. Early in the morning I worked barefooted, dabbling like a plastic artist in the dewy and crumbling sand, but later in the day the sun blistered my feet. There the sun lighted me to hoe beans, pacing slowly backward and forward over that yellow gravelly upland, between the long green rows, fifteen rods, the one end terminating in a shrub oak copse where I could rest in the shade, the other in a blackberry field where the green berries deepened their tints by the time I had made another bout. Removing the weeds, putting fresh soil about the bean stems, and encouraging this weed which I had sown, making the yellow soil express its summer thought in bean leaves and blossoms rather than in wormwood and piper and millet grass, making the earth say beans instead of grass, — this was my daily work. As I had little aid from horses or cattle, or hired men or boys, or improved implements of husbandry, I was much slower, and became much more intimate with my beans than usual. But labor of the hands, even when pursued to the verge of drudgery, is perhaps never the worst form of idleness. It has a constant and imperishable moral, and to the scholar it yields a classic result. A very *agricola laboriosus* was I to travellers bound westward through Lincoln and Wayland to nobody knows where; they sitting at their ease in gigs, with elbows on knees, and reins loosely hanging in festoons; I the home-staying, laborious native of the soil. But soon my homestead was out of their sight and thought. It was the only open and cultivated field for a great distance on either side of the road, so they made the most of it; and sometimes the man in the field heard more of travellers' gossip and comment than was meant for his ear: "Beans so late! peas so late!" — for I continued to plant when others had begun to hoe, — the ministerial husbandman had not suspected it. "Corn, my boy, for fodder; corn for fodder." "Does he *live* there?" asks the black bonnet of the gray coat; and the hard-featured farmer reins up his grateful dobbin to inquire what you are doing where he sees no manure in the furrow, and recommends a little chip dirt, or any little waste stuff, or it may be ashes or plaster. But here were two acres and a half of furrows, and only a hoe for cart and two hands to draw it, — there being an aversion to other carts and horses, — and chip dirt far away. Fellow-travellers as they rattled by compared it aloud with the fields which they had passed, so that I came to know how I stood in the agricultural world. This was one field not in Mr. Colman's report. And, by the way, who estimates the value of the crop which nature yields in the still wilder fields unimproved by man? The crop of

English hay is carefully weighed, the moisture calculated, the silicates and the potash; but in all dells and pond-holes in the woods and pastures and swamps grows a rich and various crop only unreaped by man. Mine was, as it were, the connecting link between wild and cultivated fields; as some states are civilized, and others half-civilized, and others savage or barbarous, so my field was, though not in a bad sense, a half-cultivated field. They were beans cheerfully returning to their wild and primitive state that I cultivated, and my hoe played the *Ranz des Vaches* for them. . . .

Those summer days which some of my contemporaries devoted to the fine arts in Boston or Rome, and others to contemplation in India, and others to trade in London or New York, I thus, with the other farmers of New England, devoted to husbandry. Not that I wanted beans to eat, for I am by nature a Pythagorean, so far as beans are concerned, whether they mean porridge or voting, and exchanged them for rice; but, perchance, as some must work in fields if only for the sake of tropes and expression, to serve a parable-maker one day. It was on the whole a rare amusement, which, continued too long, might have become a dissipation. Though I gave them no manure, and did not hoe them all once, I hoed them unusually well as far as I went, and was paid for it in the end, "there being in truth," as [English diarist John] Evelyn says, "no compost or lætation whatsoever comparable to this continual motion, repastination, and turning of the mould with the spade." "The earth," he adds elsewhere, "especially if fresh, has a certain magnetism in it, by which it attracts the salt, power, or virtue (call it either) which gives it life, and is the logic of all the labor and stir we keep about it, to sustain us; all dungings and other sordid temperings being but the vicars succedaneous to this improvement." Moreover, this being one of those "worn-out and exhausted lay fields which enjoy their sabbath," had perchance, as Sir Kenelm Digby thinks likely, attracted "vital spirits" from the air. I harvested twelve bushels of beans.

Rebecca Harding Davis on Pollution and Human Life in the Iron Mills, 1861

> Is this the end?
> O Life, as futile, then, as frail!
> What hope of answer of redress?

A cloudy day: do you know what that is in a town of iron-works? The sky sank down before dawn, muddy, flat, immovable. The air is thick, clammy with the breath of crowded human beings. It stifles me. I open the window, and, looking out, can scarcely see through the rain the grocer's shop opposite, where a crowd of drunken Irishmen are puffing Lynchburg tobacco in their pipes. I can detect the scent through all the foul smells ranging loose in the air.

The idiosyncrasy of this town is smoke. It rolls sullenly in slow folds from the great chimneys of the iron-foundries, and settles down in black, slimy pools on the muddy streets. Smoke on the wharves, smoke on the dingy boats, on the yellow river, — clinging in a coating of greasy soot to the house-front, the two faded poplars, the faces of the passers-by. The long train of mules, dragging masses of pig-iron through the narrow street, have a foul vapor hanging to their reeking sides. Here, inside, is a little broken figure of an angel pointing upward from the mantel-shelf; but even its wings are covered with smoke, clotted and black. Smoke everywhere! A dirty canary chirps desolately in a cage beside me. Its dream of green fields and sunshine is a very old dream, — almost worn out, I think.

From the back-window I can see a narrow brick-yard sloping down to the river-side, strewed with rain-butts and tubs. The river, dull and tawny-colored, (*la belle riviere!*) drags itself sluggishly along, tired of the heavy weight of boats and coal-barges. What wonder? When I was a child, I used to fancy a look of weary, dumb appeal upon the face of the negro-like river slavishly bearing its burden day after day. Something of the same idle notion comes to me today, when from the street-window I look on the slow stream of human life creeping past, night and morning, to the great mills. Masses of men, with dull, besotted faces bent to the ground, sharpened here and there by pain or cunning; skin and muscle and flesh begrimed with smoke and ashes; stooping all night over boiling caldrons of metal, laired by day in dens of drunkenness and infamy; breathing from infancy to death an air saturated with fog and grease and soot, vileness for soul and body. What do you make of a case like that, amateur psychologist? You call it an altogether serious thing to be alive: to these men it is a drunken jest, a joke, — horrible to angels perhaps, to them commonplace enough. My fancy about the river was an idle one: it is no type of such a life. What if it be stagnant and slimy here? It knows that beyond there waits for it odorous sunlight, — quaint old gardens, dusky with soft, green foliage of apple-trees, and flushing crimson with roses, — air, and fields, and mountains. The future of the Welsh puddler passing just now is not so pleasant. To be stowed away, after his grimy work is done, in a hole in the muddy graveyard, and after that, — *not* air, nor green fields, nor curious roses.

* * * *

If you could go into this mill where Deborah lay, and drag out from the hearts of these men the terrible tragedy of their lives, taking it as a symptom of the disease of their class, no ghost Horror would terrify you more. A reality of soul-starvation, of living death, that meets you every day under the besotted faces on the street, — I can paint nothing of this, only give you the outside outlines of a night, a crisis in the life of one man: whatever muddy depth of soul-history lies beneath you can read according to the eyes God has given you.

ESSAYS

The ambivalence expressed in the documents over the value of nature versus civilization stems from deeper conflicts within an emerging industrial-capitalist society. More than in colonial society, capitalism in the nineteenth century split culture from nature, public from private, reason from emotion, and male from female. The public sphere of production and politics was dominated by men; the private sphere of the home and emotion was culturally assigned to women. Science and technology became instruments of capitalist development; nature, a refuge for spirit and emotion.

The three essays that follow consider the relationships between nature and civilization. Michael Heiman, a geographer at Dickinson College, argues in the opening selection that civilization (exemplified by capitalist production) was of primary importance to nineteenth-century elites. Nature was secondary to civilization as both a commodity and a refuge for humans. The primary reality of the Hudson Valley lay in its use for commodity production through lumbering, tanning, mining, quarrying, brewing, brick and cement making, and the manufacture of textiles and detachable shirt collars. Those "blemishes" were ignored by artists and tour guides, who instead painted and promoted an ideal nature as a refuge for humans. Both viewpoints had a homocentric orientation: civilization was the ultimate reality.

The second essay, by historian Robert Kuhn McGregor of Sangamon State University, suggests that a few nineteenth-century Americans recognized the primacy of nature over civilization. Preeminent among them was Henry David Thoreau. Thoreau's biocentric, or life-centered, vision included the activities of mammals and plants and other organisms as living actors. Humans were part of nature; animals had their own civilizations. To write a biocentric history, McGregor argues, "scholars must discard the notion that human beings are the center of all things." In the long term, nature is the ultimate reality.

In the third essay, Annette Kolodny, a professor of English at the University of Arizona at Tuscon, raises the issue of gender in relation to nature and civilization. In view of the fact that many American writers represented nature as a female, wife, or mother, what is the implication for men and women's roles in relationship to the environment and its transformation? Here she discusses the concept of nature and gender in the work of John James Audubon and James Fenimore Cooper.

As a group, the three essays explore the ways in which nineteenth-century humans assigned value to nature and civilization in the context of an emerging industrial society.

Civilization over Nature

MICHAEL HEIMAN

The identification of nature as a refuge removed from the negative social and environmental externalities accompanying industrial production is a common feature of American landscape ideology. More specifically, nature, in the form of residential and recreation space, is perceptually and physically appropriated as a subset of personal consumption space. Here, in this defended space, individuals, be they workers or owners, can attempt to escape the rigors of the workplace to consume the hard-earned fruits of their efforts. Nature, however, is also essential for commodity production, furnishing both the raw material as well as the space required for capital accumulation. As such, the defense of

Excerpts from Michael Heiman, "Production Confronts Consumption: Landscape Perception and Social Conflict in the Hudson Valley," Environment and Planning D: Society and Space 7 (1989): 165–173.

nature as residential and recreational consumption space in the form of wilderness preserves, greenbelts, and even as suburban backyards, presents serious problems for the expansion of capital.

Nature as a Refuge from, and as an Input to, Commodity Production

Although not exclusive to capitalism, the interpretation of nature as a refuge from the workplace is a basic expression of underlying structural contradiction for capitalism. . . . In an expanding economy the conceptual partitioning of space into production zones and consumption zones (or what are perceived as nature zones) is acceptable. This is because the separation, whether conceptual or through the actual practice of land use, permits the development of production zones (and of the resources contained or utilized within) as inputs into commodity production for exchange value, while reserving those areas set aside from commodity production, and defended against the attending environmental degradation and social conflict, as places for biological, psychological, and social rejuvenation. Places for social rejuvenation typically encompass areas where we reside and recreate.

The Hudson Valley . . . since the colonial period . . . was, and continues as, one of the most significant battlegrounds between the forces of production and those seeking protection of leisure and residential consumption amenities. Having given birth and inspiration to artistic, literary, and design schools that dominated nineteenth-century landscape perceptions and continue to inspire contemporary land use battles, the Hudson Valley experience is at once unique yet commonplace and is therefore of value in an examination of capitalist landscape ideology.

Images of Nature in the [Hudson] Valley: The Ideal and the Reality

Today, with the Valley's industries and cities oriented toward onshore transportation routes and away from the river, one can scarcely imagine that the calm waters of the majestic river 150 years ago supported one of the most intensively utilized commercial routes in the nation. With a bed lying below sea level, the broad lower half of the Hudson River could accommodate ocean-going vessels as far as the Albany–Troy area (Figure 1). Here, goods were exchanged for transport on the famous Erie Canal, completed in 1825 through the Mohawk Valley to Buffalo on Lake Erie. Taken together, the Hudson–Mohawk valleys provided the only navigable break through the Appalachian Mountains in the United States.

From the 1780s until the 1830s, travel on the river was dominated by the slow, broad-bottom Hudson River sailing sloop. Averaging 100 tons in capacity, the ships would take from a few days to a week to make the 150-mile run from Albany to New York City, depending upon wind and tides. Every Hudson village had its own fleet, and at the height of sloop use in the 1830s over a hundred could be spotted from a single vantage on the River's broad Tappen Zee section. In 1807, however, Robert Fulton's *Clermont* made the first steam voyage up the Hudson from New York to Albany in just over 32 hours. Soon

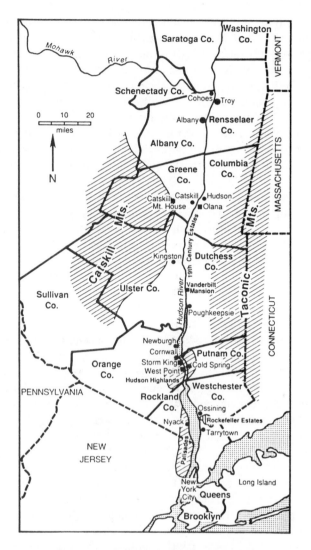

Figure 1.   Hudson Valley Landmarks.

thereafter steam became the preferred mode of passenger travel, with the sloops reserved for bulk cargo. By 1840 over a hundred steamboats and several hundred sloops were active day and night on the river, and flotillas of up to 50 barges, fastened together and with a steamtug in the middle for propulsion, were beginning to appear.

The Hudson Valley also gave birth and inspiration to the young nation's first indigenous school of painting. Beginning in 1825 with Thomas Cole's arrival in New York City and his initial trip by steamboat up the Hudson, the Hudson River School of Landscape Painting lasted until the 1870s. Impressed by Alexander von Humboldt, Louis Agassiz, and by other naturalists, Cole and his colleagues were pioneering in the exactitude of their geological and botanical depictions. Nonetheless, the popular acceptance of the Hudson River

School as portraying a wilderness condition actually found in the Valley and in the adjoining Catskill Mountains was itself mistaken. Thus the Hudson's 'wild shores' already ran through the heart of what was referred to as the 'breadbasket of the nation' from the close of the Revolutionary War until the 1820s, when the Erie Canal provided access to newer wheat-growing regions in western New York and, later, in the Midwest USA. At the peak of the school's influence in the 1830s and 1840s, the intensely settled Valley swarmed with Europeans on the Grand Tour of America's 'wild wonders'. Judging from their diaries as they steamed up the river, most appeared oblivious to intense shore-line resource extraction and to the squalid living conditions of adjoining tenant farmers.

A closer examination of the discrepancy between the ideal, as depicted by nineteenth-century artists and essayists, and the reality, at least as recorded in gazetteers and by more discerning travelers, is enlightening. This is because it illuminates the tension in bourgeois landscape perception as first fashioned in the Valley. Moreover, it underscores the increasing futility of private efforts to maintain a distance between landscapes of production and consumption in the years prior to state assistance for that purpose.

Although tenancy, and the violence of the French, the Indian, and the Revolutionary wars retarded settlement in the Valley, development resumed with the subsequent peace. Production greatly accelerated during the War of 1812, when the Valley emerged as an important manufacturing center to supply the goods no longer available from Britain. Already by 1830 most of the Valley's once-thick forest cover had been cut at least once, and usually several times, to supply the fuel and raw material for the numerous forges, steamboats, and tanneries active in the region. At the scenic Hudson Highlands, straddling the river at West Point 40 miles north of New York City, the forest cover upon Cole's first passage was already greater than it had been 20 years earlier, when the entire area had been cleared to fuel nearby iron foundries. To the north, deforestation was so severe in Rensselaer County that according to one observer the remaining "woodlands [were] . . . worth more than the same quality of land under tolerable cultivation, including buildings, fences and every improvement. . . ."

On the west bank, the Catskill counties were alive by the 1820s with lumbering, tanning, and mining activities. The mountainous terrain had been opened for commercial exploitation through an intricate system of canals and turnpikes. Between 1824 and 1850 the mountain valleys above Cole's studio in the village of Catskill supported the largest tanning industry in the nation. Hides were brought in from as far away as Patagonia. Throughout the Catskills thousands of acres of hemlock were cleared and stripped for the tannin in the bark, and once-pristine mountain streams now ran rancid with hair, grease, acids, and other tanning wastes.

Downriver the west bank areas around Nyack, Haverstraw, and Kingston were already leading quarrying and brick manufacturing centers by the 1820s, supplying much of the material used to pave and build New York City. With the completion of the Delaware and Hudson Canal in 1828, designed to bring in coal from the Pennsylvania fields, the Kingston (Rondout) terminus became a major shipping and manufacturing center. Kingston was also the center of the state's cement production following discovery of deposits through canal construction. Miles of shaft were sunk to quarry Rosendale Cement, world-famous for its capacity to harden under water. By mid-century, 30 miles north of New York City, Haverstraw's brick trade had expanded to cover several miles of waterfront with clay quarries, drying racks, kilns, and shipment wharves. Here labor militancy was a perennial issue, with scabs commonly brought in from Quebec. At about the same time, nearby, at Rockland Lake on a ledge above the Hudson, several thousand people were employed at ice production just to serve the cooling requirements of the city downriver.

With its shallow slope, the eastern bank of the river supported most of the agriculture and even more settlement than the western shore. Here major iron foundries and forges were established at Troy, Hudson, Poughkeepsie, Cold Spring, and Peekskill. On the east bank, 30 miles south of Albany, Hudson was the fourth largest city in the state in 1820 and an international port of trade noted for woollen manufacturing, whaling, and quarrying. Poughkeepsie, 40 miles farther downriver, was also known for its textiles and as an important brewing and limestone center.

Founded by Yankees in the 1780s, Troy was the quintessential manufacturing boom town. In 1827 the wife of a cobbler, fed up with repeated washing of her husband's shirts just to clean the collar, cut off the soiled section and invented the detachable shirt collar. Lasting until the invention of the washing machine in the early twentieth century, the US shirt collar industry at its height employed 15,000 workers in over 20 factories spread throughout the city.

Back on the west bank, Albany, chartered in 1686, was already the state capital and an important brewing and lumber market by the time the Erie Canal opened. The city's 4300-foot-long mooring basin was the principal transshipment center for canal traffic. Already by the mid-1830s, at the height of European fascination with the Valley's natural wonders, the city's dozen steamboats provided daily service to New York City, with 700,000 passengers arriving and departing yearly.

On both banks the river cities and towns were shipment points for densely settled hinterlands. The 10 Valley-counties north of New York City (Westchester, Putnam, Dutchess, Columbia, Rensselaer, Albany, Greene, Ulster, Orange, and Rockland) contained 271,000 inhabitants in 1820. No doubt this was quite low by British standards. The greater London area already had over 1,250,000 people by this period, almost 10 times that of New York City, by then the largest city in the USA. Nonetheless, the Hudson Valley was certainly not the rural semiwilderness depicted by the artists and fancied by itinerant European visitors.

Veiling the disagreeable facts of production in this celebrated landscape required a careful sleight of hand. In their rush to fulfill the growing European and American demand for views of a romantic wilderness, Cole and his contemporaries, including Asher B. Durand, Frederick E. Church, and poet William Cullen Bryant, often overlooked or screened out with vegetation the burnt-over fields, stinking tanneries, polluted streams, clamorous sawmills, and other production intrusions. Deeply religious, Cole avoided urban scenes because he considered urban social life as lacking in those wholesome qualities which allowed art to be a source of moral inspiration. When they did address human habitation in the valley, Cole and the other artists typically preferred Sunday scenes so as to avoid signs of work and the harsher realities of tenant farming.

The artists were not, however, oblivious to the desecration of their cherished landscape. With patrons actually admonishing him for not putting enough wild nature into his scenes, Cole's lament over the destruction of his favored sketching places in the Catskills was restricted to his prose and, later, to his allegorical canvasses. In a letter of 1836 he complained that the tanneries and a railroad then under construction along Catskill Creek above his studio were "cutting down all of the trees in the beautiful valley on which I have looked so often with a loving eye." "Tell this to [Asher B] Durand—not that I wish to give him a pain, but that I want him to join with me in maledictions on all dollar-godded utilitarians."

Certainly the discord was nowhere near the extent found in Britain, where Manchester's 'satanic mills' and pale of soot had already been used as symbols of fear and apprehension by poets and artists some decades earlier. For many the Hudson region, by comparison, represented a fresh slate, a landscape where wilderness might still give way to a more harmonious and even sublime pattern when viewed from the proper perspective.

The Recreational Escape to Nature

Eagerly sought out by wealthy collectors in New York and London, the Hudson River artists enjoyed an unusual degree of success and exposure. In the Hudson Highlands and along the Catskill escarpment luxurious mountaintop hotels were erected to provide a comfortable experience for the would-be wilderness traveler in search of the scenes made famous by the artists. Many river travelers on the Grand Tour sought out the Catskill Mountain House.

Established in 1823 this fabled resort was one of the nation's first major vacation destinations not tied to medicinal waters. Here, perched 2250 feet above the Valley on the hotel's veranda, the wealthy guests could imagine an idealized rural landscape devoid of social struggle. According to a noted Catskill historian:

> Pilgrims en route to the Mountain House might hold their noses as tanner's wagons passed by or rub their eyes when the smoke of forestfires made the mountain air thick and biting, yet they could console themselves by reflecting that they were in the midst of what the best authorities certified to be a wilderness Garden of Eden into which only the famous Mountain House intruded.

Apparently the charade was too much for one jaded visitor who, upon visiting Katterskill Falls, the most famous cataract in the state after Niagara, astutely recorded the consumption of nature:

The proprietor of the bar-room is also the genius of the Fall, and drives a trade both with his spirits and his water. In fact, if your romantic nerves can stand the steady truth, the Catskill Fall is *turned on* to accommodate poets and parties of pleasure.

The process of "doing" the sight, for those who are limited in time, is very methodical. You leave the [Mountain House] hotel and drive in a coach to the bar-room. You "refresh." You step out upon the balcony, and look into the abyss. The proprietor of the Fall informs you that the lower plunge is eighty feet high. It appears to you to be about ten. You laugh incredulously — he smiles in return the smile of a *mens conscia recti.* "Would you step down and have the water turned on?" You do step down a somewhat uneven but very safe staircase. You reach the bottom. "Look! now it comes!" and the proud cascade plunges like a free force into the air and slips, swimming in foam, away from your gaze. . . .

This is ludicrous. But most of us are really only shop-keepers, and natural spectacles are but shopwindows on a grand scale.

Most of the Catskill visitors came for the season to marvel at, and perhaps sketch or record in their diaries, the scenes made famous by the artists. They also came to escape the riots, congestion, heat, malaria, yellow fever, and other environmental and social discomforts of the valley lowlands and the crowded metropolis downriver. Clutching the ubiquitous guidebooks, visitors were advised of exact times and positions when best to view God's creation so as to avoid the disagreeable facts of production owing to tanning, mining, logging, and subsistence farming. In this manner the American literati and bourgeoisie did not so much return to the land, for they rarely had agrarian roots, as they actually turned toward an idealized nature for spiritual inspiration and emotional release.

The escape to nature through recreation in the Hudson Valley was closely related to the social history of New York City. By 1880 over 2 million people lived within a day's travel of the Valley. Nonetheless, insufficient means and overt ethnic discrimination largely limited resort use to wealthy Anglo-Protestants. Beginning in the 1880s, however, union victories in wage and hour demands succeeded in allowing organized labor at least a Sunday outing by steamboat to numerous picnic sites at the foot of the Catskill, Highland, and Palisade cliffs. Here, much to the chagrin of more refined travelers and Sunday prohibitionists, the working-class immigrants feasted and drank to oblivion, attempting as best they could to escape, if only for a few hours. As with the bourgeoisie, nature was also a refuge from production for the workers. However, for the working class nature was less a source of passive contemplation and aesthetic appreciation than it was a resource for active recreational consumption.

Residential Consumption of Nature

During the 1830s and 1840s a new breed of landowner emerged in the Hudson Valley, one whose fortune was derived from industrial and financial activity rather than from land inheritance. The new estate owners were only marginally concerned with Hudson property for rent or for productive investment. Instead, they acquired land for their own residence and leisure consumption.

Many of the larger estates were located atop the more level eastern shore of the River, in Dutchess and Columbia counties. This permitted stunning views across to the rugged Catskill Mountains. The most lavish estates were erected between the 1870s and the 1890s when the Vanderbilts, Harrimans, Rockefellers, and others acquired Hudson property in addition to holdings at Newport (Rhode Island) in the Adirondacks, and at other fashionable resorts.

Famed landscape architect Andrew Jackson Downing was closely identified with the design of the Hudson River estate as a place for residential consumption of nature. Moreover, he was one of the first to publicize the concept of a suburb as a planned community where successful citizens who labored all day in commerce could retire amidst a cultivated, parklike nature. As was evident on his own estate, Highland Gardens, Downing banished all signs of work from the residences. He went so far as to prescribe the placement of pens, portfolios, and other instruments in the library for effect only.

Following completion of the first rail line along the eastern bank of the River in 1851 the lower Hudson, from the Highlands south, fell within the commute shed of New York City, and the suburban dream of Downing became a reality. The very first train up the Hudson to the Greenbush terminal across from Albany completed the run in just under 4 hours, a rate that compares favorably with rail travel today. On the opposite shore a line from Jersey City reached Albany in 1883. On both banks construction had been slow owing to opposition from steamboat lines and from existing estate owners, across whose front lawns the trains would run.

With year-round transit now available, wealthy merchants, bankers, and others whose presence in New York was a daily or weekly requirement moved north from Manhattan abodes to estates clustered along the Westchester and Putnam heights and around Nyack and Cornwall on the western shore. Here they created a privileged landscape, removed from the social turmoil and industrial pollution of their urban workplace, and defended against the intrusion of adjoining production zones.

Nature over Civilization

ROBERT KUHN McGREGOR

On the night of February 5, 1854, two red foxes emerged from the swampy bottomlands southeast of the Assabet River in the town of Concord, Massachusetts. Moving eastward, the pair crossed open meadows until they reached the skirts of Nut Meadow Brook where they split up. One fox continued east,

---

From Robert Kuhn McGregor, "Deriving a Biocentric History: Evidence From the Journal of Henry David Thoreau," *Environmental Review*, 12, No. 2 (Summer 1988): 117–124. Reprinted with permission from *Environmental History Review*, © 1988, the American Society for Environmental History.

following the course of the brook through open fields and into a wood. The night was cold, but fortunately only a little snow lay on the ground. White-footed mice, the fox's principal food source, burrow beneath deep snow, making them difficult to catch. Foxes must eat regularly and cache food against the remaining hard days of winter, if possible.

The fox climbed a hillside, momentarily dragging its white-tipped tail in the snow, then struck out across a potato field and into another meadow. Her course intersected the tracks of mice, rabbits, and her chief enemies: dogs and people. South of a bridge, she crossed a road and the brook and came at last to the edge of the Sudbury River. Game seems to have been scarce that night, because she continued on across the river to examine the muskrat houses dotting the marsh on the eastern side. One by one, the fox jumped on the fibrous mounds attempting to frighten out the inhabitants. She urinated on each lodge, marking the site with her strong, musky scent. Thus far she had travelled more than a mile in her search for prey. Because February is the peak of the fox mating season, she needed to build up her food cache in anticipation of the pups, due in six to eight weeks.

Most professionals would deem the nocturnal activities of a fox in the vicinity of the Assabet River in 1854 a matter of little historical concern. Although this incident may have occurred, there seems little reason to attach importance to the journey, or to engage in further research. According to conventional argument, it is not history. The purpose of this essay is to contend that these occurrences are in fact history, and that they are of fundamental importance to the future direction of the discipline. . . . This essay advocates the development of a biocentric history.

To recreate the activities of a historic fox, I employed the familiar methods known to historians, in this case the impeccable *Journal* of Henry David Thoreau. The Concord writer induced the activities of the fox in question by following the animal's foot tracks on the afternoon of February 5, 1854. I supplemented that material with other observations Thoreau made concerning foxes over the course of a dozen years. I turned next to standard technical sources to flesh out my understanding of the habits of the red fox. There is every indication that my description encapsulates a real incident.

In the eyes of colleagues, my history founders on the test of significance. What is so important about a fox? It farmed no soil, practiced no religion, sold no goods, nor did it ever run for Congress. Its journey is a simple occurrence in nature, one that undoubtedly happened countless times in many places.

The first significant point about this fox is the record of its travels. Although it could leave no records of its own, Thoreau believed the fox's activities important enough to enter in his journal. In addition to the movements of foxes, Thoreau recorded the actions of every other creature he encountered, including the behavior of thousands of plants. Those records comprise a wealth of primary material for a history of all the forms of life in Concord during Thoreau's time there. The significance of the fox lies in the role it played in the environmental whole, a part equally important to that of various quadrupeds, insects, birds, fish, and humans. Thoreau generally made daily entries in his journal between 1850 and 1861, recording all the phenomena necessary to understand the nature of life. We might advance our own comprehension by undertaking to write a history of all life in a particular place and time.

To research and develop such a meaningful history, scholars must first discard the notion that human beings are the center of all things. Humans, after all, walk the earth in the company of myriad other creatures, each with its own requirements for survival and well-being. Although humans have exercised tremendous influence on the world's ecologies, they do not control the world, nor do other creatures exist for their benefit. To understand the manner in which life on earth functions, it is necessary to look at things from a holistic point of view; modern ecologists and philosophers have called that intellectual process "biocentrism."

In the biocentric world view all species of life are effectively equal because they depend upon others for survival, for food, shelter, air, and water. The human belief that we live a separate, superior realm of existence is simple anthropocentric self-delusion; humans are, as Aldo Leopold observed, "plain citizens" of the biotic community. . . .

Thoreau recorded a wealth of information concerning the rivers, meadows, woods, hilltops, and bogs of Concord. His journals record in minute detail the activities of the hundreds of living species associated with each landform. He attempted to develop an understanding of the complex relationships and the interdependencies among the living beings of the region. The journals, therefore, provide the basic raw material for a comprehensive history of all species of life in a small town during the nineteenth century. Although his view of that world may have been an involved melding of the transcendental and the scientific, he never wavered in his ultimate determination: to discover truth.

In the late summer of 1846 Thoreau stood atop Mount Katahdin and asked "*Who* are we? *where* are we?" Other scholars have detected a note of despair in the passage, a measured rejection of his earlier commitment to wildness. That is debatable. Those lines are merely agonizingly simple questions posed to himself. He spent the remainder of his life searching for the answers. "The poet says the proper study of mankind is man," Thoreau observed. "I say, study to forget all that; take wider views of the universe." Over time, the scope of his search altered, his methods changed, but the determination to know who and where we are never diminished.

All his life Thoreau considered himself a transcendentalist. He confided a definition of that philosophy to his journal in 1840: transcendentalism was essentially a romantic belief, a rejection of inductive science in favor of self-perceived truth. The material world mattered little, it existed merely as a pale reflection of a higher, spiritual plane. "My thought is a part of the meaning of the world," he stated, "and hence I use part of the world as a symbol to express my thought."

Thoreau did not always express his transcendental belief so clearly. He observed in the spring of 1854 that "the man of most science is the man most alive, whose life is the greatest event." Thoreau employed the scientific method to an extraordinary degree in his search for a sense of place in the universe. By the 1850s, he was a botanist of considerable repute, not merely in identifying species, but in tracking their life cycles through the year. He also recorded the activities of birds, insects, amphibians, reptiles, and fish; and he struggled to understand the manner in which they interacted with one another and with the climate and geography of Concord.

The inherent conflict between transcendental belief and scientific method Thoreau recognized at once: "If you would be wise, learn science and then forget it." At times, especially during winter or during moments of personal tragedy, he heeded that advice, forsaking inductive knowledge to "commune with the spirit of the universe." More often, usually in spring and summer, the lush abundance of nature would overwhelm his spiritual side. Only direct observation and year-to-year record keeping could satisfy his desire to know. For every journal entry expressing transcendental belief, there are a thousand scientific observations of nature at work.

The seeming contradiction between romantic philosophy and inductive science was not an inconsistency on Thoreau's part. "The fact is," he wrote, "I am a mystic, a transcendentalist, and a natural philosopher to boot. . . . I probably stand as near to nature as any of them, and am by constitution as good an observer as most." Thoreau was searching both for the activities that took place in nature and for a sense of the spirit in nature: "There is a civilization going on among brutes as well as men." He believed the forests were sacred and was willing to allow trees the possibility of reaching heaven. Every occurrence in nature, he maintained, "is a parable of the Great Teacher."

More startling to Thoreau was the existence of humanity in nature, "a fact which few have realized." But what exactly was the human place in nature? He readily acknowledged that human beings stood apart from the rest of nature in many ways. His fellow beings were steeped in the exploitive views dominant in Western culture and assumed that God created the world for their benefit. "What is a shrub oak good for?" a neighbor asked him. Often, that narrow self-centered attitude repelled Thoreau. He fumed over government's lack of comprehension or interest in the natural world: "Children are attracted by the beauty of butterflies, but their parents and legislators deem it an idle pursuit."

Thoreau also recognized that most species were suspicious of the humans in their midst: "Birds certainly are afraid of man," he observed. "They [allow virtually] all other creatures — cows, horses, etc. . . . to come near them, but not man. . . . Is he, then, a true lord of creation, whose subjects are afraid of him, and with reason?"

Certainly in Thoreau's view humans had done much to earn the emnity of other creatures. So-called "improvements" had closed the Concord River to several species of fish, and the urge to shoot everything that moved had driven away many birds and mammals. People did not seem to care; they failed to perceive the activities of those creatures still remaining or even to hear the song of the toads in the spring. Humans were far more adept at overuse and misuse of nature's species. "What right has my neighbor to burn ten cords of wood, when I burn only one?" Thoreau demanded. "He who burns the most wood on his hearth is the least warmed by the sight of it growing."

For all that, Thoreau remained convinced that nature's children included human beings. "How plainly we are a part of nature! For we live like the animals around us." He believed that humanity would be far better off living in harmony with nature, rather than attempting to dominate it. "To be serene and successful we must be at one with the universe," he wrote in 1854. "The least conscious and needless injury inflicted on any creature is to its extent a suicide. What peace — or life — can a murderer have?" His belief that "in wildness is the preservation of the world" is well known. People depend upon nature for life itself. To Thoreau, human beings must "live more naturally, and so more safely."

To apply Thoreau's perspective to the writing of history requires a broader point of view, one that encompasses all that goes on in the world, not merely the role that humans play. A biocentric history must include an accounting of all the forces of life pertinent to a specific place and time, and it must place human beings firmly within that context. If people are not separate from the rest of nature, historians should not treat them separately in environmental history. Thoreau's journals provide a few thoughts that might be applied to the process.

The Concord transcendentalist complained in 1857: "How much is written about Nature as somebody has portrayed her, how little about Nature as she is." The task for environmental historians in that context, therefore, is to distance themselves from the habit of examining nature from a solely human perspective. Other species are not merely resources, or impediments, or even objects of beauty; they are each unique individuals, living and attempting to pass life on through their progeny. "Every child should be encouraged to study not man's system of nature, but nature's," Thoreau advised.

A sense of perspective is the place to commence the process of writing such a history. But it is only a beginning, because the problems of source and method still confront those who embark on a project in biocentric history. What is to be the locus of such a story? Necessarily, the initial subjects must be limited in terms of time and space. Researchers who study the lives of common people have adopted a community approach; broadening that perspective to include the rest of nature can only complicate the work. Hence, it will be necessary to focus at first on the microcosm, on a small, biologically inclusive area, concentrating on a limited time span. When scholars have mastered the ability to write histories that see human beings as a part of nature, they may begin the work of synthesis. The problem of sources is perhaps the most difficult challenge to the creation of biocentric history. Although much of the material familiar to historians includes some clues pertinent to the condition of the environment in a particular place, a truly biocentric history requires greater detail than most sources provide. The vast majority of the authors, reporters, correspondents, diarists, and census takers shared the anthropocentric view that is still dominant in the world. Their observations of nature often are little more than background for their genuine interest: the activities of humans.

To create a biocentric version of the past, historians will need an accurate reportage of the myriad activities of a host of species including humans in a given place and time. Only a few sources, however, have demonstrated the breadth of vision sufficient to make a biocentric history possible.

But why do this? Why is it important to create a biocentric history of Concord, Massachusetts, or of anywhere else, for that matter?

The reasons for crafting such a history fall into several categories: the politically immediate, the educational, the scientific, and the metaphysical. A reading of the daily newspapers is enough to drive home the urgent need for such an approach. Greed and the false assumption that the world exists for the exclusive use of humans are rapidly destroying large numbers of species, ruining whole ecosystems, and endangering humanity. A biocentric view will draw attention to the abuse of the earth and the place of humans within its ecosystem. Such histories may serve to educate people to the necessity of considering the needs of other species.

Good biocentric history may also provide perspective for scientific inquiry. Ecological scientists share an inability to conduct effective research and analysis because of the dynamic nature of existing ecosystems. How does one analyze an environment undergoing constant change without treating the system in static terms (and therefore inaccurately)? By studying the actions of previous environments, historians may describe all the interactions of the species resident in a particular place over a period of time, thereby providing scientists a basis for comparison to existing systems.

History is not science, nor should it have such pretensions. Historians stand midway between science and art, commanding a view of both. They are not cold-blooded inductivists, collecting facts with cool rationality; nor are they starry-eyed romantics, ignoring the hard facts in order to paint historical pictures in broad artistic splashes. Yet historians possess the capacity to be a little of each; they have the ability to craft a holistic view of the past that embodies the hard facts. So much of what they create depends entirely on their historical point of view. For that reason, a few of them need to adopt a biocentric approach toward their subject. If the profession truly stands between science and art, it has much to offer to each. Both scientists and artists may profit from a perspective that encompasses the needs of all earth's creatures. Historians can and should assist in that process.

A final word of caution: a biocentric point of view is well outside the mainstream of Western cultural thought. Historians attempting to adopt such an approach will discover that they are walking a very lonely path. Thoreau understood the nature of the problem: "The mind that perceives clearly any natural beauty is in that instant withdrawn from human society. My desire for society is infinitely increased; my fitness for any actual society is diminished."

Thoreau's Aunt Maria looked at the matter from another perspective: "Think of it!" she said. "He stood half an hour to-day to hear the frogs croak, and he wouldn't read the life of Chalmers."

May our condemnations be no worse.

Nature, Civilization, and Gender
ANNETTE KOLODNY

Among those who first wandered across the borderlands and frontier communities of the Ohio and Mississippi valleys was the artist-naturalist, John James Audubon. What resulted from those travels were not only the famous illustrations of birds and small mammals, but, just as important, the unique written record of a man whose memory and imagination remained committed to that brief moment when he and others first "arrived on the banks of the broad stream [of the Mississippi], gaze[d] in amazement on the dark, deep woods around them." . . .

Originally published as short chapters scattered throughout the first three volumes of the *Ornithological Biography*, the "Episodes" were finally collected and brought together in a single volume, in 1926, under the title, *Delineations of American Scenery and Character*. Though probably composed several years later from notes and from memory, all the chapters center around "the year 1808." . . .

The very first sketch suggests the inevitably disruptive outcome of human movement into comparatively untouched natural areas that then echoes, like a nervous refrain, through the subsequent fifty-eight chapters. The piece opens with Audubon and his family slowly making their way in a skiff up the Ohio River in search of new specimens to capture and paint.

But all too quickly the cacophony of civilization invades the "more mellow" harmonies of this pastoral landscape, and the lazy navigation of the river is halted abruptly. . . . Each human interruption of a pastoral mood immediately leads Audubon to consider the meaning of "the destruction of the forest, and [the] transplanting [of] civilization into its darkest recesses." Setting the tone for what is to follow, then, this first chapter ends with a disturbed and disturbing ambivalence:

> When I think of these times, and call back to my mind the grandeur and beauty of those almost uninhabited shores; when I picture to myself the dense and lofty summits of the forest, that everywhere spread along the hills, and overhung the margins of the stream, unmolested by the axe of the settler; when I know how dearly purchased the safe navigation of that river has been by the blood of many worthy Virginians; when I see that no longer any Aborigines are to be found there, and that the vast herds of elks, deer and buffaloes which once pastured on these hills and in these valleys, making for themselves great roads to the several saltsprings, have ceased to exist; when I reflect that all this grand portion of our Union, instead of being in a state of nature, is now more or less covered with villages, farms, and towns, where the din of hammers and machinery is constantly heard; that the woods are fast disappearing under the axe by day, and the fire by night; that hundreds of steam-boats are gliding to and fro, over the whole length of the majestic river, forcing commerce to take

Reprinted, by permission of the author and publisher, from *The Lay of the Land: Metaphor as Experience and History in American Life and Letters*, by Annette Kolodny. © 1975 The University of North Carolina Press.

root and to prosper at every spot; when I see the surplus population of Europe coming to assist in the destruction of the forest, and transplanting civilization into its darkest recesses; — when I remember that these extraordinary changes have all taken place in the short period of twenty years, I pause, wonder, and although I know all to be fact, can scarcely believe its reality. . . .

In an effort to limit the scope of such depredations and, perhaps, the scope of his own involvement in the trek westward, Audubon locates most of his sketches in a semipopulated, only partially cultivated, rural landscape, its human inhabitants still in close touch with nature. . . . Trying . . . to expunge what was perhaps only a barely conscious experience of masculine aggression into a feminine ambience, Audubon sets up, in each of the settlers' cabins, a compensatory and virtually archetypal balance of masculine and feminine components. . . . |The feminine is always depicted as both wife and mother, and the planting or hunting activities of the male are experienced not as a violation, but rather as a means of protecting and providing for the feminine| Obviously, this is humankind playing what were, until this century, its most archetypal roles. Rarely are individual personalities depicted in these episodes, but, instead, immediately identifiable gendered polarities, compatible within their cabin and, together, in harmony with the landscape outside. . . . The cabins . . . seem to provide a refuge where he may experience himself, as it were, as a member of the family. But, as his own vocabulary choices reveal, he finds no permanent or legitimate role in such scenes and remains, inevitably, the "stranger," as much an intruder inside the cabin as he has been in the landscape without, where, violating his intimacy even as he seeks to preserve it, he kills or maims the "beautiful birds" and small mammals that nature had provided for his admiration. . . .

Of the fifty-nine sketches that make up *The Delineations of American Scenery and Character*, only five focus on events in which nature is either harmful or threatening. . . . Two of these involve the threat of flood along the Mississippi, "A Flood" and "The Force of the Waters," while the other three deal with an earthquake, a hurricane, and a forest fire. The danger of these disasters is mediated, however, since in each case the story is related either about or by those who have survived and now sit in the comfort of a new home, before a hearth that "sends forth a blaze of light over the happy family." . . .

In effect, the real threats to Audubon's pastoral impulse are not, as we might expect, natural disasters such as earthquake or flood, but, instead, the acquisitional strivings of "the man who, with his family, removed to the [new territories], . . . assured that, in that land of exuberant fertility, he could not fail to provide amply for all his wants." . . . Audubon is . . . attempting to reconcile the conflicting pastoral impulses that motivate the frontier woodsman, "felling and squaring the giant trees," and the frontier naturalist, trying to preserve his beloved animals in pen and ink, to not only enjoy and accept nature's bounties passively, but to control and use them in such a way as to threaten the conditions under which they were supplied. The felled trees will provide planks for the ships that navigate the rivers and facilitate the advance of settlers onto the frontier; and the naturalist kills the very animals he is attempting to preserve for posterity.

To James Fenimore Cooper . . . must go the credit for giving the first major, and successful, literary coherence to the pastoral impulse in America. . . . Once having admitted, though reluctantly, that a nonexploitive white community, living happily and harmoniously within the embrace of nature, was no longer even a possibility — its demise there, in the first of the Leatherstocking tales, with the settlement of Templeton — Cooper turned to the possibility of a lone frontiersman, Natty Bumppo, living out the pastoral impulse.

If the first of the Leatherstocking novels, *The Pioneers*, published in 1823, explores the inevitable conflict between the individual and the community, the impulse to freedom versus the need for social organization, it does so within a context structured by the two conflicting aspects of the pastoral impulse. On the one hand, there is Natty Bumppo, the man who claims himself " 'form'd for the wilderness,' " desperate to leave the settlements and " 'go where my soul craves to be' " — into the woods. And, on the other hand, there are the settlers of Templeton, variously represented by Judge Temple, determined to awaken the land lying " 'in the sleep of nature . . . to supply the wants of man' "; by Billy Kirby, intent upon hacking and burning his way out of every enclosure, opening up "the depths of the woods" to the "daylight"; and by Cousin Richard Jones, whose gadget-oriented technology, in the course of the novel, intrudes upon all of nature's precincts — lake, land, and sky. . . . Reminding us of those whom Audubon had described "sporting" with a mother bear and her cubs or cruelly taunting pitted wolves, Cooper's fictionalized settlers appear to be a people who grasp only weapons of destruction. . . . Natty parallels the maternal response of nature, mourning for the pigeons shot in flocks, or the fish hauled in by seine, the trees felled by axe and fire. . . .

We are forced . . . to reassess what Natty's stance as a lone hunter and a reputed dead shot actually implies. His anger at the " 'wasty ways' " of the settlers clearly suggests that he is not to be regarded as one of those whom Crèvecoeur criticized for having taken advantage of "the unlimited freedom of the woods." In fact, though we are constantly reminded of Natty's hunting skills throughout the novels, we rarely see him aim at anything. . . . Instead, it is generally the restraint of his hunting instincts and the frugality of his meals that are emphasized. He never takes " 'more than can be eat,' " and his notion of a hunt is to give the game " 'some chance for . . . life.' " Still, even if his skill as a hunter can be kept within unabusive bounds, the very fact of Natty's being a white man, skilled in tracking and woodlore, and having, as a result, at least *some* ties to advancing settlement, puts him always in danger of somehow aiding that settlement's violating progress into nature's enclosures. It is precisely this dilemma that Cooper attempts to resolve by his choice of phrasing at the end of the novel, placing Natty "foremost" and thereby suggestively apart from "that band of Pioneers, who are opening the way for the march of our nation across the continent." . . . By its very definition, civilization in this novel *is* the destruction of the wilderness. The man whose eye looks forward to bridges, canals, mines, and towns, as does Judge Temple's, will never, like Natty, live happily " 'five years at a time without seeing the light of a clearing bigger than a wind-row in the trees.' " It is therefore difficult to imagine Natty willingly participating in any "opening [of] the way for the march of our nation across the continent." . . . [He] declare[s], " 'I love the woods, and ye relish the face of man; . . . I'm form'd for the wilderness; if ye love me, let me go where my soul craves to be ag'in!' "

Clearly, Cooper had attempted at least three impossible tasks, and, in the course of the novel, resolved to abandon two of them. The possibility of a human settlement harmonious with nature is rejected as early as the opening chapter; the possibility that a man could serve both as spokesman for civilization and as a protector of the natural world proved unworkable, and Judge Temple stands as the first and the last character whom Cooper attempted to fit into that role, . . . but the possibility that a single man might be able to live happily and harmoniously within nature's embrace without either losing his human identity or abusing the nurturing ambience he could not abandon. . . .

The Prairie (1827) . . . is really the end of a dream. Though Natty still insists upon the possibility of experiencing a primal pastoral harmony between man and the natural world, we realize that he himself has abandoned the garden and chosen, instead, to spend his last days on "the naked prairies." No longer does Cooper even pretend that Natty could willingly take a place "in that band of Pioneers who are opening the way for the march of our nation across the continent." Rather, as though in self-punishment for his former guilt and in a final attempt to escape its repetition, Natty has cut himself off entirely from white civilization — the necessity of which had become painfully obvious by the end of the second novel — and sequestered himself within nature's most uninviting domain. Not only do the prairies' distance from the settlements make the arrival of the axe and the "chopper" highly improbable, but, more important, their very terrain renders that aggression impotent.

. . . Natty has fled, hoping to escape forever, in " 'these vast and naked fields,' " all association with the aggressions of the "Long-knives." But even here he is to hear, once again before his death, " 'the sound of axes, and the crash of falling trees,' " and to know, once and for all, his own inescapable complicity in that violation. Though . . . he himself never directly violates nature's precincts — talking of trapping but never actually shown doing so, aiming at a charging buffalo but missing his shot — he does lead the Bush family to a campsite, shares a meal with them, and then watches, "with a melancholy" and discontented gaze, as Ishmael's sons destroy a grove of cottonwoods. . . . If . . . Natty could not be entirely dissociated from the brutal raping of nature's precincts, he had nevertheless been the first character in American fiction to at least *promise* entry without violation. As mid-century approached, moreover, American writers began to express a kind of urgency on the subject, fearing . . . that "the various charms of scenery which our country possesses" might, indeed, go unsung and forgotten in the wake of "progress."

❦ *F U R T H E R   R E A D I N G*

Catherine Albanese, *Nature Religion in America: From the Algonkian Indians to the New Age* (1990)

Everett Dick, *The Lure of the Land: A Social History of the Public Lands from the Articles of Confederation to the New Deal* (1970)

Arthur A. Ekirch, Jr., *Man and Nature in America* (1963)

Robert Gangewere, ed., *The Exploited Eden: Literature on the American Environment* (1972)

Sam D. Gill, *Mother Earth: An American Story* (1987)

William H. Goetzmann, *New Lands, New Men: America and the Second Great Age of Discovery* (1986)

E. Richard Hart, ed., *That Awesome Space: Human Interaction with the Intermountain Landscape* (1981)

John K. Howat, *The Hudson River and Its Painters* (1972)

————, ed., *American Paradise: The World of the Hudson River School* (1988)

Hildegard Binder Johnson, *Order upon the Land: The U.S. Rectangular Land Survey and the Upper Mississippi Country* (1976)

Annette Kolodny, *The Lay of the Land* (1975)

James McIntosh, *Thoreau as Romantic Naturalist: His Shifting Stance Toward Nature* (1974)

Leo Marx, *The Machine in the Garden: Technology and the Pastoral Ideal in America* (1964)

Lee Clark Mitchell, *Witnesses to a Vanishing America: The Nineteenth-Century Response* (1981)

Roderick Nash, *Wilderness and the American Mind*, 3d ed. (1982)

————, *The Rights of Nature: A History of Environmental Ethics* (1989)

Barbara Novak, *American Painting of the Nineteenth Century: Realism, Idealism and the American Experience* (1969)

————, *Nature and Culture: American Landscape and Painting, 1825–1875* (1980)

Raymond J. O'Brien, *American Sublime: Landscape and Scenery of the Lower Hudson Valley* (1981)

Roy M. Robbins, *Our Landed Heritage: The Public Domain, 1776–1970*, 2d ed. (1970)

Peter J. Schmitt, *Back to Nature: The Arcadian Myth in Urban America* (1969)

Henry Nash Smith, *Virgin Land* (1950)

Henry David Thoreau, *The Natural History Essays* (1980)

————, *In the Woods and Fields of Concord* (1982)

————, *Walden* (1854)

Cecelia Tichi, *New World, New Earth: Environmental Reform in American Literature from the Puritans Through Whitman* (1979)

Frederick Turner, *Beyond Geography: The Western Spirit Against the Wilderness* (1980)

David Scofield Wilson, *In the Presence of Nature* (1978)

Donald Worster, *Nature's Economy: A History of Ecological Ideas* (1977)

CHAPTER 7

The Cotton South Before and
After the Civil War

❦

This chapter explores the environmental history of the Cotton South as an interaction between its climate, soil, pests, and fertilizers on the one hand and the capitalist system of slave agriculture on the other hand.

In the late eighteenth and early nineteenth centuries, textile-production technologies (spinning mills, power looms, and steam engines) introduced in England and New England combined with Eli Whitney's invention of the cotton gin (1793) to make cotton culture profitable. Sea Island cotton, with its long fibers and smooth, easily removed seeds, had grown well along the coast of Georgia and South Carolina during the colonial era, but the upland long- and short-staple cotton varieties, with their shorter fibers and sticky seeds, were well adapted to the inland valleys and the Gulf coastal plain. The cotton gin (which separated seeds from lint), the growth and spread of slavery, and expanding markets made the mass production of these upland varieties feasible. Cotton, which requires a 200-day frost-free growing season and 50–60 inches of rainfall a year, could be raised as far north as Virginia, Tennessee, and northern Arkansas and Oklahoma and in eastern Texas as well. Georgia, Alabama, and Mississippi experienced cotton booms in the 1830s, as did Louisiana and Texas in the 1850s, when people migrated west, pushing Native Americans off the Gulf lands. By 1860 the South was producing 7 million bales of cotton a year, along with other staple crops—sugar, corn, rice, and tobacco. In contrast to the North, the region remained largely rural and heavily forested throughout the nineteenth century, with plantations often separated by a day's travel along poor roads.

The environmental history of the South before the Civil War was shaped by an interaction between a labor-intensive system of agriculture based on slavery and the resultant soil degradation. In 1860 only 25 percent of the South's white population owned slaves (about 10,000 families), and 88 percent of these had fewer than twenty slaves. Two-thirds of the whites were independent, nonslaveowning farmers who farmed and herded in the hills and woods. Free blacks and mulattoes made up the remainder of the southern population. Slaves typically worked in the cotton fields in gangs, hoeing, plowing, planting, weeding, and picking, and as house servants, cooks, and child caretakers. They often were whipped for failure to perform. The intensity of southern agricultural production resulted in degraded, exhausted soils — a deterioration only partially mitigated by corn-cotton rotations, the practice of grazing livestock in the harvested fields, and labor-intensive methods of weed and pest control (to remove the cotton bollworm, a moth larva).

The years following the Civil War saw the rise of sharecropping, in which landowners furnished land, tools, mules, seed, a cabin, and food in return for a share of the crop; tenant farming, in which farmers owned their own tools and mules but rented the land by returning a percentage of the crop; and the crop-lien system, in which farmers borrowed supplies from a merchant at interest in return for a portion of the forthcoming crop. One-third of all farmers, usually blacks and poor whites, were sharecroppers or tenants in 1880, and two-thirds were sharecroppers by 1920. The northward migration of the cotton boll weevil (a beetle) from Mexico after 1892 severely damaged cotton-crop yields and led to the expansion of the U.S. Agricultural Extension Service to assist farmers with methods of controlling the weevil and improving soil fertility.

ᴪ D O C U M E N T S

The documents look at the ways in which planters and slaves used the lands of the Lower South in the nineteenth and early twentieth centuries to produce marketable crops. Frances Anne Kemble, author of the first document, was an English actress who married the Philadelphian Pierce Butler, the heir to a Georgia plantation that began producing Sea Island cotton in the late eighteenth century. In the first document, taken from a journal of letters written in 1838–1839 to her friend Elizabeth Dwight Sedgwick of Massachusetts, Kemble describes her visit to her husband's holdings and her revulsion toward the slave system of cotton production in which, by virtue of her marriage, she participated. Her horror at the treatment of slaves contrasts sharply with her joy at the beauties of nature in the South. In the second document, Georgia planter John B. Lamar, in letters written in 1847 to his brother-in-law Howell Cobb, a member of Congress, discusses his acquisition of fertile cotton lands in newly settled Sumpter County, about sixty miles southwest of his headquarters in Macon, and his excitement at the prospect of huge cotton profits.

The third document comes from the travel accounts of New York landscape architect Frederick Law Olmsted, published in 1861. Olmstead covered several thousand miles in the southern states over fourteen months. He portrays a well-managed cotton plantation, as well as abandoned plantations and exhausted soils in Mississippi. The fourth document contains sharecroppers' contracts made after the Civil War between landowner A. T. Mial of Wake County, North Carolina, and croppers A. Robert Medlin in 1876 and Fenner Powell in 1886. Mial furnished each man the supplies and tools to grow crops in exchange for a portion of the forth-coming harvest.

The techniques of cotton planting, pest control, harvesting, and ginning are seen through the eyes of ex-slave Louis Hughes in the fifth document, excerpted from his book *Thirty Years a Slave* (1897). Prior to the use of pesticides, slave labor controlled the cotton bollworm, a moth larva, that destroyed cotton plants. The boll weevil, a beetle, invaded the Cotton South from Mexico beginning in 1892, moving northward in waves across Texas, Louisiana, Mississippi, Arkansas, and Oklahoma by 1910. In the sixth document, dating from 1903, the Louisiana

Boll Weevil Convention raises the alarm and advocates methods for arresting the weevil's progress, most of them ultimately to no avail. Despite the weevil's destruction and the reduction of yields by as much as 50 percent, cotton remained profitable in the Lower South into the early twentieth century.

During the Great Depression of the 1930s, the Federal Writers' Project of the WPA (Work Projects Administration) funded the interviewing of former slaves concerning their life experiences. In the seventh document, published in 1937, freed slaves Monroe Brackins, Andy J. Anderson, and Ellen Payne of Texas and Sarah Felder, Della Buckley, and John Belcher of Mississippi describe their reliance on fishing, hunting, poultry raising, and gardening to supplement their daily rations. In the final selection, part of the Folklore edition of the Federal Writers' Project, published in 1945, an anonymous ex-slave proposes an alternative "ecological" explanation of why the boll weevil came.

The documents as a whole suggest that the environmental history of the Cotton South could be told from several different perspectives: from that of a cotton planter, a slave, a particle of soil, — or even a boll weevil!

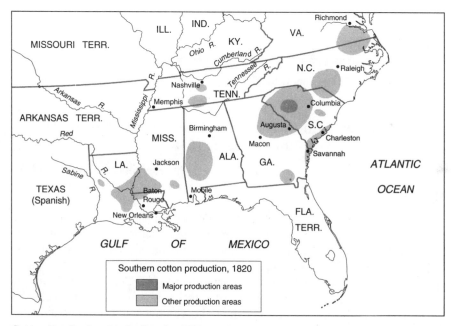

Cotton Production in the South, 1820

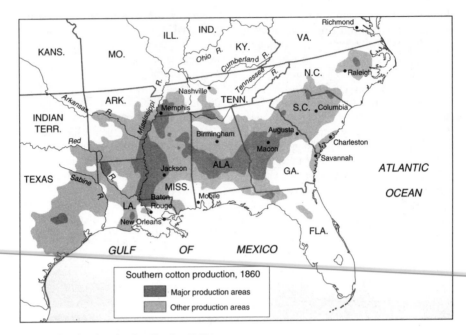

Cotton Production in the South, 1860

Frances Anne Kemble on Slavery and Nature in Georgia, 1838

[Philadelphia. December, 1838]

My dear E[lizabeth],

I return you Mr. _____'s letter. I do not think it answers any of the questions debated in our last conversation at all satisfactorily: the *right* one man has to enslave another, he has not the hardihood to assert; but in the reasons he adduces to defend that act of injustice, the contradictory statements he makes appear to me to refute each other. He says, that to the Continental European protesting against the abstract iniquity of slavery, his answer would be, "the slaves are infinitely better off than half the Continental peasantry"; to the Englishman, "they are happy compared with the miserable Irish." But supposing that this answered the question of original injustice, which it does not, it is not a true reply. Though the Negroes are fed, clothed, and housed, and though the Irish peasant is starved, naked, and roofless, the bare name of freemen — the lordship over his own person, the power to choose and will — are blessings beyond food, raiment, or shelter; possessing which, the want of every comfort of life is yet more tolerable than their fullest enjoyment without them. . . .

Mr. _____, and many others, speak as if there were a natural repugnance in all whites to any alliance with the black race; and yet it is notorious, that almost every Southern planter has a family more or less numerous of illegitimate colored children. Most certainly, few people would like to assert that such connections are formed because it is the *interest* of these planters to increase the number of their human property, and that they add to their revenue by the closest intimacy with creatures that they loathe, in order to reckon among their wealth the children of their body. . . . Now it appears very evident that there is no law in the white man's nature which prevents him from making a colored woman the mother of his children, but there *is* a law on his statute books forbidding him to make her his wife. . . . It seems almost as curious that laws should be enacted to prevent men marrying women toward whom they have an invincible natural repugnance, as that education should by law be prohibited to creatures [presumed] incapable of receiving it.

As for the exhortation with which Mr. _____ closes his letter, that I will not "go down to my husband's plantation prejudiced against what I am to find there," I know not well how to answer it. Assuredly I *am* going prejudiced against slavery, for I am an Englishwoman, in whom the absence of such a prejudice would be disgraceful. Nevertheless, I go prepared to find many mitigations in the practice to the general injustice and cruelty of the system — much kindness on the part of the masters, much content on that of the slaves; and I feel very sure that you may rely upon the carefulness of my observation, and the accuracy of my report, of every detail of the working of the thing that comes under my notice; and certainly, on the plantation to which I am going, it will be more likely that I should some things extenuate, than set down aught in malice.

St. Simons Island, [Georgia]
[Feburary 18, 1839]

Dearest E[lizabeth],

The cotton crop [here] is no longer by any means as paramount in value as it used to be, and the climate, soil, and labor of St. Simons are better adapted to old, young and feeble cultivators than the swamp fields of the rice island. I wonder if I ever told you of the enormous decrease in value of this same famous sea-island, long-staple cotton. When Major [Butler], Mr. [Butler]'s grandfather, first sent the produce of this plantation where we now are to England, it was of so fine a quality that it used to be quoted by itself in the Liverpool cotton market, and was then worth half a guinea a pound; it is now not worth a shilling a pound. This was told me by the gentleman in Liverpool who has been factor for this estate for thirty years. Such a decrease as this in the value of one's crop, and the steady increase at the same time of a slave population, now numbering between seven hundred and eight hundred bodies to clothe and house, mouths to feed, while the land is being exhausted by the careless and wasteful nature of the agriculture itself, suggests a pretty serious prospect of declining prosperity; and, indeed, unless these Georgia cotton planters can command more land, or lay abundant capital (which they have not, being almost all of them over head and ears in debt) upon that which has already spent its virgin vigor, it is a very obvious thing that they must all very soon be eaten up by their own property. The rice plantations are a great thing to fall back upon under these circumstances, and the rice crop is now quite as valuable, if not more so, than the cotton one on Mr. [Butler]'s estates, once so famous and prosperous through the latter.

[February 28–March 2, 1839]

Dear E[lizabeth],

[Today] I detained Louisa, whom I had never seen but in the presence of her old grandmother, whose version of the poor child's escape to, and hiding in the woods, I had a desire to compare with the heroine's own story.

She told it very simply, and it was most pathetic. She had not finished her task one day, when she said she felt ill, and unable to do so, and had been severely flogged by driver Bran, in whose "gang" she then was. The next day, in spite of this encouragement to labor, she had again been unable to complete her appointed work; and Bran having told her that he'd tie her up and flog her if she did not get it done, she had left the field and run into the swamp.

"Tie you up, Louisa!" said I; "what is that?"

She then described to me that they were fastened up by their wrists to a beam or a branch of a tree, their feet barely touching the ground, so as to allow them no purchase for resistance or evasion of the lash, their clothes turned over their heads, and their backs scored with a leather thong, either by the driver himself, or, if he pleases to inflict their punishment by deputy, any of the men he may choose to summon to the office; it might be father, brother, husband, or lover, if the overseer so ordered it. I turned sick, and my blood curdled listening to these details from the slender young slip of a lassie, with her poor piteous face and murmuring, pleading voice.

"Oh," said I, "Louisa; but the rattlesnakes — the dreadful rattlesnakes in the swamps; were you not afraid of those horrible creatures?"

"Oh, missis," said the poor child, "me no tink of dem; me forget all 'bout dem for de fretting."

"Why did you come home at last?"

"Oh, missis, me starve with hunger, me most dead with hunger before me come back."

"And were you flogged, Louisa?" said I, with a shudder at what the answer might be.

"No, missis, me go to hospital; me almost dead and sick so long, 'spec driver Bran him forgot 'bout de flogging."

I am getting perfectly savage over all these doings, E[lizabeth], and really think I should consider my own throat and those of my children well cut if some night the people were to take it into their heads to clear off scores in that fashion. . . .

I am helped to bear all that is so very painful to me here by my constant enjoyment of the strange, wild scenery in the midst of which I live, and which my resumption of my equestrian habits gives me almost daily opportunity of observing. I rode today to some new-cleared and plowed ground that was being prepared for the precious cotton crop. I crossed a salt marsh upon a raised causeway that was perfectly alive with land crabs, whose desperately active endeavors to avoid my horse's hoofs were so ludicrous that I literally laughed alone and aloud at them. The sides of this road across the swamp were covered with a thick and close embroidery of creeping moss, or rather lichens of the most vivid green and red: the latter made my horse's path look as if it was edged with an exquisite pattern of coral; it was like a thing in a fairy tale, and delighted me extremely.

I suppose, E[lizabeth], one secret of my being able to suffer as acutely as I do, without being made either ill or absolutely miserable, is the childish excitability of my temperament, and the sort of ecstasy which any beautiful thing gives me. No day, almost no hour, passes without some enjoyment of the sort this coral-bordered road gave me, which not only charms my senses completely at the time, but returns again and again before my memory, delighting my fancy, and stimulating my imagination. . . .

After my crab and coral causeway I came to the most exquisite thickets of evergreen shrubbery you can imagine. If I wanted to paint Paradise I would copy this undergrowth, passing through which I went on to the settlement at St. Annie's, traversing another swamp on another raised causeway. The thickets through which I next rode were perfectly draped with the beautiful wild jasmine of these woods. Of all the parasitical plants I ever saw, I do think it is the most exquisite in form and color, and its perfume is like the most delicate heliotrope.

I stopped for some time before a thicket of glittering evergreens, over which hung, in every direction, streaming garlands of these fragrant golden cups, fit for Oberon's banqueting service. These beautiful shrubberies were resounding with the songs of mockingbirds. I sat there on my horse in a sort of dream of enchantment, looking, listening, and inhaling the delicious atmosphere of those flowers.

A Georgia Planter Tells Why Cotton Pays, 1847

To Howell Cobb

Macon [Georgia], Jan. 10, 1847

. . . I have established a large planting interest in Sumpter, having purchased 2500 acres. Of this I have paid for one place 5500 $ already & have 1 & 2 years to pay 4000 for the other. Now you see at one extremity of this land & joining the first place I bought, I have a neighbor owning 600 acres of most superior land, which I shall buy to add to my last purchase, which will make me one place of unequalled fertility. And at the other extremity I have a chance of buying from an estate 1200 acres, joining the second purchase, which added to it will make a plantation scarcely inferior to the above named. All put together will make an investment of 24,000 $. I have already paid 5500 $. I shall be able to pay say 5000 $ out of the crop of this year. And then I shall have 14,000 $ to pay in one & two years. This is pretty extensive business for one so scary as I am about pecuniary responsibility. But I have ciphered it out and it can be done without risk. With the arable land I already have and what is on the two places to be purchased, considering the quality, for it is all fresh & rich as river bottoms, I can pay through easy. I have made my calculations safely. I have estimated my crops at 1/3rd less than an average & calculated on 6 cents per pound for cotton, & I can pay out & have a surplus. After this recital you see I shall be too heavy laden to take on the Baker place for the Trust estate until I get through with Sumpter.

Lord, Lord, Howell you and I have been too used to poor land to know what crops people are making in the rich lands of the new counties. I am just getting my eyes open to the golden view. On those good lands, when cotton is down to such a price as would starve us out, they can make money. I have moved 1/3rd of my force to Sumpter. I shall move another 1/3rd this fall or winter, leaving the remaining 1/3rd to cultivate the best lands on my Bibb place. This year I shall do better than I ever have done, & next year I shall do better than I ever expected to do. This year I shall cultivate very little poor land & next year I shall not waste labour on a foot of unprofitable soil. All will be of the 1st quality. When I work through I will try & help you onward to the promised land. But for 2 years after the present one, I shall be up to my chin in responsibility. I hate responsibility, but I have figured it out, that unless I take some as other prudent folks do I shall be like John Grier of Chack farm cultivating poor land all my life, which I am resolved not to do.

[John B. Lamar]

To Howell Cobb

Macon, May 16, 1847

. . . I have been asleep to my interests for 10 years. I have just woke up from a regular Rip Van Winkle nap & found every body round me advancing & I just holding my own on poor lands, that were (most of them) exhausted before I ever saw them. In my zeal of a new convert to the doctrine of "progress" — I went down to Sumpter and bought 17,500 $ worth of choice land while cotton was selling at 6 cents & land low in proportion. I have paid $5500 of that amount & if my crop this year don't pay the balance of 12,000 & leave me a handsome surplus I shall think myself very unlucky. And my planting arrangements are not this year fully developed either, as I do not get possession of one plantation (included in the above named purchase) until next Christmas. When I get that & divide my force into three plantations & cultivate lands as rich as any in Georgia, I shall begin to reap the benefits of my new energy.

[John B. Lamar]

Frederick Law Olmsted Describes Cotton Production and Environmental Deterioration, 1861

A Well-Managed Cotton Plantation

We had a good breakfast in the morning, and immediately afterward mounted and rode to a very large cotton-field, where the whole field-force of the plantation was engaged.

It was a first-rate plantation. On the highest ground stood a large and handsome mansion, but it had not been occupied for several years, and it was more than two years since the overseer had seen the owner. He lived several hundred miles away, and the overseer would not believe that I did not know him, for he was a rich man and an honorable, and had several times been where I came from — New York.

The whole plantation, including the swamp land around it, and owned with it, covered several square miles. It was four miles from the settlement to the nearest neighbor's house. There were between thirteen and fourteen hundred acres under cultivation with cotton, corn, and other hoed crops, and two hundred hogs running at large in the swamp. It was the intention that corn and pork enough should be raised to keep the slaves and cattle. This year, however, it has been found necessary to purchase largely, and such was probably usually the case, though the overseer intimated the owner had been displeased, and he "did not mean to be caught so bad again."

There were 135 slaves, big and little, of which 67 went to field regularly — equal, the overseer thought, to 60 able-bodied hands. Beside the field-hands, there were 3 mechanics (blacksmith, carpenter and wheelwright), 2 seamstresses, 1 cook, 1 stable servant, 1 cattle-tender, 1 hog-tender, 1 teamster, 1 house servant (overseer's cook), and one midwife and nurse. These were all first-class hands; most of them would be worth more, if they were for sale, the overseer said, than the best of field-hands. There was also a driver of a hoe-gang who did not labor personally, and a foreman of the plow-gang. These two acted as petty officers in the field, and alternately in the quarters.

There was a nursery for sucklings at the quarters, and twenty women at this time who left their work four times each day, for half an hour, to nurse their young ones, and whom the overseer counted as half-hands — that is, expected to do half an ordinary day's work.

Abandoned Plantations

I passed during the day four or five large plantations, the hill-sides gullied like icebergs, stables and negro quarters all abandoned, and given up to decay.

The virgin soil is in its natural state as rich as possible. At first it is expected to bear a bale and a half of cotton to the acre, making eight or ten bales for each able field-hand. But from the cause described its productiveness rapidly decreases.

Originally, much of this country was covered by a natural growth of cane, and by various nutritious grasses. A good northern farmer would deem it a crying shame and sin to attempt to grow any crops upon such steep slopes, except grasses or shrubs which do not require tillage. The waste of soil which attends the practice is much greater than it would be at the North, and, notwithstanding the unappeasable demand of the world for cotton, its bad economy, considering the subject nationally, can not be doubted.

If these slopes were thrown into permanent terraces, with turfed or stone-faced escarpments, the fertility of the soil might be preserved, even with constant tillage. In this way the hills would continue for ages to produce annual crops of greater value than those which are at present obtained from them at such destructive expense — from ten to twenty crops of cotton rendering them absolute deserts. But with negroes at $1000 a head and fresh land in Texas at $1 an acre, nothing of this sort can be thought of. The time will probably come when the soil now washing into the adjoining swamps will be brought back by our descendants, perhaps on their heads, in pots and baskets, in the manner Huc describes in China, which may be seen also in the Rhenish vineyards, to be relaid on the sunny slopes, to grow the luxurious cotton in.

Sharecroppers' Contracts, 1876–1886

STATE OF NORTH CAROLINA, Wake County

Articles of Agreement, Between *Alonzo T. Mial* of said County and State, of the first part, and *A. Robert Medlin* of the County and State aforesaid, of the second part, to secure an Agricultural Lien according to an Act of General Assembly of North Carolina, entitled "An Act to secure advances for Agricultural purposes":

Whereas, the said *A. R. Medlin* being engaged in the cultivation of the soil, and being without the necessary means to cultivate his crop, *The Said A. T. Mial* has agreed to furnish goods and supplies to the said *A. R. Medlin* to an amount not to exceed *One Hundred and fifty* Dollars, to enable him to cultivate and harvest his crops for the year 1876.

And in consideration thereof, the said *A. R. Medlin* doth hereby give and convey to the said *A. T. Mial* a LIEN upon all of his crops grown in said County in said year, on the lands described as follows: *The land of A. R. Medlin adjoining the lands of Nelson D. Pain Samuel Bunch & others*.

And further, in Consideration thereof, the said *A. R. Medlin* for One Dollar in hand paid, the receipt of which is hereby acknowledged, have bargained and sold, and by these presents do bargain, sell and convey unto the said *A. T. Mial his* heirs and assigns forever, the following described Real and Personal Property to-wit: *All of his Stock horses, Cattle Sheep and Hogs — Carts and Wagons House hold and kitchen furnishings*. To Have and to Hold the above described premises, together with the appurtenances thereof, and the above described personal property, to the said *A. T. Mial his* heirs and assigns.

The above to be null and void should the amount found to be due on account of said advancements be discharged on or before the *1st* day of *November* 1876: otherwise the said *A. T. Mial his* executors, administrators or assigns, are hereby authorized and empowered to seize the crops and Personal Property aforesaid, and sell the same, together with the above Real Estate, for cash, after first advertising the same for fifteen days, and the proceeds thereof apply to the discharge of this Lien, together with the cost and expenses of making such sale, and the surplus to be paid to the said *A. R. Medlin*, or his legal representatives.

IN WITNESS WHEREOF, The said parties have hereunto set their hands and seals this *29th* day of *February*, 1876.

his

A. Robert × Medlin, [seal]

mark

Witness: *L. D. Goodloe* [signed]   A. T. Mial [signed], [seal]

This contract made and entered into between A. T. Mial of one part and Fenner Powell of the other part both of the County of Wake and State of North Carolina —

Witnesseth — That the Said Fenner Powell hath bargained and agreed with the Said Mial to work as a cropper for the year 1886 on Said Mial's land on the land now occupied by Said Powell on the west Side of Poplar Creek and a point on the east Side of Said Creek and both South and North of the Mial road, leading to Raleigh, That the Said Fenner Powell agrees to work faithfully and dilligently without any unnecessary loss of time, to do all manner of work on Said farm as may be directed by Said Mial, And to be respectful in manners and deportment to Said Mial. And the Said Mial agrees on his part to furnish mule and feed for the same and all plantation tools and Seed to plant the crop free of charge, and to give the Said Powell One half of all crops raised and housed by Said Powell on Said land except the cotton seed. The Said Mial agrees to advance as provisions to Said Powell fifty pound of bacon and two sacks of meal pr month and occationally Some flour to be paid out of his the Said Powell's part of the crop or from any other advance that may be made to Said Powell by Said Mial. As witness our hands and seals this the 16th day of January A.D. 1886

A. T. Mial [signed] [Seal]

his

Fenner × Powell [Seal]

mark

Witness

W. S. Mial [signed]

Freed Slave Louis Hughes on Cotton and Cotton Worms, 1897

Cotton Raising

After the selection of the soil most suitable for cotton, the preparation of it was of vital importance. The land was deeply plowed, long enough before the time for planting to allow the spring rains to settle it. Then it was thrown into beds or ridges by turning furrows both ways toward a given center. The seed was planted at the rate of one hundred pounds per acre. The plant made its appearance in about ten days after planting, if the weather was favorable. Early planting, however, followed by cold, stormy weather frequently caused the seed to rot. As soon as the third leaf appeared the process of scraping commenced, which consisted of cleaning the ridge with hoes of all superfluous plants and all weeds and grass. After this a narrow plow known as a "bull tongue," was used to turn the loose earth around the plant and cover up any grass not totally destroyed by the hoes. If the surface was very rough the hoes followed, instead of preceding, the plow to unearth those plants that may have been partially covered. The slaves often acquired great skill in these operations, running plows within two inches of the stalks, and striking down weeds within half an inch with their hoes, rarely touching a leaf of the cotton. Subsequent plowing, alternating with hoeing, usually occurred once in twenty days. There was danger in deep plowing of injuring the roots, and this was avoided, except in the middle of rows in wet seasons when it was necessary to bury and more effectually kill the grass. The implements used in the culture of cotton were shovels, hoes, sweeps, cultivators, harrows and two kinds of plows. It required four months, under the most favorable circumstances, for cotton to attain its full growth. It was usually planted about the 1st of April, or from March 20th to April 10th, bloomed about the 1st of June and the first balls opened about August 15th, when picking commenced. The blooms come out in the morning and are fully developed by noon, when they are a pure white. Soon after meridian they begin to exhibit reddish streaks, and next morning are a clear pink. They fall off by noon of the second day.

The Cotton Worm

A cut worm was troublesome sometimes; but the plants were watched very carefully, and as soon as any signs of worms were seen work for their destruction was commenced. The majority of the eggs were laid upon the calyx and involucre. The worm, after gnawing through its enclosed shell, makes its first meal upon the part of the plant upon which the egg was laid, be it leaf, stem or involucre. If it were laid upon the leaf, as was usually the case, it might be three days before the worm reached the boll; but were the eggs laid upon the involucre the worm pierced through within twenty-four hours after hatching. The newly hatched boll worm walks like a geometrical larva or looper, a measuring worm as it was called. This is easily explained by the fact that while in the full grown worm the abdominal legs, or pro legs, are nearly equal in length, in the newly hatched worm the second pair are slightly shorter than the third, and the first pair are shorter and slenderer than the second — a state of things approaching that in the full grown cotton worm, though the difference in size in the former case is not nearly so marked as in the latter. This method of walking is lost with the first or second molt. There is nothing remarkable about these young larvæ. They seem to be thicker in proportion to their length than the young cotton worms, and they have not so delicate and transparent an appearance. Their heads are black and their bodies seem already to have begun to vary in color. The body above is furnished with sparse, stiff hairs, each arising from a tubercle. I have often watched the newly hatched boll while in

The cotton bollworm.

the cotton fields. When hatched from an egg which had been deposited upon a leaf, they invariably made their first meal on the substance of the leaf, and then wandered about for a longer or shorter space of time, evidently seeking a boll or flower bud. It was always interesting to watch this seemingly aimless search of the young worm, crawling first down the leaf stem and then back, then dropping a few inches by a silken thread and then painfully working its way back again, until, at last, it found the object of its search, or fell to the ground where it was destroyed by ants. As the boll worms increase in size a most wonderful diversity of color and marking becomes apparent. In color different worms will vary from a brilliant green to a deep pink or dark brown, exhibiting almost every conceivable intermediate stage from an immaculate, unstriped specimen to one with regular spots and many stripes. The green worms were more common than those of any other color — a common variety was a very light green. When these worms put in an appearance it raised a great excitement among the planters. We did not use any poison to destroy them, as I learn is the method now employed.

The Cotton Harvest

The cotton harvest, or picking season, began about the latter part of August or first of September, and lasted till Christmas or after, but in the latter part of July picking commenced for "the first bale" to go into the market at Memphis. This picking was done by children from nine to twelve years of age and by women who were known as "suckers," that is, women with infants. The pickers would pass through the rows getting very little, as the cotton was not yet in full bloom. From the lower part of the stalk where it opened first is where they got the first pickings. The season of first picking was always a great time, for the planter who brought the first bale of cotton into market at Memphis was presented with a basket of champagne by the commission merchants. This was a custom established throughout Mississippi. After the first pickings were secured the cotton developed very fast, continuing to bud and bloom all over the stalk until the frost falls. The season of picking was exciting to all planters, every one was zealous in pushing his slaves in order that he might reap the greatest possible harvest. The planters talked about their prospects, discussed the cotton markets, just as the farmers of the north discuss the markets for their products. I often saw Boss so excited and nervous during the season he scarcely ate. The daily task of each able-bodied slave during the cotton picking season was 250 pounds or more, and all those who did not come up to the required amount would get a whipping. When the planter wanted more cotton picked than usual, the overseer would arrange a race. The slaves would be divided into two parties, with a leader for each party. The first leader would choose a slave for his side, then the second leader one for his, and so on alternately until all were chosen. Each leader tried to get the best on his side. They would all work like good fellows for the prize, which was a tin cup of sugar for each slave on the winning side. The contest was kept up for three days whenever the planter desired an extra amount picked. The slaves were just as interested in the races as if they were going to get a five dollar bill.

Preparing Cotton for Market

The gin-house was situated about four hundred yards from "the great house" on the main road. It was a large shed built upon square timbers, and was similar to a barn, only it stood some six feet from the ground, and underneath was located the machinery for running the gin. The cotton was put into the loft after it was dried, ready for ginning. In this process the cotton was dropped from the loft to the man who fed the machine. As it was ginned the lint would go into the lint room, and the seed would drop at the feeder's feet. The baskets used for holding lint were twice as large as those used in the picking process, and they were never taken from the gin house. These lint baskets were used in removing the lint from the lint room to the place where the cotton was baled. A bale contained 250 pounds, and the man who did the treading of the cotton into the bales would not vary ten pounds in the bale, so accustomed was he to the packing. Generally from fourteen to fifteen bales of cotton were in the lint room at a time.

Other Farm Products

Cotton was the chief product of the Mississippi farms and nothing else was raised to sell. Wheat, oats and rye were raised in limited quantities, but only for the slaves and the stock. All the fine flour for the master's family was bought in St. Louis. Corn was raised in abundance, as it was a staple article of food for the slaves. It was planted about the 1st of March, or about a month earlier than the cotton. It was, therefore, up and partially worked before the cotton was planted and fully tilled before the cotton was ready for cultivation. Peas were planted between the rows of corn, and hundreds of bushels were raised. These peas after being harvested, dried and beaten out of the shell, were of a reddish brown tint, not like those raised for the master's family, but they were considered a wholesome and nutritious food for the slaves. Cabbage and yams, a large sweet potato, coarser than the kind generally used by the whites and not so delicate in flavor, were also raised for the servants in liberal quantities. No hay was raised, but the leaves of the corn, stripped from the stalks while yet green, cured and bound in bundles, were used as a substitute for it in feeding horses.

Farm Implements

Almost all the implements used on the plantation were made by the slaves. Very few things were bought. Boss had a skilled blacksmith, uncle Ben, for whom he paid $1,800, and there were slaves who were carpenters and workers in wood who could turn their hands to almost anything. Wagons, plows, harrows, grubbing hoes, hames, collars, baskets, bridle bits and hoe handles were all made on the farm and from the material which it produced, except the iron. The timber used in these implements was generally white or red oak, and was cut and thoroughly seasoned long before it was needed. The articles thus manufactured were not fine in form or finish, but they were durable, and answered the purposes of a rude method of agriculture. Horse collars were made from corn husks and from poplar bark which was stripped from the tree, in the spring, when the sap was up and it was soft and pliable, and separated into narrow strips which were plaited together. These collars were easy for the horse, and served the purpose of the more costly leather collar. Every season at least 200 cotton baskets were made. One man usually worked at this all the year round, but in the spring he had three assistants. The baskets were made from oak timber, grown in the home forests and prepared by the slaves. It was no small part of the work of the blacksmith and his assistant to keep the farm implements in good repair, and much of this work was done at night. All the plank used was sawed by hand from timber grown on the master's land, as there were no saw mills in that region. Almost the only things not made on the farm which were in general use there were axes, trace chains and the hoes used in cultivating the cotton.

The Clearing of New Land

When additional land was required for cultivation the first step was to go into the forest in summer and "deaden" or girdle the trees in a given tract. This was cutting through the bark all around the trunk about thirty inches from the ground. The trees so treated soon died and in a year or two were in condition to be removed. The season selected for clearing the land was winter, beginning with January. The trees, except the larger ones, were cut down, cut into lengths convenient for handling and piled into great heaps, called "log heaps," and burned. The undergrowth was grubbed out and also piled and burned. The burning was done at night and the sight was often weird and grand. The chopping was done by the men slaves and the grubbing by women. All the trees that blew down during the summer were left as they fell till winter when they were removed. This went on, year after year, until all the trees were cleared out. The first year after the new land was cleared corn was put in, the next season cotton. As a rule corn and cotton were planted alternately, especially if the land was poor, if not, cotton would be continued year after year on the same land. Old corn stalks were always plowed under for the next year's crop and they served as an excellent fertilizer. Cotton was seldom planted on newly cleared land, as the roots and stumps rendered it difficult to cultivate the land without injury to the growing plant.

I never saw women put to the hard work of grubbing until I went to McGee's and I greatly wondered at it. Such work was not done by women slaves in Virginia. Children were required to do some work, it mattered not how many grown people were working. There were always tasks set for the boys and girls ranging in age from nine to thirteen years, beyond these ages they worked with the older slaves. After I had been in Pontotoc [Mississippi] two years I had to help plant and hoe, and work in the cotton during the seasons, and soon learned to do everything pertaining to the farm.

A Louisiana Convention Declares War on the Boll Weevil, 1903

At noon on the 30th Nov., the Convention was called to order in the Odd Fellows Hall, in the City of New Orleans, by the temporary chairman, Abe Brittin, President of the N. O. Cotton Exchange, who spoke as follows:

"I bring you

GREETINGS FROM THE COTTON EXCHANGE

which extends you its privileges while you are in the city, and will co-operate with you in any movement for the extermination of the Mexican cotton boll weevil.

"You are called upon to consider ways and means for arresting the further progress of the pest. More than this, you are expected to devise means to permanently exterminate the weevil. It is folly to say that this cannot be accomplished. It can be accomplished; it must be accomplished; it will be accomplished. When the vineyards of France were threatened, France produced her Pasteur, and the vineyards were saved. America will produce her Pasteur, and the cotton fields will be saved.

"Last September I said that the most momentous peril involved in the cotton outlook was the Mexican cotton boll weevil. The evil is spreading, and eventually it will spread from Texas to other States. The seriousness of the situation should be brought to the attention of the Government.

"With the increased acreage, improved fertilizers and methods of culture, we are to-day five years away from the production of a maximum crop. This has not occurred in twenty-five years, and, if we except the period of the Civil War, it has never occurred in the history of the South. Production is not keeping pace with consumption, and if this condition be not relieved, some other section of the world will produce the cotton needed. This should not be. This may be a time for the States to hedge the weevil in or out, but the paramount responsibility rests upon the National Government. And we need not go to Congress as mendicants, but, with heads erect, present the situation, and say that if it would protect the industry, a remedy must be found. . . ."

At the conclusion of his remarks, Mr. Brittin introduced the permanent Chairman,

HON. CHAS. SCHULER,

who spoke as follows:

"Gentlemen of the Convention and Brother Farmers Interested in the Culture of Cotton: This Convention has been called by His Excellency, the Governor of this State, with a view to consulting with the people most interested in the welfare of the State and the cotton industry, to see whether it is necessary to call an extra session of the Legislature to take steps and pass laws by which to check the progress of the insect that is threatening the welfare not only of the State, but of the country.

"The State of Louisiana is threatened on the west by an insect known as the Mexican cotton-boll weevil. It has been a mystery to me that the great State of Texas, with its immense territory from west to east, would permit an insect to destroy millions of its property without any effort, so far as I know, on the part of the State to check its course. How was it that the veterans who sacrificed their property and their lives to drive back the human vermin that infested their State would suffer this insect to overwhelm them? If we consider the amount of money that is in circulation; if we consider the number of people that live upon the production and handlings of this staple, we can realize the immense importance of the crop.

VALUE OF COTTON

during the month of October, in this last year—one month, no more—amounted to $60,000,000. Does any individual, knowing this, think that the

National Government could afford to keep hands off and not render help in this crisis? Some of us who are old enough remember the effect on the National Treasury when the exportation of cotton was prohibited by blockade.

"Sometimes we hear of men saying that it will be a blessing in disguise; that we cotton planters ought to learn to plant lettuce, cabbage, onions, etc., in order to make a profit. Now, every cotton planter here present knows how absolutely foolish this is. Others say that it will prove a blessing in disguise, because we can get 50 cents a pound for cotton. But they forget that the balance of the world is making heroic efforts to grow this very staple in other portions of the world. . . .

The next speaker was

PROF. H. A. MORGAN,

Station Entomologist. He said:

HOW TO PROTECT LOUISIANA AGAINST THE INVASION OF THE BOLL WEEVIL.

We are confronted to-day with a problem of very difficult solution. To successfully overcome, or even to retard for a few years, the entrance of the Mexican boll weevil into Louisiana will require the united efforts of every one interested in Louisiana's future.

All effective preventive and remedial measures used against the injurious insects of the world are the outcome of careful investigation and study of life-cycles and habits and of the conditions peculiar to the locality where these remedies are put into operation. Unless the work against the weevil is based upon all the known facts of its habits and development, and upon the conditions peculiar to the section of country where the warfare is to be carried on, the results will be disappointing and harmful. . . .

The weevil belongs to that division of insects which have complete metamorphoses — i.e., there are four stages in the existence of each weevil, viz: the egg, the grub or worm stage, the pupa, sometimes called "the kicker," stage, and finally the adult or sexually mature form — the weevil. The adults, or

The mature boll-weevil. Note the *two* projections at the outer end of the first joint of the front legs.

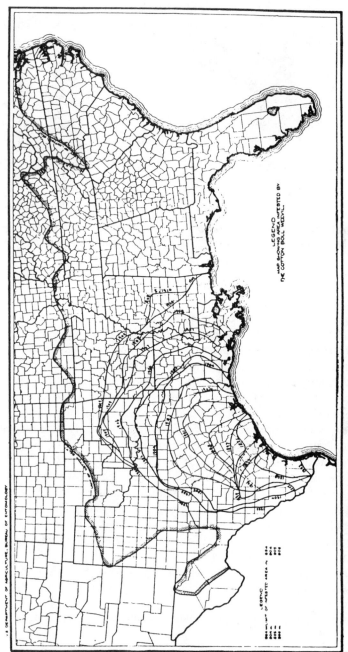

Map showing the areas infested by the boll-weevil each year from 1892 to August 1910

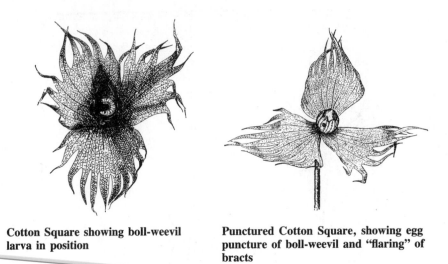

Cotton Square showing boll-weevil larva in position

Punctured Cotton Square, showing egg puncture of boll-weevil and "flaring" of bracts

weevils, live through the winter among material of various kinds. Grass, leaves, bark of trees and trash of any kind in the cotton field or in close proximity to it, offer suitable hibernating quarters. That weevils do not migrate far is clearly indicated in the great saving to a cotton crop where fall plowing of all infected cotton fields is practiced after the cotton stalks and other trash have been raked up and thoroughly burned. The weevils that survive the hibernating period emerge from winter quarters in the spring and feed upon volunteer or planted cotton. In the forms or squares eggs (one in each square) are deposited. The eggs hatch in a day or two into the worms (grubs or larvae), which feed upon the contents of the squares for from eight to twenty days, depending upon the temperature. The grubs at the end of the existence of this stage assume the pupa or kicker condition, and in from five to twelve days the weevils emerge from the pupae and are soon ready to lay eggs. Two facts must be here emphasized, viz: that the entire early life is completely concealed in the square or boll, and that the length of the cycle of development depends upon food and temperature conditions. In early and late summer thirty or more days may be consumed in the transformation from egg to weevil, while in midsummer only fifteen to twenty are required.

During winter the weevil does not require food, but in spring, summer and fall, when life's functions are active, food is essential.

COTTON IS THE ONLY KNOWN FOOD PLANT

In the . . . absence of cotton the weevils die in summer. . . .

When squares are punctured and eggs deposited in them they invariably fall to the ground, where, in the shade of the plant, the weevil goes on developing until its life cycle is completed. The sun's heat frequently dries up fallen squares before the weevils are mature, and hence the value of planting cotton in wide rows and plenty of distance between the plants in the row in weevil-infected cotton lands.

In the presence of sufficient food the boll weevil does not range extensively, and hence cultural methods that will limit the number of weevils during the active breeding season is of the utmost importance in checking the migration of the weevil to other fields and States. It therefore seems plain that the wide distribution of the weevil each year is not due so much to the ranging or migratory habits of the weevil itself, but to the distribution of material such as cotton, cottonseed, hay and other products from infected lands, in and upon which the weevil may be resting or hibernating. The cotton gin is a focal point for weevils, which are gathered in seed cotton, and the cottonseed a distributing medium, especially in the spring of the year.

Among the suggestions as to how best to protect Louisiana against the invasion of the boll weevil, none seem more important than the one whereby every planter in the State shall become conversant with all the known facts associated with the life and habits of the weevil in order that he may scrupulously avoid its importation and understand the very best means of eradicating it, should isolated outbreaks appear. For a number of years the United States Department of Agriculture and the Experiment Station authorities of Texas have been earnestly at work to develop methods of successfully combatting the weevil. The result of these investigations have so far established that insecticides are useless, and that the clean culture of early varieties of cotton make it possible to grow a profitable crop. The number of weevils in infected fields is limited by these cultural methods until the cotton plants have had time to mature their fruit. When these cultural methods are adopted the natural range or overflow of the weevil is minimized, but, unfortunately for Texas, and to the great regret of the planters of Louisiana, these suggestions have not been universally put into practice, and the consequent increase of the infected area has become alarming. The weevil area of Texas has spread until it is only a few miles from the western border of our State, and from this time out it behooves us to guard zealously our borders, quarantine against infected products and to adopt reasonable methods of preventing the natural and general spread of this pest throughout Louisiana.

A NON-INFECTED COTTON ZONE

lies between the borders of Louisiana and the weevil fields of Texas. This zone will protect us in a very great measure from gross infection next year, provided the utmost care is exercised in preventing infected products, particularly cotton seed, hulls, hay and corn, from entering our State. The most serious impediment to the prosecution of preventive measures is the indifference of many of our farmers and planters as to the seriousness and extreme gravity of the situation, and hence I wish again to emphasize the great need of an educational campaign along the western border of our State that will arouse every man to the necessity of intelligent, uniform and immediate action.

Should the weevil appear next spring and summer in isolated fields of the western border of this State, such fields should be immediately quarantined, and all infected plants destroyed. The adult weevils may be gathered from a few trap plants left for this purpose. Upon this area and on adjacent fields no cotton should be grown the following year, in order to completely starve out any forms that may have escaped.

Ex-Slaves Describe Their Means of Subsistence, 1937
Monroe Brackins

We had possums and coons to eat sometimes. My father, he generally cooked the coons; he would dress them and stew them and then bake them. My mother would eat them. There were plenty of rabbits, too. Sometimes when they had taters, they cooked them with them. I remember one time they had just a little patch of blackhead sugar cane. After the freedom, my mother had a kind of garden, and she planted snap beans and watermelons pretty much every year.

The master fed us tolerably well. Everything was wild; beef was free, just had to bring one in and kill it. Once in a while, on a Sunday morning, we'd get biscuit flour bread to eat. It was a treat to us. They measured the flour out, and it had to pan out just like they measured. He gave us a little something every Christmas and something good to eat. I heard my people say coffee was high, at times, and I know we didn't get no flour, only Sunday morning. We lived on cornbread, mostly, and beef and game out of the woods. That was during the [Civil] war and after the war, too.

Andy J. Anderson

I'm going to explain how it was managed on Master Haley's plantation. It was sort of like a little town, because everything we used was made right there. There was the shoemaker, and he was the tanner and made the leather from the hides. Master had about a thousand sheep, and he got the wool, and the niggers carded and spinned, and wove it, and that made all the clothes. Then master had cattle and such to provide the milk and the butter and beef meat for eating. Then he had the turkeys and chickens and the hogs and the bees. With all that, we never were hungry.

The plantation was planted in cotton, mostly, with the corn and wheat a little, because master didn't need much of them. He never sold anything but the cotton.

Ellen Payne

I mostly minded the calves and chickens and turkeys. Massa Evans used an overseer, but he didn't allow him to cut and slash his niggers, and we didn't have a hard taskmaster. There were about thirty slaves on the farm, but I am the only one living now. I loved all my white folks, and they were sweet to us.

The hands worked from sun to sun and had a task at night. Some spun or made baskets or chair bottoms or knitted socks. Some of the young ones courted and some just rambled around most all night.

Excerpts from Sarah Felder, Della Buckley, and John Belcher reprinted by permission of Greenwood Publishing Group, Inc., Westport, CT, from *The American Slave: A Composite Autobiography.* Vols. 6, 7 of *Mississippi Narratives* edited by George P. Rawick, excerpts from pp. 46–7, 300–302, 110–113. Copyright © 1977.

There was always plenty to eat, and one nigger didn't do anything but raise gardens. They hunted coon and possum and rabbits with dogs, and the white folks killed deer and big game like that. My daddy always had some money because he made baskets and chair bottoms and sold them, and massa Evans gave every slave a patch to work, and they could sell what it produced and keep the money.

Sarah Felder

I allus planted my garden in de moon, an' iffen you plant beans or cucumbers when de sign is in de arm yer will allus hev big bunches of beans ter cum at one time, cause dat is when de sign means twins.

Iffen you want good luck ter cum ter you, when you see er white mule, jes stamp him, by wettin' yer finger an' hittin de palm uf yer hand an' yer will hev good luck fur dat day; an' iffen yer see a bussard dat same day yer will hev good luck all dat week.

When we wus chulluns old Mandy uster mek 'teas an' give us ter keep us well, an' I larnt how ter doctor my chaps dat same way, an' dat beats eny doctor you ebery seed. Iffen dar is whoopin' cough in de neighborhood, jes tie er lil'l 'asfiddy' in er rag an' tie it round yer neck an' yer wont hev whoppin' cough.

I am old now an' de young folks doan think we old folks hev eny sense, but dar is er lotter things I culd tell dem iffen I wuld, but when dey git sick dey hev ter buy store bought medicine.

I am not able ter wurk now, but I hev seed de time when I culd beat eny uf de niggers wurkin' in de fiel' an' doin' all my wurk at de house, an' tendin' ter de chaps as well. None uf dese young one can do dat now.

We allus walked whar eber we wint an' dese young folks say dey cant walk now er day, an' de want er fine car an' go in debt fur it ter git it.

Della Buckley

I aint never studied 'bout how old I is; that's sumpen I aint never paid any 'tention to. I was bornd in Montgomery on the East'ley plantation, kinder out in the country, you know. The lady I nuss'd fer was all time travelin' back an' fofe ter Mer-*ree*-dian ter see her husband; he worked in an' outer there; an' fine-ly she 'come on' ter Mer-*ree*-dian fer good an' I come with her.

When I was 'bout grown, I started cookin' but I learned ter cook good befo' I started workin' fer Boss Williams an' Ol' Miss. I 'speck I was 'bout thirty-five then. I mar'ied right here in my own house in they backyard, mar'ied Pretty. Yas'm, that's what they calls him, 'cause he's so ugly, I reckon. I been had fo' chullen but they all dead.

They do say I cooks right good, must er been cookin' fer 'em might 'nigh forty years. They all time havin' comp'ny. When Boss's gent'mun friends comes from New York an' Baltimore, they brags right smart on my spoon-bread an' sech. But they aint but one sho' 'nough way ter cook a possum. I'll tell you jes how I does it.

Firs', you gits the boy ter clean him fer you, scrape him twell he git white. Then you soaks him all night in salten water; take him out in the mornin' an' *dreen* him an' wipe him off nice an' dry; then you par-boils him a while. Then you takes him out an' grease him all over with butter an' rub flour all over him an' rub pepper in with it. Then you bas'e him with some er the juice what you par-boiled him in. Then you puts him in the stove an' lets him bake. Ever' time you opens the stove do', you bas'es him with he gravy. Peel yo sweet pertaters an' bake along with him twell they is nice an' sof' an' brown like the possum hisse'f. Sprinkle in flour ter thicken yo gravy jes' like you was makin' reg'lar chicken gravy. When he's nice an' brown, you puts a pertater in he mouf an' one on each side, an' yo possum is ready ter eat.

Yas'm, I been sailin' right high all my life. When you comin' ter dinner with us again?

John Belcher

I fishes wid a pole and line all together. I got no license but I sells all I cotch. I jes walks up an down de river bank an fishes. Once I cotch a 59 pound cat fish. I wuz livin on a farm, on Mr. Duncan McCloud's place, bout ten years ago. I had set my pole and gone back to de house fer supper. 'fore goin to bed I sont one of de boys down to see effen dere wuz any thing on de line and after a while hearin' so much fuss down dar I lit de lamp and went down to see bout it. I shore wuz 'sprised; we did'n know, for sho, what wux on dat line. I got a boat and 'tween us we bringed dat fish in. It took us two hours to land him as he weighed 59 pounds. We et fish fer three or four days and give all de folks roun fish, too.

Fer catchin' Buffalo now I uses flour dough an a little corn meal, mixed wid a little cotton worked in it, fer bait. Durin de time I'm not fishin I puts two or three "Draws" out in different places on de river. To make dese "Draws" I puts chops, corn meal, or bread, in a crocker sack making a roll bout 12 inches long by 10 inches wide. I attach a wire to dis and anchor de wire to a stob long de river bank. I leaves dis here fer bout 8 days to toll de fish to dis spot. When I gits ready to fish dere I partly draws dis wire in den drap in my line and I really catches dem buffaloe.

In de spring an summer I uses earth worms and chicken entrails fer bait. But the best trick of all, I doan want no one to know dis trick, Mis is dis. Git ten cents worth of olive oil, mix wid a pint of waste oil from a filling station, mix wid about 1/2 pint of coal oil. Put all dis in a big fruit jar and shake rale good. Drap yo fish line and hooks in dis den put a little bait on yo hook and when de fish smells dis dey sho come.

Yas'm I used to hunt lots. De way I cotch wild turkeys I'd roost him at night, you know when you hears em settlin on a limb, sorta rustlin dere wings, I'd spot him and git dere fore he left nex mornin and shoot him, fore day light.

I use to set traps fer deer. You take a stick 'bout 3 feet long sharpen it at one end and put it in de ground leanin toward a rail fence. One stick on the inside and one on the outside. When de deer jumped over dat fence the stob snagged him. I'se cot several dat way. A old Indian taught me dat trick when I lived in Florida. I fergits de name of dat swamp but dere wuz lots of Indians dere and Deer, too.

We use to cotch seven or eight possums a night. We used dogs, to tree em den we'd shake em out on de ground and de dogs would catch em. Effen one uf us had to clamb a tree we'd allus leave one man on de ground to catch em. Sometimes we'd git mixed up wid a coon and a coon can whip two or three good dogs.

One wild cat could run a set (4) of dogs down any time. We used to take after a cat and as fast as one would run one set of dogs down we'd set another set on him. It took bout twelve hours to run a cat down. After the dogs would bay him den we'd shoot him or kill him some way. Once a wild cat runned a white lady, school teacher, and most scared her to death. He wuz a big one and we had a time catchin him. Dis wuz in Monroe County, Alabama.

In Clark County, Alabam between the Alabama and Tombigbee Rivers Mr. Allan Holder used to set his double barrel shot gun, lay it in a way and setting the trigger wid a string tied to it. He'd load dat gun wid 12 or 18 buck shot and some powder, in each barrel. He killed bear dis way. Dat bear would trip over de string and de gun would go off an kill him. I'se helped him bring in, sometimes, two and three a week dat he killed dis way.

A Freed Slave Explains "Why That Boll Weevil Done Come," 1945

I knows why that boll weevil done come. They say he come from Mexico, but I think he always been here. Away back yonder a spider live in the country, 'specially in the bottoms. He live on the cotton leaves and stalks, but he don't hurt it. These spiders kept the insects eat up. They don't plow deep then, and plants cotton in February, so it made 'fore the insects git bad.

Then they gits to plowing deep, and it am colder 'cause the trees all cut, and they plows up all the spiders and the cold kill them. They plants later, and there ain't no spiders left to eat up the boll weevil.

⚲ *E S S A Y S*

The essays emphasize different aspects of Cotton South agriculture, soils, and pests. Albert Cowdrey, an environmental historian of the South from the U.S. Army Center of Military History, in the first essay takes up the soils and environmental conditions of the Lower South that made cotton production feasible, as well as the row-crop monocultures of corn and cotton that resulted in soil erosion and toxicity, parasites, and pest outbreaks. Whereas Cowdrey associates soil degradation with the technological characteristics of row-crop cultivation, Eugene Genovese, a historian at the University Center of Georgia, in the second essay ascribes it to the slave system of production. "Slavery and the plantation system," he argues, "led to agricultural methods that depleted the soil." Slavery was not conducive to the care and attention that the application of fertilizers required, and the use of cotton-corn rotations alone did not return sufficient fertility to the soil. Yet ending slavery did not lead to the restoration of soil fertility, as historian Peter Daniel of the Smithsonian Institution argues in the third essay. Sharecropping, farm tenancy, and the crop-lien systems that replaced slavery perpetuated soil degradation as power was consolidated in the hands of landlords, merchants, banks, and loan companies. Government assistance provided by the U.S. Department of

Agriculture and its Cooperative Extension Service introduced agricultural improvements and pest controls while educating farmers about better methods. Despite the additional efforts of black extension agents to aid African-American farmers, however, agricultural improvement primarily reached only well-to-do black and white farmers.

Soils Used

ALBERT COWDREY

The expansion of the South across the Appalachians and the Mississippi River to the fringes of the high plains was one of the great American folk wanderings. Motivated by the longing for fresh and cheap land, and by obscurer urges, such as simple restlessness and the large human capacity for dissatisfaction, southerners completed their occupation of a region as large as western Europe. Despite the variety of the land — which contained regions of pine barrens and prairies, of hardwood forests and limey plateaus, of some of the world's oldest mountains and a considerable part of its third longest river — and the variety of the societies from which they came, the settlers of the Southwest had certain broad similarities. They might be farmers large or small, but most farmed or lived by serving the needs of farmers. Their way of dealing with the wild assumed each man's right to use beasts and timber as he saw fit. Not all owned or ever would own slaves, but most accepted slavery as a mode of holding and creating wealth. Throughout the Southwest a burgeoning democracy amplified the folk voice for both good and ill. . . .

In 1803 the Louisiana Purchase added to the South a new city, a new culture, and a new physiographic region. Indeed, several regions, for beyond the western escarpment of the alluvial valley stretched forested hills giving way to treeless plains which were to mark for the white and black South, as they had for the red, an indefinite yet enduring cultural boundary.

Dominating the immediate area of settlement was the Mississippi, which had created the alluvial valley. From Missouri's Commerce Hills to the sea 600 miles to the south, the river expanded during floodtime to cover vast areas of bottomland, precipitating its heavier alluvium to form natural levees, and carrying finely-divided clays back into the swamps. Human settlement gravitated to these natural levees to be safe from floods, to exploit their fertility, and to use the river for transport. The Franco-Spanish Creole culture of the valley showed in this respect certain similarities to the Mississippian Indian culture, whose remnants it encountered among the Natchez and helped to destroy.

The settlers grew rice because the land behind the levees was easily flooded, and maize, which as usual established itself as the food of the poor. A modest tobacco industry grew up, and indigo, as well, until destroyed in the 1790s by Asian competition and local insects. Experiments began with sugar cane, a much-travelled plant, which had been carried from India to Spain by the

Excerpts from Albert E. Cowdrey. *This Land, This South: An Environmental History*, 1983, reprinted by permission of the University of Kentucky Press.

Muslims, by the Spanish to the New World, and by the French from Haiti to Louisiana. . . .

Across much of the new territory south and east of the Appalachians rose the phenomenon of the Cotton Kingdom. The development in the late eighteenth century of an efficient gin for separating the lint and seeds of short-staple cotton is a justly famous example of the impact of technology on culture. It is also true that the culture was in search of the technology. To fuel an expansion of the character and speed that occurred between 1790 and 1837, the South needed some commercial crop adapted to the climate, demanded by the overseas market, and suitable for production in circumstances ranging from the frontier farm to the great plantation. The fact that the English textile industry was already mechanizing made this crop particularly timely. Cotton as a great staple was invented as much as grown, made to order for the place and time. Early in the nineteenth century Mexican cotton was introduced, because its "large wide-open bolls" facilitated picking and greatly increased the amount that a worker could gather in a day. . . .

Like the crop itself, the boundaries of the Cotton Kingdom were determined by tacit agreement between [humans] and nature. Antebellum opinion sometimes held that, roughly speaking, the southern border of Pennsylvania, extended west, marked the limit of profitable production. With few exceptions, however, the actual dimensions of the region were smaller. A better boundary was the 77°F summer isotherm. This line runs roughly from the northeastern border of North Carolina, dipping south of the Appalachian massif, and rising to the northwestern border of Tennessee. West of the Mississippi it skirts the Ozark highlands and rises again to north-central Oklahoma. On occasion cotton was grown commercially north of this line in response to high prices — notably in southern Virginia and the Nashville basin. Noncommercial production for household use was also common. But in general terms, this was the boundary of the Cotton Kingdom. Northward, cotton grew well enough in mild years but poorly in cool ones; in short, it was not a money crop that could be depended upon. The line was a limit defined partly by the human need for consistency in a commercial undertaking, partly by the nature of the plant itself. . . .

Between 1800 and 1860 Georgia's white population increased about nine times, Louisiana's and Tennessee's about ten times, Mississippi's about one hundred times, Arkansas's over four hundred times, and Alabama's about one thousand times. (Such figures of course indicate not only the rapidity of settlement but the initial lack of a white populace in the middle Gulf region.) . . .

The Cotton Kingdom made rapid conquests, not only in the middle Gulf region, but along the lower Mississippi River and its tributaries. Prior to the War of 1812 cotton production in Louisiana had been comparatively small (two million pounds estimated for 1811). But the fiber was already being grown in the Natchez area, and between 1810 and 1820 it made rapid progress in Louisiana, as well, spreading into the Attakapas and Opelousas regions and up the Red River. Soon settlers, led by squatters and harassed by federal troops trying to protect Indian lands, were entering the region where Louisiana, Arkansas, and Texas later met.

* * * *

As long as prices held and erosion was a process only beginning, the Cotton Kingdom throve. Acreage, production, and yield all grew, and would continue to do so until 1890 or so. Especially during the 1850s the mood of the cotton planters was ebullient, as reflected in their journals. Profits were good and "slavery itself was generally returning high profits to those who invested in that peculiar institution." The question of whether the antebellum South was able, in the face of its commercial commitments, to feed itself remains in doubt. A complex of many subregions, the South defies summary on this point; by and large it probably did so, though considerable food was imported from the West, as well.

Triumphant agriculture took out heavy liens against the natural dower. Row crops bared the soil, the rows made watercourses for the rains, which were heavy, and the colonial practice of plowing straight up and down hills was by no means extirpated. Further, any system which covers too many fields with the same plant falls afoul of the ecological principle which states that the simplest systems are apt to be the most unstable. Natural systems, almost always complex, contain multitudes of checks which prevent any single event from threatening the whole with destruction. In any great center of monoculture, soil toxins develop and parasites of many sorts are encouraged to multiply explosively. The South was not unique in planting great areas to a few basic plants, but no more than the Ireland of the 1840s was it exempt from the dangers inherent in such dependence.

Few can view without sympathy the extraordinary achievements of the black and white pioneers and settlers who created the row-crop empire in a few generations of prodigious effort. To make a living from the land without injuring it is nowhere easy, and in much of the South probably harder than elsewhere in America. It does appear, however, that the westward movement had imposed a burden on the southern environment which neither wisdom nor good will would be able to lighten significantly for generations to come.

Soils Abused

EUGENE GENOVESE

Soil Exhaustion as a Historical Problem

The South, considered as a civilization, found itself locked in an unequal, no-quarter struggle with the more modern and powerful capitalist civilization of the free states. The concentration of wealth in the hands of an aristocratic ruling class retarded the accumulation of capital and the evolution of a home market and thereby spelled defeat for the South's efforts at matching the North's industrial progress. Paradoxically, the agrarian South could not keep pace with

Reprinted from *The Political Economy of Slavery*, by Eugene Genovese, excerpts from pp. 85, 88–97. © 1989 by Eugene D. Genovese, Wesleyan University Press, by permission of University Press of New England.

the North in agricultural advancement, and the attempt to break the pattern of one-crop farming and colonial dependence on the export trade largely ended as a failure. The South's inability to combat soil exhaustion effectively proved one of the most serious economic features of its general crisis. . . .

The essence of soil exhaustion is not the total exhaustion of the land, nor merely "the progressive reduction of crop yields from cultivated lands," for the reduction may be arrested at a level high enough to meet local needs. An acceptable general theory of the social effects of soil exhaustion must be sufficiently flexible to account for the requirements of different historical epochs. The rise of capitalism requires a theory that includes the inability of the soil to recover sufficient productivity to maintain a competitive position. The main problem lies in the reaction of social institutions, rather than in the natural deterioration of the soil. The Old South, specifically, had to compete in economic development with the exploding capitalist power of the North, but its basic institution, slavery, rendered futile its attempts to fight the advance of soil exhaustion and economic decline.

The Role of Slavery

Although the land of the Black Belt ranked among the finest in the world and although cotton was not an especially exhausting crop, the depletion of Southern soil proceeded with a rapidity that frightened and stirred to action some of the best minds in the South. Many of the principles of soil science have only recently come to be understood, and many misleading ideas prevailed during the nineteenth century. Several important points had nevertheless been settled by the mid-1850s: that crops require phosphates and salts of alkalis; that nonleguminous crops require a supply of nitrogenous compounds; that artificial manures may maintain soil fertility for long periods; and that fallowing permits an increase in the available nitrogen compounds in the soil. Southern reformers, especially the talented Edmund Ruffin, had discovered these things for themselves and were particularly concerned with counteracting soil acidity. Southern agricultural periodicals and state geological surveys repeatedly stressed the need for deep plowing, crop rotation, the use of legumes, manuring, and so forth.

Although the results of the agricultural reform movement were uneven at best and although John Taylor of Caroline, the South's first great agricultural reformer, had called slavery "a misfortune to agriculture incapable of palliation," later agronomists denied that slavery contributed to the deterioration of the soil. Ruffin, for example, attributed soil exhaustion to the normal evolution of agriculture in a frontier community and assumed that economic pressures would eventually force farmers and planters to adopt new ways. Ruffin's attitude has been resurrected and supported by many historians, who have held that slavery did not prevent the adoption of better methods and that the Civil War interrupted a general agricultural reformation. . . .

Slavery contributed to soil exhaustion by preventing the South from dealing with the problem after the frontier conditions had disappeared. [William Chandler] Bagley [Jr.] argues that "the slaveowner cannot because of slavery escape wearing out the soil," but the greater weakness lay in the slaveholders' inability to restore lands to competitive levels after they had become exhausted naturally in a country with a moving frontier. The one-crop system perpetuated by slavery prevented crop rotation; the dearth of liquid capital made the purchase of fertilizer difficult; the poor quality of the implements that planters could entrust to slaves interfered with the proper use of available manures; and the carelessness of slaves made all attempts at soil reclamation or improved tillage of doubtful outcome.

The Use of Fertilizers

The direct and indirect effects of slavery greatly restricted the use of fertilizers. For cotton and corn the application of fertilizers to hills or rows is far superior to spreading it broadcast, and considerable care must be taken if the labor is not to be wasted. The planter had to guarantee maximum supervision to obtain minimum results. Planters did not have the equipment to bury fertilizers by deep plowing, and the large estates, which inevitably grew out of the slave economy, made fertilization almost a physical and economic impossibility. In certain parts of the Upper South planters solved the problem by selling some of their slaves and transforming them into liquid capital with which to buy commercial fertilizers. The smaller slave force made possible greater supervision and smaller units. This process depended upon the profitable sale of slaves to the Lower South and was therefore applicable only to a small part of the slave region. In the Southeast the use of fertilizers proceeded, as did reform in general, slowly and painfully. Despite the pleas of the reformers, the reports of state geologists, and the efforts of local or state agricultural societies, county after county reported to the federal Patent Office, which was then responsible for agricultural affairs, that little fertilization of any kind was taking place.

Many planters used cottonseed, which was most effective in the cornfields, as fertilizer in the 1850s, but the cotton fields had to depend largely on barnyard manure. This dependence need not have been bad, for barnyard manure probably supplies plants with needed iron, but planters did not keep sufficient livestock and did not feed their animals well enough to do much good. To be of use barnyard manure requires considerable care in storage and application, and even today much of it is lost. In 1938 experts in the Department of Agriculture estimated that one-half was dropped on uncultivated land and that the valuable liquid portion of the remainder was often lost. Improper application rendered much of the rest useless, for manure must be applied at the right time according to soil conditions and climate. This fertilizer requires all the time, care, supervision, and interest that farmers can provide and that slaves cannot or will not. Overseers or even planters themselves hardly had the desire to watch their laborers with the unrelenting vigilance that was needed. . . .

The difficulties in accumulating barnyard manure stirred a growing interest in marl, which Ruffin recommended so highly as an agent capable of counteracting soil acidity and of "deepening the soil" by lowering the level of good earth. In 1853 he claimed that properly marled land in Virginia had increased in value by 200 per cent. . . .

Yet by 1860 few in Mississippi used either guano or marl. Perhaps in time more of these fertilizers would have been used, but not many planters could possibly have borne the cost of transporting enough marl for their huge estates, much less the cost of buying and transporting enough guano. Planters and farmers in Alabama and Georgia used little marl before 1850, and there is no evidence of an appreciable improvement in the fifties. When they did use marl, they generally had it applied so badly that Ruffin despaired of ever teaching them to do it properly. To make matters worse, errant planters only succeeded in convincing themselves that Ruffin was, after all, only a "book farmer."

Peruvian guano emerged as the great hope of planters and farmers with exhausted lands. The desire for guano reached notable proportions during the 1840s and 1850s: whereas less than 1,000 tons were imported from Peru during 1847–1848, more than 163,000 tons were imported during 1853–1854. . . .

Guano, like other fertilizers, required considerable care in application; if not used intelligently, it could damage the land. The less expensive American guano required more attention than the Peruvian, especially since it contained hard lumps that had to be thoroughly pulverized.

When guano did come into use in the Lower South indications are that wealthy coastal planters applied it to their badly exhausted fields. . . .

According to the *Report on Agriculture* submitted by the Commissioner of Patents in 1854, about 300 pounds of Peruvian guano had to be applied to fertilize an acre of exhausted land, with a second dressing of 100 to 200 pounds recommended for land planted to Southern staples. That is, cotton land required about 450 pounds of guano per acre. Although the American Guano Company claimed that 200 to 350 pounds of its brand would do, the more objective De Bow's *Industrial Resources* insisted on 900 pounds of this inferior but adequate guano. At forty dollars per ton a planter with 250 acres would have had to spend somewhere between $500 and $2,500 for this second-rate guano; and since its effects were not lasting he would have had to spend it regularly. Whatever the advantages of the relatively inexpensive American variety, it required more cash than all but a few planters had. . . .

When one considers the size of the plantations of the Cotton Belt and the careless, wasteful way in which the slaves worked, planters cannot be blamed for ignoring the results of neat experiments conducted by a few unusual men like David Dickson of Georgia or Noah B. Cloud of Alabama. James S. Peacocke of Redwood, Louisiana, summed up some of the planters' problems:

In respect to our worn out lands, it is almost useless for anyone to waste paper and ink to write the Southern planter telling him to manure. It is well enough for Northern farmers to talk; they can well afford to fertilize their little spots of ten or a dozen acres; but a Southern plantation of 500 or 600 acres in cultivation would require all the manure in the parish and all the force to do it justice . . . Again, we have no time to haul the large quantities of manure to the field, for it generally takes until January to get all our cotton, and we have to rush it then, to get time to make repairs before we go to plowing for our next crop.

Peacocke was writing about barnyard manure, but all that he needed to add to account for other fertilizers was that few planters, and fewer farmers, could afford to buy them.

Crop Rotation

Rotation of staple crops with alfalfa, clover, and other legumes might have protected and restored Southern soils. Rotation helps counteract the effects of leaching and erosion, and green manure, although probably less useful than barnyard manure, increases the supply of nitrogen in the soil. Ebenezer Emmons, state geologist of North Carolina, pointed out that marl could be harmful if too much was applied and that proper crop rotation and plowing under the peas could offset the danger of excessive lime.

The South is not the best grass country, although in recent years its share of the nation's grassland has risen remarkably. There was no natural obstacle to the production of more alfalfa, oats, rye, cowpeas, clover, hairy vetch, and other soil-improving crops. Although nitrogenous manuring for cereals tends to encourage the growth of straw relative to grain, the reverse is true for cotton and corn. . . . The cotton-corn-cowpea sequence did not return enough elements to the soil to prevent a steady decline of fertility.

Exceptions to the no-rotation rule appeared only here and there. Ruffin used a fine six-field system, and a fellow Virginian, Colonel Tulley, rotated his wheat with clover and got excellent results. Most planters, especially in the Cotton Belt, were unwilling and more often economically unable to take land away from their cash crop. . . . In 1860, Eugene W. Hilgard, Mississippi state geologist, wrote that the only rotation practiced on a large scale was that of cotton and corn, and similar reports came from throughout the Lower South.

The Exhaustion of the Soils of the Lower South

Daniel Lee, editor of the *Southern Cultivator*, estimated in 1858 that 40 per cent of the South's cotton land was already exhausted, and he was given considerable support by other competent observers. . . . As early as 1842 the *Southern Planter* had reported worn-out lands across the interior of Mississippi, and the soil deteriorated steadily thereafter. . . .

Fertilizers absorbed more than 7 per cent of the South's farm income, compared with 1 per cent for the rest of the country, although only fifteen bushels of corn were produced per acre, compared with forty-three bushels in New England and thirty-six in the Middle Atlantic states. Parts of South Carolina in 1920 required about 1,000 pounds of fertilizer per acre of cotton land, and the general requirements of Mississippi ranged from 200 to 1,000 pounds. The South still grows cotton only because of tremendous expenditures for the fertilizers with which to strengthen its exhausted soils.

Slavery and the plantation system led to agricultural methods that depleted the soil. In this respect the results did not differ much from those experienced on the Northern frontier, but slavery forced the South into continued dependence on exploitative methods after the frontier had passed. Worse, it prevented the reclamation of the greater part of the worn-out land. The planters had too much land under cultivation; they lacked the necessary livestock; they could practice crop rotation only with difficulty; and they had to rely on a labor force of poor quality. Under such circumstances, notwithstanding successes in some areas, the system could not reform itself. When reforms did come to Maryland, Virginia, and certain counties of the Lower South, it was either at the expense of slavery altogether or by a reduction in the size of slaveholdings and the transformation of the surplus slaves into liquid capital. The South faced a dilemma of which the problem of soil exhaustion formed only a part. On the one hand, it needed to develop its economy to keep pace with that of the free states, or the proud slaveholding class could no longer expect to retain its hegemony. On the other hand, successful reform meant the end of slavery and of the basis for the very power the planters were trying to preserve.

Soils Infested

PETE DANIEL

For a century and a half cotton farming dominated the southern United States. Indeed, the invention of the cotton gin followed by only four years the establishment of the government; the cotton culture and the fledgling nation grew up together. Between 1793 and 1861 the cotton culture expanded from the Atlantic seaboard across the Mississippi River. The cotton gin was such a simple machine that it was endlessly replicated in each settlement as cotton marched west from county to county. A way of life moved across the land—a class-bound society run by planters, acknowledged by white farmers, and fueled by slave labor. Dynamic and expansive, the short staple cotton culture literally burst upon South Carolina and paused only briefly to gather young sons and additional slaves before moving through the Black Belt of Georgia and Alabama and into Mississippi and Louisiana.

The peculiar needs of the crop dictated the way cotton farmers ordered their lives. Cotton had its cycle of land preparation, sowing, chopping, and harvest. After breaking the land in the late winter, rows were run and then the cotton was planted. After it sprouted, the workforce passed through the fields, thinning the plants and chopping out the weeds. Plowing alternated with chopping until around July, when workers laid the crop by—a term that simply meant they ended fieldwork. Then there was time for fishing, religious revivals, and leisure. In September or October the bolls filled out and burst into white puffs of lint, and then workers moved through the fields with sacks, picking out the cotton. As additional bolls burst, the task continued throughout the fall until the field had yielded its crop. The cotton gin separated the seeds from the lint, which was baled and sold. Until the 1880s seeds were discarded, except for enough to plant the next year. This annual work cycle persisted from the late eighteenth century well into the twentieth.

Excerpts from Pete Daniel, *Breaking the Land: The Transformation of Cotton, Tobacco, and Rice Cultures since 1880*, 1985. Reprinted by permission of the University of Illinois Press.

Although cultivation practices changed little for a century and a half, the end of slavery revolutionized tenure arrangements in the cotton culture. Most former slaves as well as increasing numbers of white yeomen became share-croppers who worked on yearly contracts and received housing, food, fuel, and the right to hunt and fish in exchange for their labor. Much of the subsequent history of the rural South revolved around the localized relations between landlord and tenant. By the turn of the twentieth century the United States Department of Agriculture (USDA) attempted to reconfigure traditional tillage. While leading the fight against the boll weevil, the USDA also introduced the latest ideas on diversification and mechanization. Unless all aspects of cotton farming were mechanized, however, owners needed seasonal labor, so the old farming practices and sharecropping endured through the 1930s.

The evolution of the new tenure system, characterized by sharecropping and tenancy, spanned the thirty years after the Civil War and became an incredibly complex mixture of law and custom, freedom and slavery, prosper-ity and ruin. Throughout those years landownership became concentrated into fewer hands. As King Cotton reorganized his realm, merchants, landlords, banks, loan companies, and life insurance companies controlled increasing expanses of southern cotton land. . . .

Even as the number of sharecroppers increased and proscriptive laws eroded their status, other harbingers of change in the 1890s suggested the development of southern agriculture in the next half-century. In 1894 the boll weevil crossed the Rio Grande and infested the cotton fields of Texas, begin-ning an invasion that would ultimately doom the old cotton kingdom. The federal government reported the progress of the weevil and educated farmers on how to combat it, but those efforts did not halt its thirty-year conquest of the Cotton South. The weevil not only ravaged the cotton fields but also set in motion a demonstration program and the federal Extension Service run by the U.S. Department of Agriculture. Extension agents educated farmers and, more important, stressed commercial farming with the latest machinery and methods. This well-intended government intrusion helped the more educated and aggres-sive farmers to survive, while those who were marginal gradually disappeared from the land. . . .

More than any other factor, however, the fight against the boll weevil heralded government intervention. It upset the traditional culture enough so that southern farmers were willing to look up from their almanacs and listen to agricultural experts. Ultimately the weevil would force cotton into western growing areas that were less vulnerable to the pest. In 1894 C. H. DeRyee of Corpus Christi, Texas, wrote to the USDA calling attention to a weevil that destroyed cotton bolls. The Agriculture Department assessed the situation, perceived grave problems, and suggested that the Texas legislature halt cotton planting for a year in the infested area. Failing to bring about legislative action, department entomologists suggested that farmers pick up and destroy the punc-tured squares, or young buds, that fell from the plant and served as nests for young weevils, and that they also use Paris Green as an insecticide. Experts later suggested that farmers destroy the cotton stalks immediately after picking and, during cultivation, that they use a plow with a crossbar that would knock the infested squares from the plant. As the weevil spread, some Texas farmers and businessmen put a bounty on the head of the boll weevil, from ten to twenty-five cents per hundred.

When the insect neared the Mississippi River, alarmed farmers on the east side suggested a fifty-mile cotton-free zone along its banks. The USDA, unable to calculate how to reimburse farmers for their sacrifice, never made a decision on this plan. Failing to halt the spread of the weevil, the agency instead instructed farmers on how to cope with the insect. This plan was an outgrowth of farmers' institutes, correspondence courses, and other outreach plans that preceded it. In 1902 the Department of Agriculture hired Seaman A. Knapp as "Special Agent for the Promotion of Agriculture in the South." A year later, on the Walter C. Porter farm near Terrell, Texas, Knapp set up a demonstration farm to show farmers how to defeat the weevil with good cultivation practices. While restoring production, the new methods drove up the cost of cotton farming east of the Mississippi River and pushed cotton growing to less infested western areas. . . .

By 1908 the boll weevil had eaten its way northward into Arkansas and leaped over the Mississippi River. Agents fanned out over the area, giving farmers basic training for combat. Some planters and sharecroppers adjusted to the emergency, but others moved from infested areas. Farmers in Concordia Parish, Louisiana, started growing rice in 1909, dismantled the old cotton gins and oil mills, and built a rice mill in Vidalia. After several years farmers discovered that, even with the weevil, it was more profitable to grow cotton, so the cotton culture reemerged and the rice culture lapsed. Such shifts in crop cultures easily escaped censustakers. Yet the weevil did push some farmers toward diversification, and Louisiana farmers tried peanuts, truck crops, livestock, and dairy herds. In the decade following 1910, however, farmers increasingly turned back to cotton, learning from extension agents that they could cope with the weevil although they would have less production. In that sense the Extension Service stunted diversification by concentrating on maintaining cotton production. It would not be the last contradiction in government agricultural policy. . . .

The boll weevil did not discriminate by the race of the farmer, and Seaman A. Knapp acted in conjunction with Booker T. Washington to aid black farmers. Washington, of course, attempted to educate not only those who wanted to farm scientifically but also traditional farmers who lived around Tuskegee Institute. In 1892 he inaugurated the Tuskegee Negro Conference, and he later sponsored farmers' institutes, short courses in agriculture, county fairs, a farm newspaper, and miscellaneous leaflets. In 1906, after securing backing from a New York banker named Morris K. Jesup and the John F. Slater Fund, Washington sent forth the "Jesup Agricultural Wagon" to tour the countryside near the school.

Despite this reluctance to engage black agricultural agents, Seaman Knapp realized that the wagon was the perfect vehicle to carry information to black farmers, and he cooperated with Washington. Thomas M. Campbell took over the mule team that pulled the wagon and drove off to begin a career that spanned a half-century. Tuskegee Institute's parent school, Hampton Institute, also sponsored an agent, John B. Pierce. At first restricted to Macon County, Alabama, and to Norfolk County, Virginia, the agricultural wagon idea performed so well that Knapp hired additional black agents. Although never equal in number or funding to the whites, black agents by 1919 were in all southern extension programs. The Smith-Lever Act of 1914 encouraged the sponsorship of black agents, but these men and women were always closely supervised by whites. Although most black agents were dedicated to their work, the task before them proved immense. Indeed, with their dependence upon the white agricultural complex for funds, they could never innovate plans to reform the sharecropping system.

From the beginning, black extension agents did not concentrate on helping the poor sharecroppers and marginal farmers who most needed instruction, but instead sought out more prosperous farmers. They had a delicate task. First they made peace with local white landlords and merchants; then they selected their clientele from among the most respectable black farmers. Black agents had no choice but to abide by the dictates of white administrators, but white agents also concentrated on the better class of farmers. Thus the bottom strata of both races faltered before the weevil, just as they had under other natural and manmade calamities.

The job proved difficult for even the most dedicated agent. Eugene A. Williams wrote to Thomas M. Campbell in June 1916 of his work among black farmers in Georgia. . . . He had not taken a day's vacation during the past year; he slept in his clothes for five days at a stretch, and he worked at night. "I found when I entered the work most of the negro farmers were discouraged, and I have had to spend considerable time trying to convince a number that their white neighbor was his friend and desired to see him improve."

By 1917 many southern whites realized the significance of the black exodus, and the Extension Service mobilized to pacify would-be immigrants. "Thousands of negroes have left this State and gone north during the past two months," the director of extension work in Mississippi complained. "The labor problem, I fear, will materially affect crop production in this State." The migration made planters more conscious of conditions among black sharecroppers. H. E. Savely attended the Delta Community Congress in Clarksdale in June 1917 and admitted that diseases such as tuberculosis, pellagra, malaria, and typhoid were widespread. . . . Many blacks had left the rural areas, he wrote, and he feared that not enough would remain to harvest the cotton crop. . . .

Southern farmers studied the boll weevil carefully. In *All God's Dangers: The Life of Nate Shaw*, Theodore Rosengarten transcribed the words of the real Ned Cobb as he described his personal study of the boll weevil. When the weevil first appeared, Cobb said, "these white folks down here told the colored people if you don't pick them cotton squares off the ground and destroy them boll weevils, we'll quit furnishin you. Told em that—putting the blame on the colored man for the boll weevil comin in this country." Cobb put his children into the fields picking up squares. "I was industrious enough to do somethin about the boll weevil without bein driven to it," he bragged. He did not believe that picking up the squares, as the Extension Service suggested, destroyed all the weevils. "You couldn't keep your fields clean — boll weevil schemin to eat your crop faster than you workin to get him out." It was the weevil that led Cobb to make the statement used in the title of his autobiography: "Yes, all God's dangers aint a white man."

The weevil laid eggs in the squares, and "in a few days, one weevil's got a court of young uns hatchin." Cobb carefully observed the life cycle of the insect. "I've pulled them squares open and caught em in all their stages of life: found the old egg in there, and I've found him just hatched out and he's right white like a worm, just a little spot in there, that's him; and if he's a little older he looks green-colored and sappy; and after he gets grown he's a old ashy-colored rascal, his wings is gray like ash. I've known him from the first to the last. I've picked him up and looked at him close. He's just an insect, but really, he's unusual to me. I can't thoroughly understand the nature of a boll weevil." He grew to the size of a fly, Cobb revealed. "And he's a very creepin fellow, he gets about too; he'll ruin a stalk of cotton in a night's time." Cobb walked through his fields and knocked weevils off the plants when he saw them. "And he'll get up — he aint quick about it, but he'll get up from there and fly off, you looking at him."

Understanding the insect's habits and interrupting the life cycle by destroying squares did not get rid of the weevil. "When I seed I couldn't defeat the boll weevil by pickin up squares, I carried poison out to the field and took me a crocus sack, one of these thin crocus sacks, put my poison in there enough to poison maybe four or five rows and just walk, walk, walk; shake that sack over the cotton when I'd look back, heap of times, that dust flyin every whichway and the breeze blowin, that cotton would be white with dust, behind me." He wore a cloth over his mouth; still the dust bothered him. If the weevil returned, Cobb would dust again until the boll got "too far advanced for him to handle it and that boll will open with healthy locks." He concluded that poison was "the only way to beat the devil, run him out the field." But the battle renewed every year. "Everything, every creature in God's world, understands how to try to protect itself. And I believe that scoundrel goes right into the forests and finds his appointed place to wait; spring of the year, he right back in the field, soon as your cotton comes up, he right back on it."

There were larger implications for the old cotton-growing areas of the South. The center of cotton production would have shifted westward anyway, as it always had, but the weevil "accelerated the process." Texas and Oklahoma doubled their acreage from 1910 to 1930, and Mississippi, Arkansas, and Louisiana increased theirs by 40 percent. Alabama, Georgia, South and North Carolina only increased acreage by 5 percent. Thus the weevil had set in motion a westward movement that would accelerate during the 1920s and the New Deal.

❦ *F U R T H E R   R E A D I N G*

William Andrews, *Six Women's Slave Narratives* (1988)

Samuel Batchelder, *Introduction and Early Progress of the Cotton Manufacture in the United States* (1863)

Hugh Hammond Bennett, *The Soils and Agriculture of the Southern States* (1921)

John W. Blassingame, *The Slave Community: Plantation Life in the Antebellum South* (1979)

W. J. Cash, *The Mind of the South* (1941)

Sydney John Chapman, *The Cotton Industry and Trade* (1905)

Albert E. Cowdrey, *This Land, This South: An Environmental History* (1983)

Pete Daniel, *Breaking the Land: The Transformation of Cotton, Tobacco, and Rice Cultures Since 1880* (1985)

John Frederick Duggar, *Southern Field Crops [Exclusive of Forage Plants]* (1911)

Elizabeth Fox-Genovese, *Within the Plantation Household: Black and White Women of the Old South* (1989)

Eugene D. Genovese, *Roll, Jordan, Roll: The World the Slaves Made* (1972)

————, *The Political Economy of Slavery* (1965)

Lewis Cecil Gray, *History of Agriculture in the Southern United States to 1860* (1958)

E. W. Hilgard, *General Discussion of the Cotton Production of the United States* (1884)

Frances Anne Kemble, *Journal of a Residence on a Georgian Plantation in 1838–1839* (1863, 1961)

John Hebron Moore, *The Emergence of the Cotton Kingdom in the Old Southwest: Mississippi, 1770–1860* (1987)

James Oscar Morgan, *Field Crops for the Cotton-Belt* (1917)

Frederick Law Olmsted, *The Slave States* (1959)

John Solomon Otto, *The Southern Frontiers, 1607–1860: The Agricultural Evolution of the Colonial and Antebellum South* (1989)

Ulrich B. Phillips, *Life and Labor in the Old South* (1956)

George P. Rawick, ed., *The American Slave: A Composite Autobiography* (1977)

Theodore Rosengarten, *All God's Dangers: The Life of Nate Shaw* (1974)

————, *Tombee: Portrait of a Cotton Planter* (1986)

Susan Dabney Smedes, *Memorials of a Southern Planter* (1965)

Kenneth Stampp, *The Peculiar Institution: Slavery in the Ante-Bellum South* (1956)

Rupert Bayless Vance, *Human Factors in Cotton Culture: A Study in the Social Geography of the American South* (1929)

Deborah Gray White, *Ar'n't I a Woman?* (1985)

Charles Reagan Wilson and William Ferris, *Encyclopedia of Southern Culture* (1989)

C. Vann Woodward, *American Counterpoint: Slavery and Racism in the North-South Dialogue* (1964)

Gavin Wright, *The Political Economy of the Cotton South* (1978)

CHAPTER 8

Mining California's Earth
in the Nineteenth Century

ψ

Scientific conceptions of the earth as inanimate — and thus a source of nonrenewable metallic resources — is a nineteenth-century development. In contrast, Native American peoples and most eighteenth-century Euramericans believed that rocks and metals were alive and grew in a living earth. If miners extracted a vein (an organic term) of ore, it eventually would grow back. Probably many of the forty-niners who swarmed over California's sunny Sierra pinelands with their pans, cradles, and pickaxes still believed that gold "grew" in the "mother" lode as an inexhaustible source of wealth.

The forty-niners had diverse ethnic and racial roots. Comprising Americans (including blacks and Indians), Europeans, Canadians, Asians, Hispanics, Mexicans, and others, they carried a variety of cultural traditions and beliefs to the gold fields, mining towns, farms, and young cities of northern and central California. California's early history uniquely reflects the United States' cultural and racial diversity.

This demographic diversity brought both strength and tension to Gold Rush society. Indians, at first a welcome source of labor in the gold fields, soon experienced prejudice, massacre, and relocation. Some free blacks and even some slaves found gold, and some managed to purchase freedom for themselves and their families, but all felt the deep-seated prejudices of white society. Chinese miners, buoyed by their cultural traditions, founded Chinacamps and Chinatowns, worked river bottoms abandoned by whites, and provided labor for mining and railroad entrepreneurs but soon fell victim to vigilante violence and the Chinese exclusion act of 1882. Mexicans, who imported their own architectural, religious, and culinary traditions, increasingly contributed the stoop labor for California's farms. White society meanwhile cast aside its egalitarian dreams for class-based realities as mining gold and other minerals required ever more costly and sophisticated hydraulic nozzles and hoses, iron-stamp mills, grinders, and amalgamation techniques for exploiting river bottoms, gravel deposits, and quartz rock formations. Most whites who stayed in mining became laborers for the few who made lucky strikes or who pooled their wealth to found companies. Others invested in trades that supported mining communities or abandoned mining for fishing, farming, or lumbering.

Mining had severe environmental repercussions. Miners' camps polluted the air and water. Hydraulic mining washed so much debris into the Sacramento River and San Francisco Bay that valley farmers brought suit against mountain miners and successfully halted hydraulic mining in 1884. Fishing and spawning were affected not only by the debris but also by the mercury used as an amalgam to capture gold and silver in the sluice boxes. Soils suffered from runoff, flooding, and erosion. This chapter probes how peoples of diverse racial and ethnic groups interacted with each other and with the environment in mining California's earth in the nineteenth century.

♀ D O C U M E N T S

The documents in this chapter view the Gold Rush and its evolving mining technologies from a variety of perspectives, illustrating the impact of the gold rush on the natural environment and on the lives of and relationships among a diversity of peoples. The selections raise questions about the possible connections between a healthy natural environment and a healthy social environment.

During the 1840s, Euramerican society leapfrogged across the Great Plains to settle Oregon Territory (which the United States officially acquired in 1846 after the settlement of disputes with Great Britain located the northern U.S. border at the 49th parallel) and California (which the nation acquired in 1848, at the end of the Mexican War). The first document is a speech made by Missouri senator Thomas Hart Benton to Congress in 1846 in which he urges the U.S. settlement of Oregon and justifies settlement of the Pacific lands on grounds of the superiority of the "white" race over the "red, yellow, black, and brown" races. In the second document, black slave Alvin Coffey describes his journey from St. Louis to San Francisco during the 1849 Gold Rush. Coffey later purchased his and his family's freedom with the money he earned in the mining of placer (glacial gravel) deposits (page 279).

The one hundred thousand Indians who lived in California in 1849 were reduced to fifteen thousand by 1900 through disease, massacre, and loss of subsistence resources. The third document features an 1853 letter from a federal agent to his superintendent in the San Francisco Bureau of Indian Affairs describing the impact of the gold mines on Indian subsistence.

In the fourth document, excerpted from an 1857 article for *California Magazine*, James Marshall recalls his 1848 discovery of gold near Sutter's Fort outside Sacramento. News of the discovery spread like wildfire around the world, sparking the 1849 Gold Rush. The fifth selection is an extract from *Sunset Land*, a promotional settlement account, written in 1870 by New England minister John Todd, who traveled to California during the Gold Rush. He explains to prospective settlers the techniques for mining gold, silver, and mercury that will enable them to make their fortunes.

The sixth document focuses on the fate of the gold country around Mount Shasta. Taken from Joaquin Miller's 1890 book *My Life Amongst the Modocs*, the passages reveal the simultaneous demise of the Indians and deterioration of their environment under the impact of mining. In the seventh document, dating from 1925, Wintu Indian Kate Luckie prophesies that waters from the north will destroy the miners who had abused the trees, rocks, and grasses.

The mining camps are recalled in the eighth document by pioneer woman Sarah Royce, who journeyed west on the Overland Trail in 1849. Her memoirs were recorded in the 1880s at the request of her son, the philosopher Josiah Royce, and published in 1932.

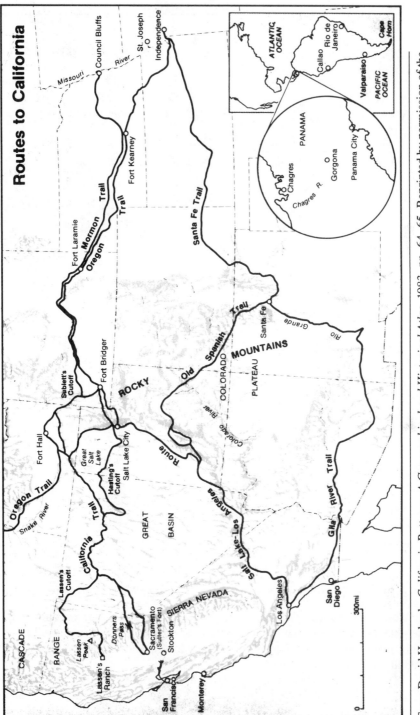

Routes to California

From David Hornbeck, *California Patterns: A Geographical and Historical Atlas*, 1983, pp. 64, 65. Reprinted by permission of the Mayfield Publishing Company. Copyright © 1983 by Mayfield Publishing Company.

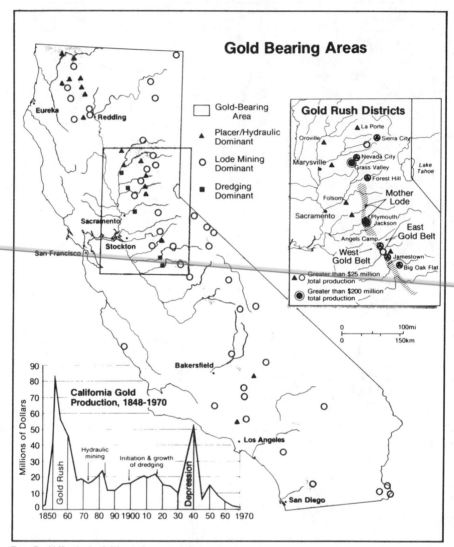

From David Hornbeck, *California Patterns: A Geographical and Historical Atlas*, 1983, pp. 64, 65. Reprinted by permission of the Mayfield Publishing Company. Copyright © 1983 by Mayfield Publishing Company.

Senator Thomas Hart Benton on Manifest Destiny, 1846

It would seem that the White race alone received the divine command, to subdue and replenish the earth: for it is the only race that has obeyed it — the only race that hunts out new and distant lands, and even a New World, to subdue and replenish. . . .

The Red race has disappeared from the Atlantic coast; the tribes that resisted civilization met extinction. This is a cause of lamentation with many. For my part, I cannot murmur at what seems to be the effect of divine law. I cannot repine that this Capitol has replaced the wigwam — this Christian people, replaced the savages — white matrons, the red squaws. . . . Civilization, or extinction, has been the fate of all people who have found themselves in the trace of the advancing Whites, and civilization, always the preference of the Whites, has been pressed as an object, while extinction has followed as a consequence of its resistance. . . .

The van of the Caucasian race now top the Rocky Mountains, and spread down on the shores of the Pacific. In a few years a great population will grow up there, luminous with the accumulated lights of European and American civilization. Their presence in such a position cannot be without its influence upon eastern Asia. . . .

The Mongolian, or Yellow race is there, four hundred millions in number spreading almost to Europe; a race once the foremost of the human family in the arts of civilization, but torpid and stationary for thousands of years. It is a race far above the Ethiopian, or Black — above the Malay, or Brown, (if we admit five races) — and above the American Indians, or Red; it is a race far above all these, but still far below the White and like all the rest, must receive an impression from the superior race whenever they come in contact. . . .

The sun of civilization must shine across the sea; socially and commercially the van of the Caucasians, and the rear of the Mongolians, must intermix. They must talk together, and trade together, and marry together. . . . Moral and intellectual superiority will do the rest; the White race will take the ascendant, elevating what is susceptible of improvement — wearing out what is not. . . . And thus the youngest people, and the newest land, will become the reviver and the regenerator of the oldest. . . .

It is in this point of view, and as acting upon the social, political, and religious condition of Asia, and giving a new point of departure to her ancient civilization, that I look upon the settlement of the Columbia river by the van of the Caucasian race as the most momentous human event in the history of man since his dispersion over the face of the earth.

Alvin Coffey's Experiences as a Black Forty-Niner, 1849

I started from St. Louis, Mo., on the 2nd day of April in 1849. There was quite a crowd of the neighbors who drove through the mud and rain to St. Joe to see us off. About the first of May we organized the train. There were twenty wagons in number and from three to five men to each wagon.

We crossed the Missouri River at Savanna Landing on about the sixth of May. There were several trains ahead of us. At twelve o'clock three more men took our place and we went to camp. At six in the morning, there were three more who went to relieve those on guard. One of the three that came in had cholera so bad that he was in lots of misery. Dr. Bassett [Coffey's owner], the captain of the train, did all he could for him, but he died at ten o'clock and we buried him. We got ready and started at eleven the same day and the moon was new just then.

From *Reminiscences of Alvin Coffey* as found in Sue Bailey Thurman, *Pioneers of Negro Origin in California*, 1952, pp. 11–15. Reprinted by permission of Alice Phelan Sullivan Library and Archives at The Society of California Pioneers.

We got news every day that people were dying by the hundreds in St. Joe and St. Louis. It was alarming. When we hitched up and got ready to move, Dr. said, "Boys, we will have to drive day and night."

There were only three saddle horses in the train, Dr. Bassett, Mr. Hale, Sr., and John Triplet owning them. They rode with the Dr. to hunt camping places. We drove night and day and got out of reach of the cholera. There was none ahead of us that we knew of.

Dave and Ben Headspeth's train was ahead of us. They had fourteen or fifteen wagons in the train and three to five men to a wagon. Captain Camel had another such train. When we caught up with them, we never heard of one case of cholera on their trains.

We got across the plains to Fort Laramie, the sixteenth of June, and the ignorant driver broke down a good many oxen on the trains. There were a good many ahead of us, who had doubled up their trains and left tons upon tons of bacon and other provisions.

When we got well down Humboldt to a place called Lawson's Meadow, which was quite a way from the sink of the Humboldt, the emigrants agreed to drive there. There was good grass at Lawson's Meadow. We camped there a day and two nights, resting the oxen, for we had a desert to cross to get to Black Rock where there was grass and water.

Starting to cross the desert to Black Rock at four o'clock in the evening, we traveled all night. The next day it was hot and sandy. When within twenty miles of Black Rock, we saw it very plainly.

A great number of cattle perished before we got to Black Rock. When about fifteen miles from Black Rock, a team of four oxen was left on the road just where the oxen had died. Everything was left in the wagon.

I drove one oxen all the time and I knew about how much an ox could stand. Between nine and ten o'clock a breeze came up and the oxen threw up their heads and seemed to have new life. At noon, we drove into Black Rock.

Before we reached Sacramento Valley, we had poor feed a number of nights. The route by the way of Humboldt was the oldest and best known to Hangtown. We crossed the South Pass on the Fourth of July. The ice next morning was as thick as a dinner plate. About two days before we got to Honey Lake we were in a timbered country. We camped at a place well known as Rabbit Hole Springs. An ox had given out and was down, and not able to get up, about one hundred yards from the spring. A while after it got dark as it was going to be, the ox commenced bawling pitifully. Some of the boys had gone to bed. I said, "Let us go out and kill the ox for it is too bad to hear him bawl." The wolves were eating him alive. None would go with me, so I got two double-barreled shot-guns which were loaded. I went out where he was. The wolves were not in sight, although I could hear them. I put one of the guns about five or six inches from the ox's head and killed him with the first shot. The wolves never tackled me. I had reserved three shots in case they should.

When we got in Deer Creek in Sacramento Valley, we divided up wagons. Some went to Sacramento Valley to get provisions for the winter and came up to Redding Springs later. We camped several days at Honey Lake but the grass on Madeline Plains was not very good. While Headspeth and a guide we had were hunting the best path to Sacramento road, the cattle recruited up nicely. We took several days to go from Honey Lake to Sacramento Valley.

Those that kept on from Deer Creek to Redding Springs camped at Redding Springs the thirteenth day of October, 1849. Eight to ten miles drive was a big one for us at the latter end. The last four miles the cattle had nothing to eat but poison-oak brush. We cut down black oaks for them to browse on, and got to Redding Springs the next day at four o'clock. We watered the oxen out of buckets that night and morning. The next day we gathered them up, drove them down to Clear Creek where they had plenty of poison oak to eat.

On the morning of the fifteenth we went to dry-digging mining. We dug and dug to the first of November. At night it commenced raining, and rained and snowed pretty much all the winter. We had a tent but it barely kept us all dry. There were from eight to twelve in one camp. We cut down pine trees for shakes to make a cabin. It was a whole week before we had a cabin to keep us dry.

The first week in January, 1850, we bought a hundred pounds of bear meat at one dollar per pound. I asked the man how many pounds he had sold, and he said, "I've sold thirteen hundred pounds and have four hundred to five hundred pounds left in camp yet. I gave the men considerable for helping me dress it."

A Federal Agent Assesses Mining's Impact on the Indians, 1853

Diamond Springs
El Dorado County
December 31st 1853

The Indians in this portion of the State are wretchedly poor, having no horses, cattle or other property. They formerly subsisted on game, fish, acorns, etc., but it is now impossible for them to make a living by hunting or fishing, for nearly all the game has been driven from the mining region or has been killed by the thousands of our people who now occupy the once quiet home of these children of the forest. The rivers or tributaries of the Sacramento formerly were clear as crystal and abounded with the finest salmon and other fish. I saw them at Salmon Falls on the American river in the year 1851, and also the Indians taking barrels of these beautiful fish and drying them for winter. But the miners have turned the streams from their beds and conveyed the water to the dry diggings and after being used until it is so thick with mud that it will scarcely run it returns to its natural channel and with it the soil from a thousand hills, which has driven almost every kind of fish to seek new places of resort where they can enjoy a purer and more natural element. And to prove the old adage that misfortunes never come singly the oaks have for the last three years refused to furnish the acorn, which formed one of the chief articles of Indian food. They have often told me that the white man had killed all their game, had driven the fish from the rivers, had cut down and destroyed the trees and that what were now standing were worthless for they bore no acorns. In their superstitious imaginations they believe that the White man's presence among them has caused the trees (that formerly bore plentifully) to now be worthless and barren. In concluding this brief report I deem it my duty to recommend to your favorable consideration the early establishment of a suitable reservation and the removal of these Indians thereto, where they can receive medical aid and assistance which at the present time they so much require.

All of which is very respectfully submitted.

E. A. Stevenson
Spec. Indian Agent

Hon. Thos. J. Henley
Supt. of Indian Affairs
San Francisco Cal.

James Marshall Tells How He Discovered Gold, 1857

While we were in the habit at night of turning the water through the tail race we had dug for the purpose of widening and deepening the race, I used to go down in the morning to see what had been done by the water through the night; and about half past seven o'clock on or about the 19th of January — I am not quite certain to a day, but it was between the 18th and 20th of that month — 1848, I went down as usual, and after shutting off the water from the race, I stepped into it, near the lower end, and there, upon the rock, about six inches beneath the surface of the water, I discovered the gold. I was entirely alone at the time. I picked up one or two pieces and examined them attentively; and having some general knowledge of minerals, I could not call to mind more than two which in any way resembled this — *sulphuret of iron*, very bright and brittle; and *gold*, bright, yet malleable; I then tried it between two rocks, and found that it could be beaten into a different shape, but not broken. I then collected four or five pieces and went up to Mr. Scott (who was working at the carpenter's bench making the mill wheel) with the pieces and said, "I have found it."

"What is it?" inquired Scott.

"Gold," I answered.

"Oh! no," returned Scott, "that can't be."

I replied positively — "I know it to be nothing else."

Mr. Scott was the second person who saw the gold. W. J. Johnston, A. Stephens, H. Bigler, and J. Brown, who were also working in the mill yard, were then called up to see it. Peter L. Wimmer, Mrs. Jane Wimmer, C. Bennet, and I. Smith, were at the house; the latter two of whom were sick; E. Persons and John Wimmer, (a son of P. L. Wimmer), were out hunting oxen at the same time. About 10 o'clock the same morning, P. L. Wimmer came down from the house, and was very much surprised at the discovery, when the metal was shown him; and which he took home to show his wife, who, the next day, made some experiments upon it by boiling it in strong lye, and saleratus; and Mr. Bennet by my directions beat it very thin.

Four days afterwards, I went to the Fort for provisions, and carried with me about three ounces of the gold, which Capt. Sutter and I tested with *nitric acid*. I then tried it in Sutter's presence by taking three silver dollars and balancing them by the dust in the air, then immersed both in water, and the superior weight of the gold satisfied us both of its nature and value.

An Advocate Publicizes the California Gold Mines, 1870

Captain Sutter had a large Spanish grant, on the Sacramento River, and there he planted himself, built a fort, and called it New Helvetia. The fruit was ripening, and was ready to fall into the hands of those who were ready to catch it. In 1845, Congress declared . . . Texas to be annexed to our country. The war which followed clinched the nail, and the American flag was planted in California. But not until terrible battles had been fought, and vast wisdom and courage had been shown by John C. Fremont and Commodore Stockton, did the land have rest.

No novel could be more thrilling than the history of the fearful struggles to decide the question who should own California? In 1845, it was estimated that the population of California was eight thousand whites, perhaps ten thousand domesticated Indians, and from one to three hundred thousand wild Indians. In 1847, the emigrating wagons over the mountains had poured in a great stream, while confidence in the safety which the American flag gave, had drawn in people from all nations till the population had increased to twelve or fifteen thousand in the whole State. But now an event was to take place which, beyond all others unparalleled, was suddenly to change the face of a country, electrify the world, and jerk forward the progress of civilization, at the rate of a century in a few years.

In the winter of 1847–8, Sutter was building a saw-mill on the south branch of the American River, a branch of the Sacramento. Mr. James W. Marshall, the contractor to build the mill, one day let water into the tail-race, in order to deepen the channel. The water carried sand and mud, which it soon deposited. On looking down, Marshall discovered something bright among the sand. At once, on feeling of its weight, he was convinced that it was gold. Eager with excitement, he hastened to tell Sutter. On seeing his excitement, and hearing his story, Sutter thought he had gone mad, and kept his eye on his loaded rifle. Marshall tossed an ounce of gold on the table, and they were equally excited: they hastened to the spot, vowing secrecy. But as they continued to search under an excitement they could not conceal, a Mormon soldier watched them, and soon possessed the secret. He told his companions, who had been with him in the Mexican war; and now the cat was fairly out of the bag. Warm rumors flew in every direction — exaggerated, of course. Gold — gold was to be had for the picking up, on "the Rio de los Americanos." The population rushed in a swarm. In a few days, more than twelve hundred people were at the saw-mill, digging with shovels, spades, knives, sticks, wooden bowls, and everything else. Infants were turned out of cradles, that the cradles might be used for washing gold. The husband left his wife; American, Spaniard, and all rushed, helter-skelter, to the diggings. Towns were depopulated, ships left sailorless, — everything thrown away — all feeling sure, if they could only reach the diggings, they would return *millionnaires*. In the mean time, other streams and gulches were found to contain gold. It seemed as if the whole Nevadas might be only a thin crust over mountains of gold. A few ships got away, and letters and gold dust went with them: the excitement widened its circle. On rushed the nearest people, the Mexicans; then all the nooks and corners of California poured out their population. Oregon on the north, the Sandwich Islands on the west, Peru and Chili on the south, poured in their eager diggers. Then China felt the thrill, and her people flocked over. Australia sent her convicts and rascals; and adventurers from all parts of the earth, having nothing to lose, flew to California. The Mexican war had just been closed, and thousands of young men from the soldiery went to the land of gold. The East caught the fever, and emigrant wagons uncounted, hastened over the deserts, leaving the bones of men and of animals to bleach along their path. . . .

It was a far-off land, where there were neither houses, nor clothing, nor food. As a rare luxury, a saloon, composed of cloth only, could now and then hang out the sign "potatoes this day;" and it was crowded. Apples sold at five dollars apiece in gold. Everybody had a flush of gold. Fortunes were made in a day, and lost in gambling at night. It was mean not to spend all as it came. Every man was loaded with gold, revolvers, and bowie-knives. Nothing was valued; nothing was sacred. It will be readily seen how it was that this mining population could be so easily excited by rumors of new and rich diggings. Tell them that at such diggings every man can obtain, at the lowest mark, five hundred dollars a day, and all would rush thither. . . .

In mining, the first requisite and essential, after finding evidences of gold, is water — water to wash out the soil and sand, leaving the gold behind. When they first began, they carried the earth on their backs, or on pack-horses, two or three miles to the nearest water.

You are a miner, we will suppose, of the poorest and simplest working power. In that case, you have a pan in which you shovel the earth, and then wash it till the soil is out, and the gold left on the bottom. But the gold, for the most part, is very fine. It is mere dust. Then you put quicksilver in the bottom of your pan; that attracts the gold, and forms what is called an amalgam. If you have got beyond the simple pan, you have the rocker, — a larger vessel, round on the bottom, and long, like a hollow log split lengthwise; this you put under running water, and while one shovels in the earth, you rock and wash it. Or, you make a trough, with little slats nailed across the bottom inside. Here, above the slats, you put your quicksilver, and let in a stream of running water, while you shovel in the earth. All the day long you do this, and at night gather out your amalgam. Now, the gold is scattered through all the gulches of the foot-hills, and the necessity of running water has created Water Companies, who bring it along on the sides of the mountains in ditches, and across ravines in troughs held up on trestle-work. Sometimes this water is brought one hundred and forty miles, and the right to use it is sold to the miner by the square inch. A more productive way is what is called the hydraulic method. This is now the most expensive, and for the placer mining the most profitable.

Suppose you are to get the gold out of a hill or flat where the soil is sixteen or twenty feet deep before you come to the bed-rock, which underlies all the hills. You bring water from any distance, however great, and let it fall, say fifty feet, through a hose six inches in diameter. This hose must be encased in iron rings, — rings, so that you can bend it, — and very near each other, to prevent its bursting. Or, better still, in place of the hose, you have iron pipes, through which the water rushes, and which is safer than the hose, which is apt to "buck," as they call it; i.e., twitch and jerk as would a live buck, if held by the hind leg. Let in a stream through your pipe, as big as your wrist, upon the bank, and it washes it down with amazing rapidity. Being dissolved, it flows through the long trough, where the quicksilver lies in wait to court and embrace, and retain it. The more soil you can thoroughly dissolve, the more gold you get. After all, with your utmost skill, you lose at least thirty-three per cent. of all the gold you move in the soil. . . .

Nothing can be more dreary than a territory where the soil has been washed out as low as the water will run off. Ten thousand rocks of all shapes, and forms, and sizes are left; acres and acres, and even miles, of the skeletons of beauty, with the flesh all gone, and nothing but hideousness remaining. I have heard it asserted, that the placer mines are about exhausted, and that, hereafter, nothing but the rich companies, who have great mills to crush the quartz rock, can gain a living. I do not believe this is true. While capital and skill can gain much faster in quartz-mining, I have no doubt that it will take generations, if not a thousand years, before the gold is so washed out of the soil of California, that mining will not be a paying business. In the quartz mines, a very huge water-wheel, made to turn by the smallest amount of water possible, pumps the water from the mine as fast as it accumulates; the ore is then dug or blasted out, broken into pieces about as large as the fist, then put into an iron mortar, and stamped with iron pestles, till it is so reduced to powder, that water will wash it out in the trough, where the quicksilver lies in wait to catch the gold. This amalgam, quicksilver and gold, is next put into a covered retort of iron, with a pipe allowing the fumes of the quicksilver to escape, which pipe is cooled by passing through cold water, till the quicksilver fumes are condensed, and it drops down, the pure metal it was, leaving the gold in the retort. In this process, about twenty-five per cent. of the quicksilver is lost. There are about four hundred and fifty quartz mills already in operation in the State, and the number is constantly increasing. In the placer mines the poorest man may go to work, only paying for the use of water. In the quartz-mining, vast capital can and must be employed. When the little claims on mining land have been staked out, the spirit of speculation comes in to buy and sell these claims. I have seen many houses bought for the sake of the soil that might be dug out under them. The useless house is left standing on sticks.

As I have mentioned quicksilver, this will be the proper place to lead you to its source. Leaving San Francisco, and going south in the Santa Clara valley, nearly seventy miles, you come to the Almaden mines, the largest quicksilver mines in the world. It is a wild, weird-looking place. Up, up the round hills, three miles from the gorge, are the mines, nine hundred and forty feet perpendicular height.

The history of this mine is curious. In 1845, a Mexican officer met a tribe of Indians, with their faces painted with vermilion, which they had obtained from the cinnabar or quicksilver ore. By bribery he induced the Indians to show him the place. The mines are on a spur of the Coast Range of mountains. The

Indians had dug fifty or sixty feet into the mountain, when first discovered by Captain Castellero, with their hard-wood sticks. Probably they had known the mines for many generations. A quantity of skeletons were found in a passage, where life had undoubtedly been lost by the caving in of the earth. Up the mountain, and near the mouth of the mines, are the cabins of the miners — all Mexicans. For a time after the discovery, it was supposed the ore contained gold, or at least silver; but a gentleman who procured a retort, and applied fire at the bottom, soon found, by the pernicious effects of the fumes on his system, that he had caught a tiger. . . .

From this greatest of quicksilver mines comes the metal that enables the miners to gather the silver and gold all through California and Nevada. There are several other quicksilver mines in California, the united produce of which was, previous to the last year, six hundred thousand flasks of seventy-six and a half pounds each, and in the aggregate worth over eighteen million dollars at wholesale.

The silver mining is of more recent date in these parts than the gold. The silver belt lies on the east side of the Nevadas, commencing, probably up in Alaska, and running south, down through Mexico, and into South America. This belt is about three hundred miles wide, and may be two thousand, and even more, in length. It is quarried, broken, and crushed very much as the gold quartz. Like all that is money, it is very uncertain. You may have a claim to-day, that is rich and promises well, and you could sell it for a hundred thousand dollars; but to-morrow the rock may stop, or you lose the lode. You may find it again after you have excavated your mine one hundred or three hundred feet, and you may never find it. In seeking for it you may expend all you have in the world, and never find it, and you are a poor man. You rush to find another claim, but you may try twenty and not find silver. So you buy claims, and probably not one in hundreds is of any possible worth. Indeed, those who understand the thing — and there is scarcely a man in California who does not understand it by bitter experience, first or last — say that it is like a lottery where there is one prize to about five thousand blanks.

As to the amount of precious metals that have been dug out of the soil of California during the twenty years, it is difficult to form an estimate on which you can rely. As near as I can judge, I should put the gold at one thousand millions of dollars. This, if all brought together, would weigh just about two hundred tons. The silver mining is now in its infancy, but the yield is enormous. You go into the express office on the arrival of the daily steamer, and you are amazed at the enormous amount of huge silver bars that have just come in, — sometimes three tons of these in a single day! These are almost all sent off in the bars to China, and other parts of the world.

* * * *

The discovery of gold, and the amount obtained, have given a stimulus to commerce, to agriculture, to every department of life. They have created impulses that have advanced civilization, and shaken up nations, and poured one country into another, till we hardly know what will be next. The arts have advanced, architecture has made new discoveries in applying its skill, manufactures have been called upon to supply more people, and with better garments; and if a few have played the fool by sudden riches, the great mass of the people have been greatly benefited. . . .

Since this outpouring of the silver and the gold from the mines, we are every way improved; we have better clothing, better houses, better carriages, better school-houses and churches, and schools and colleges, better books and libraries, better ships and steamboats, better goods manufactured, and everything better. Not only so, but where one used to have these good things, ten have them now. The whole plane of human comforts and enjoyments has been raised up many degrees.

Joaquin Miller on Environmental Deterioration in the Gold Country, 1890

As lone as God, and white as a winter moon, Mount Shasta starts up sudden and solitary from the heart of the great black forests of Northern California.

You would hardly call Mount Shasta a part of the Sierras; you would say rather that it is the great white tower of some ancient and eternal wall, with nearly all the white walls overthrown.

* * * *

Ascend this mountain, stand against the snow above the upper belt of pines, and take a glance below. Toward the sea nothing but the black and unbroken forest. Mountains, it is true, dip and divide and break the monotony as the waves break up the sea; yet it is still the sea, still the unbroken forest, black and magnificent. To the south the landscape sinks and declines gradually, but still maintains its column of dark-plumed grenadiers, till the Sacramento Valley is reached, nearly a hundred miles away. Silver rivers run here, the sweetest in the world. They wind and wind among the rocks and mossy roots, with California lilies, and the yew with scarlet berries dipping in the water, and trout idling in the eddies and cool places by the basketful. On the east, the forest still keeps up unbroken rank till the Pitt River Valley is reached; and even there it surrounds the valley, and locks it up tight in its black embrace. To the north, it is true, Shasta Valley makes quite a dimple in the sable sea, and men plow there, and Mexicans drive mules or herd their mustang ponies on the open plain. But the valley is limited, surrounded by the forest, confined and imprisoned.

Look intently down among the black and rolling hills, forty miles away to the west, and here and there you will see a haze of cloud or smoke hung up above the trees; or, driven by the wind that is coming from the sea, it may drag and creep along as if tangled in the tops.

These are mining camps. Men are there, down in these dreadful cañons, out of sight of the sun, swallowed up, buried in the impenetrable gloom of the forest, toiling for gold. Each one of these camps is a world of itself. History, romance, tragedy, poetry, in every one of them. They are connected together, and reach the outer world only by a narrow little pack trail, stretching through the timber, stringing round the mountains, barely wide enough to admit of footmen and little Mexican mules, with their apparajos, to pass in single file.

But now the natives of these forests. I lived with them for years. You do not see the smoke of their wigwams through the trees. They do not smite the mountain rocks for gold, nor fell the pines, nor roil up the waters and ruin them for the fishermen. All this magnificent forest is their estate. The Great Spirit made this mountain first of all, and gave it to them, they say, and they have possessed it ever since. They preserve the forest, keep out the fires, for it is the park for their deer.

This narrative, while the thread of it is necessarily spun around a few years of my early life, is not of myself, but of this race of people that has lived centuries of history and never yet had a historian; that has suffered nearly four hundred years of wrong, and never yet had an advocate.

Yet I must write of myself, because I was among these people of whom I write, though often in the background, giving place to the inner and actual lives of a silent and mysterious people, a race of prophets, poets without the gift of expression — a race that has been often, almost always, mistreated, and never understood — a race that is moving noiselessly from the face of the earth; dreamers that sometimes waken from their mysteriousness and simplicity, and then, blood, brutality, and all the ferocity that marks a man of maddened passions, women without mercy, men without reason, brand them with the appropriate name of savages.

I have a word to say for the Indian. I saw him as he was, not as he is. In one little spot of our land, I saw him as he was centuries ago in every part of it perhaps, a Druid and a dreamer — the mildest and tamest of beings. I saw him as no man can see him now. I saw him as no man ever saw him who had the desire and patience to observe, the sympathy to understand, and the intelligence to communicate his observations to those who would really like to understand him. He is truly "the gentle savage;" the worst and the best of men, the tamest and the fiercest of beings. The world cannot understand the combination of these two qualities. For want of truer comparison let us liken him to a woman — a sort of Parisian woman, now made desperate by a long siege and an endless war.

A singular combination of circumstances laid his life bare to me. I was a child, and he was a child. He permitted me to enter his heart. . . .

All this city [Sacramento] had been built, all this country opened up, in less than two years. Twenty months before, only the Indian inhabited here; he was lord absolute of the land. But gold had been found on this spot by a party of roving mountaineers; the news had gone abroad, and people poured in and had taken possession in a day, without question and without ceremony.

And the Indians? They were pushed aside. At first they were glad to make the strangers welcome; but, when they saw where it would all lead, they grew sullen and concerned. . . .

I hurried on a mile or so to the foot-hills, and stood in the heart of the placer mines. Now the smoke from the low chimneys of the log cabins began to rise and curl through the cool, clear air on every hand, and the miners to come out at the low doors; great hairy, bearded, six-foot giants, hatless, and half-dressed.

They stretched themselves in the sweet, frosty air, shouted to each other in a sort of savage banter, washed their hands and faces in the gold-pans that stood by the door, and then entered their cabins again, to partake of the eternal beans and bacon and coffee, and coffee and bacon and beans.

The whole face of the earth was perforated with holes; shafts sunk and being sunk by these men in search of gold, down to the bed-rock. Windlasses stretched across these shafts, where great buckets swung, in which men hoisted the earth to the light of the sun by sheer force of muscle.

The sun came softly down, and shone brightly on the hillside where I stood. I lifted my hands to Shasta, above the butte and town, for he looked like an old acquaintance, and again was glad.

An Indian Woman Deplores the Soreness of the Land, Recorded in 1925

Prophecy of Kate Luckie (ten years ago). — People talk a lot about the world ending. Maybe this child [pointing to her eldest child] will see something, but this world will stay as long as Indians live. When the Indians all die, then God will let the water come down from the north. Everyone will drown. That is because the white people never cared for land or deer or bear. When we Indians kill meat, we eat it all up. When we dig roots, we make little holes. When we build houses, we make little holes. When we burn grass for grasshoppers, we don't ruin things. We shake down acorns and pine nuts. We don't chop down the trees. We only use dead wood. But the white people plow up the ground, pull up the trees, kill everything. The trees say, "Don't. I am sore. Don't hurt me." But they chop it down and cut it up. The spirit of the land hates them. They blast out trees and stir it up to its depths. They saw up the trees. That hurts them. The Indians never hurt anything, but the white people destroy all. They blast rocks and scatter them on the earth. The rock says, "Don't! You are hurting me." But the white people pay no attention. When the Indians use rocks, they take little round ones for their cooking. The white people dig deep long tunnels. They make roads. They dig as much as they wish. They don't care how much the ground cries out. How can the spirit of the earth like the white man? That is why God will upset the world — because it is sore all over. Everywhere the white man has touched it, it is sore. It looks sick. So it gets even by killing him when he blasts. But eventually the water will come.

This water, it can't be hurt. The white people go to the river and turn it into dry land. The water says: "I don't care. I am water. You can use me all you wish. I am always the same. I can't be used up. Use me. I am water. You can't hurt me." The white people use the water of sacred springs in their houses. The water says: "That is all right. You can use me, but you can't overcome me." All that is water says this. "Wherever you put me, I'll be in my home. I am awfully smart. Lead me out of my springs, lead me from my rivers, but I came from the ocean and I shall go back into the ocean. You can dig a ditch and put me in it, but I go only so far and I am out of sight. I am awfully smart. When I am out of sight I am on my way home."

Sarah Royce Recalls the Mining Camps, Recorded in 1932

And now began my first experience in a California mining camp. The sense of safety that came from having arrived where there was no danger of attacks from Indians, or of perishing of want or of cold on the desert, or in the mountains, was at first so restful, that I was willing, for awhile, to throw off anxiety; and, like a child fixing a play-house I sang as I arranged our few comforts in our tent. Indeed, part of the time it was fixing a play-house; for Mary was constantly pattering about at my side; and often, things were arranged for her convenience and amusement.

Still, there was a lurking feeling of want of security from having only a cloth wall between us and out of doors. I had heard the sad story (which, while it shocked, reassured us) of the summary punishment inflicted in a neighboring town upon three thieves, who had been tried by a committee of citizens and, upon conviction, all hung. The circumstances had given to the place the name of Hang-Town. We were assured that, since then, no case of stealing had occurred in the northern mines; and I had seen, with my own eyes, buck-skin purses half full of gold-dust, lying on a rock near the road-side, while the owners were working some distance off. So I was not afraid of robbery; but it seemed as if some impertinent person might so easily intrude, or hang about, in a troublesome manner.

But I soon found I had no reason to fear. Sitting in my tent sewing, I heard some men cutting wood up a hill behind us. One of them called out to another "Look out not to let any sticks roll that way, there's a woman and child in that tent." "Aye, aye, we won't frighten them" was the reply, all spoken in pleasant, respectful tones. A number of miners passed every morning and afternoon, to and from their work; but none of them stared obtrusively. One, I observed, looked at Mary with interest a time or two, but did not stop, till one day I happened to be walking with her near the door, when he paused, bowed courteously and said, "Excuse me madam, may I speak to the little girl? We see so few ladies and children in California, and she is about the size of a little sister I left at home." "Certainly," I said, leading her towards him. His gentle tones and pleasant words easily induced her to shake hands, and talk with him. He proved to be a young physician, who had not long commenced practice at home, when the news of gold discovery in California induced him to seek El Dorado, hoping thus to secure, more speedily, means of support for his widowed mother and the younger members of the family. His partner in work was a

Text from Sarah Royce, *A Frontier Lady: Recollections of the Gold Rush.* Lincoln, Neb.: University of Nebraska Press, 1977 [1932], pp. 79–85. Yale University Press.

well educated lawyer; and another of their party was a scientist who had been applying his knowledge of geology and mineralogy, in exploring; and had lately returned from a few miles south with a report so favorable they intended in a day or two to go and make a claim on his newly discovered ground. Here, then, was a party of California miners, dressed in the usual mining attire, and carrying pick, shovel and pans to and from their work; who yet were cultured gentlemen.

I soon found that this was by no means a solitary instance. But a much larger number of the miners belonged to other very valuable classes of society. Merchants, mechanics, farmers were all there in large numbers. So that in almost every mining camp there was enough of the element of order, to control, or very much influence, the opposite forces. . . .

During my short residence, of only two months, in Weaverville I had but a few brief glimpses of the objectionable phases of society. Indeed, I ought not to say *glimpses*, for it was almost wholly through the ear, that anything of this kind came to me. There was on the opposite side of the ravine, some rods down, a large tent, or rather, two tents irregularly joined, which, at first, I heard called a boarding house, then found was a public stopping place for travelers; and afterwards it turned out to include a full fledged drinking and gambling saloon. . . .

The . . . sound I caught . . . came through a woman, the only one besides myself in the town. There had been another when I first came, a delicate, lovely invalid who, away back on the Platte River, had for awhile traveled in the same company with us, riding much on horseback in hope of benefiting her health. She and her husband stayed in Weaverville a short time but, when the rains began they sought the valleys farther to the south. This other woman who remained was a plain person who, with her husband, had come from one of the eastern states, and was acquainted only with country life. She was probably between thirty and thirty-five years of age, and the idea of "shining in society" had evidently never dawned upon her mind, when I first used to see her cooking by her out-door camp fire, not far from our tent. Ordinary neighborly inter-course had passed between us, but I had not seen her for some time, when she called one day and in quite an exultant mood told me the man who kept the boarding-house had offered her a hundred dollars a month to cook three meals a day for his boarders, that she was to do no dishwashing and was to have someone help her all the time she was cooking. She had been filling the place some days, and evidently felt that her prospect of making money was very enviable. Her husband, also, was highly pleased that his wife could earn so much. Again I saw nothing of her for some time, when again she called; this time much changed in style. Her hair was dressed in very youthful fashion; she wore a new gown with full trimmings, and seemed to feel in every way elevated. She came to tell me there was to be a ball at the public house in a few days; that several ladies who lived at different camps within a few miles, chiefly at Hang-Town, were coming; and she came to say that I might expect an invitation as they would like very much to have me come. I laughingly declined, as being no dancer, and entirely unfitted to adorn any such scene. The assembly I think came off, but I did not get even a glimpse of its glories; and as she, soon after, left the town, I never saw her again. I only remembered the circumstance because it amused me as being my first invitation into "Society" in California; and also as it gave me a glimpse of the ease with which the homeliest if not the oldest, might become a "belle" in those early days, if she only had the ambition; and was willing to accept the honor, in the offered way.

Soon after arriving in Weaverville, my husband had met with an acquaintance who had been a traveling companion in the early part of our long journey. He had washed out a little gold, and was desirous to go into business. He had made two or three acquaintances who also thought this new mining settlement presented an opening for a store; but none of them were accustomed to trading. They understood that my husband was; so they proposed to him to enter into partnership with them, proceed immediately to Sacramento City to purchase goods, and they, by the time he returned, would have a place prepared to open a store.

An effort was made to get a house built. The plan was, to hew out timber for the frame, and to split shakes for the roof and sides. But when they tried to get men to help them; so that the building could be done in anything like reasonable time, they found it impossible. All were so absorbed in washing out gold, or hunting for some to wash, that they could not think of doing anything else. On all sides the gold-pans were rattling, the cradles rocking, and the water splashing. So the best that could be done was, to hew out some strong tent poles and ridges, and erect two good sized tents, one behind the other; the back one for dwelling, the front for a store. An opportunity occurred to buy a large cook stove, which was placed near the junction of the two tents. The back part of the back tent was curtained off for me, leaving a space round the cook stove for kitchen and dining room. One of the men slept in the store, and the other two had a small tent on one side. They managed to buy some packing boxes, and other odds and ends of lumber, and so made shelves and a counter, which did very well for those primitive times.

We were soon fixed in our new quarters, the goods arrived from Sacramento, and business was opened. As one of the partners had formerly been in the meat business, some fat cattle were purchased, and beef was added to the other articles sold. This drew quite a crowd every morning; for fresh meat had not yet become very plentiful in the mines. It had not been thought necessary for all the men of the firm to devote their time to the store. Two of them continued mining; so, when a large number of customers came together, I helped to serve them.

❦ E S S A Y S

The essays explore the contributions of and conflicts among people of different races, ethnicities, and classes who lived in California during the Gold Rush years of the nineteenth century. The first, by George H. Phillips, a historian at the University of Colorado, Boulder, describes Indian life before and after the Gold Rush and details the Indians' initial resistance and eventual accommodation to California's newer immigrants. The second essay, by Robert Kelley, a historian at the

University of California, Santa Barbara, depicts environmental deterioration under hydraulic mining and analyzes the ensuing legal battle between farmers defending their property from debris and miners defending their right to make profits. In the third essay, Rudolph Lapp, a historian at the College of San Mateo, discusses opportunities and problems encountered by African-Americans who went west either as free blacks from the northern states or as slaves from the South. Finally, the fourth selection, by Sylvia Sun Minnick, a historian from Stockton, California, analyzes the lives of the Chinese who immigrated to California, worked in the mines, and then suffered the effects of prejudice and violence. As a group, the essays spotlight some different ways in which people of diverse races and classes reconstructed California's environment and contributed to its ecological transformation.

Indians Encounter Miners

GEORGE H. PHILLIPS

Archaeologists generally agree that Asian peoples first migrated into the Western Hemisphere across the Bering Strait from Siberia to Alaska sometime between 50,000 and 20,000 B.C. Following the large game upon which they subsisted, they crossed the strait because at different periods during the Pleistocene epoch, commonly called the Ice Age, a land bridge connected Siberia and Alaska. When glacial ice locked up immense amounts of the planet's ocean water, the bridge appeared; when meltage poured water back into the oceans, the bridge disappeared.

The main route into the present United States was probably along an ice-free corridor that extended from the Arctic Ocean southwards through Canada. From this route, which lay just east of the Rocky Mountains, some groups branched off to the west. By 9,000 B.C., or perhaps much earlier, their descendants had reached the Pacific Coast. . . .

By the sixteenth century, the Indians of California had acquired considerable knowledge about their environment. They hunted deer, tule elk, Roosevelt elk, and pronghorn antelope as well as small animals, including rabbits, rodents, squirrels, ducks, songbirds, quail, and mice. Bows and arrows, snares, throwing sticks, pitfalls, and nets were employed to kill or capture the game.

Coastal Indians exploited a variety of marine life, such as the king and silver salmon and the steelhead trout. As attested by the numerous shell mounds and bones found at many coastal sites, Indians eagerly sought mollusks and sea mammals. Sea mussel, oyster, scallop, and California venus clam were particularly abundant along the southern coast, and sea mussel, bentnose macoma, and oyster were found along the northern coast. The peoples of the Santa Barbara Channel and nearby islands relied heavily on the sea lion, sea otter, and harbor seal.

On the Sacramento and San Joaquin rivers and their tributaries, fishing was a most rewarding economic activity. The salmon semiannually spawned

---

From George H. Phillips, *The Enduring Struggle: Indians in California History*. San Francisco: Boyd and Fraser, 1981, pp. 5–13, 43–52. Reprinted by permission of Boyd & Fraser Publishing Company.

upstream in great numbers, so a concentrated fishing effort often brought great return. Weirs and traps were placed in streams but only for a limited number of days, thus allowing some of the salmon to pass through to be caught by groups residing upriver. Because political boundaries often encompassed river and stream fronts, inter-lineage disputes were probably frequent as groups vied with one another for preferred fishing territories.

Indians also collected a variety of plant foods, such as the buckeye, sage seed (chia), the epos root, and different kinds of berries. But the acorn was the most important plant staple in California, and Indians ranked in order of preference at least ten species of oak. Indians gathered the acorns in the fall while still on the trees, the harvesting continuing until a winter's supply had been acquired.

The acorn became an essential food staple once Indians mastered the process of grinding the nut into a meal and leaching the tannic acid. Pouring hot water through the meal placed either in a basket or a sand-lined depression in the ground eliminated the poison. The meal was then roasted, baked, or boiled.

So economically important was the acorn that the territory controlled by each society was often determined by the number and productivity of oak trees. Failure of an acorn crop could cause severe hardships, even starvation. Crises of this kind often led to conflicts in which territorial aggrandizement resulted. Those regions containing the most productive oak trees carried the largest populations and were the most contested.

Gaining knowledge of their environment required a persistent effort over a long period and indicates that Indians, contrary to established opinion, were not passive occupants of the land. Rather, they experimented actively in developing techniques of land management. For example, in the five ecological zones exploited (grasslands, woodlands, woodland-grass, chaparral, and coniferous forest), Indians practiced controlled burning. Within the woodland-grass and grassland zones, fires reduced brush cover, which lessened the hazards of wildfires and increased plant and animal productivity. In the chaparral zone, fire, by destroying the upper portions of shrub species, allowed new growth to emerge that attracted browsing animals. Select fires in the woodlands and coniferous forest zones created parklike conditions which gave Indians easy access in their search for plants and animals.

Techniques of land management are also evident in proto-horticultural activities. The Ipai, Tipai, Cahuilla, Wintu, Maidu, Miwok, Yokuts, Panamint, Hupa, Yurok, and Karok planted tobacco. The Ipai and Tipai sometimes transplanted wild plants to areas where they could be better tended, and the Cahuilla regularly pruned mesquite to improve growth.

By the first decade of the nineteenth century, some groups in the interior of southern California—the Cahuilla, Ipai, Tipai, and Chemehuevi in particular—were raising corn and other crops. Since agriculture was not well established at the Spanish coastal missions in southern California until the 1770s, it is unlikely that knowledge of crop growing could have diffused eastward in so short a period. Indeed, this period of some thirty years (1770s to early 1800s) must be weighed against the hundreds of years in which knowledge of farming could have spread westward from the Colorado River where horticulture long preceded the arrival of Europeans. . . .

After 1769 and the establishment of permanent Spanish settlements, Indian culture came under enormous pressure. But the first Californians did not readily submit to foreign domination as is sometimes thought. Rather, they implemented strategies of evasion, selective acculturation, and military resistance. Indians possessing prior experience with Europeans were better able to assess the intentions of the settlers than were those who had remained outside the contact zones. This experience may account for the open hostility demonstrated by southern California societies shortly after the Spanish arrived.

In 1848 when gold was discovered in northern California, rancheros in the area quickly transferred their Indian workers from ranching to mining. Moreover, during the first two years of the gold boom, a large part of the independent Indian population of the Sierra foothills, from the Feather to the Merced rivers, engaged in some form of mining activity. A government report of 1848 estimated that more than half of the four thousand miners were Indians. Most worked for whites, but increasing numbers mined on their own.

The arrival of thousands of newcomers from outside California during 1849 dramatically altered relations between Indians and whites in the gold-bearing regions. Whereas the Mexican and Anglo miners of 1848 considered Indians an important economic asset, the forty-niners viewed them as a savage barrier to their own financial advancement. They were outraged that some of their fellow miners could muster large numbers of Indian workers while they had to pan in small groups. Direct economic competition with Indians was outside their experience. To them the Indian was not a worker but a warrior, not an economic unit to be exploited but a physical threat to be eliminated.

To illustrate: in early 1849 a party of Oregonians prospecting on the American River took over a Maidu village and raped several women and shot a number of men who tried to intervene. A short time later, Indians retaliated by killing five miners on the Middle Fork of the American River. The Oregonians, in turn, attacked a village near Weber's Creek where they killed a dozen Indians and captured several more, some being employees of local whites. In Coloma they executed seven of the prisoners. Since no evidence linked the executed Indians with the killing of the five miners, they may have been chosen simply because they were mine workers. Shortly after this incident, Indians began leaving the gold fields, and by the early 1850s few remained.

The cycle of violent escalation that characterized Indian-white interaction in the north is further demonstrated by an incident known as the Clear Lake Massacre. In 1849 Pomo Indians killed two white men, Andrew Kelsey and Charles Stone, who had established a ranch in the Clear Lake area and had abused and even murdered some of their Indian laborers. The following year an army unit confronted the Indians and, to use modern military jargon, engaged in obvious "overkill." According to the San Francisco *Daily Alta California*,

The troops arrived in the vicinity of the Lake, and came unexpectedly upon a body of Indians numbering between two and three hundred. — They immediately surrounded them and as the Indians raised a shout of defiance and attempted escape, poured in a destructive fire indiscriminately upon men, women, and children. "They fell," says our informant,"as grass before the sweep of the scythe." Little or no resistance was encountered, and the work of butchery was of short duration. The shrieks of the slaughtered victims died away, the roar of muskets. . . ceased, and stretched lifeless upon the sod of their native valley were the bleeding bodies of these Indians. . . .

Also causing Indian anguish and hatred were Anglo slave raiders. Because Indian children were in demand as servants and workhands, a new business emerged in the early 1850s that continued for over a decade. Although blatantly illegal, slave raiding was stimulated by "An Act for the Government and Protection of Indians," which the California legislature had approved in April 1850. Section three of the act provided for the indenturing of Indians to whites. . . .

Between 1852 and 1867, three to four thousand children were taken. Added to these figures must be the hundreds of Indian women who were seized for concubinage and adult men apprehended for field labor. In April 1863 section three of the 1860 act was repealed, probably because the question of slavery was then being decided by the Civil War. The damage had been done, however, and the Indians who had lost their children were left with a lingering bitterness. . . .

In early 1850 James Savage established a trading post and mining camp on the Merced River, some twenty miles from the entrance to the [Yosemite] valley. Indians, probably Miwok-speaking Yosemites, attacked the post in the spring but were driven off. Savage withdrew from the area and erected posts on the Mariposa and Fresno rivers. There he gained dominance over local Indians and monopolized the gold trade with Indian and white miners.

It was not long before local Indian leaders realized the danger Savage and the miners posed to Indian sovereignty. A Chowchilla Yokuts, José Rey, attempted to unite various groups to drive the whites from the region. At a meeting with Savage in late 1850, Rey stunned the trader by admitting that war was imminent.

My people are now ready to begin a war against the white gold diggers. If all the tribes will be as one tribe, and join with us, we will drive all the white men from our mountains. If all the tribes will go together, the white men will run from us, and leave their property behind them. The tribes who join in with my people will be the first to secure the property of the gold diggers.

Shortly after this meeting, Indians who worked at the Mariposa camp deserted, and the following day the Fresno post was attacked. Indians killed three white men, plundered the store, and drove off horses and mules. Several other attacks occurred in the vicinity, igniting what the Americans called the Mariposa Indian War.

In response to the outbreak, the governor of California authorized the formation of a volunteer military unit. Known as the Mariposa Battalion and commanded by James Savage, it consisted of 200 men and officers. The governor also encouraged the three Indian commissioners to proceed at once to the trouble spot and negotiate with the disaffected groups. They arrived on the Mariposa River in early March and quickly concluded a treaty with six Indian societies. The Indians were given land at the base of the foothills between the Merced and Tuolumne rivers.

The Yosemites and their chief Tenaya, however, failed to attend the conference, and the commissioners ordered the Mariposa Battalion to bring them in. A few days later Savage captured a village on the south fork of the Merced. Indian messengers were dispatched into the Yosemite Valley, and the following day Tenaya appeared alone and convinced Savage that his people would arrive shortly. Tenaya could not understand why his people had to give up their mountain homeland for territory in the San Joaquin Valley.

> My people do not want anything from the "Great Father" you tell me about. The Great Spirit is our father, and he has always supplied us with all we need. We do not want anything from white men. Our women are able to do our work. Go, then; let us remain in the mountains where we were born; where the ashes of our fathers have been given to the winds. . . . My people do not want to go to the plains. The tribes who go there are some of them very bad. They will make war on my people. We cannot live on the plains with them. Here we can defend ourselves against them. . . .

The Yosemites were relocated to territory on the Fresno River, but individually and in small groups they slipped away at the first opportunity. "I remained in the Fresno Camp for twelve days," recalled María Lebrado. "After that I went farther and farther for acorns. Finally, I ran away from camp along with the other Indians and came back to Yosemite Valley."

Their freedom was of short duration. In May 1852, when Indians killed two prospectors in the valley, federal troops rushed in. They captured five Indians wearing the clothes of the miners and executed all on the spot. Tenaya and his people fled east across the Sierra Nevada to the Mono Lake Paiutes.

The Indian commissioners continued their work, eventually negotiating eighteen treaties with over a hundred Indian societies. They set aside about one-seventh of the state for Indian occupation, a land allotment considered too generous by most whites. Public pressure on the state's U.S. senators caused them to oppose ratification, and in early June 1852 the Senate rejected the treaties. Indians who had given up their homelands in exchange for territories promised in the treaties now had neither.

In the meantime, Congress had established an independent Indian superintendency for California. . . . In theory, Indians would be persuaded, not forced, to settle on reservations where they would receive seeds, farm animals, and instruction in farming methods. A garrison of soldiers would be stationed at each reservation to maintain order and protect the Indians from unscrupulous whites. . . .

[But by 1867] only five [sic] reservations were functioning—Hoopa Valley, about twenty miles northeast of Eureka; Round Valley, some sixty miles south and slightly east of Hoopa Valley; Smith River, near the Oregon line; and Tule River, some thirty miles north and slightly east of Bakersfield. Of an Indian population that had dropped precipitously to only 34,000, fewer than

3,000 resided on reservations. As a substitute for traditional society, the reservation obviously had failed.

Miners Encounter Farmers

ROBERT KELLEY

The floor of the Sacramento Valley is flat, almost featureless, and quite close to sea level. Meandering rivers cross it to empty into the cluster of bays which center upon San Francisco. The longest and deepest of these rivers is the Sacramento, which emerges from the high country at Redding and flows down the middle of the 150-mile long valley, swinging past the city of Sacramento and then losing itself in the complex of islands and channels in the delta lands. To the west of the valley are the lumpy hills and low eminences of the coast ranges; to the north Mount Shasta dominates a vast complex of uplands, and to the east is the Sierra Nevada, the most imposing single geographic feature of California. For four hundred miles it stands as a great, shaggy barrier between the fertile Sacramento and San Joaquin valleys and the Nevada deserts. . . .

Down the long western slope of the northern Sierra Nevada rush four rivers: the Feather, the Yuba, the Bear, and the American. They do not drop from such great heights as those in the southern reaches of the Sierra, but they are powerful, torrential streams, especially in the spring when the great snow pack above them melts. They have trenched themselves in deep canyons, and flow far below the horizon formed by the gently sloping strata which form the Sierra Nevada. The farthest north and longest of these rivers is the Feather, whose forks rise in the remote wilds of Plumas County. . . .

About midway in its course from Oroville to the Sacramento, the Feather receives the waters of the second of the four northern rivers, the Yuba. Its forks, whose wide watersheds of conifer forest in the mountains encompass most of Nevada and Sierra counties, join just before leaving the foothills at Smartville. A vigorous, swiftly-moving stream, the Yuba hurries out of the mountains, . . . joining the Feather where Marysville sits within its great levees. . . . The Feather receives the third of these rivers; the Bear. . . .

The last of the four rivers is the long, winding American, a stream heavy with history. In its south fork James Marshall, in 1848, found the dull flakes which set off the rush to the golden Sierra. The broad ridge paralleling its north fork has borne, in turn, the argonauts who came in search of wealth, the Chinese building the first railroad to vault the Sierra, and now the endless flow of immigration which coasts down this long ridge on the major transcontinental highway. It was where the American joins the Sacramento that John Sutter decided to build the fort which grew into California's capital city. . . .

When the gravel hills were first discovered at Nevada City, miners left the stream bed with a rush. Rising and falling picks glinted all over the valley as

Text from Robert Kelley, *Gold vs. Grain: The Hydraulic Mining Controversy in California's Sacramento Valley*, Arthur H. Clark, 1959, pp. 21–28, 57–82, 229–42. Reprinted by permission of Arthur H. Clark Co.

miners planted claims on the hillside and attacked it vigorously. They tore up the underbrush, stripped off overburden, and even uprooted soaring pines in their search for gold. . . .

. . . Men came flocking to the new diggings from all over the Sierra, for stream placers were giving out and river towns were dying. Several thousand men were soon digging and washing pay dirt on the hill above Nevada City. Pick and shovel tore up the entire valley, yet few claims paid enough to warrant all the toil. The technical problem was apparently insoluble. But in the spring of 1852, a miner named Anthony Chabot, who was working a claim on the side of Buckeye Hill above Nevada City, devised a tolerable solution. He built a set of inclined wooden penstocks, strengthened by iron clamps so that they could hold a fifty-foot column, or "head" of water without bursting. To this he attached a four-inch canvas hose which he laid upon his claim. The water gushing out of it created an artificial stream strong enough to tear up the soil. It soon excavated a ditch into which Chabot fed pay dirt by breaking the ground on either side and shoveling it into the water. He periodically shut off the water to recover the gold which had collected on the bed of the ditch. This process, called "ground-sluicing," was much more efficient than older methods, and spread rapidly as a step to an economical system for working Tertiary gravels.

Early the following year, in March of 1853, Edward E. Matteson began mining on American Hill, just north of Nevada City. . . . He suggested to his partners that they try breaking down the bank of a cut they had made into the hillside not by pick, but by a stream of water. . . . Chabot, a sail-maker by trade, constructed a hose for them, and Eli Miller, Matteson's partner and a tinsmith, made a tapered nozzle of sheet iron. Hose and nozzle were attached to a barrel on top of the bank to regulate the head of water which was carried to it by Chabot's wooden penstocks. . . .

To their delight, the jet of water turned the bank into sliding mud and washed it into and through their sluice. The gold, being much heavier than gravel and dirt, settled behind riffle boards in the bottom of the sluice. Given water, ground, drainage, and the proper equipment, one man could do in a day what dozens could hardly do in weeks. They had revolutionized gold mining and invented a process which was eventually to spread all over the world.

The results were immediate and profound. An entirely new industry was born. Wherever Tertiary gravels were being worked, rudimentary water systems were hastily enlarged, claims were fitted up with hoses and nozzles, and the roar of hurtling water filled the air. . . .

The northern Sierra boomed with prosperity. During the 1870's, Nevada City grew from a town of roughly four thousand people to one of fifty-four hundred. The townships along the Ridge and in the upper Bear watershed all increased in the same proportion, while Grass Valley, the quartz mining town, dropped a few hundred from its population of a bit over seven thousand in 1870. . . .

But though the mines were prosperous, they were in deep trouble. Down in the Sacramento Valley, where the rivers draining the mines crossed broad, flatland counties, the farms and cities had been bitterly complaining for years about what the miners were doing. The Yuba and its sister streams, as they rushed down their mountain canyons to the Valley floor, carried enormous quantities of mining debris. In their beds lay vast heaps of tailings which slowly moved downstream as the torrential rivers sought to scour out their beds. Abruptly levelling out on the flatlands, the rivers dropped their silt, thereby laying down rapidly-growing fan deposits of tailings. . . .

When the boom swept the mountains in the late sixties and great companies began dumping debris directly into the canyons instead of into slow-moving upland creeks where most of the tailings remained fairly permanently lodged, concern mounted again. Farmers talked of how the rivers were filling, how each small rise in the water produced flood, how hundreds of acres of fruit orchard along the rivers were dying as debris spread slowly, imperceptibly, out into the valley. Their problem was the more ominous because the rivers were undiked and untended. At no level of government was there any agency charged with controlling the Sacramento and its tributaries, or for that matter any other river in the state. River management was completely in the hands of private individuals, and this could only produce chaos, for the rivers overwhelmed the pathetic efforts of isolated individuals to protect themselves. As channels filled with debris and rivers were forced out of their beds, the Sacramento Valley entered a protracted state of siege.

The towns of Marysville and Yuba City were in an especially dangerous situation. Sitting on either side of the Feather where it is joined by the Yuba, they were assaulted not only by the debris coming down from the mines near Oroville, but also by the great flow coming out of the upper Yuba basin. By 1868, the beds of the two rivers were higher than Marysville's streets, and in that year the town began building the levees which eventually encircled the city as high as the housetops. Within the next decade Marysville was to spend hundreds of thousands of dollars on these great walls; their cost eventually soared well over a million dollars. . . .

In early January of 1875 a storm moved in over the valley and deluged mountains and flatlands for a week with snow, rain, thunder and lightning. By the morning of the nineteenth the swollen brown waters of the Yuba were rushing along near the top of Marysville's levees. With the fire house bell ringing in their ears, men rushed out of their homes and flung themselves into a nightmare struggle to save the city. Near the cemetery, despite frantic efforts, the river began slipping over the levee and pouring down into town. By nightfall people were rushing wildly for safety; at eight o'clock the levee broke near the hospital, and a torrent of water rushed into the streets. In wild confusion women and children were rescued, barns, sheds and frame houses began floating about, and a little boy drowned. By the following noon the city had filled like a bowl. Not until the evening of the twenty-first did the cold and hungry citizens of Marysville get aid, with the steamer "Flora" breasting the flood from Sacramento. . . .

By [the] time the legislature was beginning its 1876 session, a cloud of resolutions, bills, and sundry proposals of all sorts descended upon it. . . . On the eighth of January, 1876, Campbell Berry, Sutter County's assemblyman, added to these proposals a recommended concurrent resolution which he hoped the legislature would send to Congress. It condemned the hydraulic mining industry in terms by then familiar, and asked that Congress do two things: prevent the opening of any more hydraulic claims until the operators took steps to impound their debris; and send out an engineering team to examine the situation and make recommendations to Congress. . . .

Miners fought desperately in their attempt to convince a people in transition that gold production was essential to the state's prosperity, and at all costs must be protected. The report of the Committee on Mines and Mining pointed out that agriculture was called into existence in California by the needs of the mining population, and insisted that one-fifth of the farmers' customers still lived in the mountains. Indeed, an excessive concentration on farming would be inimical, for "It is a well-known historical fact, that every country which has largely exported its cereals for many consecutive years, has, in the end, impoverished itself, and finally fallen into decay." Above all, a local market should be fostered and this could best be done by increasing the hydraulic mining industry, not decreasing it. Anything undertaken to cripple hydraulic mining would injure the farmer, not help him.

The Committee on Agriculture submitted a . . . brief recommendation. No man should use his property, it insisted, so as to damage that of others, yet this had been done for years in spite of the fact that the gold yield was steadily declining and the mines were less valuable to the state at large. Where "once stood fine mansions, pleasant homes, rich orchards, and fields smiling with golden grain, is now to be seen only barrenness and desolation." Furthermore, hydraulic mining was only in its infancy, and devastation of farm lands would become far worse in the near future. The farms faced utter destruction, as did also the city of Marysville. Farm production far exceeded in value the gold extracted even in the best years of the mines; on "agriculture, and its kindred pursuits, . . . the wealth and strength of states and nations are founded; it is our great reliance in the future." Moreover, navigable streams were filling, and the state would be delivered completely into the greedy hands of the railroads. The Bay of San Francisco would shoal, its entrance would fill, and San Francisco's prosperity would be ruined. . . .

The mines continued to operate at peak capacity despite all that had gone on previously and the farmers resolved to carry their fight further. . . .They decided to take the controversy into the federal courts, on the supposition that their great power and prestige would be adequate to enforce any injunctions which might be issued.

On the nineteenth of September, 1882, Edwards Woodruff, a citizen of New York state and a property owner in Marysville and its surrounding countryside, entered the Ninth United States Circuit Court in San Francisco and filed suit against the North Bloomfield and all other mines along the Yuba, asking for a perpetual injunction. Judge Lorenzo Sawyer notified the defendants that they must show cause why a temporary injunction to be effective during the suit should not be issued, basing his action on affidavits submitted by Woodruff's attorney, George Cadwalader.

The Woodruff case extended over the better part of a year and a half; not until January of 1884 did Sawyer render his decision. In the meantime, the case remained close to the center of public interest. . . .

On several occasions, Judge Sawyer made trips up the rivers, over the farms, and into the mines. These trips were usually made by steamer so that he could see for himself how the rivers had changed since he had tramped along them thirty years earlier. . . .

On Thursday, January 6, 1884, word came to Marysville that the decision would be given the next day. The townspeople, tremendously excited, rushed about preparing for a celebration. . . .

At 11:00 A.M. the following morning in San Francisco, Judge Sawyer entered his courtroom, which was packed by a large audience of attorneys and interested parties, and began reading his decision. He described at great length the injurious effect of mining debris, pointing out that two state-built dams, costing about $500,000, proved utterly ineffective and were eventually destroyed. Those dams which the miners themselves constructed had rapidly filled with debris, breached, and become ineffective. Since mining debris was doing such widespread damage, he held that unless dumping tailings into the rivers was authorized by law it constituted a general, far-reaching and most destructive public and private nuisance in both common and statutory law. Furthermore, the generality of action by one against the other was justified, since the suits were actually between the mining and valley counties interested. As proof, he pointed to the formation of organizations on both sides which paid all expenses.

Three and a half hours after he had started reading his decision, which covered two hundred and twenty-five pages, Sawyer stated that the defendant companies were "perpetually enjoined and restrained from discharging or dumping into the Yuba river . . . [or its tributaries] any of the tailings, bowlders [*sic*], cobble stones, gravel, sand, clay, debris or refuse matter. . . ." Furthermore, the companies enjoined, who owned most of the ditches and dams in the Yuba basin, were enjoined from allowing anyone to use their water supplies for hydraulic mining. No longer could they look the other way while their workmen engaged in clandestine operations. Every possible legal loophole had been closed. The miners were absolutely forbidden to allow any of their tailings to get into the rivers. . . .

The mining counties received the news as they would a death sentence. Smartville was sunk in gloom; Grass Valley reported a general feeling of "profound sorrow;" in Nevada City there was "universal dissatisfaction and regret;"a Dutch Flat resident laconically remarked, "Most of us will pack our gripsacks."

In San Francisco, the *Bulletin* expressed what might well have been a majority view when it remarked that, after all, the mines were no longer the mainstay of California. This distinction had shifted to agriculture: "The wheat field produces year after year, and wine and oil and wool are perennial." California's values were passing through a crucial transition. The farmer was taking the place of eminence long held by the miner.

Black Miners in California

RUDOLPH LAPP

When the gold rush began in 1848, the black population in California was no more than a few dozen. They were a blend of the earlier, pre-American period, arrivals and those who came with the American conquerors of Mexican California. By the end of 1848, their numbers were augmented by the deserters from New England ships, mostly whalers from New Bedford, Massachusetts, and by the Afro-Latin Americans who came from Mexico, Chile, and Peru. By the end of 1849, the great wave of gold seekers brought blacks from every region of the United States and the West Indies. California played host to the broadest representation of Afro-Americans in the western hemisphere. Black New Englanders met slaves from Missouri, New York blacks met black Jamaicans, and free blacks from Ohio met free Spanish-speaking blacks from south of the border. American blacks were by far the largest group, and more of them were free than slave.

According to the census of 1850, there were 962 persons of color in California, including some Sandwich Islanders (often called *Kanakas*). The majority of those called black in the census, between 600 and 700 living in the gold rush counties, were of North American origin. The others, who included Latin-American blacks, were distributed throughout the state, with some concentrations in San Francisco and Sacramento. Many of the Latin-American blacks, however, soon left California to return to their homes, chiefly in Mexico and Chile.

Well over half of the Afro-Americans in the Mother Lode counties by the beginning of 1850 were free persons. The overwhelming majority, whether free or slave, were classified as miners.

Blacks from the United States who were in the mines by 1850 came from three geographic regions: the free states, chiefly New York and Massachusetts (134); the slave states of the lower and Deep South (91); and the border states of the South, to which Virginia was the greatest contributor (374). More than half of this latter group may well have been free, because the border states had the largest free Negro populations. Also, many of these black men and women, born in border states of the South, had resided in the North prior to their departure for California.

The unceasing flow of people to California had, by 1852, more than doubled the black population of the state, although blacks remained about one percent of the population. There were more than 2,000 Negroes in California by then. While the black communities of San Francisco and Sacramento became somewhat larger, the black population increase was greater in the mining communities. There were over 1,000 blacks in the Mother Lode country, while San Francisco and Sacramento had 444 and 338 black residents respectively. In Los Angeles County there were only 45 blacks. Most of these had come with Mississippi Mormons, their former masters, to found and build the town of San Bernardino.

Gold rush maps of the Mother Lode bear witness to the presence of the Afro-Americans in those frenzied years. One finds, for instance, the place names Negro Hill or Nigger Hill, Negro Bar, and Negro Flat. They represent sites where a black man made a lucky strike or where groups of black men lived and mined. Erwin G. Gudde, historian of California place names, found over thirty locations in the state that used the term *Nigger* or *Negro* and in some cases *Negros* where the Spanish recognized the presence or importance of some black man. In addition to the above, there were sites named Negro Butte, Negro Run, Nigger Bill Bend, Nigger Jack Slough, and Arroyo de los Negros. While the word *Negro* has evaporated from current maps of California, the story of the black gold miners has survived. From splinters of information scattered among obscure sources there emerge tales of good fortune, bad luck, courage, and despair.

Many black miners tried their luck in the gold fields, but only those whose luck was exceptional gained any notice. Perhaps the first of these fortunate gold hunters was a cook named Hector, who deserted the naval squadron ship *Southhampton* in Monterey in 1848. An on-the-spot observer was present when Hector returned to Monterey with $4,000 in gold. One of the richest strikes made by anyone was that of a black man known only as Dick, who mined $100,000 worth of gold in Tuolumne County in 1848, only to lose it by gambling in San Francisco.

The stories of the two Negro Hills tell much of the black experience in gold rush California. The first Negro Hill was located on the American River, not far from where gold was originally discovered on the south fork of the river. The hill was first mined by blacks in 1849. According to one source, these men were a Massachusetts black named Kelsey and a black Methodist minister. Digging in that area continued to prove rewarding, as new finds were being made into the following year. Early in 1850 the San Francisco *Daily Alta California* reported:

> About four miles below Mormon Island on the American River, there have been new diggings discovered which prove to yield exceedingly well. They are called "Nigger Diggings" from the fact that some colored gentlemen first discovered them.

Two years later another strike was made nearby. Its proximity to Negro Hill was felt by miners to insure that a long run of profit would follow.

The original success of the two black men resulted in the growth of a Negro mining community around the hill, as well as on a nearby hill that came to be called Little Negro Hill. In 1852 two Massachusetts blacks opened a store and boardinghouse, around which a concentration of black residences grew up. Since the diggings continued to be sufficiently rewarding, the Negro Hill community continued to survive and was even stable enough to deserve the attentions of a minister. By 1854, a white Methodist clergyman was offering Sunday evening services on a regular basis. A young white New Englander, who attended these services occasionally, commented that the majority of the congregation was black. He wrote to his sister that he would have attended more consistently if he did not have to fight his prejudices every time. By 1855 the Negro Hill community had grown to about 400. Other minority peoples, particularly Chinese and Portuguese miners, became residents of this village. In 1855 Negro Hill was still described as an area with "scores of hardy miners making good wages." However, trouble soon appeared because many of the Negro Hill community were white and prejudiced. That year drunken whites looking for a fight attacked the Negro quarters and killed one black man. They were arrested, tried, and set free by a Coloma court.

The experience of blacks in nearby Massachusetts Flat stands in contrast to that of Negro Hill. This mining community, founded by New Englanders in 1854, was composed largely of Negroes and Portuguese by the following year. Here blacks were never harassed. In the presidential election of 1856, further evidence of the contrast between Negro Hill and Massachusetts Flat is found in the voting returns. The racist Negro Hill community gave Fremont only 22 percent of their vote, while Massachusetts Flat gave this antislavery candidate 75 percent of their vote.

The second Negro Hill story took place in 1851, in the southern mines near Mokelumne Hill, not far from the Mokelumne River. Unlike the Negro Hill of the northern mines, this area had many white miners working there before a black man's lucky strike. The history of this strike is associated with legend that has the ring of truth to it. As the story goes, a black man wandering into the Mokelumne Hill area looking for a claim was told by white miners to keep moving, as every spot he started to prospect was claimed to be some white man's diggings. Finally, some jokester told the black prospector to go to a high point nearby where everyone "knew" there was no gold. It was here, by digging deep enough, that he made an incredibly rich strike. The news of this find spread far and wide. The lucky black (never named in the press) soon had a black partner. As the local paper put it:

A couple of negroes who had been at work at the cayote diggings of Mokelumne Hill went home in one of the steamers . . . with eighty thousand dollars that they took out of one hole during the past four months.

Thus "Negro" or "Nigger Hill" got its name and immediately became the object of a rush of miners, both black and white.

In the environment of the gold rush it was inevitable that a mythology emerge about blacks and gold. News of black men making lucky strikes took on an aura of almost superstitious inevitability. The mythology was fed by true tales like that of the white prospector whose slave told him that in a dream he had found gold underneath their cabin. The unbelieving miner finally dug under the cabin and came upon a rich find. . . . However, given the American attitudes toward the Negro in the nineteenth century, most white minds could only conceive of superstitious insights rather than equal ability, tenacity, and luck as an explanation for blacks' exceptional gold strikes.

Black miners, like the whites, from time to time formed associations among themselves for purposes of mutual aid. While there is only one group of this kind recorded, the New York company organized in that city, the evidence suggests there were others in the gold country. They probably came together in the same informal way that so many white groups formed and reformed in the Mother Lode counties. In that uncertain and overwhelmingly white world blacks had a real need for mutual aid. Undoubtedly such organizations existed on the two Negro Hills previously described. The manuscript census clearly suggests that groups such as the eighteen blacks on the middle fork of the American River in 1850 were organized into a company. Eleven of these black miners were from Massachusetts, a state where skills in organizing had long been known by Negroes.

Organized black companies became even more visible when they occasionally associated themselves with whites. Such associations not only served the usual purposes, but for the blacks they sometimes worked as an umbrella of protection against hostile whites. . . .

* * * *

All miners in the wilds of the Sierra had to deal with the hazards of nature and the back-breaking toil of the search for gold, but the free black miner had an additional hazard—the racial attitudes of white miners in a setting of frequent lawlessness. The more hooliganlike Americans in the mines were notorious for driving people of color from well-paying claims. In the early lawless years "decent" white men would deplore this practice but only infrequently do something about it. A black man who discovered rich diggings on Long's Bar on the Feather River was soon "crowded from his claim." Daniel Langhorne, who came to California as a slave from Virginia, recalled that when he went gold prospecting to buy his freedom, he did well but had to defend his claim on the Yuba River against a white man. He was fortunate in coming before a fair-minded judge who ruled in his favor. Another black man found the harassment so intolerable that, although he was doing well, he decided to leave for the "Islands." One group of white miners near Volcano, in Amador County, tried to call a miners' meeting to organize the expulsion of black miners nearby who had well-paying claims.

* * * *

Eastern newspapers published rumors of large numbers of slaves and many slaveholders coming to California. Available evidence suggests, however, that the great majority of those who entered California as slaves came with their masters in groups of three at the most. . . . It is reasonable to estimate that there were at any given time in the early 1850s between 200 and 300 black men and women in the mining country held as slaves. Including those who returned to the slave states, there were probably between 500 and 600 slaves involved in the gold rush. This guess is ventured cautiously, because it is known that census takers in the wilds of the Sierra Nevada were themselves not sure that they had reached all persons. Some slaveowners, worried about the possible loss of their human property, tried to stay out of sight. One Mississippi white with his slave was advised to seek remote mining areas in order not to be seen using slave labor. . . .

Little is known about the black men who came as slaves to the mining country and returned to slave states. More is known about those who achieved freedom in California and remained to become permanent residents of the state. Whether free or slave, the daily lives of blacks in California were probably very similar to that of the average white miner, with the exception of their servile status. Few could have had the experience of "little Harry," held by a group of white Arkansans on the Trinity River, who watched men play poker for the right to his labor. The winner had Harry's labor for one week. In another unusual case, a black lad on board a Sacramento River boat was asked to whom he belonged. He said that he would have to wait until a poker game on board had ended to be able to answer the question. His original master had lost him to a ship's clerk, and he, in turn, had lost him to another player. The game was still going. . . .

Some slaves with genuinely kindly masters felt greater personal security in returning with them than in seeking permanent residence in the uncertain and unstable world of gold rush California. Southern contemporary observers were inclined to note such cases. The *New Orleans Picayune* reported the story of a Georgian who had taken his slaves to the gold mines and, after several years of profitable mining, offered them their freedom and a grubstake. According to this account they all refused the offer. . . .

It is certain that many slaves were kept in bondage by force. A correspondent to a New York newspaper wrote that he heard one slaveowner remark that he would shoot one of his Negroes if he tried to run away. A black man named Sam, who made his break for freedom upon returning from California with his master via New York, noted that he could not think seriously about such a move in California because he was surrounded there by so many Southerners and their supporters. . . .

The only black member of the prestigious Society of California Pioneers, Alvin Coffey, came to California in 1849 as a slave. He was twenty-seven years old, the property of Dr. Bassett, a Missourian. Freedom purchase was obviously in Coffey's mind. He dug gold to the value of $5,000 for Bassett and, in his spare time over a two-year period, earned $700 washing clothes for nearby miners. However, Dr. Bassett decided to return to Missouri and Coffey had to go with him; he had a wife and two daughters held as slaves by Bassett back in Missouri. Evidently Bassett did not have any sympathy for black men who yearned for freedom, and so he sold Alvin Coffey to another Missourian, after taking Coffey's $700 from him. The new master seems to have been a different kind of Missourian. He allowed Coffey to return to California to mine gold for his freedom. This Coffey did, paying $1,500 for himself and, in time, similar amounts to Dr. Bassett for his wife and daughters, who eventually joined him in California. He did all this by placer mining around Redding and Red Bluff.

Alvin Coffey is perhaps the best-known black who purchased his own and his family's freedom, but hundreds more accomplished this feat. One elderly black man named Isadore, who had gained his freedom before coming to California, went to work mining for Franklin Morse near Grass Valley in 1850.

Morse recalled that the ex-slave "was saving most of the eight dollars per day wages I paid him to buy his wife's liberty." . . .

In the early years of the gold rush there was a fragile and spotty democracy that prevailed between free black men and white men in the mines. It occasionally extended to the slave. Frederick Jackson Turner's descriptions of frontier conditions as a wellspring for democracy in America explain this momentary egalitarianism only in part. Men in the mines did face circumstances that muted their concerns about caste or class; but racism on frontiers was rarely totally absent. In the Turner model, frontiersmen were carving out communities that they planned to make into their permanent homes, while the miners of the early years of the gold rush rarely had permanent settlement in mind. White miners did not view their river- and gulch-side neighbors as potential lifetime acquaintances. Their nearly unanimous objective was to return home and resume their former lives, much wealthier than they were before.

Chinese Miners in California

SYLVIA SUN MINNICK

In the mid-nineteenth century, thousands of young Chinese men stared fixedly at the horizon beyond their village and, with trepidation and excitement, envisioned a sojourn to foreign lands. The reasons for their travel were many. Some felt the weight of their family's financial strain pressing on their shoulders. Others felt only relief at the prospect of escaping from the devastations in China. Many were simply exhilarated by the thought of a voyage and the opportunity to prove their abilities as fortune hunters. Those who journeyed eastward followed a dream across the Pacific Ocean to the gold-filled mountains of the California Sierra. . . .

Emigration seemed the only solution to many problems in South China. In the mid-nineteenth century, China, and more particularly Guangdong Province, suffered not only from a series of natural and social disasters, but from the oppression of a decaying feudal system as well.

The nearly 2,000 square mile Toishan District in Guangdong Province lies between 800 and 1,000 feet above sea level. The terrain is rocky, and by 1853 the meager farms produced only enough food to feed its population of 680,000 for four months of the year. Wherever possible, farmers concentrated on growing rice, sweet potatoes, peanuts, vegetables and small livestock, but with the scarcity of land and poor soil conditions, many abandoned agricultural work and sought other occupations to feed their families. Some journeyed to the cities and became peddlers, shopkeepers, merchants; others with skills became carpenters, fish farmers, or basketweavers. For many, competition became too difficult, and living in the overcrowded urban areas presented new and even more rigorous hardships than in the country. . . .

Excerpts from *Samfow: The San Joaquin Chinese Legacy*, by Sylvia Sun Minnick, Panorama West Publishing, 1988, pp. 1–23. Reprinted by permission of the author.

Civil strife, with its attendant social dislocation and distress, caused many thousands to migrate from the Pearl River Delta region. The seaport towns of Canton and Hongkong became release valves and jumping-off centers for thousands of young sojourners seeking a solution to hunger and want for themselves and their families.

The waning days of 1848 proved propitious for those who would seek their fortunes. In San Francisco, the Mormon store proprietor Sam Brannan shouted news of the gold discovery at Sutter's Mill on the American River. Chum Ming, a Chinese merchant who arrived in that city in 1847, became the first of his race to join the gold rush. Ming sent word of California's el dorado to fellow villager Cheong Yum in Guangdong Province; the excited Yum spread the news further before he too departed for the California gold mountains. By 1849, 323 Chinese arrived to capitalize on the fortune to be had. The next year 450 other countrymen followed. . . .

Almost without exception, the Chinese who entered California came from twenty-four districts of the Guangdong Province. Greatest in number were the three major dialect groups, the *Sam Yup, Sze Yup*, and *Heungshan* people. These would ultimately have the greatest influence in California. . . .

For a brief period in the early 1850s and 1860s other Cantonese companies, based both in California and Hong Kong, operated a contract labor system which actively recruited workers. These laborers were expected to work a specific period of time in payment for their passage. The flow of immigrants under this system was controlled by those in California and the worker-volume depended on the companies' ability to find employment needs. When no work was available the number of ticket offers declined. . . .

Upon arrival in *Dai Fow* (the "big city" — the Chinese name for San Francisco), interpreters and representatives from the various *hui kuens* (associations) were at the embarcadero to greet the new arrivals. Although differences in dialects among the Chinese passengers made communications virtually impossible during the voyage, most quickly recognized the shouts and screams of individuals on the pier trying to catch the attention of travelers hailing from the various locales of Guangdong Province. This first contact, coming as it did in an accustomed dialect, brought quick acknowledgment and also uplifted the spirit of each newcomer. . . .

Here in San Francisco's Chinatown, in the area surrounding present-day Portsmouth Square, the Chinese found an ambience similar to their homeland: the aroma of Chinese food filtering from the restaurant kitchens, the native sausages tied in bundles and slabs of pork suspended on meat hooks in front of grocery stores. Other shops carried vegetables, hardware, wicker baskets and sun hats stacked in neat piles, and clerks unpacked newly-arrived imported packages of dried fish, shrimp and other meat products from the nest of straw in the packing crates.

Chinatown bustled with activity wherever one looked: merchants tended their businesses, traders hurried between shops checking on merchandise, restaurants and gambling houses hawked for customers and pushed those who had nearly finished their meals out the door to make room for new arrivals. There was a sea of Chinese faces. Men wore the familiar dark-colored pajama trousers and loose-fitting, front-buttoned overshirts. Some trotted briskly down the streets as they carried their wares suspended from their shoulder poles. Brightly-painted wooden placards written in familiar characters hung over doorways, announcing agents and consultants ready to sell information and maps to specific areas in the California hinterland, gold or work opportunities supposedly being plentiful in these locations. Herb shops did a thriving business selling medication to those who became ill on the long sea voyage, and temple attendants sold incense and punks to new arrivals who felt the desire to thank their gods for a safe passage. As the newcomer wandered through Chinatown, its sights and sounds were so similar to his homeland that these reminders gave him a sense of inner peace even though he was in a strange new land. . . .

After consulting with his district association and perhaps looking for others who were interested in pooling resources to work a claim, the sojourner gathered his necessities and once again headed for the docks. From there many types of vessels — sailing ships, sidewheelers and paddle-wheelers — traveled to the inland ports. Those traveling to the northern mines purchased a ticket to Sacramento. To reach the southern Mother Lode regions one boarded ships destined for Stockton, gateway to the southern mines. . . .

After purchasing necessary picks, shovels, pans, baskets and poles and assembling their supplies, the Chinese eagerly made their way to the foothills and, at long last, to the mountain streams lined with gold.

The Chinese were primarily engaged in placer mining and used tools such as the Long Tom and rocker or cradle. Instructions for using the rocker were simple. It involved shoveling auriferous dirt from a nearby riverbed or stream into a hopper at the top of the machine, then flushing water through a series of sieve-like boxes in the unit. While the water flowed the length of the machine, the miner gently rocked the device, dividing earth from gold; the heavier metal stuck to riffles in the box and was then removed. The inexperienced quickly became adept in this simple but tedious process.

In a few short years placer mining depleted the surface gold and different techniques were employed to penetrate the earth farther, in search of a rich vein. Quartz mining became the next accepted method, followed by hydraulic mining and then dredging. By the time placer mining ended most Chinese had already begun to look elsewhere for other work opportunities. A few remained in the goldfields and found employment in quartz mines and stamp mills owned by white companies. . . .

There were two types of Chinese habitations in the goldfields: Chinese camps and Chinese quarters in mining towns. The former, the more numerous, was located generally on the bank of a stream. The camps, consisting of up to six men in a tent, served as convenient shelters for the men doing the actual digging. These camps, inhabited by kinsmen, clan or fellow villagers, maintained their distance from other Chinese groups. . . .

Numbers of Chinese in mining camps fluctuated according to the gold's availability and the social and political conditions in the region. Visitors to the mining areas noted many Chinese camps throughout the Mother Lode. For example, traveler J. D. Borthwick described the conditions at Mississippi Bar on the Yuba River: "There were about 150 [Chinese] living in a perfect village of small tents, all clustered together on the rocks. . . ." Other historians have cited 200 Chinese at Mormon Bar and 400 at Horsehoe Bar on the American River, while "a whole bevy" inhabited Weaver Creek in Placerville. These and other descriptions provide us with clear images of the numbers and appearance of Chinese encampments. . . .

Prior to 1852, when the number of Chinese in the mining region was minimal, they were regarded as a curious lot and were generally tolerated. But with the increased Chinese mining population after 1852, they were chased out of the rich claims and relegated to isolated regions or areas that had already been mined out. The Chinese were willing, however, to rework patiently those tailings abandoned by previous argonauts for they felt the earlier miners had worked the earth too quickly and carelessly.

Although their mining locations and campsites were not the best and their high visibility generated animosity among other miners, the Chinese closeness yielded immeasurable benefits. There was companionship and cooperation. The commonality of bonding, mutual investment and trust was far more valuable than gold itself.

Even in the most remote mining areas the Chinese had little difficulty obtaining food items in keeping with their diet such as rice, dried fish and shrimp, and tea. Chinese merchants in nearby mining towns played a major role in these gold seekers' life. Aside from providing the necessary supplies and food, the storekeeper was a vital link in the Chinese network. Oftentimes a shareholder in the nearest Chinese diggings, the merchant held the group's yield in safekeeping until it could be safely transported to San Francisco; at times, he financed the miners' needs and kept an account of their debts. His store served as a message and postal center for the highly transient Chinese, ready to move their camps at a moment's notice when a new strike was announced or when the surface dirt offered up its last speck of gold.

By the mid-1850s, one of every five miners was Chinese and major mining towns such as Marysville, Oroville, Auburn and Weaverville boasted as high a percentage of Chinese in their population as San Francisco. Even smaller towns witnessed a proportionate increase in the number of Chinese stores and businesses ready to serve the miners' needs. . . .

When placer mining began to fail the scramble for gold created a natural cleavage between men of different skin color and cultures. The first to feel the political sting of the white miners' actions were the dark-skinned foreign miners, Chileans, Mexicans and Peruvians. Passage of a Foreign Miner's Tax of twenty dollars per month in 1850 and its enforcement quickly forced most of the Latin miners from the region. At this time there were comparatively few Chinese in the mines and of these, many worked productive areas and were able to pay the high tariff. . . .

While taxes were a political form of harassment, physical violence endured by the Chinese occurred randomly, and as the years progressed, more frequently. Frustrated, and often liquor-filled, white miners began simply to roust them from their diggings. Chinese miners fleeing from such wrath often fled to nearby mining towns in the hope that local law enforcement and the proximity of more civilized, level-headed citizens would serve to dampen the violence. In some towns, such hopes were vain, and the persecutors became encouraged by their successes. Beginning around 1860 and lasting well through the 1880s, violent white citizens joined by workingmen and lumbermen in small Mother Lode towns and surrounding areas took to driving out the Chinese miners. In addition, they also called for eviction of local Chinese laundrymen and restaurant workers, even though these individuals did not participate in any sort of mining activity and their businesses were considered necessary to the growing communities. Many of those who acted in violence had been patrons of the Chinese businesses. In many instances angry mobs burned down the Chinese sections of towns giving no thought to the lives or property of others. The furor in the mining communities waxed and waned; like dominoes, when one community struck out against its Chinese, residents in the neighboring towns did likewise within a matter of days. . . .

Displaced from the placer mines by force and by changing mining techniques, the confirmed Chinese miner found other parts of the world. . . . In California today there is little evidence of the many Chinese gold camps, largely due to the temporary nature of the shelters. Yet a number of sites of early Chinese quarters exist in the old mining towns such as Angel's Camp, Fiddletown, Chinese Camp, and Folsom. . . .

Despite rumors filtering back to the Guangdong Province that the easy way of gold-gathering had ended and that racism had given way to violence, the Chinese impulse to immigrate did not cease.

Once in California, the agrarian-oriented Heungshan and Toishan Cantonese headed for the coastline and the central valley, seeking to work the earth and to fish the waters of the California shores. Instinctively, they realized the Delta region of the great Central Valley was as close as they could come to finding conditions and climate similar to those of their native homeland.

❦ *F U R T H E R   R E A D I N G*

M. A. Baumhoff, *Ecological Determinants of Aboriginal California Populations* (1963)

Sucheng Chan, *The Bittersweet Soil: The Chinese in California Agriculture, 1860–1910* (1986)

Jack Chen, *The Chinese of America: From the Beginnings to the Present* (1981)

Douglas Henry Daniels, *Pioneer Urbanites: A Social and Cultural History of Black San Francisco* (1980)

Raymond F. Dasmann, *California's Changing Environment* (1988)

James R. Gibson, *Farming the Frontier: The Agricultural Opening of the Oregon Country, 1786–1846* (1985)

William H. Goetzmann, *Army Exploration in the American West, 1803–1863* (1959)

Marion S. Goldman, *Gold Diggers and Silver Miners: Prostitution and Social Life on the Comstock Lode* (1981)

LeRoy R. Hafen, ed., *Mountain Men and Fur Traders of the Far West* (1965)

Robert F. Heizer and Albert B. Elsasser, *The Natural World of the California Indians* (1980)

Robert F. Heizer and M. A. Whipple, *The California Indians: A Source Book*, 2d ed. (1971)

Robert Kelley, *Gold vs. Grain: The Hydraulic Mining Controversy in California's Sacramento Valley* (1959)

_____, *Battling the Inland Sea: American Political Culture, Public Policy, and the Sacramento Valley, 1850–1986* (1989)

Rudolph Lapp, *Blacks in Gold Rush California* (1977)

Henry T. Lewis, *Patterns of Indian Burning in California: Ecology and Ethnohistory* (1973)

Malcolm Margolin, *The Ohlone Way: Indian Life in the Monterrey–San Francisco Bay Area* (1978)

_____, ed., *The Way We Lived: California Indian Reminiscences, Stories, and Songs* (1981)

Ruth B. Moynihan et al., eds., *So Much to Be Done: Women Settlers on the Mining and Ranching Frontier* (1990)

George H. Phillips, *The Enduring Struggle: Indians in California History* (1981)

T. A. Rickard, *A History of American Mining* (1932)

Fayette Robinson and Franklin Street, *The Gold Mines of California: Two Guidebooks* (rpt. 1974)

Sarah Royce, *A Frontier Lady: Recollections of the Gold Rush and Early California* (1977)

Carl P. Russell, *Firearms, Traps, and Tools of the Mountain Men* (1967)

Mari Sandoz, *The Beaver Men* (1964)

Duane Smith, *Colorado Mining: A Photographic History* (1977)

_____, *Mining America: The Industry and the Environment, 1800–1980* (1987)

Mark Twain, *Roughing It* (1902)

Jack R. Wagner, *Gold Mines of California* (1970)

Ralph T. Wattenburger, *The Redwood Lumbering Industry on the Northern California Coast, 1850–1900* (1931)

Otis E. Young, Jr., *Western Mining* (1970)

CHAPTER 9

Great Plains Grasslands Exploited

ψ

Travel west from the oak openings and tall-grass prairies of Illinois, to the short-grass plains of western Kansas and Nebraska, to the sagebrush deserts of Nevada, and you travel from a land of plentiful rain to a land of little rain. Move forward through time from an era of waving seas of perennial grama grasses, thundering herds of buffalo, and horse-mounted Indians to a time of acres of introduced cheatgrass, stockyards of steers, and chapped and spurred cowboys, and you move through a century of changing grassland history. The story of the Great Plains can be told as a tale of human progress and technological triumph over buffalo, Indian, and drought (from chaos to garden) or as a saga of human decline and ecological deterioration (from garden to chaos). Each story reveals the perspectives of the storyteller, the listener, and the time of telling. Each leaves out some of the facts and some of the actors to create a particular plot for a particular audience.

The Kiowa Indians tell the story of the grasslands from a unique viewpoint—that of the buffalo. "There was war between the buffalo and the white men. . . . The white men hired hunters to do nothing but kill the buffalo. Up and down the plains those men ranged, shooting sometimes as many as a hundred buffalo a day. . . . The buffalo saw that their day was over. . . . Sadly, the last remnant of the great herd gathered in council, and decided what they would do. . . . Straight to Mount Scott the leader of the herd walked. Behind him came the cows and their calves, and the few young males who had survived. . . . The face of the mountain opened. Inside Mount Scott the world was green and fresh. . . . The rivers ran clear, not red. The wild plums were in blossom, chasing the redbuds up the inside slopes. Into this world of beauty the buffalo walked, never to be seen again."*

---

*Richard Erdoes and Alfonso Ortiz, eds., *American Indian Myths and Legends* (New York: Pantheon, 1984), pp. 490–491.

What story do the documents and essays of this chapter suggest to you? What is its plot? Who are the actors? Whom have you left out? What alternative stories can you tell?

ψ D O C U M E N T S

The documents reveal changing perceptions and uses of the Great Plains over 150 years. The speakers and writers provide elements for a number of possible stories of the grasslands' environmental history.

Beginning with the Lewis and Clark expedition of 1804–1806, explorers mapped the land and cataloged the plants and animals of the Mississippi and Missouri river systems. Capture of beaver from Rocky Mountain streams and along the shallow tributaries that fed these two great rivers followed rapidly in the wake of these explorations. One of the largest fortunes ever amassed from the fur trade was that of John Jacob Astor. The first document concerns the status of Astor's American Fur Company as detailed in a letter of 1827 from Astor to one of his field superintendents, Ramsey Crooks. Settlers traveling west on the overland trail to Oregon and California in the 1840s were followed by cowboys, sheepmen, and farmers who stopped short of the West Coast and settled on the plains. In the second document, James Beckwourth, a black mountain man renowned for his explorations of the trans-Mississippi West, describes (through his recorder Thomas Bonner) his trading post, an important emigrant stopover near the California-Nevada border, in 1852.

Although sometimes stereotyped as reluctant pioneers, women often were eager settlers, as well as astute observers and chroniclers of life on the plains. The third selection features some women's perceptions of the grasslands environment and its challenges during the settlement of Kansas in the period from 1860 to 1886. The Homestead Act of 1862, excerpted in the fourth document, did not restrict homestead entry — possession through settlement — to men. Although land speculators often abused the law's provisions, any single person over twenty-one years of age, any head of a household, or any immigrant intending to become a citizen could file for entry and make final proof of his or her claim after five years of living on and improving 160 acres of land. Single, divorced, widowed, and even married women (who illegally filed in their maiden names) became landowners through the Homestead Act.

The short-grass plains west of the hundredth meridian, a region where rainfall usually did not reach the twenty inches a year necessary for reliable farming, were ideal for cattle ranching. Until depleted by overgrazing, perennial grasses provided nutritious forage for herds of Texas longhorned and eastern shorthorned cattle. Eventually, the open range became a realm of fenced ranches watered by wells and seeded with annual grasses that supported far fewer head per acre than the native perennials. The fifth document is excerpted from the autobiography of entrepreneur Joseph McCoy, founder of the first cowtown in Abilene, Kansas, in 1866. He describes the cattle drives northward along the Chisholm Trail that brought steers directly to the newly completed east-west Kansas Pacific Railroad for shipment to midwestern slaughterhouses. Such was the unregulated growth of the meatpacking industry that by 1905 muckraker Upton Sinclair was documenting labor exploitation and cattle abuse in the packinghouses. The revelations in his exposé *The Jungle*, excerpted in the sixth document, shocked the nation.

Just as cattle competed with buffalo for grassland nourishment, white settlers competed with Indians for claims to the land. Whites' unchecked slaughter of buffalo for their hides, which were used in such products as machine belts and robes, released the grasslands for cattle grazing and reduced the Indians' sources of subsistence. As Crow Indian chief Plenty-Coups tells it in the seventh document, recounted in 1950, the Indian way of life passed away with the passing of the buffalo. What was a tragic story for Indians, however, was a triumph for European Americans, as is emphasized in the eighth document, a 1979 newspaper editorial.

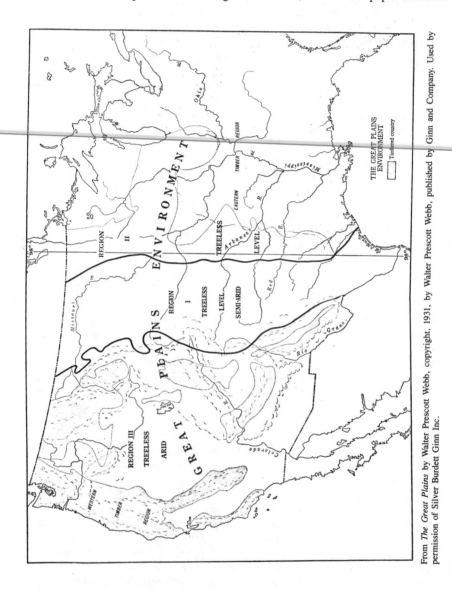

From *The Great Plains* by Walter Prescott Webb, copyright, 1931, by Walter Prescott Webb, published by Ginn and Company. Used by permission of Silver Burdett Ginn Inc.

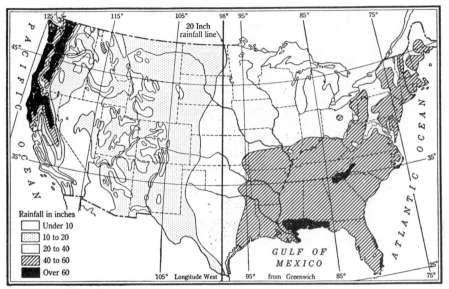

Approximate average annual precipitation

From *The Great Plains* by Walter Prescott Webb, copyright, 1931, by Walter Prescott Webb, published by Ginn and Company. Used by permission of Silver Burdett Ginn Inc.

John Jacob Astor on the Western Fur Trade, 1827

New York, 12 April, 1827

Dear Sir:-

I recieved yesterday your letter of 21st Ulto. [*ultimo*: previous month] and was rejoiced to see your health was better (take care of it) We had a sale 4 Int. [*instant*: this month] and sold about 80 M. [*M*: one thousand] Muskrats at 35 1/8 Cents; besides those I sold about 100 M at a private sale at 35 Cents, so that here we have about 120,000 to sell and I expect not to get less than 35 for them.

Beaver sold very low. Rocky Mountain 4 1/2 Missouri 3 1/2 to 375 [*sic*] — Lake Superior 5 to 5 1/2 Mackinacs 4 to 4 1/4 — About 5000 good Hatters. Racoon at 15 to 16 Cents.

Sampson had a large sale of Beaver 2 days before ours — The Beaver bought of Ashley is not good and if I had it I could not get 4$ for it. —

I have no doubt Muskrats good will be 36 to 37 next Autumn, Beaver I think will keep about as it is.

We have no good accounts from Europe not for any one single article.

Mr Munson is here, and I have bought him and Mr Stone out. Mr Bastwick is interested, but some of the others not yet decided, no doubt they will come in.

Valle is here and tells me he wants no more good than the triffling order they gave us, so I suppose gets them by other means. he has here some few good deer skins, but says he wants to sell all they get together & I will not buy without seeing them nor would I recommend you to meddle with them except it be for good heavy skins, only I think they will not rise in Europe as we have still more than 300 Bales there unsold and have just now nearly as many going

Deer goods not yet arrived but we expect them next week, they come still pretty high, but not so high as last year. Otter skins sold well in Canton, we had none there. I recommend your attention to them.

I think you may take Berthold & Co.'s Bear at 3$ and the Rocky Mountain at 3 1/2 or thereabouts as the quantity may be.

About Buffalo, I think they will do if you can get the whole and not otherwise, when I speak of the whole I mean something like it, at least 5/6 of them, so as to have the command of the market.

Deer skins I think we can buy them better here unless you meet some good heavy skins.

Mathews has his men and will be in time.

I am Dear Sir Respectfully
Your ob. Servt.

R. Crooks Esq.   John Jacob Astor, Prest.
Agent Am. Fur Co.   Am. Fur Co.

Mountain Man James Beckwourth Describes Travel in the West, 1852

In the spring of 1852 I established myself in Beckwourth Valley, and finally found myself transformed into a hotel-keeper and chief of a trading-post. My house is considered the emigrant's landing-place, as it is the first ranch he arrives at in the golden state, and is the only house between this point and Salt Lake. Here is a valley two hundred and forty miles in circumference, containing some of the choicest land in the world. Its yield of hay is incalculable; the red and white clovers spring up spontaneously, and the grass that covers its smooth surface is of the most nutritious nature. When the weary, toil-worn emigrant reaches this valley, he feels himself secure; he can lay himself down and taste refreshing repose, undisturbed by the fear of Indians. His cattle can graze around him in pasture up to their eyes, without running any danger of being driven off by the Arabs of the forest, and springs flow before them as pure as any that refreshes this verdant earth.

When I stand at my door, and watch the weary, way-worn travelers approach, their wagons holding together by a miracle, their stock in the last stage of emaciation, and themselves a perfect exaggeration of caricature, I frequently amuse myself with imagining the contrast they must offer to the *tout ensemble* and general appearance they presented to their admiring friends when they first set out upon their journey.

We will take a fancy sketch of them as they start from their homes. We will fancy their strong and well-stored wagon, bran-new for the occasion, and so

Excerpts from *The Life and Adventures of James P. Beckwourth*, as told to Thomas D. Bonner (Lincoln: University of Nebraska Press, 1972), pp. 519–20, 525–28.

firmly put together that, to look at it, one would suppose it fit to circumrotate the globe as many times as there are spokes in the wheels; then their fat and frightened steers, so high-spirited and fractious that it takes the father and his two or three sons to get each under the yoke; next, the ambitious emigrant and his proud family, with their highly-raised expectations of the future that is before them: the father, so confident and important, who deems the Eastern States unworthy of his abilities, and can alone find a sufficiently ample field in the growing republic of the Pacific side; the mother, who is unwilling to leave her pleasant gossiping friends and early associations, is still half tempted to believe that the crop of gold that waits their gathering may indemnify her for her labors; so they pull up stakes, and leave town in good style, expecting to return with whole cart-loads of gold dust, and dazzle their neighbors' eyes with their excellent good fortune. . . .

Much stock is lost in crossing the Plains, through their drinking the alkali water which flows from the Sierra Nevada, becoming impregnated with the poisonous mineral either in its source or in its passage among the rocks. There are also poisonous herbs springing up in the region of the mineral water, which the poor, famishing animals devour without stint. Those who survive until they reach the Valley are generally too far gone for recovery, and die while resting to recruit their strength. Their infected flesh furnishes food to thousands of wolves, which infest this place in the winter, and its effect upon them is singular. It depilates their warm coats of fur, and renders their pelts as bare as the palm of a man's hand. My faithful dogs have killed numbers of them at different times, divested entirely of hair except on the extremity of the nose, ears, and tail. They present a truly comical and extraordinary appearance.

This general loss of cattle deprives many of the poor emigrants of the means of hauling their lightened wagons, which, by the time they reach my ranch, seldom contain any thing more than their family clothing and bedding. Frequently I have observed wagons pass my house with one starveling yoke of cattle to drag them, and the family straggling on foot behind. Numbers have put up at my ranch without a morsel of food, and without a dollar in the world to procure any. They never were refused what they asked for at my house; and, during the short space that I have spent in the Valley, I have furnished provisions and other necessaries to the numerous sufferers who have applied for them to a very serious amount. Some have since paid me, but the bills of many remain unsettled. Still, although a prudent business man would condemn the proceeding, I can not find it in my heart to refuse relief to such necessities, and, if my pocket suffers a little, I have my recompense in a feeling of internal satisfaction.

My pleasant valley is thirty-five miles at its greatest breadth. It is irrigated by two streams, with their various small tributaries. These form a junction about ten miles from my house up the valley, which, as you remount it, becomes the central fork of the Feather River. All these streams abound with trout, some of them weighing seven or eight pounds. In the main one there are also plenty of otter. Antelopes and deer are to be found the entire year, unless the winter is unusually severe, when they cross the mountains to the eastern slope. Grizzly bears come and disappear again, without asking leave of any man. There are wolves of every species, together with foxes, hares, rabbits, and other animals. Of the feathered tribe, we have wild geese, ducks, sage-hens, grouse, and a large variety of smaller birds. Service-berries and cherries are the only kinds of fruit that grow from nature's cultivation.

The growth of timber about the valley is principally pitch-pine, although there is a considerable intermixture of cedar. I have never yet sown any grain, but I have cultivated a small kitchen-garden, and raised cabbages, turnips, and radishes of great size. I have never known the snow to fall to a greater depth than three feet, and when the storms are over it dissolves very rapidly, notwithstanding the elevation is many thousand feet above the level of the Pacific. The snow clings to the mountain peaks that overlook the valley to the eastward the year round, and as it is continually melting and feeding the streams, it keeps the water icy cold all the summer through. About a mile and a half distant from my house there is a large sulphur spring, and on the eastern slope, in the desert, there are copious hot springs, supplying the traveler with boiling water for his coffee without the cost of fuel.

The Truchy rises on the summit of the Sierra Nevada, opposite the head-waters of the Yuba, and runs in an easterly direction until it loses itself in Pyramid Lake, about fifty miles east of this valley. This lake is a great natural curiosity, as it receives not alone the waters of the Truchy, but numerous other streams, and has no visible outlet; its surcharge of water probably filtering into the earth, like St. Mary's River, and some others I have met with. There is no place in the whole state that offers so many attractions for a few weeks' or months' retirement; for its charms of scenery, with sylvan and piscatorial sports, present unusual attractions.

Pioneer Women Portray the Plains Environment, 1860–1886

Matilda Steele

My father, Rev. John Armstrong Steele, and my mother, Catherine Hampton Steele, came to Topeka with their family of eight children in 1860 from Illinois. . . . There was not a tree nor shrub nor fence. Our house seemed to be in the open prairie and around it was that yellow clay soil so noticeable to strangers and so well remembered by old settlers. No spear of grass grew there. No shade, no fruit, no flowers, and worst of all, no rain, for this was the year of the great drouth in Kansas. It needs no descriptive adjectives, and no dates to make any old Kansan know what it meant. Since then dry spells have destroyed this crop and that, sometimes at one end of the season and sometimes at the other, but the drouth of 1860 swept the calendar.

Hattie Wilson

My father's and brother's first work was to build a log house . . . and when they had gotten the logs all out for the walls and "shakes" (long shingles) split from logs of oak wood and "puncheon" (long thin boards hewed out with an adz from logs) for the floor, they had a "house raising" and all the men in the country, for they had gathered in quickly, were invited to help raise it.

I remember we had eaten most of our provisions up and were waiting to go out to the nearest railroad town to get more, so the only food they had to give the men was cornbread and black coffee with sugar, but they were all in the same situation so they enjoyed and relished it all.

Aura St. John

I had a puncheon floor, . . . and I think but few of you know what that is. They would take a section of saw log about four feet long and split off slabs as thin as they could, from one to four inches thick, and they made a much better floor than dirt. I scrubbed them with a splint broom made from a piece of hickory and they would look so bright and grateful after it. This broom was made by shaving fine splints from the bottom up about eight or ten inches, removing the very center, then shaving from the same distance above down near these at the bottom, turning these down and tying them.

Mrs. F. M. Pearl

Oh, what flavor and fragrance! . . . Blackberries were plentiful over in Doniphan County along Missions Bluff, also some wonderful plums. Supposition was that roving Indians brought them from the east and dropped the seed at one of their camps, for they were by no means wild. One variety in size, shape and color was that of a small lemon, another very large red and all told were several distinct varieties.

There were also wild gooseberries, wild grapes, chokeberries, pawpaws, wild crab apples, hazel nuts, and hickory nuts, if you went far enough to get them, but the one lone fruit on the prairie was the globe apple, which was made into preserves and was very much appreciated on account of the scarcity of fruit.

Some of the other necessary things gathered was the Mullen plant to be made into candy to ward off winter colds, also horsemint and catnip for teas.

Sarah Hammond White

Many years ago, . . . the resources of this new country were Buffalo, Deer, Wild Turkey and Antelope, Prairie Chicken, Quail and many fur-bearing animals. The settlers subsisted on wild game for meat, particularly Buffalo and Prairie Chicken. The Buffalo roamed at will in western Kansas and woe to the travelers who encountered a herd of them when they decided to go south in the fall of the year as was their custom. In the fall the men usually went west and killed our winter supply. Some of it was dried and hung up to be used as we needed it, and the best parts of the animals were allowed to freeze and put away for winter use. We needed no expensive butcher shops at this time as each family was provided with this buffalo meat, and the prairie chicken was an agreeable change. I can still hear that peculiar noise the prairie chicken made when they went forth in the early morning for their morning meal. But the prairie chicken, like the buffalo, were ruthlessly slain and it is no wonder that after sixty-five years have elapsed they are almost extinct.

Susan Proffitt

I remember driving over to the [Groves] ranch one beautiful day in early spring. . . . The great acres gave promise of an unusual harvest of feed for the thousands of white-faced cattle grazing contentedly in the pastures. A more beautiful scene I never saw.

Spring gave into summer, and in August at the close of a hot day when the grasses seemed to wither and the cattle bunched up near the creek and well and no air seemed to stir the leaves on the trees, all nature seemed still with an ominous stillness. A mass of black clouds loomed up in the west, distant thunder rumbled, the clouds gathered fast, taking on a greenish hue, thunder boomed and lightning streaked the sky and cut through the landscape and then with a rush and roar came the hail, devastating everything.

Mary Lyon

August 1, 1874, . . . is a day that will always be remembered by the then inhabitants of Kansas. . . . For several days there had been quite a few hoppers around, but this day there was a haze in the air and the sun was veiled almost like Indian summer. They began, toward night, dropping to earth, and it seemed as if we were in a big snowstorm where the air was filled with enormous-size flakes. . . .

They devoured every green thing but the prairie grass. . . . They ate the leaves and young twigs off our young fruit trees, and seemed to relish the green peaches on the trees, but left the pit hanging. They went from the corn fields as though they were in a great hurry, and there was nothing left but the toughest parts of the bare stalks. Our potatoes had to be dug and marketed to save them.

I thought to save some of my garden by covering it with gunny sacks, but the hoppers regarded that as a huge joke, and enjoyed the awning thus provided, or if they could not get under, they ate their way through. The cabbage and lettuce disappeared the first afternoon; by the next day they had eaten the onions. They had a neat way of eating onions. They devoured the tops, and then ate all of the onion from the inside, leaving the outer shell.

The garden was soon devoured, and when all of these delicacies were gone, they ate the leaves from the fruit trees. They invaded our homes, and if our baking was not well guarded by being enclosed in wood or metal, we would find ourselves minus the substantial part of our meals; and on retiring to bed, we had to shake them out of the bedding, and were fortunate if we did not have to make a second raid before morning.

The Homestead Act, 1862

An Act to secure Homesteads to actual Settlers on the Public Domain.

Be it enacted by the Senate and House of Representatives of the United States of America in Congress assembled, That any person who is the head of a family, or who has arrived at the age of twenty-one years, and is a citizen of the United States, or who shall have filed his declaration of intention to become such, as required by the naturalization laws of the United States, and who has never borne arms against the United States Government or given aid and comfort to its enemies, shall, from and after the first January, eighteen hundred and sixty-three, be entitled to enter one quarter section or a less quantity of unappropriated public lands, . . . *Provided*, That any person owning and residing on land may, under the provisions of this act, enter other land lying contiguous to his or her said land, which shall not, with the land so already owned and occupied, exceed in the aggregate one hundred and sixty acres.

SEC. 2. *And be it further enacted*, That the person applying for the benefit of this act shall, upon application to the register of the land office in which he or she is about to make such entry, make affidavit before the said register or receiver that he or she is the head of a family, or is twenty-one years or more of age, or shall have performed service in the army or navy of the United States, and that he has never borne arms against the Government of the United States or given aid and comfort to its enemies, and that such application is made for his or her exclusive use and benefit, and that said entry is made for the purpose of actual settlement and cultivation, and not either directly or indirectly for the use or benefit of any other person or persons whomsoever; and upon filing the said affidavit with the register or receiver, and on payment of ten dollars, he or she shall thereupon be permitted to enter the quantity of land specified: *Provided, however*, That no certificate shall be given or patent issued therefor until the expiration of five years from the date of such entry; and if, at the expiration of such time, or at any time within two years thereafter, the person making such entry; or, if he be dead, his widow; or in case of her death, his heirs or devisee; or in case of a widow making such entry, her heirs or devisee, in case of her death; shall prove by two credible witnesses that he, she, or they have resided upon or cultivated the same for the term of five years immediately succeeding the time of filing the affidavit aforesaid, and shall make affidavit that no part of said land has been alienated, and that he has borne true allegiance to the Government of the United States.

Joseph G. McCoy on the Chisholm Trail and Abilene Stockyards, 1874

We left the herd fairly started upon the trail for the northern market. Of these trails there are several: one leading to Baxter Springs and Chetopa; another

---

Excerpts from *Historic Sketches of the Cattle Trade of the West and Southwest*, by Joseph G. McCoy (Glendale, Calif.: Arthur H. Clark, 1940 [1874]), pp. 162–68, 173–77.

called the "Old Shawnee trail," leaving Red river and running eastward, crossing the Arkansas not far above Fort Gibson, thence bending westward up the Arkansas river. But the principal trail now traveled is more direct and is known as "Chisholm trail," so named from a semicivilized Indian who is said to have traveled it first. It is more direct, has more prairie, less timber, more small streams and less large ones, and altogether better grass and fewer flies (no civilized Indian tax or wild Indian disturbances) than any other route yet driven over, and is also much shorter in distance because direct from Red river to Kansas. Twenty-five to thirty-five days is the usual time required to bring a drove from Red river to the southern line of Kansas, a distance of between two hundred and fifty and three hundred miles and an excellent country to drive over. So many cattle have been driven over the trail in the last few years that a broad highway is tread out, looking much like a national highway; so plain, a fool could not fail to keep in it.

One remarkable feature is observable as being worthy of note, and that is how completely the herd becomes broken to follow the trail. Certain cattle will take the lead, and others will select certain places in the line, and certain ones bring up the rear; and the same cattle can be seen at their post, marching along like a column of soldiers, every day during the entire journey, unless they become lame, when they will fall back to the rear. A herd of one thousand cattle will stretch out from one to two miles whilst traveling on the trail, and is a very beautiful sight, inspiring the drover with enthusiasm akin to that enkindled in the breast of the military hero by the sight of marching columns of men. Certain cowboys are appointed to ride beside the leaders and so control the herd, whilst others ride beside and behind, keeping everything in its place and moving on, the camp wagon and caviyard bringing up the rear.

Few occupations are more cheerful, lively, and pleasant than that of the cowboy on a fine day or night; but when the storm comes, then is his manhood and often his skill and bravery put to test. When the night is inky dark and the lurid lightning flashes its zigzag course athwart the heavens, and the coarse thunder jars the earth, the winds moan fresh and lively over the prairie, the electric balls dance from tip to tip of the cattle's horns — then the position of the cowboy on duty is trying, far more than romantic. When the storm breaks over his head, the least occurrence unusual, such as the breaking of a dry weed or stick, or a sudden and near flash of lightning, will start the herd as if by magic, all at an instant, upon a wild rush, and woe to the horse or man or camp that may be in their path. The only possible show for safety is to mount and ride with them until you can get outside the stampeding column. It is customary to train cattle to listen to the noise of the herder, who sings in a voice more sonorous than musical a lullaby consisting of a few short monosyllables. A stranger to the business of stock driving will scarce credit the statement that the wildest herd will not run, so long as they can hear distinctly the voice of the herder above the din of the storm.

But if by any mishap the herd gets off on a real stampede, it is by bold, dashing, reckless riding in the darkest of nights, and by adroit, skillful management that it is checked and brought under control. The moment the herd is off, the cowboy turns his horse at full speed down the retreating column and seeks to get up beside the leaders, which he does not attempt to stop suddenly, for such an effort would be futile, but turns them to the left or right hand and gradually curves them into a circle, the circumference of which is narrowed down as fast as possible until the whole herd is rushing wildly round and round on as small a piece of ground as possible for them to occupy. Then the cowboy begins his lullaby note in a loud voice, which has a great effect in quieting the herd. When all is still and the herd well over its scare, they are returned to their bed ground, or held where stopped until daylight. Often a herd becomes scattered and run in different directions, in which case the labor is great to collect them; some will run a distance of twenty or thirty miles before stopping and turning out to rest, after which they will travel on at a rapid rate. Many times great loss in numbers and condition is sustained by a single stampede; and a herd, when once the habit of running is formed, will do but little good in thrift — if they do not become poor and bony and get the appearance of grey-hounds. And the habit, once contracted, is next to impossible to break up and get the cattle to be quiet and thrifty, save by putting them in small herds or fenced pastures, and this will not always remedy the evil or break up the habit.

* * * *

After a drive of twenty-five to one hundred days the herd arrives in western Kansas, whither, in advance, its owner has come, and decided what point at which he will make his headquarters. Straightway a good herding place is sought out, and the herd, upon its arrival, placed thereon, to remain until a buyer is found, who is dilligently sought after; but if not found as soon as the cattle are fat, they are shipped to market. But the drover has a decided preference for selling on the prairie, for there he feels at home and self-possessed; but when he goes on the cars he is out of his element and doing something he doesn't understand much about and doesn't wish to learn, especially at the price it has cost many cattle shippers.

* * * *

Of the 35,000 cattle that arrived in 1867 at Abilene, about 3,000 head were bought and shipped to Chicago by the parties owning the stockyards; of the balance, much the larger portion was sent to Chicago and either sold on the market or packed for the account of the drovers. The latter proved more [un]fortunate for the drover. The cattle were thin in flesh and made only the lower grades of beef, for which there was but little demand at ruinously low figures. Those who sold on the market did better than those who packed, yet they lost money heavily. Another portion of the drive of 1867 went into winter quarters. A few were taken north to the Platte country for the Indians, but quite a large number were packed at Junction City, where an enterprising firm of citizens, headed by a now well-known cattleman, but then late of Indianapolis, Indiana, had erected a temporary packing house, in which several thousand cattle were slaughtered, the product thereof being shipped direct to New York.

But this experiment resulted unsatisfactorily to both packers and drovers. The cattle were not as good or fat as both parties had anticipated, and it proved a disastrous loss to all concerned. A few cattle were packed at the same place the following season, but the establishment was soon abandoned and finally torn down. Had the drovers of 1867 gone into winter quarters and kept their stock until the following season, a fine profit instead of a loss would have been realized. But it was upon the tongue of nearly everyone that the cattle would not stand the rigors of a northern winter, and inasmuch as there was no precedent by which to be governed, it was thought best to sell and pack them as before described.

The summer season of 1867 was one of extreme sultry weather, and [of] great rainfall flooding the country and producing an immense growth of grass, which was soft and washy, utterly failing to produce any tallow in the animal consuming it; and when the hot weather set in, the grass became hard and uneatable; and when the first frosts touched it, not a single bit of nutriment was left in it—but little better than dry shavings for food. In addition to poor grass, the rainstorms by day, the bellowing thunder and vivid lightning of the often-recurring storms at night, got all the cattle on the prairie in the way of stampeding. When this habit becomes chronic, it is impossible to fatten the herd, often impossible to keep them together. All these causes, and others not enumerated, combined to make the final wind-up of the cattle market of 1867 at Abilene unsatisfactory, and to none more so than the parties who expended so much money in creating the necessary facilities for conducting a cattle market.

* * * *

But we will close this chapter with [a] brief sketch of [a] widely known and universally liked [drover] and [trader], . . . J. D. Reed, a resident of Texas for twenty-three years but an Alabamian by birth. Upon entering Texas, he went straightway on a stock ranch of his own selection on the frontier of his adopted state. Notwithstanding he devotes much of his time and attention to driving and trading in cattle, he keeps up his stocks in Texas. Of cattle he has about ten thousand head, and of horses a stock sufficiently large to keep good the supply of saddle ponies with which to care for his cattle stocks. Although his ranch consists of fully one thousand acres of land, his stock ranges over an immense area of country, mostly belonging to the state of Texas. . . . In 1871 he changed his plans of operation and turned his herds toward western Kansas. Each year since has witnessed on an average fully thirty-five hundred head of beeves en route for western Kansas driven by Mr. Reed's cowboys. Whatever frontier cattle town can secure his patronage and influence, regards him a host in its behalf. He drives none but good beeves, and is, upon arrival, ready to sell out all or in part; or if prices do not suit him to sell, he will turn about and buy. He is not particular which he does, so he is doing something, for he is a man of fine energy and great perseverance; a man who is familiar with all phases of life and is always in to see, know, and learn everything that may be going on, among the highest to the lowest, where he may be stopping. He is one of that type of men that makes friends in all spheres of life, and few there are who have a larger list of warm admirers than J. D. Reed, of Goliad, Texas. During the year 1872 he handled fully eight thousand head of beeves and put fourteen hundred head into winter quarters the same fall. During the year 1873 he drove about three thousand head, and selling out soon after arriving in western Kansas, was in good shape to join his friend, A. H. Pierce, in buying seven thousand head at panic prices to put into winter quarters. Certainly money in large amounts was made upon the cattle bought during the months of October and November, 1873. In 1871, Mr. Reed wintered about sixteen hundred head of cattle in western Kansas. It matters little in what country he comes in contact with the cattle trade, so thorough is his practical knowledge of the business and so unerring his judgment that he seldom fails to meet with success in all his live stock operations.

Upton Sinclair on the Chicago Stockyards, 1905

It was in the stockyards that Jonas' friend had gotten rich, and so to Chicago the party was bound. They knew that one word, Chicago — and that was all they needed to know, at least, until they reached the city. . . .

A full hour before the party reached the city they had begun to note the perplexing changes in the atmosphere. It grew darker all the time, and upon the earth the grass seemed to grow less green. Every minute, as the train sped on, the colors of things became dingier; the fields were grown parched and yellow, the landscape hideous and bare. And along with the thickening smoke they began to notice another circumstance, a strange, pungent odor. They were not sure that it was unpleasant, this odor; some might have called it sickening, but their taste in odors was not developed, and they were only sure that it was curious. Now, sitting in the trolley car, they realized that they were on their way to the home of it — that they had traveled all the way from Lithuania to it. It was now no longer something far off and faint, that you caught in whiffs; you could literally taste it, as well as smell it — you could take hold of it, almost, and examine it at your leisure. They were divided in their opinions about it. It was an elemental odor, raw and crude; it was rich, almost rancid, sensual, and strong. There were some who drank it in as if it were an intoxicant; there were others who put their handkerchiefs to their faces. The new emigrants were still tasting it, lost in wonder, when suddenly the car came to a halt, and the door was flung open, and a voice shouted — "Stockyards!" . . .

Then the party became aware of another strange thing. This, too, like the odor, was a thing elemental; it was a sound, a sound made up of ten thousand little sounds. You scarcely noticed it at first — it sunk into your consciousness, a vague disturbance, a trouble. It was like the murmuring of the bees in the spring, the whisperings of the forest; it suggested endless activity, the rumblings of a world in motion. It was only by an effort that one could realize that it was made by animals, that it was the distant lowing of ten thousand cattle, the distant grunting of ten thousand swine. . . .

There is over a square mile of space in the yards, and more than half of it is occupied by cattle pens; north and south as far as the eye can reach there stretches a sea of pens. And they were all filled — so many cattle no one had ever dreamed existed in the world. Red cattle, black, white, and yellow cattle; old cattle and young cattle; great bellowing bulls and little calves not an hour born; meek-eyed milch cows and fierce, long-horned Texas steers. The sound of them here was as of all the barnyards of the universe; and as for counting them — it would have taken all day simply to count the pens. . . .

"And what will become of all these creatures?" cried Teta Elzbieta.

"By tonight," Jokubas answered, "they will all be killed and cut up; and over there on the other side of the packing houses are more railroad tracks, where the cars come to take them away."

There were two hundred and fifty miles of track within the yards, their guide went on to tell them. They brought about ten thousand head of cattle every day, and as many hogs, and half as many sheep — which meant some eight or ten million live creatures turned into food every year. One stood and watched, and little by little caught the drift of the tide, as it set in the direction of the packing houses. There were groups of cattle being driven to the chutes, which were roadways about fifteen feet wide, raised high above the pens. In these chutes the stream of animals was continuous; it was quite uncanny to watch them, pressing on to their fate, all unsuspicious — a very river of death.

* * * *

They climbed a long series of stairways outside of the building, to the top of its five or six stories. Here was the chute, with its river of hogs, all patiently toiling upward; there was a place for them to rest to cool off, and then through another passageway they went into a room from which there is no returning for hogs.

It was a long, narrow room, with a gallery along it for visitors. At the head there was a great iron wheel, about twenty feet in circumference, with rings here and there along its edge. Upon both sides of this wheel there was a narrow space, into which came the hogs at the end of their journey; in the midst of them stood a great burly Negro, bare-armed and bare-chested. He was resting for the moment, for the wheel had stopped while men were cleaning up. In a minute or two, however, it began slowly to revolve, and then the men upon each side of it sprang to work. They had chains which they fastened about the leg of the nearest hog, and the other end of the chain they hooked into one of the rings upon the wheel. So, as the wheel turned, a hog was suddenly jerked off his feet and borne aloft.

At the same instant the ear was assailed by a most terrifying shriek; the visitors started in alarm, the women turned pale and shrank back. The shriek was followed by another, louder and yet more agonizing — for once started upon that journey, the hog never came back; at the top of the wheel he was shunted off upon a trolley, and went sailing down the room. And meantime another was swung up, and then another, and another, until there was a double line of them, each dangling by a foot and kicking in frenzy — and squealing. The uproar was appalling, perilous to the eardrums; one feared there was too much sound for the room to hold — that the walls must give way or the ceiling crack. There were high squeals and low squeals, grunts, and wails of agony; there would come a momentary lull, and then a fresh outburst, louder than ever, surging up to a deafening climax. It was too much for some of the visitors — the men would look at each other, laughing nervously, and the women would stand with hands clenched, and the blood rushing to their faces, and the tears starting in their eyes.

Plenty-Coups Mourns the Vanishing Buffalo, Recorded in 1950

"One day when the chokecherries were black and the plums red on the trees, my grandfather rode through the village, calling twenty of us older boys by name. The buffalo-runners had been out since daybreak, and we guessed what was before us. 'Get on your horses and follow me,' said my grandfather, riding out on the plains.

"We rode fast. Nothing was in sight until Grandfather led us over a hill. There we saw a circle of horsemen about one hundred yards across, and in its center a huge buffalo bull. We knew he had been wounded and tormented until he was very dangerous, and when we saw him there defying the men on horseback we began to dread the ordeal that was at hand.

"The circle parted as we rode through it, and the bull, angered by the stir we made, charged and sent us flying. The men were laughing at us when we returned, and this made me feel very small. They had again surrounded the bull, and I now saw an arrow sticking deep in his side. Only its feathers were sticking out of a wound that dripped blood on the ground.

" 'Get down from your horses, young men,' said my grandfather. 'A cool head, with quick feet, may strike this bull on the root of his tail with a bow. Be lively, and take care of yourselves. The young man who strikes, and is himself not hurt, may count coup.'

"I was first off my horse. Watching the bull, I slipped out of shirt and leggings, letting them fall where I stood. Naked, with only my bow in my right hand, I stepped away from my clothes, feeling that I might never see them again. I was not quite nine years old.

"The bull saw me, a human being afoot! He seemed to know that now he might kill, and he began to paw the ground and bellow as I walked carefully toward him.

"Suddenly he stopped pawing, and his voice was still. He came to meet me, his eyes green with anger and pain. I saw blood dropping from his side, not red blood now, but mixed with yellow.

"I stopped walking and stood still. This seemed to puzzle the bull, and he too stopped in his tracks. We looked at each other, the sun hot on my naked

Excerpts from Frank B. Linderman, *American: The Life Story of a Great Indian*, New York: John Day, 1950, pp. 29–31, 48–9, 55–7, HarperCollins Publishers, Inc.

back. Heat from the plains danced on the bull's horns and head; his sides were panting, and his mouth was bloody.

"I knew that the men were watching me. I could feel their eyes on my back. I must go on. One step, two steps. The grass was soft and thick under my feet. Three steps. 'I am a Crow. I have the heart of a grizzly bear,' I said to myself. Three more steps. And then he charged!

"A cheer went up out of a cloud of dust. I had struck the bull on the root of his tail! But I was in even greater danger than before.

"Two other boys were after the bull now, but in spite of them he turned and came at me. To run was foolish. I stood still, waiting. The bull stopped very near me and bellowed, blowing bloody froth from his nose. The other boys, seeing my danger, did not move. The bull was not more than four bows' lengths from me, and I could feel my heart beating like a war-drum.

"Two large gray wolves crossed the circle just behind him, but the bull did not notice them, did not move an eye. He saw only me, and I was growing tired from the strain of watching him. I must get relief, must tempt him to come on. I stepped to my right. Instantly he charged—but I had dodged back to my left, across his way, and I struck him when he passed. This time I ran among the horsemen, with a lump of bloody froth on my breast. I had had enough."

At this ending Coyote-runs spoke up. "I saw him do that," he said proudly. "I was younger than he, but I was there and saw Plenty-coups strike the bull twice. No other boy struck him at all." . . .

* * * *

"Our country is the most beautiful of all. Its rivers and plains, its mountains and timber lands, where there was always plenty of meat and berries, attracted other tribes, and they wished to possess it for their own.

"To keep peace our chiefs sent out clans to the north, east, south, and west. They were to tell any who wished to come into our country that they were welcome. They were told to say, 'You may hunt and may gather berries and plums in our country, but when you have all you can carry you must go back to your own lands. If you do this all will be well. But if you remain overlong, we will warn you to depart. If you are foolish and do not listen, your horses will be stolen; and if even this does not start you homeward, we will attack you and drive you out.' "

The country belonging to the Crows was not only beautiful, but it was the very heart of the buffalo range of the Northwest. It embraced endless plains, high mountains, and great rivers, fed by streams clear as crystal. No other section could compare with the Crow country, especially when it was untouched by white men. Its wealth in all kinds of game, grass, roots, and berries made enemies for the Crows, who, often outnumbered, were obliged continually to defend it against surrounding tribes.

"These clans did not go to the other people, but camped near the boundaries of our domain so that they might speak to any visitor coming from any direction and give him the message from our chiefs. But little heed was paid to what we said. There was almost continual war with those who coveted our country.

"The Lacota [Sioux], Striped-feathered-arrows [Cheyennes], and Tattooed-breasts [Arapahoes] kept pushing us back, away from the Black Hills, until finally when I was a young man we were mostly in the country of the Bighorn and Little Bighorn rivers. These tribes, like the Pecunies [Piegans], Bloods, and Blackfeet [all Blackfeet], had many guns which they had obtained from white traders, while we had almost no guns in the tribe. The northern tribes could easily trade with the Hudson's Bay people, while the tribes eastward of us traded furs and robes to the American Fur Company for guns, powder, and lead.

"There is no better weapon than the bow for running buffalo, but in war the gun is often the best. All tribes were against us, the Blackfeet north and west, the Cheyennes and Sioux east, the Shoshones and Arapahoes on the south; and besides these there was often war with the Flatheads, Assinniboines, and Hairy-Noses [Gros Ventres of the prairies]." . . .

To count coup a warrior had to strike an armed and fighting enemy with his coup-stick, quirt, or bow before otherwise harming him, or take his weapons while he was yet alive, or strike the first enemy falling in battle, no matter who killed him, or strike the enemy's breastworks while under fire, or steal a horse tied to a lodge in an enemy's camp, etc. The first named was the most honorable, and to strike such a coup a warrior would often display great bravery. An eagle's feather worn in the hair was a mark of distinction and told the world that the wearer had counted coup. He might wear one for each coup he counted "if he was that kind of man," Plenty-coups said. But if a warrior was wounded in counting coup, the feather he wore to mark the event must be painted red to show that he bled. Strangely enough from our point of view, this was not considered so great an honor as escaping unharmed. After a battle, or exploit, by one or more individuals there ensued the ceremony of counting coup, relating adventures. This is the custom that led the white man to declare the Indian a born boaster. Some of the tribes of the Northwest added an eagle's feather to their individual coup-stick for each coup counted. But the Crows did not follow this custom.

"We feasted there," said Plenty-coups. "Fat meat of bighorn, deer, and elk was plentiful. The hunters had killed many of these animals because they knew there would soon be a very large village to feed. Besides, light skins were always needed for shirts and leggings. Even the dogs found more than they could eat near that village, and our horses, nearly always feasting on rich grass, enjoyed the change the mountains gave them. All night the drums were beating, and in the light of fires that smelled sweet the people danced until they were tired.

Author's [Frank B. Linderman] Note

Plenty-coups refused to speak of his life after the passing of the buffalo, so that his story seems to have been broken off, leaving many years unaccounted for. "I have not told you half that happened when I was young," he said, when urged to go on. "I can think back and tell you much more of war and horse stealing. But when the buffalo went away the hearts of my people fell to the ground, and they could not lift them up again. After this nothing happened. There was little singing anywhere. Besides," he added sorrowfully, "you know that part of my life as well as I do. You saw what happened to us when the buffalo went away."

I do know that part of his life's story, and that part of the lives of all the Indians of the Northwestern plains; and I did see what happened to these sturdy, warlike people when the last of the buffalo was finally slaughtered and left to decay on the plains by skin-hunting white men.

The Indian's food supply was now gone; so too were the materials for his clothes and sheltering home. Pitched so suddenly from plenty into poverty, the Indian lost his poise and could not believe the truth.

An Editor Bids Good Riddance to Buffalo, 1979

Gone are the millions of American buffalo. Their wanton slaughter brought temporary profit and sport. But their departure opened the North American continent for human development.

The bison known as the plains buffalo in America well could serve as a national symbol for the concept that human progress requires environmental alterations, whether in mining ore, building factories, plowing ground or controlling wild beasts.

From vast crops in the heartlands of the United States and Canada, the modern farmer produces enough food and fiber for his needs and 55 other persons, making ours the richest agricultural area of the world. Thundering herds of buffalo no longer exist to trample down the seas of grain.

Domestic animals bred to highest qualities of dinner-plate tastes and cost-efficiency graze in peace across America without fear of attack from stampeding buffalo. A hiker can stroll unafraid of buffalo assault in any urban area from Atlanta to Butte to Grand Forks.

The buffalo have almost disappeared as a result of one of the remarkable wild-animal eradication programs recorded in human history. The benefit is mankind's. Few should weep over buffalo. America never would have blossomed to its current status in world leadership unless buffalo were removed from the land.

The oxlike grazing animal of family Bovidae weighs a ton or more when mature. Long-lived, agile, fast and unpredictable, an estimated 60 million

From *The Daily Chronicle*, Centralia–Chehalis, Washington, September 10, 1979. Reprinted by permission of The Daily Chronicle.

buffalo were roaming over North America when the white man arrived. Unimpeded by sentimental environmentalists having short-range vision, early settlers found that buffalo were commercially worthless when compared with domestic animals.

As the white civilization pushed westward from the Allegheny Mountains, vast herds of buffalo were slaughtered purposely to permit farms to be created, railroads to be built, housewives to pluck carrots without being trampled. Short term profits from buffalo slaughter came from tough meat, hides and sport. The beasts existed for private enterprise to consume, to clear the land for superior breeds, crops, cities, human growth and progress.

William F. Cody (Buffalo Bill) among others was renowned for the number of bison he killed. Around 1900, as buffalo neared extinction, action by cattlemen and conservationists led to their protection on government preserves in fortified paddocks.

By coincidence, a thriving buffalo herd today thunders about a heavily fenced mountain ranch at Cody, Wyo., as a tourist tribute to Buffalo Bill Cody. Other Western buffalo paddocks are in Colorado, Oregon and at Banff, Canada. There are a few buffalo on private ranches in Washington.

With some 60 million of the awesome beasts virtually wiped from the face of North America, human ingenuity and hard work rapidly converted the Great Plains and rolling hills into modern miracles of agricultural production, thriving cities, hearty commerce and vigorous Americans.

When we pat the nose of a precious animal, we are thankful it's a Polled Hereford or a brown-eyed Jersey instead of horned buffalo defying domestication. Gone are the millions of American buffalo, thanks to visionary settlers of the 18th and 19th Centuries.

✹ *E S S A Y S*

Like the documents, the essays tell different stories about the grasslands. In the first essay, Walter Prescott Webb, an eminent historian of the Great Plains, constructs his history as a triumph of white settlers and their technologies over a formidable arid environment and fierce horse-mounted Indian tribes. Donald Worster, an environmental historian at the University of Kansas, in the second selection, presents the region's history as a tragedy of environmental deterioration at the hands of capitalist ranchers. Finally, in the third essay, William Cronon, an environmental historian at the University of Wisconsin, Madison, analyzes the characteristics of storytelling, showing how histories are stories of the past with a beginning, middle, and end. Progressive histories often depict what might be considered human triumphs, such as Europeans' conquest of the American wilderness, in an upward or ascending plot. Conversely, environmental histories often have downward or declining plots that portray nature as destroyed by humans. These ascensionist and declensionist plots are ways in which humans inevitably impose order on the world. There may be alternative stories with other plots, actors, and settings, but human cognition, and even science itself, necessarily may take the form of storytelling.

Great Plains Ecology

WALTER PRESCOTT WEBB

The Great Plains area, as the term will be used in this [selection], does not conform in its boundaries to those commonly given by geographers and historians. The Great Plains comprise a much greater area than is usually designated, — an area which may best be defined in terms of topography, vegetation, and rainfall.

A plains environment, such as that found in the western United States, presents three distinguishing characteristics:

1. It exhibits a comparatively level surface of great extent.
2. It is a treeless land, an unforested area.
3. It is a region where rainfall is insufficient for the ordinary intensive agriculture common to lands of a humid climate. The climate is sub-humid.

In the region west of the Mississippi River, the region under consideration here, these three characteristics of a plains environment are not coextensive or coterminal. The three are not found in conjunction except in a portion of what is commonly called the Central Great Plains; that is, in the High Plains, or the Plains proper. In the High Plains the land is relatively level and unscored, it is barren of timber, and the climate is sub-humid, semi-arid, or arid. The High Plains constitute the heart of what may be called the Great Plains, and exemplify to the highest degree the features of a plane surface, a treeless region, and a sub-humid one. . . .

This area, with its three dominant characteristics, affected the various peoples, nations as well as individuals, who came to take and occupy it, and was affected by them. . . . The historical truth that becomes apparent in the end is that the Great Plains have bent and molded Anglo-American life, have destroyed traditions, and have influenced institutions in a most singular manner.

The Great Plains offered such a contrast to the region east of the ninety-eighth meridian, the region with which American civilization had been familiar until about 1840, as to bring about a marked change in the ways of pioneering and living. For two centuries American pioneers had been working out a technique for the utilization of the humid regions east of the Mississippi River. They had found solutions for their problems and were conquering the frontier at a steadily accelerating rate. Then in the early nineteenth century they crossed the Mississippi and came out on the Great Plains, an environment with which they had had no experience. The result was a complete though temporary breakdown of the machinery and ways of pioneering. They began to make adjustments. . . .

As one contrasts the civilization of the Great Plains with that of the eastern timberland, one sees what may be called an institutional *fault* (comparable to a geological fault) running from middle Texas to Illinois or Dakota, roughly following the ninety-eighth meridian. At this *fault* the ways of life and of living changed. Practically every institution that was carried across it was either broken and remade or else greatly altered. The ways of travel, the weapons, the method of tilling the soil, the plows and other agricultural implements, and even the laws themselves were modified. When people first crossed this line they did not immediately realize the imperceptible change that had taken place in their environment, nor, more is the tragedy, did they foresee the full consequences which that change was to bring in their own characters and in their modes of life. In the new region — level, timberless, and semi-arid — they were thrown by Mother Necessity into the clutch of new circumstances. Their plight has been stated in this way: east of the Mississippi civilization stood on three legs — land, water, and timber; west of the Mississippi not one but two of these legs were withdrawn, — water and timber, — and civilization was left on one leg — land. It is small wonder that it toppled over in temporary failure. . . .

The distinguishing climatic characteristic of the Great Plains environment from the ninety-eighth meridian to the Pacific slope is a deficiency in the most essential climatic element — water. Within this area there are humid spots due to local causes of elevation, but there is a deficiency in the average amount of rainfall for the entire region. This deficiency accounts for many of the peculiar ways of life in the West. It conditions plant life, animal life, and human life and institutions. In this deficiency is found the key to what may be called the Plains civilization. It is the feature that makes the whole aspect of life west of the ninety-eighth meridian such a contrast to life east of that line. . . . The line representing twenty inches of annual precipitation follows approximately the hundredth meridian. In no appreciable area between that line and the Pacific slopes does the rainfall run far above twenty inches. Over great stretches it falls below twenty to fifteen, to ten, and, in the true desert, to five inches.

It is generally agreed that wherever precipitation is less than twenty inches the climate is deficient. This means, or has come to mean, that the land in such areas cannot be utilized under the same methods that are employed in the region where precipitation is more than twenty inches. . . .

Five weather phenomena — hot winds and chinooks, northers, blizzards, and hailstorms — are all localized in the Great Plains country. . . . They are a significant part of the unusual conditions which civilization had to meet and overcome in the Great Plains. . . .

The ninety-eighth meridian separates the vegetation of the East from that of the West. In its primeval state practically the entire region east of this line was heavily timbered, truly a forest land. West of the line (excepting the northern Pacific slope and the islands in the mountains) there is a scarcity or a complete absence of timber. . . . The non-forested area, the Great Plains environment, falls into three subdivisions: the tall grass, or prairie; the short grass, or Plains; and the desert shrub. . . .

In the prairie country the tall grass falls into three subdivisions, or communities: the blue-stem sod, the blue-stem bunch grass, and the needle grass and slender wheat grass. The blue-stem sod is found in Illinois, Iowa, eastern Kansas, in parts of Missouri, Oklahoma, and Texas, and in western Minnesota, eastern North Dakota, South Dakota, and Nebraska. The whole region is rich, and the central portion forms what is known as the corn belt.

The short, or Plains, grasses are the grama, galleta, buffalo, and mesquite. All these types occur west of the ninety-eighth meridian.

West of the grasslands lies the desert-shrub area, the intermountain region. This vegetation belongs to three general types: sagebrush, or northern-desert shrub; creosote bush, or southern-desert shrub; greasewood, or salt-desert shrub. In all this region the desert type of vegetation prevails over the grassland. . . .

The Plains animals exhibit certain common characteristics:

1. All, save the coyote and the wolf, are grass-eaters.
2. Two types, the antelope and the jack rabbit, are noted for their speed, and both stick to the open country, depending primarily on speed for safety.
3. All can get along with little or no actual water supply. The prairie dog and the jack rabbit need none. The antelope exhibits great ingenuity in finding water and, by virtue of its speed, can travel far for its supply.
4. All these animals are extremely shy, and must be hunted with long-range guns, a fact that had a marked influence on the development of weapons in the United States. . . .

The buffalo had few qualities, save massive size and gregariousness, that fitted it to the Plains. It is described by all observers, from [George] Catlin on, as a stupid animal, the easiest victim to the hunter, whether the redman with bow and arrow or the white man with his long-range buffalo gun. The buffalo was slow of gait, clumsy in movement, and had relatively poor eyesight and little fear of sound. Though it had a fairly keen sense of smell, this sense was useless to it when it was approached from down the wind.

Historically the buffalo had more influence on man than all other Plains animals combined. It was life, food, raiment, and shelter to the Indians. The buffalo and the Plains Indians lived together, and together passed away. The year 1876 marks practically the end of both. . . .

The contrast between the East and the West . . . extending through the plant and animal kingdoms may be continued by the contrast between the timber Indians and the Plains Indians. . . .

The Plains Indians constituted for a much longer time than we realize the most effectual barrier ever set up by a native American population against European invaders in a temperate zone. For two and a half centuries they maintained themselves with great fortitude against the Spanish, English, French, Mexican, Texan, and American invaders, withstanding missionaries, whisky, disease, gunpowder, and lead. . . . The Plains culture area coincides with the grassland and the buffalo range and has nearly twice the extent, from north to south, of any other area. By way of further simplification the cultural areas may be reduced to three, designated as eastern woodland, central plains, and western mountain. . . . A still simpler classification is that of the native-food areas. The eastern maize area lies east of the Mississippi, the salmon and wild-seeds area lies on the Pacific, and the bison area lies in the Great Plains. . . .

Within the Plains area dwelt thirty-one tribes of Indians. Eleven of these are typical Plains tribes, possessing in common, in the highest degree, the characteristic Plains culture. These eleven tribes are the Assiniboin, Arapaho, Blackfoot, Cheyenne, Comanche, Crow, Gros Ventre, Kiowa, Kiowa-Apache, Sarsi, and Teton-Dakota. They occupied the region from southern Canada to Mexico. The . . . tribes to the east and west possessed many characteristics of the Plains culture, but they exhibited also characteristics of the non-Plains tribes; that is to say, they represented a transition from one culture to another, a transition found in both vegetation and animal life. . . . The following are the significant facts:

1. The Plains Indians were nomadic and nonagricultural.
2. They depended for their existence on the wild cattle or buffalo, and were often called buffalo Indians. The buffalo furnished them with all the necessities and luxuries of life.
3. They used weapons especially adapted to the hunting of big game, particularly the buffalo.
4. They used beasts of burden for transportation, an indication of their nomadic character. They were the only Indians in North America occupying land in a temperate climate who used a beast of burden. First they used the dog and later the horse.
5. They adopted the horse long before white civilization came in contact with them, and their use of the horse effected a far-reaching revolution in their ways of life. The Plains Indians became the horse Indians, and the Plains area might then well have been called the horse area of America. . . .

Fossil remains indicate that horses roamed over both North America and South America, to disappear before Columbus came and probably before the Indians themselves arrived. . . . The association of man and horse apparently arose in an environment very similar to the Great Plains; that is, in the steppes of Asia.

[The] . . . horsemen of the steppes extended their forays in every direction. The Huns came west into Europe; other tribes passed eastward into China, compelling the Chinese to erect the Great Wall on their northern border. . . .

To put the matter briefly, there arose in Europe two traditions of horsemanship, or horse culture — the one that of a settled people with whom horses were but one of the incidents of life, and the other the tradition of the nomadic people to whom horses were vital. Both traditions found their way to America, and each found its appropriate environment. The "civilized" culture came through Europe to England and found lodgment in the English colonies of the Atlantic coast; the nomadic horse culture came from the Asiatic steppes to the plains of Arabia, thence across northern Africa to Spain, and with the Spaniards to the pampas of South America and to the Plains of the United States. . . . It is generally accepted by anthropologists that these herds originated from the horses lost or abandoned by De Soto about 1541. Whether they came from De Soto's horses, or from those of Coronado, or from other explorers is not material; we know that the Kiowa and Missouri Indians were mounted by 1682; the Pawnee, by 1700; the Comanche, by 1714; the Plains Cree and Arikara, by 1738; the Assiniboin, Crow, Mandan, Snake, and Teton, by 1742; and the most northern tribe, the Sarsi, by 1784. How much earlier these Indians rode horses we do not know; but we can say that the dispersion of horses which began in 1541 was completed over the Plains area by 1784. . . .

The Indians had horses for all purposes. The buffalo horse was merely a trained cow pony; he bore a special mark or nick in his ear to distinguish him. He had to be alert, intelligent, willing to follow the game and press close to the side of the running animal, yet able to detect its intention and swerve from it so as not to become entangled, and all with no more guidance than the Indian exerted by pressure of his knees. The war horse and the buffalo were renowned for their speed, intelligence, and endurance. They were prize possessions and were valued above all else. . . .

The horsemanship of the Plains Indian aroused the wonder and admiration of all who observed it. The following account of the prairie warrior's equestrian skill is by Captain Marcy.

> His only ambition consists in being able to cope successfully with his enemy in war and in managing his steed with unfailing adroitness. He is in the saddle from boyhood to old age, and his favorite horse is his constant companion. It is when mounted that the prairie warrior exhibits himself to the best advantage; here he is at home, and his skill in various manœuvres which he makes available in battle — such as throwing himself entirely upon one side of his horse and discharging his arrows with great rapidity toward the opposite side from beneath the animal's neck while he is at full speed — is truly astonishing. Many of the women are equally expert, as equestrians, with the men. . . .

Of the horsemanship of the Comanches, Catlin says:

> Amongst their feats of riding, there is one that has astonished me more than anything of the kind I have ever seen, or expect to see, in my life: — a stratagem of war, learned and practiced by every young man in the tribe; by which he is able to drop his body upon the side of his horse at the instant he is passing, effectually screened from his enemies' weapons as he [lies] in a horizontal position behind the body of his horse, with his heel hanging over the horse's back; by which he has the power of throwing himself up again, and changing to the other side of the horse if necessary. In this wonderful condition, he will hang whilst his horse is at fullest speed, carrying with him his bow and his shield, and also his long lance of fourteen feet in length, all or either of which he will wield upon his enemy as he passes; rising and throwing his arrows over the horse's back, or with ease and equal success under the horse's neck. . . .

It should be pointed out here that Catlin was accompanied by a cavalry troop whose members should have been familiar with all the feats of horsemanship that are known to military science or to the people of the Eastern states. It was a case of the two horse cultures coming into contact in the West. . . .

Thus armed, equipped, and mounted the Plains Indians made both picturesque and dangerous warriors. . . . They were far better equipped for successful warfare in their own country than the white men who came against them,
and presented to the European or American conqueror problems different from
those found elsewhere on the continent. . . .

Let us visualize the American approach to the Great Plains by imagining
ourselves standing on the dividing line between the timber and plain, say at the
point where the ninety-eighth meridian cuts the thirty-first parallel. As we gaze
northward we see on the right side the forested and well-watered country and on
the left side the arid, treeless plain. On the right we see a nation of people
coming slowly but persistently through the forests, felling trees, building
cabins, making rail fences, digging shallow wells, or drinking from the numerous springs and perennial streams, advancing shoulder to shoulder, pushing
the natives westward toward the open country. They are nearing the Plains.
Then, in the first half of the nineteenth century, we see the advance guard of
this moving host of forest homemakers emerge into the new environment,
where there are no forests, no logs for cabins, no rails for fences, few springs
and running streams. Before them is a wide land infested by a fierce breed of
Indians, mounted, ferocious, unconquerable, terrible in their mercilessness.
They see a natural barrier made more formidable by a human barrier of
untamed savagery. Upon this barrier of the Great Plains the pioneers threw
themselves, armed and equipped with the weapons, tools, ideas, and institutions which had served them so long and so well in the woods that now lay
behind them. Inevitably they failed in their first efforts, and they continued to
fail until they worked out a technique of pioneering adapted to the Plains rather
than to the woodland. . . . Their effort constitutes a gigantic human experiment with an environment.

* * * *

Undoubtedly the Texans needed a new weapon, something with a reserve
power and capable of "continuous" action — a weapon more rapid than the
Indian's arrows, of longer reach than his spear, and, above all, one adapted to
use on horseback. The man who supplied the weapon that fulfilled all these
necessities was a Connecticut Yankee by the name of Samuel Colt. . . . Those
who went into the West went on horseback with six-shooters in their
belts. . . . It should be borne in mind that its introduction, rapid spread, and
popularity throughout the Plains area, the Indian and cattle country, were in
response to a genuine need for a horseman's weapon. Whatever sins the six-
shooter may have to answer for, it stands as the first mechanical adaptation
made by the American people when they emerged from the timber and met a set
of new needs in the open country of the Great Plains. It enabled the white man
to fight the Plains Indian on horseback.

* * * *

New inventions and discoveries had to be made before the pioneer farmer could go into the Great Plains and establish himself. . . . In the interval of awaiting the Industrial Revolution there arose in the Plains country the cattle kingdom.

The cattle kingdom was a world within itself, with a culture all its own, which, though of brief duration, was complete and self-satisfying. . . .

The cattle kingdom had its origin in Texas before the Civil War. After the war it expanded, and by 1876 it had spread over the entire Plains area. The physical basis of the cattle kingdom was grass, and it extended itself over all the grassland not occupied by farms. Within a period of ten years it had spread over western Texas, Oklahoma, Kansas, Nebraska, North and South Dakota, Montana, Wyoming, Nevada, Utah, Colorado, and New Mexico; that is, over all or a part of twelve states. For rapidity of expansion there is perhaps not a parallel to this movement in American history.

After the panic of 1873 the range cattle industry began to struggle upward once more, though the drives from Texas were less frequent owing to the approaching saturation of the range and the fact that the railroads were extending into the West and diverting the cattle from the trails. . . .

By 1876 the cattle industry was recovering from the panic of three years before, and there was a steady demand for cattle, with a rising market — premonitory symptom of the cattle boom of the eighties. During the last four years of the seventies (1876–1880) the cattle business expanded on a steady or rising market. In the last year two million head were marketed. A well-matured Northwestern ranger would bring about $60 in the Northern markets, and a Texan steer about $50. Grass was still free, the range was open, and the farmer was far away. Again, it could not last.

Then came the great boom of the early eighties. "It was a time of golden visions in a blaze of glory that led on to riotous feastings on the rim of the crater of ruin — a brief era of wild extravagance in theories and in practices." There were many contributing factors to explain the boom; and, given the boom, the collapse was inevitable. . . .

Analyzing the situation about 1885 we find the following factors present. . . .

1. Several railroads had by this time crossed the Plains or had gone far out on them.
2. These railroad companies were laying out and booming towns, doing all they could to get settlers into the region out of which they hoped to obtain a revenue both from the use of the road and from the sale of the bounty lands.
3. Money was plentiful in the country as a whole and was seeking an outlet for investment.
4. The eastern part of the United States was becoming more crowded, and farmers were pushing farther and farther into the cattle country. . . .
5. The Indians had all been reduced, and people were no longer held back from the Plains by fear of the scalping knife and the tomahawk.

6. Some of the ranges were being fenced, and this alarmed those who had hoped that the free range would last, causing them to grab for more land.

We have noted that the agricultural frontier came to a standstill about 1850, and that for a generation it made but little advance into the sub-humid region of the Great Plains. It was barbed wire and not the railroads or the homestead law that made it possible for the farmers to resume, or at least accelerate, their march across the prairies and onto the Plains. . . .

The invention of barbed wire revolutionized land values and opened up to the homesteader the fertile Prairie Plains, now the most valuable agricultural land in the United States. With cheap fencing the farmers were enabled to stake out their free homesteads, and the agricultural frontier moved rapidly across the prairie to the margin of the dry plains, where the farmers were again checked until further adaptations could be made. The homestead law was not a success in the High Plains and the more arid country, as will be shown later; but it served as an effective bait which lured the farmers on beyond the tall-grass country, where agriculture could be carried on successfully, into the short-grass country, where the occupation was extremely hazardous. In the wet years the farmers pushed across the dead line into the Plains country and took up homesteads which they could now fence. In this way they encroached on the cattlemen and forced all land under fence. Without barbed wire the Plains homestead could never have been protected from the grazing herds and therefore could not have been possible as an agricultural unit.

Th[e] first inroad of farmers synchronized with the cattle boom of the eighties and the general conditions of prosperity at that time, and was accompanied or preceded by the deceptive wet years which led the people to conclude that the rainfall would increase.

It was . . . experiences growing out of the droughts that led the men who remained in the Plains country to enter upon countless hundreds of experiments with the windmill. . . . It was the acre or two of ground irrigated by the windmill that enabled the homesteader to hold on when all others had to leave.

The effects of the windmill in Nebraska, which may be considered typical for most of the Great Plains, are set forth eloquently by [Erwin Hinckley] Barbour [Professor at the University of Nebraska, 1898]:

What a contrast may be presented by two farms — one with cattle crowding around the well, waiting for some thoughtless farm hand to pump them their scanty allowance of water, the other where the cattle are grazing and the tanks and troughs are full and running over . . . .

Thus did the West carry on its search for water by means of the windmill. Extravagant hopes were entertained — hopes which could never be realized; but still the whirling wheel made life on the Great Plains possible in hitherto untenable places. It was an important agent in transforming the so-called Great American Desert into a land of homes.

Cowboy Ecology

DONALD WORSTER

Ask almost any group of people in the world, from Peoria to Perth, and they will say that the American West is about the cowboy and his life of chasing cows on the range. They may add, without much encouragement, that that West has come to symbolize the national identity of the United States. Instead of seeing in that response a measure of truth, historians have tended to dismiss it as popular myth-making, a fashion of mass culture, essentially false and insignificant. Those who write the history of the nation have more or less ignored the life on the range (as they have the life in the trans-Mississippi West generally). A survey of fourteen popular American history textbooks shows that the range industry, cowboy, and ranch receive, on the average, less than two pages' worth of attention out of almost a thousand pages of text. The historians say one thing about what is important in our past, the popular intuition says another. In this case, I believe, the popular intuition is worth heeding, though not for all the popular reasons.

One prominent exception to the academic trend to scant the West is Daniel Boorstin, who opens the third volume of his survey of the American experience with a celebration of the "go-getters," a generation of entrepreneurs who, in the aftermath of the Civil War, "went in search of what others had never imagined was there to get," men who "made something out of nothing." Prominent among them were cowboys in the broad sense of the term: western cattle drovers like Charles Goodnight and cattle shippers like Joseph McCoy, two among many who saw the possibility of extracting meat out of the unlikely environment of the "desert." Boorstin regards such men as the archetypes of a new America that refuses to be constrained by traditional, rigid morality but plunges ahead into modern ambiguity and makes up its own rules as it goes. Others, less persuaded that free enterprise has made old morals obsolete, have called those cowboy entrepreneurs thugs and rustlers. Most academic historians have come to regard the whole saga of cowpunchers, cattlemen, the beef and wool industry with some boredom, if not distaste, and deny its relevance to the mainstream of social change and conflict.

The low status of ranching history, and with it western history, strikes one with special force when compared to the status of the plantation history of the American South. Even at this late point in the twentieth century, after so much urbanization and economic growth, the plantation still stands at the very center of southern studies. Moreover, unlike the ranch, it occupies a distinctly prominent place in the textbooks. Yet the ranch and the plantation were alike spawned by the capitalist revolution in agriculture. Each institution has been a powerful determinant of a regional identity. The critical difference between them lies, of course, in the fact that the plantation practiced an especially heinous form of labor exploitation, which has left an enduring mark on race

From the book, *Under Western Skies: Nature and History in the American West* by Donald Worster (New York: Oxford University Press, 1992). Reprinted by permission of the author.

relations, not only in the United States but in a number of other societies, mainly in the warmer latitudes where Europeans came to force nonwhites to raise exotic foods and fiber for them on a large scale. The plantation has been a critical instrument in the European conquest of people of color, and historians seeking to understand that long story of racial conquest, exploitation, and injustice have rightly given it careful attention.

But out on the western range, human relations have always seemed a lot more open, sunny, unrepressive, and therefore forgettable. True, every ranch involved, somewhere in the past, a dispossession of native peoples. And on the typical ranch there was a poorly paid work crew and it was partly nonwhite: Indian, Mexican, African-American, and if one includes the Hawaiian range, even Asian and Polynesian. The European languages spoken out West included Spanish, German, Danish, and the Gaelic dialects; far more often than the southern plantation, the range was a microcosmic league of nations under white hegemony. We have tended, through the influence of too many John Wayne movies, to assume otherwise; the full history of the diverse racial and ethnic relations on the range has yet to be written. All the same, compared to chattel slavery, the work relationships there seem to be pretty ordinary and even benign, more egalitarian than exploitative. The system was one of wage la-borers' selling their services freely, sometimes for only a season or two, then moving on. With the job necessarily went a lot of autonomy. Since chasing after steers often took one far away from the scrutiny of a foreman, since the work in fact required a great deal of self-directedness and initiative, and since hired men were allowed to ride big horses and carry big guns across a big space, there was relatively more personal freedom for workers in the ranching industry than in, say, the eastern textile factory or the cotton field. Conse-quently, the idea of a "cowboy proletariat" is a seed that has been sown a few times by historians but always fallen on stony ground.

However, if labor and racial exploitation did not occur on the range to the same terrible degree they did on the plantation, there is another aspect that stands out as distinctive, compelling, and historically significant. This is an issue that is absolutely crucial to the course of western American development. It is one that has much to teach the rest of the nation. And, above all, it is an issue that is vital to much of today's world, particularly the developing nations of Asia, Africa, and Latin America. I mean the question of how we are to get a living from a fragile, vulnerable earth without destroying it — or put otherwise, how we are to lead a sustainable life that does not deplete the natural environ-ment or ourselves. For this issue the West, because so much of it is ecologically marginal for many human purposes, has represented one of the preeminent laboratories on the planet. It is, as Walter Prescott Webb once noted, a semi-desert with a desert at its heart. Compared to the North and South, the western environment did not yield easily to agriculture or urban growth, and only in recent decades, with the aid of modern, sophisticated technology to pump the water and cool the air, has the region acquired much population. Such is also the condition of much of the Third World: they too face the challenge of marginal lands — lands that are too hot, too cold, too dry, too mountainous — lands that defy human ambitions; but lands that today, under the pressure of explosive population growth, are being brought under cultivation or husbandry and being settled.

Compounding those environmental challenges is the question of what form of tenure or property rights will best ensure a sustainable future: individual or communal, private or bureaucratic? Here again, the history of ranching in the American West offers a relevant experience, for it has been wracked from its earliest days by debate over the question.

But in order to be useful in these ways western history has to be presented more forcefully than it has in terms of comparative human ecology, emphasizing the relation of people to other animals, of animals to vegetation, and of vegetation to patterns of tenure. In the rest of this brief essay I want to sketch that alternative approach and suggest lines of research that can bring the region's significance home to scholars from all over the world. We ought to begin by getting outside our regional provincialisms, overcoming our insistence on American uniqueness, and try to situate the cowboy and his ranch in the broad panorama of human adaptation to the earth.

Except in California, where everything is a ranch (avocado ranches, tomato ranches, golf ranches, retired president ranches), a ranch is an extensive farm that specializes in raising cows, sheep, goats, or horses. But it is also a modern reworking of an ancient pastoral way of life, and we need to understand what it replaced in order to comprehend fully what it has been and what it is becoming.

Pastoralism, an adaptation involving the herding of livestock, seems to have begun as a variant on agriculture, with its mixed economy of plants and animals. Possibly it appeared in response to the pressure of a growing population on a limited space; some people may have been excluded from farming, by whatever method of selection, and forced to find a living in more marginal lands — that is, they were forced out of river valleys onto broad uplands or high mountains or steppes, often where only scrub brush grew and the rainfall was scanty and erratic. Here they had to abandon much of their old life, limiting their subsistence base mainly to various ruminants. Apparently, the earliest people to be, so to speak, thrown out into the wasteland were the nomads of the Middle East, the children of Ishmael, who took to roaming the deserts with their camels, goats, and sheep, though maintaining a mutualistic relationship with the agrarian settlements, now trading with them, now raiding them, maintaining that uncertain relationship well down into recent times.

The anthropologist Brian Spooner has identified . . . [these] broad cultural regions emerging from this ancient history of nomadic pastoralism: the region of sub-Saharan Africa, where people's livelihood came to be based on herding cattle; the region of the vast desert belt that stretches from the Sahara across Arabia to India, a zone where the camel has been the key animal; the region of the mountain plateaus of Iberia, Italy, Greece, Turkey, and Afghanistan, based on sheep mainly; the region of the Central Asian Steppe, also sheep based; and the far northern region, from Norway to the Bering Sea, where the reindeer has long been the principal herd animal, the chief source of clothing and food.

Perhaps the most important inquiry for a modern western historian to make of that long nomadic tradition is how all those peoples, living with a diversity of animals in so many different places, managed to sustain their way of life before the modern age. In east Africa, for example, tribes have been following their flocks and herds for up to 10,000 years; though, in the accounts of some authorities, they have had a profound effect on the flora of the continent in that period, they have nonetheless managed to achieve a state of fluctuating equilibrium, at least until very recently. Whatever damages to nature they may have done, whatever tragedies they may have experienced over those ten millennia, they have survived down to the days of note-taking anthropologists. How did they do it? How did they regulate their impact on the land to keep it producing? How successful were they in conserving the graze or browse on which their stock depended? What kind of land degradation could one find among pastoral peoples in the past, and how severe was it?

There are as many answers to those questions as there are — or I should say, were — nomadic pastoral societies. In some cases, it would seem, particularly in extensive dry areas, the herding life often produced a highly independent-minded folk who relied on constant mobility to preserve their ecological base. It was a regular thing to squabble amongst themselves and make war against rival tribes. Among the Qashga'i of southwestern Iran, for instance, each extended household traditionally kept its herds separate from others in the tribe, grazed them on pasture allocated by the headmen, and managed with few communal rules. Each household tried to build its herds as large as it could, keeping a steady high pressure on the range, demanding more room from the headmen to accommodate their surplus; the tribe in turn asserted control of as much land as it could through force and defended it against competitors. A rough — and sometimes it got very rough — balance of power among area tribes determined who had winter and summer pasture access. Within each tribe a hierarchy based on livestock wealth existed, though private property in land was unknown.

Generally, nomads show little interest in resource conservation or pasture improvement, though they are incredibly knowledgeable about the lands they exploit. They have to know where there will be grass in the months ahead, how many head of animals it will support, where there will be waterholes, when to expect drought. As they deplete their supplies locally, they go looking for more, sometimes entering upon the territory of others, where they use diplomacy if they can to gain access but take by arms if they must. Eventually, when the abandoned pastures have recovered, they bring their stock back to chew it all up again. So long as their human numbers remain limited by war and disease and their herd sizes are regularly culled by drought, hunger, predation, theft, and infertility, they manage to stay within the carrying capacity of their range, the vegetation evolving toward resilience and tenacity.

In other cases, however, the history of pastoralism took an altogether different direction; the strategy of survival was not one of wandering impermanently from one site to another, in an endless cycle of nomadism, but of learning to stay in one place and adjusting to its limits. The circumalpine environment of Europe furnishes many examples of this more intensive, sedentary form of pastoralism. There the herders traditionally spent a part of the year grazing their animals in nearby alpine meadows — practicing a kind of vertical and partial nomadism called transhumance. At summer's end they trailed their stock down to established villages, where they fed them through the winter on stored hay; thus, they lived much of the year like other farmers, but harvested milk and cheese rather than grain. The high summer pastures of this region have been used since Neolithic times, and since the Middle Ages there has "gradually evolved what would appear to be the most stable and finely balanced form of peasant society and culture in the European area." Similar patterns of settled village life, limited pastoral movement, and cautious environmental control can be found in the Andean region of South America and in the Himalayas.

The classic ecological study of mountain pastoralism is Robert Netting's *Balancing on an Alp*, which examines the still-thriving Swiss community of Törbel, located above the Rhone Valley toward Zermatt and the Italian border. For at least seven centuries daily life there has been hedged about with precise written rules and regulations that no desert nomad would find tolerable; the earliest of them, an ancient scrap of parchment written in Latin, dates as far back as 1224 A.D. Mainly, the regulations deal with land use. They specify, for example, exactly who in the village has the right to graze livestock, who in effect owns a share in this community pasture. So strict is the observance of the rules that no outsiders have ever been allowed to break into that closed circle. Each family is also limited to the number of cattle they can winter over on their individual hay crop, which is raised on their private landholdings; there are 5,000 such parcels in the community, and a family may own as many as 100 of them, scattered among everyone else's, along with a piece of the many large storage barns. It is a close-knit, egalitarian community, where there are neither rich nor poor families. The feudal ages never entered to disrupt the social and ecological order, nor has the modern capitalist economy succeeded yet in breaking it down. It strikes a balance between communal and individual owner-ship. It is a thoroughly local system, and it reflects local needs. Above all, the pastoral life in Törbel is based on a strong, persistent, widely shared sense of natural limits; otherwise, the regulations would cease to be acceptable. As Netting puts it, "The centuries-long survival and continued productivity of both alp and forest testify to the effectiveness of communal management, the wis-dom of conservation measures, and the continued enforcement of rules against overgrazing and indiscriminate timber cutting."

One could travel on and on around the world examining these pastoral ways of life. My point in making only a quick discursus is to suggest that the student of the American West has a vast history to become at least passingly familiar with and has a wealth of possibilities for comparative analysis. The cowboy in an important sense belongs to this greater world of human ecology, not merely to Wyoming.

The North American ranch began to emerge as an institution in the southern part of Texas during the 1860s, and its history belongs completely to the post–Civil War era of the nation. Though it adopted terms, tools, and animal lore going back into the dim past, drawing on Iberian and Celtic pastoral anteced-ents, the ranch was unmistakably a modern capitalist institution. It specialized in raising cattle or other animals to sell in the marketplace, furnishing meat, hides, and wool to the growing metropolises in the East and their armies of laborers. Livestock became a form of capital in this innovative system, and that capital was made to earn a profit and increase itself many times over, without limit. But the animals were only one part of the capital — a mere mechanism for processing the more essential capital, the western grasslands, into a form suitable for human consumption; the cattle carried the grass, as it were, to the Chicago or Kansas City stockyards, where they were slaughtered by the millions and carved into beefsteak. From the beginning, the scale of this industry was continental, growing up as it did with the national railroad lines; and, then following the invention of the refrigerated ship in 1879, it became transoceanic and global.

In the place of the Swiss and the Maasai cowherd, the Berber and Baluchistan shepherd, the Peruvian llama, and Yemeni camel tender, the American cowboy steps forth, a brand-new figure in the long tradition. But like his predecessors, he must confront the fundamental questions: What is his relationship to the land to be, and how long can he sustain himself in comparison with the others?

The first quarter-century of American livestock ranching was, according to every historian who has written on the subject, an unmitigated disaster — colorful, exciting, fabulous, yes, but a disaster all the same. From Texas to the Canadian plains and all the way westward to the Pacific, thousands of entrepreneurs assembled their herds and drove them onto the public lands, millions of acres lying open to enterprise. They had no tribal headmen to guide them, no ancient parchments to spell out their rights and responsibilities, little or no knowledge of the landscapes they were invading, and no willingness to wait for any of these to appear. The range belonged to no one, they claimed; therefore, it belonged to everyone. The first individuals to arrive simply appropriated what they wanted and, without legal title, began to take off the grass. Others soon arrived and claimed the same right. Then there was a multitude, some of them individuals, some of them corporations, not a few of them cowboys living in Edinburgh or London. Let one of the most prominent of these newfangled pastoralists, Granville Stuart, describe the frenzied scene in Montana in the boom years:

> In 1880, the country was practically uninhabited. One could travel for miles without seeing so much as a traveler's bivouac. Thousands of buffalo darkened the rolling plains. There were deer, elk, wolves and coyotes on every hill and in every ravine and thicket. . . .
>
> In the fall of 1883, there was not a buffalo remaining on the range, and the antelope, elk, and deer were indeed scarce. In 1880 no one had heard tell of a cowboy in "this niche of the woods" and Charlie Russell had made no pictures of them; but in the fall of 1883, there were 600,000 head of cattle on the range. The cowboy . . . had become an institution.

But a mere five years later, in 1888, he might have added, much of the western ranching industry was lying in ruins, the victim of severe overgrazing and desperately cold winters. Many thousands of animals were lying dead all over the range, starved and frozen; others were riding in boxcars to the stockyards for rapid liquidation by their owners. Even faster than it had boomed, the new American pastoralism busted. It would take decades for it to recover.

That collapse — or what we might call the "tragedy of the laissez-faire commons" — was one of the greatest in the entire history of pastoralism, as measured in the loss of animal life. It has been told many times in western history courses, and probably forgotten as often, for Americans do not like to remember that they once failed abysmally in a form of husbandry where illiterate African tribesmen have succeeded. My purpose in recalling it here, though, is not to emphasize the failure of our early cowboy capitalists but rather to draw out of it the difficult predicament it left us with in the United States. We had acquired a vast public domain, and a large part of it would never be suitable for agriculture; it was as marginal as they come. What it offered was a pasture of considerable potential for livestock, a pasture covering several hundred million acres. But who would own it? Who would manage it? Was there any safe, permanent, humane way to turn the grass and the poor, dumb, hoofed animals on that acreage into modern dreams of unlimited personal wealth?

For a hundred years now there have been two competing answers to that set of questions, and neither has so far managed to make its case convincing enough to settle the matter once and for all. I should add that neither answer has much continuity with that long tradition of Old World pastoralism; indeed, they are both based on a rejection of tradition, on a confidence in the new, and perhaps it is that fact which has made neither of them quite an acceptable solution.

One of the answers that came quickly out of the debacle of the 1880s was predictable in a nation devoted to the principles of free enterprise: turn the whole public domain over to the ranchers as their private property and let them manage it without hindrance. If farmers could get free homesteads of 160 acres, why should the stockmen not get free ranches of 1,600 or 16,000 acres, get whatever they needed to raise their herds and flocks? In the eyes of many, it was a highly ethical question, a matter of fairness and rights for those who lived by herds instead of crops. But when the claim of a right to a freehold of 16,000 acres did not seem to get much recognition, another, more compelling argument emerged, based on economics and ecology. Privatizing the range, it was argued, would give the western grazier a real incentive to manage the land better and avoid the kind of irresponsible free-for-all of the 1880s. With a fee simple title in hand, he would be more likely to invest his capital in long-term improvements, especially fencing. The fences were all important: a set of fences, it was said, would provide a far greater return from the land, for they would allow the stockman to bring in a better grade of animal, free of the fear that they would breed uncontrollably with lesser stock. Fences would also make possible a system of pasture rotations, confining the animals to areas where the vegetation was in good shape, keeping them off areas that needed to recover. There would be less erosion, depletion, and weed invasion. Under a program of privatization the range could be made to yield a higher economic return while, simultaneously, remaining a more healthy and productive environment.

Such was the answer that began to be heard in congressional hearings from the first part of the twentieth century on to the present, an answer one can follow among individual stockmen, their lobbying groups (the National Livestock Association, the National Wool Growers Association, the various state versions of the same), their senators and representatives, and an odd resource economist or two. In 1929 President Herbert Hoover, impressed by this collective din, proposed to turn over the federal lands to the western states, permitting them to dispose of them in turn to individual parties. The measure failed when it was learned that he did not mean to include mineral rights with the grass. More recently, between 1979 and 1981, a number of western states, beginning with Nevada, have tried to claim federal lands within their borders, with the idea of putting them into the hands of stockmen; this was the so-called Sagebrush Rebellion, but eventually it too fizzled out.

The other, opposing answer came from conservationists and government officials, along with a number of scientists. The great western pastures had been acquired at the price of considerable blood and money by the federal government on behalf of all the American people, it was argued, and they should stay public. Though almost everything else had been disposed of into private hands, these lands ought to continue in a state of federal ownership. Here again there was a moral dimension to the argument, an appeal to social democratic ideals of equality and commonwealth. There was also an effort to refute the claim that only privatization could produce the greatest economic return; on the contrary, it was insisted, public ownership would ensure the greatest return to the greatest number of people. But perhaps the most effective part of the argument, though it was never put too starkly, was that the private entrepreneur simply could not be trusted to look out for the long-term ecological health of the range resource. He would tend to exploit rather than conserve it; making the pastures private would not be a reliable way to protect them for posterity. A much better solution would be to create a centralized bureaucracy of disinterested, scientifically trained professionals to oversee the public range.

In 1934 Congress, leaning toward this second proposal, passed the Taylor Grazing Act, which for the first time established a significant measure of control over the unappropriated public domain. The declared purpose of the act was "to stop injury to the public grazing lands by preventing overgrazing and soil deterioration, to provide for their orderly use, improvement, and development, to stabilize the livestock industry dependent upon the public range, and for other purposes." The legislation set up a National Grazing Service to carry out those purposes through a scheme of leasing acreage for a fee; together with the Forest Service, which administers grazing leases within the national forest system, the Grazing Service (later the Bureau of Land Management) would supervise ranchers over a domain encompassing the largest part of the rural West. Some stockmen would have their entire ranch on the public lands, but the average lessee would mix private holdings with public leases in about a 4:6 ratio. The leases were almost but not quite a rancher's private property. They could be traded in the market, could serve as bank collateral, and could be fenced. But always, in the corner of the rancher's eye, there would be standing a federal bureaucrat with a mandate to protect the public's interest in the land.

During the 1960s and 1970s, after a long era of benign neglect and under rising pressure from conservationists, the bureaucrats began to assert their mandate in modest but galling ways. They contended that many leases were badly over-grazed and stock would have to be removed. In the eyes of many rancher-lessees that ever-present bureaucracy was from the beginning, but particularly has become in recent years, an unacceptable infringement on their freedom and a threat to their security of tenure.

The long contest between these two rivals in modern pastoralism has given much of the American West a peculiar set of property and managerial arrange-ments: a hybrid of capitalist and bureaucratic regimes, each assuming it knows what is best for the nation's pocketbook and for nature. The significance of the struggle is immense. In a century where land everywhere has been put under more and more intensive use, the West speaks directly to the issue of where we can find the ideal manager. Is it the man or woman dressed in Stetson hat and boots, claiming to belong to the land and to know it intimately but speaking the language of private property, business, and profit maximization? Or is it the government official, also likely to be dressed in the traditional western garb, as much a local resident as the other but trained in the discourse of biology or range management? Does the self-interest of the capitalist really lead to rational land use, as many claim, or is it destructive of self, society, and the land? Can those who have no immediate economic stake in the land be trusted to make better decisions about its use? Has either the capitalist or the bureaucrat the capacity to match the Old World pastoralists' ability to sustain themselves on the margins of the good earth? The West offers millions of acres and decades of experience in which to find answers for those questions.

However, that more probing kind of history of the western range has not yet been written. We have shelves and shelves of books on the general subject, but very little of that literature has systematically addressed the critical ques-tions of tenure, environment, and managerial strategies. What is needed is a full ecological history of the western range that will examine comparatively the condition of the range under private and public (or quasi-public) ownership, that will explore the impact of rangeland science on management, that will test the claims made by the rival parties and help resolve the old debate, and that will frame such an inquiry in terms of a broad world of people, animals, and arid lands.

I am aware that most folks, when they think of cowboys and the West, do not have in mind all that I have touched on here. They imagine a life of freedom in an open country, as the East Germans once looked across the Berlin Wall, dreaming of a west beyond restraint. Pastoralism has always had that effect on people toiling in fields and cities; more poor, more primitive, more uncouth than village or city folk, the herders are nonetheless admired for their oppor-tunity to trek the high mountains, the distant savannas, the endless deserts, to possess the richness of space. But in America we have added to that old set of associations some new ones. The cowboy-rancher stands, somewhat paradox-ically, for the ideal of free enterprise and for the institution of private property. Historians need to take all those images and associations seriously—more seriously than they have—but they will also have to insist that the public understand the full, complex ideological and ecological story behind them. Moreover, it is historians, familiar with the hundred years of ranching in the West, familiar with the much longer span of pastoral life on the planet, who can help resolve the unsettled question of how we are most likely to find a sustainable future.

Telling Stories About Ecology*

WILLIAM CRONON

In 1979, two books were published about the long drought that struck the Great Plains during the 1930s. The two had nearly identical titles: one, by Paul Bonnifield, was called *The Dust Bowl*; the other, by Donald Worster, *Dust Bowl*. The two authors dealt with virtually the same subject, had researched many of the same documents, and agreed on most of their facts, and yet their conclusions could hardly have been more different.

Bonnifield's closing argument runs like this:

> The story of the dust bowl was the story of people, people with ability and talent, people with resourcefulness, fortitude, and courage. . . . The people of the dust bowl were not defeated, poverty-ridden people without hope. They were builders for tomorrow.

Worster, on the other hand, paints a bleaker picture:

> The Dust Bowl was the darkest moment in the twentieth-century life of the southern plains, . . . one of the three worst ecological blunders in history. . . . It cannot be blamed on illiteracy or overpopulation or social disorder. It came about because the culture was operating in precisely the way it was supposed to. . . . The Dust Bowl . . . was the inevitable outcome of a culture that deliberately, self-consciously, set itself [the] task of dominating and exploiting the land for all it was worth.

For Bonnifield, the dust storms of the 1930s were mainly a natural disaster; when the rains gave out, people had to struggle for their farms, their homes, their very survival. Their success in that struggle was a triumph of individual and community spirit: nature made a mess, and human beings cleaned it up. Worster's version differs dramatically. Although the rains did fail during the 1930s, their disappearance expressed the cyclical climate of a semiarid environment. The story of the Dust Bowl is less about the failures of nature than about the failures of human beings to accommodate themselves to nature. . . .

Whichever of these interpretations we are inclined to follow, they pose a dilemma for scholars who study past environmental change — indeed, a

---

*This essay is an abridged version of the original article. Readers interested in the history of Great Plains narratives and postmodern criticism are urged to read the longer version.

Excerpts from Cronon, William, "A Place for Stories: Nature, History, and Narrative," *Journal of American History*, 78 (March 1992), 1347–1376. Reprinted with permission.

dilemma for all historians. As often happens in history, they make us wonder how two competent authors looking at identical materials drawn from the same past can reach such divergent conclusions. But it is not merely their *conclusions* that differ. Although both narrate the same broad series of events with an essentially similar cast of characters, they tell two entirely different *stories*. In both texts, the story is inextricably bound to its conclusion, and the historical analysis derives much of its force from the upward or downward sweep of the plot. So we must eventually ask a more basic question: where did these stories come from?

The question is trickier than it seems, for it transports us into the much contested terrain between traditional social science and postmodernist critical theory. As an environmental historian who tries to blend the analytical traditions of history with those of ecology, economics, anthropology, and other fields, I cannot help feeling uneasy about the shifting theoretical ground we all now seem to occupy. On the one hand, a fundamental premise of my field is that human acts occur within a network of relationships, processes, and systems that are as ecological as they are cultural. To such basic historical categories as gender, class, and race, environmental historians would add a theoretical vocabulary in which plants, animals, soils, climates, and other nonhuman entities become the coactors and codeterminants of a history not just of people but of the earth itself. . . .

And yet scholars of environmental history also maintain a powerful commitment to narrative form. When we describe human activities within an ecosystem, we seem always to tell *stories* about them. Like all historians, we configure the events of the past into causal sequences — stories — that order and simplify those events to give them new meanings. We do so because narrative is the chief literary form that tries to find meaning in an overwhelmingly crowded and disordered chronological reality. When we choose a plot to order our environmental histories, we give them a unity that neither nature nor the past possesses so clearly. In so doing, we move well beyond nature into the intensely human realm of value. There, we cannot avoid encountering the postmodernist assault on narrative, which calls into question not just the stories we tell but the deeper purpose that motivated us in the first place: trying to make sense of nature's place in the human past. . . .

If we consider the Plains in the half millennium since Christopher Columbus crossed the Atlantic, certain events seem likely to stand out in any long-term history of the region. If I were to try to write these not as a *story* but as a simple *list* . . . the resulting chronicle might run something like this.

Five centuries ago, people traveled west across the Atlantic Ocean. So did some plants and animals. One of these — the horse — appeared on the Plains. Native peoples used horses to hunt bison. Human migrants from across the Atlantic eventually appeared on the Plains as well. People fought a lot. The bison herds disappeared. Native peoples moved to reservations. The new immigrants built homes for themselves. Herds of cattle increased. Settlers plowed the prairie grasses, raising corn, wheat, and other grains. Railroads moved people and other things into and out of the region. Crops sometimes failed for lack of rain. Some people abandoned their farms and moved else-where; other people stayed. During the 1930s, there was a particularly bad drought, with many dust storms. Then the drought ended. A lot of people began to pump water out of the ground for use on their fields and in their towns. Today, Plains farmers continue to raise crops and herds of animals. Some have trouble making ends meet. Many Indians live on reservations. It will be interesting to see what happens next. . . .

How do we discover a story that will turn the facts of Great Plains history into something more easily recognized and understood? The repertoire of historical plots we might apply to the events I've just chronicled is endless and could be drawn not just from history but from all of literature and myth. To simplify the range of choices, let me start by offering two large groups of possible plots. On the one hand, we can narrate Plains history as a story of improvement, in which the plot line gradually ascends toward an ending that is somehow more positive — happier, richer, freer, better — than the beginning. On the other hand, we can tell stories in which the plot line eventually falls toward an ending that is more negative — sadder, poorer, less free, worse — than the place where the story began. The one group of plots might be called "progressive," given their historical dependence on eighteenth-century En-lightenment notions of progress; the other might be called "tragic" or "declensionist," tracing their historical roots to romantic and antimodernist reactions against progress.

If we look at the ways historians have actually written about the changing environment of the Great Plains, the upward and downward lines of progress and declension are everywhere apparent. The very ease with which we recog-nize them constitutes a warning about the terrain we are entering. However compelling these stories may be as depictions of environmental change, their narrative form has less to do with nature than with human discourse. . . .

Take, for instance, the historians who narrate Great Plains history as a tale of frontier progress. The most famous of those who embraced this basic plot was of course Frederick Jackson Turner, for whom the story of the nation recapitulated the ascending stages of European civilization to produce a uniquely democratic and egalitarian community. Turner saw the transformation of the American landscape from wilderness to trading post to farm to boom-town as the central saga of the nation. If ever there was a narrative that achieved its end by erasing its true subject, Turner's frontier was it: the heroic encounter between pioneers and "free land" could only become plausible by obscuring the conquest that traded one people's freedom for another's. By making Indians the foil for its story of progress, the frontier plot made their conquest seem natural, commonsensical, inevitable. But to say this is only to affirm the narrative's power. . . . In its ability to turn ordinary people into heroes and to present a conflict-ridden invasion as an epic march toward enlightened democratic na-tionhood, it perfectly fulfilled the ideological needs of its late-nineteenth-century moment.

The Great Plains would eventually prove less tractable to frontier progress than many other parts of the nation. . . . One of Dakota Territory's leading missionaries, Bishop William Robert Hare, prophesied in the 1880s that the plot of Dakota settlement would follow an upward line of migration, struggle, and triumph:

> You may stand ankle deep in the short burnt grass of an uninhabited wilderness — next month a mixed train will glide over the waste and stop at some point where the railroad has decided to locate a town. Men, women and children will jump out of the cars. . . . The courage and faith of these pioneers are something extraordinary. Their spirit seems to rise above all obstacles.

For Hare, this vision of progress was ongoing and prospective, a prophecy of future growth, but the same pattern could just as easily be applied to retrospective visions. . . . Ordinary people saw such descriptions as the fulfillment of a grand story that had unfolded during the course of their own lifetimes. As one Kansas townswoman, Josephine Middlekauf, concluded,

> After sixty years of pioneering in Hays, I could write volumes telling of its growth and progress. . . . I have been singularly privileged to have seen it develop from the raw materials into the almost finished product in comfortable homes, churches, schools, paved streets, trees, fruits and flowers.

Consider these small narratives more abstractly. They tell a story of . . . linear progress, in which people struggle to transform a relatively responsive environment. There may be moderate setbacks along the way, but their narrative role is to play foil to the heroes who overcome them. Communities rapidly succeed in becoming ever more civilized and comfortable. The time frame of the stories is brief, limited to the lifespan of a single generation, . . . just after invading settlers first occupied Indian lands. Our attention as readers is focused on local events. . . . All of these framing devices . . . compel us toward the conclusion that this is basically a happy story.

If the story these narrators tell is about the drama of settlement and the courage of pioneers, it is just as much about the changing stage on which the drama plays itself out. The transformation of a Kansas town is revealed not just by its new buildings but by its shade trees, apple orchards, and gardens. . . . As the literary critic Kenneth Burke long ago suggested, the scene of a story is as fundamental to what happens in it as the actions that comprise its more visible plot. Indeed, Burke argues that a story's actions are almost invariably consistent with its scene. . . .

If the way a narrator constructs a scene is directly related to the story that narrator tells, then this has deep implications for environmental history, which after all takes scenes of past nature as its primary object of study. If the history of the Great Plains is a progressive story about how grasslands were turned into ranches, farms, and gardens, then the end of the story requires a particular kind of scene for the ascending plot line to reach its necessary fulfillment. Just as important, the closing scene has to be different from the opening one. If the story ends in a wheatfield that is the happy conclusion of a struggle to transform the landscape, then the most basic requirement of the story is that the earlier form of that landscape must either be neutral or negative in value. It must *deserve* to be transformed.

It is thus no accident that these storytellers begin their narratives in the midst of landscapes that have few redeeming features. Bishop Hare's Dakota Territory begins as "an uninhabited wilderness," and his railroad carries future settlers across a "waste." . . . Josephine Middlekauf perceived the unplowed Kansas grasslands chiefly as "raw materials." Even so seemingly neutral a phrase as this last one — "raw materials" — is freighted with narrative meaning. Indeed, it contains buried within it the entire story of progressive development in which the environment is transformed from "raw materials" to "finished product." In just this way, story and scene become entangled — with each other, and with the politics of invasion and civilized progress — as we try to understand the Plains environment and its history.

Now in fact, these optimistic stories about Great Plains settlement are by no means typical of historical writing in the twentieth century. The problems of settling a semiarid environment were simply too great for the frontier story to proceed without multiple setbacks and crises. Even narrators who prefer an ascending plot line in their stories of regional environmental change must therefore tell a more complicated tale of failure, struggle, and accommodation in the face of a resistant if not hostile landscape.

Among the most important writers who adopt this narrative strategy are Walter Prescott Webb and James Malin. . . . For Webb, the Plains were radically different from the more benign environments that Anglo-American settlers had encountered in the East. Having no trees and little water, the region posed an almost insurmountable obstacle to the westward march of civilization. After describing the scene in this way, Webb sets his story in motion with a revealing passage:

> In the new region — level, timberless, and semi-arid — [settlers] were thrown by Mother Necessity into the clutch of new circumstances. Their plight has been stated in this way: east of the Mississippi civilization stood on three legs — land, water, and timber; west of the Mississippi not one but two of these legs were withdrawn, — water and timber, — and civilization was left on one leg — land. It is small wonder that it toppled over in temporary failure.

It is easy to anticipate the narrative that will flow from this beginning: Webb will tell us how civilization fell over, then built itself new legs and regained its footing to continue its triumphant ascent. The central agency that solves these problems and drives the story forward is human invention. Unlike the simpler frontier narratives, Webb's history traces a dialectic between a resistant landscape and the technological innovations that will finally succeed in transforming it. Although his book is over five hundred pages long and is marvelously intricate in its arguments, certain great inventions mark the turning points of Webb's plot. Because water was so scarce, settlers had to obtain it from the only reliable source, underground aquifers, so they invented the humble but revolutionary windmill. Because so little wood was available to build fences that would keep cattle out of cornfields, barbed wire was invented in 1874 and rapidly spread throughout the grasslands. These and other inventions — railroads, irrigation, new legal systems for allocating water rights, even six-shooter revolvers — eventually destroyed the bison herds, created a vast cattle kingdom, and broke the prairie sod for farming.

Webb closes his story by characterizing the Plains as "a land of survival where nature has most stubbornly resisted the efforts of man. Nature's very stubbornness has driven man to the innovations which he has made." Given the scenic requirements of Webb's narrative, his Plains landscape must look rather different from that of earlier frontier narrators. For Webb, the semiarid environment is neither a wilderness nor a waste, but itself a worthy antagonist of civilization. It is a landscape the very resistance of which is the necessary spur urging human ingenuity to new levels of achievement. Webb thus spends much more time than earlier storytellers describing the climate, terrain, and ecology of the Great Plains so as to extol the features that made the region unique in American experience. Although his book ends with the same glowing image of a transformed landscape that we find in earlier frontier narratives, he in no way devalues the "uncivilized" landscape that preceded it. Quite the contrary: the more formidable it is as a rival, the more heroic become its human antagonists. In the struggle to make homes for themselves in this difficult land, the people of the Plains not only proved their inventiveness but built a regional culture beautifully adapted to the challenges of their regional environment. . . .

Webb's story of struggle against a resistant environment has formed the core of most subsequent environmental histories of the Plains. We have already encountered one version of it in Paul Bonnifield's *The Dust Bowl*. It can also be discovered in the more ecologically sophisticated studies of James C. Malin, in which the evolution of "forest man" to "grass man" becomes the central plot of Great Plains history. Malin's prose is far less story-like in outward appearance than Webb's, but it nonetheless narrates an encounter between a resistant environment and human ingenuity. Malin's human agents begin as struggling immigrants who have no conception of how to live in a treeless landscape; by the end, they have become "grass men" who have brought their culture "into conformity with the requirements of maintaining rather than disrupting environmental equilibrium." . . . Human inhabitants have become one with an environment that only a few decades before had almost destroyed them. . . .

Most interestingly, the human subject of these stories has become significantly broader than the earlier state and local frontier histories. Rather than focus primarily on individual pioneers and their communities, these new regional studies center their story on "civilization" or "man." The inventions that allowed people to adapt to life on the Great Plains are thus absorbed into the broader story of "man" and "his" long conquest of nature. No narrative centered on so singular a central character could be politically innocent. More erasures are at work here: Indians, yes, but also women, ethnic groups, underclasses, and any other communities that have been set apart from the collectivity represented by Man or Civilization. The narrative leaves little room for them, and even less for a natural realm that might appropriately be spared the conquests of technology. These are stories about a progress that, however hard-earned, is fated; its conquests are only what common sense and nature would expect. For Webb and Malin, the Great Plains gain significance from their ties to a world-historical plot, Darwinian in shape, that encompasses the entire sweep of human history. The ascending plot line we detect in these stories is in fact connected to a much longer plot line with the same rising characteristics. Whether that longer plot is expressed as the Making of the American Nation, the Rise of Western Civilization, or the Ascent of Man, it still lends its grand scale to Great Plains histories that outwardly appear much more limited in form. . . .

But there is another way to tell this history, one in which the plot ultimately falls rather than rises. The first examples of what we might call a "declensionist" or "tragic" Great Plains history began to appear during the Dust Bowl calamity of the 1930s. The dominant New Deal interpretation of what had gone wrong on the Plains was that settlers had been fooled by a climate that was sometimes perfectly adequate for farming and at other times disastrously inadequate. Settlement had expanded during "good" years when rainfall was abundant, and the perennial optimism of the frontier had prevented farmers from acknowledging that drought was a permanent fact of life on the Plains. In this version, Great Plains history becomes a tale of self-deluding hubris and refusal to accept reality. Only strong government action, planned by enlightened scientific experts to encourage cooperation among Plains farmers, could prevent future agricultural expansion and a return of the dust storms. . . .

Whatever the scientific or political merits of this description, consider its narrative implications. The New Deal planners in effect argued that the rising plot line of our earlier storytellers not only was false but was itself the principal cause of the environmental disaster that unfolded during the 1930s. The Dust Bowl had occurred because people had been telling themselves the wrong story and had tried to inscribe that story — the frontier — on a landscape incapable of supporting it. The environmental rhythms of the Plains ecosystem were cyclical, with good years and bad years following each other like waves on a beach. The problem of human settlement in the region was that people insisted on imposing their linear notions of progress on this cyclical pattern. Their perennial optimism led them always to accept as "normal" the most favorable part of the precipitation cycle, and so they created a type and scale of agriculture that could not possibly be sustained through the dry years. In effect, bad storytelling had wreaked havoc with the balance of nature. . . . [James] Malin wrote in the wake of the New Deal and was a staunch conservative opponent of everything it represented. His narratives of regional adaptation expressed his own horror of collectivism by resisting the New Deal story at virtually every turn. The planners, he said, had exaggerated the severity of the Dust Bowl to serve their own statist ends and had ignored the fact that dust storms had been a natural part of the Plains environment as far back as anyone remembered. Their scientistic faith in ecology had grave political dangers, for the ecologists had themselves gone astray in viewing the Plains environment as a stable, self-equilibrating organism in which human action inevitably disturbed the balance of nature. Ecosystems were dynamic, and so was the human story of technological progress: to assert that nature set insurmountable limits to human ingenuity was to deny the whole upward sweep of civilized history. The New Dealers' affection for stories in which nature and society were metaphorically cast as organisms only revealed their own hostility to individualism and their flirtation with communist notions of the state. . . .

It is James Malin's anti–New Deal narrative that informs Paul Bonnifield's *The Dust Bowl*. Writing in the late 1970s, at a time when conservative critiques of the welfare state were becoming a dominant feature of American political discourse, Bonnifield argues less urgently and polemically than Malin, but he tells essentially the same story. . . . When the Dust Bowl hit, it was the people who lived there, not government scientists, who invented new land-use practices that solved earlier problems. New Deal planners understood little about the region and were so caught up in their own ideology that they compounded its problems by trying to impose their vision of a planned society. . . . In fact, Bonnifield argues, the Plains contained some of the best farming soil in the world. The landscape was difficult but ultimately benign for people who could learn to thrive upon it. Their chief problem was less a hostile nature than a hostile government. The narrative echoes Malin's scenic landscape but gains a different kind of ideological force when placed at the historical moment of its narration — in the waning years of the Carter administration just prior to Ronald Reagan's triumphant election as president. Bonnifield's is a tale of ordinary folk needing nothing so much as to get government off their backs.

If Bonnifield elaborates the optimistic Dust Bowl narrative of a conservative critic of the New Deal, Donald Worster returns to the New Deal plot and deepens its tragic possibilities. Worster, who is with Webb the most powerful narrator among these writers, accepts the basic framework of Roosevelt's planners — the refusal of linear-minded Americans to recognize and accept cyclical environmental constraints — but he shears away its statist bias and considerably expands its cultural boundaries. . . . Worster . . . argues instead that the Plains were actually a paradigmatic case in a larger story that might be called "the rise and fall of capitalism."

For Worster, the refusal to recognize natural limits is one of the defining characteristics of a capitalist ethos and economy. He is therefore drawn to a narrative in which the same facts that betokened progress for Webb and Malin become signs of declension and of the compounding contradictions of capitalist expansion. The scene of the story is world historical only this time the plot leads toward catastrophe:

That the thirties were a time of great crisis in American, indeed, in world, capitalism has long been an obvious fact. The Dust Bowl, I believe, was part of that same crisis. It came about because the expansionary energy of the United States had finally encountered a volatile, marginal land, destroying the delicate ecological balance that had evolved there. We speak of farmers and plows on the plains and the damage they did, but the language is inadequate. What brought them to the region was a social system, a set of values, an economic order. There is no word that so fully sums up those elements as "capitalism." . . . Capitalism, it is my contention, has been the decisive factor in this nation's use of nature.

By this reading, the chief agent of the story is not "the pioneers" or "civilization" or "man"; it is capitalism. The plot leads from the origins of that economic system, through a series of crises, toward the future environmental cataclysm when the system will finally collapse. The tale of Worster's Dust Bowl thus concerns an intermediate crisis that foreshadows other crises yet to come; in this, it proclaims an apocalyptic prophecy that inverts the prophecy of progress found in earlier frontier narratives. Worster's inversion of the frontier story is deeply ironic, for it implies that the increasing technological "control" represented by Webb's and Malin's human ingenuity leads only toward an escalating spiral of disasters. He also breaks rank with the New Dealers at this point, for in his view their efforts at solving the problems of the Dust Bowl did nothing to address the basic contradictions of capitalism itself. For Worster, the planners "propped up an agricultural economy that had proved itself to be socially and ecologically erosive."

Given how much his basic plot differs from Webb's and Malin's, the scene Worster constructs for his narrative must differ just as dramatically. Since Worster's story concerns the destruction of an entire ecosystem, it must end where the frontier story began: in a wasteland. His plot must move downward toward an ecological disaster called the Dust Bowl. Whereas the frontier narratives begin in a negatively valued landscape and end in a positive one, Worster begins his tale in a place whose narrative value is entirely good. . . . Delicate and beautiful, the Plains were an ecosystem living always on the edge of drought, and their survival depended on an intricate web of plants and animals that capitalism was incapable of valuing by any standard other than that of the marketplace. From this beginning, the story moves down a slope that ends in the dust storms whose narrative role is to stand as the most vivid possible symbol of human alienation from nature.

The very different scenes that progressive and declensionist narrators choose as the settings for their Great Plains histories bring us to another key observation about narrative itself: where one chooses to begin and end a story profoundly alters its shape and meaning. . . . If we shift time frames to encompass the Indian past, we suddenly encounter a new set of narratives, equally tragic in their sense of crisis and declension, but strikingly different in plot and scene. As such, they offer further proof of the narrative power to reframe the past so as to include certain events and people, exclude others, and redefine the meaning of landscape accordingly.

[For example], Plenty Coups, a Crow Indian chief, tells in his 1930 autobiography of a boyhood vision sent him by his animal Helper, the Chickadee. In the dream, a great storm blown by the Four Winds destroyed a vast forest, leaving standing only the single tree in which the Chickadee — smallest but shrewdest of animals — made its lodge. The tribal elders interpreted this to mean that white settlers would eventually destroy not only the buffalo but also all tribes who resisted the American onslaught. On the basis of this prophetic dream, the Crows decided to ally themselves with the United States, and so they managed to preserve a portion of their homelands. Saving their land did not spare them from the destruction of the bison herds, however, and so they shared with other Plains tribes the loss of subsistence and spiritual communion that had previously been integral to the hunt. As Plenty Coups remarks at the end of his story, "when the buffalo went away the hearts of my people fell to the ground, and they could not lift them up again. After this nothing happened."

Few remarks more powerfully capture the importance of narrative to history than this last of Plenty Coups: "After this nothing happened." For the Crows as for other Plains tribes, the universe revolved around the bison herds, and life made sense only so long as the hunt continued. When the scene shifted — when the bison herds "went away" — that universe collapsed and history ended. Although the Crows continued to live on their reservation and although their identity as a people has never ceased, for Plenty Coups their subsequent life is all part of a different story. The story he loved best ended with the buffalo. Everything that has happened since is part of some other plot, and there is neither sense nor joy in telling it. . . .

And just what *is* a narrative? As the evidence of my Great Plains chronicle would imply, it is not merely a sequence of events. To shift from chronicle to narrative, a tale of environmental change must be structured so that, as Aristotle said, it "has beginning, middle, and end." What distinguishes stories from other forms of discourse is that they describe an action that begins, continues over a well-defined period of time, and finally draws to a definite close, with consequences that become meaningful because of their placement within the narrative. Completed action gives a story its unity and allows us to evaluate and judge an act by its results. The moral of a story is defined by its ending: as Aristotle remarked, "the end is everywhere the chief thing."

Narrative is a peculiarly human way of organizing reality, and this has important implications for the way we approach the history of environmental change. . . . Many natural events lack [a] linear structure. Some are cyclical: the motions of the planets, the seasons, or the rhythms of biological fertility and reproduction. Others are random: climate shifts, earthquakes, genetic mutations, and other events the causes of which remain hidden from us. One does not automatically describe such things with narrative plots, and yet environmental histories, which purport to set the human past in its natural context, all have plots. Nature and the universe do not tell stories; we do. Why is this?

Two possible answers to this question emerge from the work that philosophers and post-structuralist literary critics have done on the relationship between narrative and history. One group, which includes Hayden White and the late Louis Mink as well as many of the deconstructionists, argues that narrative is so basic to our cultural beliefs that we automatically impose it on a reality that bears little or no relation to the plots we use in organizing our experience. Mink summarizes this position nicely by asserting that "the past is not an untold story." The same could presumably be said about nature: we force our stories on a world that doesn't fit them. The historian's project of recovering past realities and representing them "truly" or even "fairly" is thus a delusion. . . .

An alternative position, most recently defended by David Carr but originally developed by Martin Heidegger, is that although narrative may not be intrinsic to events in the physical universe, it is fundamental to the way we humans organize our experience. Whatever may be the perspective of the universe on the things going on around us, our human perspective is that we inhabit an endlessly storied world. . . . Our very habit of partitioning the flow of time into "events," with their implied beginnings, middles, and ends, suggests how deeply the narrative structure inheres in our experience of the world. As Carr puts it, "Narrative is not merely a possibly successful way of describing events; its structure inheres in the events themselves. . . . "

Carr's position will undoubtedly be attractive to most historians, since it argues that, far from being arbitrary, our narratives reflect one of the most fundamental properties of human consciousness. It also gives us a way of absorbing the lessons of narrative theory without feeling we have abandoned all ties to an external reality. Insofar as people project their wills into the future, . . . they live their lives as if they were telling a story. It is undoubtedly true that we all constantly tell ourselves stories to remind ourselves who we are, how we got to be that person, and what we want to become. The same is true not just of individuals but of communities and societies: we use our histories to remember ourselves, just as we use our prophecies as tools for exploring what we do or do not wish to become. As Plenty Coups's story implies, to recover the narratives people tell themselves about the meanings of their lives is to learn a great deal about their past actions and about the way they *understand* those actions. Stripped of the story, we lose track of understanding itself. . . .

It is because we care about the consequences of actions that narratives — unlike most natural processes — have beginnings, middles, and ends. Stories are intrinsically teleological forms, in which an event is explained by the prior events or causes that lead up to it. This accounts for one feature that all these Great Plains histories have in common: all are designed so that the plot and its changing scene — its environment — flow toward the ultimate end of the story. In the most extreme cases, if the tale is of progress, then the closing landscape is a garden; if the tale is of crisis and decline, the closing landscape (whether located in the past or the future) is a wasteland. As an obvious but very important consequence of this narrative requirement, opening landscapes must be different from closing ones to make the plot work. A trackless waste must become a grassland civilization. Or: a fragile ecosystem must become a Dust Bowl. The difference between beginning and end gives us our chance to extract a moral from the rhetorical landscape. Our narratives take changes in the land and situate them in stories whose endings become the lessons we wish to draw from those changes.

However serious the epistemological problems it creates, this commitment to teleology and narrative gives environmental history — all history — its moral center. Because stories concern the consequences of actions that are potentially valued in quite different ways, whether by agent, narrator, or audience, we can achieve no neutral objectivity in writing them. Historians may strive to be as fair as they can, but as these Plains examples demonstrate, it remains possible to narrate the same evidence in radically different ways. Within the field of our narratives we too — as narrators — are moral agents and political actors. As storytellers we commit ourselves to the task of judging the consequences of human actions, trying to understand the choices that confronted the people whose lives we narrate so as to capture the full tumult of their world. In the dilemmas they faced we discover our own, and at the intersection of the two we locate the moral of the story. If our goal is to tell tales that make the past meaningful, then we cannot escape struggling over the values that define what meaning is. . . .

The stories we tell about the past do not exist in a vacuum, and our storytelling practice is bounded in at least three ways that limit its power. First, our stories cannot contravene known facts about the past. This is so much a truism of traditional historical method that we rarely bother even to state it, but it is crucial if we wish to deny that all narratives do an equally good job of representing the past. At the most basic level, we judge a work bad history if it contradicts evidence we know to be accurate and true. Good history does not knowingly lie. A history of the Great Plains that narrated a story of continuous progress without once mentioning the Dust Bowl would instantly be suspect, as would a history of the Nazi treatment of Jews that failed to mention the concentration camps. Historical narratives are bounded at every turn by the evidence they can and cannot muster in their own support.

Environmental historians embrace a second set of narrative constraints: given our faith that the natural world ultimately transcends our narrative power, our stories must make ecological sense. You can't put dust in the air—or tell stories about putting dust in the air—if the dust isn't there. Even though environmental histories transform ecosystems into the scenes of human narratives, the biological and geological processes of the earth set fundamental limits to what constitutes a plausible narrative. The dust storms of the 1930s are not just historical facts but natural ones: they reflect the complex response of an entire ecosystem—its soils, its vegetation, its animals, its climate—to human actions. Insofar as we can know them, to exclude or obscure these natural "facts" would be another kind of false silence, another kind of lying. . . .

Finally, historical narratives are constrained in a third important way as well. Historians do not tell stories by themselves. We write as members of communities, and we cannot help but take those communities into account as we do our work. Being American, being male, being white, being an upper-middle-class academic, being an environmentalist, I write in particular ways that are not all of my own choosing, and my biases are reflected in my work. But being a scholar, I write also for a community of other scholars—some very different from me in their backgrounds and biases—who know nearly as much about my subject as I do. They are in a position instantly to remind me of the excluded facts and wrong-headed interpretations that my own bias, self-delusion, and lack of diligence have kept me from acknowledging. . . .

The danger of postmodernism, despite all the rich insights it offers into the contested terrain of narrative discourse, is that it threatens to lose track of the very thing that makes narrative so compelling a part of history and human consciousness both. After all, the principal difference between a chronicle and a narrative is that a good story makes us *care* about its subject in a way that a chronicle does not. My list of "significant Great Plains events" surely had no effect on anyone's emotions or moral vision, whereas I doubt anyone can read Donald Worster's *Dust Bowl* without being moved in one way or another. More powerfully still, the nothingness at the end of Plenty Coups's story suggests that even silence — the ability of narrative to rupture the flow of time in the service of its meaning — can touch us deeply with its eloquence. When a narrator honestly makes an audience care about what happens in a story, the story expresses the ties between past and present in a way that lends deeper meaning to both. . . . At its best, however, historical storytelling helps keep us morally engaged with the world by showing us how to care about it and its origins in ways we had not done before.

If this is true, then the special task of environmental history is to assert that stories about the past are better, all other things being equal, if they increase our attention to nature and the place of people within it. They succeed when they make us look at the grasslands and their peoples in a new way. This is different from saying that our histories should turn their readers into environmentalists or convince everyone of a particular political point of view. Good histories rarely do this. But if environmental history is successful in its project, the story of how different peoples have lived in and used the natural world will become one of the most basic and fundamental narratives in all of history, without which no understanding of the past could be complete. . . .

Because I care so much about nature and storytelling both, I would urge upon environmental historians the task of telling not just stories about nature, but stories about stories about nature. I do so because narratives remain our chief moral compass in the world. Because we use them to motivate and explain our actions, the stories we tell change the way we act in the world. They are not just passive accounts: in a very literal sense, the frontier stories helped *cause* the Dust Bowl, just as the New Deal stories helped cause the government response to that disaster. We find in such stories our histories and prophecies both, which means they remain our best path to an engaged moral life. In organizing ecological change into beginnings, middles, and ends — which from the point of view of the universe are fictions, pure and simple — we place human agents at the center of events that they themselves may not fully understand but that they constantly affect with their actions. The end of these human stories creates their unity, the telos against which we judge the efficacy, wisdom, and morality of human actions.

Historians and prophets share a common commitment to finding the meaning of endings. However much we understand that an ecosystem transcends mere humanity, we cannot escape the valuing process that defines our relationship to it. To see how much this is so, one has only to consider the various labels Americans have attached to the Great Plains since 1800: the Land of the Buffalo; the Great American Desert; the Great Plains; the Wheat Belt; the Dust Bowl; the Breadbasket of the World; the Land Where the Sky Begins. These are not simply names or descriptive phrases. Each implies a different possible *narrative* for environmental histories of the region, and different possible endings for each of those stories. Narrative is thus inescapably bound to the very names we give the world. Rather than evade it — which is in any event impossible — we must learn to use it consciously, responsibly, self-critically. To try to escape the value judgments that accompany storytelling is to miss the point of history itself, for the stories we tell, like the questions we ask, are all finally about value. So it is with questions that I will end:

What do people care most about in the world they inhabit?

How do they use and assign meaning to that world?

How does the earth respond to their actions and desires?

What sort of communities do people, plants, and animals create together?

How do people struggle with each other for control of the earth, its creatures, and its meanings?

And on the grandest scale: what is the mutual fate of humanity and the earth?

Good questions all, and starting points for many a story. . . .

❦ F U R T H E R   R E A D I N G

Larry Barsness, *Heads, Hides and Horns: The Compleat Buffalo Book* (1985)

Black Elk (Oglala Lakota), *Black Elk Speaks,* ed. John Neihardt (1932)

Allan G. Bogue, *From Prairie to Corn Belt: Farming on the Illinois and Iowa Prairies in the Nineteenth Century* (1963)

Paul Bonnifield, *The Dust Bowl: Men, Dirt, and Depression* (1979)

Willa Cather, *O Pioneers* (1913)

————, *My Antonía* (1918)

David F. Costello, *The Prairie World* (1969)

Bernard DeVoto, ed., *The Journals of Lewis and Clark* (1953)

Philip Durham and Everett L. Jones, *The Negro Cowboy* (1965)

John Mack Faragher, *Women and Men on the Overland Trail* (1979)

Arlen L. Fowler, *The Black Infantry in the West, 1869–1891* (1971)

Josiah Gregg, *The Commerce of the Prairies* ([1926] 1967)

Mary Wilma M. Hargreaves, *Dry Farming in the Northern Great Plains, 1900–1925* (1957)

R. Douglas Hurt, *The Dust Bowl: An Agricultural and Social History* (1981)

William Loren Katz, *The Black West* (1987)

Annette Kolodny, *The Land Before Her: Fantasy and Experience of the American Frontiers, 1630–1860* (1984)

John (Fire) Lame Deer, *Lame Deer: Seeker of Visions,* ed. Richard Erdoes (1972)

Tom McHugh, *The Time of the Buffalo* (1972)

Russell McKee, *The Last West: A History of the Great Plains in North America* (1974)

James C. Malin, *The Grassland of North America: Prolegomena to Its History,* 4th ed. (1967)

————, *History and Ecology: Studies of the Grassland,* ed. Robert Swierenga (1984)

John S. Milloy, *The Plains Cree: Trade, Diplomacy and War, 1790 to 1870* (1988)

Sandra L. Myres, *Westering Women and the Frontier Experience, 1800–1915* (1982)

Francis Parkman, *The Oregon Trail* (1950)

Sheryll Patterson-Black, "Women Homesteaders on the Great Plains Frontier," *Frontiers* 1, 2 (Spring 1976), 67–88

————, *Western Women in History and Literature* (1978)

Plenty-coups (Crow), *Plenty-coups: Chief of the Crows,* ed. Frank B. Linderman (1962)

Pretty-Shield (Crow), *Pretty-Shield, Medicine Woman of the Crows,* ed. Frank B. Linderman (1974)

John F. Reiger, *The Passing of the Great West* (1972)

Osborne Russell, *Journal of a Trapper, 1834–1843* (1955)

Sherman W. Savage, *Blacks in the West* (1976)

Lillian Schlissel, *Women's Diaries of the Westward Journey* (1982)

James C. Shaw, *North from Texas* (1952)

Luther Standing Bear (Sioux), *Land of the Spotted Eagle,* ed. E. A. Brininstool (1933)

Joanna L. Stratton, *Pioneer Women: Voices from the Kansas Frontier* (1981)
Frederick Jackson Turner, "The Significance of the Frontier in American History" (1893)
Walter Prescott Webb, *The Great Plains* (1931)
Richard White, *The Roots of Dependency: Subsistence, Environment, and Social Change Among the Choctaws, Pawnees, and Navajos* (1983)
————, *The Middle Ground: Indians, Empires, and Republics in the Great Lakes Region, 1650–1850* (1991)
Jim Whitewolf (Kiowa Apache), *Jim Whitewolf: The Life of a Kiowa Apache Indian*, ed. Charles S. Brant (1969)
David Wishart, *The Fur Trade of the American West, 1807–1840* (1979)
Donald Worster, *Dust Bowl* (1979)

Resource Conservation
in an Industrializing Society

ψ

By the late nineteenth century, most of the land composing the contiguous United States had been settled. The 1890 census announced the closing of the frontier and the declining availability of free land. As scientists, writers, and politicians brought attention to decreasing stocks of natural resources needed for an industrializing society, a conservation consciousness arose. Laissez-faire capitalism, which had left resource development to individuals and private enterprise, was challenged by a Progressive Era politics of natural-resource conservation through government regulation. An egocentric (individualistic) ethic, centered on the notion that what was good for the individual was good for society as a whole, was challenged by a homocentric (utilitarian) ethic based on the greatest good for the greatest number of people. Politics and political institutions thus responded to a perception of limited renewable and nonrenewable resources in an era of closing frontier opportunities and expanding industrialization.

Spawned by the demand for reliable sources of water in the arid western states, by deteriorating rangelands, and by the rapid depletion of forests, a nationwide movement to preserve watersheds, build dams, replant trees, and reseed grasslands took shape. Bringing the progressive emphasis on technological efficiency to bear, engineers designed dams and irrigation systems, foresters developed selective harvesting and planting techniques, and ranchers planted new forage mixtures, fenced rangelands, and introduced pure-bred stock. At the grassroots level, schoolchildren planted trees, women's clubs cleaned up towns and harbors, and Audubon societies campaigned to save endangered birds. During the first decade of the twentieth century, under the presidency of Theodore Roosevelt, these disparate strands were united under the term conservation, *defined as "the use of natural resources for the greatest good of the greatest number for the longest time." However, even as the movement was coming together under the banner of conservation, it also was splintering into utilitarian conservation and wilderness preservationist camps (see Chapter 11). Changing political theories and political alignments during this era of an emerging national conservation policy provide the focus of this chapter.*

❦ D O C U M E N T S

The first five documents convey the growing awareness of natural-resource depletion in the United States by the late nineteenth century; they feature proposals for
government development and regulation of water, rangelands, and forests. The last
four selections concern the shaping of a national conservation policy and the rise of
a popular conservation movement.

When Vermont statesman George Perkins Marsh published *Man and Nature* in
1864, no one predicted that within a decade the book would be an international
classic. In exhaustive detail, Marsh wrote a history of human despoliation of nature
from the ancient civilizations of the Mediterranean world to the nineteenth century,
with abundant comparisons between Europe and the United States. Excerpted in the
opening document are passages in which Marsh depicts nature in the female gender, strong and stable when left alone but vulnerable and transformable by "man"
and "his" technologies. Humans' proper ethical role, Marsh argues, is to cooperate
with nature to repair the damage and restore lost harmonies.

In 1878 John Wesley Powell, a one-armed Civil War veteran, explorer, and
ethnographer, published his *Report on the Lands of the Arid Region of the United
States*, excerpted in the second document. Following Powell's extensive exploration
of the West, featuring a hair-raising expedition down the Colorado River in four
wooden boats and ascents up some of the region's most hazardous peaks, his
Report put forth a radical, democratic plan for developing the arid West within the
constraints set by the environment. Lowlands around streams could be irrigated
through cooperative labor and farmed, the forested mountain highlands could be
used for watershed and timber, and the rangelands between could be developed as
communal pasturage for cattle.

The third document presents excerpts from historian Frederick Jackson Turner's
famous essay of 1893 on the significance of the frontier in American history. In
contrast to Powell's vision that the West's arid environment encouraged cooperative
farming and new social institutions, Turner argued that the region's frontier conditions produced rugged individualism and democracy. Plentiful furs, nutritious
grasses, and rich soils lured successive waves of trappers, ranchers, and farmers
westward who wrested civilization from the wilderness. The environment thus determined American character and social institutions, Turner maintained.

In 1902, the federal government implemented some of Powell's recommendations when it passed the Reclamation Act, excerpted in the fourth document. This
law established a reclamation fund for the construction of dams and irrigation
works in the arid western states. Individuals could receive water from federal projects to irrigate a maximum of 160 acres, provided that they lived on or near the
land. Like the acreage restrictions of the Homestead Act (see page 295), however,
the limits specified by the Reclamation Act were never strictly enforced, a lapse
that allowed land and water speculators to thwart the law's democratic intentions.

Forest resources became another major concern of the Progressive Era. The
fifth document is taken from *Economics of Forestry*, published in 1902 by Bernhard
Fernow, first chief of the government's Division of Forestry, which had been created in 1886. In contrast to Turner, Fernow saw the individualism of a frontier
society as destructive of natural resources because it asserted the rights of the few.
He argued that the state's function was to guard the interests of the many, including those of future generations, by restricting laissez-faire development. Forests
should not be exploited for immediate individual gain but should be managed as
watershed and soil cover for present and future generations.

These efforts to develop and use water, range, and forest resources more wisely and frugally were brought together under the concept of conservation in 1908. Launched at a White House conference of governors through a speech by President Theodore Roosevelt (see the sixth document), the movement to conserve natural resources soon became a national cause célèbre. The Roosevelt administration's program, however, was opposed by laissez-faire capitalists, as is illustrated in the seventh document, taken from George L. Knapp's 1910 article, published in the prestigious, conservative *North American Review*. Women's groups such as the General Federation of Women's Clubs (GFWC) and the Daughters of the American Revolution (DAR) enthusiastically promoted conservation, as the eighth document, a speech by Mrs. Marion Crocker of the GFWC at the Fourth National Conservation Congress in 1912, reveals. In the last document, forest administrator Gifford Pinchot, one of the primary architects of Roosevelt's conservation program, recalls the birth of the term *conservation*.

George Perkins Marsh on Man and Nature, 1864

Stability of Nature

Nature, left undisturbed, so fashions her territory as to give it almost unchanging permanence of form, outline, and proportion, except when shattered by geologic convulsions; and in these comparatively rare cases of derangement, she sets herself at once to repair the superficial damage, and to restore, as nearly as practicable, the former aspect of her dominion. In new countries, the natural inclination of the ground, the self-formed slopes and levels, are generally such as best secure the stability of the soil. They have been graded and lowered or elevated by frost and chemical forces and gravitation and the flow of water and vegetable deposit and the action of the winds, until, by a general compensation of conflicting forces, a condition of equilibrium has been reached which, without the action of man, would remain, with little fluctuation, for countless ages. . . .

Two natural causes, destructive in character, were, indeed, in operation in the primitive American forests, though, in the Northern colonies, at least, there were sufficient compensations; for we do not discover that any considerable permanent change was produced by them. I refer to the action of beavers and of fallen trees in producing bogs, and of smaller animals, insects, and birds, in destroying the woods. . . .

I am disposed to think that more bogs in the Northern States owe their origin to beavers than to accidental obstructions of rivulets by wind-fallen or naturally decayed trees; for there are few swamps in those States, at the outlets of which we may not, by careful search, find the remains of a beaver dam. . . . I do not know that we have any evidence of the destruction or serious injury of American forests by insects, before or even soon after the period of colonization; but since the white man has laid bare a vast proportion of the earth's surface, and thereby produced changes favorable, perhaps, to the multiplication of these pests, they have greatly increased in numbers, and, apparently, in voracity also.

In countries untrodden by man, the proportions and relative positions of land and water, the atmospheric precipitation and evaporation, the thermometric mean, and the distribution of vegetable and animal life, are subject to change only from geological influences so slow in their operation that the geographical conditions may be regarded as constant and immutable. These arrangements of nature it is, in most cases, highly desirable substantially to maintain, when such regions become the seat of organized commonwealths. It is, therefore, a matter of the first importance, that, in commencing the process of fitting them for permanent civilized occupation, the transforming operations should be so conducted as not unnecessarily to derange and destroy what, in too many cases, it is beyond the power of man to rectify or restore.

Restoration of Disturbed Harmonies

In reclaiming and reoccupying lands laid waste by human improvidence or malice, and abandoned by man, or occupied only by a nomade or thinly scattered population, the task of the pioneer settler is of a very different character. He is to become a co-worker with nature in the reconstruction of the damaged fabric which the negligence or the wantonness of former lodgers has rendered untenantable. He must aid her in reclothing the mountain slopes with forests and vegetable mould, thereby restoring the fountains which she provided to water them; in checking the devastating fury of torrents, and bringing back the surface drainage to its primitive narrow channels; and in drying deadly morasses by opening the natural sluices which have been choked up, and cutting new canals for drawing off their stagnant waters. He must thus, on the one hand, create new reservoirs, and, on the other, remove mischievous accumulations of moisture, thereby equalizing and regulating the sources of atmospheric humidity and of flowing water, both which are so essential to all vegetable growth, and, of course, to human and lower animal life.

Destructiveness of Man

Man has too long forgotten that the earth was given to him for usufruct alone, not for consumption, still less for profligate waste. Nature has provided against the absolute destruction of any of her elementary matter, the raw material of her works; the thunderbolt and the tornado, the most convulsive throes of even the volcano and the earthquake, being only phenomena of decomposition and recomposition. But she has left it within the power of man irreparably to derange the combinations of inorganic matter and of organic life, which through the night of æons she had been proportioning and balancing, to prepare the earth for his habitation, when, in the fulness of time, his Creator should call him forth to enter into its possession.

Apart from the hostile influence of man, the organic and the inorganic world are, as I have remarked, bound together by such mutual relations and adaptations as secure, if not the absolute permanence and equilibrium of both, a long continuance of the established conditions of each at any given time and place, or at least, a very slow and gradual succession of changes in those conditions. But man is everywhere a disturbing agent. Wherever he plants his foot, the harmonies of nature are turned to discords. The proportions and accommodations which insured the stability of existing arrangements are over-thrown. Indigenous vegetable and animal species are extirpated, and sup-planted by others of foreign origin, spontaneous production is forbidden or restricted, and the face of the earth is either laid bare or covered with a new and reluctant growth of vegetable forms, and with alien tribes of animal life. These intentional changes and substitutions constitute, indeed, great revolutions; but vast as is their magnitude and importance, they are . . . insignificant in com-parison with the contingent and unsought results which have flowed from them.

The fact that, of all organic beings, man alone is to be regarded as essentially a destructive power, and that he wields energies to resist which, nature — that nature whom all material life and all inorganic substance obey — is wholly impotent, tends to prove that, though living in physical nature, he is not of her, that he is of more exalted parentage, and belongs to a higher order of existences than those born of her womb and submissive to her dictates. . . .

The earth was not, in its natural condition, completely adapted to the use of man, but only to the sustenance of wild animals and wild vegetation. These live, multiply their kind in just proportion, and attain their perfect measure of strength and beauty, without producing or requiring any change in the natural arrangements of surface, or in each other's spontaneous tendencies, except such mutual repression of excessive increase as may prevent the extirpation of one species by the encroachments of another. In short, without man, lower animal and spontaneous vegetable life would have been constant in type, distribution, and proportion, and the physical geography of the earth would have remained undisturbed for indefinite periods, and been subject to revolu-tion only from possible, unknown cosmical causes, or from geological action. . . .

Purely untutored humanity, it is true, interferes comparatively little with the arrangements of nature, and the destructive agency of man becomes more and more energetic and unsparing as he advances in civilization, until the impoverishment, with which his exhaustion of the natural resources of the soil is threatening him, at last awakens him to the necessity of preserving what is left, if not of restoring what has been wantonly wasted.

John Wesley Powell Advocates Reclamation, 1878

The Arid Region is the great Rocky Mountain Region of the United States, and it embraces something more than four-tenths of the whole country, excluding Alaska. In all this region the mean annual rainfall is insufficient for agriculture, but in certain seasons some localities, now here, now there, receive more than their average supply. . . .

Irrigable Lands

Within the Arid Region only a small portion of the country is irrigable. These irrigable tracts are lowlands lying along the streams. On the mountains and high plateaus forests are found at elevations so great that frequent summer frosts forbid the cultivation of the soil. Here are the natural timber lands of the Arid Region — an upper region set apart by nature for the growth of timber necessary to the mining, manufacturing, and agricultural industries of the country. Between the low irrigable lands and the elevated forest lands there are valleys, mesas, hills, and mountain slopes bearing grasses of greater or less value for pasturage purposes. . . . In discussing the lands of the Arid Region, three great classes are recognized — the irrigable lands below, the forest lands above, and the pasturage lands between.

Advantages of Irrigation.   There are two considerations that make irrigation attractive to the agriculturist. Crops thus cultivated are not subject to the vicissitudes of rainfall; the farmer fears no droughts; his labors are seldom interrupted and his crops rarely injured by storms. This immunity from drought and storm renders agricultural operations much more certain than in regions of greater humidity. Again, the water comes down from the mountains and plateaus freighted with fertilizing materials derived from the decaying vegetation and soils of the upper regions, which are spread by the flowing water over the cultivated lands. . . . It may be anticipated that all the lands redeemed by irrigation in the Arid Region will be highly cultivated and abundantly productive, and agriculture will be but slightly subject to the vicissitudes of scant and excessive rainfall.

Coöperative Labor or Capital Necessary for the Development of Irrigation.   Small streams can be taken out and distributed by individual enterprise, but coöperative labor or aggregated capital must be employed in taking out the larger streams.

The diversion of a large stream from its channel into a system of canals demands a large outlay of labor and material. To repay this all the waters so taken out must be used, and large tracts of land thus become dependent upon a single canal. It is manifest that a farmer depending upon his own labor cannot undertake this task. . . . When farming is dependent upon larger streams such men are barred from these enterprises until coöperative labor can be organized or capital induced to assist. . . .

In Utah Territory coöperative labor, under ecclesiastical organization, has been very successful. Outside of Utah there are but few instances where it has been tried; but at Greeley, in the State of Colorado, this system has been eminently successful. . . .

Timber Lands

Throughout the Arid Region timber of value is found growing spontaneously on the higher plateaus and mountains. These timber regions are bounded above and below by lines which are very irregular, due to local conditions. Above the upper line no timber grows because of the rigor of the climate, and below no timber grows because of aridity. Both the upper and lower lines descend in passing from south to north; that is, the timber districts are found at a lower altitude in the northern portion of the Arid Region than in the southern. The forests are chiefly of pine, spruce, and fir, but the pines are of principal value. Below these timber regions, on the lower slopes of mountains, on the mesas and hills, low, scattered forests are often found, composed mainly of dwarfed piñon pines and cedars. . . . The protection of the forests of the entire Arid Region of the United States is reduced to one single problem — Can these forests be saved from fire? . . .

In the main these fires are set by Indians. Driven from the lowlands by advancing civilization, they resort to the higher regions until they are forced back by the deep snows of winter. Want, caused by the restricted area to which they resort for food; the desire for luxuries to which they were strangers in their primitive condition, and especially the desire for personal adornment, together with a supply of more effective instruments for hunting and trapping, have in late years, during the rapid settlement of the country since the discovery of gold and the building of railroads, greatly stimulated the pursuit of animals for their furs — the wealth and currency of the savage. On their hunting excursions they systematically set fire to forests for the purpose of driving the game. This is a fact well known to all mountaineers. Only the white hunters of the region properly understand why these fires are set, it being usually attributed to a wanton desire on the part of the Indians to destroy that which is of value to the white man. The fires can, then, be very greatly curtailed by the removal of the Indians. . . .

Lumbermen and woodmen will furnish to the people [in the lands] below their supply of building and fencing material and fuel. In some cases it will be practicable for the farmers to own their timber lands, but in general the timber will be too remote, and from necessity such a division of labor will ensue.

Pasturage Lands

The irrigable lands and timber lands constitute but a small fraction of the Arid Region. Between the lowlands on the one hand and the highlands on the other is found a great body of valley, mesa, hill, and low mountain lands. To what extent, and under what conditions can they be utilized? Usually they bear a scanty growth of grasses. These grasses are nutritious and valuable both for summer and winter pasturage. Their value depends upon peculiar climatic conditions; the grasses grow to a great extent in scattered bunches, and mature seeds in larger proportion perhaps than the grasses of the more humid regions. . . .

The Farm Unit for Pasturage Lands.   The grass is so scanty that the herdsman must have a large area for the support of his stock. In general a quarter section of land alone is of no value to him; the pasturage it affords is entirely inadequate to the wants of a herd that the poorest man needs for his support.

Four square miles may be considered as the minimum amount necessary for a pasturage farm, and a still greater amount is necessary for the larger part of the lands; that is, pasturage farms, to be of any practicable value, must be of at least 2,560 acres, and in many districts they must be much larger.

Farm Residences Should Be Grouped.   These lands will maintain but a scanty population. The homes must necessarily be widely scattered from the fact that the farm unit must be large. That the inhabitants of these districts may have the benefits of the local social organizations of civilization — as schools, churches, etc., and the benefits of coöperation in the construction of roads, bridges, and other local improvements, it is essential that the residences should be grouped to the greatest possible extent. This may be practically accomplished by making the pasturage farms conform to topographic features in such manner as to give the greatest possible number of water fronts.

The great areas over which stock must roam to obtain subsistence usually prevents the practicability of fencing the lands. It will not pay to fence the pasturage fields, hence in many cases the lands must be occupied by herds roaming in common; for poor men coöperative pasturage is necessary, or communal regulations for the occupancy of the ground and for the division of the increase of the herds. Such communal regulations have already been devised in many parts of the country.

Frederick Jackson Turner on the Significance of the Frontier in American History, 1893

In a recent bulletin of the Superintendent of the Census for 1890 appear these significant words: "Up to and including 1880 the country had a frontier of settlement, but at present the unsettled area has been so broken into by isolated bodies of settlement that there can hardly be said to be a frontier line. In the discussion of its extent, its westward movement, etc., it can not therefore, any longer have a place in the census reports." This brief official statement marks the closing of a great historic movement. Up to our own day American history has been in a large degree the history of the colonization of the Great West. The existence of an area of free land, its continuous recession, and the advance of American settlement westward, explain American development.

Behind institutions, behind constitutional forms and modifications, lie the vital forces that call these organs into life and shape them to meet changing conditions. The peculiarity of American institutions is, the fact that they have been compelled to adapt themselves to the changes of an expanding people — to the changes involved in crossing a continent, in winning a wilderness, and in developing at each area of this progress out of the primitive economic and political conditions of the frontier into the complexity of city life. . . . American social development has been continually beginning over again on the frontier. This perennial rebirth, this fluidity of American life, this expansion westward with its new opportunities, its continuous touch with the simplicity of primitive society, furnish the forces dominating American character. The true point of view in the history of this nation is not the Atlantic coast, it is the great West. . . .

The frontier is the line of most rapid and effective Americanization. The wilderness masters the colonist. It finds him a European in dress, industries, tools, modes of travel, and thought. It takes him from the railroad car and puts him in the birch canoe. It strips off the garments of civilization and arrays him in the hunting shirt and the moccasin. It puts him in the log cabin of the Cherokee and Iroquois and runs an Indian palisade around him. Before long he has gone to planting Indian corn and plowing with a sharp stick; he shouts the war cry and takes the scalp in orthodox Indian fashion. In short, at the frontier the environment is at first too strong for the man. He must accept the conditions which it furnishes, or perish, and so he fits himself into the Indian clearings and follows the Indian trails. Little by little he transforms the wilderness, but the outcome is not the old Europe, not simply the development of Germanic germs, any more than the first phenomenon was a case of reversion to the Germanic mark. The fact is, that here is a new product that is American. At first, the frontier was the Atlantic coast. It was the frontier of Europe in a very real sense. Moving westward, the frontier became more and more American. . . .

In these successive frontiers we find natural boundary lines which have served to mark and to affect the characteristics of the frontiers, namely: The "fall line"; the Alleghany Mountains; the Mississippi; the Missouri, where its direction approximates north and south; the line of the arid lands, approximately the ninety-ninth meridian; and the Rocky Mountains. The fall line marked the frontier of the seventeenth century; the Alleghanies that of the eighteenth; the Mississippi that of the first quarter of the nineteenth; the Missouri that of the middle of this century (omitting the California movement); and the belt of the Rocky Mountains and the arid tract, the present frontier. Each was won by a series of Indian wars. . . .

The Atlantic frontier was compounded of fisherman, fur-trader, miner, cattle-raiser, and farmer. Excepting the fisherman, each type of industry was on the march toward the West, impelled by an irresistible attraction. Each passed in successive waves across the continent. Stand at Cumberland Gap and watch the procession of civilization, marching single file — the buffalo following the trail to the salt springs, the Indian, the fur-trader and hunter, the cattle-raiser, the pioneer farmer — and the frontier has passed by. Stand at South Pass in the Rockies a century later and see the same procession with wider intervals between. The unequal rate of advance compels us to distinguish the frontier into the trader's frontier, the rancher's frontier, or the miner's frontier, and the farmer's frontier. . . .

The exploitation of the beasts took hunter and trader to the west, the exploitation of the grasses took the rancher west, and the exploitation of the virgin soil of the river valleys and prairies attracted the farmer. Good soils have been the most continuous attraction to the farmer's frontier. . . .

But the most important effect of the frontier has been in the promotion of democracy. . . . The frontier is productive of individualism. Complex society is precipitated by the wilderness into a kind of primitive organization based on the family. The tendency is anti-social. It produces antipathy to control, and particularly to any direct control. The tax gatherer is viewed as a representative of oppression. . . . The frontier individualism has from the beginning promoted democracy. . . .

So long as free land exists, the opportunity for a competency exists, and economic power secures political power. But the democracy born of free land, strong in selfishness and individualism, intolerant of administrative experience and education, and pressing individual liberty beyond its proper bounds, has its dangers as well as its benefits. Individualism in America has allowed a laxity in regard to governmental affairs. . . . [But] . . . steadily the frontier of settlement advanced and carried with it individualism, democracy, and nationalism, and powerfully affected the East and the Old World. . . .

Never again will such gifts of free land offer themselves. For a moment, at the frontier, the bonds of custom are broken and unrestraint is triumphant. There is not *tabula rasa*. The stubborn American environment is there with its imperious summons to accept its conditions; the inherited ways of doing things are also there; and yet, in spite of environment, and in spite of custom, each frontier did indeed furnish a new field of opportunity. . . . And now, four centuries from the discovery of America, at the end of a hundred years of life under the Constitution, the frontier has gone, and with its going has closed the first period of American history.

The Reclamation Act, 1902

An Act Appropriating the receipts from the sale and disposal of public lands in certain States and Territories to the construction of irrigation works for the reclamation of arid lands.

Be it enacted by the Senate and House of Representatives of the United States of America in Congress assembled, That all moneys received from the sale and disposal of public lands in Arizona, California, Colorado, Idaho, Kansas, Montana, Nebraska, Nevada, New Mexico, North Dakota, Oklahoma, Oregon, South Dakota, Utah, Washington, and Wyoming . . . shall be, and the same are hereby, reserved, set aside, and appropriated as a special fund in the Treasury to be known as the "reclamation fund," to be used in the examination and survey for and the construction and maintenance of irrigation works for the storage, diversion, and development of waters for the reclamation of arid and semiarid lands in the said States and Territories, and for the payment of all other expenditures provided for in this Act: . . .

Sec 3 . . . that public lands which it is proposed to irrigate by means of any contemplated works shall be subject to entry only under the provisions of the homestead laws in tracts of not less than forty nor more than one hundred and sixty acres, . . .

Sec. 5. That the entryman upon lands to be irrigated by such works shall, in addition to compliance with the homestead laws, reclaim at least one-half of the total irrigable area of his entry for agricultural purposes, and before receiving patent for the lands covered by his entry shall pay to the Government the charges apportioned against such tract, as provided in section four. No right to the use of water for land in private ownership shall be sold for a tract exceeding one hundred and sixty acres to any one landowner, and no such sale shall be made to any landowner unless he be an actual bona fide resident on such land, or occupant thereof residing in the neighborhood of said land, and no such right shall permanently attach until all payments therefor are made.

Bernard Fernow on the Economics of Forestry, 1902

The natural resources of the earth have in all ages and in all countries, for a time at least, been squandered by man with a wanton disregard of the future, and are still being squandered wherever absolute necessity has not yet forced a more careful utilization.

This is natural, as long as the exploitation of these resources is left unrestricted in private hands; for private enterprise, private interest, knows only the immediate future—has only one aim in the use of these resources, namely, to obtain from them the greatest possible personal and present gain. . . .

From the fact that within any aggregation of people inimical interests arise, that the interests of one set of individuals may clash with those of another set, or that the welfare of the whole may be jeopardized by the unrestricted exercise of the rights of the few, the necessity for the limitation of the rights of the members arises, which, as far as the exercise of property rights goes, finds expression in the old Roman law, "*Utere tuo ne alterum noccas*," namely, such use of the property as shall not entail damage to another party.

This ancient restrictive principle, which is recognized in all civilized states, was at first probably applied only to interferences between private interests; but finally the protection of the interests of the aggregation against those of the individual must have necessitated its application, whenever a communal interest would suffer by the unrestricted exercise of individual rights.

This restrictive function of the state, in addition to that of defending the aggregation against outsiders, will probably be admitted by all parties and schools as elementary and essential to the existence of the state. Divergence of opinion arises, however, not only when additional, more positive, and directive functions are claimed for the state,—as, for instance, when the *laissez-faire* policy is to be supplanted by a *faire-marcher* promotive policy,—but also in the interpretation of the meaning of the terms of the mere restrictive function, when the question arises, what is to be considered damage and who the other is that is to be protected.

The very nature of the modern civilized government necessitates the very widest interpretation of these terms. Civilized states of to-day are intended and built for permanency; they are not held together by mere compacts of the single members of society, which may be broken at any time. While forms of government may change, the organization, the state idea, promises to be permanent. This conception of the permanency of the state, the realization that it is not a thing of to-day and for a limited time, but forever, widens its functions and extends its sphere of action; for it is no longer to be regarded as merely the arbiter between its present members, but it becomes the guardian of its future members; government becomes the representative, not only of present communal interests, as against individual interests, but also of future interests as against those of the present. Its object is not only for the day, but includes the *perpetuity* of the well-being of society, and the *perpetuity* of such favorable conditions as will conduce to the *continued* welfare and improvement of the same; in short, its activity must be with regard to continuity, it must provide for the future, it must be *providential*. We do not create this special providence for the individual, but for society; the individual will have to work out his own salvation to a large extent, with the opportunities for advancement offered by society, but society itself can only act through the state; and, as the representative of the future as well as the present, the state cannot, like the individual, "let the future take care of itself." . . .

Only those nations who develop their natural resources economically, and avoid the waste of that which they produce, can maintain their power or even secure the continuance of their separate existence. A nation may cease to exist as well by the decay of its resources as by the extinction of its patriotic spirit. While we are debating over the best methods of disposing of our wealth, we gradually lose our very capital without even realizing the fact. As [George Perkins] Marsh points out in his classical work, man is constantly modifying the earth and making it more and more uninhabitable; he goes over its rich portions and leaves behind a desert. . . .

Whether fertile lands are turned into deserts, forests into waste places, brooks into torrents, rivers changed from means of power and intercourse into means of destruction and desolation — these are questions which concern the material existence itself of society; and since such changes become often irreversible, the damage irremediable, and at the same time the extent of available resources becomes smaller in proportion to population, their consideration is finally much more important than those other questions of the day. Increase of population and increased requirements of civilization call for a continual increase of our total economic forces, and increased "*intensity*" in the management of our resources; and this requires such continued care and administration, that it is not safe to leave it entirely to the incentive of private competition, which always means wasteful use.

There are, then, enough precedents established to show that, whatever the greed and selfishness of the individual may dictate, society recognizes its right to interfere with the individual in the use of resources, not only for its present objects, but even for considerations of the future. . . .

We shall recognize that to the individual it is the timber, the accumulated growth of centuries, which is of interest, and which he exploits for the purpose of making a profit on his labor and outlay without any interest in the future of the exploited area. The relation of the forest to other conditions, direct or indirect, immediate or future, hardly ever enters into his calculations.

On the other hand, the function of the forest, which it exercises as a soil cover by preventing erosion of the soil, by regulating water flow, changing surface drainage into subsoil drainage, and thereby influencing the water stages of rivers, and its possible relation to the local climatic conditions, preëminently renders it an object of government consideration. . . .

The forest resource is one which, under the active competition of private enterprise, is apt to deteriorate, and in its deterioration to affect other conditions of material existence unfavorably; that the maintenance of continued supplies as well as of favorable conditions is possible only under the supervision of permanent institutions with whom present profit is not the only motive. It calls preëminently for the exercise of the providential functions of the state to counteract the destructive tendencies of private exploitation.

Theodore Roosevelt Publicizes Conservation, 1908

Governors of the several States; and Gentlemen:

I welcome you to this Conference at the White House. You have come hither at my request, so that we may join together to consider the question of the conservation and use of the great fundamental sources of wealth of this Nation. . . .

This Conference on the conservation of natural resources is in effect a meeting of the representatives of all the people of the United States called to consider the weightiest problem now before the Nation; and the occasion for the meeting lies in the fact that the natural resources of our country are in danger of exhaustion if we permit the old wasteful methods of exploiting them longer to continue.

With the rise of peoples from savagery to civilization, and with the consequent growth in the extent and variety of the needs of the average man, there comes a steadily increasing growth of the amount demanded by this average man from the actual resources of the country. And yet, rather curiously, at the same time that there comes that increase in what the average man demands from the resources, he is apt to grow to lose the sense of his dependence upon nature. He lives in big cities. He deals in industries that do not bring him in close touch with nature. He does not realize the demands he is making upon nature. . . .

In [George] Washington's time anthracite coal was known only as a useless black stone; and the great fields of bituminous coal were undiscovered. As steam was unknown, the use of coal for power production was undreamed of. Water was practically the only source of power, save the labor of men and animals; and this power was used only in the most primitive fashion. But a few small iron deposits had been found in this country, and the use of iron by our countrymen was very small. Wood was practically the only fuel, and what lumber was sawed was consumed locally, while the forests were regarded chiefly as obstructions to settlement and cultivation. The man who cut down a tree was held to have conferred a service upon his fellows.

Such was the degree of progress to which civilized mankind had attained when this nation began its career. It is almost impossible for us in this day to realize how little our Revolutionary ancestors knew of the great store of natural resources whose discovery and use have been such vital factors in the growth and greatness of this Nation, and how little they required to take from this store in order to satisfy their needs.

Since then our knowledge and use of the resources of the present territory of the United States have increased a hundred-fold. Indeed, the growth of this Nation by leaps and bounds makes one of the most striking and important chapters in the history of the world. Its growth has been due to the rapid development, and alas that it should be said! to the rapid destruction, of our natural resources. Nature has supplied to us in the United States, and still supplies to us, more kinds of resources in a more lavish degree than has ever been the case at any other time or with any other people. Our position in the world has been attained by the extent and thoroughness of the control we have achieved over nature; but we are more, and not less, dependent upon what she furnishes than at any previous time of history since the days of primitive man. . . .

The wise use of all of our natural resources, which are our national resources as well, is the great material question of today. I have asked you to come together now because the enormous consumption of these resources, and the threat of imminent exhaustion of some of them, due to reckless and wasteful use, . . . calls for common effort, common action.

We want to take action that will prevent the advent of a woodless age, and defer as long as possible the advent of an ironless age. . . .

Natural resources . . . can be divided into two sharply distinguished classes accordingly as they are or are not capable of renewal. Mines if used must necessarily be exhausted. The minerals do not and can not renew themselves. Therefore in dealing with the coal, the oil, the gas, the iron, the metals generally, all that we can do is to try to see that they are wisely used. The exhaustion is certain to come in time. We can trust that it will be deferred long enough to enable the extraordinarily inventive genius of our people to devise means and methods for more or less adequately replacing what is lost; but the exhaustion is sure to come.

The second class of resources consists of those which can not only be used in such manner as to leave them undiminished for our children, but can actually be improved by wise use. The soil, the forests, the waterways come in this category. Every one knows that a really good farmer leaves his farm more valuable at the end of his life than it was when he first took hold of it. So with the waterways. So with the forests. In dealing with mineral resources, man is able to improve on nature only by putting the resources to a beneficial use which in the end exhausts them; but in dealing with the soil and its products man can improve on nature by compelling the resources to renew and even reconstruct themselves in such manner as to serve increasingly beneficial uses — while the living waters can be so controlled as to multiply their benefits. . . .

In the past we have admitted the right of the individual to injure the future of the Republic for his own present profit. In fact there has been a good deal of a demand for unrestricted individualism, for the right of the individual to injure the future of all of us for his own temporary and immediate profit. The time has come for a change. As a people we have the right and the duty, second to none other but the right and duty of obeying the moral law, of requiring and doing justice, to protect ourselves and our children against the wasteful development of our natural resources, whether that waste is caused by the actual destruction of such resources or by making them impossible of development hereafter.

Finally, let us remember that the conservation of our natural resources, though the gravest problem of today, is yet but part of another and greater problem to which this Nation is not yet awake, but to which it will awake in time, and with which it must hereafter grapple if it is to live—the problem of national efficiency, the patriotic duty of insuring the safety and continuance of the Nation. [Applause.] When the People of the United States consciously undertake to raise themselves as citizens, and the Nation and the States in their several spheres, to the highest pitch of excellence in private, State, and national life, and to do this because it is the first of all the duties of true patriotism, then and not till then the future of this Nation, in quality and in time, will be assured. [Great applause]

George L. Knapp Opposes Conservation, 1910

For some years past, the reading public has been treated to fervid and extended eulogies of a policy which the eulogists call the "conservation of our natural resources." In behalf of this so-called "conservation," the finest press bureau in the world has labored with a zeal quite unhampered by any considerations of fact or logic; and has shown its understanding of practical psychology by appealing, not to popular reason, but to popular fears. We are told by this press bureau that our natural resources are being wasted in the most wanton and criminal style; wasted, apparently, for the sheer joy of wasting. We are told that our forests are being cut at a rate which will soon leave us a land without trees; and Nineveh, and Tyre, and any other place far enough away are cited to prove that a land without trees is foredoomed to be a land without civilization. We are told that our coal-mines would be exhausted within a century; that our iron ores are going to the blast-furnace at a rate which will send us back to the stone age within the lifetime of men who read the fearsome prophecy. In short, we are assured that every resource capable of exhaustion is being exhausted; and that the resource which cannot be exhausted is being monopolized. . . .

I propose to speak for those exiles in sin who hold that a large part of the present "conservation" movement is unadulterated humbug. That the modern Jeremiahs are as sincere as was the older one, I do not question. But I count their prophecies to be baseless vaporings, and their vaunted remedy worse than the fancied disease. I am one who can see no warrant of law, of justice, nor of necessity for that wholesale reversal of our traditional policy which the advocates of "conservation" demand. I am one who does not shiver for the future at the sight of a load of coal, nor view a steel-mill as the arch-robber of posterity. I am one who does not believe in a power trust, past, present or to come; and who, if he were a capitalist seeking to form such a trust, would ask nothing better than just the present conservation scheme to help him. I believe that a government bureau is the worst imaginable landlord; and that its essential nature is not changed by giving it a high-sounding name, and decking it with home-made haloes. I hold that the present forest policy ceases to be a nuisance only when it becomes a curse. . . .

The terrors from which "conservation" is to save us are phantoms. The evils which "conservation" brings us are very real. Mining discouraged, homesteading brought to a practical standstill, power development fined as criminal, and, worst of all, a Federal bureaucracy arrogantly meddling with every public question in a dozen great States — these are some of the things which result from the efforts of a few well-meaning zealots to install themselves as official prophets and saviors of the future, and from that exalted station to regulate the course of evolution.

It is no more a part of the Federal Government's business to enter upon the commercial production of lumber than to enter upon the commercial production of wheat, or breakfast bacon, or hand-saws. . . .

Our natural resources have been used, not wasted. Waste in one sense there has been, to be sure; in that a given resource has not always been put to its best use as we now see that use. But from Eden down, knowledge has been the costliest thing that man could covet; and the knowledge of how to make the earth best serve him seems well-nigh the most expensive of all. But I think we have made a fair start at the lesson; and considering how well we have already done for ourselves, the intrusion of a Government schoolmaster at this stage seems scarcely needed. The pine woods of Michigan have vanished to make the homes of Kansas; the coal and iron which we have failed — thank Heaven! — to "conserve" have carried meat and wheat to the hungry hives of men and gladdened life with an abundance which no previous age could know. We have turned forests into villages, mines into ships and sky-scrapers, scenery into work. Our success in doing the things already accomplished has been exactly proportioned to our freedom from governmental "guidance," and I know no reason to believe that a different formula will hold good in the tasks that lie before. If we can stop the governmental encouragement of destruction, conservation will take care of itself. . . . There is just one heritage which I am anxious to transmit to my children and to their children's children — the heritage of personal liberty, of free individual action, of "leave to live by no man's leave underneath the law." And I know of no way to secure that heritage save to sharply challenge and relentlessly fight every bureaucratic invasion of local and individual rights, no matter how friendly the mottoes on the invading banners.

Mrs. Marion Crocker on the Conservation Imperative, 1912

Madam Chairman, and Mr. President and Members of the Convention: Conservation is a term so apt that it has been borrowed and made to fit almost all lines of public work, but Conservation as applied to that department bearing its name in the General Federation [of Women's Clubs] means conservation of natural resources only. . . . If we do not follow the most scientific approved methods, the most modern discoveries of how to conserve and propagate and renew wherever possible those resources which Nature in her providence has given to man for his use but not abuse, the time will come when the world will not be able to support life, and then we shall have no need of conservation of health, strength or vital force, because we must have the things to support life or else everything else is useless.

We will begin with the forests, because in our natural conservation we consider that the foundation of the fundamental principle of the conservation of natural resources. And what does the forest for us? What is the purpose of the forest? Why must we have them? Well, the forest makes soil in a way; that is, it makes humus matter, which is so large a portion of the soil that it may well be termed the soil. The forest is the only crop that grows that gives to the soil more than it takes from the soil. It also conserves the mineral in the soil that it takes Nature ages to produce by its slow processes of disintegration, and at the same time prevents the filling up of reservoirs, lakes and streams, and to that extent prevents the pollution of the waters. The forest is a great health resort, and why? Because it actually purifies the air. Its action is just the reverse of animals. It gives the air what we need and takes from it that which is detrimental to our health.

We must look a little into plant life and see what nature does that we may fully appreciate that point. I cannot take time tonight because of the late hour to go into the whole life of the tree, but I will say that its principal constituent is carbon, and it takes from the air the carbonic acid gas which is so detrimental to human beings and to all animals. It has a way of converting it into its own life blood in combination with the sap taken up from the roots, by the marvelous process in the leaves, by this little understood substance called chlorophyll, that has the power of converting this poisonous substance for us into the life of the tree, and then taking so much from it and giving it to the soil. That is a most important factor which is so often overlooked.

Then the forest is valuable as a wind shield for crops. And for the wood supply. Wood is demanded in all the industries or the arts, for almost all things we use.

These are the fundamental things the forest does for us. Are we not working for conservation of strength and health and human life when we are working for the forest?

While the General Federation takes up many phases of water Conservation, perhaps I may just say that we have irrigation, drainage, waterways, the deep canals for transportation, we have water power, which is the coming thing. This is something to be conserved, and which conserves our coal, which conserves the purity of our atmosphere by not having all the gases turned into it by the burning of the coal.

And then the very last and most vital is the pure continuous supply of water, which all human beings and which all animals demand. It is, next to the air we breathe, the most important factor in animal existence. . . .

The soil is indirectly our staff of life. From it does not come our bread? Must not this seed fall into the ground, spring from the earth and be protected until it reaches maturity, and we have food? Many other instances might I bring forward had I time.

Then the animal kingdom is much more nearly related to human existence than we would think at the outset; but when we come to look more deeply into it we find this close relationship.

I so often come up against the saying, "Oh, I am so much interested in human life. I have no time, no thought, no desire to give to the animal kingdom. It is all right enough for you sentimentalists, but I am not interested." Yes, but even from a selfish point of view, if we do not care at all for any suffering, or anything which may come to the animal kingdom beside ourselves, it is of economic value to us.

I will choose but one example of the animal kingdom, and that is the birds, because it is said that all vegetation from the earth would cease if the birds existed no longer. . . .

This very conservation of bird life is one of the things that is the great new problem of conservation of natural resources, and one in which you women take a hand and have the real control. I know you have heard so much about that I am not going to give you statistics as to what the birds do for agriculture. I am going to ask you a personal favor: that this fall when you choose your fall millinery, will you not think of your Chairman of your Conservation Department of the General Federation, and I beg you choose some other decoration for your hats. This is not sentiment. It is pure economics. You have no idea what you do when you wear these feathers, until you think really deeply into it. . . .

Now, I want to say just a few words about the way to go to work to do some of these things. I will not go into the larger fields of forestry, or even into shade trees, except to emphasize the fact that while the shade tree is a very important one, and especially in the cities, we must never lose sight of the larger fact that after all it is not forestry, it does not stand for that, and that our arbor day, where we plant the one tree, should extend far beyond that. . . . There is a great work to be done with the children, in making the school garden, and then the home garden; to teach the children to know what the soil is made of and how it should be treated, to make them love the growing flower and to make them respect the property of others. There we are laying the foundation of things for the next generation. . . .

I am going to tell you a little story of how I became interested in these things. It was before I was out of school myself, although pretty nearly so. It was when the welfare work began of taking the children out in the country from the slums in the north end. I was personally acquainted with one of the teachers, who was among the first to take the children out in the fresh air to breathe and see the grass and flowers and trees that they had never seen before. One little boy, after he had looked around in amazement — it was in the fall of the year — saw the bright red apples on the trees, and he looked up and said, "Apples on trees, by God!" . . .

I will say to you this one message, while you are working for this thing of prime importance, the conservation of life, for which this Congress has stood at this fall meeting, do not forget that the conservation of life itself must be built on the solid foundation of conservation of natural resources, or it will be a house built upon the sands that will be washed away. It will not be lasting. I thank you. (Great applause.)

Gifford Pinchot Recalls
the Origins of the Conservation Movement, 1947

It was my great good luck that I had more to do with the work of more bureaus than any other man in Washington. This was partly because the Forest Service was dealing not only with trees but with public lands, mining, agriculture, irrigation, stream flow, soil erosion, fish, game, animal industry, and a host of other matters with which other bureaus also were concerned. The main reason, however, was that much of T.R.'s [Theodore Roosevelt's] business with the natural resources bureaus was conducted through me.

It was therefore the most natural thing in the world that the relations of forests, waters, lands, and minerals, each to each, should be brought strongly to my mind. But for a long time my mind stopped there. Then at last I woke up. And this is how it happened:

In the gathering gloom of an expiring day, in the moody month of February, some forty years ago, a solitary horseman might have been observed pursuing his silent way above a precipitous gorge in the vicinity of the capital city of America. Or so an early Victorian three-volume novelist might have expressed it.

In plain words, a man by the name of Pinchot was riding a horse by the name of Jim on the Ridge Road in Rock Creek Park near Washington. And while he rode, he thought. He was a forester, and he was taking his problems with him, on that winter's day of 1907, when he meant to leave them behind.

The forest and its relation to streams and inland navigation, to water power and flood control; to the soil and its erosion; to coal and oil and other minerals; to fish and game; and many another possible use or waste of natural resources — these questions would not let him be. What had all these to do with Forestry? And what had Forestry to do with them?

Here were not isolated and separate problems. My work had brought me into touch with all of them. But what was the basic link between them?

Suddenly the idea flashed through my head that there was a unity in this complication — that the relation of one resource to another was not the end of the story. Here were no longer a lot of different, independent, and often antagonistic questions, each on its own separate little island, as we had been in the habit of thinking. In place of them, here was one single question with many parts. Seen in this new light, all these separate questions fitted into and made up the one great central problem of the use of the earth for the good of man.

To me it was a good deal like coming out of a dark tunnel. I had been seeing one spot of light ahead. Here, all of a sudden, was a whole landscape. Or it was like lifting the curtain on a great new stage.

There was too much of it for me to take it all in at once. As always, my mind worked slowly. From the first I thought I had stumbled on something really worth while, but that day in Rock Creek Park I was far from grasping the full reach and swing of the new idea.

Excerpts from *Breaking New Ground*, by Gifford Pinchot (Washington, D.C.: Island Press, 1947), pp. 322–323, 326.

It took time for me to appreciate that here were the makings of a new policy, not merely nationwide but world-wide in its scope — fundamentally important because it involved not only the welfare but the very existence of men on the earth. I did see, however, that something ought to be done about it. . . .

The first man I carried it to was Overton Price. Within a few days I told him the story as we rode our horses together on the Virginia side of the Potomac, and asked what he thought of it. He saw it as I did. I was glad of that, for my reliance on his judgment was very great.

After Overton, I discussed my brain child not only with my Father and Mother, whose interest in my work never flagged, but with geologist and philosopher WJ McGee, [U.S. Geological Survey Chief, Frederick] Newell, . . . and others. It was McGee who grasped it best. He sensed its full implication even more quickly than I had done, and saw its future more clearly.

McGee became the scientific brains of the new movement. With his wide general knowledge and highly original mind we developed, as I never could have done alone, the breadth and depth of meaning which lay in the new idea. McGee had constructive imagination.

It was McGee, for example, who defined the new policy as the use of the natural resources for the greatest good of the greatest number for the longest time. It was McGee who made me see, at long last and after much argument, that monopoly of natural resources was only less dangerous to the public welfare than their actual destruction.

Very soon after my own mind was clear enough to state my proposition with confidence, I took it to T.R. And T.R., as I expected, understood, accepted, and adopted it without the smallest hesitation. It was directly in line with everything he had been thinking and doing. It became the heart of his Administration.

Launching the Conservation movement was the most significant achievement of the T.R. Administration, as he himself believed. It seems altogether probable that it will also be the achievement for which he will be longest and most gratefully remembered.

Having just been born, the new arrival was still without a name. There had to be a name to call it by before we could even attempt to make it known, much less give it a permanent place in the public mind. What should we call it?

Both Overton and I knew that large organized areas of Government forest lands in British India were named Conservancies, and the foresters in charge of them Conservators. After many other suggestions and long discussions, either Price or I (I'm not sure which and it doesn't matter) proposed that we apply a new meaning to a word already in the dictionary, and christen the new policy Conservation.

During one of our rides I put that name up to T.R., and he approved it instantly. So the child was named, and that bridge was behind us.

Today, when it would be hard to find an intelligent man in the United States who hasn't at least some conception of what Conservation means, it seems incredible that the very word, in the sense in which we use it now, was unknown less than forty years ago.

⚘ E S S A Y S

The essays focus on the politics and institutions that provided both cohesion and tension in the conservation movement during the period of swift American industrialization. In the first essay, Samuel Hays, a professor of history at the University of Pittsburgh and one of the foremost historians of the conservation movement, argues that conservation was spearheaded by scientists and engineers to promote efficiency in resource use. According to the second essayist, Carl Moneyhon, a historian at the University of Arkansas, Little Rock, conservation was a political movement representing several factions — conservationists, preservationists, ecologists, and laissez-faire capitalists — who often disagreed on means and ends. The third essay, by journalist Marc Reisner, depicts conservation as a failed movement that attempted to promote the democratic distribution of resources, particularly water, in the arid West. Finally, Carolyn Merchant, an environmental historian at the University of California, Berkeley, argues in the fourth selection that although conservation as a popular movement owed its inspiration and major accomplishments to women's work, women ultimately broke ranks with Roosevelt and Pinchot over conflicts between the goals of conservation and those of preservation.

Conservation as Efficiency

SAMUEL HAYS

Conservation neither arose from a broad popular outcry, nor centered its fire primarily upon the private corporation. Moreover, corporations often supported conservation policies, while the "people" just as frequently opposed them. In fact, it becomes clear that one must discard completely the struggle against corporations as the setting in which to understand conservation history, and permit an entirely new frame of reference to arise from the evidence itself.

Conservation, above all, was a scientific movement, and its role in history arises from the implications of science and technology in modern society. Conservation leaders sprang from such fields as hydrology, forestry, agrostology, geology, and anthropology. Vigorously active in professional circles in the national capital, these leaders brought the ideals and practices of their crafts into federal resource policy. Loyalty to these professional ideals, not close association with the grass-roots public, set the tone of the Theodore Roosevelt conservation movement. Its essence was rational planning to promote efficient development and use of all natural resources. The idea of efficiency drew these federal scientists from one resource task to another, from specific programs to comprehensive concepts. It molded the policies which they proposed, their administrative techniques, and their relations with Congress and the public. It is from the vantage point of applied science, rather than of democratic protest, that one must understand the historic role of the conservation movement.

The new realms of science and technology, appearing to open up unlimited opportunities for human achievement, filled conservation leaders with intense optimism. They emphasized expansion, not retrenchment; possibilities, not limitations. True, they expressed some fear that diminishing resources would create critical shortages in the future. But they were not Malthusian prophets of despair and gloom. The popular view that in a fit of pessimism they withdrew vast areas of the public lands from present use for future development does not stand examination. In fact, they bitterly opposed those who sought to withdraw resources from commercial development. They displayed that deep sense of hope which pervaded all those at the turn of the century for whom science and technology were revealing visions of an abundant future.

The political implications of conservation, it is particularly important to observe, grew out of the political implications of applied science rather than from conflict over the distribution of wealth. Who should decide the course of resource development? Who should determine the goals and methods of federal resource programs? The correct answer to these questions lay at the heart of the conservation idea. Since resource matters were basically technical in nature, conservationists argued, technicians, rather than legislators, should deal with them. Foresters should determine the desirable annual timber cut; hydraulic engineers should establish the feasible extent of multiple-purpose river development and the specific location of reservoirs; agronomists should decide which forage areas could remain open for grazing without undue damage to water supplies. Conflicts between competing resource users, especially, should not be dealt with through the normal processes of politics. Pressure group action, logrolling in Congress, or partisan debate could not guarantee rational and scientific decisions. Amid such jockeying for advantage with the resulting compromise, concern for efficiency would disappear. Conservationists envisaged, even though they did not realize their aims, a political system guided by the ideal of efficiency and dominated by the technicians who could best determine how to achieve it.

This phase of conservation requires special examination because of its long neglect by historians. Instead of probing the political implications of the technological spirit, they have repeated the political mythology of the "people versus the interests" as the setting for the struggle over resource policy. This myopia has stemmed in part from the disinterestedness of the historian and the social scientist. Often accepting implicitly the political assumptions of elitism, rarely having an axe of personal interest to grind, and invariably sympathetic with the movement, conservation historians have considered their view to be in the public interest. Yet, analysis from outside such a limited perspective reveals the difficulty of equating the particular views of a few scientific leaders with an objective "public interest." Those views did not receive wide acceptance; they did not arise out of widely held assumptions and values. They came from a limited group of people, with a particular set of goals, who played a special role in society. Their definition of the "public interest" might well, and did, clash with other competing definitions. The historian, therefore, cannot understand conservation leaders simply as defenders of the "people." Instead, he must examine the experiences and goals peculiar to them; he must describe their role within a specific sociological context.

Conservation as Politics

CARL MONEYHON

The late nineteenth century saw four major ideas concerning society and environment develop, each with a wide following. These major modes of thought may be characterized as conservation, preservation, ecology, and laissez faire. While adherents to each concept recognized the general problem, their goals varied, indeed were often contradictory, and, therefore, a general reform movement to solve environmental problems was virtually impossible. Even within these groups general agreement concerning goals and means to ends proved difficult. For Americans, therefore, there was a general perception of a crisis, but little agreement on its definition or on measures to alleviate it.

Of the four major ideologies, conservationism received the greatest publicity during this period. Its spokesmen were the most vocal and political. The concept promised to meet the crisis with minimal modification of existing American society. Conservationists emphasized the role of scientific and rational institutions in achieving a solution. Proper application of these techniques, they believed, would abate the problem by providing new resources to avoid shortages and making more efficient use of the natural wealth that was already available. This particular approach found its strongest adherents among scientists, professionals such as physicians and scholars, and some industrialists — men who possessed the technical knowledge that they believed would save the nation. Elements of conservationist thought were found in a host of programs developed during the late nineteenth century. Typical was the effort of Bernhard E. Fernow and Gifford Pinchot to bring scientific methods of tree farming into currency in the timber industry. Through careful cultivation, development of new kinds of timber, and proper harvesting, they believed the nation's timber resources could be preserved practically intact for future generations as well as the current. Perhaps no better statement exists of the kind of thought that embraced the conservationists than that of the economist Simon Patten. In *The New Basis of Civilization* he indicated his belief that science and technology would provide the ultimate means for man to overcome the limits of environment. He wrote:

> Artificial culture and experimental science have already fundamentally altered the elemental relations existing two hundred years ago between population and environment. Yet to say that the methods which have made man physically independent of the local food supply are artificial is to underrate the powers of the new forces by implying that they are constantly opposed by fundamental natural forces which in the end must again triumph. The final victory of man's machinery over nature's materials is the next logical process in evolution, as nature's control of human society was the transition from anarchic and puny individualism to the group acting as a powerful, intelligent organism.

From Carl H. Moneyhon, "The Environmental Crisis and American Politics, 1860–1920," in Lester J. Bilsky, ed. *Historical Ecology: Essays on Environmental and Social Change*, Port Washington, NY: Kennikat Press, 1980, pp. 143–155.

Machinery, science, and intelligence moving on the face of the other may well affect it as the elements do, upbuilding, obliterating, and creating; but they are man's forces and will be used to hasten his dominion over nature.

The conservationists believed that promised shortages could be avoided, that the social status quo could consequently be maintained, with the innovation made possible by science and technology.

As a practical program, a variety of governmental agencies designed to apply the conservationist solution to problems appeared after the 1870s. The first of these was the United States Fish Commission created in 1871. Congress created it specifically to discover what was happening to the coastal fisheries and what might be done to prevent their destruction. Its first commissioner, Spencer Fullerton Baird, was a scientist who pushed the commission into a general study of marine biology and fish culture. As a result of these studies, Congress funded programs to replenish fish stocks and also moved to restrict fishing. Conservationism was also apparent in the work of the Division of Forestry created in 1881 within the Department of Agriculture. Under Franklin B. Hough, Bernhard E. Fernow, and Gifford Pinchot the division collected information on scientific tree culture and disseminated that information throughout the United States. At the request of the nation's chief foresters, Congress passed laws to preserve timber resources. Typical of these was the 1891 legislation allowing the president to set aside parts of the public domain for forest reserves. The most encompassing legislation passed through Congress in 1897, and authorized a system of management for these national forests under the direction of the Department of the Interior.

By 1900, however, conservationists confronted a dilemma. Their piecemeal approach to conservation provided only limited results. While they could respond to problems as they arose, the number of crisis situations continued to mount. Further, they became aware of the interrelationship of environmental problems. Realizing that the situation required a broad approach, conservationists, encouraged by the leadership of President Theodore Roosevelt, attempted to expand their ideal into a general reform. Roosevelt became the center of this movement when he brought to his administration prominent advocates of conservation, such as Gifford Pinchot, W. J. McGee, and Charles Van Hise. In 1908 the president called together a conference of governors to secure broad support for various conservation measures that he hoped to push through Congress. The general thrust of these measures would be to create a general conservation policy, the first step of which would be the organization of a National Conservation Commission to inventory resources that would allow better planning. Roosevelt further envisioned annual conservation conferences in Washington to help develop a broad national policy. Emphasizing his concern, Roosevelt told the assembled governors that the conservation of natural resources was "the weightiest problem now before the Nation." He warned them that without quick measures, the nation's natural wealth was "in danger of exhaustion." . . .

The move to a general policy split the conservationists for development of a program raised major questions as to means and ends. All could agree that the environment must be managed, but they could not agree as to who should do the managing and whose purpose should be served by it. In short, there was no agreement as to who constituted society or what defined social interest. As a result two major groups emerged among the conservationists. The first, consisting of Roosevelt, Pinchot, Van Hise and others, came to believe that planning and definition must be in the hands of society through government. The second pushed the view that the response must be by society through individuals and private interests of the community. As a result, the conservationists, even though they agreed on the nature of the environmental problem and the solution to the problem, split over the question of social welfare. . . .

Divisions within the conservationist camp created problems, and these were further complicated by the opposition of people who saw the crisis but had an alternative solution—the preservationists. This group represented a large number of Americans who viewed the environment somewhat romantically. Some were outright reactionaries. They believed that physical development did not always lead to progress. They argued that the best in life might be found in nature rather than in the words of man. Preservationism was not a new idea in the United States; in fact, it had a long tradition that could be traced in the ideas of Thoreau, George Catlin, and others. By the late nineteenth century men like Frederick Law Olmsted, Charles W. Eliot, and John Muir had become its carriers. They believed that nature possessed a spiritual quality necessary for the survival of mankind and argued for wilderness, for the preservation of the undeveloped. Muir wrote, "Everybody needs beauty as well as bread, places to play in and pray in, where nature may heal and cheer and give strength to body and soul alike." Eliot, president of Harvard and chairman of the National Conservation Congress in 1909, cooperated with the conservationists but believed nature was more than a resource for human utilization; it was worth preserving for itself. To him the city and the factory system created evils too great for the human body to endure and which only a resort to nature could cure. Frederick Law Olmsted, whose career included laying out natural sanctuaries in the heart of cities, suggested that the contemplation of nature was necessary for the health and vigor of mankind. Without it man had, "softening of the brain, paralysis, palsy, monomania, insanity, mental and nervous excitability, moroseness, melancholy or irascibility, and incapacitation of the individual for proper exercise of intellectual and moral forces."

The preservationists' position was not an easy one for an individual at the turn of the century. To adopt it usually involved serious problems, for many could appreciate the advantages made possible by urban and industrial civilization. Yet at the same time they feared it and looked to the past, to a natural order for solace in the face of the upheaval of the industrial age. The paradoxes involved in the preservationist view appear prominently in the thought of John Burroughs. In *The Summit of the Year* he criticized the conservationist approach, the scientific way of looking at the world. It provided a mixed blessing:

> Well, we can gain a lot of facts, such as they are, but we may lose our own souls. This spirit has invaded school and college. Our young people go to the woods with pencil and note-book in hand; they drive sharp bargains with every

flower and bird and tree they meet; they want tangible assets that can be put down in black and white. Nature as a living joy, something to love, to live with, to brood over, is now, I fear, seldom thought of. It is only a mine to be worked and to be through with, a stream to be fished, a tree to be shaken, a field to be gleaned. With what desperate thoroughness the new men study the birds; and about all their studies yield is a mass of dry, unrelated facts.

However, Burroughs could not see a way out of the dilemma. He did not like what was happening, but he did not believe the world could forget what it had now learned. He concluded that men ultimately "must face and accept the new situation. . . .We shall write less poetry, but we ought to live saner lives; we shall tremble and worship less, but we shall be more at home in the universe." All preservationists were not as willing as Burroughs to accept compromise with "progress." In political battles of the Roosevelt and Taft years they would frequently stand against the conservationists and their opposition, as the internal split within conservationism, would work to preclude the development of a broad approach to ecological crisis.

A third approach to the apparent crisis of the late nineteenth century embraced elements and values of both conservationism and preservationism but had its unique elements. Its uniqueness would make its adherents uncooperative with those of the other two ideas. This approach may be called ecological. The concept of ecology involved the idea that man was integrally involved with nature in an interdependent relationship. Ecologists, therefore, argued that the demands of nature must play as great a role in determining a proper course for society to follow as the needs of man. The earliest spokesman for this view in the United States was George P. Marsh, a diplomat who had served in Europe and witnessed first-hand the devastation that resulted from ignoring the demands of nature. In 1864 he published *Man and Nature* in which he warned Americans that they were creating problems for themselves by destroying their environment and cautioned them not to interfere with the "spontaneous arrangements of the organic and inorganic world." Marsh believed that nature possessed a natural balance and that man, if he dealt unknowingly with it, could destroy that balance and make the world unfit for life. Looking at what Italians had done to their mountains, the destruction of timber and the resulting erosion and flooding, Marsh saw ample proof of his view's validity. He told Americans that they must stop. "We are even now breaking up the floor and wainscoting and doors and window frames of our dwelling, for fuel to warm our bodies and to seethe our pottage, and the world cannot afford to wait till the slow and sure progress of exact science has taught it better economy."

Marsh presented a strong challenge to the entire American concept of life and nature. He suggested that man might not have the right to do with nature what he wanted but rather that he needed to understand what nature wanted. Perhaps it was too radical a departure for the time; consequently its adherents remained a small group, generally confined to the academy. Still, it was a point of view important among a potentially influential group of people. Unfortunately, it provided another approach to the American environmental problem and thus fragmented social response. The ecologists, because of their definition of the problem, had to move slowly. They had to discover what the correct relationship with the world should be. Nathaniel Shaler argued for education, for only through the study of nature would an answer to environmental problems be discovered. Shaler, however, found this goal hindered by the very institutions designed for study. He wrote of scientific education in the United States:

> We now present the realm to beginners as a group of fragments labeled astronomy, geology, chemistry, physics, and biology, each, as set forth, appearing to him as a little world in itself, with its own separate life, having little to do with its neighbors. It is rare, indeed, in a very considerable experience with youths to find one who has gained any inkling as to the complex unity of nature. Seldom it is, even with those who attain mastery in some one of these learnings, that we find a true sense as to the absolute oneness of the realm, or the place of man as the highest product of its work.

The ecologists perceived themselves in an adversary relationship with the rest of the community, including conservationists and preservationists, and believed that they had the only answer to the situation.

Conservationism, preservationism, and ecology represented activist approaches to environmental pressures. A fourth approach was the adoption of a wait-and-see attitude, a belief in laissez faire—let the situation develop and find out what happens. Accompanying this point of view was a basic optimism, a trust that nature or God would work things out. Its exponents adopted basic hostility toward those groups seeking to intervene in the process. George L. Knapp condemned the conservationists as "unadulterated humbugs" who sought to undermine the best in American life. In an article for the *North American Review* he wrote:

> That the modern Jeremiahs are as sincere as was the older one I do not question. But I count their prophesies to be baseless vaporings, and their vaunted remedy worse than the fancied disease. I am one who can see no warrant of law, or justice, nor of necessity for that wholesale reversal of our traditional policy which the advocates of "conservation" demand. I am one who does not shiver for the future at the sight of a load of coal, nor view a steel-mill as the arch-robber of posterity.

While there might be immediate shortages, existing institutions would meet the crisis. The optimism of the advocates of laissez faire was strikingly expounded by Congressman Martin Dies of Texas before Congress on August 30, 1913. Dies strongly opposed efforts to prevent the construction of a dam across the Hetch Hetchy Valley in California, and speaking to the point he said:

> I sympathize with my friends in California who want to take a part of the public domain now. . . . I am willing to let them have it.
> That is what the great resources of this country are for. They are for the American people. I want them to open the coal mines in Alaska. I want them

to open the reservations of this country. I am not for preservations or parks. I would have the great timber and mineral and coal resources of this country opened to the people. . . . Let California have it, and let Alaska open her coal mines. God Almighty has located the resources of this country in such form as that His children will not use them in disproportion, and your Pinchots will not be able to controvert and circumvent the laws of God Almighty.

The ideology of the advocates of laissez faire appears clearly in the statements of both Knapp and Dies. It represented, at least in part, a reassertion of two traditional American ideas. The environment existed for man to subdue and develop, and to be subdued and developed by private initiative, by the individual whose pursuit of his own interests worked in the interest of the American people. In addition, God had a special concern with the people of the United States, and he would not allow anything bad to happen. While a crisis might exist, there was no need to change American ways.

Resources were diminishing. Wild life was disappearing. Everybody could see that something was happening. Something had gone wrong. But no consensus emerged as to what should be done. If planning was to be done, who would be responsible? If technological innovation was necessary, who would sponsor it? What approach should be taken? The problem raised by the crisis was no longer one of science. What had emerged was a political dilemma in which a variety of views contested for acceptance and no one could claim majority support. Everyone claimed to speak for public interest, for the national good and welfare, but the various groups proposing solutions offered different definitions of both the public interest and how to secure it. Consequently, reform efforts ran into trouble in the national political arena. In one episode after another environmental reformers found themselves unable to cooperate with one another. As a result, perhaps, the forces for laissez faire won the day. . . . No broad reform plan emerged, no directed solution to the problem. Instead the nation met crises as it had in the past, piecemeal and responsively. This placed adjustments in each case in the hands of those directly tied to specific shortages. Thus, power companies developed waterways, steel companies sought new sources of iron ore, and so on. In the short run this probably averted the crisis. Private industry and enterprise was interested in efficient utilization of resources. It also managed to develop alternative sources for the energy and raw materials whose destruction had been feared.

But in the long run what took place? The discovery of new sources of diminishing materials spurred American growth, and the American population quickly expanded to consume whatever could be produced. Thus, society was still tied to the same pattern of utilization of resources that had created the initial crisis. That portion of the problem had only been delayed. However, in addition the crisis had prompted less visible change in the American community. The status quo had not been maintained; change had not been stopped. In fact, Americans confronted the very crisis feared by Frederick Jackson Turner. By the success they achieved in solving the immediate problems, private entrepreneurs secured greater control over the resources that they needed and, consequently, greater economic and political power. Within this situation the chance of the individual either to gain economic power or exercise power outside of these corporations was diminished. The crisis forced change, whether Americans planned for it or not.

Conservation as Reclamation

MARC REISNER

One hundred and sixty acres. If anything unifies the story of the American West — its past and its present, its successes and its dreadful mistakes — it is this mythical allotment of land. Its origins are found in the original Homestead Act of 1862, which settled on such an amount — a half-mile square, more often referred to as a quarter section — as the ideal acreage for a Jeffersonian utopia of small farmers. The idea was to carve millions of quarter sections out of the public domain, sell them cheaply to restless Americans and arriving immigrants, and, by letting them try to scratch a living out of them, develop the nation's resources and build up its character.

In the West, the Homestead Act had several later incarnations. The Desert Lands Act, the Timber Culture Act, and the Timber and Stone Act were the principal ones. Neither Congress nor the General Land Office, which was responsible for administering the acts, could ever comprehend that the relative success of the land program east of the Mississippi River had less to do with the perseverance of the settlers or the wisdom of the legislation than with the forgiving nature of the climate. In the East, virtually every acre received enough rainfall, except during years of extraordinary drought, to grow most anything that didn't mind the soil and the temperature. (Unlike much of the West, which suffers through months of habitual drought, the East gets precipitation year-round; in the spring and early summer, when crops need water most, much of the East is exceptionally wet.) Since the growing season, except in the extreme north, was at least five months long, even an ignorant or lazy farmer could raise *some* kind of crop.

In the West, even if you believed that the rainfall was magically increasing, you still had to contend with high altitudes (the western plains, the Snake River Valley, and most of the irrigable lands in the Great Basin would float over the tops of all but the highest Appalachian Mountains) and, as a result, chronic frost danger even in May and September. Then there were the relentless winds, hailstones bigger than oranges, tornadoes, and breathtaking thunderstorms. There were sandy lands that would not retain moisture and poorly drained lands that retained too much; there were alkaline lands that poisoned crops.

The General Land Office bureaucrats sat in Washington pretending that such conditions did not exist. Their job, as they perceived it, was to fill little squares with people. They extended no credit, provided no water, offered no services. And the permutations of the Homestead Act that found their way into the western versions of the law sometimes *added* to the farmers' burdens.

Under the Timber Culture Act, for example, you had to plant one-quarter of your quarter section with trees, a stipulation inserted because it was thought that trees increased the rainfall. In West Texas, where, meteorologically speaking, all that is predictable is the wind, you would have to spend most of your time replanting your fallen-down trees. Under the Desert Lands Act, which applied to land so arid even the government realized that farming was hopeless without irrigation, you had to demonstrate "proof of irrigation" before you could own the land. Unless you owned reasonably flat land immediately adjacent to a relatively constant stream which did not, as most western rivers do for much of their length, flow in a canyon, complying with the Desert Lands Act was almost out of the question. A mutual irrigation effort by the inhabitants of a valley was, perhaps, a possibility. That was what the Mormons had done, but they were a close-knit society linked by a common faith and a history of persecution.

The members of Congress who wrote the legislation, the land office agents who doled out land, and the newspaper editors who celebrated the settlers' heroism had, in a great many cases, never laid eyes on the land or the region that enclosed it. They were unaware that in Utah, Wyoming, and Montana — to pick three of the colder and drier states — there was not a single quarter section on which a farmer could subsist, even with luck, without irrigation, because an unirrigated quarter section was enough land for about five cows. The Indians accepted things as they were; that is why they were mostly nomadic, wandering toward greener grass and fuller herds and flowing water. If whites were going to insist on living there — fixed, settled, mortgaged, fenced — the best they could do with the land was graze it. But in those three states, an economical grazing unit was, say, twenty-five hundred to five thousand acres, depending on the circumstances. To amass that much land you had to cheat — on a magnificent scale. If you didn't, you had to overgraze the land and ruin it, and many millions of acres were damaged or ruined in exactly this way. Many settlers were tasting property ownership for the first time in their lives, and all they had in common was greed.

Speculation. Water monopoly. Land monopoly. Erosion. Corruption. Catastrophe. By 1876, after several trips across the plains and through the Rocky Mountain states, John Wesley Powell was pretty well convinced that those would be the fruits of a western land policy based on wishful thinking, willfulness, and lousy science. And by then everything he predicted was happening, especially land monopoly, water monopoly, graft, and fraud.

Homesteads fronting on streams went like oranges aboard a scurvy-ridden ship. The doctrine of riparian rights, which had been unthinkingly imported from the East, made it possible to monopolize the water in a stream if you owned the land alongside it. But if the stream was anything larger than a creek, only the person who owned land upstream, where it was still small, could manage to build a dam or barrage to guarantee a summer flow; then he could divert all he wanted, leaving his downstream neighbors with a bed of dry rocks. Riparian doctrine alone, therefore, made it possible for a tiny handful of landowners to monopolize the few manageable rivers of the West. When their neighbors saw their predicament and sold out, they could monopolize the best land, too.

As for the Desert Land Act and the Timber and Stone Act, they could not have promoted land monopoly and corruption more efficiently if they had been expressly designed for that purpose. A typical irrigation scene under the Desert Land Act went as follows: A beneficiary hauled a hogshead of water and a witness to his barren land, dumped the water on the land, paid the witness $20, and brought him to the land office, where the witness swore he had seen the land irrigated. Then, with borrowed identification and different names, another land application was filed, and the scene was repeated. If you could pull it off six or seven times, you had yourself a ranch. Foreign sailors arriving in San Francisco were offered a few dollars, a jug of whiskey, and an evening in a whorehouse in exchange for filing a land claim under the Timber and Stone Act. Before shipping out, the sailors abdicated title; there were no restrictions on transfer of ownership. Whole redwood forests were acquired in such a manner.

Then there was the Swamplands Act, or Swamp and Overflow Act—a Desert Lands Act of the bulrushes. If there was federal land that overflowed enough so that you could traverse it at times in a flat-bottomed boat, and you promised to reclaim it (which is to say, dike and drain it), it was yours. Henry Miller, a mythical figure in the history of California land fraud, acquired a large part of his 1,090,000-acre empire under this Act. According to legend, he bought himself a boat, hired some witnesses, put the boat and witnesses in a wagon, hitched some horses to it, and hauled the boat and witnesses over county-size tracts near the San Joaquin River where it rains, on the average, about eight or nine inches a year. The land became his. The sanitized version of the story, the one told by Miller's descendants, has him benefiting more from luck than from ruse. During the winter of 1861 and 1862, most of California got three times its normal precipitation, and the usually semiarid Central Valley became a shallow sea the size of Lake Ontario. But the only difference in this version is that Miller didn't need a wagon for his boat; he still had no business acquiring hundreds of thousands of acres of the public domain, yet he managed it with ease.

One of the unforeseen results of the homestead legislation was a high rate of employment among builders of birdhouses. In most instances, you were required to display an "erected domicile" on your land. The Congress, after all, was much too smart to give people land without requiring them to live on it. In a number of instances, the erected domicile was a birdhouse, put there to satisfy a paid witness with a tender conscience. It is quite possible that the greatest opportunity offered by the homestead legislation in the West was the opportunity to earn a little honest graft. By conservative estimates, 95 percent of the final proofs under the Desert Land Act were fraudulent. "Whole townships have been entered under this law in the interest of one person or firm," thundered Binger Hermann, a commissioner of the General Land Office, about the Timber and Stone Act. Not long afterward, Hermann himself was fired for allowing unrestricted fraud.

Mark Twain might have written it off to the human condition, but [John Wesley] Powell, who subscribed to a more benevolent view of humanity, wrote it off to the conditions of the desert and the failure to understand them.

Americans were making a Procrustean effort to turn half a continent into something they were used to. It was a doomed effort. Even worse, it was unscientific.

The document that Powell hoped would bring the country to its senses was called *A Report on the Lands of the Arid Region of the United States, with a More Detailed Account of the Lands of Utah*. Published in 187[8], the volume was seven years in preparation — though Powell took time out for a second expedition down the Colorado, in 1871, and for his usual plethora of intermittent pursuits. Powell's *Report* is remarkably brief, a scant two hundred pages in all. Unlike many of his rivals, such as the bombastic Ferdinand V. Hayden, Powell was more interested in being right than in being long. But his portrait of the American West has revolutionary implications even today.

At the beginning, Powell reconfirmed his view, which he had already submitted to an unbelieving Congress, that two-fifths of the United States has a climate that generally cannot support farming without irrigation. On top of that, irrigation could reclaim only a fraction of it. "When all the waters running in the streams found in this region are conducted on the land," Powell said, "there will be but a small portion of the country redeemed, varying in the different territories perhaps from *one to three percent*" (emphasis added). Powell regarded the theory that increased rainfall accompanied human settlement as bunk, but, typically, he disposed of it in a sympathetic and felicitous way: "If it be true that increase of the water supply is due to increase in precipitation, as many have supposed, the fact is not cheering to the agriculturalist of the arid region. . . . Any sudden great change [in climate] is ephemeral, and usually such changes go in cycles, and the opposite or compensating change may reasonably be anticipated. . . . [W]e shall have to expect a speedy return to extreme aridity, in which case a large portion of the agricultural industries of these now growing up would be destroyed."

The whole problem with the Homestead Acts, Powell went on, was that they were blind to reality. In the West, a 160-acre *irrigated* farm was too *large*, while a 160-acre *unirrigated* farm was too *small*. Most western valley soil was fertile, and a good crop was a near certainty once irrigation water was applied; in the milder regions the growing season was very long and two crops were possible, so one could often subsist on eighty irrigated acres or less. That, in fact, was about all the irrigated land one family could be expected to work. Remove the irrigation water, however, and things were drastically different. Then even a whole section was too small a piece of land. Under most circumstances, Powell claimed, no one could make a living through dryland ranching on fewer than 2,560 acres — four full sections. And even with that much land, a settler's prospects would be dicey in times of drought, because the land might lie utterly bare. Therefore, every pasturage farm should ideally have a water right sufficient to irrigate twenty acres or so during emergencies.

Having thrown over the preeminent myths about agriculture in the American West, Powell went on to the truly revolutionary part of his report. Under riparian water law, to give everyone a water right for twenty irrigated acres was impossible if you gave everyone a neat little square of land. Some squares would contain much greater stream footage than others, and their owners would have too much water compared with the others. The property boundaries would therefore have to be gerrymandered to give everyone a sufficient piece of the stream. That was one way you could help avert the monopolization of water. Another way was to insist that people *use* their water rights, not hold on to them in the hope that cities would grow up and one could make a killing someday selling water to them. An unused water right should revert — let us say after five years — to the public trust so someone else could claim it.

Doing all this, Powell reasoned, might help assure that water would be used equitably, but not necessarily efficiently. Ideally, to get through drier months and times of drought, you needed a reservoir in a good location — at a low altitude, and on the main branch of a stream. That way you could get more efficient storage of water — a dam only twice as large, but lower down, might capture five times as much water as a smaller one upstream. Also, you could then irrigate the lower valley lands, which usually have better soil and a longer growing season. In any event, an on-stream storage reservoir was, from the point of view of irrigation, preferable to small shallow ponds filled with diverted streamwater, the typical irrigation reservoirs of his day; the ponds evaporated much greater amounts of water and displaced valuable cropland.

But who, Powell asked, was building on-stream reservoirs? Practically no one. Homesteaders couldn't build them at all, let alone build them right, nor could groups of homesteaders — unless perhaps they were Mormons. Such dams required amounts of capital and commitment that were beyond the limits of aggregations of self-interested mortals. Private companies probably couldn't build good irrigation projects either, nor even states. Sooner or later, the federal government would have to get into the irrigation business or watch its efforts to settle the West degenerate into failure and chaos. Once it realized that, it would have to undertake a careful survey of the soil characteristics so as not to waste a lot of money irrigating inferior land with drainage problems. And (he implied rather than stated) the government ought to put J. W. Powell in charge; the General Land Office, which would otherwise be responsible, was, as anyone could see, "a gigantic illustration of the evils of badly directed scientific work."

Having gone this far, Powell figured he might as well go the whole route. Fences, for example, bothered him. What was the sense of every rancher enclosing his land with a barbed-wire fence? Fenced lands tended to be un-evenly grazed, and fences were obvious hazards to cattle in winter storms. Fencing was also a waste of time and money, especially in a region where rainfall could skid from twenty to six inches in successive years and someone was lucky to survive at all, let alone survive while constantly repairing and replacing fences. Individually fenced lands were a waste of resources, too; it takes a lot more tin, Powell reasoned, to make five eight-ounce cans than to make one forty-ounce can. The sensible thing was for farms to be clustered together and the individually owned lands treated as a commons, an *ejido*, with a single fence around the perimeter.

States bothered Powell, too. Their borders were too often nonsensical. They followed rivers for convenience, then struck out in a straight line, bisect-ing mountain ranges, cutting watersheds in half. Boxing out landscapes, sneering at natural reality, they were wholly arbitrary and, therefore, stupid. In the West, where the one thing that really mattered was water, states should logically be formed around watersheds. Each major river, from the glacial drip at its headwaters to the delta at its mouth, should be a state or semistate. The great state of Upper Platte River. Will the Senator from the state of Rio Grande yield? To divide the West any other way was to sow the future with rivalries, jealousies, and bitter squabbles whose fruits would contribute solely to the nourishment of lawyers.

While Powell knew that his plan for settling the American West would be considered revolutionary, he saw a precedent. After all, what was the difference between a cooperative irrigation district and a New England barn-raising? One was informal, the other organized and legalized, but otherwise they were the same thing. Communal pasturelands might be a gross affront to America's preoccupation with private property rights, but they were common in Europe. In the East, where inland navigation was as important as irrigation was in the West, you already had a strong federal presence in the Corps of Engineers. If anything was revolutionary, it was trying to graft English common law and the principles and habits of wet-zone agriculture onto a desert landscape. There was not a desert civilization in the world where that had been tried — and most of those civilizations had withered even after following sensible rules.

Powell was advocating cooperation, reason, science, an equitable sharing of the natural wealth, and — implicitly if not explicitly — a return to the Jeffersonian ideal. He wanted the West settled slowly, cautiously, in a manner that would work. If it was done intelligently instead of in a mad, unplanned rush, the settlement of the West could help defuse the dangerous conditions building in the squalid industrial cities of the East. If it was done wrong, the migration west might go right into reverse.

The nation at large, however, was in no mood for any such thing. It was avid for imperial expansion, and the majority of its citizens wanted to get rich. New immigrants were arriving, dozens of boatloads a day, with that motive burning in their brains. To them America was not so much a democratic utopia as a gold mine. . . .

The unpeopled West, naturally, was where a great many immigrants hoped to find their fortunes. They didn't want to hear that the West was dry. Few had ever seen a desert, and the East was so much like Europe that they imagined the West would be, too. A tiny bit semiarid, perhaps, like Italy. But a desert? Never! They didn't want to hear of communal pasturelands — they had left those behind, in Europe, in order that they could become the emperors of Wyoming. They didn't want the federal government parceling out water and otherwise meddling in their affairs; that was another European tradition they had left an ocean away. . . .

The result, in the end, was that Powell got some money to conduct his Irrigation Survey for a couple of years — far less than he wanted, and needed — and then found himself frozen permanently out of the appropriations bills. The excuse was that he was moving too slowly, too deliberately; the truth was that he was forming opinions the West couldn't bear to hear. There was inexhaustible land but far too little water, and what little water there was might, in many cases, be too expensive to move. Having said this, held to it, and suffered for it, Powell spent his last years in a kind of ignominy. Unable to participate in the settlement of the West, he retreated into the Bureau of Ethnology, where his efforts, ironically, helped prevent the culture of the West's original inhabitants from being utterly trampled and eradicated by that same settlement. On September 23, 1902, he died at the family compound near Haven, Maine, about as far from the arid West as he could get. . . .

The passage of the Reclamation Act of 1902 was such a sharp left turn in the course of American politics that historians still gather and argue over why it was passed. To some, it was America's first flirtation with socialism, an outgrowth of the Populist and Progressive movements of the time. To others, it was a disguised reactionary measure, an effort to relieve the mobbed and riotous conditions of the eastern industrial cities—an act to save heartless capitalism from itself. To some, its roots were in Manifest Destiny, whose incantations still held people in their sway; to others, it was a military ploy to protect and populate America's western flank against the ascendant Orient.

What seems beyond question is that the Reclamation Act, or some variation of it, was by the end of the nineteenth century, inevitable. To resist a federal reclamation program was to block all further migration to the West and to ensure disaster for those who were already there—or for those who were on their way. Even as the victims of the great white winter and the drought of the 1880s and 1890s were evacuating the arid regions, the trains departing Chicago and St. Louis for points west were full. The pull of the West reached deep into the squalid slums of the eastern cities; it reached back to the ravined, rock-strewn farms of New England and down into the boggy, overwet farmlands of the Deep South. No matter what the government did, short of erecting a wall at the hundredth meridian, the settlement of the West was going to continue. The only way to prevent more cycles of disaster was to build a civilization based on irrigated farming.

As soon as Roosevelt was in the White House, [Nevada Representative Francis] Newlands introduced a bill creating a federal program along the lines suggested by Powell. But the bitterness he felt over huge financial loss[es] was so strong that he described his bill in language almost calculated to infuriate his western colleagues, who were clinging to the myth that the hostile natural forces of the West could be overcome by individual initiative. In a long speech on the floor of the Congress, Newlands said outright that the legislation he was introducing would "nationalize the works of irrigation"—which was like saying today that one intended to nationalize the automobile industry. Then he launched into a long harangue about the failures of state reclamation programs, blaming them on "the ignorance, the improvidence, and the dishonesty of local legislatures"—even though many of his listeners had recently graduated from such legislatures themselves. . . . New lands bill . . . ran into immediate opposition . . . Roosevelt intervened. . . . On June 17, 1902, the Reclamation Act became law.

Women and Conservation

CAROLYN MERCHANT

In his book *The Fight For Conservation* (1910), Gifford Pinchot praised the women of the progressive era for their substantial contributions to conservation. He cited the conservation committee of the Daughters of the American Revolution (chaired by his mother), the Pennsylvania Forestry Association, "founded by ladies," which carried out some of the earliest work done in that state, the National Forests preserved by Minnesota women, and the Calaveras Big Trees set aside by the women of California after a nine year fight.

Writing his definitive history of the progressive conservation campaign in 1959, Samuel Hays also acknowledged the enthusiasm of women's organizations for conservation and their staunch support, until 1913, for Pinchot as leader of the movement. Historians Robert Welker and Stephen Fox amplified other female contributions, especially to the Audubon movement and the hiking clubs, while admitting that much remains to be learned regarding women's role in conservation.

Who were the women of the conservation crusade? What were their accomplishments, objectives, and ideals? How did they interact with the men who promoted conservation? What ideological framework did they bring to the crusade and to the conflicts that developed within it?

In the nineteenth century, women had developed interests and organizations that paved the way for their work in the conservation and reform movements of the progressive era. Literary clubs oriented toward culture drew women together for mutual improvement and shared experiences, while the women's rights and abolition movements exposed them to the political process and the public arena. Leisure time had afforded middle and upper-class women opportunities for botanizing, gardening, birdlore, and camping. Women visited the National Parks and scenic wonderlands of the West or, sometimes casting off skirts and donning Turkish pants, joined the Appalachian Mountain Club (founded in 1876) or the Sierra Club (founded in 1892).

Propelled by a growing consciousness of the panacea of bucolic scenery and wilderness, coupled with the need for reform of the slums and squalor of the cities, women burst vividly into the public arena in the early twentieth century as a force in the progressive conservation crusade. Behind the brief tributes by historians to their substantial contributions lies an untold story of immense energy, achievement, and dedication by thousands of women to the cause of conservation. Although only the most prominent women appear in the archives of history, without the input of women in nearly every locale in the country, conservation gains in the early decades of the century would have been fewer and far less spectacular.

From Carolyn Merchant, "The Women of the Progressive Conservation Crusade, 1900–1915," in Kendall E. Bailes, ed. *Environmental History: Critical Issues in Comparative Perspective*, 1985, pp. 153–170. Reprinted by permission of University Press of America.

Feminist Conservation: The General Federation of Women's Clubs

In 1900, Mrs. Lovell White of San Francisco, the brilliant, dynamic, and resourceful founder and president of the California Club, took up the cause of forestry. Founded at the home of Mrs. White on a cold rainy evening in 1897 in the wake of the first and abortive California suffrage campaign — a campaign "brilliant, rich in experiences" with "a spirit of wholesome comradeship," — the California Club merged in January of 1900 with women's clubs throughout the state to form the California Federation of Women's Clubs. With Mrs. Robert Burdette of Pasadena as president and Mrs. White as vice-president at large, the first meeting was steeped in conservation ideals.

"The preservation of the forests of this state is a matter that should appeal to women," declared Mrs. Burdette in her opening address. "While the women of New Jersey are saving the Palisades of the Hudson from utter destruction by men to whose greedy souls Mount Sinai is only a stone quarry, and the women of Colorado are saving the cliff dwellings and pueblo ruins of their state from vandal destruction, the word comes to the women of California that men whose souls are gang-saws are meditating the turning of our world-famous Sequoias into planks and fencing worth so many dollars." The forests of the state, she went on, were the source of the state's waters and together they made possible the homes and health of the people of California. "Better one living tree in California, than fifty acres of lumberyard. Preserve and replant them and the State will be blessed a thousandfold in the development of its natural resources. . . ."

Nationally, the General Federation of Women's Clubs (G.F.W.C.), founded in 1890, had been active in forestry since the turn of the century as part of women's civic obligation to become informed on the most urgent political, economic, and social issues of the day. Selecting women in each state who were familiar with the principles of forestry to head the clubs' forestry committees, local members first conducted cosmetic campaigns to save waste paper and clean up their towns and cities. They formed coalitions with civic organizations which engaged in the beautification of yards, vacant lots, school yards, and public buildings through planting trees and shrubs. Following the example of German women, with whom they corresponded, they planted long avenues of shade trees. They also worked toward the acquisition and preservation of wooded tracts of land wherein "Nature should be left unrestrained."

Local forestry committees formed study groups that emphasized both the aesthetic and utilitarian aspects of forestry and the conservation of wood and water. The Forest Service provided literature and sent guest lecturers on trees and forestry to club meetings. *Century* magazine supplied them with articles on conservation, while local libraries were encouraged to acquire books on the principles of forestry.

In addition to keeping 800,000 members informed of the conservation policies and achievements of Roosevelt and Pinchot, the General Federation's Forestry Committee played an influential role in the passage of legislation to protect forests, waters, and birdlife. Under the direction of Mrs. Lydia Phillips

Williams (for 1904–6), an enthusiastic conservationist who had learned forestry at the family's Peterson Nursery in Chicago and on her numerous excursions to forests in Norway, Sweden, and Germany; Mrs. F. W. Gerard (1908–10) from Connecticut, and Mrs. Lovell White (1910–1912), who had established a national reputation in saving the Calaveras Big Trees of California, the committee coordinated efforts to support such projects as the creation of national forest reserves in New Hampshire and the Southern Appalachians and passage of the Weeks Bill for protection of the watersheds of navigable streams. In 1910, 233 clubs reported that they had sent letters and petitions for state and national legislation on forest fire laws, tax remission for reforestation, and the appropriation of demonstration forests, while 250 were active in the movement for bird and plant protection.

In 1909, under the leadership of Mrs. John Wilkinson of Louisiana the Federation formed a Waterways Committee to promote the development of water power, clean water, and cheaper, higher volume transportation. The rationale for women's involvement lay in the effect of waterways on every American home: Pure water meant health; impure meant disease and death. Additionally, beautification of waterfronts, as had occurred in the watertowns of Europe, would lead to patriotism and love of one's country.

Joseph Ransdell, chair of the National Rivers and Harbors Committee speaking to the Tenth Biennial Convention of the Federation in 1910, acknowledged the important contributions of the women's clubs to conservation. "I appeal to you as a representative of the men who need and wish the help of women. We know that nothing great or good in this world ever existed without the women. We consider our movement one of the greatest and best ever inaugurated in the union and we know that women can help us."

In 1910 the Federation reorganized its forestry and waterways committees under a Department of Conservation headed by Mrs. Emmons Crocker of Fitchburg, Massachusetts, and added a birdlife representative, Mrs. Francis B. Hornbrooke, also of Massachusetts. This new Department sent representatives to the Second National Conservation Congress in St. Paul, Minnesota, in 1910 and the National Irrigation Congress at Pueblo, Colorado.

During the period 1907–1912, women contributed notices, news items, reports, and articles to *Forestry and Irrigation*, the journal of the American Forestry Association. They pointed out women's work to save forests in places such as Colorado, Vermont, Maine, and New York, printed lengthy summaries of progress in conservation as reported at the Federation's biennial meetings, and announced protest actions such as that taken by Mrs. D. M. Osborne of Auburn, New York who, outraged by telephone pole workers who had mercilessly trimmed her trees without permission, "drove off the workmen and cut down the poles."

Mrs. Lydia Adams-Williams, a self-styled feminist conservation writer and member of the Women's National Press Association was particularly vociferous in her efforts to popularize women's accomplishments. Her article "Conservation — Women's Work" (1908), in which she characterized herself as the first woman lecturer and writer on conservation, complained that "man has been too busy building railroads, constructing ships, engineering great projects, and exploiting vast commercial enterprises" to consider the future. Man the moneymaker had left it to woman the moneysaver to preserve resources. She placed women's roles in conservation squarely in the context of feminist history:

> To the intuition of Isabella of Spain, to her tenacious grasp of a great idea, to her foresight and her divine sympathy the world is indebted for the discovery of a great continent, for the civilization we enjoy today and for the great wealth of resources. . . . And as it was the intuitive foresight of a woman which brought the light of civilization to a great continent, so in great measure, will it fall to woman in her power to educate public sentiment to save from rapacious waste and complete exhaustion the resources upon which depend the welfare of the home, the children, and the children's children.

In "A Million Women for Conservation" (1908), again taking liberal notice of her own accomplishments, Mrs. Adams-Williams discussed the resolutions passed by the women's clubs in support of the conservation efforts of Roosevelt, Pinchot, the Inland Waterways Commission, the Forest Service, the Geological Survey, and the American Mining Congress. The Federation in Washington, D.C., of which she was a member, was the first to pass these resolutions followed by four other national women's organizations the combined membership of which totalled one million.

By 1908, the General Federation had begun to play an important role in the national conservation movement. Mrs. Philip N. Moore, president of the Federation from 1908–1910, was a member of the executive committee of the National Conservation Congress during its first four years, was a presiding officer in 1912, and became its vice-president in 1913. Tribute was paid by the president of the Congress to her "rare ability" to organize and preside over large numbers of enthusiastic women. Mrs. Moore of St. Louis, Missouri, a leader in educational and philanthropic work, was born in Rockford, Illinois, graduated from Vassar College, and later became one of its trustees. She had been active for many years at the local, state, and national levels of the Federation. The voice of Mrs. Moore and dozens of other women were heard loudly and forcefully at the National Conservation Congresses held from 1909–1912.

Women's National Rivers and Harbors Congress.   In 1908, seven women in Shreveport, Louisiana, banded together to form the Women's National Rivers and Harbors Congress that would cooperate with the National Rivers and Harbors Congress then headed by Joseph E. Ransdell. Within fourteen months, under the leadership of its president, Mrs. Hoyle Tomkies, it had grown to 20,000 members and had held a national congress in Washington, D.C. at which twenty states were represented. As Mrs. Tomkies expressed it, "Our work is mainly to educate upon the subject. . . . We are putting forth all the energy and influence we can muster for the cause, lest the enemy come while we are sleeping and sow in the peoples' minds the tares of 'individualism' and non-conservation."

The Daughters of the American Revolution. In 1909 Mrs. Matthew T. Scott was elected President General of the 77,000 member Daughters of the American Revolution. A representative of the more liberal wing of the D.A.R. who had recently defeated the conservatives in a national election, Mrs. Scott was an enthusiastic conservationist who encouraged the maintenance of a conservation committee consisting of 100 members representing every state. The chair of this committee was Mrs. James Pinchot, mother of Gifford Pinchot, who by that token as well as her conservation efforts was said to have "done more for the cause of conservation than any other woman."

Pinchot himself addressed the 18th D.A.R. Congress in Washington in 1909 praising the members for their efforts against "land grabbers" and suggesting certain conservation projects for further action. At the 1912 convention Pinchot thanked the women for their efforts in aiding the passage of the Alaska coal bill and the LaFollette legislation regulating grazing, and invited them to take up the cause of water power. The D.A.R., Pinchot said on another occasion, "spells only another name for the highest form of conservation, that of vital force and intellectual energy."

Other conservation efforts of the D.A.R. were directed toward the preservation of the Appalachian watersheds, the Palisades, and Niagara Falls (then threatened by over usage of water by power companies). In fact, as Mrs. Carl Vrooman pointed out to the National Conservation Congress of 1911, "these 77,000 women do indeed represent a perfect Niagara of splendid ability and force—enough, if intelligently directed, to furnish the motive power to keep revolving all the wheels of progress in this country." In 1905–6 women nationwide had responded to Horace MacFarland of the American Civic Association whose editorials in the *Ladies' Home Journal* on the preservation of Niagara Falls had produced tens of thousands of letters to Congress.

The Audubon Movement. The post–Civil War resurgence of high fashion for ladies had, by the end of the century, taken an immense toll on American bird-life in the creation of exotic styles in millinery. Bird feathers and whole birds nestled atop the heads of society's upper and middle-class women. The first Audubon societies, organized in 1886, protested the "abominable" habit of wearing feather fashions. Women who sought to educate their sisters to the peril of birds formed Audubon clubs, such as the one at Smith College where two young female students developed a plan to protect plume birds.

In 1898 "a score of ladies met in Fairfield," Connecticut, to form the Audubon society of the State of Connecticut, electing as president Mrs. Mabel Osgood Wright. With the publication in 1899, of the first issue of the Audubon Societies' official journal, *Bird Lore*, Mrs. Wright took on the task of editing the magazine's Audubon section and of reporting the latest developments in the politics of bird preservation. She requested that the secretaries of the initial nineteen state societies, all but one of whom were women, send news and notes to broaden and strengthen the movement.

In 1905 the Audubon Society appealed to the National Federation of Women's Clubs for help: "The club women of America with their powerful influence should take a strong stand against the use of wild birds' plumage, and especially against the use of the Aigrette. . . . A close affiliation between this Association and the National Federation of Women's clubs would be mutually helpful." . . .

In cooperation with the request made by the Audubon Society, Mrs. Gerard, Chair of the General Federation of Women's Clubs' Forestry Committee appealed to women at the Federation's 1910 Biennial Convention: "Our work for the Audubon Society is not as active as it should be. Can we logically work for conservation and expect to be listened to, while we still continue to encourage the destruction of the song birds by following the hideous fashion of wearing song birds and egrets upon our hats?"

And speaking to the 1912 Conservation Congress, Mrs. Crocker of the GFWC's Conservation Committee asked a personal favor of the women present: "This fall when you choose your fall millinery . . . I beg you to choose some other decoration for your hats. . . . "

After a long campaign, in October 1913, a new Tariff Act was passed that outlawed the importing of wild bird feathers into the United States. It was so vigorously enforced that newspapers were filled with accounts of "the words and actions of indignant ladies who found it necessary to give up their aigrettes, paradise plumes, and other feathers upon arriving from Europe. Two days after the new law went into effect, Audubon Save the Birds Hats were being advertised in New York for $15 to $45 apiece. Congratulations poured in from all over the world for the Audubon Society's great victory. . . .

So rare as to be on the verge of extermination a few years before, by 1915 egrets in guarded rookeries in the southern United States, numbered 10,580 along with 50,000 Little Blue Herons, and an equal number of Ibis. Owing to the combined efforts of the Audubon Societies and the women's clubs, public opinion had shifted so far toward bird protection that far fewer "bad bird-laws" were being introduced into state legislatures. The work of a decade and a half had begun to show results. . . .

Conservation Ideology

The Conservation Trilogy.   Although the women of the organizations represented at the National Conservation Congresses were public activists in their local communities, they nevertheless accepted the traditional sex roles assigned to them by late nineteenth century American society as caretakers of the nation's homes, husbands, and offspring, supporting rather than challenging the two spheres ideology of the nineteenth century.

At the National Congresses, women repeatedly called on the traditions assigned them by society in justifying the public demands they were making. Unwilling and unable to break out of these social roles, and supported by the men of the Congresses, they drew on a trilogy of slogans — conservation of womanhood, the home, and the child.

The Conservation of True Womanhood. The "conservation of true woman-hood" was a subject repeatedly stressed by women at the Conservation Congresses. Mrs. Scott of the D.A.R. pleaded "as the representative of a great National organization of the women of the land, for the exalting, for the lifting up in special honor, of the Holy Grail of Womanhood." Just as the agricultural college prepared prospective farmers, so schools of domestic science would produce prospective housewives.

Speaking to the Conservation Congress of 1909, Mrs. Overton Ellis of the General Federation of Women's Clubs, called conservation "the surest weapon with which women might win success." Centuries of turning last night's roast into hash, remaking last year's dress and controlling the home's resources had given women a heightened sense of the power of the conservation idea in creating true womanhood. "Conservation in its material and ethical sense is the basic principle in the life of woman. . . ."

In her presidential address to the General Federation's Tenth Biennial Meeting in 1910, Mrs. Philip N. Moore set conservation in its context for women as "no new word, no new idea," but a unifying theme for the contributions of women to society as the conservors of life. "There is a 'new woman,' the product of evolution the result of social and commercial changes. She rebels, however, when she sees woman spelled with capital letters or harnessed to the word 'Career.' "

Mrs. Carl Vrooman, also of the D.A.R., emphasized the ideal woman's subservience to the man in conservation. "We may not, it is true, formulate any new policies for you, or launch any issues, or make any very original contributions to your program, but there is one thing women can bring to a movement of this kind — an atmosphere that makes ideas sprout and grow, and ideals expand and develop and take deeper root in the subsoil of the masculine mind."

The Conservation of the Home. The home as the domain of true woman-hood became the second theme in the conservation trilogy. The National Congress of Mothers, represented by Mrs. Orville Bright of Chicago, dedicated itself to the conservation of natural resources for "the use, comfort, and benefit of the homes of the people." "Life, health and character all depend on the home and its efficiency." Mrs. Bright adopted the utilitarian philosophy of the progressives in stressing that conservation primarily benefitted human life rather than that of other organisms, since the fate of forests, land, waters, minerals, or food would be of little consequence were there "no men, women, and children to use and enjoy them."

Margaret Russell Knudsen of Hawaii, of the Women's National Rivers and Harbors Congress argued (at the 1909 Conservation Congress) that the conservation of the home was the special mission of woman. The "mark of civilization was the arrival of woman on the scene. . . . In no national movement has there been such a spontaneous and universal response from women as in this great question of conservation. Women from Maine to the most Western shore of the Hawaiian Islands are alive to the situation, because the home is woman's domain. She is the conserver of the race."

Conservation of the Child.   Third in the trilogy was the link between the conservation of natural resources and the conservation of the children and future generations of the United States. According to Mrs. John Walker, a member of the Kansas City chapter of Daughters of the American Revolution, woman's role in conservation was dedicated to the preservation of life, while man's role was the conservation of material needs. "Woman, the transmitter of life" must therefore care for the product of life—future generations. The children of the nation should not be sacrificed to "factories, mills, and mines," but must be allowed "to enjoy the freedom of the bird and the butterfly . . . and all that the sweet breast of Nature offers so freely."

Mrs. Overton Ellis of the General Federation of Women's Clubs promoted the conservation of children's lives at the 1909 Congress: "Women's supreme function as mother of the race gives her special claim to protection not so much individually as for unborn generations."

Males active in the movement helped to reinforce the role of woman as "guardian of the child," "consecrated utterly to conservation." Reverend Charles Goss of Cincinnati, speaking to the Federation of Women's Clubs' Biennial Convention in 1910 on "Conservation in its Broadest Sense," assured them that "woman was designed by God to be the great Conservator." . . .

Denouement.   The Fifth National Conservation Congress opened in Washington, D.C., on November 18, 1913, and proceeded for three days. Its vicepresident, Mrs. Philip N. Moore of the General Federation of Women's Clubs, did not speak. Nor did any other woman from the Federation, the D.A.R., the Country Women's Clubs or the Women's National Rivers and Harbors Congress. The sole female voice heard was Miss Mabel Boardman from the American Red Cross who lectured on "Conservation of Life in the Lumber Camps."

American Forestry (the new name of the journal of the American Forestry Association) carried a full report on the meeting in its November issue. Descriptions of the activities of the Congress were accompanied by the portraits of fifty men who had chaired or worked on the committees. A photograph taken the night of the Forestry Banquet on November 19 showed some 160 men seated at round tables before a speaker's platform. Mrs. Philip N. Moore was not among them.

A brief note in the Forestry Committee's report to the Congress seems to provide the explanation for the absence of women:

> The desirability of . . . an organization [to represent the mutual forestry and lumbering interests] was emphasized by the presence at [the Fourth National Congress in] Indianapolis [1912] of a number of men who were no longer in need of the general educational propaganda relative to the conservation of natural resources, but attended the Congress for the purpose of meeting progressive men in their own and related lines and securing specific information helpful in the solution of their own problems.

Conservation and forestry had come of age as technical professions. As such they were no longer accessible to women. After 1912 the American Forestry Association ceased to print articles or news items on the work of women in forestry. Lydia Adams-Williams disappeared from the scene.

A second explanation for the disappearance of women also seems plausible. That same year the popular nationwide struggle for the preservation of Hetch Hetchy Valley, a part of California's Yosemite National Park, reached its conclusion. With the passage of the Raker Act by Congress in 1913, the City of San Francisco won its long battle for a public water supply. The women of the conservation crusade had worked hard to preserve the valley as an integral part of the park.

Gifford Pinchot, the women's early inspiration and supporter in conservation efforts, had taken the opposing side, recommending at the congressional hearings that a dam be constructed across the valley to serve the interests of thousands of city people rather than accommodate the needs of the few who camped and hiked in the area.

Soon after a City of San Francisco referendum in November 1903 favored construction of the dam, John Muir had taken the Hetch Hetchy issue to the nation. Preservationists rallied to support its retention in the park through letters and telegrams to the House Committee on Public Lands which held hearings in January 1909. Among them were women who had camped in the valley, who were members of the Sierra Club or Appalachian Mountain Club, or who were opposed to the commercial use of such a scenic wonderland. . . .

In 1913, the National Committee for the Preservation of Yosemite National Park headed by Robert Underwood Johnson, editor of *The Century*, and Charles Eliot, president of the First Conservation Congress, circulated brochures on "The Hetch Hetchy Grab" and "The Invasion of Yosemite National Park" documenting opposition from over 100 newspapers. Among the prominent citizens listed as preservationists for the park were Mrs. Emmons Crocker, chair of the Conservation Committee of the General Federation of Women's Clubs. On the committee, which represented most of the states of the union were twenty-five women, some of whom, like Mrs. Philip N. Moore, were General Federation leaders now openly opposed to Pinchot.

Although preservationists lost the battle over Hetch Hetchy in December 1913, they had aroused the nation. The passage of the National Parks Act in 1916 that established an administration in the Department of the Interior for the numerous parks created since 1862, gave them some compensation for its loss. . . .

During the decade and a half that introduced the century, women's organizations had helped the nation to achieve enormous gains in the conservation of natural resources and the preservation of scenic landscapes. Yet the platform for promoting these objectives had been a mixed one. Working closely with the men of the movement, women frequently saw themselves as ideologically opposed to what they perceived as commercial and material values. Feminist and progressive in their role as activists for the public interest, they were nevertheless predominantly conservative in their desire to uphold traditional values and middle-class life styles rooted in these same material interests. These contradictions within the women's conservation movement, however, were in reality manifestations of the similar mixture of progressive and conservative tendencies that characterized the Progressive Era itself.

☙ F U R T H E R   R E A D I N G

Kendrick A. Clements, "Engineers and Conservationists in the Progressive Era," *California History* 58 (1979–1980), 282–303

Henry E. Clepper, *Crusade for Conservation: The Centennial History of the American Forestry Association* (1975)

Samuel Dana and Sally Fairfax, *Forest and Range Policy: Its Development in the U.S.* (1980)

Arthur A. Ekirch, *Man and Nature in America* (1963)

Susan L. Flader, ed., *The Great Lakes Forest: An Environmental and Social History* (1983)

Emanuel Fritz, *The Development of Industrial Forestry in California* (1960)

Michael Frome, *Whose Woods These Are: The Story of the National Forests* (1962)

Samuel P. Hays, *Conservation and the Gospel of Efficiency: The Progressive Conservation Movement, 1890–1920* (1959)

George Michael McCarthy, *Hour of Trial: The Conservation Conflict in Colorado and the West, 1891–1907* (1977)

Roderick Nash, "John Muir, William Kent, and the Conservation Schism," *Pacific Historical Review* 36 (1967), 423–433

———, ed., *The American Environment: Readings in the History of Conservation* (1976)

James Penick, Jr., *Progressive Politics and Conservation* (1968)

John Wesley Powell, *The Exploration of the Colorado River and Its Canyons,* introduction by Wallace Stegner (1987)

Marc Reisner, *Cadillac Desert* (1986)

Elmo R. Richardson, *The Politics of Conservation: Crusades and Controversies, 1897–1913* (1962)

William G. Robbins, *Lumberjacks and Legislators: Political Economy of the U.S. Lumber Industry, 1890–1941* (1982)

Glen O. Robinson, *The Forest Service: A Study in Land Management* (1975)

Theodore Roosevelt, *Wilderness Writings* (1986)

William D. Rowley, *U.S. Forest Service Grazing and Rangelands: A History* (1985)

Harold K. Steen, *The U.S. Forest Service: A History* (1976)

Wallace Stegner, *Beyond the Hundredth Meridian: John Wesley Powell and the Second Opening of the West* (1954)

Donald C. Swain, *Federal Conservation Policy, 1921–1933* (1963)

James A. Tober, *Who Owns the Wildlife: The Political Economy of Conservation in Nineteenth Century America* (1981)

James Whorton, *Before Silent Spring: Pesticides and Public Health in Pre-DDT America* (1974)

Peter Wild, *Pioneer Conservationists of Western America* (1979)

Donald Worster, ed., *American Environmentalism: The Formative Period, 1860–1915* (1973)

William K. Wynant, *Westward in Eden: The Public Lands and the Conservation Movement* (1982)

CHAPTER 11

Wilderness Preservation

at the Turn of the Century

᯽

Burgeoning cities, steep population growth, a flood of immigration, and brisk industrialization changed Americans' perception of wilderness by the turn of the century. As open land and forest receded from easy urban access, wilderness took on a positive value as a source of the rugged pioneer spirit that had built America. As cities became polluted by soot, garbage, and noise, and as their working-class neighborhoods mushroomed, they took on a negative value as urban wildernesses. The inspiration to save wild nature grew out of romantic and Transcendentalist art and literature, middle-class desires to seek solace in the countryside, and male needs to recapture pioneer vigor. The politics of wilderness preservation emerged from the interests of railroad promoters in establishing parks for tourists; of city planners in creating safe, "moral" spaces for both elites and working classes; and of politicians in reclaiming wild areas devoid of human habitation. This chapter looks at the political and class interests at stake in the turn-of-the-century movement to preserve wilderness.

᯽ D O C U M E N T S

Along with his descriptions of the southern United States, landscape architect Frederick Law Olmsted is known for his designs of city parks, among them Central Park in New York City, as well as for his efforts to create state parks and national parks such as Yosemite in California. In the first document, from 1865, Olmsted sets out a rationale for the preservation of natural scenery for human psychological and social benefit, especially for the poor, who otherwise would have no relief from the tensions of the industrial workplace.

Camping excursions, field trips, and tourism ranked high among the many reasons cited for nature preservation in these years. Women were a major force in the preservation movement. Isabella Bird, an Englishwoman who suffered from a spinal illness, found that exercise and travel in remote areas of the world (including parts of Canada, the United States, Hawaii, Japan, India, and Tibet) relieved her symptoms. Her letter describing the Rocky Mountains in the second document derives from an extended trip she took alone on horseback in 1873. Her appreciation of a personified female Nature contrasts with contemporary perceptions of nature as a source of commodities and profits, as revealed in the next document.

The third selection presents the perspective of the lumbering industry on the California redwoods. Writer C. G. Noyes prepared the text for an 1884 series of photographs publicizing the enormous size and commercial potential of the coastal redwood groves. He discussed the projected value of the redwoods in terms of their total board feet and forecast their demise within a few years. Such predictions inspired preservationists to create redwood parks.

Women were prominent among the early nature preservationists. In the fourth document, Florence Merriam Bailey, an Audubon Society activist and one of the country's foremost popular writers on bird life, reveals some techniques that women used to dissuade other women from purchasing hats decorated with the feathers of endangered bird species. Mary Austin, author of the fifth document, was one of the earliest nature writers to depict the western deserts and their Native American inhabitants sympathetically. The vastness, stark beauty, and climatic extremes of the desert humbled humans and dwarfed individual significance.

The differing rationales of utilitarian conservation and aesthetic preservation came to a head through a nationwide controversy over the damming of California's Hetch Hetchy Valley as a water supply for the city of San Francisco. John Muir's arguments, presented in the sixth document, written in 1912, popularized the preservationists' reasons for saving the valley, whereas Gifford Pinchot's utilitarian arguments for water conservation ultimately persuaded Theodore Roosevelt to side with San Francisco. The passage of the 1913 Raker Act authorizing San Francisco to dam Hetch Hetchy temporarily defeated Muir and the preservationists but ultimately led to the passage of the National Parks Act in 1916. This act, excerpted in the seventh document, created the National Park Service within the Department of the Interior to administer the separately created national parks. It represented a notable victory for the preservationists.

In the seventeenth century, William Bradford had described New England as a place full of wild men and wild beasts. By the twentieth century, European Americans had redefined wilderness as a place without Indians. But to Indians, as Chief Luther Standing Bear points out in document eight, the land had never been a wilderness, only a home. Wilderness was an ethnocentric idea—a European creation.

Frederick Law Olmsted on the Value of Parks, 1865

It is a scientific fact that the occasional contemplation of natural scenes of an impressive character, particularly if this contemplation occurs in connection with relief from ordinary cares, change of air and change of habits, is favorable to the health and vigor of men and especially to the health and vigor of their intellect beyond any other conditions which can be offered them, that it not only gives pleasure for the time being but increases the subsequent capacity for happiness and the means of securing happiness. The want of such occasional recreation where men and women are habitually pressed by their business or

From Frederick Law Olmsted, "The Yosemite Valley and the Mariposa Big Trees," *Landscape Architecture*, 43 (1952), pp. 17–21. Reprinted with permission of American Society of Landscape Architects.

household cares often results in a class of disorders the characteristic quality of which is mental disability, sometimes taking the severe forms of softening of the brain, paralysis, palsy, monomania, or insanity, but more frequently of mental and nervous excitability, moroseness, melancholy or irascibility, incapacitating the subject for the proper exercise of the intellectual and moral forces. . . .

If we analyze the operation of scenes of beauty upon the mind, and consider the intimate relation of the mind upon the nervous system and the whole physical economy, the action and reaction which constantly occur between bodily and mental conditions, the reinvigoration which results from such scenes is readily comprehended. Few persons can see such scenery as that of the Yosemite and not be impressed by it in some slight degree. All not alike, all not perhaps consciously, and amongst all who are consciously impressed by it, few can give the least expression to that of which they are conscious. But there can be no doubt that all have this susceptibility, though with some it is much more dull and confused than with others.

* * * *

The enjoyment of the choicest natural scenes in the country and the means of recreation connected with them is . . . a monopoly, in a very peculiar manner, of a very few, very rich people. The great mass of society, including those to whom it would be of the greatest benefit, is excluded from it. In the nature of the case private parks can never be used by the mass of the people in any country nor by any considerable number even of the rich, except by the favor of a few, and in dependence on them.

Thus without means are taken by government to withhold them from the grasp of individuals, all places favorable in scenery to the recreation of the mind and body will be closed against the great body of the people. For the same reason that the water of rivers should be guarded against private appropriation and the use of it for the purpose of navigation and otherwise protected against obstruction, portions of natural scenery may therefore properly be guarded and cared for by government. To simply reserve them from monopoly by individuals, however, it will be obvious, is not all that is necessary. It is necessary that they should be laid open to the use of the body of the people.

Isabella Bird Describes Nature in the Rockies, 1873

Estes Park, Colorado Territory, *October 2*

How time has slipped by I do not know. This is a glorious region, and the air and life are intoxicating. I live mainly out of doors and on horseback, wear my half-threadbare Hawaiian dress, sleep sometimes under the stars on a bed of

From *A Lady's Life in the Rocky Mountains* by Isabella L. Bird. New edition copyright © 1960 by the University of Oklahoma Press.

pine boughs, ride on a Mexican saddle, and hear once more the low music of my Mexican spurs.

. . . "What is Estes Park?" Among the striking peculiarities of these [Rocky] mountains are hundreds of high-lying valleys, large and small, at heights varying from 6,000 to 11,000 feet. The most important are North Park, held by hostile Indians; Middle Park, famous for hot springs and trout; South Park is 10,000 feet high, a great rolling prairie seventy miles long, well grassed and watered, but nearly closed by snow in winter. But parks innumerable are scattered throughout the mountains, most of them unnamed, and others nicknamed by the hunters or trappers who have made them their temporary resorts. They always lie far within the flaming Foot Hills, their exquisite stretches of flowery pastures dotted artistically with clumps of trees sloping lawnlike to bright swift streams full of red-waistcoated trout, or running up in soft glades into the dark forest, above which the snow peaks rise in their infinite majesty. Some are bits of meadow a mile long and very narrow, with a small stream, a beaver dam, and a pond made by beaver industry. Hundreds of these can only be reached by riding in the bed of a stream, or by scrambling up some narrow canyon till it debouches on the fairy-like stretch above. These parks are the feeding grounds of innumerable wild animals, and some, like one three miles off, seem chosen for the process of antler-casting, the grass being covered for at least a square mile with the magnificent branching horns of the elk. . . .

[Estes] The park is most irregularly shaped, and contains hardly any level grass. It is an aggregate of lawns, slopes, and glades, about eighteen miles in length, but never more than two miles in width. The Big Thompson, a bright, rapid trout stream, snow born on Long's Peak a few miles higher, takes all sorts of magical twists, vanishing and reappearing unexpectedly, glancing among lawns, rushing through romantic ravines, everywhere making music through the still, long nights. Here and there the lawns are so smooth, the trees so artistically grouped, a lake makes such an artistic foreground, or a waterfall comes tumbling down with such an apparent feeling for the picturesque, that I am almost angry with Nature for her close imitation of art. But in another hundred yards Nature, glorious, unapproachable, inimitable, is herself again, raising one's thoughts reverently upwards to her Creator and ours. Grandeur and sublimity, not softness, are the features of Estes Park. . . .

The wild flowers are gorgeous and innumerable, though their beauty, which culminates in July and August, was over before I arrived, and the recent snow flurries have finished them. The time between winter and winter is very short, and the flowery growth and blossom of a whole year are compressed into two months. Here are dandelions, buttercups, larkspurs, harebells, violets, roses, blue gentian, columbine, painter's brush, and fifty others, blue and yellow predominating; and though their blossoms are stiffened by the cold every morning, they are starring the grass and drooping over the brook long before noon, making the most of their brief lives in the sunshine. . . . The timber line is at a height of about 11,000 feet, and is singularly well defined. The most attractive tree I have seen is the silver spruce, *Abies Englemanii*, near of kin to what is often called the balsam fir. Its shape and color are both beautiful. My heart warms towards it, and I frequent all the places where I can find it. It looks as if a soft, blue, silver powder had fallen on its deep-green needles, or as if a bluish hoar-frost, which must melt at noon, were resting upon it. Anyhow, one can hardly believe that the beauty is permanent, and survives the summer heat and the winter cold. The universal tree here is the *Pinus ponderosa*, but it never attains any very considerable size, and there is nothing to compare with the red-woods of the Sierra Nevada, far less with the sequoias of California.

. . . Estes Park is thirty miles from Longmount, the nearest settlement, and it can be reached on horseback only by the steep and devious track by which I came, passing through a narrow rift in the top of a precipitous ridge, 9,000 feet high, called the Devil's Gate. Evans takes a lumber wagon with four horses over the mountains, and a Colorado engineer would have no difficulty in making a wagon road. In several of the gulches over which the track hangs there are the remains of wagons which have come to grief in the attempt to emulate Evans's feat, which without evidence, I should have supposed to be impossible. It is an awful road. The only settlers in the park are Griffith Evans, and a married man a mile higher up. "Mountain Jim's" cabin is in the entrance gulch, four miles off, and there is not another cabin for eighteen miles toward the Plains. The park is unsurveyed, and the huge tract of mountainous country beyond is almost altogether unexplored.

A Lumberer's Perspective on the California Redwoods, 1884

Twenty-five or thirty years ago—long before the era of Continental Railways—our Eastern and trans-Atlantic cousins read in letters from our people of California, of its wonderful scenery, climate and productions, with incredulity; they believing, perhaps, that the then wanderers from the old homes and hearthstones to the jumping off place on the American continent had produced a sort of epidemic in the way of boasting of the new Eldorado. . . .

Of all that has been told or written by travellers and correspondents concerning California scenery, its huge growth of beets, melons, squash, pears, and fruits of all descriptions, the least attention has been called to our grand forests of Redwood. This, however, is not much a matter of surprise, as the facilities for a careful inspection of this favorite building material are quite or nearly as primitive as during the early settlement of the State. Especially is this the case in the northern section of the State, where the redwood belt has greater width, and from climatic causes has developed a heavier growth of timber. Not only are the trees in this northern section larger in circumference, but they attain a much greater height, and withal give a product to the millmen that is far superior in quality to that obtained in the southern extremity of the redwood belt. . . .

The California Redwood Company (the largest in this line on the coast) has already taken the initiative step looking to a supply of clear seasoned lumber for the Eastern market. At Tormey Station just below Port Costa, and convenient for shipping both by rail and sea to all parts of the world, they have built wharves and opened a yard covering some twenty acres, where their lumber can be seasoned properly before being offered to the markets abroad. . . . Once let builders at the East be thoroughly convinced, as we are, that redwood is superior for interior finish, and our local market will seldom become glutted with an over-product.

Many will argue — and justly, too — that it would be better for the country that a demand which causes such a draft upon its lumber resources should, by some manner of means, be restricted, and that if high rates of freight will prevent the rapid denudation of our forests, they had better be maintained by the railroad corporations. Others can argue, however, that owners of timber lands can assist in reproduction by a slight effort in the way of timber culture, and thereby extend the supply to an indefinite period. . . . We have often thought that should the Government offer as great inducements in the reproduction of redwoods as it is doing to encourage timber culture in parts where it is unnatural for forests to thrive, that the redwoods would never become exterminated, as has so frequently been predicted. One must confess, however, that the matter of cultivating this tree with a view to growing timber like anything of its present size, would require a people possessing a higher regard for generations a hundred or more years hence than the mind of an average American can comprehend.

The Government map . . . shows that the really valuable portion of the belt (from Russian River to the northern limit) covers about two hundred and seventy miles from north to south. . . . The Government estimate (board measure) of timber standing in this belt in the census year 1880 was 25,825,000,000 feet. This was made up from estimates furnished by a few lumbermen, whose opportunities for making a fair estimate cannot be questioned. But it is also true that many others, including millmen and lumbermen, estimate from 50 to 100 per cent higher; and taking the estimated area of the belt from Russian River to the Oregon line with the estimate of timber standing, we shall find even their figures largely increased. The 275 miles covered by this portion of the belt multiplied by the least estimated width (15 miles) gives 4125 miles. A square mile contains 640 acres, and the average yield per acre (according to government estimate) is 50,000 feet, which would give 32,000,000 feet to the square mile. This would give us a total for the 4125 square miles 132,000,000,000 feet of standing timber. . . .

Economy in the manufacture of redwood lumber is a matter in which the pioneer millmen of the Pacific Coast have taken but little interest until within the past three or four years. This could hardly be expected to have been otherwise, for the reason that the supply seemed to them unlimited and inexhaustible. The interest manifested by foreign investors and eastern capitalists in the timber reserves of America, however, has of late checked the inclination to waste which our old lumbermen inconsiderately indulged in for years. This check upon waste is commendable, more especially in the redwoods, because of its adaptability for building purposes, where white pine and the softer woods of the eastern forests are considered indispensable. And that the redwood is largely to fill the demand which has caused the almost entire destruction of the pineries of Maine, Michigan, Wisconsin, and Canada, there is not the least doubt among observant lumbermen of the eastern States. As corroboration of this statement, we may here refer to the large number of agents sent into the counties of Humboldt and Mendocino during the past two years by eastern capitalists, as well as from England and Scotland, to purchase tracts of redwood timber ranging from three thousand to ten thousand acres. . . .

Almost the first thought passing in one's mind, as he enters a virgin forest of redwoods, is one of pity that such a wonderful creation of nature should be subject to the greed of man for gold. The same feelings of awe pervade one's being upon his first introduction to this apparently exhaustless army of giants, that impress the beholder of Niagara, Yosemite, and the near relatives of the redwoods — the Big Trees of Calaveras and Merced. . . .

When transportation facilities are complete, either by rail or by water, . . . as they certainly will be within a few years, it needs no prophet to predict that the California Redwood will, in the near future, have no rival in the lumber marts of the world.

Within a generation to come the question will be asked: "How long will the Redwoods last? A few years at most. But in that brief time men will build their castles and their thrones of power upon the mighty race of giants, with the one regret that there are no more to conquer."

Florence Merriam Bailey on the Early Audubon Women, 1900

As far back as 1886, when the Audubon movement was just beginning, the Smith College girls took to 'birding.' Before the birding began, however, behind the scenes, the two amateur ornithologists of the student body had laid deep, wily schemes. "Go to," said they; "we will start an Audubon Society. The birds must be protected; we must persuade the girls not to wear feathers on their hats." "We won't say too much about hats, though," these plotters went on. "We'll take the girls afield, and let them get acquainted with the birds. Then, of inborn necessity, they will wear feathers never more." So these guileful persons, having formally organized a Smith College Audubon Society for the Protection of Birds, put on their sunhats and called, "Come on, girls!" This they did with glee in their hearts, for it irked them to proclaim, "Behold, see, meditate upon this monster evil," while it gave them joy to say, "Come out under the sun-filled heavens and open your soul to the song of the Lark."

This, then, was the inspiration of the bird work that started up and spread so surprisingly, and was carried on with such eager enthusiasm in those early days at Smith. And this must be the inspiration of all successful field work, wherever it is done. A list of species is good to have, but without a knowledge of the birds themselves, it is like Emerson's Sparrow brought home without the river and sky. The true naturalist, like Audubon, will ever go to nature with open heart as well as mind.

Feeling this, the organizers of the Smith work persuaded John Burroughs to come to give it an impetus. When he took the girls to the woods at five o'clock in the morning, so many went that the bird had often flown before the rear guard arrived, but the fine enthusiasm of the man's spirit could not be missed.

No one could come in touch with it without realizing that there was something in nature unguessed before, and worth attending to. And when the philosopher stood calmly beside a stump in the rain, naming unerringly each bird that crossed the sky, the lesson in observation, impressive as it was, was not merely one in keenness of vision. His attitude of stillness under the heavens made each one feel that 'by lowly listening' she too might hear the right word — the message nature holds for each human heart.

Mary Austin on the Wonders of the Desert, 1903

East away from the Sierra, south from Panamint and Amargosa, east and south many an uncounted mile, is the Country of Lost Borders.

Ute, Paiute, Mojave, and Shoshone inhabit its frontiers, and as far into the heart of it as man dare go. Not the law, but the land sets the limit. Desert is the name it wears upon the maps, but the Indian's is the better word. Desert is a loose term to indicate land that supports no man; whether the land can be bitted and broken to that purpose is not proven. Void of life it never is, however dry the air and villainous the soil.

This is the nature of that country. There are hills, rounded, blunt, burned, squeezed up out of chaos, chrome and vermilion painted, aspiring to the snow-line. Between the hills lie high level-looking plains full of intolerable sun glare, or narrow valleys drowned in blue haze. . . .

The sculpture of the hills here is more wind than water work, though the quick storms do sometimes scar them past many a year's redeeming. In all the Western desert edges there are essays in miniature at the famed, terrible Grand Canyon, to which, if you keep on long enough in this country, you will come at last.

Since this is a hill country one expects to find springs, but not to depend upon them; for when found they are often brackish and unwholesome, or maddening, slow dribbles in a thirsty soil. Here you find the hot sink of Death Valley, or high rolling districts where the air has always a tang of frost. Here are the long heavy winds and breathless calms on the tilted mesas where dust devils dance, whirling up into a wide, pale sky. Here you have no rain when all the earth cries for it, or quick downpours called cloudbursts for violence. A land of lost rivers, with little in it to love; yet a land that once visited must be come back to inevitably. If it were not so there would be little told of it.

This is the country of three seasons. From June on to November it lies hot, still, and unbearable, sick with violent unrelieving storms; then on until April, chill, quiescent, drinking its scant rain and scanter snows; from April to the hot season again, blossoming, radiant, and seductive. These months are only approximate; later or earlier the rain-laden wind may drift up the water gate of the Colorado from the Gulf, and the land sets its seasons by the rain. . . .

If you have any doubt about it, know that the desert begins with the creosote. This immortal shrub spreads down into Death Valley and up to the lower timber-line, odorous and medicinal as you might guess from the name, wandlike, with shining fretted foliage. . . .

Nothing the desert produces expresses it better than the unhappy growth of the tree yuccas. Tormented, thin forests of it stalk drearily in the high mesas, particularly in that triangular slip that fans out eastward from the meeting of the Sierras and coastwise hills where the first swings across the southern end of the San Joaquin Valley. The yucca bristles with bayonet-pointed leaves, dull green, growing shaggy with age, tipped with panicles of fetid, greenish bloom. . . .

Above the lower tree-line, which is also the snow-line, mapped out abruptly by the sun, one finds spreading growth of piñon, juniper, branched nearly to the ground, lilac and sage, and scattering white pines. . . .

Go as far as you dare in the heart of a lonely land, you cannot go so far that life and death are not before you. Painted lizards slip in and out of rock crevices, and pant on the white hot sands. Birds, hummingbirds even, nest in the cactus scrub; woodpeckers befriend the demoniac yuccas; out of the stark, treeless waste rings the music of the night-singing mockingbird. If it be summer and the sun well down, there will be a burrowing owl to call. . . .

If one is inclined to wonder at first how so many dwellers came to be in the loneliest land that ever came out of God's hands, what they do there and why stay, one does not wonder so much after having lived there. None other than this long brown land lays such a hold on the affections. The rainbow hills, the tender bluish mists, the luminous radiance of the spring, have the lotus charm. They trick the sense of time, so that once inhabiting there you always mean to go away without quite realizing that you have not done it. Men who have lived there, miners and cattle-men, will tell you this, not so fluently, but emphatically, cursing the land and going back to it. For one thing there is the divinest, cleanest air to be breathed anywhere in God's world. Some day the world will understand that, and the little oases on the windy tops of hills will harbor for healing its ailing, house-weary broods. . . .

For all the toll the desert takes of a man it gives compensations, deep breaths, deep sleep, and the communion of the stars. It comes upon one with new force in the pauses of the night that the Chaldeans were a desert-bred people. It is hard to escape the sense of mastery as the stars move in the wide clear heavens to risings and settings unobscured. They look large and near and palpitant; as if they moved on some stately service not needful to declare. Wheeling to their stations in the sky, they make the poor world-fret of no account. Of no account you who lie out there watching, nor the lean coyote that stands off in the scrub from you and howls and howls.

John Muir Advocates Wilderness Preservation, 1912

Yosemite is so wonderful that we are apt to regard it as an exceptional creation, the only valley of its kind in the world; but Nature is not so poor as to have only one of anything. Several other yosemites have been discovered in the Sierra that occupy the same relative positions on the Range and were formed by the same forces in the same kind of granite. One of these, the Hetch Hetchy Valley, is in the Yosemite National Park about twenty miles from Yosemite and is easily accessible to all sorts of travelers by a road and trail that leaves the Big Oak Flat road at Bronson Meadows a few miles below Crane Flat, and to mountaineers by way of Yosemite Creek basin and the head of the middle fork of the Tuolumne.

It is said to have been discovered by Joseph Screech, a hunter, in 1850, a year before the discovery of the great Yosemite. After my first visit to it in the autumn of 1871, I have always called it the "Tuolumne Yosemite," for it is a wonderfully exact counterpart of the Merced Yosemite, not only in its sublime rocks and waterfalls but in the gardens, groves and meadows of its flowery park-like floor. The floor of Yosemite is about 4000 feet above the sea; the Hetch Hetchy floor about 3700 feet. And as the Merced River flows through Yosemite, so does the Tuolumne through Hetch Hetchy. The walls of both are of gray granite, rise abruptly from the floor, are sculptured in the same style and in both every rock is a glacier monument.

Standing boldly out from the south wall is a strikingly picturesque rock called by the Indians, Kolana, the outermost of a group 2300 feet high, corresponding with the Cathedral rocks of Yosemite both in relative position and form. On the opposite side of the Valley, facing Kolana, there is a counterpart of the El Capitan that rises sheer and plain to a height of 1800 feet, and over its massive brow flows a stream which makes the most graceful fall I have ever seen. From the edge of the cliff to the top of an earthquake talus it is perfectly free in the air for a thousand feet before it is broken into cascades among talus boulders. It is in all its glory in June, when the snow is melting fast, but fades and vanishes toward the end of summer. The only fall I know with which it may fairly be compared is the Yosemite Bridal Veil; but it excels even that favorite fall both in height and airy-fairy beauty and behavior. . . .

Hetch Hetchy Valley, far from being a plain, common, rock-bound meadow, as many who have not seen it seem to suppose, is a grand landscape garden, one of Nature's rarest and most precious mountain temples. As in Yosemite, the sublime rocks of its walls seem to glow with life, whether leaning back in repose or standing erect in thoughtful attitudes, giving welcome to storms and calms alike, their brows in the sky, their feet set in the groves and gay flowery meadows, while birds, bees, and butterflies help the river and waterfalls to stir all the air into music — things frail and fleeting and types of permanence meeting here and blending, just as they do in Yosemite, to draw her lovers into close and confiding communion with her.

Sad to say, this most precious and sublime feature of the Yosemite National Park, one of the greatest of all our natural resources for the uplifting joy and peace and health of the people, is in danger of being dammed and made into a reservoir to help supply San Francisco with water and light, thus flooding it from wall to wall and burying its gardens and groves one or two hundred feet deep. This grossly destructive commercial scheme has long been planned and urged (though water as pure and abundant can be got from sources outside of the people's park, in a dozen different places), because of the comparative cheapness of the dam and of the territory which it is sought to divert from the great uses to which it was dedicated in the Act of 1890 establishing the Yosemite National Park. . . .

The first application to the Government by the San Francisco Supervisors for the commercial use of Lake Eleanor and the Hetch Hetchy Valley was made in 1903, and on December 22nd of that year it was denied by the Secretary of the Interior, Mr. [Ethan] Hitchcock, who truthfully said:

> Presumably the Yosemite National Park was created such by law because of the natural objects of varying degrees of scenic importance located within its boundaries, inclusive alike of its beautiful small lakes, like Eleanor, and its majestic wonders, like Hetch Hetchy and Yosemite Valley. It is the aggregation of such natural scenic features that makes the Yosemite Park a wonderland which the Congress of the United States sought by law to reserve for all coming time as nearly as practicable in the condition fashioned by the hand of the Creator — a worthy object of National pride and a source of healthful pleasure and rest for the thousands of people who may annually sojourn there during the heated months. . . .

In 1907 when Mr. [James] Garfield became Secretary of the Interior the application was renewed and granted; but under his successor, Mr. [Walter] Fisher, the matter has been referred to a Commission, which as this volume goes to press still has it under consideration.

That any one would try to destroy such a place seems incredible; but sad experience shows that there are people good enough and bad enough for anything. The proponents of the dam scheme bring forward a lot of bad arguments to prove that the only righteous thing to do with the people's parks is to destroy them bit by bit as they are able. Their arguments are curiously like those of the devil, devised for the destruction of the first garden — so much of the very best Eden fruit going to waste; so much of the best Tuolumne water and Tuolumne scenery going to waste. Few of their statements are even partly true, and all are misleading.

Thus, Hetch Hetchy, they say, is a "low-lying meadow." On the contrary, it is a high-lying natural landscape garden. . . .

"It is a common minor feature, like thousands of others." On the contrary it is a very uncommon feature; after Yosemite, the rarest and in many ways the most important in the National Park.

"Damming and submerging it 175 feet deep would enhance its beauty by forming a crystal-clear lake." Landscape gardens, places of recreation and worship, are never made beautiful by destroying and burying them. The beautiful sham lake, forsooth, would be only an eyesore, a dismal blot on the landscape, like many others to be seen in the Sierra. For, instead of keeping it at the same level all the year, allowing Nature centuries of time to make new shores, it would, of course, be full only a month or two in the spring, when the snow is melting fast; then it would be gradually drained, exposing the slimy sides of the basin and shallower parts of the bottom, with the gathered drift and waste, death and decay of the upper basins, caught here instead of being swept on to decent natural burial along the banks of the river or in the sea. Thus the

Hetch Hetchy dam-lake would be only a rough imitation of a natural lake for a few of the spring months, an open sepulcher for the others.

"Hetch Hetchy water is the purest of all to be found in the Sierra, unpolluted, and forever unpollutable." On the contrary, excepting that of the Merced below Yosemite, it is less pure than that of most of the other Sierra streams, because of the sewerage of camp grounds draining into it, especially of the Big Tuolumne Meadows camp ground, occupied by hundreds of tourists and mountaineers, with their animals, for months every summer, soon to be followed by thousands from all over the world.

These temple destroyers, devotees of ravaging commercialism, seem to have a perfect contempt for Nature, and, instead of lifting their eyes to the God of the mountains, lift them to the Almighty Dollar.

Dam Hetch Hetchy! As well dam for water-tanks the people's cathedrals and churches, for no holier temple has ever been consecrated by the heart of man.

The National Parks Act, 1916

August 25, 1916. [H. R. 15522.]

An Act To establish a National Park Service

Be it enacted by the Senate and House of Representatives of the United States of America in Congress assembled, That there is hereby created in the Department of the Interior a service to be called the National Park Service, which shall be under the charge of a director, who shall be appointed by the Secretary. . . . The service thus established shall promote and regulate the use of the Federal areas known as national parks, monuments, and reservations hereinafter specified by such means and measures as conform to the fundamental purpose of the said parks, monuments, and reservations, which purpose is to conserve the scenery and the natural and historic objects and the wild life therein and to provide for the enjoyment of the same in such manner and by such means as will leave them unimpaired for the enjoyment of future generations. . . .

SEC. 3. That the Secretary of the Interior shall make and publish such rules and regulations as he may deem necessary or proper for the use and management of the parks, monuments, and reservations under the jurisdiction of the National Park Service. . . . He may also, upon terms and conditions to be fixed by him, sell or dispose of timber in those cases where in his judgment the cutting of such timber is required in order to control the attacks of insects or diseases or otherwise conserve the scenery or the natural or historic objects in any such park, monument, or reservation. He may also provide in his discretion for the destruction of such animals and of such plant life as may be detrimental to the use of any of said parks, monuments, or reservations. He may also grant privileges, leases, and permits for the use of land for the accommodation of visitors in the various parks, monuments, or other reservations herein provided for, but for periods not exceeding twenty years; and no natural curiosities, wonders, or objects of interest shall be leased, rented, or granted to anyone on such terms as to interfere with free access to them by the public: *Provided, however*, That the Secretary of the Interior may, under such rules and regulations and on such terms as he may prescribe, grant the privilege to graze live stock within any national park, monument, or reservation herein referred to when in his judgment such use is not detrimental to the primary purpose for which such park, monument, or reservation was created, except that this provision shall not apply to the Yellowstone National Park.

Chief Luther Standing Bear Gives an Indian View of Wilderness, Recorded in 1933

"We did not think of the great open plains, the beautiful rolling hills, and winding streams with tangled growth, as 'wild.' Only to the white man was nature a 'wilderness' and only to him was the land 'infested' with 'wild' animals and 'savage' people. To us it was tame. Earth was bountiful and we were surrounded with the blessings of the Great Mystery. Not until the hairy man from the east came and with brutal frenzy heaped injustices upon us and the families we loved was it 'wild' for us. When the very animals of the forest began fleeing from his approach, then it was that for us the 'Wild West' began."

❦ *E S S A Y S*

The essays examine wilderness values from a range of perspectives. In the first selection, Roderick Nash, an environmental historian, argues that wilderness preservation emerged primarily from the concerns of eastern urbanites, and he delineates eight reasons why wilderness should be saved. Alfred Runte, an environmental historian at the Institute for Pacific Northwest Studies, instead suggests in the second essay that the railroads' interests in promoting tourism underlay the movement to establish national parks. The third essay, by environmental ethicist J. Baird Callicott of the University of Wisconsin, Stevens Point, criticizes the idea of wilderness as a Western, European, elite construct alien to Native Americans and rooted in false modern assumptions of the timeless stability of ecosystems and the separation of people from nature. This chapter explores the history of the movement to appreciate and save natural areas and asks whose interests are at stake when nonhuman nature is defined and preserved as wilderness.

The Value of Wilderness

RODERICK NASH

Historians believe that one of the most distinguishing characteristics of American culture is the fact that it emerged from a wilderness in less than four

---

From Roderick Nash, "The Value of Wilderness," *Environmental Review*, 3 (1977), pp. 14–25. Reprinted with permission from *Environmental History Review*, © 1977, the American Society for Environmental History.

centuries. The Europeans who migrated to North America in the seventeenth century settled in a wilderness. The so-called Indians, who had occupied the region for some 20,000 years, were unfortunately regarded as wild animals. The pioneers, as they were called, were principally concerned with transforming wilderness into civilization. They were the vanguard of a westward-moving empire, and they referred to the continually moving line at which their civilization abutted the wilderness as the "frontier." Clearly this term signifies in the United States something quite different from in Europe, where a "frontier" is taken to be the boundary between nations. The American frontier was the boundary between the wild and the civilized. It existed in the United States as recently as 1890. In that year the federal census published a report showing that settlement of the continent had proceeded to such an extent that the term frontier no longer had meaning. Significantly, 1890 was also the year of the last major war of Indian resistance in the American West. The white man's control of the continent and its aboriginal occupants was complete.

The early American attitude toward wilderness was highly unfavorable. Wild country was the enemy. The pioneer saw as his mission the destruction of wilderness. Protecting it for its scenic and recreational values was the last thing frontiersmen desired. The problem was too much raw nature rather than too little. Wild land had to be battled as a physical obstacle to comfort and even to survival. The country had to be "cleared" of trees; Indians had to be "removed;" wild animals had to be exterminated. National pride arose from transforming wilderness into civilization, not preserving it for public enjoyment. But by 1872, the year of the creation of Yellowstone National Park, the world's first, the attitude of some Americans toward undeveloped land had sufficiently shifted to permit the beginnings of appreciation. So Yellowstone National Park was designated on March 1, 1872 as "a public park or pleasuring ground" in which all the features of this 3,000 square-mile wilderness in northwestern Wyoming would be left "in their natural condition." . . .

The appreciation of wilderness . . . appeared first in the minds of sophisticated Americans living in the more civilized East. George Catlin, American painter of Indians and landscapes, and the father in 1832 of the idea of a national park, made the point clearly and succinctly. "The further we become separated from pristine wildness and beauty, the more pleasure does the mind of enlightened man feel in recurring to those scenes." Catlin was himself an example. He lived in Philadelphia, an Eastern city in one of the original thirteen states, Pennsylvania. Catlin was civilized enough to appreciate wilderness. Living in a city, he did not have to battle wild country on a day-to-day basis like a pioneer. For him it was a novelty and a place for a vacation. Indeed Catlin looked forward each summer in the 1830's to escaping from his Eastern artist's studio to the wilderness along the upper Missouri River.

All the nineteenth-century champions of wilderness appreciation and national parks in the United States were products of either urban Eastern situations or of one of the West's most sophisticated cities, such as San Francisco. Lumbermen, miners, and professional hunters did not, as a rule, advocate

scenic and recreational conservation. They lived too close to nature to appreciate it for other than its economic value as raw material. Let one additional
example suffice to make the point. Henry David Thoreau, American nature
philosopher, went to Harvard University and lived near Boston in the highly
civilized Eastern seaboard state of Massachusetts. Thoreau believed that a
certain amount of wildness (which he regarded as synonymous with freedom,
vigor, and creativity) was essential to the success of a society as well as an
individual. Neither a person nor a culture should, in Thoreau's opinion, become totally civilized. For this reason Thoreau advocated national parks as
reservoirs of physical and intellectual nourishment. "Why should not
we . . . have our national preserves," he wondered in 1858, ". . . not for idle
sport or food, but for inspiration and our own true recreation?" Of course
Thoreau approved of the idea of large national parks in the West, although he
did not live to see the concept realized, but he also advocated reserving wild
places in settled areas. Every Massachusetts town or village, he argued in 1859,
"should have a park, or rather a primitive forest, of five hundred or a thousand
acres." The public would own such places, according to Thoreau's plan, and
they would be guarded against economic exploitation of any kind. With natural
landscapes disappearing rapidly from the environment of the eastern portions of
the United States, arguments like those of Thoreau made increasing sense. The
special American relationship to wilderness — having it, being shaped by it, and
then almost eliminating it — was working to create the most persuasive case for
Yellowstone and the other national parks that followed. . . .

The first legal preservation for public use of an area with scenic and
recreational values occurred in 1864 when the federal government granted the
Yosemite Valley to the state of California "for public use, resort and recreation." Technically, the Yosemite grant of 1864 was not the first federal act. In
1832 some hot springs in the state of Arkansas were set aside as a national
reservation. The area was tiny, however, heavily developed, hardly scenic, and
very much in the tradition of public spas and baths common, for example, in
Europe. Carved by glaciers and the Merced River into the western slope of a
mountain range in California called the Sierra, Yosemite ranks among the
world's most spectacular scenic wonders. It was discovered by white men less
than two decades before the act of 1864. The area reserved was only the valley
floor, about ten square miles. The larger national park that also bears the name
"Yosemite" did not exist until 1891.

The landscape architect Frederick Law Olmsted proved most perceptive in
understanding the principles which justified the 1864 reservation of Yosemite
Valley as a state park. Olmsted's 1865 report also illustrates how social ownership of scenic and recreational resources could be enthusiastically supported in
a nation that, especially in the late nineteenth century, valued private property
and a minimum of government interference with the development of natural
resources by an unrestrained capitalist economy. Olmsted began by observing
that exceptional natural environments, such as Yosemite Valley, should not
become private property. He explained that it was the duty of a democratic
government "to provide means of protection for all its citizens in the pursuit of

happiness against the obstacles . . . which the selfishness of individuals or combinations of individuals is liable to interpose to that pursuit." Until the 1860's, few political philosophers had understood this protective function of government to extend beyond economic, military, and educational consideration to those involving the enjoyment of nature. Nowhere in the documents and commentary associated with the establishment of the United States in 1776 and 1787 did the concept of "pursuit of happiness" appear to include the provision by the government of opportunities to enjoy natural scenery and outdoor recreation. Olmsted, however, argued that this was a justifiable extension of the central principle of the democratic-republican theory on which the nation stood. . . .

Besides a favorable attitude toward undeveloped nature and a democratic political tradition, the final factor explaining the American invention of national parks was simply affluence. The wealth of the United States subsidized national parks. We were and have remained rich enough to afford the luxury of setting aside some land for its non-material values. Had the United States been struggling at the subsistence level, scenic and recreational conservation would have, at the least, demanded a much harder decision. Probably they would not have occurred at all. Ironically, American success in exploiting the environment increased the likelihood of its protection. The axiom seems to hold that nature protection is a full-stomach phenomenon.

Since the time of Catlin, Thoreau, and Olmsted, American thinkers have substantially expanded the justification for scenic and recreational conservation. They have been aided considerably by changing circumstances. To a far greater extent than in 1864 and 1872, when the Yosemite and Yellowstone reservations were made, the United States is urbanized and industrialized. About 75 per cent of the population lives in cities. The amount of wilderness (both protected and unprotected and not counting the state of Alaska) is, by generous reckoning, about 180,000 square miles out of three million, or 6 per cent of the forty-eight contiguous states. Close to the same amount of land is *paved!*

In this context, so new to Americans who once believed the wilderness beyond the frontier to be endless, several arguments have emerged to become the staples in the contemporary defense of nature protection in the United States. While they are presented here in terms of wilderness, such as exists in the larger national parks like Yellowstone and Yosemite, they may be applied in slightly altered form to any open space or nature reserve. They might also be applied, with appropriate alteration, to Italy or any other nation. The summary that follows is in outline form.

Argument 1: Wilderness as a Reservoir of Normal Ecological Processes

Aldo Leopold, wildlife manager and philosopher whose efforts led in 1924 to creation of the first reserved wilderness on National Forest land in the United States, once said that wilderness reveals "what the land was, what it is, and what it ought to be." He added that nature reserves conceivably had more importance for science than they did for recreation. What Leopold meant was that wilderness is a model of healthy, ecologically balanced land. At a time when so much of the environment is disturbed by technological man, wilderness has vital importance as a criterion against which to measure the impact of civilization. Without it we have no way of knowing how the land mechanism functions under normal conditions. The science of ecology needs nature reserves as medical science needs healthy people.

Argument 2: Wilderness as a Sustainer of Biological Diversity

It is axiomatic in the biological sciences that there is strength in diversity. The whole evolutionary miracle is based on the presence over time of an almost infinite diversity of life forms. Maintenance of the full evolutionary capacity that produced life as we know it and, we may suppose, will continue to shape life on earth, means that the size of the gene pool should be maximized. But with his agriculture and urban growth, modern man has made extensive inroads on biological diversity. Some of the changes, to be sure, have been desirable. But many are carried too far. More species have been exterminated in the last three hundred years than in the previous three million. Many other species, including some of the most awesome life forms on earth, are threatened. The whales fall into this category. The problem is that man in his shortsighted pursuit of what he believes to be his self-interest has branded some forms of life as "useless" and therefore expendable. The creative processes that produced these life forms in the first place did not regard them as such. Modern man frequently appears to be a clumsy mechanic, pounding on a delicate and complex machine with a sledgehammer. . . .

Argument 3: Wilderness as Formative Influence on American National Character

It was not until the census report of 1890 pronounced the frontier era ended that many Americans began to ponder the significance of wilderness in shaping them as individuals and as a society. The link between American character or identity, and wilderness, was forged, as historian Frederick Jackson Turner argued so persuasively in 1893, during three centuries of pioneering. Independence and individualism were two heritages; a democratic social and political theory and the concept of equal opportunity were other frontier traits. So was the penchant for practical achievement that marks the American character so distinctly.

If wilderness shaped our national values and institutions, it follows that one of the most important roles of nature reserves is keeping those values and institutions alive. Theodore Roosevelt, President of the United States from 1901 to 1909 and the leader of the first period of great achievement in conservation, was keenly aware of this relationship. "Under the hard conditions of life in the wilderness," Roosevelt wrote, those who migrated to the New World "lost all remembrance of Europe" and became new men "in dress, in customs, and in mode of life." But the United States by 1900 was becoming increasingly like the more civilized and longer settled parts of the world. Consequently Roosevelt declared that "as our civilization grows older and more complex, we need a greater and not a less development of the fundamental frontier virtues." The Boy Scouts of America was just one of the responses of Roosevelt's contemporaries to the problem he described. Without wilderness areas in which successive generations can relearn the values of their pioneer ancestors, the American culture will surely change. Perhaps it should, but many remain concerned about cutting off the roots of their national character. And merely from the standpoint of safeguarding an historical document, a part of the national past, we should save wilderness. Once all America was wild; without remnants to refresh our memories we run the risk of cultural amnesia.

Argument 4: Wilderness as Nourisher of American Arts and Letters

Time and again in the course of history the native land has been the inspiration for great works of music, painting, and literature. What the American painter, Alan Gussow, calls "a sense of place" is as vital to the artistic endeavor as it is to patriotism and national pride. And "place," it should be clear, has to do with the natural setting. Subdivisions, factories, and used car lots rarely inspire artistic excellence. Nature commonly does. Parks and reserves, as reservoirs of scenic beauty that touches the soul of man, have a crucial role in the quality of a nation's culture.

Certainly the United States would have a poorer artistic heritage without the existence of wild places of inspiring beauty. James Fenimore Cooper in literature, Thomas Cole and Albert Bierstadt in painting, and, to take a recent example, John Denver in music, have based their art on wilderness. In the case of the United States, wilderness had a special relationship to culture. It was the one attribute the young nation had in abundance, the characteristic that set it apart from Old World countries. Ralph Waldo Emerson and Henry David Thoreau were among the many who, by the mid-nineteenth century, called on America to attain cultural self-reliance by basing its art on the native landscape. Nature, for these philosophers, was intellectual fertilizer. Blended in the proper proportion with civilization, it produced cultural greatness. Thoreau was fond of pointing out that the grandeur that was Rome at its zenith had its beginnings in the rearing of Romulus and Remus by that symbol of the wild, a wolf. When these wild roots became buried beneath too much civilization, Rome declined and fell. The conquerers, significantly, were wilder people — barbarians from the forests and the steppes. . . .

Cole's [1836 five panel painting, "The] Course of Empire" contained a clear lesson for the United States. If it was to avoid the cyclical pattern of rise and fall, the inspiring qualities of nature had best be made a permanent part of the American environment. The point was to avoid becoming *over* civilized and decadent. One means to that end, Cole advised his countrymen, was to preserve parts of the American wilderness while civilization grew up around them. Cultural greatness, indeed cultural survival, depended on this blending of environments.

Argument 5: Wilderness as a Church

With the aid of churches and religions, people attempt to find solutions to, or at least live with, the weightiest mental and emotional problems of human existence. One value of wilderness for some people is its significance as a setting for what is, essentially, religious activity. In nature, as in a church, they attempt to bring meaning and tranquility to their lives. They seek a sense of oneness, of harmony, with all things. Wilderness appeals as a place to knot together the unity that civilization tends to fragment. Contact with the natural world shows man his place in systems that transcend civilization and inculcates reverence for those systems. The result is peace.

The Transcendental philosophers, Ralph Waldo Emerson and Henry David Thoreau, were among the first Americans to emphasize the religious importance of nature. Moral and aesthetic truths seemed to them to be more easily observed in wild places than in regions where civilization interposed a layer of artificiality between man and nature. John Muir, a leading force in the preservation of Yosemite National Park and first president of the Sierra Club, also believed that to be closer to nature was to be closer to God. The wild Sierra that he explored and lived in was simply a "window opening into heaven, a mirror reflecting the Creator." Leaves, rocks, and lakes were "sparks of the Divine Soul." Muir spent little time in a building called a church, but his enjoyment of wilderness was religious in every sense of the word.

Argument 6: Wilderness as a Guardian of Mental Health

Sigurd Olson, veteran guide and interpreter of the canoe country extending northward from Lake Superior, noted in 1946 that "civilization has not changed emotional needs that were ours long before it arose." Sigmund Freud had the same idea when he said that civilization bred "discontents" in the form of repressions and frustrations. One of the most distressing for modern man is the bewildering complexity of events and ideas with which civilization obliges him to deal. The price of failing to cope with the new "wilderness" of people and paper is psychological problems. The value of wilderness and outdoor recreation is the opportunity it extends to civilized man to slip back, occasionally, into what Olson calls "the grooves of ancestral experience." The leading advocate of wilderness protection in the 1930's, Robert Marshall, spoke of the "psychological necessity" for occasional escape to "the freedom of the wilderness."

Olson and Marshall were referring to the fact that wild country offers people an alternative to civilization. The wilderness is different. For one thing, it simplifies. It reduces the life of those who enter it to finding basic human needs and satisfactions, such as unmechanized transportation, water, food, and shelter. Civilization does not commonly permit us this kind of self-sufficiency and its dividend, self-confidence. A hike of ten miles has more meaning in this respect than a flight of ten thousand. Wilderness also reacquaints civilized people with pain and fear. Surprising to some, these are ancient energizing forces — springboards to achievement long before monetary success and status were even conceived. The gut-level fears associated with survival drove the wheels of evolution. At times, of course, they hurt and even killed, but we pay a price in achievement for entering the promised land of safety and comfort. For many it is horribly dull. They turn to crime or drugs or war to fill their needs for risk and challenge. Others find beds in mental institutions the only recourse. Wilderness recreation is a better alternative.

Argument 7: Wilderness as a Sustainer of Human Diversity

Just as it promotes biological diversity (see Argument 2), the preservation of wilderness helps to preserve human dignity and social diversity. Civilization means control, organization, homogenization. Wilderness offers relief from these dehumanizing tendencies; it encourages individuality. Wild country is an arena where man can experiment, deviate, discover, and improve. Was not this the whole meaning of the New World wilderness for those settlers who migrated to it from Europe? Wilderness meant freedom. Aldo Leopold put it this way: "of what avail are forty freedoms without a blank spot on the map?" For novelist Wallace Stegner wild country was "a place of perpetual beginnings." . . .

There is another sense in which wilderness preservation joins hands with the perpetuation of human diversity. The very existence of wilderness is evidence of respect for minority rights. Only a fraction, although a rapidly growing one, of the American people seek scenic beauty and wilderness recreation. Only a fraction care about horse racing or opera or libraries. The fact that these things can exist is a tribute to nations that cherish and defend minority interests as part of their political ideology. Robert Marshall of the United States Forest Service made it plain in the 1930's that protection of minority rights is one of the hallmarks of a successful democracy. The majority may rule, said Marshall, but that does not mean it can impose its values universally. Otherwise art galleries (a minority interest) would be converted into hamburger stands and amusement parks. The need was for a fair division — of land, for instance — to accommodate a variety of tastes and values.

Argument 8: Wilderness as an Educational Asset in Developing Environmental Responsibility

To experience wilderness is to discover natural processes and man's dependency upon them. It is to discover man's vulnerability and, through this realization, to attain humility. Life in civilization tends to promote antipodal qualities: arrogance and a sense of mastery. Not only children believe that milk comes from bottles and heat from radiators. "Civilization," Aldo Leopold wrote, "has so cluttered [the] elemental man-earth relation with gadgets and middlemen that awareness of it is growing dim. We fancy that industry supports us, forgetting what supports industry." Contact with wilderness is a corrective that modern man desperately needs if he is to achieve long-term harmony between himself and his environment.

Wilderness can also instruct man that he is a member, not the master, of a community that extends to the limits of life and the earth itself. Because wild country is beyond man's control, because it exists apart from human needs and interests, it suggests that man's welfare is not the primary reason for or purpose of the existence of the earth. This seemingly simple truth is not easily understood in a technological civilization whose basis is control and exploitation. In wilderness we appreciate other powers and interests because we find our own limited.

A final contribution of wilderness to the cause of environmental responsibility is a heightened appreciation of the meaning and importance of restraint. When we establish a wilderness reserve or national park we say, in effect, thus far, and no farther to development. We establish a limit. For Americans self-limitation does not come easily. Growth has been our national religion. But to maintain an area as wilderness is to put other considerations before material growth. It is to respect the rights of non-human life to habitat. It is to challenge the wisdom and moral legitimacy of man's conquest and transformation of the entire earth. This acceptance of restraint is fundamental if people are to live within the limits of the earth.

The United States developed its present system of scenic and recreational conservation because of public acceptance of the eight arguments just presented. So it is that attitudes and values can shape a nation's environment just as do bulldozers and chain saws. Nature reserves exist and will continue to exist under republican forms of government only because they are valued by society.

Railroads Value Wilderness

ALFRED RUNTE

Among the methods of conservation in the United States, the national park idea has been heralded as America's purest expression of landscape democracy. As a result, the mere suggestion that an institution so famous for its idealism and philanthropy would receive a crucial boost from industry may seem almost sacrilegious. According to popular tradition, the explorers who opened Yellowstone in 1870 conceived the national park idea while unraveling the mysteries of the region. But at best, ecology and altruism were afterthoughts of the Yellowstone Park campaign. From the outset, establishment of the park owed far more to the financier Jay Cooke and to officials of the Northern Pacific Railroad—all

---

From *Trains of Discovery: Western Railroads and the National Parks*, by Alfred Runte (Niwot, Colorado: Roberts Reinhart Publishers, 1990). Copyright © 1990 by Alfred Runte. Reprinted with the permission of the publisher.

of whom, upon completion of the line, expected to profit from the territory as a great tourist resort.

As the more patriotic and unselfish account, the popular depiction of the origins of Yellowstone National Park has obviously been less difficult to embrace. According to this version, the national park idea was not born in a corporate boardroom; instead, it came into being on the night of September 19, 1870, when members of the celebrated Washburn Expedition settled down around their campfire to share impressions of the wonderland that they had just finished exploring. Apparently, one of the men proposed that each member of the party claim a tract of land surrounding the canyon or the geyser basins for personal gain. Cornelius Hedges, a young lawyer from Helena, Montana, strongly disagreed, and pleaded with the explorers to abandon any private ambitions in the interest of promoting Yellowstone as a great national park for all Americans to own and enjoy. Nathaniel Pitt Langford, the noted publicist of the expedition, recorded the following in his diary: "His suggestion met with an instantaneous and favorable response from all—except one—of the members of our party, and each hour since the matter was first broached, our enthusiasm has increased." Thus, Langford concluded his entry for September 20, "I lay awake half of last night thinking about it; and if my wakefulness deprived my bed-fellow (Hedges) of any sleep, he has only himself and his disturbing National Park proposition to answer for it."

There is only one nagging doubt about the accuracy of this statement: Langford did not publish these words until 1905, fully thirty-five years after the event. By then, of course, he and his colleagues had had numerous opportunities to amend their accounts of the expedition in light of the growing fame of the national park idea. Certainly there is something suspicious in the fact that, despite their reported enthusiasm, not one of the eighteen men present around that Yellowstone campfire ever mentioned the national park idea in the articles and speeches prepared immediately afterward. In either case, even if Langford's account were credible, some very important names would still be missing from his story, most notably Jay Cooke, promoter and financier of the Northern Pacific Railroad extension project, and Cooke's office manager, A. B. Nettleton.

Indeed, the explorers' discussion around their campfire that mid-September evening could not have taken place in ignorance of the plans of the Northern Pacific Railroad. Langford must have informed all of the men about Jay Cooke's intentions, including Henry D. Washburn, the surveyor general of Montana and nominal leader of the expedition. Three months prior to the venture, Langford had met personally with Cooke at the latter's estate just outside Philadelphia. Not only did Cooke retain Langford to promote Yellowstone as part of a publicity campaign to secure funding for the railroad, he probably suggested the Washburn Expedition itself. By then, Cooke realized that his right-of-way through south-central Montana would bring him within forty or fifty miles of Yellowstone. Obviously, with such a great wonderland lying along his main line to the Pacific, Cooke stood to become the direct beneficiary of any publicity aimed at introducing the region to prospective travelers.

Meanwhile, following the expedition of 1870, Nathaniel Langford returned east to lecture in New York, Philadelphia, and Washington, D.C., on behalf of the Northern Pacific. Here again, his writings and statements reveal that he acted more as a promoter rather than as a concerned private citizen speaking only for the protection of Yellowstone. At every opportunity, Langford trumpeted the building of the Northern Pacific Railroad, specifically noting that completion of the line would make Yellowstone "speedily accessible" to tourists.

As a scientist, Professor Ferdinand V. Hayden, a geologist and government surveyor, found Langford's descriptions of Yellowstone's thermal features especially fascinating. Accordingly, he petitioned Congress for extra funding to take his own survey into the region during the summer of 1871. Congress agreed and appropriated $40,000 to ensure that the expedition would be the most complete and systematic ever.

Once more, the office of Jay Cooke intervened in planning for the Hayden survey on behalf of the Northern Pacific Railroad. Cooke's office manager, A. B. Nettleton, wrote directly to Hayden to request that Thomas Moran, a landscape artist of growing renown, be permitted to accompany the expedition as a private citizen. "Please understand that we do not wish to burden you with more people than you can attend to," Nettleton began his letter, "but I think that Mr. Moran will be a very desirable addition to your expedition. . . ." On a personal note, Nettleton also stressed that the favor would "be a great accommodation" to Jay Cooke and the interests of the railroad. "[Moran], of course, expects to pay his own expenses, and simply wishes to take advantage of your cavalry escort."

In reality, Moran needed financial assistance; like Nathaniel P. Langford, his distant benefactor was none other than Jay Cooke, from whom the artist borrowed the five hundred dollars required to supplement his own meager resources. In this manner, Cooke's endorsement (and funds) directly led to the production of Moran's most famous oil painting, *The Grand Canyon of the Yellowstone*, now housed in the National Museum of American Art, Smithsonian Institution, in Washington, D.C.

As late as September 1871, however, when the Hayden Survey returned from the Yellowstone wilderness, no public campaign to protect the region as a national park had yet been formed. For this reason, the Yellowstone campfire story of 1870 is even more suspect. Certainly, if the explorers of the preceding expedition had pledged themselves to such a grand scheme, they would not have sacrificed another perfect opportunity — in this instance, the publicity generated by the Hayden Survey — to once more introduce the national park idea to the American people. No one came forward, not even Professor Hayden, who had achieved great distinction in the public eye.

Credit for proposing the introduction of legislation to protect Yellowstone as a public park actually rests with officials of the Northern Pacific Railroad project. The clue is to be found in a letter Professor Hayden received on October 28, 1871, from A. B. Nettleton, written on the stationery of Jay Cooke & Co., Bankers, Financial Agents, Northern Pacific Railroad Company. The letter began:

Dear Doctor:

Judge Kelley has made a suggestion which strikes me as being an excellent one, viz: Let Congress pass a bill reserving the Great Geyser Basin as a public park forever—just as it has reserved that far inferior wonder the Yosemite valley and big trees. If you approve this would such a recommendation be appropriate in your official report?

Judge Kelley was Congressman William Darrah Kelley of Philadelphia, a prominent Republican sympathetic to Cooke and his railroad enterprises. Kelley learned about Yellowstone through the published congressional report of Lieutenant Gustavus C. Doane, commander of the cavalry escort for the Washburn Expedition. Nettleton's reference to "Yosemite valley and the big trees" was also significant, for it underscored the crucial matter of precedent. In 1864, Congress had granted Yosemite Valley and the Mariposa Grove of Giant Sequoias to the state of California "for public use, resort, and recreation," to be held "inalienable for all time." Although Yosemite was a state park, its congressional origin was not overlooked by Yellowstone's own champions. Management considerations aside, Nettleton, for one, appreciated that Congress, through the Yosemite grant, had already established a procedure for setting aside unique scenery in the national interest.

Not until Professor Hayden received the letter in question, however, did he or any of the other explorers—including Nathaniel Langford and Cornelius Hedges— actually begin working to have Yellowstone protected as a public park similar to Yosemite. So again, the intervention of the Northern Pacific Railroad, not the latent sympathies of Yellowstone's actual discoverers, was crucial.

From the perspective of the Northern Pacific, the campaign itself was anticlimactic. Having entrusted the idea for a park to Professor Hayden, officials of the railroad stayed out of the limelight on Capitol Hill, confident that Hayden's fame and credibility as a government geologist would guarantee a favorable outcome. They were not to be disappointed, for on March 1, 1872, only three months after being introduced in Congress, the Yellowstone Park Act was signed into law by President Ulysses S. Grant.

Unfortunately for Jay Cooke, his own hopes of opening the Yellowstone country to tourists were dashed by the depression of 1873. Ten years later and under new management, the Northern Pacific Railroad lines across Montana and the spur track to Yellowstone, which headed due south from Livingston, were completed. Nevertheless, the initial efforts of Jay Cooke and A. B. Nettleton had clearly been instrumental, first in launching the Yellowstone Park campaign itself, and later, in securing public sympathy to retain the park until significant numbers of tourists could in fact begin visiting its wonders.

After 1883, the Northern Pacific Railroad spared no expense to promote Yellowstone National Park. As early as 1886, for example it underwrote the construction of a series of hotels located near primary attractions. Charles S. Fee, general passenger agent in St. Paul, Minnesota, sought to publicize both the railroad and its accommodations by commissioning a colorfully written and illustrated series of guidebooks, beginning with his personal compilation, *Northern Pacific Railroad: The Wonderland Route to the Pacific Coast, 1885.*

By utilizing quotations from articulate travelers and well-known personalities, these guidebooks introduced Americans not only to Yellowstone, but to Mount Rainier, the Columbia River Gorge, the Cascade Mountains, and similar landmarks made accessible via the Northern Pacific. Even at this early date, Mount St. Helens, visible from the trains approaching Portland, Oregon, was featured for its appeal to observers as "the great Sugar Loaf" of the Pacific Northwest.

Obviously, what modern Americans would recognize as ecological awareness was rarely evident in these guidebook testimonials. After all, the primary objective was to publicize those features of the West which were experiencing growing popularity among tourists. More visitors, in turn, promised the Northern Pacific Railroad greater revenues from hotels, transcontinental trains, and its other passenger-related operations.

Commercial motives aside, the long-range impact of this publicity on the preservation movement in the United States was positive and significant. The railroad's dependence on unspoiled scenery to attract tourists tempered its purely extractive aims, such as logging, mining, and land development. The passenger department, at the very least, became one of the first and most outspoken defenders of Yellowstone National Park. Barely had the railroad come to the gates of the wonderland than Charles S. Fee declared on behalf of his employers:

> We do not want to see the Falls of the Yellowstone driving the looms of a cotton factory, or the great geysers boiling pork for some gigantic packinghouse, but in all the native majesty and grandeur in which they appear to-day; without, as yet, a single trace of that adornment which is desecration, that improvement which is equivalent to ruin, or that utilization which means utter destruction.

As if to underscore the pledge, in 1893 the Northern Pacific adopted a new logo, patterned after the Chinese yin-yang symbol of the balanced universe, and suspended it above the caption, "Yellowstone Park Line."

By the turn of the century, as interest in wildlife conservation grew in importance, representatives of the Northern Pacific again spoke out strongly in defense of Yellowstone. More Americans now recognized that the protection of natural wonders, as opposed to wild animals, required only limited amounts of land. Wildlife populations paid no heed to park boundaries laid out to preserve scenery, but instead seasonally followed their traditional migration routes. For the first time, Yellowstone's ecological shortcomings were dramatically apparent. Despite its great size, the park lacked sufficient territory to protect its larger mammals, particularly elk, deer, and antelope. Every autumn, as these species deserted the park for their winter ranges in the lower elevations, they were forced to run a gauntlet of poachers and sportsmen who had no respect for bag limits. For Yellowstone to support its native wildlife effectively, either the park would have to be greatly enlarged or the animals themselves better protected when wandering outside its borders.

The Northern Pacific, through another of its authors, Olin D. Wheeler, enthusiastically supported both park expansion and wildlife protection measures. "In order . . . to properly preserve these fast-disappearing relics of wild animal life to future generations," Wheeler wrote in the *Wonderland* guidebook of 1902, "additional territory should be added either to the park proper or to the forest reserve about it, so that absolute protection can be maintained. . . ." Poachers and "game hogs" cared "only for their own selfish pleasure in killing as many deer or elks as they can," he bitterly noted. Perhaps the only solution lay in "the boys and girls" of America, those with the greatest stake in the destiny of Yellowstone. Wheeler concluded that from their "irresistible" efforts, their "vim and enthusiasm," might spring the "national movement," a movement that would finally compel Congress to "arrange for game protection in the Yellowstone Park region for all future time."

Actually, another half century would pass before the addition of Jackson Hole to Grand Teton National Park, lying just to the south, complemented Yellowstone as a wildlife preserve. Again, the delay did not compromise the significance of that first crucial step — of stating unequivocally the need for park expansion. Through its agent, Olin D. Wheeler, the Northern Pacific Railroad fully shared in the credit for that endorsement.

Meanwhile, the national park idea was winning converts nationwide; at the turn of the century, Mount Rainier in Washington state was among the natural wonders proposed for park status. The Northern Pacific Railroad played a major role in establishing this reserve as well. Approved by Congress in 1899, the park was carved from square-mile sections on the peak; alternate sections were owned by the Northern Pacific, and the balance by the federal government. The railroad's sections dated back to its original land grant, awarded in 1864. Agreeing that these properties were best suited for scenic enjoyment, the government exchanged with Northern Pacific federally held public lands elsewhere in the Pacific Northwest. . . .

Soon after the turn of the century, every major western railroad was playing a crucial role in the establishment, protection, and improvement of national parks. The managers of these lines were motivated more by a desire to promote tourism and increase profits than by altruism or environmental concern. Nevertheless, preservationists like John Muir came to recognize the value of forming an alliance with a powerful corporate group committed to similar goals, if not from similar ideals. Tourism at the time, however encouraged, provided the national parks with a solid economic justification for their existence. No argument was more vital in a nation still unwilling to pursue scenic preservation at the cost of business achievement.

The Northern Pacific, as the first company to become involved with the national parks, set an example for the other railroads to follow. Across the West, railroad companies learned to appreciate the publicity and profits that could be won by sponsoring scenic preservation in their particular spheres of influence. Among the earliest to respond to the opportunity was the Southern Pacific Railroad in California, which lobbied in 1890 for the establishment of Yosemite, Sequoia, and General Grant national parks, all located in the High Sierra. "Even the soulless Southern Pacific R.R. Co., never counted on for anything good, helped nobly in pushing the bill for [Yosemite] park through Congress." With these words, John Muir recorded the initial astonishment among preservation interests.

The Grand Canyon of Arizona provided the Atchison, Topeka & Santa Fe Railway with a similar golden opportunity. Travel to the canyon was considerably improved with the completion in 1901 of a spur track to the South Rim from Williams, Arizona, a distance of approximately sixty miles. Visitors were no longer forced to endure long and tiring stagecoach rides in the desert heat. Similarly, in January 1905, the Santa Fe dedicated its luxurious El Tovar Hotel, also on the canyon brink. Here, too, the publicity of the railroad and its structural improvements contributed immeasurably to the protection of the Grand Canyon, for not until 1908 was it set aside as a national monument by order of President Theodore Roosevelt. . . .

Louis W. Hill [Great Northern's president] took great personal pride in opening Glacier National Park as his own unique gift to the nation. From the outset, visitors to the park detected his dedication to the project. Mary Roberts Rinehart, for example, writing for *Collier's* magazine, informed her readers in 1916: "Were it not for the Great Northern Railway, travel through Glacier Park would be practically impossible." Of course, the railroad was "not entirely altruistic," the popular novelist confessed, "and yet I believe that Mr. Louis Warren Hill, known always as 'Louie' Hill, has had an ideal and followed it — followed it with an enthusiasm that is contagious." . . .

National park conferences, called in 1912 and 1915 by the Department of the Interior . . . reaffirmed the unanimous support for a Park Service among the western railroads. The opposition in the federal bureaucracy, once confident of success, could no longer withstand this powerful tide of enthusiasm from such a prestigious quarter. On August 25, 1916, preservationists cleared their last potential hurdle when President Woodrow Wilson signed the National Park Service Act into law.

The Ethnocentricity of Wilderness Values

J. BAIRD CALLICOTT

A Three Point Critique of the Received Concept of Wilderness

Upon close scrutiny, the simple, popular wilderness idea dissolves before one's gaze. First, the concept perpetuates the pre-Darwinian Western metaphysical dichotomy between "man" and nature, albeit with an opposite spin. (Fully aware that it is gender-biased, I use the term "man" both deliberately and apologetically to refer globally and collectively to the species *Homo sapiens*, because no other term carries the same connotation and flavor, a connotation and flavor that I wish to evoke in the course of this critique, including its

From "The Wilderness Idea Revisited: The Sustainable Development Alternative," *The Environmental Professional*, 13 (1991), pp. 236–45. Reprinted by permission of *The Environmental Professional*.

decided sexism.) In fact, one of the principal psycho-spiritual benefits of wilderness experience is said to be contact with the radical "other," and wilderness preservation the letting be of the nonhuman other in its full otherness. . . .

The Wilderness Act of 1964 beautifully reflects the conventional understanding of wilderness. It reads: "A wilderness, in contrast with those areas where man and his works dominate the landscape, is hereby recognized as an area where the earth and its community of life are untrammeled by man, where man himself is a visitor who does not remain."

This definition assumes, indeed it enshrines, a bifurcation of man and nature. That the man-nature dichotomy insidiously infects even our well-intentioned and noble efforts to limit our own grasp should not be surprising. A major theme both in Western philosophy, going back to the ancient Greeks, and in Western religion, going back to the ancient Hebrews, is how man is unique and set apart from the rest of nature. . . .

Second, . . . the popular wilderness idea is ethnocentric. More than anyone else, Nash has molded the popular idea of wilderness in the contemporary American mind. He acknowledges, but skates rapidly over, American Indian complaints that the very concept of wilderness is a racist idea, and he expresses no doubt that the first European settlers of North America encountered a "wilderness condition." In the recent (and excellent) Wilderness Idea film by Hott and Garey (1989), Nash is even more emphatic. He says that the pilgrims literally stepped off the Mayflower into a wilderness of continental dimensions.

Upon the eve of European landfall, most of temperate North America was not, *pace* Nash, in a wilderness condition — not undominated by the works of man — unless one is prepared to ignore the existence of its aboriginal inhabitants and their works or to insinuate that they were not "man," *i.e.*, not fully human human beings. In 1492, Antarctica was the only true wilderness land mass on the planet. (And by now, even a good bit of it has come under the iron heel of industrial man.) . . . The incredible abundance of wildlife encountered in the western hemisphere by the first European intruders was not, however, a concomitant of a universal wilderness condition, that is, not due to the absence of inherently destructive *Homo sapiens* in significant numbers everywhere. Rather, the biological wealth of North America on the eve of European landfall is more attributable to the bioregional management programs of the indigenous human population than to low numbers. Further, the ubiquity of grizzly bears throughout the west and big cats and wolves throughout the continent indicates a mutual tolerance of these species with *Homo sapiens americana* that was, apparently, disrupted when *Homo sapiens europi* began to persecute them as varmints.

Third . . ., wilderness preservation, as the popular conservation alternative to destructive land use and development, suggests that, untrammeled by man, a wilderness will remain "stable," in a steady state. However, nature is inherently dynamic; it is constantly changing and ultimately evolving. Today, most of the pitifully small fenced-off patches of designated wilderness areas of temperate North America lack major components of their Holocene ecological complement — notably their large predators. Not only that, a fence, or the policy equivalent thereof, will not exclude all the exotic species that have accompanied or followed the migration of *Homo sapiens europi* to North America. Designated wilderness areas, paradoxically, must be restored and managed actively if they are to remain fit habitat for native species, but the necessity of means raises a question of ends, of values. Is maintaining "vignettes of primitive America" the most important and defensible goal of biological conservation? (Here, again, let me be clear. I am excluding from consideration biologically-destructive economic desiderata such as hydroelectric impoundment.) Since we must manage nature actively and invasively to preserve the ecological status quo ante, the possibility of managing nature for more direct, less incidental conservation goals arises. . . .

The wilderness idea has not only made conservation convenient, . . . allowing us to enjoy the benefits of industrial development and over consumption, while salving our consciences by setting aside a few undeveloped remnants for nature — but it also has made conservation philosophy simple and easy. If we conceive of wilderness as a static benchmark of pristine nature in reference to which all human modifications may be judged to be more or less degradations, then we can duck the hard intellectual job of specifying criteria for land health in four-dimensional, inherently dynamic landscapes long inhabited by *Homo sapiens* as well as by other species. The idea of healthy land maintaining itself is more sensitive to the dynamic quality of ecosystems than is the conventional idea of preserving vignettes of primitive America. Moreover, if the concept of land health replaces the popular, conventional idea of wilderness as a standard of conservation, then we might begin to envision ways of creatively reintegrating man and nature.

Conservation via Sustainable Development

The new idea in conservation today is called "sustainable development," a term that can mean different things to different people. Under the essentially economic interpretation of the Brundtland Report (1987), it means little more than what it says: initiation of human economic activity that can be sustained indefinitely, quite irrespective of whether such development is ecologically salubrious. Worse still, some economists would denominate a development path "sustainable," even if it leaves subsequent generations a depauperate natural environment, but sufficient technological know-how and investment capital to invent and manufacture an ersatz world. . . . I would like to mean by "sustainable development" initiation of human economic activity that is limited by ecological exigencies; economic activity that does not compromise ecological integrity seriously; and, ideally, economic activity that positively enhances ecosystem health. However, is sustainable development, so understood, possible? The surest proof of possibility is actuality.

* * * *

The symbiotic win-win philosophy of conservation gradually is replacing the bifurcated zero-sum approach as the 20th century gives way to the 21st. For example, one of the most promising conservation stratagems in the Amazon rainforest today is the designation not of nature reserves from which people are excluded to protect the forest and its wildlife, but of so-called "extractive reserves." (1989). An extractive reserve is an area where traditional patterns of human-nature symbiosis — such as those evolved by the Amazonian Indians and more recently by the rubber tappers — are protected from loggers, cattle ranchers, miners, and hydroelectric engineers. . . .

Can we generalize this particular example of the sustainable development alternative to either conventional development, like intensive stock grazing, or wilderness designation and restoration (where none existed before)? Can we envision and work to create an eminently livable, systemic, postindustrial technological society well adapted to, and at peace and in harmony with, its organic environment? . . .

Can't a civilized, technological society also live, not merely in peaceful coexistence, but in benevolent symbiosis with nature? Is our current industrial civilization the only one imaginable? Aren't there more appropriate, alternative technologies? Can't we be good citizens of the biotic community, . . . drawing an honest living from nature and giving back as much or more than we take?

F U R T H E R   R E A D I N G

Horace M. Albright, as told to Robert Cahn, *The Birth of the National Park Service* (1985)

Craig W. Allin, *The Politics of Wilderness Preservation* (1982)

Donald N. Baldwin, *The Quiet Revolution: Grass Roots of Today's Wilderness Preservation Movement* (1972)

Frank Bergon, ed., *The Wilderness Reader* (1957)

Paul Brooks, *The Pursuit of Wilderness* (1971)

————, *Speaking for Nature: How Literary Naturalists from Henry Thoreau to Rachel Carson Have Shaped America* (1980)

Kendrick A. Clements, "Politics and the Park: San Francisco's Fight for Hetch Hetchy, 1908–1913," *Pacific Historical Review* 48 (1979), 185–215

Michael P. Cohen, *The Pathless Way: John Muir and the American Wilderness* (1984)

Thomas Dunlap, *Saving America's Wildlife* (1988)

Susan Flader, *Thinking like a Mountain: Aldo Leopold and the Evolution of an Ecological Attitude Toward Deer, Wolves, and Forests* (1974)

Steven Fox, *John Muir and His Legacy: The American Conservation Movement* (1981)

Michael Frome, *Battle for the Wilderness* (1974)

Hans Huth, *Nature and the American: Three Centuries of Changing Attitudes* (1957)

John Ise, *Our National Park Policy: A Critical History* (1961)

Ronald F. Lockmann, *Guarding the Forests of Southern California: Evolving Attitudes Toward Conservation of Watershed, Woodlands, and Wilderness* (1981)

John McPhee, *Encounters with the Archdruid* (1971)

Robert Ben Martin, *The Hetch Hetchy Controversy: The Value of Nature in a Technological Society* (1982)

Roderick Nash, *Wilderness and the American Mind*, 3d ed. (1982)

Max Oeschlager, *The Idea of Wilderness from Prehistory to the Age of Ecology* (1991)

Janet Robertson, *The Magnificent Mountain Women: Adventures in the Colorado Rockies* (1990)

Alfred Runte, *National Parks: The American Experience* (1979)

————, *Yosemite: The Embattled Wilderness* (1990)

————, *Trains of Discovery: Western Railroads and the National Parks* (1990)

Susan Schrepfer, *The Fight to Save the Redwoods: A History of Environmental Reform, 1917–1978* (1983)

Duane Smith, *Mesa Verde National Park* (1988)

Deborah Strom, ed., *Birdwatching with American Women: A Selection of Nature Writings* (1986)

Douglas H. Strong, *Trees—or Timber? The Story of Sequoia and Kings Canyon National Parks* (undated)

————, *Dreamers and Defenders: American Conservationists* (1988)

Donald C. Swain, *Wilderness Defender: Horace M. Albright and Conservation* (1970)

Peter Wild, *Pioneer Conservationists of Western America* (1979)

————, ed., *The Desert Reader* (1991)

Urban Pollution and Reform

in the Twentieth Century

❦

*In 1800 only 6 percent of Americans lived in cities; by 1920 the urban
population had spurted to 51 percent. Along with the growth of cities came water
pollution, smog, and disease. Writing in 1898, Robert Woods saw the city as a
social wilderness; Booth Tarkington, in his novel* The Turmoil *(1914), described
it as grimy, dingy, and dirty. Smoke, once a sign of progress, became a nuisance.
Garbage piled up along the edges of city streets; horse manure mounted down
the middle. The din of machinery, the clanking of metal, and the screeching of
whistles, bells, and sirens filled the air from early morning to late evening, and
refuse, sewage, and factory effluents poured into rivers and seeped into ground
water. Cholera, tuberculosis, and bronchitis threatened human health. These
forms of urban pollution and disease differentially affected affluent and working-
class neighborhoods. Nature within the inner-city environment differed from
rural and suburban nature, but were connected by air and water flows.*

*A movement took shape in the early twentieth century to clean up air,
water, garbage, and noise pollution. It was part of a larger urban-reform campaign focusing on health, sanitation, parks, and beautification. Members of civic
groups and women's clubs, politicians, lawyers, and engineers all participated in
efforts to improve urban environments. However, progress came slowly, owing to
industry resistance, technological problems, ineffective legislation, and lack of enforcement. And, primarily a middle-class movement to improve middle-class life,
this reform initiative embraced quality-of-life rather than social-justice issues; for
the working class, problems of racism, labor unrest, immorality, and poor living
conditions persisted. Nevertheless, urban environmental reform in this era
marked the first phase of a citizens' action movement dedicated to improving the
environment and human health.*

❦ D O C U M E N T S

The first document, excerpted from Robert Woods's *The City Wilderness* (1898),
looks at deteriorating working-class neighborhoods as threats to health and morality
whose effects could be mitigated only partially through philanthropy and social

reform. Environmental reform focused more narrowly on the impact of noise, garbage, smoke, and water on human health. In the second document, dating from
1900, the editor of the journal *Current Literature* connects city noise to problems
of psychological health. The third selection, an article written in 1901 by Mrs.
C. G. Wagner, treasurer of the Women's Health Protective Association of
Brooklyn, New York, details the problems arising from refuse accumulation and
describes citizens' cleanup efforts. In the fourth document reformer Jane Addams,
the founder of Chicago's Hull-House, a poor people's refuge, discusses women's
efforts to organize garbage-collection reforms in tenement-house neighborhoods.

In addition to noise and garbage, the smoke befouling urban skies was a major
health hazard. Herbert Wilson, chief engineer with the U.S. Geological Survey, author of the fifth document, describes the ill effects of the smoke and dust of coal-
burning furnaces on human health, trees, laundry, retail goods, and private property. In the sixth document, Mrs. Ernest Koreger, president of the Women's
Organization for Smoke Abatement of St. Louis, details women's efforts to enforce
state laws against the smoke nuisance.

The next selection, by novelist Booth Tarkington, writing in 1914, graphically
depicts city dirt as spawned by individual greed and population growth, resulting in
massive migrations of people of every color and every origin into the cities, with a
consequent rise in poverty, illness, and social turmoil. Racial and ethnic minorities,
including blacks, bore the brunt of urban pollution and social stigma. In the final
document, writer Richard Wright, an African-American migrant from the South
who arrived in Chicago in 1927, compares the blackness of urban soot to his own
blackness. To many northern urbanites, both blacks and pollution seemed invisible
and inevitable parts of the city landscape.

Robert Woods on the City Wilderness, 1898

Isolated and congested working-class quarters, with all the dangers to moral
and material well-being that they present, grow along with the growth of all our
great cities.

The course of their evolution is in nearly all cases much the same. At first
the well-to-do and the poor live near together, the poor having their abode on
the back streets. There is no absolute line of demarcation between the interests
of the two classes. Both share, to a degree, in a common life. But as time goes
on, the poor increase to such an extent, through industrial change at home and
immigration from abroad, that they become overcrowded where they are, and
begin to emerge into some of the front streets, dislodging and pushing along
their more prosperous neighbors.

Residences get into the hands of lodging-house keepers. Later, in many
cases, they undergo a few alterations and become tenements. New buildings
soon begin to spring up in nooks and corners of unoccupied land. Shops and
other places of business line the main streets more and more. Each later
immigration adds to the local population that is already taxing the housing
accommodation. Factories begin to come into those parts, increasing the crowd
and making the conditions still more complicated.

Meanwhile the well-to-do, establishing themselves elsewhere, have
opened up centres of civilizing influence in which the working people have no
share. The ties which for a time bound them to their former homes and

neighbors have been severed one by one. Although perhaps owning property or interested in business at that section of the city, they have practically forgotten it in all its social and moral aspects. Cut off as it now is in great measure from the centres of the city's life, such a quarter provides fit haunts for the depraved and vicious. Evils of all kinds find here a congenial soil and produce a rank growth. The back streets, at best, are dreary and depressing, and have dark squalid courts and alleys running in from them. The chief thoroughfares gradually take on aspects of garish picturesqueness, which, set against a mixed background of poverty and moral tragedy, give them a weird fascination.

These various conditions tend to disintegrate neighborhood life and to destroy what is best in the life of the home. Neighborhoods come to be made up of people who have no local attachments and are separated from one another by distinctions of race and religion. There is no concerted action for a better social life, no watchfulness over common interests. Such a state of things gives political corruption its best opportunity. This is precisely the place where money is to be laid out at election time. . . .

In the evolution of the crowded city quarter, . . . two periods only were described: that when the well-to-do and poor live in the same neighborhoods and their interests were in a measure bound together, and that marked by the more or less complete separation of these two classes and the abandonment of the poor to their fate. A third stage has been reached in not a few instances, brought about by a quickened social conscience among the well-to-do and cultured. Through a growing feeling of obligation on the part of those that have towards those that have not, attention has been directed with real concern to the city's social and moral wastes. As a result, charities and philanthropies have begun to invade them in growing number and variety. Such churches as are located there feel the reaction, and begin to take on new forms of activity the better to meet the situation presented by their respective neighborhoods; and other churches from without see in wholly neglected neighborhoods the fields for new missionary enterprise.

An Editor Comments on the Noise Nuisance, 1900

There seems to be no adequate regard in American cities for the sanitary virtues of quietness. Indeed to make a noise appears to be the protected right of any street loafer, huckster or hand-organ man. The police will not interfere with them, even in cases where the comfort and health of property owners is at stake. The following article, inspired by an effort made to abate the noises of Chicago, is from the Medical Journal of Philadelphia:

> The chief of police has classified noises into the tolerable, the intolerable and the unavoidable. We should be inclined to exclude the first and third classes and classify all noises as intolerable. Certainly all noises injurious to health are intolerable and avoidable. But our modern American cities are pandemoniac with avoidable noises. It is perhaps not far from the truth that the "nervousness" and waste energy of our people are due to the nerve-shattering noises of our life. The few nervous systems that can withstand such ceaseless shocks are blunted into stupid dullness. Every physician and sanitarian should use all

justifiable means to lessen the noise-nuisance and to bring such influences to bear upon executive officers of the city and town as may abate it. In Philadelphia the most disgraceful indifference to noise was found ultimately to be due to the fact that the police have found it useless to arrest and prosecute noise-makers as well as beggars, drunkards, insulters of women, etc., because the magistrates at once discharge the offenders unfined; the police are thus powerless to curb such impudence and lawlessness. The political boss is always the aider and abettor of crime. The drunkards and rowdy boys bawl and yell unrestrained, the dogs bark, the crazy whistlers do their worst, the street venders bellow and the buyers of old rags outbellow them, the street-car men bang their bells, and the street-organs add to the din. In Brooklyn recently the street venders in every street, failing to invent a more diabolic noise, were ringing cow-bells. The modern trolley-car is the very acme of atrocity. It has been made so heavy and the crossing rails are so clumsily arranged that houses are jarred for a square every minute or two day and night, and dynamo-roar and bell-thumping are added. We have taught the young for a hundred years that making the most frightful noise is the way to express joy. How long will it take us to teach the healthfulness of quiet? How soon shall we learn that one has no more right to throw noises than they have to throw stones into a house? Every physician knows the baleful effect of noise upon his patients, and every physiologist understands its pathogenic effect upon the nervous system. Above all things unnecessary noises at night should be mercilessly stopped. If all the physicians and medical societies of a city should use their influence upon the city governors, the greater part of such noises could be eliminated.

A Woman Reformer Advocates Civic Cleanliness, 1901

Because of the indifference on the part of many of our voters, combined with the exactions of business for others, and the neglect of our city officials in matters pertaining to the betterment of the city, it was forced upon the minds of a number of thinking women that something ought to be done to remedy the existing evils. For this reason, in April, 1890, the Women's Health Protective Association of Brooklyn, N.Y., was incorporated.

Its attention was first drawn to the unsanitary methods of collection and disposal of garbage and ashes. At that time the garbage was carried beyond the harbor and dumped into the sea, only to be washed back again upon the south shore, leaving an unsightly and ill-smelling beach. It was frequently placed upon the walk in paper boxes, grape boxes, and even newspapers have been used for the unfortunate collector to handle, but by constant agitation, to some extent that has been corrected; for, at present, in most localities the receptacles are more in accordance with the city ordinance: "That it should be put in unleakable vessels." The larger portion of the garbage is now cremated, and the association looks forward to the day when it shall all be disposed of in that way.

Another line of work was that of getting the householder to keep the ash cans within the fence line, and when it is complied with, is certainly an improvement on the old way of having a long row of unsightly barrels and boxes lining the edge of the walks, filled to overflowing with worn-out pots and kettles, old brooms, rubbers, umbrellas, and various articles of household waste too numerous to mention.

And now the association has secured the separate removal of rubbish, although not done to its satisfaction, yet hoping some day to reach the point it aims for. . . .

The agitation against the slovenly manner in which the street cleaning was done brought about a better state of affairs, thanks to Col. [George E.] Waring [New York City street cleaning commissioner], for surely the present system far exceeds the old, when the dirt was swept into heaps and left sometimes for days before its gathering, for the winds and wagons to scatter it again. Though fallen below Col. Waring's standard, still it is in great advance of the past.

The unsanitary plumbing in some of the public schools was brought to the notice of the association as being detrimental both to the morals and the health of the pupils. On investigating, a sad state was found in some of them and continues the same to-day. Lack of funds was the excuse given for the condition of the buildings, though languages and the higher branches could be taught at a great expense to the taxpayers. Very little has been done, and the association intends to continue its efforts until these things are remedied.

Among the minor reforms of the association was getting the piggeries removed beyond the city line. The placing of cans on the street corners for waste paper is another reform, and the overflowing condition of some show how useful they are and how much would otherwise be distributed in the streets. An uncleanly obstruction on the edge of the walk was the grocers' coal boxes; they are now placed against the house. To a great extent the association has succeeded in having carts that were left standing in the streets stabled elsewhere. The distribution of circulars on the streets has claimed its attention for years, but success in that direction has not come yet.

"The secret of success is constancy of purpose."

Jane Addams on Garbage in Chicago, 1910

One of the striking features of our neighborhood twenty years ago, and one to which we never became reconciled, was the presence of huge wooden garbage boxes fastened to the street pavement in which the undisturbed refuse accumulated day by day. The system of garbage collecting was inadequate throughout the city but it became the greatest menace in a ward such as ours, where the normal amount of waste was much increased by the decayed fruit and vegetables discarded by the Italian and Greek fruit peddlers, and by the residuum left over from piles of filthy rags which were fished out of the city dumps and brought to the homes of the rag pickers for further sorting and washing.

The children of our neighborhood twenty years ago played their games in and around these huge garbage boxes. They were the first objects that the toddling child learned to climb; their bulk afforded a barricade and their contents provided missiles in all the battles of the older boys; and finally they became the seats upon which absorbed lovers held enchanted converse. We are obliged to remember that all children eat everything which they find and that odors have a curious and intimate power of entwining themselves into our tenderest memories, before even the residents of Hull-House can understand their own early enthusiasm for the removal of these boxes and the establishment of a better system of refuse collection.

It is easy for even the most conscientious citizen of Chicago to forget the foul smells of the stockyards and the garbage dumps, when he is living so far from them that he is only occasionally made conscious of their existence but the residents of a Settlement are perforce constantly surrounded by them. During our first three years on Halsted Street, we had established a small incinerator at Hull-House and we had many times reported the untoward conditions of the ward to the city hall. We had also arranged many talks for the immigrants, pointing out that although a woman may sweep her own doorway in her native village and allow the refuse to innocently decay in the open air and sunshine, in a crowded city quarter, if the garbage is not properly collected and destroyed, a tenement-house mother may see her children sicken and die, and that the immigrants must therefore, not only keep their own houses clean, but must also help the authorities to keep the city clean.

Possibly our efforts slightly modified the worst conditions but they still remained intolerable, and the fourth summer the situation became for me absolutely desperate when I realized in a moment of panic that my delicate little nephew for whom I was guardian, could not be with me at Hull-House at all unless the sickening odors were reduced. I may well be ashamed that other delicate children who were torn from their families, not into boarding school but into eternity, had not long before driven me to effective action. Under the direction of the first man who came as a resident to Hull-House we began a systematic investigation of the city system of garbage collection, both as to its efficiency in other wards and its possible connection with the death rate in the various wards of the city.

The Hull-House Woman's Club had been organized the year before by the resident kindergartner who had first inaugurated a mothers' meeting. The members came together, however, in quite a new way that summer when we discussed with them the high death rate so persistent in our ward. After several club meetings devoted to the subject, despite the fact that the death rate rose highest in the congested foreign colonies and not in the streets in which most of the Irish American club women lived, twelve of their number undertook in connection with the residents, to carefully investigate the condition of the alleys. During August and September the substantiated reports of violations of the law sent in from Hull-House to the health department were one thousand and thirty-seven. For the club woman who had finished a long day's work of washing or ironing followed by the cooking of a hot supper, it would have been much easier to sit on her doorstep during a summer evening than to go up and down ill-kept alleys and get into trouble with her neighbors over the condition of their garbage boxes. It required both civic enterprise and moral conviction to be willing to do this three evenings a week during the hottest and most uncomfortable months of the year. Nevertheless, a certain number of women persisted. . . .

With the two or three residents who nobly stood by, we set up six of those doleful incinerators which are supposed to burn garbage with the fuel collected in the alley itself. The one factory in town which could utilize old tin cans was a window weight factory, and we deluged that with ten times as many tin cans as it could use — much less would pay for. We made desperate attempts to have the dead animals removed by the contractor who was paid most liberally by the city for that purpose but who, we slowly discovered, always made the police ambulances do the work, delivering the carcasses upon freight cars for shipment to a soap factory in Indiana where they were sold for a good price although the contractor himself was the largest stockholder in the concern. Perhaps our greatest achievement was the discovery of a pavement eighteen inches under the surface in a narrow street. . . .This pavement became the *casus belli* between myself and the street commissioner when I insisted that its restoration belonged to him, after I had removed the first eight inches of garbage. The matter was finally settled by the mayor himself, who permitted me to drive him to the entrance of the street in what the children called my "garbage phaëton" and who took my side of the controversy.

. . . Perhaps no casual visitor could be expected to see that these matters of detail seemed unimportant to a city in the first flush of youth, impatient of correction and convinced that all would be well with its future. The most obvious faults were those connected with the congested housing of the immigrant population, nine tenths of them from the country, who carried on all sorts of traditional activities in the crowded tenements. That a group of Greeks should be permitted to slaughter sheep in a basement, that Italian women should be allowed to sort over rags collected from the city dumps, not only within the city limits but in a court swarming with little children, that immigrant bakers should continue unmolested to bake bread for their neighbors in unspeakably filthy spaces under the pavement, appeared incredible to visitors accustomed to careful city regulations.

"Smoke Worse Than Fire": An Engineer Describes Smoke Pollution, 1911

The smoke nuisance is one of the greatest dangers of modern times, insidiously attacking the health of the individual, lowering his vitality, increasing the death rate, and causing untold loss and injury to property. The damage which this evil inflicts can hardly be estimated in money; it is equally impossible to estimate the amount of suffering, disease and death and the general effect of lowered vitality caused by this nuisance. . . .

The Smoke Committee of Cleveland, discussing the losses occasioned by smoke, reported:

> There are approximately 400 retail dry goods stores in Cleveland doing business of from $10,000 to $3,000,000 or $4,000,000 a year. The owners of some of these stores estimate, and the same estimate is given in other cities, that on all white goods a clear loss of 10 per cent must be figured. Taking the single items of underwear, shirt waists, linens and white dress goods for the

eleven department stores, the proprietors conservatively estimate their combined loss at \$25,000. . . .

But a greater cost than all of these must be considered in the loss to the 100,000 homes in Cleveland. The constant need of cleaning walls, ceilings, windows, carpets, rugs and draperies, for redecorating and renewing, can be realized only by the house owner or housekeeper. To this should be added the increased laundry bills for household linen, the dry cleaning for clothing, and the great additional wear resulting from this constant renovation, necessitating frequent renewal. Consider also the permanent injury to books, pictures and similar articles. Though impossible of computation, it will be seen that the total of these items aggregates millions of dollars.

The City Forester of St. Louis declared that more than 4 per cent of the city trees are killed every year by smoke. In that city it has been found impossible to grow evergreen conifers, except the dwarf juniper and the Austrian pine. Only the hardiest of roses grow in that city. The trees which suffer the greatest injury are the oaks, hickories and conifers, and these are especially ideal park trees and far more valuable for beauty and permanence than the softer wooded varieties. . . .

Turning now to the losses in fuel combustion: our present method of burning coal with smoke is costing the people of this country, unnecessarily, \$90,000,000. It is estimated that 8 per cent of the coal used in the production of power, light and heat, or in all about 20,000,000 tons of coal, are going up the chimneys each year in smoke.

The prime source of the pollution of the atmosphere is smoke. The death rate is higher in the city than in the country, and the larger the city the higher the death rate. . . .

It must be understood that smoke, aside from the looks and tangible shapes in which it presents itself, is one of the most poisonous gases polluting the very air we breathe. So apparent is this fact that physicians in our larger cities state their ability to tell at a moment's glance at the lungs in a post-mortem examination whether the man has lived more than thirty days in such a city or not. In the former case their examination proves that the blood, instead of showing red, is black as soot can make it.

Medical men the world over are unanimous in the declaration that the breathing of coal smoke predisposes the lungs to tuberculosis and even more violent lung trouble, such as pneumonia, as well as to many other acute diseases. We know that lung diseases are more prevalent in smoky cities; that the death rate of children due to diseases of the respiratory organs is especially great in coal and iron districts; that tuberculosis is more rapidly fatal in smoky regions.

In addition to all the above, there is the psychological effect of smoke. The city enveloped in a sooty fog is a gloomy city and the children reared therein are in danger of growing up with too much toleration for dirt and too little of that full enthusiasm for the beautiful and clean things of life which sunlight and God's blue sky encourage about as well as anything else in this world.

A Woman Reformer Promotes Smoke Abatement, 1912

The smoke nuisance in St. Louis had grown almost intolerable when the Wednesday Club, a strong, fine organization of five hundred women, took up the question and cast about to see what could be done. This was in December, 1910. Up to that time there had been sporadic attempts, with considerable results from these efforts, made by the Smoke Abatement Committee of the Civic League. The Missouri State Law, a strong law covering all aspects of the question excepting that of locomotives, was passed as a result of their work.

The State Law was excellent, but the work of the Civic League in enforcing the law was almost completely hampered by an ineffective City Smoke Abatement Department and indifference on the part of the public. The City Department had combined the Smoke Abatement Department with the Boiler and Elevator Department, and placed at the head of both a Chief Inspector of Boilers and Elevators, with several deputy boiler inspectors, and *no* deputy smoke inspector. The consequence was that there was no force to look after the smoke nuisance.

The Wednesday Club made tentative inquiry of the Civic League as to the necessity of energetic effort, and received in reply a cordial invitation to coöperate with its Smoke Abatement Committee to secure the enforcement of the (existing) smoke ordinance. After accepting the invitation of the Civic League, the Wednesday Club realized that the movement should be larger and more general than a club movement, and, further, felt the necessity of arousing public opinion. With this end in view a mass meeting of the women of St. Louis was called in the Auditorium of the Wednesday Club and a program provided touching on the smoke nuisance from the standpoint of health, cleanliness, housekeeping, city planning, etc. The program included men and women speakers, some of whom were city officials.

At this meeting, which was crowded, the Women's Organization for Smoke Abatement in St. Louis was formed with 250 paid members. By the next afternoon there were 400 members, and at the present time the membership numbers 1,300. An executive board of twelve women was elected and has had charge of the planning and directing of all the organization's work. These women met weekly the first season and fortnightly the second, and have been enthusiastic and tireless in their crusade against the smoke nuisance.

The first work they took up was districting the city in districts of about five square blocks with volunteer members of the organization as reporters of the smoking chimneys in their districts. Colonel James Gay Butler, one of St. Louis' most public-spirited citizens, came to the assistance of the women with an open purse, stating that he would spend $50,000 if necessary to make St. Louis a clean city. He employed a lawyer and six smoke inspectors to supplement the work of the city, and offered to coöperate with the women in securing legal evidence from their district reports.

These district reports were mailed to the Executive Board of the Women's Organization, where copies were made and forwarded to the newspapers, Colonel Butler's lawyer and the City Department. These cases were then followed up, taken into court and required to comply with the law. For fifteen months Colonel Butler's lawyer and inspectors have secured convictions against offending chimneys, until now the manufacturing districts are pretty well cleaned up. The locomotives, residences and small apartment houses are at present our greatest offenders, and the combined efforts of the women, the Civic League, Colonel Butler and the newspapers are being directed against them. The newspapers have been most powerful allies in the smoke work and have given thousands of dollars of free advertising to the campaign.

The City Department has done all that it could do to coöperate with the Civic League and the Women's Organization. About a year ago the Mayor replaced the former Inspector of Boilers and Elevators with an able man who is doing all he possibly can under his present restrictions.

Booth Tarkington Depicts Urban Growth and Pollution, 1914

There is a midland city in the heart of fair, open country, a dirty and wonderful city nesting dingily in the fog of its own smoke. The stranger must feel the dirt before he feels the wonder, for the dirt will be upon him instantly. It will be upon him and within him, since he must breathe it, and he may care for no further proof that wealth is here better loved than cleanliness; but whether he cares or not, the negligently tended streets incessantly press home the point, and so do the flecked and grimy citizens. At a breeze he must smother in whirlpools of dust, and if he should decline at any time to inhale the smoke he has the meager alternative of suicide.

The smoke is like the bad breath of a giant panting for more and more riches. He gets them and pants the fiercer, smelling and swelling prodigiously. He has a voice, a hoarse voice, hot and rapacious trained to one tune: "Wealth! I will get Wealth! I will make Wealth! I will sell Wealth for more Wealth! My house shall be dirty, my garment shall be dirty, and I will foul my neighbor so that he cannot be clean—but I will get Wealth! There shall be no clean thing about me: my wife shall be dirty and my child shall be dirty, but I will get Wealth!" And yet it is not wealth that he is so greedy for; what the giant really wants is hasty riches. To get these he squanders wealth upon the four winds, for wealth is in the smoke.

Not quite so long ago as a generation, there was no panting giant here, no heaving, grimy city; there was but a pleasant big town of neighborly people who had understanding of one another, being, on the whole, much of the same type. It was a leisurely and kindly place—"homelike," it was called—and when the visitor had been taken through the State Asylum for the Insane and made to appreciate the view of the cemetery from a little hill, his host's duty as Baedeker was done. The good burghers were given to jogging comfortably about in phaetons or in surreys for a family drive on Sunday. No one was very rich; few were very poor; the air was clean, and there was time to live.

But there was a spirit abroad in the land, and it was strong here as elsewhere—a spirit that had moved in the depths of the American soil and labored there, sweating, till it stirred the surface, rove the mountains, and

emerged, tangible and monstrous, the god of all good American hearts—
Bigness. And that god wrought the panting giant.

In the souls of the burghers there had always been the profound longing for
size. Year by year the longing increased until it became an accumulated force:
We must Grow! We must be Big! We must be Bigger! Bigness means Money!
And the thing began to happen; their longing became a mighty Will. We must
be Bigger! Bigger! Bigger! Get people here! Coax them here! Bribe them!
Swindle them into coming, if you must, but get them! Shout them into coming!
Deafen them into coming! Any kind of people; all kinds of people! We must be
Bigger! Blow! Boost! Brag! Kill the fault-finder! Scream and bellow to the
Most High: Bigness is patriotism and honor! Bigness is love and life and
happiness! Bigness is Money! We want Bigness!

They got it. From all the states the people came; thinly at first, and slowly,
but faster and faster in thicker and thicker swarms as the quick years went by.
White people came, and black people and brown people and yellow people; the
negroes came from the South by the thousands and thousands, multiplying by
other thousands and thousands faster than they could die. From the four
quarters of the earth the people came, the broken and the unbroken, the tame
and the wild—Germans, Irish, Italians, Hungarians, Scotch, Welsh, English,
French, Swiss, Swedes, Norwegians, Greeks, Poles, Russian Jews, Dalma-
tions, Armenians, Rumanians, Bulgarians, Servians, Persians, Syrians, Japa-
nese, Chinese, Turks, and every hybrid that these could propagate. And if there
were no Eskimos nor Patagonians, what other human strain that earth might
furnish failed to swim and bubble in this crucible?

With Bigness came the new machinery and the rush; the streets began to
roar and rattle, the houses to tremble; the pavements were worn under the tread
of hurrying multitudes. The old, leisurely, quizzical look of the faces was lost
in something harder and warier; and a cockney type began to emerge
discernibly—a cynical young mongrel, barbaric of feature, muscular and cunning; dressed in good fabrics fashioned apparently in imitation of the sketches
drawn by newspaper comedians. The female of his kind came with him—a pale
girl, shoddy and a little rouged; and they communicated in a nasal argot, mainly
insolences and elisions. Nay, the common speech of the people showed change;
in place of the old midland vernacular, irregular but clean, and not un-
wholesomely drawling, a jerky dialect of coined metaphors began to be heard,
held together by *gunnas* and *gottas* and much fostered by the public journals.

The city piled itself high in the center, tower on tower for a nucleus, and
spread itself out over the plain, mile after mile; and in its vitals, like benevolent
bacilli contending with malevolent in the body of a man, missions and refuges
offered what resistance they might to the saloons and all the hells that cities
house and shelter. Temptation and ruin were ready commodities on the market
for purchase by the venturesome; highwaymen walked the streets at night and
sometimes killed; snatching thieves were busy everywhere in the dusk; while
housebreakers were a common apprehension and frequent reality. Life itself
was somewhat safer from intentional destruction than it was in medieval Rome
during a faction war—though the Roman murderer was more like to pay for his

deed — but death or mutilation beneath the wheels lay in ambush at every crossing.

The politicians let the people make all the laws they liked; it did not matter much, and the taxes went up, which is good for politicians. Law-making was a pastime of the people; nothing pleased them more. Singular fermentation of their humor, they even had laws forbidding dangerous speed. More marvelous still, they had a law forbidding smoke! They forbade chimneys to smoke and they forbade cigarettes to smoke. They made laws for all things and forgot them immediately; though sometimes they would remember after a while, and hurry to make new laws that the old laws should be enforced — and then forget both new and old. Wherever enforcement threatened Money or Votes — or wherever it was too much bother — it became a joke. Influence was the law.

So the place grew. And it grew strong.

Straightway when he came, each man fell to the same worship:

> Give me of thyself, O Bigness:
> Power to get more power!
> Riches to get more riches!
> Give me of thy sweat that I may sweat more!
> Give me Bigness to get more Bigness to myself,
> O Bigness, for Thine is the Power and the Glory! And
>   there is no end but Bigness, ever and for ever!

A Black Migrant Experiences the Urban Environment, 1927

My first glimpse of the flat black stretches of Chicago depressed and dismayed me, mocked all my fantasies. Chicago seemed an unreal city whose mythical houses were built of slabs of black coal wreathed in palls of gray smoke, houses whose foundations were sinking slowly into the dank prairie. Flashes of steam showed intermittently on the wise horizon, gleaming translucently in the winter sun. The din of the city entered my consciousness, entered to remain for years to come. The year was 1927.

What would happen to me here? Would I survive? My expectations were modest. I wanted only a job. Hunger had long been my daily companion. Diversion and recreation, with the exception of reading, were unknown. In all my life — though surrounded by many people — I had not had a single satisfying, sustained relationship with another human being and, not having had any, I did not miss it. I made no demands whatever upon others.

The train rolled into the depot. Aunt Maggie and I got off and walked slowly through the crowds into the station. I looked about to see if there were signs saying: FOR WHITE — FOR COLORED. I saw none. Black people and white people moved about, each seemingly intent upon his private mission. There

Excerpt from *American Hunger*, by Richard Wright. Copyright 1944 by Richard Wright, pp. 1–3. Copyright renewed 1977 by Ellen Wright. Reprinted by permission of HarperCollins Publishers.

was no racial fear. Indeed, each person acted as though no one existed but himself. It was strange to pause before a crowded newsstand and buy a newspaper without having to wait until a white man was served. And yet, because everything was so new, I began to grow tense again, although it was a different sort of tension than I had known before. I knew that this machine-city was governed by strange laws and I wondered if I would ever learn them.

As we waited for a streetcar to take us to Aunt Cleo's home for temporary lodging, I looked northward at towering buildings of steel and stone. There were no curves here, no trees; only angles, lines, squares, bricks and copper wires. Occasionally the ground beneath my feet shook from some faraway pounding and I felt that this world, despite its massiveness, was somehow dangerously fragile. Streetcars screeched past over steel tracks. Cars honked their horns. Clipped speech sounded about me. As I stood in the icy wind, I wanted to talk to Aunt Maggie, to ask her questions, but her tight face made me hold my tongue. I was learning already from the frantic light in her eyes the strain that the city imposed upon its people. I was seized by doubt. Should I have come here? But going back was impossible. I had fled a known terror, and perhaps I could cope with this unknown terror that lay ahead.

The streetcar came. Aunt Maggie motioned for me to get on and pushed me toward a seat in which a white man sat looking blankly out the window. I sat down beside the man and looked straight ahead of me. After a moment I stole a glance at the white man out of the corners of my eyes; he was still staring out the window, his mind fastened upon some inward thought. I did not exist for him; I was as far from his mind as the stone buildings that swept past in the street. It would have been illegal for me to sit beside him in the part of the South that I had come from.

The car swept past soot-blackened buildings, stopping at each block, jerking again into motion. The conductor called street names in a tone that I could not understand. People got on and off the car, but they never glanced at one another. Each person seemed to regard the other as a part of the city landscape. The white man who sat beside me rose and I turned my knees aside to let him pass, and another white man sat beside me and buried his face in a newspaper. How could that possibly be? Was he conscious of my blackness?

✹ E S S A Y S

The essays examine the history of urban pollution and environmental reform from several social perspectives. In the first selection, Martin V. Melosi, an environmental historian at the University of Houston, discusses efforts over time to deal with city refuse through technological and engineering approaches to solid-waste management. Suellen M. Hoy, executive secretary of the Public Works Historical Society, argues in the second essay that women constituted a significant force in the movement to clean up urban environments. Finally, the third essay, written by environmental historian Andrew Hurley, looks at industrial pollution in Gary, Indiana, in the context of the city's history as a steel town employing a large black labor force.

City Wastes

MARTIN V. MELOSI

"The problems associated with hazardous waste were virtually unknown a few years ago. In a remarkably short period of time, however, they have climbed to the top of the American public opinion polls as a source of concern to the American people." This remark by Tennessee Senator Albert Gore, Jr. in 1982 is representative of the public perception of environmental issues in the United States. Most Americans, if they think about it at all, assume that the environmental movement is a product of the late 1960s and early 1970s. Some might associate modern environmental concerns with the establishment of Yellowstone Park, the presidency of Theodore Roosevelt, Gifford Pinchot's resource conservation, or John Muir's naturalism; but they fail to connect recent quality of life issues with the more obscure antismoke campaign of the 1910s or the push for sanitary sewers in the 1850s. Similarly, this dwelling on the present causes one to see the hazardous waste problem as growing out of Love Canal (1978) and to date the legislative response to the advent of Superfund in 1980. Granted, those most expert in the field acknowledge the complex origins of toxic materials, but too little attention has been paid to the antecedents of the current hazardous waste problems in the United States.

Historical perspective not only helps set the context in which to understand the scale and nature of the waste problem in America but also sheds light on the evolution of environmental liability. Preliminary research suggests that post–World War II concepts of environmental liability, as they pertain to hazardous waste, grew out of issues regarding municipal refuse collection and disposal and industrial waste disposal in the period 1880–1940. In addition, regulatory concerns about hazardous materials in recent years have been grounded in the waste problems of the past. As Bruce Piasecki and Gary A. Davis suggest, "regulatory programs have evolved in an entirely reactive fashion, building piecemeal on old assumptions about solid waste that proved insufficient in the light of technical discoveries emerging almost daily."

In an attempt to provide a historical framework for understanding environmental liability as it pertains to hazardous waste, this article will focus on the period 1880–1940, with emphasis on: (1) the nature of the municipal waste problem and the impact of collection and disposal practices; (2) the extent and nature of industrial waste disposal; and (3) [engineering and technical] . . . responses to contemporary environmental problems.* The pervasiveness of municipal waste in this period raised initial concern about refuse as a health hazard. Growing public awareness of a garbage "nuisance" in the 1880s led, by the turn of the century, to the institution of solid waste management programs in every major city. Debate over the dumping of industrial waste on land and

---

*For judicial and legislative responses, see original article.

From Martin Melosi, "Hazardous Waste and Environmental Liability: An Historical Perspective," *Houston Law Review*, 25, no. 4, July 1988, 741–53. Reprinted by permission of the Houston Law Review.

in watercourses, and a growing interest in smoke abatement, brought about the first major efforts to document the range of toxic substances utilized in the United States and pitted the desire for perpetual economic growth against an increasing demand for a clean environment. The evolution of the concept of public nuisance in the courts and the implementation of pollution abatement statutes (through local ordinances and both state and federal legislation) established important precedents for environmental liability in the post–World War II era.

Refuse is primarily an urban blight. Agrarian societies throughout history generally escaped refuse pollution, while cities and towns faced the gravest dangers. The urban refuse problem has been a result of limited space and dense population. Thus, it is modern industrial society, rather than the ancient primitive cultures, that has experienced the most intense refuse problems. With the Industrial Revolution in Europe and the United States came human concentration in and around cities, an expanding emphasis on material acquisitiveness, extraordinary amounts of mass-produced goods and their accompanying pollutants. Ironically, as industrial America became more affluent, its waste problems loomed larger.

By the late 1880s, the refuse problem was so apparent that the average citizen needed little stimulus to become concerned. In Chicago, 225 street teams gathered about 2,000 cubic yards of refuse daily. By the turn of the century in Manhattan, scavengers averaged 612 tons of garbage daily; during July and August, that volume increased to 1,100 tons.

In most of the major American cities, the per capita amount of refuse collected annually ranged from one-half to three-quarters of a ton. European city dwellers produced substantially less. A 1905 study indicated that 14 American cities averaged 860 pounds of mixed rubbish per capita annually while in 8 English cities the amount was 450 pounds per capita, and in 77 German cities, 319 pounds. In 1912, Franz Schnieder, research associate of the Sanitary Laboratory of the Massachusetts Institute of Technology, calculated that if the entire year's refuse of New York City was gathered in one place "the resulting mass would equal in volume a cube about one-eighth of a mile on an edge. This surprisingly large volume is over three times that of the great pyramid of Ghizeh, and would accommodate one hundred and forty Washington monuments with ease."

In the late nineteenth century, horses—the major means of transportation—rivaled humans in waste production. At the turn of the century, there were three to three and one-half million horses in American cities. Engineers estimated that the normal, healthy city horse produced more than twenty pounds of manure and several gallons of urine daily, most of which ended up in the streets. Cumulative totals of manure produced by horses are staggering: 26,000 horses in Brooklyn yielded about 200 tons daily, and 12,500 horses in Milwaukee produced about 133 tons. In the 1850s, the proliferation of horse-cars for mass transit exacerbated the problem. By the mid-1880s, 100,000 horses and mules were pulling 18,000 horsecars over 3,500 miles of track nationwide. The discharges not only cluttered the streets and corroded the metal streetcar tracks but also threatened the health of city dwellers. Stables and manure pits were notorious breeding grounds for disease. And since the life expectancy of a city horse was only about two years, carcasses were plentiful. New York City scavengers removed fifteen thousand dead horses in 1880.

With so much organic waste accumulating in the streets and alleys, one would have expected urbanites to recognize a major sanitation problem in the making. For many years, however, garbage and rubbish had been perceived as mere inconveniences. The connection between waste and disease was finally established with the emergence of modern health science in England in the mid-nineteenth century. In 1842, the Poor Law Commission published a report — authored primarily by the lawyer-turned-sanitarian Edwin Chadwick — concerning the sanitary condition of the working population. The most significant conclusion of the report was that communicable disease was related to filthy environmental conditions, in some way. The establishment of the Sanitary Commission in 1869 and the subsequent enactment of public health laws provided for corrective environmental sanitation measures in England, which led to reductions in urban disease. Similar programs, established later in other parts of Europe and in the United States, signaled a new "age of sanitation."

At the heart of the new sanitary science was the notion that environmental factors caused disease. The "miasmic," or filth, theory dominated American thinking on sanitation into the 1890s. According to the theory, gases emanating from putrefying matter and sewers produced contagious diseases. Environmental sanitation — including proper drainage and sewerage, adequate ventilation of buildings, and the timely collection of refuse — seemed to offer an immediate and effective hedge against epidemics. Sanitary programs based on the miasmic theory gained popular support and enjoyed several major victories, including: The writing of the New York Metropolitan Health Law (1860), the creation of state boards of health (beginning with the Massachusetts board in 1869), the founding of the American Public Health Association in 1872, and the establishment of the short-lived National Board of Health in 1879.

As the sole means of ridding the cities of disease, environmental sanitation had some serious drawbacks. In the 1880s the discovery of specific pathogenic organisms — bacteria — enabled public health officials and sanitarians to understand the actual causes of many contagious diseases. In the twentieth century, bacteriological laboratories became the chief means of controlling epidemics.

The transition from the widely accepted miasmic theory to the *germ theory* was not a simple one. Anticontagionists continued to offer strong resistance to bacteriological science through the mid-1880s. Most people were unable to comprehend that something unseen or unfelt could be the cause of disease. Even the venerable *Scientific American*, in 1878, chided the advocates of the new theory for accepting such a farfetched notion. Impressive reductions in the mortality rate between 1860 and 1880, attributable in some measure to improved sanitation practices, further weakened the case for bacteriology. The death rate in most cities fell from between twenty-five to forty persons per thousand in 1860 to between sixteen to twenty-six per thousand in 1880. Rates were especially low in cities with sound sanitary practices. Nonetheless, the tenacity of the contagionists and the inconsistent results of environmental sanitation began to mute the controversy. The verifiable successes of immunization and inoculation and the advances credited to the bacteriological laboratories in the early twentieth century were far more impressive than the erratic record of "municipal housecleaning" and other sanitation practices.

The contagionists' victory over the anticontagionists was, however, only a qualified success. Adherents of the germ theory too readily accepted bacteriology as the only way to avert epidemics and too quickly dismissed environmental sanitation as a valuable tool in disease prevention. In the eyes of many in the health field, the emphasis on the environment as the root cause of disease had been misplaced or at least exaggerated. The scientific basis of environmental sanitation was seriously flawed, but its goal of removing potential breeding grounds of disease had merit.

The demise of the filth theory led to a critical appraisal of whether environmental sanitation was a proper function of health departments. In the growing urban bureaucracies after mid-century, environmental sanitation initially had become the province of municipal health authorities. The 1880 census reveals that at least ninety-four percent of the cities surveyed had a board of health, a health commission, or a health officer. Of these authorities forty-six percent had some direct control over the collection and disposal of refuse.

Throughout the 1880s and 1890s, public health officers dominated the thinking on collection and disposal practices. Now regarded as a health problem, refuse could no longer be treated simply as an inconvenience. In 1887, citing the unsatisfactory state of collection and disposal methods throughout the nation, the American Public Health Association established a Committee on Garbage Disposal. The Committee spent ten years studying the extent of the refuse problem in the United States, gathering statistics from every major city, examining European methods, and analyzing local practices. Efforts such as these demonstrate the degree to which the health question infused refuse reform with a sense of direction and purpose.

Warnings by sanitarians and public health officers about the potential health hazards associated with accumulating waste soon began to raise public consciousness of the need for better sanitation. Concern about the waste problem was reflected in most newspapers, popular magazines, and technical and professional journals of the day. Citizens' neglect was a popular theme. One writer noted that "[t]he average citizen, accustomed to endure nuisances as a humpback carries his deformity, saunters along sublimely indifferent to foul smells, obstructed sidewalks, etc." As the refuse problem gained wider publicity, citizen groups joined sanitarians and public health officials in calling for improvement of collection and disposal practices.

But almost as soon as the public health community took center stage in identifying refuse as a health hazard and promoting environmental sanitation, it questioned the necessity of supervising or directing collection and disposal programs. Public health officials continued to regard refuse as a health problem, albeit somewhat diminished by the new adherence to the germ theory, but few believed that its solution required the active involvement of municipal health departments. Dr. Charles V. Chapin — Superintendent of Health in Providence, Rhode Island and one of the pioneers in the American public health movement—believed that the health officer "should be free to devote more energy to those things which he alone can do. He should not waste his time arguing with the owners of pigsties or compelling landlords to empty their cesspools."

By the early twentieth century, collection and disposal of refuse shifted from health departments to departments of public works. However, in most cities where health departments did not oversee collection and disposal, they did retain enforcement power over nuisances and, in some instances, supervisory power over the selection of contractors. Such compromises often led to jurisdictional disputes among municipal departments and prevented the definition of precise roles for health officers in sanitation programs. In addition, the shift of the collection and disposal functions to public works departments tended to identify refuse as more of an engineering or technical problem than as a health problem.

The municipal engineer was the obvious choice to assume responsibility for the refuse problem. The growing belief that environmental sanitation was a task primarily requiring effective administrative and technical expertise, supplemented by some basic medical and scientific knowledge, pointed directly to the engineering profession. By 1900, engineering was the second largest profession in the United States, following close behind teaching. By 1930, the engineering ranks had swelled to 226,000. The vitality of the profession was apparent not only in the increasing numbers of engineers but also in the diversity of their activities.

Inevitably, large numbers of engineers looked to the cities as their primary arenas of enterprise and opportunity. By the late nineteenth century, engineers were playing major roles as consultants to city officials or as administrators and employees in various municipal departments. The need for safe water supplies, adequate sewerage, well ventilated housing, and efficient refuse collection and disposal required the engineer's technical expertise and the public health officer's knowledge of sanitation. A hybrid profession, sanitary engineering, emerged to meet the environmental challenge of the burgeoning industrial cities.

The origins of the new profession were in Europe. During the 1870s, the emergence of sanitary engineers coincided with the development of the biological sciences and the implementation of water filtration and sewage treatment in London and other major European cities. By 1890, a few professionally trained sanitary engineers were graduating from American technical schools. By 1900, whole curricula were available at some of the leading private and public universities. Like their European counterparts, American sanitary engineers received their first practical education in developing public water supplies and constructing citywide sewerage systems.

The widespread recognition of the accomplishments of sanitary engineers and the concomitant abandonment of environmental sanitation by health departments encouraged municipal officials to look to sanitary engineers to resolve another pressing urban problem, refuse collection and disposal. Faith in technology fostered the belief that since the water carriage problem had been solved by technical means, refuse could likewise be mastered through the skills of the engineer.

Sanitary engineers were not always successful in finding solutions to the confounding problems of collection and disposal, but they produced the first comprehensive study of the refuse problem, which identified a range of possible solutions. Although some of their recommendations were criticized or ignored by municipal leaders in the politically charged atmosphere of city government, they offered realistic alternatives to the primitive methods still being practiced, such as indiscriminate land and water dumping of wastes. They also provided the first national, and even international, perspective on refuse problems which further helped discredit the shortsighted programs of the past.

Sanitary engineers understood the importance of gathering and collating data as a necessary prelude to offering possible solutions. From the late nineteenth century onward, engineering societies, often in conjunction with other groups interested in sanitation, applied their resources to conducting surveys and assembling data on collection and disposal practices in North America and abroad.

Nevertheless, sanitary engineers were not satisfied simply to collect statistics. Necessary additional steps included implementing new programs or revising old ones. This required effective administration. Sanitary engineers advised municipalities on ways of placing public works departments on a business footing. Borrowing heavily from private industry as well as from successful water and wastewater carriage programs, they sought to centralize refuse management through uniformity in organizational methods and the implementation of new accounting and recordkeeping systems.

Among the sanitary engineers' recommendations for efficient refuse management was an almost universal support for municipal control of sanitation functions. Although commitment to community responsibility in street cleaning and garbage removal was spotty during the 1880s and 1890s, the increasing emphasis on "home rule" in the larger cities and the subsequent expansion of municipal bureaucracies made municipal control of sanitation seem more practical. Most sanitary engineers had a vested interest in municipal control of sanitation, since it not only provided a greater degree of permanence and a larger capital base than contracted services, but also guaranteed job security. In their influential book *Collection and Disposal of Municpal Refuse*, Rudolph Hering and Samuel Greeley stated bluntly: "[t]he collecton of public refuse is a public utility."

Although sanitary engineers were unable to find the ultimate technical solutions to collection and disposal, they did make strides in placing in perspective the relative strengths and weaknesses of primitive methods and the potential applicability of new techniques. With the luxury of hindsight they appreciated many of the limitations of nineteenth century methods. They almost universally condemned, or at least criticized, such practices as land and sea dumping, open burning, and filling with untreated wastes.

Until World War I, the two disposal methods which received the greatest attention from sanitary engineers were incineration and reduction. The success of the English "destructor," or incinerator, led to dozens of attempts to find an application suitable to American conditions. Interest in reduction was relatively short-lived, but it emphasized the potential value in recycling used materials. The two disposal "solutions" of the late nineteenth and early twentieth centuries fell on hard times after 1930. Both methods failed to operate as efficiently as engineers had hoped, both created air pollution problems, and both required substantial capital outlays. Interest in the reduction process waned after 1910 and never recovered. Incineration fared better and continued to be a viable disposal method, but not to the same extent as in the 1910s. By the late 1930s the number of incinerators had declined sharply.

Of all the disposal methods, none captured the fancy of the engineer as did the sanitary landfill. Although the sanitary landfill did not become a primary disposal method until the 1940s, it was still considered the breakthrough that revived a nineteenth century interest in filling depressions or trenches with waste. The sanitary landfill was a more carefully supervised and maintained modification of the primitive method of garbage burial. The basic principle was to utilize all forms of waste and, at the same time, eliminate the problem of putrefaction of organic materials. Typical sanitary fills were layered: twelve inches of garbage were covered with eighteen to twenty-four inches of ashes, street sweepings, or rubbish. Then another layer of garbage was added and so forth. Chemicals were sometimes sprayed on the fill to retard putrefaction.

The method took several years to gain popularity because it was relatively expensive in the early years and it was labor intensive. The British pioneered the use of sanitary landfills in World War I, calling the process "controlled tipping." By 1935 almost forty-five percent of all English refuse was placed in tips. In the 1910s, cities as diverse as Seattle, New Orleans, and Davenport, Iowa, experimented with fills. San Francisco constructed a sanitary landfill in 1926 after abandoning its incinerators. In the 1930s, Fresno, California, and New York City developed sanitary landfills which were important models for many other disposal programs.

Often, open dumps passed for sanitary fills. After World War II, however, some care was taken to replace open dumping with better controlled sanitary fills, and the pioneering efforts in New York City and Fresno, and on military bases under the direction of the Army Corps of Engineers, brought more respectability to what became the new disposal panacea. The prevailing wisdom was that sanitary landfilling was the most economical form of disposal and, at the same time, offered an environmentally safe method which also produced reclaimed land. Proponents of sanitary landfill were zealous in their praise of the method, but as often happens, translating an idea into practice was not easy. As late as the mid-1970s, ninety-four percent of the seventeen thousand land disposal sites surveyed did not meet the minimum requirements for a sanitary fill.

The nature of the waste problem and the evolution of solid waste management in the United States is too complex to present in this paper. Nevertheless, several key issues from the historical record relate to the more recent problem of hazardous waste and modern concepts of environmental liability. First, the acknowledgment of collection and disposal as a municipal responsibility in the late nineteenth century made refuse a public, or community, issue. Second, the waste problem was transformed from an inconvenience into a health hazard, largely through the efforts of public health advocates and sanitarians. Third, by relinquishing major responsibility for environmental sanitation, resulting from the advocacy of bacteriology as a solution to communicable diseases, public health officials had accepted the idea of refuse as an engineering issue. While waste remained a health hazard, proper collection and disposal appeared achievable through the application of technology. And fourth, the growing interest in the sanitary landfill as an alternative to incineration and reduction, created the impetus for land disposal as a panacea for the increasing generation of solid wastes.

Women and City Wastes in the Early Twentieth Century

SUELLEN M. HOY

> As society grows more complicated it is necessary that woman shall
> extend her sense of responsibility to many things outside of her home,
> if only in order to preserve the home in its entirety.
>
> Jane Addams
> "Woman's Conscience and Social Amelioration"
> (1908)

During the late nineteenth and early twentieth centuries, Americans witnessed the transformation of the United States from a predominantly rural-agricultural society to a primarily urban-industrial one. Many Americans, especially those living in cities, were disturbed by the rapidity and complexity of the change and were anxious about the future of traditional American values and institutions. Women, as individuals and in groups, found themselves particularly concerned about their homes and families. It is not surprising that many of them took on the important task of improving the urban environment.

Men and women alike believed that it was only natural for women to serve as "municipal housekeepers" in their communities. George E. Waring, the well-known sanitary engineer, was convinced that "city cleansing" was above all "woman's work." It required the "sort of systematized attention to detail, especially in the constantly recurring duty of 'cleaning-up,' that grows more naturally out of the habit of good housekeeping than out of any occupation to which man is accustomed." Dr. Katherine Bement Davis, New York City's commissioner of correction, agreed. She observed that it had always been woman's responsibility "to do the spanking and the house-cleaning."

Countless women in the United States joined a multiplicity of civic leagues, women's clubs, and village improvement societies. Discussions at meetings and club publications reinforced the conviction that "city housekeeping was quite as much their vocation as taking care of the home" and that their own health and happiness as well as that of their families depended in large part

Text by Suellen M. Hoy, " 'Municipal Housekeeping': The Role of Women in Improving Urban Sanitation Practices, 1880–1917" in Martin Melosi, ed., *Pollution and Reform in American Cities, 1870–1930*, 1980, pp. 173–6, 193–4. Reprinted by permission of University of Texas Press.

on the sanitary conditions of their communities. Club officers also reminded members that women "are no less good mothers and devoted wives because they realize that many outside influences touch their domestic life." Thus, women in large numbers came to believe that "the one calling in which they were, as a body, proficient, that of housekeeping and homemaking, had its outdoor as well as its indoor application." This knowledge led them into the movement for sanitary reform.

In nearly every region of the country, groups of women became involved in activities that, among other things, included cleaning streets, inspecting markets, abating smoke, purifying water, and collecting and disposing of refuse. Several women were appointed to positions in local government and made responsible for improving the cleanliness of their cities. One woman, Caroline Bartlett Crane of Kalamazoo, Michigan, was hired as a consultant by over sixty municipalities to prepare sanitary surveys. And Mary E. McDowell, commonly referred to as the "Garbage Lady," was instrumental in effecting substantial changes in the solid waste disposal practices of Chicago, Illinois.

The early women's groups were rather exclusive, with membership ordinarily restricted to women of the upper and upper-middle classes who had extended periods of leisure, common interests, and congenial tastes. Women in these clubs typically met at each others' homes and at other social gatherings and discussed art, literature, and related subjects. Not until the late nineteenth century did they begin to concern themselves with philanthropic and civic affairs.

Middle-class housewives made up the majority of club women interested in improving urban sanitary conditions. Many were middle-aged, had children in school, and often hired servants to clean their homes. There remained, however, a strong contingent of upper- and upper-middle-class women who kept active in civic affairs and who frequently retained leadership positions in women's organizations. For example, many of the women who followed Jane Addam's example and ran settlement houses in the nation's largest cities (Mary McDowell, Mary Simkhovitch, Lillian Wald, and others) belonged to the upper class.

As early as 1894, the Civic Club of Philadelphia made its initial attack on littered and garbage-strewn gardens and streets. Established "to promote by education and active co-operation a higher public spirit and a better social order," the club obtained permission from city officials to place baskets for wastepaper and refuse in the zoological gardens, which visitors badly littered. The experiment proved so successful that the women devised a plan to place receptacles in other areas of the city. In 1896, after obtaining permission from the Philadelphia Department of Public Works, they purchased forty-five receptacles and positioned them on carefully selected street corners in the city's Seventh Ward. At the year's end, there had been a marked improvement in the appearance of the area. In June 1897, the club offered the receptacles to the city council, which accepted them with gratitude. The council also made a $400 appropriation for purchasing similar receptacles to be placed in other parts of the same district.

The work of the Civic Club did not end with the council's action. Members were encouraged to become acquainted with municipal regulations on the collection of ashes and garbage and to report infringements to the Department of Public Works. Although their complaints "received prompt and courteous attention," the women of Philadelphia did not slacken their voluntary efforts on behalf of a clean community. They were rewarded for their service in 1913 when Edith W. Pierce became the first female city inspector of street cleaning. In appointing Pierce to this position, Morris L. Cooke, the director of public works, noted that her responsibilities would be "somewhat different from that of the men inspectors." She was to inspect the entire city rather than a single district. Motivated by what she called the "three C's" — "Care, Commonsense, and Co-operation" — Pierce efficiently carried out her official assignments. She also organized sectional associations for keeping streets, sidewalks, homes, and schools clean and founded a Junior Sanitation League, modeled after George E. Waring's New York City organization.

The Civic Club of Philadelphia was not the only women's club on the eastern seaboard to educate cities to "a sense of . . . their own needs" during the late nineteenth century. In 1884 a Ladies' Health Protective Association (LHPA) was formed in New York City to confront the problem of the ever-increasing amount of garbage, manure, and rubbish left in the streets. In the introduction of an appeal to Mayor Abram S. Hewitt, the women explained why they had become involved:

> It is the climax of aggravation to the painstaking housekeeper to look out of her windows and see ash barrels standing forgotten on the sidewalk from hour to hour and often from day to day; to have those barrels toppled over by sportive boys or raked over by grimy ragpickers, and the contents left in hillocks in the street from one month's end to another; and supposing even that she personally . . . carefully sweeps and washes her own area flags and space of sidewalk, to have these covered within two hours by the sticks, loose papers and powdered manure that blow upon them from all quarters alike.

The women recommended to the mayor ways of improving the sanitary conditions of New York City's streets. They asked that the annual appropriation for street cleaning be adequate for the work; that street sweeping machines be used late in the night; that neither ashes nor garbage be allowed on pavements in front of residences; that householders be required to own galvanized iron receptacles; that crematories be built to dispose of house ashes, garbage, and street sweepings; and that the city be divided into convenient sections managed by foremen, responsible to a street commissioner-in-chief, and cleaned by laborers, paid by the piece and not by the day. The Ladies' Health Protective Association also suggested that women be appointed as inspectors, since "keeping things clean, like the training of children and the care of the sick, has ever been one of the instinctive and recognized functions of women."

The Ladies' Health Protective Association continued its drive for clean streets through programs of its own and in cooperation with another group, the Sanitary Protective League, founded in 1890. Aside from creating a greater public awareness of the problem, the group achieved few significant results until Waring was appointed street cleaning commissioner in 1894. The LHPA was far more successful in its campaign to regulate public slaughterhouses. During the winter of 1884–85, it made a thorough investigation of the city's slaughterhouses and presented its findings to the board of health. On the basis of this report, the board persuaded the legislature to pass an amendment in June 1885 restricting slaughterhouses in New York City to an area bound by the Hudson River and Eleventh Avenue between Thirty-ninth and Fortieth streets. In 1895 the New York City Department of Health gave special thanks to the LHPA for its enduring support, noting that the women had been zealous in inspecting rendering companies and in reporting unsanitary conditions.

The Woman's Municipal League of New York City followed in the tradition of the Ladies' Health Protective Association. Acting on a recommendation of the latter group and with the permission of the commissioner of street cleaning, the league's Committee on Streets raised funds to pay women to inspect the work of the Street Cleaning Department in various parts of the city and to award certificates and "Waring medals" to sweepers, drivers, and foremen who did the "best all-around work." William H. Edwards, commissioner of street cleaning, spoke warmly of the women's efforts at a conference of mayors and city officials in Binghamton, New York, in June 1913. He was grateful to the women for their "keen interest in his men" and for raising the standards of the department. . . .

The concern for the urban environment shown by individual women and groups of women in Chicago, Kalamazoo, Boston, New York, and Philadelphia was in evidence in almost every city of the United States during the late nineteenth and early twentieth centuries. In St. Louis, Cincinnati, and Pittsburgh, for example, middle-class women who considered themselves guardians of their families' health joined together and became the vanguard of the anti-smoke crusade. In St. Louis, for example, members of the Women's Organization for Smoke Abatement, known as the Wednesday Club until 1910, were tireless in their efforts to enforce existing smoke ordinances and to test new devices designed to abate the smoke nuisance.

In other parts of the country, several individual women earned the respect of their communities for their work on behalf of improved sanitary standards. In 1899 New Orleans' Kate Gordon, founder of the city's ERA [Equal Rights Association] Club and a leading suffragist in Louisiana, directed a successful campaign in favor of a bond issue that insured completion of the municipal water purification and drainage system. In Denver, Colorado, Sarah Platt Decker, president of the city's Woman's Club in 1894 and of the General Federation of Women's Clubs in 1904, became well known for her activities to secure cleaner streets and alleys. And in Portland, Oregon, Sarah A. Evans, who became president of the General Federation of Women's Clubs in 1914, led an early crusade that resulted in the nation's first municipal market sanitation ordinance and in her appointment as food and market inspector. Evans' work became a model for clubs throughout the United States.

Although their efforts have been largely overlooked, women were a significant force in the movement to improve living conditions in the industrial cities of the United States. Motivated by a desire to protect their homes and families, large numbers of women believed that they, the nation's homemakers, could make a special contribution to the housekeeping practices of their communities. In so doing, they demonstrated the importance of citizen participation in civic affairs; for they not only awakened the general public to the ways in which cities were being managed and kept, but they were also directly responsible for the passage of needed legislation and the initiation of improved sanitation practices.

In general, the movement for sanitary reform attracted women who were satisfied with their traditional societal roles as wives, mothers, and homemakers. They were women who were seeking ways to enlarge their sphere of action "without touching the sources of their inequality." They adopted goals that were conservative in nature: "to educate members, mentally and morally; to create public opinion; to secure better conditions of life." Products of their age, they characteristically employed the three-pronged Progressive method of investigation, education, and persuasion to achieve their ends. Although not every program they espoused was completely implemented, women — as individuals and in groups — were particularly instrumental in making the urban environment a healthier and more comfortable place in which to live.

Blacks and City Wastes in the Late Twentieth Century

ANDREW HURLEY

The proliferation of industrial wastes in urban America coincided with a growing public concern about environmental degradation. . . . Gary, Indiana provides an ideal setting for examining ecological change. . . . The concentration of steel manufacturing along the southern shore of Lake Michigan produced enormous quantities of airborne and waterborne industrial wastes. . . . How did . . . waste disposal patterns affect rich and poor, white and black, white collar and blue collar [between 1945 and 1980]?

The grand Calumet River divided Gary's factories from its residential population. To the north, along the Lake Michigan shoreline, sprawled the massive manufacturing plants of the United States Steel Corporation. US Steel's decision to locate between the Grand Calumet River and Lake Michigan derived from advantages of transportation, production, and waste disposal. Several rail lines passed through the site. Lake Michigan provided water transportation for the shipment of iron ore from the Mesabi Range in Minnesota and provided abundant water for cooling. Both the lake and river served as convenient repositories for waste. With the exception of a cement plant in the northwestern corner, US Steel devoted its land to making and processing steel. Among its various factories were a sheet and tin mill, a tube works, and a bridge construction plant. The central unit, Gary Works, produced coke and finished steel.

Excerpts from Andrew Hurley, "The Social Biases of Environment in Gary, Indiana, 1945–1980," *Environmental Review* (Winter 1988): pp. 1–19. Reprinted with permission from *Environmental History Review*, © 1982, The American Society for Environmental History.

Gary's residential community stretched south from the steel factories. US Steel built housing for its executives and skilled workers just beyond the mill gates. The remainder of the population settled further south. While settlement of Gary's southern, western and eastern fringes increased between 1910 and 1945, the hub of the population remained in north Gary, adjacent to the steel mills. The location of Gary's residential population in relation to the factories determined how various social groups were affected by industry's waste disposal patterns. . . .

Particulate dust constituted the most obvious and abundant source of air pollution. Small carbon particles flowed in streams of thick black smoke from coke plant smokestacks. The sintering plant and open-hearth furnaces discharged iron dust, covering the mill skyline with a bright red hue. Gary Works also emitted invisible fumes in lesser quantities, such as sulfur dioxide, nitrogen oxide, and hydrocarbons. When winds blew from the south, they dispersed dust and fumes over the lake. When they came from the north, suspended iron, cement, and coke particles hovered over the city and rained down upon its citizens. Gary's oldest neighborhoods and its downtown commercial district, which lay just south of Gary Works, were hit hardest. Industry dumped twice as much dust on these areas as on the city's remote regions. The cleanest sections were Glen Park and Miller. (See Map A.) Glen Park, six miles inland, stood furthest from the mills. The community of Miller stood several miles to the east

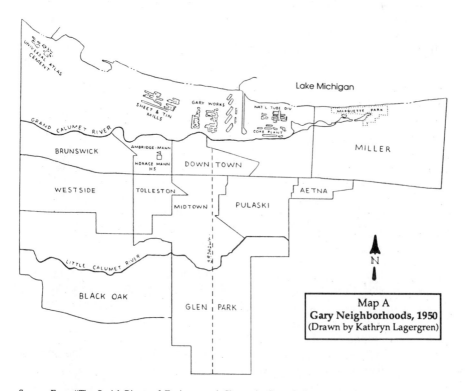

Map A
Gary Neighborhoods, 1950
(Drawn by Kathryn Lagergren)

Source: From "The Social Biases of Environmental Change in Gary, Indiana, 1944–1980, by Andrew Hurley, *Environmental Review* 12, no. 4 (Winter 1988), p. 3.

of the coke plant along the lakeshore, but received even less exposure than Glen Park as a result of wind patterns. The sparsely populated west side escaped much of Gary Works' pollution but suffered from cement plant discharges in addition to pollution from neighboring East Chicago's steel mills.

Industrial land and water use affected Gary less severely than air pollution but, once again, residents of north Gary bore the greatest burden. US Steel dumped its most toxic liquid wastes in the Grand Calumet River which flowed into Lake Michigan west of the city. Currents then carried most of these wastes northwestward to Chicago. Gary's water utility located its lake intake far to the east of the waste stream. The Grand Calumet River posed a greater threat to human health than the lake. Industrial discharges of ammonia, cyanide, phenols, and oils rendered the river uninhabitable for all life forms except blue-green algae and sludgeworms. For most of its journey through Gary it meandered through US Steel property; only in northwest Gary did the river enter residential neighborhoods. Children sometimes played on the river bank and swam in the dirty water where they risked absorbing toxic chemicals through their skin. A more serious problem affected families living near the river who were not hooked up to the city's water utility. Several thousand West Gary residents relied on well water that was probably contaminated from industrial wastes that seeped from the river through groundwater.

Prior to 1950, few industries used land as a receptacle for waste. US Steel maintained several pits on its property for the disposal of acid and mill scale, an impurity scrubbed from steel in the finishing process. For most industries, wastes usually ended up in the air or water. Land served primarily as sites for the construction of factories. . . .

Gary was a city of distinct neighborhoods. Blacks clustered together, the wealthy and poor lived apart, and working class whites often resided with others of similar ethnic background. But these cells of social activity were small and scattered indiscriminately throughout the city. Only the black community, crammed together in one neighborhood, Midtown, deviated from this pattern. . . .

Just after World War II, Gary's 39,000 blacks constituted less than 30 percent of the citizenry. They were restricted to the Midtown area, in the center of the city. Over the next thirty-five years, the number of blacks nearly tripled to make up 71 percent of Gary's population. As the black community grew and became more congested, pressure built to expand Midtown's adjacent areas. Then, in the late 1960s, Midtown burst open; its residents spilled in all directions.

Migrating blacks met varying degrees of resistance from their white neighbors. While some communities witnessed protracted battles over residential integration, others transformed from white to black neighborhoods rapidly. The path of least resistance for blacks was north and west, closer to the heart of the industrial environment. During the 1950s, West Gary was exclusively white. By 1970, the white population dwindled from 9,000 to 6,000. Ten years later, less than 1,500 whites remained. Blacks constituted 90 percent of the population while Hispanics accounted for another 8 percent.

By contrast, the areas most removed from the pathways of industrial wastes resisted black immigration most successfully. The neighborhoods of Glen Park to the south and Miller and Aetna to the east contained few waste dumps and enjoyed relatively clean air and water. After 1960 Miller became the preferred residence of Gary's wealthy whites. Many fled the affluent Horace Mann area and settled lakeshore homes in Miller. The exodus of whites from north Gary and Tolleston accounted for much of Aetna and Glen Park's new population. Although Miller, Aetna and Glen Park received an influx of several thousand blacks during the 1970s, these three neighborhoods retained a relatively high proportion of their white residents. By 1980, two-thirds of Gary's remaining 38,000 whites lived in either Glen Park, Aetna or Miller.

Racial distinctions determined who in Gary was affected most by industry's environmental impact during the 1970s. Groundwater contamination primarily affected blacks. Because many households in west Gary still relied on well water for drinking, residents who lived near dump sites encountered serious health hazards. Children in the area also faced risks when playing atop contaminated soil. Several youths reported serious burns after coming into contact with soil in the vicinity of dumping grounds. Gary's white communities were located far from hazardous waste sites and received their water from the city's utility. Similarly, sulfur dioxide pollution fell first and hardest on the black residents of west Gary. Only after making their way through Tolleston and Midtown did sulfur dioxide emissions affect the white residents of Miller, Aetna and Glen Park. Thus, many blacks escaped from the poverty of Midtown for the environmental degradation of west Gary. It is important to note, however, that west Gary's residents were financially secure. West Gary's blacks earned better than average incomes and were well represented in white collar occupations. Gary's poorest blacks either remained in Midtown or infiltrated the downtown neighborhoods adjacent to the steel mills. Although downtown particulate pollution levels remained the highest in Gary, poor blacks generally lived far from hazardous waste sites. Thus, blacks bore the brunt of recent ecological change in Gary. Within the black community, however, poor blacks suffered no worse than prosperous blacks.

Among whites, however, economic status made a major difference. By 1970, Miller's lakeshore district ranked first in median house value and in residents' income. Glen Park, at Gary's southern tip, stood just behind Miller in income and real estate values. Wealthy whites in Glen Park and Miller enjoyed clean air and water; few waste disposal sites existed in their neighborhoods. The working class residents of Aetna lived slightly closer to the steel mills and thus, encountered higher particulate pollution levels. The only white district that experienced the risks of unhealthy groundwater during the 1970s was the poorest white community, Black Oak. Located in the city's southwest corner, Black Oak only became part of Gary in 1975. Its residents sought annexation to Gary in order to receive desperately needed city services. Many residents relied on wells for drinking water; many wells lay close to hazardous waste sites. Black Oak also received more sulfur dioxide pollution than any other white neighborhood.

Although the foregoing analysis of ecological and population change has been restricted to the area within the Gary city limits, neither pollution nor population movement stopped at city borders. Especially after 1967, many whites fled Gary and relocated to towns just east and south of the city limits. Whereas Gary's blacks comprised over 70 percent of the city's population by 1980, the percentage of blacks in the communities bordering Gary on the south and east was less than one percent. The further whites moved in these directions, the further they moved from all forms of industry's environmental incursions. Beyond the city borders, air pollution levels dropped, toxic waste sites appeared less frequently, and water pollution hazards decreased.

In sum, the age of ecology coincided with changing forms of environmental degradation that discriminated along racial and class lines. Although different aspects of the industrial environment followed varying geographical courses, middle-class whites consistently escaped its worst effects. Poorer whites fared slightly worse as they lived closer to sources of air pollution and hazardous waste. Gary's blacks experienced the most significant environmental deterioration between 1945 and 1980. By the 1970s, they experienced the worst consequences of industry's air, water and land use.

The relationship between the environment and social structure changed after 1945 in Gary. The historical reasons responsible for this shift remain unclear. A far more thorough examination of the motives behind both environmental and demographic change is necessary. Why did people move? What role did shifts in the way people perceived the environment play in decisions to relocate? How did the spate of environmental reforms contribute to the precise location of new air pollution sources and waste disposal sites? Resolving these issues may illuminate the social biases of ecological change and the role played by the environmental movement itself.

❦ F U R T H E R   R E A D I N G

Ellis C. Armstrong, Michael Robinson, and Suellen Hoy, eds., *History of Public Works in the United States, 1776–1976* (1976)

Moses N. Baker, *The Quest for Pure Water: The History of Water Purification from the Earliest Records to the Twentieth Century* (1948)

Marvin Brienes, "Smog Comes to Los Angeles," *Southern California Quarterly* 58 (1976)

Robert D. Bullard, *Dumping in Dixie: Race, Class, and Environmental Quality* (1990)

Albert E. Cowdrey, "Pioneering Environmental Law: The Army Corps of Engineers and the Refuse Act," *Pacific Historical Review* 44 (1975), 331–49

William Cronon, *Nature's Metropolis* (1991)

James J. Flink, *The Car Culture* (1975)

Edward Greer, "Air Pollution and Corporate Power: Municipal Reform Limits in a Black City," *Politics and Society* 4 (1974), 483–510

Spenser W. Havlick, *The Urban Organism: The City's Natural Resources from an Environmental Perspective* (1974)

Andrew Hurley, "The Social Bases of Environmental Change in Gary, Indiana, 1945–1980," *Environmental Review* 12 (1988), 1–19

Jane Jacobs, *Death and Life of Great American Cities* (1961)

Wesley Marx, *Man and His Environment: Waste* (1971)

Martin V. Melosi, ed., *Pollution and Reform in American Cities, 1870–1930* (1980)
———, *Garbage in the Cities: Refuse, Reform, and the Environment, 1880–1980* (1981)
H. Wayne Morgan, *Industrial America: The Environment and Social Problems, 1776–1920* (1974)
Jacob Riis, *How the Other Half Lives* (1890)
George Rosen, *A History of Public Health* (1958)
Charles S. Rosenberg, *The Cholera Years: The United States in 1832, 1849, and 1866* (1962)
Barbara G. Rosenkrantz, ed., *Sewering the Cities* (1977)
Peter J. Schmitt, *Back to Nature: The Arcadian Myth in Urban America* (1969)
Upton Sinclair, *The Jungle (1905)*
Raymond W. Smilor, "Personal Boundaries in the Urban Environment: The Legal Attack on Noise, 1865–1930," *Environmental Review* 3 (1979)
Theodore Steinberg, *Nature Incorporated: Industrialization and the Waters of New England* (1991)
Bayrd Still, *Urban America: A History with Documents* (1974)
Joel A. Tarr, "Urban Pollution—Many Long Years Ago," *American Heritage* 22, no. 6 (October 1971), 65–69, 106
———, "Out of Sight, Out of Mind: A Brief History of Sewage Disposal in the United States," *American History Illustrated* 10 (1976), 40–47
———, "Historical Turning Points in Municipal Water Supply and Wastewater Disposal, 1850–1932," *Civil Engineering* 47 (1977), 82–91
Sam Bass Warner, *Urban Wilderness* (1976)
Daniel Zarin, "Searching for Pennies in Piles of Trash," *Environmental Review* 11, no. 3 (Fall 1987), 207–220

The Emergence of Ecology
in the Twentieth Century

Ψ

Although ecological modes of relating to nature have roots among indigenous as well as preindustrial peoples, the emergence of ecology as a science belongs to the industrial era. The term oekologie, from the Greek word oikos ("home"), was coined by German biologist Ernst Haeckel in 1873. In America chemist Ellen Swallow first publicized the word—changing it to oekology—in 1892, and in a book published in 1910 on sanitary chemistry, she expanded the term to human ecology.

Ecology's development as a science was not monolithic. Several schools of thought with different underlying assumptions about nature and its management have emerged in the twentieth century. For Swallow, nature was a home, and ecology described the larger home to which human homes were connected by the movements of air, water, and soil. To botanist Frederic Clements, writing in 1916, nature was organic: a plant formation was a complex organism, growing, maturing, and dying independently of humans and their activities. For British biologist Arthur Tansley, working in the 1930s, nature comprised a multitude of interconnected physical systems, from universe down to atom, of which one— the ecosystem—exhibited constant interchange among organic and inorganic components. In the view of ecologist Eugene Odum, writing in the 1950s, it was a balanced homeostatic system, much like a thermostat, stabilized and maintained through biological diversity. And for late-twentieth-century population biologists, nature is a chaotic, random series of individual events whose behavior is predictable only in unusual, narrowly defined circumstances. Imbedded in such fundamental metaphors as home, organism, machine, homeostatic system, and chaos are different ethical and political relationships between humans and nonhuman nature. This chapter's documents and essays reveal a number of possible connections between and among scientific assumptions, metaphors, policies, and ethics as the science of ecology evolved in the twentieth century. Such changing definitions of ecology pose dilemmas for environmental historians as well as for scientists, conservationists, and policymakers.

❧ *D O C U M E N T S*

In the first document, an excerpt from her *Sanitation in Daily Life* (1910), chemist Ellen Swallow defines the meaning of human ecology. The second document, from Frederic Clements's fundamental work *Plant Succession* (1916), describes ecology in terms of the similarity between the life processes of a plant community and those of a complex organism. However, in document three, botanist Henry Gleason sharply attacks Clements's organism metaphor and substitutes the individual plant association and the mosaic mixture.

The fourth document, by British botanist Arthur Tansley, likewise attacks Clements's use of the vegetative organism and substitutes the term *ecosystem*, which encompasses not only the biotic but also the inorganic, physical factors that make up the whole environment. In 1942, as discussed in the fifth document, zoologist Raymond Lindeman (using such economic metaphors as producers, consumers, productivity, and efficiency) elaborated on Tansley's concept of the ecosystem by including the food web, or trophic system, through which energy is transferred from one part to another.

In the sixth document, published in 1949 just after his death, ecologist and game manager Aldo Leopold uses Clements's concept of the biotic community to develop a land ethic. Breaking with the utilitarian conservation ethic of Gifford Pinchot that focused on commodity production to provide "the greatest good for the greatest number for the longest time," Leopold boldly asserts an ethic enlarging "the boundaries of the community to include soils, waters, plants, and animals, or collectively: the land."

The seventh selection is an excerpt from a 1969 paper by ecologist Eugene Odum on the role of humans in maintaining stable ecosystems. Drawing on Clements's concept of succession, Tansley's idea of the ecosystem, and Lindeman's views on the food chain, Odum argues that ecosystems develop toward diverse, stable systems whose balance humans may maintain or upset. Odum thus brings the concept of ecology back to Swallow's concept of the home, or *oikos* — a place in which humans must maintain clean air and water and live as a part of, not apart from, the environment.

During the 1970s and 1980s, ideas such as the diversity-stability hypothesis, equilibrium, and the "balance of nature," basic to Odum's approach to conservation, were challenged by concepts such as Gleason's patch dynamics, mosaics, disturbances, perturbations, and chaos. The final document, by ecologists S. T. A. Pickett and P. S. White, argues that equilibrium landscapes are the exception, not the rule, and that constant change poses a paradox for conservationists.

Ellen Swallow Richards on Human Ecology, 1910

Sanitary science teaches that mode of life which promotes health and efficiency.

The individual is one of a community influencing and influenced by the common environment.

Human ecology is the study of the surroundings of human beings in the effects they produce on the lives of men. The features of the environment are natural, as climate, and artificial, produced by human activity, as noise, dust, poisonous vapors, vitiated air, dirty water, and unclean food.

The study of this environment is in two chief lines:

First, what is often called municipal housekeeping—the co-operation of the citizens in securing clean streets, the suppression of nuisances, abundant water supply, market inspection, etc.

Second, family housekeeping. The healthful home demands a management of the house which shall promote vigorous life and prevent the physical deterioration so evident under modern conditions.

The close interrelation of these two parts of sanitation should be borne in mind. Even if a man has been so blessed as to be born into favorable conditions, he must nevertheless face the problem of retaining health and strength under the strain of modern progress and civilization. Formerly a man's occupation in the fields and woods kept him in health, but now he must ordinarily give what strength he has to his occupation, and rely upon other sources from which to secure a healthy body. It is possible to understand the effect that is produced by unfavorable environment, if we compare the difference in physical stature between the Scotch agricultural worker and the inhabitant of certain manufacturing towns in England. There is an average of five inches in height and thirty-one pounds in weight in favor of the Scotchman. H. G. Wells, in speaking of the responsibility for man's physical efficiency, compares the city dweller in crowded streets and tenements with the man living in the freer, more open country, and makes the difference from three and one-half to five inches in stature and from twenty to thirty pounds in weight in favor of the country dweller. The former belongs to the physically unfit for the struggle of life.

A casual observer visiting the poorer parts of one of our large cities must necessarily be impressed with the stunted appearance of the children on the streets.

Since physical strength and power have always been desired by man; and since, in these modern days, women wish to be not far behind their brothers in endurance, the facts just given should furnish food for serious thought as to the means of acquiring a body physically fit, capable of securing the greatest capacity for work and for play—for life.

Is this physical fitness and consequent mental power so good a thing, so desirable, that the pupils in our schools and colleges are ready to give their attention to habits of right living when the methods of acquiring these habits are presented to them? Is it worth their while? Let the habits be once acquired, then the attention may be turned in other directions. It has been said, "Sow a habit and reap a character." This is true of the physical and mental as of the moral. Habits become fixed. It is necessary, then, that they be good habits. Right habits of living are the foundations of health of body and mind.

To secure and maintain a safe environment there must be inculcated *habits* of using the material things in daily life in such a way as to promote and not to diminish health. Avoid spitting in the streets, avoid throwing refuse on the sidewalk, avoid dust and bad air in the house and sleeping room, etc.

It is, however, of the greatest importance that every one should acquire such habits of *belief* in the importance of this material environment as shall lead him to insist upon sanitary regulations, and to see that they are carried out.

What touches my neighbor, touches me. For my sake, and for his, the city inspector and the city garbage cart visit us, and I keep my premises in such a condition as I expect him to strive for.

The first law of sanitation requires quick removal and destruction of all wastes — of things done with.

The second law enjoins such use of the air, water, and food necessary to life that the person may be in a state of health and efficiency.

This right use depends so largely upon habit that a great portion of sanitary teaching must be given to inculcating right and safe ways in daily life.

Frederic Clements on Plant Succession, 1916

Developmental aspect. — The essential nature of [plant] succession is indicated by its name. It is a series of invasions, a sequence of plant communities marked by the change from lower to higher life-forms. The essence of succession lies in the interaction of three factors, namely, habitat, life-forms, and species, in the progressive development of a formation. In this development, habitat and population act and react upon each other, alternating as cause and effect until a state of equilibrium is reached. The factors of the habitat are the causes of the responses or functions of the community, and these are the causes of growth and development, and hence of structure, essentially as in the individual. Succession must then be regarded as the development or life-history of the climax formation. It is the basic organic process of vegetation, which results in the adult or final form of this complex organism. All the stages which precede the climax are stages of growth. They have the same essential relation to the final stable structure of the organism that seedling and growing plant have to the adult individual. Moreover, just as the adult plant repeats its development, *i.e.*, reproduces itself, whenever conditions permit, so also does the climax formation. The parallel may be extended much further. The flowering plant may repeat itself completely, may undergo primary reproduction from an initial embryonic cell, or the reproduction may be secondary or partial from a shoot. In like fashion, a climax formation may repeat every one of its essential stages of growth in a primary area, or it may reproduce itself only in its later stages, as in secondary areas. In short, the process of organic development is essentially alike for the individual and the community. The correspondence is obvious when the necessary difference in the complexity of the two organisms is recognized.

Functional aspect. — The motive force in succession, *i.e.*, in the development of the formation as an organism, is to be found in the responses or functions of the group of individuals, just as the power of growth in the individual lies in the responses or functions of various organs. In both individual and community the clue to development is function, as the record of development is structure. Thus, succession is preeminently a process the progress of which is expressed in certain initial and intermediate structures or stages, but is finally recorded in the structure of the climax formation. The process is complex and often obscure, and its component functions yield only to persistent investigation and experiment. In consequence, the student of succession must recognize clearly that developmental stages, like the climax, are only a record of what has already happened. Each stage is, temporarily at least, a stable structure, and the actual processes can be revealed only by following the development of one stage into the succeeding one. In short, succession can be studied properly only by tracing the rise and fall for each stage, and not by a floristic picture of the population at the crest of each invasion.

Henry Gleason on Plant Associations, 1926

Plant associations exist; we can walk over them, we can measure their extent, we can describe their structure in terms of their component species, we can correlate them with their environment, we can frequently discover their past history and make inferences about their future.

We attempt to classify associations, as individual examples of vegetation, into broader groups, again basing our methods on various observable features and arriving accordingly at various results. We even enter the domain of philosophy, and speculate on the fundamental nature of the association, regard it as the basic unit of vegetation, call it an organism, and compare different areas of the same sort of vegetation to a species. . . .

Let us then throw aside for the moment all our pre-conceived ideas as to the definition, fundamental nature, structure, and classification of plant associations. . . . An area of vegetation which one ecologist regards as a single association may by another be considered as a mosaic or mixture of several, depending on their individual differences in definition. Some of these variations in structure (if one takes the broader view of the association) or smaller associations (if one prefers the narrower view) may be correlated with differences in the environment.

* * * *

We know that no two areas, supposed to represent the same association-type, are exactly the same, and we do not know which one to accept as typical and which to assume as showing the effects of geographical variation. We find fragmentary associations, and usually have no solid basis for deciding whether they are mere accidental intruders or embryonic stages in a developing association which may become typical after a lapse of years. We find variation of environment within the association, similar associations occupying different environments, and different associations in the same environment. It is small wonder that there is conflict and confusion in the definition and classification of plant communities. Surely our belief in the integrity of the association and the sanctity of the association-concept must be severely shaken. Are we not justified in coming to the general conclusion, far removed from the prevailing opinion, that an association is not an organism, scarcely even a vegetational unit, but merely a *coincidence*?

* * * *

The vegetation of an area is merely the resultant of two factors, the fluctuating and fortuitous immigration of plants and an equally fluctuating and variable environment. As a result, there is no inherent reason why any two areas of the earth's surface should bear precisely the same vegetation, nor any reason for adhering to our old ideas of the definiteness and distinctness of plant associations. As a matter of fact, no herbaceous species also die. Brush fires sweep over the clearing and aid in the destruction of the original vegetation. Very soon the area grows up to a tangle of other herbaceous and shrubby species, notably *Epilobium angustifolium, Rubus strigosus*, and *Sambucus racemosa*. This persists but a few years before it is overtopped by saplings of the original hardwoods which eventually restore the forest. Is this early stage of fire-weeds and shrubs a distinct association or merely an embryonic phase of the forest? Since it has such a short duration, it is frequently regarded as the latter, but since it is caused by an entirely different type of environmental sorting and lacks most of the characteristic species of the forest, it might as well be called distinct. If it lasted for a long period of years it would certainly be called an association, and if all the forest near enough to provide seeds for immigration were lumbered, that might be the case. Again we are confronted with a purely arbitrary decision as to the associational identity of the vegetation.

* * * *

These primary causes, migration and environmental selection, operate independently on each area, no matter how small and have no relation to the process on any other area. Nor are they related to the vegetation of any other area, except as the latter may serve as a source of migrants or control the environment of the former. The effect of these primary causes is therefore not to produce large areas of similar vegetation, but to determine the plant life on every minimum area.

In conclusion, it may be said that every species of plant is a law unto itself, the distribution of which in space depends upon its individual peculiarities of migration and environmental requirements. Its disseminules migrate everywhere, and grow wherever they find favorable conditions. The species disappears from areas where the environment is no longer endurable. It grows in company with any other species of similar environmental requirements, irrespective of their normal associational affiliations. The behavior of the plant offers in itself no reason at all for the segregation of definite communities. Plant associations, the most conspicuous illustration of the space relation of plants, depend solely on the coincidence of environmental selection and migration over an area of recognizable extent and usually for a time of considerable duration. A rigid definition of the scope or extent of the association is impossible, and a logical classification of associations into larger groups, or into successional series, has not yet been achieved.

Arthur Tansley Introduces the Ecosystem, 1935

At the outset let me express my conviction that Dr. Clements has given us a theory of vegetation which has formed an indispensable foundation for the most fruitful modern work. With some parts of that theory and of its expression, however, I have never agreed. . . .

The weakness of this discussion of Clements, which is both able and ingenious, seems to me to reside . . . very largely on the assumption which governs the whole argument, and, as it seems to me, is quite illegitimate, that vegetation *is* an organism and therefore *must* obey the laws of development of what we commonly know as organisms. . . .

The usual view is that under the "typical" climatic conditions of the region and on the most favourable soils the climatic climax is reached by the succession; but that on less favourable soils of special character different kinds of stable vegetation are developed and remain in possession of the ground, to all appearance as permanently as the climatic climax. These are called *edaphic climaxes*, because the differentiating factor is a special soil type. Similarly special local climates determined by topography (*i.e.*, land relief) determine *physiographic climaxes*. But we may go farther than this and say that the incidence and maintenance of a decisive "biotic factor" such as the continuous grazing of animals may determine a *biotic climax*. And again we may speak of a *fire climax* when a region swept by constantly recurrent fires shows a vegetation consisting only of species able to survive under these trying conditions of life; or of a *mowing climax* established as a result of the regular periodic cutting of grasses or sedges. In each case the vegetation appears to be in equilibrium with *all* the effective factors present, including of course the climatic factors, and the climax is named from the special factor differentiating the vegetation from the climatic climax. . . .

I plead for empirical method and terminology in all work on vegetation, and avoidance of generalised interpretation based on a theory of what *must* happen because "vegetation is an organism." . . .

On linguistic grounds I dislike the term biotic *community*. A "community," I think it will be generally agreed, implies *members*, and it seems to me that to lump animals and plants together as *members* of a community is to put on an equal footing things which in their whole nature and behaviour are too different. Animals and plants are not common members of anything except the organic world (in the biological, not the "organicist" sense). One would not speak of the potato plants and ornamental trees and flowers in the gardens of a human community as *members* of that community, although they certainly enter into its constitution — it would be different without them. There must be some sort of *similarity*, though not of course *identity*, of nature and status between the members of a community if the term is not to be divorced too completely from its common meaning.

Excerpts from Arthur Tansley "The Use and Abuse of Vegetational Concepts and Terms," *Ecology* 16, 1935, pp. 284–5, 289–90, 292, 295–6, 299, 306. Reprinted by permission of *Ecology*.

* * * *

Animal ecologists in their field work constantly find it necessary to speak of *different* animal communities living in or on a given plant community, and this is a much more natural conception, formed in the proper empirical manner as a direct description of experience, than the "biotic community." Some of the animals belonging to these various animal communities have very restricted habitats, others much wider ones, while others again such as the larger and more active predaceous birds and mammals range freely not only through an entire plant community but far outside its limits. For these reasons also, the practical necessity in field work of separating and independently studying the animals communities of a "biome," and for some purposes the necessity of regarding them as external factors acting on the plant community—I cannot accept the concept of the *biotic* community.

This refusal is however far from meaning that I do not realise that various "biomes," the whole webs of life adjusted to particular complexes of environmental factors, are real "wholes," often highly integrated wholes, which are the living nuclei of *systems* in the sense of the physicist. Only I do not think they are properly described as "organisms" (except in the "organicist" sense). I prefer to regard them, together with the whole of the effective physical factors involved, simply as "*systems*."

I have already given my reasons for rejecting the terms "complex organism" and "biotic community." Clements' earlier term "biome" for the whole complex of organisms inhabiting a given region is unobjectionable, and for some purposes convenient. But the more fundamental conception is, as it seems to me, the whole *system* (in the sense of physics), including not only the organism-complex, but also the whole complex of physical factors forming what we call the environment of the biome—the habitat factors in the widest sense. Though the organisms may claim our primary interest, when we are trying to think fundamentally we cannot separate them from their special environment, with which they form one physical system.

It is the systems so formed which, from the point of view of the ecologist, are the basic units of nature on the face of the earth. Our natural human prejudices force us to consider the organisms (in the sense of the biologist) as the most important parts of these systems, but certainly the inorganic "factors" are also parts—there could be no systems without them, and there is constant interchange of the most various kinds within each system, not only between the organisms but between the organic and the inorganic. These *ecosystems*, as we may call them, are of the most various kinds and sizes. They form one category of the multitudinous physical systems of the universe, which range from the universe as a whole down to the atom. . . .

We must have a system of ecological concepts which will allow of the inclusion of *all* forms of vegetational expression and activity. We cannot confine ourselves to the so-called "natural" entities and ignore the processes and expressions of vegetation now so abundantly provided us by the activities of man. Such a course is not scientifically sound, because scientific analysis

must penetrate beneath the forms of the "natural" entities, and it is not practically useful because ecology must be applied to conditions brought about by
human activity. The "natural" entities and the anthropogenic derivates alike
must be analysed in terms of the most appropriate concepts we can find. Plant
community, succession, development, climax, used in their wider and not in
specialised senses, represent such concepts. They certainly involve an abstraction of the vegetation as such from the whole complex of components of the
ecosystem, the remaining components being regarded as factors. This abstraction is a convenient isolate which has served and is continuing to serve us well.
It has in fact many, though by no means all, of the qualities of an organism.
The biome is a less convenient isolate for most purposes, though it has some
uses, and it is not in the least improved by being called a "biotic community" or
a "complex organism," terms which are illegitimately derived and which introduce misleading implications. . . .

The concept of the "complex organism" as applied to the biome is objectionable both because the term is already in common use for an individual
higher animal or plant, and because the biome is not an organism except in the
sense in which inorganic systems are organisms.

The fundamental concept appropriate to the biome considered together
with all the effective inorganic factors of its environment is the *ecosystem*,
which is a particular category among the physical systems that make up the
universe. In an ecosystem the organisms and the inorganic factors alike are
components which are in relatively stable dynamic equilibrium. Succession and
development are instances of the universal processes tending towards the
creation of such equilibrated systems.

Raymond Lindeman Defines the Food Web, 1942

The *ecosystem* may be formally defined as the system composed of physical-
chemical-biological processes active within a space-time unit of any magnitude, i.e., the biotic community *plus* its abiotic environment.

Trophic Dynamics

Qualitative Food-Cycle Relationships.   Although certain aspects of food
relations have been known for centuries, many processes within ecosystems are
still very incompletely understood. The basic process in trophic dynamics is the
transfer of energy from one part of the ecosystem to another. All function, and
indeed all life, within an ecosystem depends upon the utilization of an external
source of energy, solar radiation. A portion of this incident energy is transformed by the process of photosynthesis into the structure of living organisms.
In the language of community economics introduced by [European scientist
August] Thienemann, autotrophic plants are *producer* organisms, employing
the energy obtained by photosynthesis to synthesize complex organic
substances from simple inorganic substances. Although plants again release a

Excerpts from Raymond Lindeman, "The Trophic Dynamic Aspect of Ecology," *Ecology* 23, no.
4, October 1942, pp. 400–1, 408, 415. Reprinted by permission of *Ecology*.

portion of this potential energy in catabolic processes, a great surplus of organic substance is accumulated. Animals and heterotrophic plants, as *consumer* organisms, feed upon this surplus of potential energy, oxidizing a considerable portion of the consumed substance to release kinetic energy for metabolism, but transforming the remainder into the complex chemical substances of their own bodies. Following death, every organism is a potential source of energy for saprophagous organisms (feeding directly on dead tissues), which again may act as energy sources for successive categories of consumers. Heterotrophic bacteria, and fungi, representing the most important saprophagous consumption of energy, may be conveniently differentiated from animal consumers as specialized *decomposers* of organic substance. [Selman A.] Waksman has suggested that certain of these bacteria be further differentiated as *transformers* of organic and inorganic compounds. The combined action of animal consumers and bacterial decomposers tends to dissipate the potential energy of organic substances, again transforming them to the inorganic state. From this inorganic state the autotrophic plants may utilize the dissolved nutrients once more in resynthesizing complex organic substance, thus completing the food cycle.

The Eltonian Pyramid. The general relationships of higher food-cycle levels to one another and to community structure were greatly clarified following recognition of the importance of size and of numbers in the animals of an ecosystem. Beginning with primary consumers of various sizes, there are as a rule a number of food-chains radiating outwards in which the probability is that predators will become successively larger, while parasites and hyper-parasites will be progressively smaller than their hosts. Since small primary consumers can increase faster than larger secondary consumers and are so able to support the latter, the animals at the base of a food-chain are relatively abundant while those toward the end are progressively fewer in number. The resulting arrangement of sizes and numbers of animals, termed the pyramid of Numbers by [zoologist Charles] Elton, is now commonly known as the Eltonian Pyramid. . . .

The Eltonian Pyramid may also be expressed in terms of biomass. The weight of all predators must always be much lower than that of all food animals, and the total weight of the latter much lower than the plant production. To the human ecologist, it is noteworthy that the population density of the essentially vegetarian Chinese, for example, is much greater than that of the more carnivorous English.

Summary

1. Analyses of food-cycle relationships indicate that a biotic community cannot be clearly differentiated from its abiotic environment; the *ecosystem* is hence regarded as the more fundamental ecological unit.

2. The organisms within an ecosystem may be grouped into a series of more or less discrete trophic levels ($\Lambda_1, \Lambda_2, \Lambda_3, \ldots \Lambda_n$) as producers, primary consumers, secondary consumers, etc., each successively dependent upon the

preceding level as a source of energy, with the producers (Λ_1) directly dependent upon the rate of incident solar radiation (productivity λ_0) as a source of energy.

3. The more remote an organism is from the initial source of energy (solar radiation), the less probable that it will be dependent solely upon the preceding trophic level as a source of energy.

4. The progressive energy relationships of the food levels of an "Eltonian Pyramid" may be epitomized in terms of the productivity symbol λ, as follows:

$$\lambda_0 > \lambda_1 > \lambda_2 \ldots > \lambda_n$$

5. The percentage loss of energy due to respiration is progressively greater for higher levels in the food cycle. Respiration with respect to growth is about 33 per cent for producers, 62 per cent for primary consumers, and more than 100 per cent for secondary consumers.

6. The consumers at progressively higher levels in the food cycle appear to be progressively more efficient in the use of their food supply. This generalization can be reconciled with the preceding one by remembering that increased activity of predators considerably increases the chances of encountering suitable prey.

7. Productivity and efficiency increase during the early phases of successional development. In lake succession, productivity and photosynthetic efficiency increase from oligotrophy to a prolonged eutrophic stage-equilibrium and decline with lake senescence, rising again in the terrestrial stages of hydrarch succession.

8. The progressive efficiencies of consumer levels, on the basis of very meager data, apparently tend to increase throughout the aquatic phases of succession.

Aldo Leopold Proposes a Land Ethic, 1949

The Ethical Sequence

Ethics, so far studied only by philosophers, is actually a process in ecological evolution. Its sequences may be described in ecological as well as in philosophical terms. An ethic, ecologically, is a limitation on freedom of action in the struggle for existence. An ethic, philosophically, is a differentiation of social from anti-social conduct. These are two definitions of one thing. The thing has its origin in the tendency of interdependent individuals or groups to evolve modes of co-operation. The ecologist calls these symbioses. Politics and economics are advanced symbioses in which the original free-for-all competition has been replaced, in part, by co-operative mechanisms with an ethical content. . . .

Excerpts from *A Sand County Almanac: and Sketches Here and There* by Aldo Leopold, pp. 201–4, 221–5. Copyright 1949, 1977 by Oxford University Press, Inc. Reprinted by permission.

The first ethics dealt with the relation between individuals; the Mosaic Decalogue is an example. Later accretions dealt with the relation between the individual and society. The Golden Rule tries to integrate the individual to society; democracy to integrate social organization to the individual.

There is as yet no ethic dealing with man's relation to land and to the animals and plants which grow upon it. Land, like Odysseus' slave-girls, is still property. The land-relation is still strictly economic, entailing privileges but not obligations.

The extension of ethics to this third element in human environment is, if I read the evidence correctly, an evolutionary possibility and an ecological necessity. It is the third step in a sequence. The first two have already been taken. Individual thinkers since the days of Ezekiel and Isaiah have asserted that the despoliation of land is not only inexpedient but wrong. Society, however, has not yet affirmed their belief. I regard the present conservation movement as the embryo of such an affirmation.

An ethic may be regarded as a mode of guidance for meeting ecological situations so new or intricate, or involving such deferred reactions, that the path of social expediency is not discernible to the average individual. Animal instincts are modes of guidance for the individual in meeting such situations. Ethics are possibly a kind of community instinct in-the-making.

The Community Concept

All ethics so far evolved rest upon a single premise: that the individual is a member of a community of interdependent parts. His instincts prompt him to compete for his place in that community, but his ethics prompt him also to co-operate (perhaps in order that there may be a place to compete for).

The land ethic simply enlarges the boundaries of the community to include soils, waters, plants, and animals, or collectively: the land.

This sounds simple: do we not already sing our love for and obligation to the land of the free and the home of the brave? Yes, but just what and whom do we love? Certainly not the soil, which we are sending helter-skelter downriver. Certainly not the waters, which we assume have no function except to turn turbines, float barges, and carry off sewage. Certainly not the plants, of which we exterminate whole communities without batting an eye. Certainly not the animals, of which we have already extirpated many of the largest and most beautiful species. A land ethic of course cannot prevent the alteration, manage-ment, and use of these 'resources,' but it does affirm their right to continued existence, and, at least in spots, their continued existence in a natural state.

In short, a land ethic changes the role of *Homo sapiens* from conqueror of the land-community to plain member and citizen of it. It implies respect for his fellow-members, and also respect for the community as such. . . .

Land Health and the A-B Cleavage

A land ethic, then, reflects the existence of an ecological conscience, and this in turn reflects a conviction of individual responsibility for the health of the land.

Health is the capacity of the land for self-renewal. Conservation is our effort to understand and preserve this capacity.

Conservationists are notorious for their dissensions. Superficially these seem to add up to mere confusion, but a more careful scrutiny reveals a single plane of cleavage common to many specialized fields. In each field one group (A) regards the land as soil, and its function as commodity-production; another group (B) regards the land as a biota, and its function as something broader. How much broader is admittedly in a state of doubt and confusion.

In my own field, forestry, group A is quite content to grow trees like cabbages, with cellulose as the basic forest commodity. It feels no inhibition against violence; its ideology is agronomic. Group B, on the other hand, sees forestry as fundamentally different from agronomy because it employs natural species, and manages a natural environment rather than creating an artificial one. Group B prefers natural reproduction on principle. It worries on biotic as well as economic grounds about the loss of species like chestnut, and the threatened loss of the white pines. It worries about a whole series of secondary forest functions: wildlife, recreation, watersheds, wilderness areas. To my mind, Group B feels the stirrings of an ecological conscience.

In the wildlife field, a parallel cleavage exists. For Group A the basic commodities are sport and meat; the yardsticks of production are ciphers of take in pheasants and trout. Artificial propagation is acceptable as a permanent as well as a temporary recourse — if its unit costs permit. Group B, on the other hand, worries about a whole series of biotic side-issues. What is the cost in predators of producing a game crop? Should we have further recourse to exotics? How can management restore the shrinking species, like prairie grouse, already hopeless as shootable game? How can management restore the threatened rarities, like trumpeter swan and whooping crane? Can management principles be extended to wildflowers? Here again it is clear to me that we have the same A-B cleavage as in forestry.

In the larger field of agriculture I am less competent to speak, but there seem to be somewhat parallel cleavages. Scientific agriculture was actively developing before ecology was born, hence a slower penetration of ecological concepts might be expected. Moreover the farmer, by the very nature of his techniques, must modify the biota more radically than the forester or the wildlife manager. Nevertheless, there are many discontents in agriculture which seem to add up to a new vision of 'biotic farming.'

Perhaps the most important of these is the new evidence that poundage or tonnage is no measure of the food-value of farm crops; the products of fertile soil may be qualitatively as well as quantitatively superior. We can bolster poundage from depleted soils by pouring on imported fertility, but we are not necessarily bolstering food-value. The possible ultimate ramifications of this idea are so immense that I must leave their exposition to abler pens.

The discontent that labels itself 'organic farming,' while bearing some of the earmarks of a cult, is nevertheless biotic in its direction, particularly in its insistence on the importance of soil flora and fauna.

The ecological fundamentals of agriculture are just as poorly known to the public as in other fields of land-use. For example, few educated people realize that the marvelous advances in technique made during recent decades are improvements in the pump, rather than the well. Acre for acre, they have barely sufficed to offset the sinking level of fertility.

In all of these cleavages, we see repeated the same basic paradoxes: man the conqueror *versus* man the biotic citizen; science the sharpener of his sword *versus* science the searchlight on his universe; land the slave and servant *versus* land the collective organism. Robinson's injunction to Tristram may well be applied, at this juncture, to *Homo sapiens* as a species in geological time:

> Whether you will or will not
> You are a King, Tristram, for you are one
> Of the time-tested few that leave the world,
> When they are gone, not the same place it was.
> Mark what you leave.

The Outlook

It is inconceivable to me that an ethical relation to land can exist without love, respect, and admiration for land, and a high regard for its value. By value, I of course mean something far broader than mere economic value; I mean value in the philosophical sense.

Perhaps the most serious obstacle impeding the evolution of a land ethic is the fact that our educational and economic system is headed away from, rather than toward, an intense consciousness of land. Your true modern is separated from the land by many middlemen, and by innumerable physical gadgets. He has no vital relation to it; to him it is the space between cities on which crops grow. Turn him loose for a day on the land, and if the spot does not happen to be a gold links or a 'scenic' area, he is bored stiff. If crops could be raised by hydroponics instead of farming, it would suit him very well. Synthetic substitutes for wood, leather, wool, and other natural land products suit him better than the originals. In short, land is something he has 'outgrown.'

Almost equally serious as an obstacle to a land ethic is the attitude of the farmer for whom the land is still an adversary, or a taskmaster that keeps him in slavery. Theoretically, the mechanization of farming ought to cut the farmer's chains, but whether it really does is debatable.

One of the requisites for an ecological comprehension of land is an understanding of ecology, and this is by no means co-extensive with 'education'; in fact, much higher education seems deliberately to avoid ecological concepts. An understanding of ecology does not necessarily originate in courses bearing ecological labels; it is quite as likely to be labeled geography, botany, agronomy, history, or economics. This is as it should be, but whatever the label, ecological training is scarce.

The case for a land ethic would appear hopeless but for the minority which is in obvious revolt against these 'modern' trends.

The 'key-log' which must be moved to release the evolutionary process for an ethic is simply this: quit thinking about decent land-use as solely an economic problem. Examine each question in terms of what is ethically and esthetically right, as well as what is economically expedient. A thing is right when it tends to preserve the integrity, stability, and beauty of the biotic community. It is wrong when it tends otherwise.

It of course goes without saying that economic feasibility limits the tether of what can or cannot be done for land. It always has and it always will. The fallacy the economic determinists have tied around our collective neck, and which we now need to cast off, is the belief that economics determines *all* land-use. This is simply not true. An innumerable host of actions and attitudes, comprising perhaps the bulk of all land relations, is determined by the land-users' tastes and predilections, rather than by his purse. The bulk of all land relations hinges on investments of time, forethought, skill, and faith rather than on investments of cash. As a land-user thinketh, so is he.

I have purposely presented the land ethic as a product of social evolution because nothing so important as an ethic is ever 'written.' Only the most superficial student of history supposes that Moses 'wrote' the Decalogue; it evolved in the minds of a thinking community, and Moses wrote a tentative summary of it for a 'seminar.' I say tentative because evolution never stops.

The evolution of a land ethic is an intellectual as well as emotional process. Conservation is paved with good intentions which prove to be futile, or even dangerous, because they are devoid of critical understanding either of the land, or of economic land-use. I think it is a truism that as the ethical frontier advances from the individual to the community, its intellectual content increases.

The mechanism of operation is the same for any ethic: social approbation for right actions; social disapproval for wrong actions.

By and large, our present problem is one of attitudes and implements. We are remodeling the Alhambra with a steam-shovel, and we are proud of our yardage. We shall hardly relinquish the shovel, which after all has many good points, but we are in need of gentler and more objective criteria for its successful use.

Eugene P. Odum on the Stability of the Ecosystem, 1969

The principles of ecological succession bear importantly on the relationships between man and nature. The framework of successional theory needs to be examined as a basis for resolving man's present environmental crisis. . . .

Ecological succession may be defined in terms of the following three parameters. (i) It is an orderly process of community development that is reasonably directional and, therefore, predictable. (ii) It results from modification of the physical environment by the community; that is, succession is community-controlled even though the physical environment determines the pattern, the rate of change, and often sets limits as to how far development can

Excerpts from Eugene P. Odum, "The Strategy of Ecosystem Development," *Science*, 164 (1969), pp. 262–70. Copyright 1969 by the American Association for the Advancement of Science.

go. (iii) It culminates in a stabilized ecosystem in which maximum biomass (or high information content) and symbiotic function between organisms are maintained per unit of available energy flow. In a word, the "strategy" of succession as a short-term process is basically the same as the "strategy" of long-term evolutionary development of the biosphere — namely, increased control of, or homeostasis with, the physical environment in the sense of achieving maximum protection from its perturbations. . . .

As the ecosystem develops, subtle changes in the network pattern of food chains may be expected. The manner in which organisms are linked together through food tends to be relatively simple and linear in the very early stages of succession, as a consequence of low diversity. . . . In contrast, food chains become complex webs in mature stages, with the bulk of biological energy flow following detritus pathways. . . .

There can be little doubt that the net result of community actions is symbiosis, nutrient conservation, stability, a decrease in entropy, and an increase in information. The overall strategy is . . . directed toward achieving as large and diverse an organic structure as is possible within the limits set by the available energy input and the prevailing physical conditions of existence (soil, water, climate, and so on).

[There is] a basic conflict between the strategies of man and of nature. . . . Man has generally been preoccupied with obtaining as much "production" from the landscape as possible, by developing and maintaining early successional types of ecosystems, usually monocultures. But, of course, man does not live by food and fiber alone; he also needs a balanced CO_2-O_2 atmosphere, the climatic buffer provided by oceans and masses of vegetation, and clean (that is, unproductive) water for cultural and industrial uses. Many essential life-cycle resources, not to mention recreational and esthetic needs, are best provided man by the less "productive" landscapes. In other words, the landscape is not just a supply depot but is also the *oikos* — the home — in which we must live. Until recently mankind has more or less taken for granted the gas-exchange, water-purification, nutrient-cycling, and other protective functions of self-maintaining ecosystems, chiefly because neither his numbers nor his environmental manipulations have been great enough to affect regional and global balances. Now, of course, it is painfully evident that such balances are being affected, often detrimentally. The "one problem, one solution approach" is no longer adequate and must be replaced by some form of ecosystem analysis that considers man as a part of, not apart from, the environment.

Pickett and White on Patch Dynamics, 1985

Ecologists have always been aware of the importance of natural dynamics in ecosystems, but historically, the focus has been on successional development

---

Excerpts from *The Ecology of Natural Disturbance and Patch Dynamics*, by S. T. A. Pickett and P. S. White (Orlando, Fla.: Academic Press, 1985), pp. xiii, 5, 12.

of equilibrium communities. While this approach has generated appreciable understanding of the composition and functioning of ecosystems, recently many workers have turned their attention to processes of disturbance themselves and to the evolutionary significance of such events. This shifted emphasis has inspired studies in diverse systems. We use the phrase "patch dynamics" to describe their common focus.

Focus on patch dynamics leads workers to explicit studies of disturbance-related phenomena — the conditions created by disturbance; the frequency, severity, intensity, and predictability of such events; and the responses of organisms to disturbance regimes. The phrase "patch dynamics" embraces disturbances external to the community as well as internal processes of change. Patch dynamics includes not only such coarse-scale, infrequent events as hurricanes, but also such fine-scale events as the shifting mosaic of badger mounds in a prairie. . . . The most basic theme is an evolutionary one: How does the dynamic setting of populations influence their evolution? What are the implications for communities and ecosystems? [This approach] form[s] an alternative to equilibrium concepts of the evolution of populations, composition of communities, and functioning of ecosystems. . . .

The sources of variation in disturbances include differences in ecosystem scale, differences in kinds of disturbances, and differences in disturbance regimes. Even for a single ecosystem and disturbance event, effects vary at different trophic levels and occur over a wide range of biological levels from suborganismal (e.g., physiological effects) and organismal (e.g., behavioral changes) to ecosystem-wide (e.g., nutrient availability). Most disturbances produce heterogeneous and patchy effects; these effects may themselves depend on the state of the community prior to the disturbance.

We have adopted the term "patch dynamics" . . . for the following reasons:

1. "Patch" implies a relatively discrete spatial pattern, but does not establish any constraint on patch size, internal homogeneity, or discreteness.
2. "Patch" implies a relationship of one patch to another in space and to the surrounding, unaffected or less affected matrix.
3. "Patch dynamics" emphasizes patch change. . . .

Equilibrium landscapes would . . . seem to be the exception, rather than the rule (for example, most North American landscapes have probably been influenced by changing disturbance regimes in the last several thousand to tens of thousands of years).

Patch dynamics has implications for applied ecology. . . . Preservation of natural systems necessarily involves a paradox: we seek to preserve systems that change. Success in a conservation effort thus requires an understanding of landscape patch structure and dynamics.

ᵠ E S S A Y S

The first essay, by writer Robert Clarke, credits scientist Ellen Swallow with the founding of American ecology, defined as the maintenance of a healthy environment by and for humans. In the second essay, Donald Worster, an environmental historian at the University of Kansas, explores the role of metaphors — organism, economy, and chaos — in relation to the ethics and policies of environmental management. Ecology as a science is not distinct from human society but is given meaning through human responses to disasters such as the Dust Bowl of the 1930s and the environmental crisis of the 1970s. In the chapter's concluding essay, Nathan Hare, of the Black Think Tank, in San Francisco, California, extends the social meaning of ecology to the concerns of urban blacks through a critique of "white" meanings embedded in ecology.

Ellen Swallow's Human Ecology

ROBERT CLARKE

November 30, 1892. In seven years and thirty-one days the twentieth century would begin. The complexities of a new era would replace the simple existence of the old.

Ellen Swallow had worked at an unbelievable pace to develop the inter-disciplines of an environmental science she believed the next 100 years required. She knew work alone was no guarantee of permanence for the knowledge she had pulled together. If anything, the changing world — specialized, mechanized, cosmetic — seemed to take things apart.

The world is whole, like the environment. But in working with that world, the specialists of science and technology, government and industry were fragmenting it. Focused on their own individual fields, burying deeper and deeper in their respective niches, they seemed oblivious to the environment around them.

The First Lady of Science had gone in the opposite direction, putting sciences together to nurture the roots of environment. But to perpetuate her conglomerate body of knowledge and its applications, a permanent structure was required. Ernst Haeckel had been right when he suggested the name for a science of everybody's home. Ellen Swallow began to fill the void that accompanied Oekologie's 1873 proposal with her collection of old knowledge cross-fertilized with new to build "home science" for environment and life within it.

Since 1873, she had laid the foundations and aligned the interconnecting walls of that "house." Gradually, surreptitiously at times, she opened the structure — inviting, pleading, scheming — for others to enter and occupy it. Now the time had come to open it completely.

In four days she would be fifty. The nineteenth century that had molded her was running out. The new one would be very different from anything mankind

---

Excerpts from *Ellen Swallow: The Woman Who Founded Ecology*, by Robert Clarke (New York: Follett, 1973), pp. 113–120.

had ever known. She believed, since mankind had become both the provider and the product of his environment, he could meet the challenges of a changing environment by shaping it the right way. It was changing in any case. He must be prepared for that change.

At the end of the nineteenth century, the environment was still essentially held in human hands. But from her vantage point at MIT, Ellen Swallow could see that environment was being transferred to technology. It must not be turned over completely, she believed. *People* must retain some control over the shape and change of their environment. The only way they could, she saw, was to be equipped for that function—the man on the street or at work, the woman in the home or in the community, the child in school. *All* must have the knowledge required to retain their traditional relationship with environment.

If Ellen Swallow had learned one thing in her fifty years, it was the need first to know, to understand the substance one worked with. Chemistry was a good teacher that way. That's how she felt about environment. She didn't see environment always in the terms used to describe it today. It was a different environment then. But she believed if people would work with the environmental principle superimposed on their daily lives, they would grow more conscious of what the environment is and what to do—and not do—with it.

She intended exactly that on the November evening in 1892 when she christened the science she had nurtured through nineteen years.

It was Thursday, a crisp, chilly, early winter day in Boston. As the sun began its slow slide behind the trees and brownstones on the Boston side of the Charles River, a parade of carriages carrying well dressed ladies and gentlemen began arriving at the corner of Commonwealth Avenue and Exeter Street. In less than an hour, some 300 fashionable people climbed the ornate staircase to the elegant Vendome Hotel. This was the annual meeting of the prestigious Boot & Shoe Club, the *creme de la creme* of the footwear industry in Boston, industrial capital of the world.

* * * *

Ellen Swallow entered the hotel on the arm of her tall husband. They had walked the two short blocks from MIT. Now they moved down the deep-pile carpeted hall to where a reception was in process. Gentlemen and ladies exchanged greetings. Introductions were made. Voices, a mandolin, punch cups, and the rustle of expensive silks and velvets mixed in an elegance of sound. . . .

At each setting, an engraved parchment listed the characters in this drama, its theme captured by the words of the club's poet laureate, Ralph Waldo Emerson:

> Is it not plain that not in the Senates or Courts nor in Chambers of Commerce, but in the dwelling place must the true character and hope of the time be consulted?

. . . Club President F. H. Nazro "rapped the spoons into silence." Opening the program from the long, elevated head table, Nazro responded to Emerson's question:

"The days of the present are better than the days of the past. We are optimists, and we claim that the days of the future may be better than those of today." Even an optimist said "may."

As the nineteenth century draws to a close, he observed, humanity has not solved the problem of living. "Pray God, the twentieth century may." Then Nazro introduced the woman who would propose *how* the new century should solve *what* problems, another optimist: "Mrs. Robert Richards, Instructor in Sanitary Chemistry in the Massachusetts Institute of Technology."

Rising to face the distinguished audience, Ellen paused. This, she thought, is what it's all been about. Now is the time, the place. She began.

NEW SCIENCE, headlined *The Boston Globe* the next day. "Mrs. Richards Names It Oekology." Just below, "Tis the Art of First-Class Living." Either the word environment was too long for the typesetter or too abstract for a nineteenth century reporter. Perhaps his editor felt the concept too broad for the reader to grasp. In any event, "environment" was conspicuously scarce in the story that captured the more common interpretation of women's work, even for women of science.

The story did, however, take up the best part of the page, with its drawn illustrations of the evening, an account of the fashions, and a portrait of Alice Freeman Palmer, who had come all the way from the University of Chicago to attend the unveiling of Oekology. The former president of Wellesley was a dean at the University of Chicago.

"Speaking without notes and with convincing seriousness lightened by many touches of humor," Ellen Swallow threw open environmental science to the public.

> I would like to have the gift of mind reading for a while, for I think the very best speech would be to know what each one present expected to hear, here tonight. As your president has said, we have not come to talk over the science of domestics. A Domestic Science is something broader. It is a comfort to know [however] that you believe there [can be] a science for the home.
>
> But before there can be a science, there must be an art. The art of living has been given a good deal of consideration, and for some time there has been formulating a science of living.
>
> Perhaps no one is to blame for the fact that the science to teach people how to live [in their environment] has been so long in getting any attention. . . . Men built houses long before they knew how to live in them safely.

The implication was clear. Before people build a new environment, they had better learn to live in this one. Otherwise, the very base of what is built will be flawed.

She suggested, subtly, that perhaps the real reason why man built houses without knowing how to live in them was that woman, the traditional caretaker of that environment, had been denied the education that would have augmented man's knowledge. Rather, knowledge was imbalanced and "has created many victims," as well as progress, she said. Woman is man's balancing factor, especially when it comes to environment. Together, they can live right, in a right environment, she said. But first man would have to let his counterpart catch up with the knowledge creating a new environment.

There will be more "victims of science" in the future if we do not educate woman with knowledge that will allow her to manage space, time, and technology and to educate her children on how to live in a rapidly changing environment, Ellen warned.

In the words of the *Globe* reporter, ". . . she wittily reviewed man's endeavor to make life easier for women."

"To relieve women from drudgery, fathers formerly sent [daughters] to finishing schools and gave them lessons in the fine arts. But all of these semi-polite accomplishments turned to dust and ashes literally and figuratively in the crucible of life . . ." that is the home environment.

"They walled up the beneficient fireplaces and introduced airtight stoves and put washbowls in rooms to save steps, but they forgot to make the plumbing safe. The result has been to kill off all the delicate men, women and children . . . in greater numbers than any war has ever done," she said.

Then she "scathingly" attacked, not only the educational system that would permit this ignorance among men and women, but also the ignorance by which the learning environment itself was allowed to exist—"erecting improperly ventilated and unsanitary buildings" in which children are supposed to learn. "They do learn, you know. But they learn to grow up and create more of the same kind of environment in which they learned.

"If that is the environment in which they learn, then that is the environment they learn to live in. How can we expect them to know, let alone teach or live a better way?"

Then she made her appeal:

And now I ask you here tonight to stand sponsors of the christening of a new science and to give the same your fostering care and generous support. . . .

For this knowledge of right living, we have sought a new name. . . . As theology is the science of religious life, and biology the science of [physical] life . . . so let *Oekology* be henceforth the science of [our] normal lives . . . the worthiest of all the applied sciences which *teaches the principles on which to found . . . healthy . . . and happy life.*

And, she might have added, to assure future environmental quality.

It was done. Acknowledging the comments and good wishes of the audience, Ellen and Robert thanked their friends and left the Vendome. Walking the quarter mile to Back Bay station for a train to Jamaica Plain, she felt satisfaction. She had invested the labors of nineteen years in her presentation of Oekology.

Organic, Economic, and Chaotic Ecology

DONALD WORSTER

*Organic Ecology**

On a typical afternoon the wind on the Great Plains blows at a steady fifteen miles per hour. It is a constant presence, pressing down with relentless will the grasses and row crops, whistling with an eerie whine around the farmer's barn and fences. In the spring of 1934, however, the wind suddenly turned demonic. On April 14, a vast black blizzard of earth came rolling out of the north toward Texas, whirling and spinning in a giant bowl, darkening the sun and blanketing the land with drifts up to twenty feet high. Then less than a month later, on May 10, another great storm moved east toward Chicago. Twelve million tons of plains dirt were dumped on that city. Two days later the storm reached the eastern seaboard. Dust sifted into the White House and fell on ships standing out to sea.

The wind often carried dust over the land: that was a familiar enough sight to settlers on the plains. They had even seen a few serious dust storms in 1932, in 1913, and further back in 1894 and 1886. But none of these had been of more than local significance, and nothing in the past prepared them for the frequency or terror of these new storms: 22 of regional extent in 1934, 40 in 1935, 68 in 1936, 72 in 1937, before at last they began to drop off. By then it was obvious to the entire nation that something was wrong on the western plains. Soil scientists for the Department of Agriculture estimated in 1938 that one-half of the region — some 500,000 square miles — had been seriously damaged by wind erosion. As a farmer wrote to the *Dallas Farm News* the following year: "The prairie, once the home of the deer, buffalo, and antelope, is now the home of the Dust Bowl and the WPA [Works Progress Administration]."

For a full half century the pioneers had advanced with the good years onto the plains in recurring tides of optimism, only to fall back when the dry spells appeared. But during World War I and through the 1920's man seemed at last to lay permanent hold on this defiant, intractable landscape. Much of the western grassland quickly became a vast machine-age frontier, mass-producing wheat and cotton. Thousands of new Ford tractors were put to work breaking the virgin sod, even when the nation could not absorb all the crop output. As farmers habitually do, the High Plains settlers fixed their eyes on only one factor in nature, rainfall. Rain, or the lack of it, could send the tractors out or hold them back, and during a good year of precipitation the farmer would plow and plant, regardless of the market. In this simple, single-factor way of think-ing only of the weather lay the sodbuster's unpreparedness for the Dust Bowl disaster. When the thirties brought severe drought to his fields, the most serious problem for the settler proved to be not too little rain but too much dust — the loss of his topsoil, which once had been held in place by the native sod. All

---

*Excerpts from Donald Worster, "Grass to Dust: The Great Plains in the 1930's," *Environmental Review* 3 (1977), pp. 3–9. Reprinted with permission from *Environmental History Review*, © 1977, the American Society for Environmental History.

along the farmer had ignored the essential grass that shielded the soil from the constant wind. His mastery over the land, consequently, was turned once more into defeat. . . .

"The meaning of the dust storms," wrote Archibald MacLeish in 1935, "was that grass was dead." It had died, not of drought, but of plowing. When the dry years came, there was no tough-rooted sod to hold the soil in place. The grass, it was discovered by scientists in the thirties, was more than an indication of an unpredictable, low-rainfall climate; it was a necessary buffer between man and that climate. It was a complicated ecological system, a unique community of plants and animals, that worked to moderate and even tame the harsh physical forces. Destroy that community, as the sodbusters did, and man had to face all unprepared and naked the full brute force of wind and drought. . . . But in the thirties, largely as a consequence of the Dust Bowl, other Americans began to think about the land and its human meaning increasingly in ecological terms.

During this decade the plains experience helped provoke a reevaluation of the nation's entire approach to conservation. It was no longer adequate to talk separately about forests or wildlife, grasslands or soils in resource management; all elements were discovered to be bound together in a single equation. Undoubtedly this shift in outlook owed something to the collapse of the Wall Street markets. The ensuing depression, so starkly coincidental with the Dust Bowl, put Americans in a more communal, integrative mood. It also engendered a new willingness to subordinate economic criteria to broader standards of value, including ecological sanctity. Hence this decade, so tragic for the landscape as well as for personal security, saw such initiatives as the Tennessee Valley Authority headed by David Lilienthal, the wildlife management work of Aldo Leopold, and the environmental philosophy of Lewis Mumford — all ecology-oriented departures from previous conservation thinking.

Another evidence of this shift toward ecology, and at the highest levels of public resource policy, was the report submitted by the Great Plains Committee to President Franklin Roosevelt in December, 1936. The committee's chairman was Morris Cooke, head of the Rural Electrification Administration. The other members were Hugh Bennett of the Soil Conservation Service, Harry Hopkins of the Works Progress Administration, and Secretary Henry Wallace of the Department of Agriculture. Without qualification, the committee agreed that the Dust Bowl was a wholly man-made disaster produced by a history of misguided efforts to "impose upon the region a system of agriculture to which the Plains are not adapted." The essence of the tragedy as they understood it was a failure to heed the common sense lessons of ecology. "Nature," they argued, "has established a balance in the Great Plains by what in human terms would be called the method of trial and error. The white man has disturbed this balance; he must restore it or devise a new one of his own." Unless this were done, the committee warned, the land would become a desert, and the government would have on its hands a perennial, costly problem of relief and salvage. . . .

More influential than any of these in the shaping of an ecological approach to conservation in this formative decade was Frederic Clements. A native of

Nebraska, the son of pioneers, he had studied ecology during the 1890's at the state university in Lincoln, and by the thirties was a research fellow at the Carnegie Institute in Washington. No one had been more important than he in getting ecology on its feet as an academic discipline during the first decades of the twentieth century. He had helped to introduce the avant-garde German ecologists to American readers, and he had trained a number of young scholars in this emerging field. More important, he had developed, even before 1910, a persuasive model of how nature works, an ecological paradigm that dominated this science in America, as well as Great Britain, for over three decades. So widely adopted was it that Anglo-American ecology until the 1940's was commonly identified in international circles as a unique, distinguishable tradition: the so-called historical or dynamic school. The central theme of this school was Clements's theory of the climax state of vegetation. On this particular model scientists and conservationists in the thirties would attempt to build a new land-use program, one that would have special relevance to the Great Plains.

According to Clements's model of nature, every region of the earth must pass through a series of vegetational changes, or a process of "ecological succession." From a youthful, unstable, pioneering stage, the plant life of any area evolves eventually toward a more complex, mature equilibrium state, the "climax." Deflect or disturb this pattern of succession, and nature will struggle mightily to get back on the right track. Leave nature alone, and she will produce at last a plant community of near-perfect adaptation that will go on reproducing itself through thousands of years. In the Clementsian model this climax stage is the child of climate: the final outcome of succession is almost wholly determined by the prevailing patterns of rainfall, wind currents, and temperature over any large expanse of space.

In the case of the Great Plains the climax vegetation was the primeval grass, curling and billowing over hundreds of millions of acres of land. Only this grass had proved capable of surviving the periodic droughts of this region and the perennially sparse rainfall. As Clements maintained, this grassland climax had endured for millennia, perhaps as far back as the upthrust of the Rocky Mountains. "There is no basis," he cautioned, "for assuming either that the earth itself or the life upon it will ever reach final stability." But within the span of human time-consciousness at least, nature could be said to achieve long periods of stasis that could be taken as proof of her superior workmanship. And this end product, the grass, deserved as much attention from man as the climate that produced it. . . .

Such recommendations mark an important shift in American perception of the land. In the climax model of Clements environmentalists had at last an apparently objective, scientifically calibrated yardstick by which man's intrusions into nature could be measured. From the thirties on they began to rely on it more and more in discussing both the Dust Bowl crisis and subsequent environmental problems. Generally the view gaining support was that land-use policy should leave the climax vegetation as undisturbed as possible. Whenever interference by man was necessary — and hardly anyone maintained that it was not, unless the population dropped abruptly and humans reverted to a hunting economy — then the best that could be done was to stick as tightly as possible to nature's design. . . .

Frederic Clements died in 1945, and the science of ecology has since then moved in radically different directions. The discipline is no longer dominated by the succession-climax model, with its emphasis on an evolutionary or historical perspective. Even before Clements's death, during the thirties, a few dissidents challenged his thinking and the strong respect for the natural order it implied. This "anti-climax" group, which centered around [Henry] . . . Gleason of the University of Michigan and Arthur Tansley of Oxford, found more adherents in science and beyond as the difficulties of applying Clements's approach to land policies became more apparent. The Kansas historian James Malin, for example, levelled an especially fierce blast against the Clementsian tradition and its implied criticism of plains farmers for creating the Dust Bowl.

Economic Ecology*

The scientist who laid the foundations for the New [Economic] Ecology was the Cambridge University zoologist Charles Elton. In 1927 Elton published his first major work, *Animal Ecology*, which Julian Huxley introduced to the scientific world as a tool of great promise in the more effective management of the plant and animal "industry." . . . In every community, plants, through the photosynthetic conversion of sunlight to food, form the first link in a chain of nutrition. Food, one might say, is the essential capital in the natural economic order. The remaining links — usually no more than two or three, and almost never more than four — include the herbivorous animals and their predators. A typical food chain in a North American oak woods might link acorns, quail, and foxes, or acorns, mice, and weasels; with some 200 species of birds and mammals alone feeding on the oaks, the potential number of food chains is extraordinarily large. Possibly the idea of a food chain had its source in the eighteenth century's favorite metaphor, the "Great Chain of Being." Note, however, that the older notion ranked all species on a single grand staircase, those at the top of the stairs being the most noble and honored. Elton's chains, in contrast, were exclusively economic; they had nothing at all to do with taxonomy. They could be found in nature by the thousands, all showing a common pattern but no two alike in every respect. And the bottom of the chain, rather than the top, is the most important link: The plants make the whole system possible. Elton referred to the sum total of chains in any community as the "food web" — an exceedingly complex design of crisscrossed lines of economic activity. Such webs are easiest to analyze in the relatively unpopulated arctic zones and almost impossible to untangle in the warm, humid tropics, where life forms abound.

In every food chain certain roles must be performed. The plants, for example, are all "producers." Animals can be described as either first- or second-order "consumers," depending on whether they eat plants or other

---

*Excerpts from Donald Worster, *Nature's Economy*, Cambridge University Press 1985, orig. pub. 1977, pp. 295–311, Cambridge University Press.

animals. Those animals that feed on the most numerous plants in a habitat, like the bison on prairie grasses, or copepods on diatoms in the sea, are the "key industries" in those economies. In 1926, August Thienemann had introduced the terms "producer," "consumer," and "reducer," or "decomposer," to describe ecological roles in a specific ecological setting; Elton now generalized them for every food chain in nature. These labels emphasized the nutritional interdependence that binds species together — the corporateness of survival — and they became the cues from which ecology would increasingly take an economic direction. . . .

A second long step toward the New Ecology was taken by A. G. Tansley, the Oxford botanist. In a 1935 essay, Tansley attempted to rid ecology of all the lingering traces of organismic philosophy, expressed most recently in Clements's description of vegetation as a single living organism. Although Tansley himself had once gone so far as to describe the human community as a "quasi-organism," he now decided that this organismic talk had exceeded the bounds of legitimate scientific inquiry. The often-repeated notion that the plant assemblage is more than the sum of its parts, that it forms a whole which resists reductive analysis, he took to be a fiction worked up by an overexcited imagination. These "wholes," he wrote, "are *in analysis* nothing but the synthesized actions of the components in associations." A mature science, in his view, must isolate "the basic units of nature" and must "split up the story" into its individual parts. It must approach nature as a composite of strictly physical entities organized into a mechanical system. The scientist who knows all the properties of all the parts studied separately can accurately predict their combined result. In addition, Tansley wanted to strike the word "community" from his science's vocabulary because of connotations that he considered misleading and anthropomorphic; some, he feared, might conclude from such language that human associations and those in nature were parallel. Plants and animals in a locale cannot constitute a genuine community, he argued, for no psychic bond can exist between them, and thus they can have no true social order. In short, Tansley hoped to purge from ecology all that was not subject to quantification and analysis, all those obscurities that had been a part of its baggage at least since the Romantic period. He would rescue it from the status of a vaguely mysterious, moralizing "point of view" and make of it instead of hard-edged, mechanistic, nothing-but discipline, marching in closed ranks with the other sciences.

To replace these fuzzy analogies with the organism or the human community, Tansley came up with a new model of organization: the "ecosystem." It was an idea strongly influenced by that masterful science of physics, which early in the twentieth century had begun to talk about energy "fields" and "systems" as a way of getting a more precise handle on natural phenomena than was possible in traditional Newtonian science. Organisms indeed live in closely integrated units, Tansley agreed, but these can best be studied as physical systems, not "organic wholes." Using the ecosystem, all relations among organisms can be described in terms of the purely material exchange of energy and of such chemical substances as water, phosphorus, nitrogen, and other nutrients that are the constituents of "food." These are the real bonds that hold the natural world together; they create a single unit made up of many smaller units — big and little ecosystems. The outmoded concept of an ecological community suggested a sharp disjunction between the living and nonliving substances on earth (part of the Romantic legacy). In contrast, Tansley's ecosystem brought all nature — rocks and gases as well as biota — into a common ordering of material resources. It was more inclusive, paradoxically, because it was first more reductive. Tansley was saying, in fact, that ecologists were stagnating in scientific adolescence precisely because they had not yet succeeded in reducing their subject matter to the laws of physicochemical activity, which alone could bring about genuine progress toward positive knowledge. . . .

All ecological kinships thereafter had to be reworked in terms of energy relations. No energy is created or destroyed by the ecosystem, but only transformed and re-transformed before escaping. Most important, the ecologist had to be tutored in the Second Law of Thermodynamics, first formulated by Rudolph Clausius in 1850. According to this law, all energy tends to disperse or become disorganized and unavailable for use, until at last the energy system reaches maximum entropy: a state of total randomness, total equilibrium, death. The ecosystem of the earth, considered from the perspective of energetics, is a way-station on a river of no return. Energy flows through it and disappears eventually into the vast sea of space; there is no way to get back upstream. And unlike water in the hydrological cycle, energy once passed through nature is forever, irretrievably lost. By collecting solar energy for their own use, plants retard this entropic process; they can pass energy on to animals in repackaged or reconcentrated form — some of it at least — and the animals in turn hold it temporarily in organized availability. Put another way, the ecosystem is comparable both to a chain of reservoirs that store running water, and to the dams that make it work before it is released again to rush downstream. But all along the way, some of that flow seeps into the ground and some evaporates into the air, and all that remains must at some point be released. So long as the sun goes on supplying a current of energy, the ecosystem can endure. When that supply runs out, however, the system will collapse.

What remained was to merge these overlapping ideas . . . into a comprehensive account of the energy-based economics of nature. That final step was taken in 1942, when a postgraduate student at Yale, Raymond Lindeman, published a scientific paper entitled "The Trophic-Dynamic Aspect of Ecology." This event may serve to mark the full-blown arrival of the New Ecology. It also coincided roughly with the beginnings of the "Age of Ecology" in postwar Anglo-American culture, the appearance of a wide consciousness of ecological concepts in popular environmental thought. But there was no real connection between the two; indeed, it is safe to say that few in the general public would ever hear of Lindeman or understand what he had accomplished. When his paper was published, he would have been only twenty-seven years old. But shortly before its appearance he died, following a long illness, and the scientific community lost one of its most brilliant new minds. . . .

The specific environment Lindeman studied was Cedar Bog Lake in Minnesota. Such lacustrine systems again and again proved to be the best exemplars of the processes of energy capture and use, chiefly because of the simplified plant populations and the ease of biomass measurement there. But Lindeman's paper was much more than a report on this lake as an isolated example; he wanted to pull together all the major ecological theorizing of the past several decades, including Clements's notion of succession toward climax, into one grand model of "energy-availing" relationships in nature. And he succeeded brilliantly. "Trophic-Dynamic" in the paper's title meant the ecosystem's food or energy cycle, the metabolism of the whole. All resident organisms, he pointed out, may be grouped into a series of more or less discrete "trophic levels": the familiar producers, primary consumers, secondary consumers, decomposers. Other terms might also be used here, such as "autotrophs" for the plants, which generally create their own food by photosynthesis, and "heterotrophs" for animals and bacteria, which must feed on other organic tissues. In the Minnesota lake, the producers were the macrophytic pond weeds and, more important, the microphytic phytoplankton. On these fed the browsers — tadpoles, ducks, certain fishes and insects, tiny copepods and other zooplankton — filling a niche similar to that occupied by terrestrial herbivores. On the browsers in turn depended the second-order consumers, which included other fish, crustaceans, turtles, frogs, and birds. A snapping turtle or an osprey, both carnivorous predators, might represent the third-order consumer. Last came the countless millions of decomposers, bacteria and fungi, which lived in the slimy bottom mud and worked to break down organic substance into recyclable nutrients.

The single most important fact about these trophic levels, in Lindeman's view, was that the energy in use at one level can never be passed on in its entirety to the next higher level. A portion is always lost in the transfer as heat escaping into the atmosphere. The chief goal of Lindeman's ecology was to quantify these losses: to make precise measurements of the shrinkage in available energy as it passes through the ecosystem. He wanted to know, that is, the "productivity" of each level in the food chain and the "efficiency" of energy transfers. Productivity in this case referred not to the numbers of a given species but to the accumulated biomass at any trophic level and the caloric energy required to support that amount of organic matter. . . . .

Once the ecologist had these productivity figures in hand for all the trophic levels, he could discover what happens to the captured solar energy as it moves through the ecosystem. He could calculate, that is, the "ecologic efficiencies" of organisms: how much energy they are able to utilize from lower levels and how much of that they in turn pass on, as well as how much they use up in metabolism. . . .

These then are the formative episodes in the development of the New Ecology, an energy-economic model of the environment that began to emerge in the 1920s and was virtually complete by the mid-forties. It is safe to say that this model is overwhelmingly the dominant one followed now in Anglo-American ecology. Since Lindeman, a new breed of like-minded mathematical ecologists has appeared on the academic scene, and they have pushed their subject to the front ranks of the "hard sciences." Among the postwar leaders in this surge toward respectability have been Lindeman's teacher at Yale, G.

Evelyn Hutchinson, as well as Edward Deevy, David Gates, John Phillipson, George Woodwell, Robert MacArthur, and probably most important of all, Eugene Odum. . . .

Chaotic Ecology*

In 1953 Odum published the first edition of his famous textbook, *The Fundamentals of Ecology*. In 1966 he became president of the Ecological Society of America.

By now anyone in the United States who regularly reads a newspaper or magazine has come to know at least a few of Odum's ideas, for they furnish the main themes in our popular understanding of ecology, beginning with the sovereign idea of the ecosystem. Odum defined the ecosystem as "any unit that includes all of the organisms (i.e., the 'community') in a given area interacting with the physical environment so that a flow of energy leads to clearly defined trophic structure, biotic diversity, and material cycles (i.e., exchange of materials between living and nonliving parts) within the system." The whole earth, he argued, is organized into an interlocking series of such "ecosystems," ranging in size from a small pond to so vast an expanse as the Brazilian rainforest.

What all those ecosystems have in common is a "strategy of development," a kind of game plan that gives nature an overall direction. That strategy is, in Odum's words, "directed toward achieving as large and diverse an organic structure as is possible within the limits set by the available energy input and the prevailing physical conditions of existence." Every single ecosystem, he believed, is either moving toward or has already achieved that goal. It is a clear, coherent, and easily observable strategy; and it ends in the happy state of order.

Nature's strategy, Odum added, leads finally to a world of mutualism and cooperation among the organisms inhabiting an area. From an early stage of competing against one another, they evolve toward a more symbiotic relationship. They learn, as it were, to work together to control their surrounding environment, making it more and more suitable as a habitat, until at last they have the power to protect themselves from its stressful cycles of drought and flood, winter and summer, cold and heat. Odum called that point "homeostasis." To achieve it, the living components of an ecosystem must evolve a structure of interrelatedness and cooperation that can, to some extent, manage the physical world—manage it for maximum efficiency and mutual benefit.

I have described this set of ideas as a break from the past, but that is misleading. Odum may have used different terms than Clements, may even have had a radically different vision of nature at times; but he did not repudiate Clements's notion that nature moves toward order and harmony. In the place of

*Excerpts from Donald Worster, "Ecology of Order and Chaos," *Environmental History Review*, 14, no. 1–2 (Spring/Summer 1990), pp. 4–16 excerpts. Reprinted with permission from *Environmental History Review*, © 1990, the American Society for Environmental History.

the theory of the "climax" stage he put the theory of the "mature ecosystem." His nature may have appeared more as an automated factory than as a Clementsian super-organism, but like its predecessor it tends toward order.

The theory of the ecosystem presented a very clear set of standards as to what constituted order and disorder, which Odum set forth in the form of a "tabular model of ecological succession." When the ecosystem reaches its end point of homeostasis, his table shows, it expends less energy on increasing production and more on furnishing protection from external vicissitudes: that is, the biomass in an area reaches a steady level, neither increasing nor decreasing, and the emphasis in the system is on keeping it that way — on maintaining a kind of no-growth economy. Then the little, aggressive, weedy organisms common at an early stage in development (the r-selected species) give way to larger, steadier creatures (K-selected species), who may have less potential for fast growth and explosive reproduction but also better talents at surviving in dense settlements and keeping the place on an even keel. At that point there is supposed to be more diversity in the community — i.e., a greater array of species. And there is less loss of nutrients to the outside; nitrogen, phosphorous, and calcium all stay in circulation within the ecosystem rather than leaking out. Those are some of the key indicators of ecological order, all of them susceptible to precise measurement. The suggestion was implicit but clear that if one interfered too much with nature's strategy of development, the effects might be costly: a serious loss of nutrients, a decline in species diversity, an end to biomass stability. In short, the ecosystem would be damaged.

The most likely source of that damage was no mystery to Odum: it was human beings trying to force up the production of useful commodities and stupidly risking the destruction of their life support system.

> Man has generally been preoccupied with obtaining as much "production" from the landscape as possible, by developing and maintaining early successional types of ecosystems, usually monocultures. But, of course, man does not live by food and fiber alone; he also needs a balanced CO_2–O_2 atmosphere, the climatic buffer provided by oceans and masses of vegetation, and clean (that is, unproductive) water for cultural and industrial uses. Many essential life-cycle resources, not to mention recreational and esthetic needs, are best provided man by the less "productive" landscapes. In other words, the landscape is not just a supply depot but is also the *oikos* — the home — in which we must live.

Odum's view of nature as a series of balanced ecosystems, achieved or in the making, led him to take a strong stand in favor of preserving the landscape in as nearly natural a condition as possible. He suggested the need for substantial restraint on human activity — for environmental planning "on a rational and scientific basis." . . . Ecology must be taught to the public and made the foundation of education, economics, and politics; America and other countries must be "ecologized."

Of course not every one who adopted the ecosystem approach to ecology ended up where Odum did. Quite the contrary, many found the ecosystem idea a wonderful instrument for promoting global technocracy. Experts familiar with the ecosystem and skilled in its manipulation, it was hoped in some quarters, could manage the entire planet for improved efficiency. "Governing" all of nature with the aid of rational science was the dream of these ecosystem technocrats. But technocratic management was not the chief lesson, I believe, the public learned in Professor Odum's classroom; most came away devoted, as he was, to preserving large parts of nature in an unmanaged state and sure that they had been given a strong scientific rationale, as well as knowledge base, to do it. We must defend the world's endangered ecosystems, they insisted. We must safeguard the integrity of the Greater Yellowstone ecosystem, the Chesapeake Bay ecosystem, the Serengeti ecosystem. We must protect species diversity, biomass stability, and calcium recycling. We must make the world safe for K-species.

That was the rallying cry of environmentalists and ecologists alike in the 1960s and early 1970s, when it seemed that the great coming struggle would be between what was left of pristine nature, delicately balanced in Odum's beautifully rational ecosystems, and a human race bent on mindless, greedy destruction. A decade or two later the situation has changed considerably. There are still environmental threats around, to be sure, and they are more dangerous than ever. The newspapers inform us of continuing disasters like the massive 1989 oil spill in Alaska's Prince William Sound, and reporters persist in using words like "ecosystem" and "balance" and "fragility" to describe such disasters. So do many scientists, who continue to acknowledge their theoretical indebtedness to Odum. For instance, in a recent British poll, 447 ecologists out of 645 questioned ranked the "ecosystem" as one of the most important concepts their discipline has contributed to our understanding of the natural world; indeed, "ecosystem" ranked first on their list, drawing more votes than nineteen other leading concepts. But all the same, and despite the persistence of environmental problems, Odum's ecosystem is no longer the main theme in research or teaching in the science. A survey of recent ecology textbooks shows that the concept is not even mentioned in one leading work and has a much diminished place in the others. . . .

Ecology is not the same as it was. A rather drastic change has been going on in this science of late — a radical shifting away from the thinking of Eugene Odum's generation, away from its assumptions of order and predictability, a shifting toward what we might call a new *ecology of chaos*.

In July 1973, the *Journal of the Arnold Arboretum* published an article by two scientists associated with the Massachusetts Audubon Society, William Drury and Ian Nisbet, and it challenged Odum's ecology fundamentally. The title of the article was simply "Succession," indicating that old subject of observed sequences in plant and animal associations. With both Frederic Clements and Eugene Odum, succession had been taken to be the straight and narrow road to equilibrium. Drury and Nisbet disagreed completely with that assumption. Their observations, drawn particularly from northeastern temperate forests, strongly suggested that the process of ecological succession does not lead anywhere. Change is without any determinable direction and goes on forever, never reaching a point of stability. They found no evidence of any progressive development in nature: no progressive increase over time in biomass stabilization, no progressive diversification of species, no progressive movement toward a greater cohesiveness in plant and animal communities, nor toward a greater success in regulating the environment. Indeed, they found none of the criteria Odum had posited for mature ecosystems. The forest, they insisted, no matter what its age, is nothing but an erratic, shifting mosaic of trees and other plants. In their words, "most of the phenomena of succession should be understood as resulting from the differential growth, differential survival, and perhaps differential dispersal of species adapted to grow at different points on stress gradients." In other words, they could see lots of individual species, each doing its thing, but they could locate no emergent collectivity, nor any strategy to achieve one.

Prominent among their authorities supporting this view was the nearly forgotten name of Henry A. Gleason, a taxonomist who, in 1926, had challenged Frederic Clements and his organismic theory of the climax in an article entitled, "The Individualistic Concept of the Plant Association." Gleason had argued that we live in a world of constant flux and impermanence, not one tending toward Clements's climaxes. There is no such thing, he argued, as balance or equilibrium or steady-state. Each and every plant association is nothing but a temporary gathering of strangers, a clustering of species unrelated to one another, here for a brief while today, on their way somewhere else tomorrow. "Each . . . species of plant is a law unto itself," he wrote. We look for cooperation in nature and we find only competition. We look for organized wholes, and we can discover only loose atoms and fragments. We hope for order and discern only a mishmash of conjoining species, all seeking their own advantage in utter disregard of others.

Thanks in part to Drury and Nisbet, this "individualistic" view was reborn in the mid-1970s and, during the past decade, it became the core idea of what some scientists hailed as a new, revolutionary paradigm in ecology. To promote it, they attacked the traditional notion of succession; for to reject that notion was to reject the larger idea that organic nature tends toward order. In 1977 two more biologists, Joseph Connell and Ralph Slatyer, continued the attack, denying the old claim that an invading community of pioneering species, the first stage in Clements's sequence, works to prepare the ground for its successors, like a group of Daniel Boones blazing the trail for civilization. The first comers, Connell and Slatyer maintained, manage in most cases to stake out their claims and successfully defend them; they do not give way to a later, superior group of colonists. Only when the pioneers die or are damaged by natural disturbances, thus releasing the resources they have monopolized, can latecomers find a foothold and get established.

As this assault on the old thinking gathered momentum, the word "disturbance" began to appear more frequently in the scientific literature and be taken far more seriously. "Disturbance" was not a common subject in Odum's heyday, and it almost never appeared in combination with the adjective "natural." Now, however, it was as though scientists were out looking strenuously for signs of disturbance in nature — especially signs of disturbance that were not caused by humans — and they were finding it everywhere. During the past decade those new ecologists succeeded in leaving little tranquility in primitive nature. Fire is one of the most common disturbances they noted. So is wind, especially in the form of violent hurricanes and tornadoes. So are invading populations of microorganisms and pests and predators. And volcanic eruptions. And invading ice sheets of the Quaternary Period. And devastating droughts like that of the 1930s in the American West. Above all, it is these last sorts of disturbances, caused by the restlessness of climate, that the new generation of ecologists have emphasized. As one of the most influential of them, Professor Margaret Davis of the University of Minnesota, has written: "For the last 50 years or 500 or 1,000 — as long as anyone would claim for 'ecological time' — there has never been an interval when temperature was in a steady state with symmetrical fluctuations about a mean. . . . Only on the longest time scale, 100,000 years, is there a tendency toward cyclical variation, and the cycles are asymmetrical, with a mean much different from today."

One of the most provocative and impressive expressions of the new post-Odum ecology is a book of essays edited by S. T. A. Pickett and P. S. White, *The Ecology of Natural Disturbance and Patch Dynamics* (published in 1985). I submit it as symptomatic of much of the thinking going on today in the field. Though the final section of the book does deal with ecosystems, the word has lost much of its former meaning and implications. Two of the authors in fact open their contribution with a complaint that many scientists assume that "homogeneous ecosystems are a reality," when in truth "virtually all naturally occurring and man-disturbed ecosystems are mosaics of environmental conditions." "Historically," they write, "ecologists have been slow to recognize the importance of disturbances and the heterogeneity they generate." The reason for this slowness? "The majority of both theoretical and empirical work has been dominated by an equilibrium perspective." Repudiating that perspective, these authors take us to the tropical forests of South and Central America and to the Everglades of Florida, showing us instability on every hand: a wet, green world of continual disturbance — or as they prefer to say, "of perturbations." Even the grasslands of North America, which inspired Frederic Clements's theory of the climax, appear in this collection as regularly disturbed environments. One paper describes them as a "dynamic, fine-textured mosaic" that is constantly kept in upheaval by the workings of badgers, pocket gophers, and mound-building ants, along with fire, drought, and eroding wind and water. The message in all these papers is consistent: The climax notion is dead, the ecosystem has receded in usefulness, and in their place we have the idea of the lowly "patch." Nature should be regarded as a landscape of patches, big and little, patches of all textures and colors, a patchwork quilt of living things, changing continually through time and space, responding to an unceasing barrage of perturbations. The stitches in that quilt never hold for long. . . .

Nature, many have begun to believe, is *fundamentally* erratic, discontinuous, and unpredictable. It is full of seemingly random events that elude our models of how things are supposed to work. As a result, the unexpected keeps hitting us in the face. Clouds collect and disperse, rain falls or doesn't fall, disregarding our careful weather predictions, and we cannot explain why. Cars suddenly bunch up on the freeway, and the traffic controllers fly into a frenzy.

A man's heart beats regularly year after year, then abruptly begins to skip a beat now and then. A Ping Pong ball bounces off the table in an unexpected direction. Each little snowflake falling out of the sky turns out to be completely unlike any other. Those are ways in which nature seems, in contrast to all our previous theories and methods, to be chaotic. If the ultimate test of any body of scientific knowledge is its ability to predict events, then all the sciences and pseudo-sciences — physics, chemistry, climatology, economics, ecology — fail the test regularly. They all have been announcing laws, designing models, predicting what an individual atom or person is supposed to do; and now, increasingly, they are beginning to confess that the world never quite behaves the way it is supposed to do.

Making sense of this situation is the task of an altogether new kind of inquiry calling itself the science of chaos. Some say it portends a revolution in thinking equivalent to quantum mechanics or relativity. Like those other 20th-century revolutions, the science of chaos rejects tenets going back as far as the days of Sir Isaac Newton. In fact, what is occurring may be not two or three separate revolutions but a single revolution against all the principles, laws, models, and applications of classical science, the science ushered in by the great Scientific Revolution of the 17th century. For centuries we have assumed that nature, despite a few appearances to the contrary, is a perfectly predictable system of linear, rational order. Give us an adequate number of facts, scientists have said, and we can describe that order in complete detail — can plot the lines along which everything moves and the speed of that movement and the collisions that will occur. Even Darwin's theory of evolution, which in the last century challenged much of the Newtonian worldview, left intact many people's confidence that order would prevail at last in the evolution of life; that out of the tangled history of competitive struggle would come progress, harmony, and stability. Now that traditional assumption may have broken down irretrievably. For whatever reason, whether because empirical data suggest it or because extrascientific cultural trends do — the experience of so much rapid social change in our daily lives — scientists are beginning to focus on what they had long managed to avoid seeing. The world is more complex than we ever imagined, they say, and indeed, some would add, ever can imagine.

Despite the obvious complexity of their subject matter, ecologists have been among the slowest to join the cross-disciplinary science of chaos. I suspect that the influence of Clements and Odum, lingering well into the 1970s, worked against the new perspective, encouraging faith in linear regularities and equilibrium in the interaction of species. Nonetheless, eventually there arrived a day of conversion. In 1974 the Princeton mathematical ecologist Robert May published a paper with the title, "Biological Populations with Nonoverlapping Generations: Stable Points, Stable Cycles, and Chaos." In it he admitted that the mathematical models he and others had constructed were inadequate approximations of the ragged life histories of organisms. They did not fully explain, for example, the aperiodic outbreaks of gypsy moths in eastern hardwood forests or the Canadian lynx cycles in the subarctic. Wildlife populations do not follow some simple Malthusian pattern of increase, saturation, and crash.

More and more ecologists have followed May and begun to try to bring their subject into line with chaotic theory. William Schaefer is one of them; though a student of Robert MacArthur, a leader of the old equilibrium school, he has been lately struck by the same anomaly of unpredictable fluctuations in populations as May and others. Though taught to believe in "the so-called 'Balance of Nature'," he writes, " . . . the idea that populations are at or close to equilibrium," things now are beginning to look very different. He describes himself as having to reach far across the disciplines, to make connections with concepts of chaos in the other natural sciences, in order to free himself from his field's restrictive past.

The entire study of chaos began in 1961, with efforts to simulate weather and climate patterns on a computer at MIT. There, meteorologist Edward Lorenz came up with his now famous "Butterfly Effect," the notion that a butterfly stirring the air today in a Beijing park can transform storm systems next month in New York City. Scientists call this phenomenon "sensitive dependence on initial conditions." What it means is that tiny differences in input can quickly become substantial differences in output. A corollary is that we cannot know, even with all our artificial intelligence apparatus, every one of the tiny differences that have occurred or are occurring at any place or point in time; nor can we know which tiny differences will produce which substantial differences in output. Beyond a short range, say, of two or three days from now, our predictions are not worth the paper they are written on.

The implications of this "Butterfly Effect" for ecology are profound. If a single flap of an insect's wings in China can lead to a torrential downpour in New York, then what might it do to the Greater Yellowstone Ecosystem? What can ecologists possibly know about all the forces impinging on, or about to impinge on, any piece of land? What can they safely ignore and what must they pay attention to? What distant, invisible, minuscule events may even now be happening that will change the organization of plant and animal life in our back yards? This is the predicament, and the challenge, presented by the science of chaos, and it is altering the imagination of ecologists dramatically.

John Muir once declared, "When we try to pick out anything by itself, we find it hitched to everything else in the universe." For him, that was a manifestation of an infinitely wise plan in which everything functioned with perfect harmony. The new ecology of chaos, though impressed like Muir with interdependency, does not share his view of "an infinitely wise plan" that controls and shapes everything into order. There is no plan, today's scientists say, no harmony apparent in the events of nature. If there is order in the universe — and there will no longer be any science if all faith in order vanishes — it is going to be much more difficult to locate and describe than we thought.

For Muir, the clear lesson of cosmic complexity was that humans ought to love and preserve nature just as it is. The lessons of the new ecology, in contrast, are not at all clear. Does it promote, in Ilya Prigogine and Isabelle Stenger's words, "a renewal of nature," a less hierarchical view of life, and a set of "new relations between man and nature and between man and man"? Or does it increase our alienation from the world, our withdrawal into postmodernist doubt and self-consciousness? What is there to love or preserve in a universe of chaos? How are people supposed to behave in such a universe? If such is the kind of place we inhabit, why not go ahead with all our private ambitions, free of any fear that we may be doing special damage? What, after all, does the phrase "environmental damage" mean in a world of so much natural chaos? Does the tradition of environmentalism to which Muir belonged, along with so many other nature writers and ecologists of the past — people like Paul Sears, Eugene Odum, Aldo Leopold, and Rachel Carson — make sense any longer? I have no space here to attempt to answer those questions or to make predictions but only issue a warning that they are too important to be left for scientists alone to answer. Ecology today, no more than in the past, can be assumed to be all-knowing or all-wise or eternally true.

Black Ecology

NATHAN HARE

The emergence of the concept of ecology in American life is potentially of momentous relevance to the ultimate liberation of black people. Yet blacks and their environmental interests have been so blatantly omitted that blacks and the ecology movement currently stand in contradiction to each other.

The legitimacy of the concept of black ecology accrues from the fact that: (1) the black and white environments not only differ in degree but in nature as well; (2) the causes and solutions to ecological problems are fundamentally different in the suburbs and ghetto (both of which human ecologists regard as "natural [or ecological] areas"); and (3) the solutions set forth for the "ecological crisis" are reformist and evasive of the social and political revolution which black environmental correction demands.

In the realm of white ecology, pollution "closes your beaches and prevents your youngsters from wading, swimming, boating, water-skiing, fishing, and other recreation close to home." And, "we want clear water, for boating, and swimming, and fishing — and clean water just to look at."

Similar involvement includes the planting of redwood trees, saving the American eagle, and redeeming terrestrial beauty. Thus it is seen that ecologists aimed at the hearts and purse strings of industrialists and hit the eyeballs of the white bourgeoisie.

Ecology accordingly has come to refer for the most part to chemical and physical or esthetic conditions only, while professional ecologists themselves have been known to differ in their definition of ecology.

> . . . the concept is borrowed from biology, where it means the study of relations between organisms and environment. In biological usage it includes relations between individual organisms and environment (autecology) and between groups and environment (synecology). In social science it is restricted to human synecology, that is, the study of relations between human

---

Excerpts from K. S. Shrader–Frechette, ed., *Environmental Ethics*, Boxwood Press, 1981, pp. 229–33, from *The Black Scholar* 2 (April) 2–8 and Nathan Hare. Reprinted by permission of the Black World Foundation.

groups (or populations) and their respective environments, especially their
physical environments.

A recent U.S. Department of Health, Education and Welfare report defines
environment as "the aggregate of all the external conditions and influences
affecting the life and development of an organism, human behavior, society,
etc." It is imperative therefore for us to understand how both the physical and
social environments of blacks and whites have increasingly evolved as
contrasts.

With the industrialization and urbanization of American society, there
arose a relatively more rapid and drastic shift of blacks from Southern farms to
Northern factories, particularly during periods when they were needed in war
industries. Moreover, urban blacks have been increasingly imprisoned in the
physical and social decay in the hearts of major central cities, an imprisonment
which most emphatically seems doomed to continue. At the same time whites
have fled to the suburbs and the exurbs, separating more and more the black and
white worlds. The "ecology crisis" arose when the white bourgeoisie, who have
seemed to regard the presence of blacks as a kind of pollution, discovered that a
sample of what they and their rulers had done to the ghetto would follow them
to the suburb.

But there is a greater degree of all varieties of pollutants in the black
ghetto, which also lies extremely exposed to the most final variety of environmental destruction imaginable — the "sneak atom bomb attack peril" . . .
reported by an authoritative study made by Great Britain's Institute for Strategic Studies.

> Say Russia does drop a 10-megaton bomb on Washington, D.C. or Chicago,
> for example. Up to five miles from ground zero (the point of the explosion),
> nine out of ten of all inhabitants would be killed instantly and the rest seriously
> injured or victimized by radiation. All structures would be demolished. From
> 5 to 9.7 miles out, half of the inhabitants would be killed, a third of them
> injured, all others dazed, shocked, and sickened by radiation, and all buildings
> damaged beyond repair. . . . In other words, this would just about take care
> of the Negro community.

But the ecological ordeal of the black race does not have to wait for a
nuclear attack; present conditions are deadly enough. The environmental crisis
of whites (in both its physical and social aspects) already pales in comparison to
that of blacks.

In addition to a harsher degree of industrial pollutants such as "smoke,
soot, dust, fly ash, fumes, gases, stench, and carbon monoxide" — which, as in
the black ghetto, "if there is no wind or if breezes are blocked dispersal will not
be adequate" — the black ghetto contains a heavier preponderance or ratio, for
instance, of rats and cockroaches. These creatures comprise an annoyance and
"carry filth on their legs and bodies and may spread disease by polluting food.
They destroy food and damage fabrics and bookbindings." Blacks also are
more exposed to accidents, the number four killer overall and number one in
terms of working years lost by a community.

. . . poverty amid affluence, urban squalor and decay, and alienation of young people pollute the environment as much as garbage and industrial smoke. . . . A polluted political system which enables a handful of senile Southerners to dominate, through the seniority system, the law-making body of a supposedly free people is a political system which finds racism, poverty, and poisoned rivers equally congenial in its scheme of things.

Moreover, "the ecological perspective directs attention to various kinds of phenomena. These include, among others: . . . the psychological behavior of persons (singly and in groups of various kinds). . . ." Crime, insanity and other forms of social pathology pollute the central city environment. . . .

Although it is true that blacks . . . exhibit higher rates of criminal activity, this merely stands in ecological succession to such groups as the Irish and Italians who in other eras inhabited the lower strata of the urban slums. Only a minority of blacks are criminals; more are victims of crime. Due largely to existence in a criminally infested environment, blacks are about four times as likely to fall victim to forcible rape and robbery and about twice as likely to face burglary and aggravated assault. . . .

But the residential pollution of blacks rests not alone in overcrowding and the greater prevalence of unsightly and unsanitary debris and commercial units such as factories. The very housing afforded blacks is polluted. This fact is crucial when we consider that the word "ecology" was derived by a German biologist from the word "oikos" meaning "house." A house, like the clothes we wear, is an extension of one's self. It may affect "privacy, childrearing practices, and housekeeping or study habits." Three of every ten dwellings inhabited by black families are dilapidated or without hot water, toilet, or bath. Many more are clearly fire hazards.

The shortage of adequate housing and money for rent produces high rates of black mobility which have far-reaching effects on the black social environment. It means that blacks will disproportionately live among strangers for longer periods of time and, in the case of children, attend school in strange classrooms.

The household and neighborhood environments of blacks are perhaps of greater detriment to black health. The ability to control temperature and humidity at will — climate control — in homes can affect the incidence of respiratory infections. Its impact on comfort and productivity in all seasons is without doubt. Health as a community resource is invaluable. . . .

The life expectancy of blacks is almost ten years less than that of whites, and black infant and maternal mortality rates are at the level which whites exhibited twenty years ago. Black women are more than four times as likely to die of childbirth, and black children are about three times as likely to succumb to post-natal mortality. This is because (among other factors such as dietary deficiencies) black births are about twelve times as likely to occur in a setting in which there is an "attendant not in a hospital and not specified." . . .

No solution to the ecology crisis can come without a fundamental change in the economics of America particularly with reference to blacks. Although some of the ecological differentials between blacks and whites spring directly from racism and hence defy economic correlations, many aspects of the black environmental condition are associated with basic economics. Blacks are employed in the most undesirable or polluted occupations, lagging far behind their educational attainment. About two-thirds work in unskilled and semi-skilled industries. Aggravating, and associated with, the occupational effects on the black environment is the consistently low family income of blacks which must generally support larger families. Since the turn of the century, the family income of blacks has remained about half that of whites. Six in ten of all black children must grow up in poor families. The figure is even higher for black families with a female head. Unemployment is continually at least twice as high for blacks and has been shown to affect the rate of illegitimacy and marital separation, leaving many black families fatherless. . . .

Blacks suffer the predicament wherein the colonizer milks dry the resources and labor of the colonized to develop and improve his own habitat while leaving that of the colonized starkly "underdeveloped."

> The problems of the ghetto are comparable to a colonized country. Middle city businesses and housing are owned and taxed by downtown and nothing is given in return except renewal programs that are determined by the needs of foreign interests and the transportation network that feeds downtown. . . . The job market is determined by the needs of foreign business geared to producing goods that middle city ghetto dwellers can't afford and often don't want.

The real solution to the environmental crisis is the decolonization of the black race. Blacks in the United States number more than 25,000,000 people, comprising a kidnapped and captive nation surpassed in size by only twenty other nations in the entire world. It is necessary for blacks to achieve self-determination, acquiring a full black government and a multi-billion dollar budget so that blacks can better solve the more serious environmental crises of blacks. To do so blacks must challenge and confront the very foundations of American society. In so doing we shall correct that majority which appears to believe that the solution lies in decorating the earth's landscape and in shooting at the moon.

❦ F U R T H E R   R E A D I N G

Charles C. Adams, *Guide to the Study of Animal Ecology* (1913)
Daniel Botkin, *Discordant Harmonies* (1990)
Anna Bramwell, *Ecology in the Twentieth Century: A History* (1989)
Robert Clarke, *Ellen Swallow: The Woman Who Founded Ecology* (1974)
Frederic Clements, *Plant Succession: An Analysis of the Development of Vegetation* (1916)
William Coleman, *Biology of the Nineteenth Century* (1977)
Peter Crowcroft, *Elton's Ecologists: A History of the Bureau of Animal Population* (1991)
P. K. Dayton, "Ecology: A Science and a Religion," in *Ecological Processes in Coastal and Marine Ecosystems*, ed. R. J. Livingstone (1971)

Frank Egerton, "Ecological Studies and Observations Before 1900," in Benjamin Taylor and Thurman White, eds., *Issues and Ideas in America* (1976), pp. 311–351

Susan L. Flader, *Thinking like a Mountain: Aldo Leopold and the Evolution of an Ecological Attitude Toward Deer, Wolves, and Forests* (1974)

Jean Langenheim, "The Path and Progress of American Women Ecologists," *Journal of the Ecological Society of America* 69 (1988), 184–197

Aldo Leopold, *A Sand County Almanac* (1949)

————, *The River of the Mother of God and Other Essays*, ed. Susan L. Flader and Baird Callicott (1991)

Raymond Lindeman, "The Trophic-Dynamic Aspect of Ecology," *Ecology* 23 (1942), 399–418

Robert McIntosh, *The Background of Ecology: Concept and Theory* (1985)

————, "Ecology Since 1900," in Benjamin Taylor and Thurman White, eds., *Issues and Ideas in America* (1976), pp. 353–372

George Perkins Marsh, *Man and Nature: or, Physical Geography as Modified by Human Action* (1864)

Leo Marx, "American Institutions and Ecological Ideals," *Science* 170 (1970), 945–952

Curt Meine, *Aldo Leopold: The Man and His Work* (1989)

G. Tyler Miller, Jr., *Living in the Environment: Concepts, Problems, and Alternatives* (1974)

Bernard J. Nebel, *Environmental Science: The Way the World Works*, 2d ed. (1987)

Eugene P. Odum, *Fundamentals of Ecology* (1953)

Leslie A. Real and James H. Brown, *Foundations of Ecology: Classic Papers with Commentaries* (1991)

Robert E. Ricklefs, *The Economy of Nature* (1976)

Paul Sears, *Life and Environment* (1932)

————, "Ecology — A Subversive Subject," *BioScience* 14 (1964), 11–13

Ronald C. Tobey, *Saving the Prairies* (1981)

Donald Worster, *Nature's Economy: The Roots of Ecology* (1977)

From Conservation to Environment in the Mid-Twentieth Century

Between the conservation movement of the early twentieth century and the contemporary environmental movement came the advances of the New Deal. The administration of President Franklin Delano Roosevelt from 1933 to 1945 promoted forest preservation, large dams and irrigation works such as Boulder Dam and the Tennessee Valley Authority (TVA), soil conservation, the Civilian Conservation Corps (CCC), and other public-works programs. Throughout the Great Depression and World War II, Roosevelt ardently supported farmers and workers and spiritedly lectured on behalf of conservation. During the 1950s the Cold War, the dawn of the nuclear era, and the Sputnik-initiated space age pushed science and technology to the forefront of public policy. But popular protests over radioactive fallout from atomic-bomb tests combined with outrage over the deaths of wildlife by pesticide poisoning, as well as with a growing awareness of an exploding worldwide population, to spark a major environmental movement in the 1960s. This chapter probes government conservation policies and the public response to them in the mid-twentieth century.

ψ D O C U M E N T S

The Bob Marshall Wilderness in the western Montana Rockies commemorates forester Robert Marshall's passion for forests for the people. The first document is an excerpt from Marshall's book *The People's Forests* (1933), advocating nationalization of the forests as the only way to preserve the remaining timber from devastation by private interests.

Like Marshall, President Franklin Delano Roosevelt had a zeal for reversing private exploitation of natural resources. The second document comprises excerpts from two speeches on behalf of conservation made by Roosevelt in 1935. Speaking in the Adirondacks, he recalls in the first speech how he teamed up with Gifford Pinchot to persuade the New York State legislature to conserve Adirondack forests and soils, and he praises the Civilian Conservation Corps for continuing this objective; in the second speech, made at the dedication of Boulder Dam in Colorado, Roosevelt lauds the engineering advances that brought water and electric power to the arid West in the years of drought and dust bowls. The third document, from a 1947 article by Hugh Bennett, head of the Soil Conservation Service in the U.S. Department of Agriculture, points to the irreversibility of soil erosion and the possibility of preventing it through democratically run soil-conservation districts organized by local farmers and ranchers.

The contemporary environmental movement exploded in 1962 with the publication of Rachel Carson's *Silent Spring*, excerpted in the fourth document. Carson graphically describes the transformation of life after the introduction of radioactive fallout from atomic-bomb testing and as a result of the widespread use of such pesticides as DDT, totally new to biologic experience. The following year, President John F. Kennedy helped to alert Americans to the environmental crisis through his persuasive introduction to Stewart Udall's important book *The Quiet Crisis*. Kennedy's assessment, excerpted in the fifth document, points to declining standards of environmental living and stresses the need for an expansion of the concept of conservation to meet the crisis.

During the 1960s and 1970s, a host of environmental laws were passed that regulated pesticides; set standards for clean air and water; preserved wilderness, marine mammals, and endangered species; and established procedures for waste disposal. One of the most sweeping of the new laws, the National Environmental Policy Act (NEPA) of 1969, signed into law on New Year's Day 1970 by President Richard Nixon, is excerpted in the sixth document. Although the preamble sets out goals designed to ensure a safe, healthful environment, NEPA's most significant requirement is the establishment of the environmental impact statement (EIS) for every proposed federal action that would affect the quality of the human environment. Duplicated by state legislatures throughout the country, these procedures and reports have altered or mitigated many proposed local and federal development projects.

Indian reservations, which contain natural resources such as uranium, coal, copper, and water, are leased for development by the federal government as well as by private corporations. That Indians themselves hold strongly divided opinions on whether to lease their lands is revealed in the seventh document, a 1970 letter by a group of Hopi to President Nixon. The Indians were protesting coal mining on their reservation by the Peabody Coal Company, a subsidiary of Kennecott Copper. In 1980, after heated controversy over land claims by Alaskan natives and after the construction of the Alaska Pipeline, Congress passed the Alaska National Interests Lands Act, excerpted in the eighth document. The law attempted to strike a balance among land for the conservation of wilderness and wildlife, land for the continuance of a subsistence way of life, and land that could be leased for intensive development, such as the tapping of oil and gas reserves. These last two documents illuminate some of the ongoing conflicts of interest between native peoples and the federal government over natural-resource development policies.

Robert Marshall on the People's Forests, 1933

Under their present management the American forests are drifting into constantly expanding ruin. Year by year the area of devastated land keeps mounting, until today it has reached the appalling total of 83 million acres, to which nearly a million acres are being added annually. Even more serious than the devastation is the grave deterioration which has occurred on at least 200 million additional acres. Between devastation and deterioration the American forests and all the social values which they represent are indeed in a tragic condition.

The major cause of this sorry plight is the mismanagement of privately owned forests. Fire damage, erosion, devastation, and destruction of scenic values are many times more severe on private than on public forests. This hopeless insufficiency of private ownership has obtained even though the government has carried five sixths of the burden of fire protection. When this miserable failure is contrasted with the splendid record of public forest management the moral seems inescapable. Public ownership is the only basis on which we can hope to protect the incalculable values of the forests for wood resources, for soil and water conservation, and for recreation. It is urged, therefore, that the public should acquire at least 562 million acres out of the 670 million acres of potential forest land.

Regardless of whether it might be desirable, it is impossible under our existing form of government to confiscate the private forests into public ownership. We cannot afford to delay their nationalization until the form of government changes, because if we do the forests will be so deteriorated as to be scarcely worth owning. Consequently, it will be necessary to acquire them by purchase. This purchase program cannot be consummated all at once. Pending the change from private to public ownership it will be necessary to regulate the private use of forests so that they are not too severely gutted by the time the government takes over their management. In spite of this genuine value of public regulation, it will only be an incidental to the main solution of our forest problem. This main solution, as has been stated, is public ownership. But public ownership is not a panacea. It must be backed by careful land planning, protection of the rights of those who labor on the forests, reorganization of rural government and redistribution of rural population, safeguarding of recreational values from commercial exploitation, and a great increase in the knowledge of the forest through an ambitious program of research. . . .

At present it is generally recognized that the government must provide relief for a large share of the 12 million unemployed. It seems to be a serious problem to find enough useful work for these people to do. If the government were to take over the majority of forest lands there would be enough work to keep several million people busy for many years. . . .

It is also important to consider that every year which we delay spending money to rehabilitate our forests will mean a greatly increased ultimate cost.

Excerpts from *The People's Forests,* by Robert Marshall (New York: Harrison Smith and Robert Haas, 1933), pp. 209–211, 215–218.

The deterioration of the forest is proceeding at a geometric ratio, so the sooner we put an end to it, the less we shall have to pay. Since the cost will be higher later, the only sensible way is to protect sooner, regardless of the amount which past mismanagement now demands that we must spend. . . .

In order to carry out the program of public ownership and administration which has been recommended, certain specific legislation will be needed. The following is of major importance:

1. Congress and the state legislatures should first grant authority and the appropriate funds for the purchase of the 240 million acres which have been recommended.
2. Congress and the state legislatures should make the necessary appropriations for the adequate administration of the 562 million acres of proposed public forests.
3. Congress should add to the National Forest system the 22 million acres of public domain forest lands. The government's mismanagement of these unadministered acres is the only blot on its otherwise excellent record of forest protection.
4. Laws should be passed by the federal government and the states which would automatically make tax-delinquent lands a part of the state forests if the states desire to administer them and otherwise a part of the federal forests.
5. Congress should increase the appropriations for federal research by about 1½ million dollars.
6. For those forest lands which will remain in private ownership, the federal government should pass laws giving itself the right to control fire and stop logging and grazing practice which leads to devastation.

There are two possibilities which stare us in the face with exceptional clarity. We can continue our present policy of being more solicitous of the rights of private timber owners than of the welfare of the public. There can only be one result of such a policy, the hopeless deterioration of our vitally needed forests. On the other hand, we can spend the large sums of money necessary to acquire and administer the public forests for the benefit of all the citizens. This policy will, in the long run, save us vast amounts of money, and it will preserve the unassessable value of the forest for timber production, for water and soil conservation, and for recreation. The time has come when we must discard the unsocial view that our woods are the lumbermen's and substitute the broader ideal that every acre of woodland in the country is rightly a part of the people's forests.

President Franklin D. Roosevelt Promotes Conservation, 1935

Speech by Roosevelt, Lake Placid, New York, September 14, 1935

I was very keen, after having studied the subject, to get the people of the State interested in preventing soil erosion in the Adirondacks. There were great areas which had been cut over, the tops of the trees remaining far above the ground. I wanted to get through what was known as the Top Lopping Law and I wanted to get people interested in seeing to it that the trees were preserved on the tops of our mountains. So I invited the Chief Forester of the United States, a man by the name of Gifford Pinchot, who was one of the pioneers of forestry, who had studied in Europe, [to] come up to Albany. We had a session in the Assembly Chamber and to it I succeeded in getting a large number of Senators and Assemblymen.

Gifford Pinchot put two pictures on a screen and those two pictures did more than any other thing to sell conservation to the Legislature of the State of New York. One of them, the first one he showed, was a photograph of an old Chinese painting, the painting of some place up in North China having been executed in approximately the year 1510, four hundred years before this talk that he was giving. It showed a beautiful valley, and a walled town in the valley. It was a town which, history says, had three hundred thousand people in it. There was a beautiful stream running through that valley with fields and crops on both sides of it. It was obviously a stream that was not subject to flood conditions. The mountains on each side of the valley were covered with spruce pine forests, clear to their tops. But, if you examined this old painting, you would see that up on the side of one of those mountains was a streak, and if you examined it closely, you found that it was a logging chute. In other words, those old Chinamen, four hundred years before, had begun to cut the timber off the top of the mountain and they were chuting it down to the valley for all kinds of purposes. They had never heard of conservation and history shows that for the next one hundred years the people in that valley cut off all the trees from the top of the mountain.

Then came the second picture, one that Gifford Pinchot, I think, had taken himself, had taken from the identical spot where the first painting had been made. That second picture showed a desert. It showed mountains that had rocks on them and nothing else. There was no grass, no trees, just rocks. In other words, the entire soil had been washed off those mountains and there they were, bare for all time. Down in the valley, the old, walled town was in ruins. I think there were three hundred people left in the ruins, trying to eke out a meagre existence. The stream had become a flood stream. Rocks and boulders had covered the fertile fields that once existed on both sides of the stream.

There you saw the wreck of a great civilization of four hundred years ago and nothing left except some ruins and rocks.

Well, that picture in those days, twenty-five years ago, sold conservation and forestry to the Legislature of the State of New York. And, as a result, we were enabled to get through the first important legislation for conservation. . . .

I am glad also to see these boys from the CCC [Civilian Conservation Corps] Camps. It is just two years ago when a certain person, who was entering a political campaign, suggested that for the preservation of the forests of the Nation, for the planting of acres that needed planting, for the purposes of preventing soil erosion and, incidentally, for the purpose of helping a great many unemployed families, that the Government of the United States ought to take several hundred thousand young men and ask them to go into forests all over the United States, to preserve those forests and to increase them. And I remember the comment that greeted that suggestion. Some of you who are here remember the ribald laughter about planting trees, this "crazy dream," this "political gesture."

Well, there are five hundred and ten thousand young men today in CCC Camps in every State of the Union. They are preserving the forests and the soil of the United States for generations to come. The idle dream has become a fact. And I see no reason why I should not take this occasion to tell you that, in my judgment, these Camps that do so much good in every State of the Union are not only good for future generations but are doing a lot of good for this generation. I see no reason why I should not tell you that these Camps, in my judgment, are going to be a permanent part of the policy of the United States Government. . . .

These are some of the things that Conservation has got to look forward to, and in the meantime . . . the spreading of the gospel of conservation, is something that we are succeeding in accomplishing. The people in the last two years have become more and more conscious of the practical economic effect of what we are doing. They are becoming more and more conscious of the value to themselves, city dwellers and country dwellers, in protecting these great assets of nature that God has given us.

And so, my friends, as a very old Conservationist, I am glad to be with you here today and to congratulate you on the fine work that you are doing. May it go on through all the years.

Speech by Roosevelt at the Dedication of Boulder Dam, September 30, 1935

Senator [Key] Pittman, Secretary [of the Interior, Harold] Ickes, Governors of the Colorado's States, and you especially who have built Boulder Dam: This morning I came, I saw and I was conquered, as everyone would be who sees for the first time this great feat of mankind.

Ten years ago the place where we gathered was an unpeopled, forbidding desert. In the bottom of the gloomy canyon whose precipitous walls rose to a height of more than a thousand feet, flowed a turbulent, dangerous river. The mountains on either side of the canyon were difficult of access with neither road nor trail, and their rocks were protected by neither trees nor grass from the blazing heat of the sun. The site of Boulder City was a cactus-covered waste. And the transformation wrought here in these years is a twentieth century marvel.

We are here to celebrate the completion of the greatest dam in the world, rising 726 feet above the bedrock of the river and altering the geography of a whole region; we are here to see the creation of the largest artificial lake in the world—115 miles long, holding enough water, for example, to cover the whole State of Connecticut to a depth of ten feet; and we are here to see nearing completion a power house which will contain the largest generators and turbines yet installed in this country, machinery that can continuously supply nearly two million horsepower of electric energy. All of these dimensions are superlative. They represent and embody the accumulated engineering knowledge and experience of centuries, and when we behold them it is fitting that we pay tribute to the genius of their designers. We recognize also the energy, the resourcefulness and the zeal of the builders, who, under the greatest physical obstacles, have pushed this work forward to completion two years in advance of contract requirements. But especially, my friends, we express our gratitude to the thousands of workers who gave brain and brawn in this great work of construction.

Beautiful and great as this structure is, it must also be considered in its relationship to the agricultural and industrial development and in its contribution to the health and comfort of the people of America who live in the Southwest.

To divert and distribute the waters of an arid region so that there shall be security of rights and efficiency in service, is one of the greatest problems of law and of administration to be found in any government. The farms, the cities, the people who live along the many thousands of miles of this river and its tributaries all of them depend for their permanence in value upon the conservation, regulation, and the equitable and fair division of its ever-changing water supply. What has been accomplished on the Colorado in working out such a scheme of distribution is inspiring to the whole country. Through the cooperation of the States whose people depend upon this river, and of the Federal Government which is concerned in the general welfare, there is being constructed a system of distributive works and of laws and practices which will insure to the millions of people who now dwell in this basin, and to the millions of others who will come to dwell here in future generations, a safe, just, and permanent system of water rights. In devising these policies and the means of putting them into practice the Bureau of Reclamation of the Federal Government has taken and is destined to take in the future, a leading and helpful part. The Bureau has been the instrument which gave effect to the legislation introduced into the Congress by Senator Hiram Johnson and Congressman Philip Swing.

When in flood the river was a threatening torrent. In the dry months of the year it shrank to a trickling stream. For a generation the people of Imperial Valley had lived in the shadow of disaster from this river which provided their livelihood, and which is the foundation of their hopes for themselves and their children. Every spring they awaited with dread the coming of a flood, and at the end of every summer they feared a shortage of water would destroy their crops.

The gates of these great diversion tunnels were closed here at Boulder Dam last February and in June a great flood came down the river. It came roaring down the canyons of the Colorado, through Grand Canyon, Iceberg and Boulder Canyons, but it was caught, it was caught and held safely behind Boulder Dam.

Last year a drought of unprecedented severity was visited upon the west. The watershed of this Colorado River did not escape. In July the canals of the Imperial Valley went dry. Crop losses in that Valley alone totaled $10,000,000 that summer. Had Boulder Dam been completed one year earlier, this loss would have been prevented, because the spring flood would have been stored to furnish a steady water supply for the long dry summer and fall.

Across the San Jacinto mountains southwest of Boulder Dam the cities of Southern California are constructing an aqueduct to cost $200,000,000, which they have raised, for the purpose of carrying the regulated waters of the River to the Pacific Coast 250 miles away.

And across the desert and mountains to the west and south run great electric transmission lines by which factory motors, street and household lights and irrigation pumps can be operated in Southern Arizona and California. Part of this power will be used in pumping the water through the aqueduct to supplement the domestic supplies of Los Angeles and surrounding cities.

Navigation of the river from Boulder Dam to the Grand Canyon has been made possible, a 115-mile stretch that had been traversed less than half a dozen times in all history. An immense new park has been created for the enjoyment of all of our people. And that is why, my friends, those of you who are not here today but can hear my voice, I tell you — come to Boulder Dam and see it with your own eyes.

Hugh Bennett Presses for Soil Conservation, 1947

Productive land is unlike any other natural resource. It is characterized by the element of life placed by Nature in the thin mantle of fruitful soil occurring over a limited portion of the earth's surface. It is this life-producing quality that makes some lands productive, and it is the absence of this quality that makes some barren.

Productive land is further differentiated from other natural resources in that it must be maintained and used simultaneously; that is, it must be kept intact while in use. All other natural resources, with very few exceptions, must be taken from the earth — separated from it — in order to be used by man. The exceptions are certain forms of wildlife and those natural areas which, because of their aesthetic values, are kept in their original state.

Productive land is much more limited than commonly has been supposed. It occurs only on the surface of the earth, and only on part of this surface. It is not permanent. Once the fertile topsoil is washed or blown away, it cannot be restored or replaced in any practical way for generations. And what is left — subsoil — usually is far less productive, or sterile, and less stable. There are no undiscovered reserves of productive land of any substantial area.

We cannot dig deeper into the earth and find new productive soil. We cannot pump it from wells, plant it with seeds, or dig it from mines. We must keep what we have or do without. Assorted residues of sand and gravel left stranded along streamways are of small value.

Productive land is the only natural resource without which we cannot live. We are completely dependent on it for the food we eat, except fish. We also depend on it for a very large share of our clothing and shelter. We cannot get enough to feed ourselves or provide our clothing from the oceans. On any large scale, hydroponics would be utterly impractical. We might conceivably turn

Excerpts from H. H. Bennett, "Development of Natural Resource: The Coming Technological Revolution on the Land," *Science*, 105 (January–June 1947) pp. 1–3. Copyright 1947 by the American Association for the Advancement of Science.

sometime to some form of synthetic food, as pills, plus a roughage, but this appears to be a fantastic extreme, still far away, and likely, if it ever comes, it will be decidedly unpopular.

There is no doubt about the need for protecting productive land. Year after year, for generations, man has been steadily engaged in ruining millions and millions of acres of this basic resource. Every hard rain falling on unprotected, cultivated, or overgrazed sloping land washes additional tons of soil down-slope, downstream, into the rivers, reservoirs, and oceans. There is no practical way of bringing this back. And every hard wind, blowing across bare, dry soil, whether sloping or level, adds to the damage. Wind lifts the fine soil particles into the air and often develops huge dust storms that destructively scatter the substance of the land. What is left behind, frequently, is infertile, shifting sand that smothers out vegetation on neighboring good land.

* * * *

In the United States, land technology is spreading through a new democratic device known as the soil conservation district. The district is a subdivision of State government, brought into being by a process of referendum among the landowners and operators involved. In practical application it is a legal organization of landowners and operators within a designated area for the purpose of developing and carrying forward a mutually desirable program of soil and water conservation. Its principal advantages are in the encouragement of local initiative and in the greater strength that comes with organized numbers — farmers and ranchers working together.

In soil conservation districts the farmers themselves decide what they want to do to improve their land and water resources and how they want to go about doing it. Then they proceed along this course, working together, and utilizing all the available facilities and services they can command. In almost every instance, districts are obtaining technical guidance from the Soil Conservation Service.

On August 15 there were more than 1,670 districts in the United States, voluntarily voted into existence by the farmers themselves. These districts encompassed more than 900,000,000 acres and approximately 4,000,000 farms. Farmers are continuing to organize districts at the rate of approximately 25 per month.

Although democratic soil conservation districts are being employed in the United States to further the application of land technology, other nations may choose to utilize other means. A number, however, including the Union of South Africa, Mexico, and parts of Australia, have adopted the soil conservation district method.

In the long run, the overwhelming urge of mankind for survival will dictate that every remaining productive acre be handled in such a way that it will continue to produce indefinitely. In the meantime, other factors are combining to speed up the application of technology to the land. From the standpoint of the individual and the nation alike, the development and application of soil and water conservation technology (the tool of soil conservation science) is good business. It results in greater yields and greater returns per acre for the capital and labor expended. Moreover, it maintains or improves the basic strength and self-sufficiency of individual and nation. It probably can prevent at least half the potential famines of the future.

Rachel Carson Warns of a Silent Spring, 1962

There was once a town in the heart of America where all life seemed to live in harmony with its surroundings. The town lay in the midst of a checkerboard of prosperous farms, with fields of grain and hillsides of orchards where, in spring, white clouds of bloom drifted above the green fields. In autumn, oak and maple and birch set up a blaze of color that flamed and flickered across a backdrop of pines. Then foxes barked in the hills and deer silently crossed the fields, half hidden in the mists of the fall mornings.

Along the roads, laurel, viburnum and alder, great ferns and wildflowers delighted the traveler's eye through much of the year. Even in winter the roadsides were places of beauty, where countless birds came to feed on the berries and on the seed heads of the dried weeds rising above the snow. The countryside was, in fact, famous for the abundance and variety of its bird life, and when the flood of migrants was pouring through in spring and fall people traveled from great distances to observe them. Others came to fish the streams, which flowed clear and cold out of the hills and contained shady pools where trout lay. So it had been from the days many years ago when the first settlers raised their houses, sank their wells, and built their barns.

Then a strange blight crept over the area and everything began to change. Some evil spell had settled on the community: mysterious maladies swept the flocks of chickens; the cattle and sheep sickened and died. Everywhere was a shadow of death. The farmers spoke of much illness among their families. In the town the doctors had become more and more puzzled by new kinds of sickness appearing among their patients. There had been several sudden and unexplained deaths, not only among adults but even among children, who would be stricken suddenly while at play and die within a few hours.

There was a strange stillness. The birds, for example — where had they gone? Many people spoke of them, puzzled and disturbed. The feeding stations in the backyards were deserted. The few birds seen anywhere were moribund; they trembled violently and could not fly. It was a spring without voices. On the mornings that had once throbbed with the dawn chorus of robins, catbirds, doves, jays, wrens, and scores of other bird voices there was now no sound; only silence lay over the fields and woods and marsh.

On the farms the hens brooded, but no chicks hatched. The farmers complained that they were unable to raise any pigs — the litters were small and the young survived only a few days. The apple trees were coming into bloom but no bees droned among the blossoms, so there was no pollination and there would be no fruit.

The roadsides, once so attractive, were now lined with browned and withered vegetation as though swept by fire. These, too, were silent, deserted by all living things. Even the streams were now lifeless. Anglers no longer visited them for all the fish had died.

In the gutters under the eaves and between the shingles of the roofs, a white granular powder still showed a few patches; some weeks before it had fallen like snow upon the roofs and the lawns, the fields and streams.

No witchcraft, no enemy action had silenced the rebirth of new life in this stricken world. The people had done it themselves.

This town does not actually exist, but it might easily have a thousand counterparts in America or elsewhere in the world. I know of no community that has experienced all the misfortunes I describe. Yet every one of these disasters has actually happened somewhere, and many real communities have already suffered a substantial number of them. A grim specter has crept upon us almost unnoticed, and this imagined tragedy may easily become a stark reality we all shall know. . . .

The history of life on earth has been a history of interaction between living things and their surroundings. To a large extent, the physical form and the habits of the earth's vegetation and its animal life have been molded by the environment. Considering the whole span of earthly time, the opposite effect, in which life actually modifies its surroundings, has been relatively slight. Only within the moment of time represented by the present century has one species — man — acquired significant power to alter the nature of his world.

During the past quarter century this power has not only increased to one of disturbing magnitude but it has changed in character. The most alarming of all man's assaults upon the environment is the contamination of air, earth, rivers, and sea with dangerous and even lethal materials. This pollution is for the most part irrecoverable; the chain of evil it initiates not only in the world that must support life but in living tissues is for the most part irreversible. In this now universal contamination of the environment, chemicals are the sinister and little-recognized partners of radiation in changing the very nature of the world — the very nature of its life. Strontium 90, released through nuclear explosions into the air, comes to earth in rain or drifts down as fallout, lodges in soil, enters into the grass or corn or wheat grown there, and in time takes up its abode in the bones of a human being, there to remain until his death. Similarly, chemicals sprayed on croplands or forests or gardens lie long in soil, entering into living organisms, passing from one to another in a chain of poisoning and death. Or they pass mysteriously by underground streams until they emerge and, through the alchemy of air and sunlight, combine into new forms that kill vegetation, sicken cattle, and work unknown harm on those who drink from once pure wells. As Albert Schweitzer has said, "Man can hardly even recognize the devils of his own creation."

It took hundreds of millions of years to produce the life that now inhabits the earth — eons of time in which that developing and evolving and diversifying life reached a state of adjustment and balance with its surroundings. The environment, rigorously shaping and directing the life it supported, contained elements that were hostile as well as supporting. Certain rocks gave out dangerous radiation; even within the light of the sun, from which all life draws its energy, there were short-wave radiations with power to injure. Given time — time not in years but in millennia — life adjusts, and a balance has been reached. For time is the essential ingredient; but in the modern world there is no time.

The rapidity of change and the speed with which new situations are created follow the impetuous and heedless pace of man rather than the deliberate pace of nature. Radiation is no longer merely the background radiation of rocks, the bombardment of cosmic rays, the ultraviolet of the sun that have existed before there was any life on earth; radiation is now the unnatural creation of man's tampering with the atom. The chemicals to which life is asked to make its adjustment are no longer merely the calcium and silica and copper and all the rest of the minerals washed out of the rocks and carried in rivers to the sea; they are the synthetic creations of man's inventive mind, brewed in his laboratories, and having no counterparts in nature.

To adjust to these chemicals would require time on the scale that is nature's; it would require not merely the years of a man's life but the life of generations. And even this, were it by some miracle possible, would be futile, for the new chemicals come from our laboratories in an endless stream; almost five hundred annually find their way into actual use in the United States alone. The figure is staggering and its implications are not easily grasped — 500 new chemicals to which the bodies of men and animals are required somehow to adapt each year, chemicals totally outside the limits of biologic experience.

Among them are many that are used in man's war against nature. Since the mid-1940's over 200 basic chemicals have been created for use in killing insects, weeds, rodents, and other organisms described in the modern vernacular as "pests"; and they are sold under several thousand different brand names.

These sprays, dusts, and aerosols are now applied almost universally to farms, gardens, forests, and homes — nonselective chemicals that have the power to kill every insect, the "good" and the "bad," to still the song of birds and the leaping of fish in the streams, to coat the leaves with a deadly film, and to linger on in soil — all this though the intended target may be only a few weeds or insects. Can anyone believe it is possible to lay down such a barrage of poisons on the surface of the earth without making it unfit for all life? They should not be called "insecticides," but "biocides."

The whole process of spraying seems caught up in an endless spiral. Since DDT was released for civilian use, a process of escalation has been going on in which ever more toxic materials must be found. This has happened because insects, in a triumphant vindication of Darwin's principle of the survival of the fittest, have evolved super races immune to the particular insecticide used, hence a deadlier one has always to be developed — and then a deadlier one than that. It has happened also because . . . destructive insects often undergo a "flareback," or resurgence, after spraying, in numbers greater than before. Thus the chemical war is never won, and all life is caught in its violent crossfire.

Along with the possibility of the extinction of mankind by nuclear war, the central problem of our age has therefore become the contamination of man's total environment with such substances of incredible potential for harm — substances that accumulate in the tissues of plants and animals and even penetrate the germ cells to shatter or alter the very material of heredity upon which the shape of the future depends.

Some would-be architects of our future look toward a time when it will be possible to alter the human germ plasm by design. But we may easily be doing so now by inadvertence, for many chemicals, like radiation, bring about gene mutations. It is ironic to think that man might determine his own future by something so seemingly trivial as the choice of an insect spray.

All this has been risked — for what? Future historians may well be amazed by our distorted sense of proportion. How could intelligent beings seek to control a few unwanted species by a method that contaminated the entire environment and brought the threat of disease and death even to their own kind? Yet this is precisely what we have done. We have done it, moreover, for reasons that collapse the moment we examine them. We are told that the enormous and expanding use of pesticides is necessary to maintain farm production. Yet is our real problem not one of *overproduction?* Our farms, despite measures to remove acreages from production and to pay farmers *not* to produce, have yielded such a staggering excess of crops that the American taxpayer in 1962 is paying out more than one billion dollars a year as the total carrying cost of the surplus-food storage program. And is the situation helped when one branch of the Agriculture Department tries to reduce production while another states, as it did in 1958, "It is believed generally that reduction of crop acreages under provisions of the Soil Bank will stimulate interest in use of chemicals to obtain maximum production on the land retained in crops."

All this is not to say there is no insect problem and no need of control. I am saying, rather, that control must be geared to realities, not to mythical situations, and that the methods employed must be such that they do not destroy us along with the insects.

President John F. Kennedy Assesses the Environment, 1963

The history of America is, more than that of most nations, the history of man confronted by nature. Our story has been peculiarly the story of man and the land, man and the forests, man and the plains, man and water, man and resources. It has been the story of a rich and varied natural heritage shaping American institutions and American values; and it has been equally the

Excerpt from John Kennedy, "Introduction" in *The Quiet Crisis*, by Stewart Udall, Avon Books, 1963, pp. xi–xiii. Reprinted by permission of Stewart Udall.

story of Americans seizing, using, squandering and, belatedly, protecting and developing that heritage. In telling this story [in his book *The Quiet Crisis*] and giving this central theme of American history its proper emphasis and dignity, Secretary [of the Interior Stewart] Udall puts us all in his debt.

From the beginning, Americans had a lively awareness of the land and the wilderness. The Jeffersonian faith in the independent farmer laid the foundation for American democracy; and the ever-beckoning, ever-receding frontier left an indelible imprint on American society and the American character. And Americans pioneered in more than the usual way. We hear much about "land reform" today in other parts of the world; but we do not perhaps reflect enough on the extent to which land reform, from the Northwest Ordinance through the Homestead Act of the Farm Security Administration and beyond, was an American custom and an American innovation.

Yet, at the same time that Americans saluted the noble bounty of nature, they also abused and abandoned it. For the first century after independence, we regarded the natural environment as indestructible — and proceeded vigorously to destroy it. Not till the time of [George Perkins] Marsh and [Carl] Schurz and [John Wesley] Powell did we begin to understand that our resources were not inexhaustible. Only in the twentieth century have we acted in a systematic way to defend and enrich our natural heritage.

The modern American record in conservation has been brilliant and distinguished. It has inspired comparable efforts all around the earth. But it came just in time in our own land. And, as Mr. Udall's vivid narrative makes clear, the race between education and erosion, between wisdom and waste, has not run its course. George Perkins Marsh pointed out a century ago that greed and shortsightedness were the natural enemies of a prudent resources policy. Each generation must deal anew with the "raiders," with the scramble to use public resources for private profit, and with the tendency to prefer short-run profits to long-run necessities. The nation's battle to preserve the common estate is far from won.

Mr. Udall understands this — and he understands too that new times give this battle new forms. I read with particular interest his chapter on "Conservation and the Future," in which he sets forth the implications for the conservation effort of the new science and technology. On the one hand, he notes, science has opened up great new sources of energy and great new means of control. On the other hand, new technical processes and devices litter the countryside with waste and refuse, contaminate water and air, imperil wildlife and man and endanger the balance of nature itself. Our economic standard of living rises, but our environmental standard of living — our access to nature and respect for it — deteriorates. A once beautiful nation, as Mr. Udall suggests, is in danger of turning into an "ugly America." And the long-run effect will be not only to degrade the quality of the national life but to weaken the foundations of national power.

The crisis may be quiet, but it is urgent. We must do in our own day what Theodore Roosevelt did sixty years ago and Franklin Roosevelt thirty years ago: we must expand the concept of conservation to meet the imperious problems of the new age. We must develop new instruments of foresight and protection and nurture in order to recover the relationship between man and nature and to make sure that the national estate we pass on to our multiplying descendants is green and flourishing.

I hope that all Americans understand the importance of this effort, because it cannot be won until each American makes the preservation of "the beauty and the bounty of the American earth" his personal commitment.

The National Environmental Policy Act, 1969

Pub. Law No. 91-190, 83 Stat. 852 (1970) codified at 42 U.S.C.§4331 (1982). Selected provisions.

§4331. Congressional declaration of national environmental policy

(a) The Congress, recognizing the profound impact of man's activity on the interrelations of all components of the natural environment, particularly the profound influences of population growth, high-density urbanization, industrial expansion, resource exploitation, and new and expanding technological advances and recognizing further the critical importance of restoring and maintaining environmental quality to the overall welfare and development of man, declares that it is the continuing policy of the Federal Government, in cooperation with State and local governments, and other concerned public and private organizations, to use all practicable means and measures, including financial and technical assistance, in a manner calculated to foster and promote the general welfare, to create and maintain conditions under which man and nature can exist in productive harmony, and fulfill the social, economic, and other requirements of present and future generations of Americans.

(b) In order to carry out the policy set forth in this chapter, it is the continuing responsibility of the Federal Government to use all practicable means, consistent with other essential considerations of national policy, to improve and coordinate Federal plans, functions, programs, and resources to the end that the Nation may—

(1) fulfill the responsibilities of each generation as trustee of the environment for succeeding generations;

(2) assure for all Americans safe, healthful, productive, and esthetically and culturally pleasing surroundings;

(3) attain the widest range of beneficial uses of the environment without degradation, risk to health or safety, or other undesirable and unintended consequences;

(4) preserve important historic, cultural, and natural aspects of our national heritage, and maintain, wherever possible, an environment which supports diversity and variety of individual choice;

(5) achieve a balance between population and resource use which will permit high standards of living and a wide sharing of life's amenities; and

(6) enhance the quality of renewable resources and approach the maximum attainable recycling of depletable resources.

(c) The Congress recognizes that each person should enjoy a healthful environment and that each person has a responsibility to contribute to the preservation and enhancement of the environment.

§ 4332. Cooperation of agencies; reports; availability of information; recommendations; international and national coordination of efforts

The Congress authorizes and directs that, to the fullest extent possible: (1) the policies, regulations, and public laws of the United States shall be interpreted and administered in accordance with the policies set forth in this chapter, and (2) all agencies of the Federal Government shall—

(A) utilize a systematic, interdisciplinary approach which will insure the integrated use of the natural and social sciences and the environmental design arts in planning and in decisionmaking which may have an impact on man's environment;

(B) identify and develop methods and procedures, in consultation with the Council on Environmental Quality . . . , which will insure that presently unquantified environmental amenities and values may be given appropriate consideration in decisionmaking along with economic and technical considerations;

(C) include in every recommendation or report on proposals for legislation and other major Federal actions significantly affecting the quality of the human environment, a detailed statement by the responsible official on—

(i) the environmental impact of the proposed action,

(ii) any adverse environmental effects which cannot be avoided should the proposal be implemented,

(iii) alternatives to the proposed action,

(iv) the relationship between local short-term uses of man's environment and the maintenance and enhancement of long-term productivity, and

(v) any irreversible and irretrievable commitments of resources which would be involved in the proposed action should it be implemented.

Prior to making any detailed statement, the responsible Federal official shall consult with and obtain the comments of any Federal agency which has jurisdiction by law or special expertise with respect to any environmental impact involved. Copies of such statement and the comments and views of the appropriate Federal, State, and local agencies, which are authorized to develop and enforce environmental standards, shall be made available to the President, the Council on Environmental Quality and to the public as provided by section 552 of title 5, and shall accompany the proposal through the existing agency review processes;

(D) any detailed statement required under subparagraph (C) after January 1, 1970, for any major Federal action funded under a program of grants to States shall not be deemed to be legally insufficient solely by reason of having been prepared by a State agency or official, if:

(i) the State agency or official has statewide jurisdiction and has the responsibility for such action,

(ii) the responsible Federal official furnishes guidance and participates in such preparation,

(iii) the responsible Federal official independently evaluates such
statement prior to its approval and adoption, and

(iv) after January 1, 1976, the responsible Federal official provides
early notification to, and solicits the views of, any other State or any
Federal land management entity of any action or any alternative thereto
which may have significant impacts upon such State or affected Federal
land management entity and, if there is any disagreement on such impacts,
prepares a written assessment of such impacts and views for incorporation
into such detailed statement.

The procedures in this subparagraph shall not relieve the Federal official of
his responsibilities for the scope, objectivity, and content of the entire
statement or of any other responsibility under this chapter; and further, this
subparagraph does not affect the legal sufficiency of statements prepared by
State agencies with less than statewide jurisdiction.

(E) study, develop, and describe appropriate alternatives to recommended courses of action in any proposal which involves unresolved conflicts concerning alternative uses of available resources;

(F) recognize the worldwide and long-range character of environmental
problems and, where consistent with the foreign policy of the United States,
lend appropriate support to initiatives, resolutions, and programs designed to
maximize international cooperation in anticipating and preventing a decline
in the quality of mankind's world environment;

(G) make available to States, counties, municipalities, institutions, and
individuals, advice and information useful in restoring, maintaining, and
enhancing the quality of the environment;

(H) initiate and utilize ecological information in the planning and development of resource-oriented projects; and

(I) assist the Council on Environmental Quality established by subchap-
ter II of this chapter.

Hopi Leaders on the Desecration of Their Sacred Lands, 1970

Last year [1969] the Peabody Coal Company, a subsidiary of Kennecott Copper Company, began stripping coal from 65,000 acres it has
leased from the Navajo and Hopi tribes. Company officials declared
that this mining would not damage Indian lands and in fact would
improve the lives of many Navajos and Hopis. In disagreement with
this action a group of Hopi wrote the following letter to President
Nixon:

Dear Mr. President:

We, the true and traditional religious leaders, recognized as such by the
Hopi People, maintain full authority over all land and life contained within the

Western Hemisphere. We are granted our stewardship by virtue of our instruction as to the meaning of Nature, Peace, and Harmony as spoken to our People by Him, known to us as Massau'u, the Great Spirit, who long ago provided for us the sacred stone tablets which we preserve to this day. For many generations before the coming of the white man, for many generations before the coming of the Navajo, the Hopi People have lived in the sacred place known to you as the Southwest and known to us to be the spiritual center of our continent. Those of us of the Hopi Nation who have followed the path of the Great Spirit without compromise have a message which we are committed, through our prophecy, to convey to you.

The white man, through his insensitivity to the way of Nature, has desecrated the face of Mother Earth. The white man's advanced technological capacity has occurred as a result of his lack of regard for the spiritual path and for the way of all living things. The white man's desire for material possessions and power has blinded him to the pain he has caused Mother Earth by his quest for what he calls natural resources. And the path of the Great Spirit has become difficult to see by almost all men, even by many Indians who have chosen instead to follow the path of the white man. . . .

Today the sacred lands where the Hopi live are being desecrated by men who seek coal and water from our soil that they may create more power for the white man's cities. This must not be allowed to continue for if it does, Mother Nature will react in such a way that almost all men will suffer the end of life as they now know it. The Great Spirit said not to allow this to happen even as it was prophecied to our ancestors. The Great Spirit said not to take from the Earth — not to destroy living things. The Great Spirit, Massau'u, said that man was to live in Harmony and maintain a good clean land for all children to come. All Hopi People and other Indian Brothers are standing on this religious principle and the Traditional Spiritual Unity Movement today is endeavoring to reawaken the spiritual nature in Indian people throughout this land. Your government has almost destroyed our basic religion which actually is a way of life for all our people in this land of the Great Spirit. We feel that to survive the coming Purification Day, we must return to the basic religious principles and to meet together on this basis as leaders of our people.

Today almost all the prophecies have come to pass. Great roads like rivers pass across the landscape; man talks to man through the cobwebs of telephone lines; man travels along the roads in the sky in his airplanes; two great wars have been waged by those bearing the swastika or the rising sun; man is tampering with the Moon and the stars. Most men have strayed from the path shown us by the Great Spirit. For Massau'u alone is great enough to portray the way back to Him.

It is said by the Great Spirit that if a gourd of ashes is dropped upon the Earth, that many men will die and that the end of this way of life is near at hand. We interpret this as the dropping of atomic bombs on Hiroshima and Nagasaki. We do not want to see this happen to any place or any nation again, but instead we should turn all this energy for peaceful uses, not for war.

We, the religious leaders and rightful spokesmen for the Hopi Independent Nation, have been instructed by the Great Spirit to express the invitation to the

President of the United States and all spiritual leaders everywhere to meet with us and discuss the welfare of mankind so that Peace, Unity, and Brotherhood will become part of all men everywhere.

Sincerely,

(signed) Thomas Banyacya, for
Hopi Traditional Village Leaders:
Mrs. Mina Lansa, Oraibi
Claude Kawangyawma, Shungopavy
Starlie Lomayaktewa, Mushongnovi
Dan Katchongva, Hotevilla

The Alaska National Interests Lands Act, 1980

General Provisions

§ 3101. Congressional Statement of Purpose

(a) Establishment of units. In order to preserve for the benefit, use, education, and inspiration of present and future generations certain lands and waters in the State of Alaska that contain nationally significant natural, scenic, historic, archeological, geological, scientific, wilderness, cultural, recreational, and wildlife values, the units described in the following titles are hereby established.

(b) Preservation and protection of scenic, geological, etc., values. It is the intent of Congress in this Act to preserve unrivaled scenic and geological values associated with natural landscapes; to provide for the maintenance of sound populations of, and habitat for, wildlife species of inestimable value to the citizens of Alaska and the Nation, including those species dependent on vast relatively undeveloped areas; to preserve in their natural state extensive unaltered arctic tundra, boreal forest, and coastal rainforest ecosystems; to protect the resources related to subsistence needs; to protect and preserve historic and archeological sites, rivers, and lands, and to preserve wilderness resource values and related recreational opportunities including but not limited to hiking, canoeing, fishing, and sport hunting, within large arctic and subarctic wildlands and on freeflowing rivers; and to maintain opportunities for scientific research and undisturbed ecosystems.

(c) Subsistence way of life for rural residents. It is further the intent and purpose of this Act consistent with management of fish and wildlife in accordance with recognized scientific principles and the purposes for which each conservation system unit is established, designated, or expanded by or pursuant to this Act, to provide the opportunity for rural residents engaged in a subsistence way of life to continue to do so.

(d) Need for future legislation obviated. This Act provides sufficient protection for the national interest in the scenic, natural, cultural and environmental values on the public lands in Alaska, and at the same time provides adequate opportunity for satisfaction of the economic and social needs of the State of Alaska and its people; accordingly, the designation and disposition of the public lands in Alaska pursuant to this Act are found to represent a proper balance between the reservation of national conservation system units and those public lands necessary and appropriate for more intensive use and disposition, and thus Congress believes that the need for future legislation designating new conservation system units, new national conservation areas, or new national recreation areas, has been obviated thereby.

(Dec. 2, 1980, P. L. 96-487, Title I, § 101, 94 Stat. 2374.

ψ *E S S A Y S*

The essays look at key events in U.S. environmental history from the progressive conservation movement of Theodore Roosevelt's presidency to New Deal conservation under Franklin Roosevelt to the beginnings of the contemporary environmental movement under presidents John F. Kennedy and Richard Nixon. Samuel P. Hays, an environmental historian at the University of Pittsburgh, in the first essay discusses the differing goals and policies of the conservation and environmental movements. In the second essay, Jack Lewis of the United States Environmental Protection Agency reviews the history of environmental regulation from the laissez-faire policies of the eighteenth and nineteenth centuries to the regulatory frameworks established during the twentieth century. Closing the chapter, the third essay, by Lloyd Burton of the Graduate School of Public Affairs at the University of Colorado, Denver, examines the history of Indian land and water rights and the often conflicting roles of Congress and the courts in both protecting and developing Native Americans' territory.

From Conservation to Environment

SAMUEL P. HAYS

The historical significance of the rise of environmental affairs in the United States in recent decades lies in the changes which have taken place in American society since World War II. Important antecedents of those changes, to be sure, can be identified in earlier years as "background" conditions on the order of historical forerunners. But the intensity and force, and most of the substantive direction of the new environmental social and political phenomenon can be understood only through the massive changes which occurred after the end of the War—and not just in the United States but throughout advanced industrial societies. . . .

Excerpts from Samuel P. Hays, "From Conservation to Environment: Environmental Politics in the United States Since World War II," *Environmental Review* 6, no. 2 (Fall 1982), pp. 14–29. Reprinted with permission from *Environmental History Review*, © 1982, the American Society for Environmental History.

The Conservation and Environmental Impulses

Prior to World War II, before the term "environment" was . . . used, the dominant theme in conservation emphasized physical resources, their more efficient use and development. The range of emphasis evolved from water and forests in the late 19th and early 20th centuries, to grass and soils and game in the 1930's. In all these fields of endeavor there was a common concern for the loss of physical productivity represented by waste. The threat to the future which that "misuse" implied could be corrected through "sound" or efficient management. Hence in each field there arose a management system which emphasized a balancing of immediate in favor of more long-run production, the coordination of factors of production under central management schemes for the greatest efficiency. All this is a chapter in the history of production rather than of consumption, and of the way in which managers organized production rather than the way in which consumers evolved ideas and action amid the general public.

. . . After World War I, the concern about soil erosion, from both rain and wind . . . lay in warnings about the loss of agricultural productivity. What had taken years to build up over geologic time now was threatened with destruction by short-term practices. The soil conservation program inaugurated in 1933 gave rise to a full-scale attack on erosion problems which was carried out amid almost inspired religious fervor. In the Taylor Grazing Act of 1934 the nation's grazing lands in the West were singled out as a special case of deteriorating productivity; it set in motion a long-term drive to reduce stocking levels and thereby permit recovery of the range. Also during the 1930's, scientific game management came into its own with the Pittman-Robertson Act of 1936 which provided funds. This involved concepts much akin to those in forestry, in which production and consumption of game would be balanced in such a fashion so as not to outrun food resources and hence sustain a continuous yield. . . .

State departments of "natural resources" emerged, such as in Michigan, Wisconsin and Minnesota, and some university departments of forestry became departments of natural resources — all this as the new emphasis on soils and game were added to the older ones on forests and waters. By the time of World War II a complex of professionals had come into being, with a strong focus on management as their common task, on the organization of applied knowledge about physical resources so as to sustain output for given investments of input under centralized management direction. This entailed a common conception of "conservation" and a common focus on "renewable resources," often within the rubric of advocating "wise use" under the direction of professional experts. . . . Those concerned with national parks and the later wilderness activities often used the term "conservation" to describe what they were about. In the Sierra Club the "conservation committees" took up the organization's political action in contrast with its outings. And those who formed the National Parks Association and later the Wilderness Society could readily think of themselves as conservationists, struggling to define the term quite differently than did those in the realm of efficient management. . . . [Yet] the theme of management efficiency in physical resource development dominated the scene prior to World War II and natural environment programs continued to play a subordinate role.

After the War a massive turnabout of historical forces took place. The complex of specialized fields of efficient management of physical resources increasingly came under attack amid a new "environmental" thrust. It contained varied components. One was the further elaboration of the outdoor recreation and natural environment movements of pre-War, as reflected in the Wilderness Act of 1964, the Wild and Scenic Rivers Act of 1968, and the National Trails Act of the same year, and further legislation and administrative action on through the 1970's. But there were other strands even less rooted in the past. The most extensive was the concern for environmental pollution, or "environmental protection" as it came to be called in technical and managerial circles. While smoldering in varied and diverse ways in this or that setting from many years before, this concern burst forth to national prominence in the mid-1960's and especially in air and water pollution. And there was the decentralist thrust, the search for technologies of smaller and more human scale which complement rather than dwarf the more immediate human setting. One can find decentralist ideologies and even affirmations of smaller-scale technologies in earlier years, such as that inspired by Ralph Borsodi not long before World War II. But the intensity and direction of the drive of the 1970's was of a vastly different order. The search for a "sense of place," for a context that is more manageable intellectually and emotionally amid the escalating pace of size and scale had not made its mark in earlier years as it did in the 1970's to shape broad patterns of human thought and action.

One of the most striking differences between these post-War environmental activities, in contrast with the earlier conservation affairs, was their social roots. Earlier one can find little in the way of broad popular support for the substantive objectives of conservation, little "movement" organization, and scanty evidence of broadly shared conservation values. The drive came from the top down, from technical and managerial leaders. In the 1930's one can detect a more extensive social base for soil conservation, and especially for new game management programs. But, in sharp contrast, the Environmental Era displayed demands from the grass-roots, demands that are well charted by the innumerable citizen organizations and studies of public attitudes. One of the major themes of these later years, in fact, was the tension that evolved between the environmental public and the environmental managers, as impulses arising from the public clashed with impulses arising from management. This was not a new stage of public activity per se, but of new values as well. The widespread expression of social values in environmental action marks off the environmental era from the conservation years.

It is useful to think about this as the interaction between two sets of historical forces, one older that was associated with large-scale management and technology, and the other newer that reflected new types of public values and demands. . . . Conflicts between older "conservation" and newer "environment" help to identify the nature of the change.

One set of episodes in this tension concerned the rejection of multiple-purpose river structures in favor of free flowing rivers; here was a direct case of irreconcilable objectives, one stemming from the conservation era, and another inherent in the new environmental era. There were cases galore. But perhaps the most dramatic one, which pinpoints the watershed between the old and the new, involved Hell's Canyon on the Snake River in Idaho. For many years that dispute had taken the old and honorable shape of public versus private power. Should there be one high dam, constructed with federal funds by the Bureau of Reclamation, or three lower dams to be built by the Idaho Power Company? These were the issues of the 1930's, the Truman years and the Eisenhower administrations. But when the Supreme Court reviewed a ruling of the Federal Power Commission on the issue in 1968, it pointed out in a decision written by Justice [William O.] Douglas that another option had not been considered — no dam at all. Perhaps the river was more valuable as an undeveloped, free flowing stream. The decision was unexpected both to the immediate parties to the dispute, and also to "conservationists" in Idaho and the Pacific Northwest. In fact, those conservationists had to be persuaded to become environmentalists. But turn about they did. The decision seemed to focus a perspective which had long lain dormant, implicit in the circumstances but not yet articulated, and reflected a rather profound transformation in values which had already taken place.

There were other realms of difference between the old and the new. There was, for example, the changing public conception of the role and meaning of forests. The U.S. Forest Service, and the entire community of professional foresters, continued to elaborate the details of scientific management of wood production; it took the form of increasing input for higher yields, and came to emphasize especially even-aged management. But an increasing number of Americans thought of forests as environments for home, work and play, as an environmental rather than as a commodity resource, and hence to be protected from incompatible crop-oriented strategies. Many of them bought woodlands for their environmental rather than their wood production potential. But the forestry profession did not seem to be able to accept the new values. The Forest Service was never able to "get on top" of the wilderness movement to incorporate it in "leading edge" fashion into its own strategies. As the movement evolved from stage to stage the Service seemed to be trapped by its own internal value commitments and hence relegated to playing a rear-guard role to protect wood production. Many a study conducted by the Forest Service experiment stations and other forest professionals made clear that the great majority of small woodland owners thought of their holdings as environments for wildlife and their own recreational and residential activities; yet the service forester program conducted by the Forest Service continued to emphasize wood production rather than environmental amenities as the goal of woodland management. The diverging trends became sharper with the steadily accumulating environmental interest in amenity goals in harvesting strategies and the expanding ecological emphases on more varied plant and animal life within the forest.

There were also divergent tendencies arising from the soil conservation arena. In the early 1950's, the opposition of farmers to the high-dam strategies of the U.S. Army Corps of Engineers led to a new program under the jurisdiction of the Soil Conservation Service, known as PL 566, which emphasized the construction of smaller headwater dams to "hold the water where it falls." This put the SCS in the business of rural land and water development, and it quickly took up the challenge of planning a host of such "multiple-use" projects which combined small flood control reservoirs with flat-water recreation and channel-ization with wetland drainage. By the time this program came into operation, however, in the 1960's, a considerable interest had arisen in the natural habitats of headwater streams, for example for trout fishing, and wetlands for both fish and wildlife. A head-on collision on this score turned an agency which had long been thought of as riding the lead wave of conservation affairs into one which appeared to environmentalists to be no better than the Corps — development minded and at serious odds with newer natural environment objectives.

There was one notable exception to these almost irreconcilable tensions between the old and the new in which a far smoother transition occurred — the realm of wildlife. In this case the old emphasis on game was faced with a new one on nature observation or what came to be called a "non-game" or "appre-ciative" use of wildlife. Between these two impulses there were many potential arenas for deep controversy. But there was also common ground in their joint interest in wildlife habitat. The same forest which served as a place for hunting also served as a place for nature observation. In fact, as these different users began to be identified and counted it was found that even on lands acquired exclusively for game management the great majority of users were non-game observers. As a result of this shared interest in wildlife habitat it was relatively easy for many "game managers" to shift in their self-conceptions to become "wildlife managers." Many a state agency changed its name from "game" to "wildlife" and an earlier document, "American Game Policy, 1930," which guided the profession for many years, became "The North American Wildlife Policy, 1973."

If we examine the values and ideas, then, the activities and programs, the directions of impulses in the political arena, we can observe a marked transition from the pre–World War II conservation themes of efficient management of physical resources, to the post–World War environmental themes of environ-mental amenities, environmental protection, and human scale technology. Something new was happening in American society, arising out of the social changes and transformation in human values in the post-War years. These were associated more with the advanced consumer society of those years than with the industrial manufacturing society of the late 19th and the first half of the 20th centuries. Let me now root these environmental values in these social and value changes.

The Roots of New Environmental Values

. . . We are at a stage in history when new values and new ways of looking at ourselves have emerged to give rise to new preferences. These are characteris-tic of advanced industrial societies throughout the world, not just in the United States. They reflect two major and widespread social changes. One is associ-ated with the search for standards of living beyond necessities and conve-niences to include amenities made possible by considerable increases in personal and social "real income." The other arises from advancing levels of education which have generated values associated with personal creativity and self-development, involvement with natural environments, physical and mental fitness and wellness and political autonomy and efficacy. Environmental values and objectives are an integral part of these changes. . . .

From studies specifically of environmental values, from analyses of recreational and leisure preferences undertaken by leisure research specialists, from surveys of the values expressed by those who purchase natural environment lands, and from the content of environmental action in innumerable grass-roots citizen cases one can identify the "environmental impulse" not as reactive but formative. It reflects a desire for a better "quality of life" which is another phase of the continual search by the American people throughout their history for a higher standard of living. Environmental values are widespread in American society, extending throughout income and occupational levels, areas of the nation and racial groups, somewhat stronger in the middle sectors and a bit weaker in the very high and very low groupings. There are identifiable "leading sectors" of change with which they are associated as well as "lagging sectors." They tend to be stronger with younger people and increasing levels of education and move into the larger society from those centers of innovation. They are also more associated with particular geographical regions such as New England, the Upper Lakes States, the Upper Rocky Mountain region and the Far West, while the South, the Plains States and the lower Rockies constitute "lagging" regions. Hence one can argue that environmental values have expanded steadily in American society, associated with demographic sectors which are growing rather than with those which are more stable or declining.

Within this general context one can identify several distinctive sets of environmental tendencies. One was the way in which an increasing portion of the American people came to value natural environments as an integral part of their rising standard of living. They sought out many types of such places to experience, to explore, enjoy and protect: high mountains and forests, wetlands, ocean shores, swamplands, wild and scenic rivers, deserts, pine barrens, remnants of the original prairies, places of relatively clean air and water, more limited "natural areas." Interest in such places was not a throwback to the primitive, but an integral part of the modern standard of living as people sought to add new "amenity" and "aesthetic" goals and desires to their earlier preoccupation with necessities and conveniences. These new consumer wants were closely associated with many others of a similar kind such as in the creative arts, recreation and leisure in general, crafts, indoor and household decoration, hi-fi sets, the care of yards and gardens as living space and amenity components of necessities and conveniences. Americans experienced natural environments both emotionally and intellectually, sought them out for direct personal experience in recreation, studied them as objects of scientific and intellectual interest and desired to have them within their community, their region and their nation as symbols of a society with a high degree of civic consciousness and pride.

A new view of health constituted an equally significant innovation in environmental values, health less as freedom from illness and more as physical and mental fitness, of feeling well, of optimal capability for exercising one's physical and mental powers. . . . There was an increasing tendency to adopt personal habits that promoted rather than threatened health, to engage in physical exercise, to quit smoking, to eat more nutritiously and to reduce environmental threats in the air and water that might also weaken one's wellness. Some results of this concern were the rapid increase in the business of health food stores, reaching $1.5 billion in 1979, the success of the Rodale enterprises and their varied publications such as *Prevention* and *Organic Gardening*, and the increasing emphasis on preventive medicine.

Several significant historical tendencies are integral parts of these changes. One involves consumption and the role of environmental values as part of evolving consumer values. At one time, perhaps as late as 1900, the primary focus in consumption was on necessities. By the 1920's a new stage had emerged which emphasized conveniences in which the emerging consumer durables, such as the automobile and household appliances were the most visible elements. This change meant that a larger portion of personal income, and hence of social income and production facilities were now being devoted to a new type of demand and supply. By the late 1940's a new stage in the history of consumption had come into view. Many began to find that both their necessities and conveniences had been met and an increasing share of their income could be devoted to amenities. . . .

One of the distinctive aspects of the history of consumption is the degree to which what once were luxuries, enjoyed by only a few, over the years became enjoyed by many— articles of mass consumption. In the censuses of the last half of the 19th century several occupations were identified as the "luxury trades," producing items such as watches and books which later became widely consumed. Many such items went through a similar process, arising initially as enjoyed only by a relative few and then later becoming far more widely diffused. These included such consumer items as the wringer washing machine and the gas stove, the carpet sweeper, indoor plumbing and the automobile. And so it was with environmental amenities. What only a few could enjoy in the 19th century came to be mass activities in the mid-20th, as many purchased homes with a higher level of amenities around them and could participate in outdoor recreation beyond the city. Amid the tendency for the more affluent to seek out and acquire as private property the more valued natural amenity sites, the public lands came to be places where the opportunity for such activities remained far more accessible to a wide segment of the social order. . . .

The Evolution of Environmental Action

Emerging environmental values did not make themselves felt all in the same way or at the same time. Within the context of our concern here for patterns of historical change, therefore, it might be well to secure some sense of stages of development within the post–World War II years. The most prevalent notion is to identify Earth Day in 1970 as the dividing line. There are other candidate events, such as the publication of Rachel Carson's *Silent Spring* in 1962, and the Santa Barbara oil blowout in 1969. But in any event definition of change in these matters seems to be inadequate. Earth Day was as much a result as a cause. It came after a decade or more of underlying evolution in attitudes and action without which it would not have been possible. Many environmental organizations, established earlier, experienced considerable growth in membership during the 1960's, reflecting an expanding concern. The regulatory mechanisms and issues in such fields as air and water pollution were shaped then; for example the Clean Air Act of 1967 established the character of the air quality program more than did that of 1970. General public awareness and interest were expressed extensively in a variety of public forums and in the mass media. Evolving public values could be observed in the growth of the outdoor recreation movement which reached back into the 1950's and the search for amenities in quieter and more natural settings, in the increasing number of people who engaged in hiking and camping or purchased recreational lands and homes on the seashore, by lakes and in woodlands. This is not to say that the entire scope of environmental concerns emerged fully in the 1960's. It did not. But one can observe a gradual evolution rather than a sudden outburst at the turn of the decade, a cumulative social and political change that came to be expressed vigorously even long before Earth Day. . . . A new and different concern for the adverse impact of industrial development with a special focus on air and water pollution . . . evolved slowly on a local and piecemeal basis, but emerged with national force only in the mid-1960's. In the early part of the decade air and water pollution began to take on significance as national issues and by 1965 they had become highly visible. The first national public opinion poll on such questions was taken in that year, and the President's annual message in 1965 reflected, for the first time, a full fledged concern for pollution problems. Throughout the rest of the decade and on into the 1970's these issues evolved continually. Federal legislation to stimulate remedial action was shaped over the course of these seven years, from 1965 to 1972, a distinct period which constituted the second phase in the evolution of environmental politics, taking its place alongside the previously developing concern for natural environment areas.

The legislative results were manifold. Air pollution was the subject of new laws in 1967 and 1970; water pollution in 1965, 1970 and 1972. The evolving concern about pesticides led to revision of the existing law in the Pesticides Act of 1972. The growing public interest in natural environment values in the coastal zone, and threats to them by dredging and filling, industrial siting and offshore oil development first made its mark on Congress in 1965 and over the next few years shaped the course of legislation which finally emerged in the Coastal Zone Management Act of 1972. Earth Day in the spring of 1970 lay in the middle of this phase of historical development, both a result of the previous half-decade of activity and concern and a new influence to accelerate action. The outline of these various phases of environmental activity, however, can be observed only by evidence and actions far beyond the events of Earth Day. Such more broad-based evidence identifies the years 1965 to 1972 as a well-defined phase of historical development in terms of issues, emphasizing the reaction against the adverse effects of industrial growth as distinct from the earlier emergence of natural environment issues. . . .

Beginning in the early 1970's . . . a [new] phase of environmental politics arose which brought three other sets of issues into public debate: toxic chemicals, energy and the possibilities of social, economic and political decentralization. These did not obliterate earlier issues, but as some natural environment matters and concern over the adverse effects of industrialization shifted from legislative to administrative politics, and thus became less visible to the general public, these new issues emerged often to dominate the scene. They were influenced heavily by the seemingly endless series of toxic chemical episodes, from PBB's in Michigan to kepone in Virginia to PCB's on the Hudson River, to the discovery of abandoned chemical dumps at Love Canal and near Louisville, Kentucky. These events, however, were only the more sensational aspects of a more deep-seated new twist in public concern for human health. Interest in personal health and especially in preventive health action took a major leap forward in the 1970's. It seemed to focus especially on such matters as cancer and environmental pollutants responsible for a variety of health problems, on food and diet on the one hand and exercise on the other. From these interests arose a central concern for toxic threats in the workplace, in the air and water, and in food and personal habits that came to shape some of the overriding issues of the 1970's on the environmental front. It shifted the earlier emphasis on the ecological effects of toxic pollutants to one more on human health effects. Thus, while proceedings against DDT in the late 1960's had emphasized adverse ecological impacts, similar proceedings in the 1970's focused primarily on human health.

Environmental impulses [thus] served as a major influence in shaping the newer, more "modern," economy. They brought to the fore new demand factors which in turn generated new types of production to fill them; they placed increasing pressure on greater technological efficiency in production to reduce harmful residuals and resource waste. In many aspects of the economy one can distinguish between older and newer forms of demand and supply, institutions and modes of economic analysis. The transition represents a shift from the older manufacturing to the newer advanced consumer economy. In this transition environmental influences were an integral part of the emerging economy that was struggling for a larger role in America amid more established economic institutions.

From Laissez Faire to Environmental Regulation

JACK LEWIS

Since EPA's [Environmental Protection Agency] founding in 1970, the Agency's regulatory powers and responsibilities have been the subject of intense debate. Much of that debate has been specific to EPA and the problems it handles: protection of public health and restoration of the natural environment. There is, however, a larger context: nothing less than the role of the

---

From Jack Lewis, "Looking Backward: A Historical Perspective on Environmental Regulations," *EPA Journal* 14, no. 2, March 1988, pp. 42–46. Reprinted by permission of the Environmental Protection Agency.

federal government at large, and how that role should be defined and redefined as the nation's needs change.

Before we examine the major themes of the regulatory debate as they relate specifically to EPA, let's take a . . . broad look at the historical context from which modern-day federal regulation has evolved.

The United States has come a long way since the drafting of the Constitution in 1787. . . . The heavily urbanized and industrialized world power of 1988 would be unrecognizable to the Founding Fathers. If farmers, bankers, and merchants of 1787 could be resuscitated for a debate with today's presidential candidates, nearly all would sound libertarian to modern ears: fiercely hostile to any centralization of government, and adamantly protective of the rights of private individuals and local magistrates. Still fresh in their minds was the stinging indignity of enslavement to British rulemaking and taxation.

A central theme in the writings of Tom Paine and other firebrands of the day was the youth of the American republic and its happy freedom from the complexities of law and regulation characteristic of ancient Britain. Two hundred years later, it is hardly surprising to see the United States—and its governmental bodies at all levels—exhibiting many of the traits of a polity grown old, the tendency toward "gridlock" once vilified under other names by colonial pamphleteers.

Of course, there is a clearcut difference between federal regulations and their colonial antecedents of the 1700s: ours are the products of a democratic process, forms of restraint that we as a people have chosen to assume. That they should appear alien to the average citizen, and in some cases incomprehensible, is largely a reflection of the fact that they have been written by experts for experts in a society that demands scientific standards of precision even in the statements about uncertain or unpredictable trends.

It was not always thus. Between the formulation of the U.S. Constitution and the Civil War, state and local governments were zealously protective of their prerogatives. The federal bureaucracy remained miniscule in scale, and its laws often resembled treaties among sovereign powers more than modern-day statutes. Economic expansion was the order of the day; and all levels of government hastened to distribute "sweetheart" franchises and charters to the builders of turnpikes, canals, and railroads. Virtually no effort was made to "regulate" any form of capitalist enterprise.

What little restraint the country was willing to throw in the path of progress took the form of the common law traditions the United States had inherited from its mother country, Great Britain. U.S. common law gave citizens the right to take legal action as a means of protecting themselves against nuisance or harm. If the court's ruling went in their favor, they could obtain compensation for injuries sustained. Some common law actions from this era led to judicial rulings that "regulated" the activities of isolated transgressors against the environment or the public health.

War is another way of redressing grievances, as America's Civil War illustrates: the hard-won victory of the North was the triumph of industry and city over agriculture and slavery. For the next 35 years, during the so-called

"Gilded Age," all-out competition raged among increasingly gigantic utilities, railroads, and other industries. Their lobbyists in fast-growing Washington saw to it that general and permissive grants replaced the exclusive franchises of the slower paced and more genteel antebellum world. The individual citizen was more and more a tiny David confronted with the monoliths of private enterprise.

The federal government, too, was beginning to grow, albeit at a much slower pace. Its powers were not really exercised, however, until the turn of the century when leaders, such as President Theodore Roosevelt, started using the federal statute book to shield U.S. citizens from the unbridled impact of "progress" run amok. Lawmakers decided it was impossible to turn back the clock to laissez-faire competition. Monopolies were a fact of American life, and the best that the federal government could do was to set up administrative commissions to control their worst abuses. First railroads, then public utilities, and other large-scale business entities fell under the purview of newly created federal commissions — ancestors of today's regulatory agencies.

One of President Roosevelt's favorite causes was the protection of America's wilderness territories. The conservationist mentality — given its first voice in the mid-19th century by Henry David Thoreau — had become much more popular by 1901 thanks to widely read nature writers such as John Muir. Roosevelt, himself a great outdoorsman and personal friend of Muir, used his presidential power to double the number of national parks and almost quadruple the national forest area: steps that gave a firm foundation to the conservationist tradition that, along with the parallel traditions of common law and public health, was so integral to the founding of EPA.

The public health tradition also took a giant step forward during this same period. In the first years of the 20th century, preventive statutes were written to regulate the quality of food, drinking water, and sewage treatment.

At first *de facto*, then *de jure*, the U.S. Marine Hospital Service — an organization dating back to 1798 — gradually expanded its functions to deal on a centralized basis with broad issues of public health. In 1902, Congress renamed it the "U.S. Public Health and Marine Service," a name that was further altered in 1912 to the "U.S. Public Health Service" (PHS).

A large part of the PHS's early work had to do with the prevention of waterborne disease, such as typhoid; in later years, that mission was expanded to include standard-setting for air quality in the industrial workplace. These early PHS water and workplace air standards became the prototypes for the first federal water and air programs of the 1950s and 1960s — both of which originated at the PHS. Lawmakers and health professionals in the states were also heavily influenced by precedents set by the PHS.

The Great Depression of the 1930s launched a new and even more activist phase in the evolution of the federal government. The New Deal policies of President Franklin Roosevelt caused a substantial increase in the size and power of the federal bureaucracy. Severe economic hardship opened the way for public works projects that regenerated the nation's infrastructure, and in doing so led to improvements in the quality of U.S. drinking water, sewage treatment, and other services vital to public health. The Civilian Conservation Corps put some of the jobless to work on improvement projects in wilderness and forest areas.

In addition, New Deal leaders stressed the importance of national coordination and planning, objectives that were unrealizable without an increasingly intrusive range of federal statutes and regulations . . . and ever larger and more comprehensive bureaucratic entities. For example, in 1935 President Roosevelt opted for consolidation rather than diversification by assigning federal regulation of the trucking and busing industries to the Interstate Commerce Commission, which had been established in 1885 to control the railroads. Furthermore, he decreed that the regulatory actions of all U.S. commissions should be tailored to the achievement of national policy goals.

Coordination and planning of a military and economic nature had a major trial run during World War II. To some extent, this successful experiment in federally run mobilization laid the groundwork for the ambitious environmental statutes assigned to EPA one by one in the 1970s. At the very least, the idea was driven home that the federal government could regulate and coordinate disparate types of behavior to meet national policy goals.

By the 1950s, other factors were fostering a new regulatory climate. The unbridled growth of the nation's booming chemical, plastics, petroleum, automotive, aviation, and munitions works was creating highly visible forms of pollution. As a result, the traditional method of individuals seeking redress of environmental grievances under the common law became inadequate.

The problem was not so much the quantity of environmental actions under the common law: it was their sheer difficulty from a legal standpoint. Expert witnesses could be found to argue both sides of any case, to the consternation and confusion of judges and juries. Also, quite a few cases involved tri-state and bi-state metropolitan areas, such as New York City and Chicago, with a crazy quilt of conflicting state laws and local ordinances.

Not only citizens but the industries they were suing grew impatient with the lack of *a priori* environmental standards, both legal and scientific. Some states formed advisory commissions to offer technical advice to concerned parties. From more and more quarters came the suggestion that the federal government should step in and determine exactly what were "safe" levels of various pollutants.

Several federal programs were set up both to perform research on air and water pollution and to establish national standards. Their impact was blunted by several deficiencies, some of which were immediately apparent while others came to light only later. The Federal Water Quality Administration (FWQA) was formed in 1965. The National Air Pollution Control Administration (NAPCA) — although not given that name until 1968 — originated as a research body in 1955 and had also acquired some standard-setting powers by the mid-1960s. Both FWQA and NAPCA were at first part of the Public Health Service, which was — as its name suggests — more committed to public health than to environmental protection.

The FWQA broke off from the PHS in 1966 and became part of the Department of the Interior. Since pesticides were already the concern of the

Department of Agriculture, a pattern of administrative fragmentation along the narrow lines of single media (air, water, etc.) was being perpetuated at the very time when ecological themes of inter-relatedness were arising to challenge the limitations of earlier modes of thought.

The predominant climate from which EPA's predecessor programs arose was, in fact, not ecological at all, but firmly entrenched in decades-old public health traditions. The Public Health Service had a pattern of not intervening in any problem unless invited by state officials; this did little to foster strong enforcement. The preventive, pragmatic, disease-specific nature of PHS traditions, though it had its own rationale in the public health sphere, was simply not interventionist enough to lead the fight for restoration of the biosphere. And this was a goal that had become extremely fashionable in the wake of *Silent Spring*'s publication in 1962.

The U.S. Environmental Protection Agency, formed in December 1970, was a hybrid of all these multifarious and frequently conflicting patterns. The fledgling Agency was saddled with a tremendously difficult regulatory mission: How should ecological goals be balanced with those related to public health and the common law rights of the individual? How should the atmosphere of public and media hysteria be dispelled? How should scientific findings be interpreted and correlated — and their gradations of uncertainty communicated to lawmakers, reporters, and citizens?

The regulatory challenge was so great, in fact, that it is hardly surprising that EPA quickly became and today remains involved in many of the most controversial issues in the federal government. Yet the Agency has made important progress over the past 17 years: great strides have been made in cleaning up America's air and water, especially the highly visible forms of desecration that fueled the crisis mentality of the late 1960s. The persistent, organochlorine pesticides of two decades ago, such as DDT, have been largely eliminated, and good progress is being made in dealing with abandoned hazardous waste sites.

The challenges of the future involve extremely important but less visible problems of cross-media pollution, stratospheric ozone depletion, radon contamination, and protection of air and water supplies against ever-proliferating types of toxic chemicals in trace concentrations. Continued progress on such problems will be incrementally more expensive to the U.S. government and U.S. society than the gains made during EPA's first decade and a half: a 15-year period that has coincided with economic and energy problems totally unanticipated in 1970. Crises in those areas introduced constraints that spawned the "regulatory reform" movement of the late 1970s and the 1980s: an effort to divest the federal government of many of its recently assumed regulatory responsibilities and to let state and local governments as well as business take up the slack.

Yet, despite growing concerns over the size and cost of the federal government, public-opinion polls indicate that the American people are as firmly committed as ever to the fulfillment of EPA's public health and environmental goals. Unfortunately, in many cases, the public's evaluation of what most needs fixing — an opinion EPA must under law solicit and consider — does not always square with expert scientific analyses of the most pressing dangers confronting the health of the nation's citizens and their natural environment. As a result, controversy continues over the appropriate direction and scale of EPA's future regulatory mission. . . .

Indian Land and Water Rights

LLOYD BURTON

In the study of history there is a natural tendency to organize past events into periods, patterns, and themes; to punctuate the flow of time with a concept or event perceived as having measurably affected the course of human experience. In 1983, for instance, we observed the fiftieth anniversary of the birth of the New Deal, an occasion to compare the management of past crises with the handling of our own uncertain times.

January of 1983 also marked the seventy-fifth anniversary of a legal event, almost unnoticed at its occurrence, which was in retrospect just as significant for American Indian tribes as the New Deal was for the rest of American society. In January 1908 the U.S. Supreme Court issued its seminal decision in *Winters* v. *United States*, the first case in which the federal courts explicitly affirmed the water rights of Indian reservations. The *Winters* decision would arouse little more interest now than it did three quarters of a century ago but for its impact on contemporary resource management. Armed with the reserved water rights (or "*Winters* doctrine") first articulated in this decision, over forty tribes are now locked in combat with non-Indian interests in administrative hearings and courtrooms throughout the western states, claiming their share of the water resources on which the entire economic future of the West depends. The quantities of water in controversy are huge, as are the economic benefits accruing to whichever parties eventually win.

The news media have come to recognize the magnitude and importance of Indian water-rights claims, giving the impression that the structure of current Indian-related controversies over water rights is a contemporary phenomenon. In fact, just the opposite is true: the roots of these conflicts extend at least to colonial times and the patterns of conflict emerging over the last two-hundred-fifty years may have a determinative effect on the outcome of present disputes.

Historical developments in the law of American Indian water resources have been characterized by three recurrent themes or trends. First, in entitlement disputes over natural resources, the federal judiciary has generally tended to treat North American Indian tribes as individual, nationlike entities, in accordance with the status implicitly assigned them by original provisions of the U.S. Constitution. Second, however, in keeping with the realpolitik of westward expansion, congressional and executive branch policy makers — unlike the judiciary — have come to regard the tribes not as separate, semi-autonomous nation-states with ancient rights to natural resources but collectively, as just one more ethnic minority group struggling for parity in the distribution of national wealth. This historic divergence in perspective between the courts and the more politically sensitive branches (a divergence that in modern times may be waning) has left the federal government beset by a fundamental ambivalence regarding the status, rights, and entitlements of American Indian tribes. . . .

Third, a stark parallel may be drawn between the process which created the Indian reservations in the nineteenth century, when the tribes relinquished theoretical sovereignty over vast areas in return for federally protected control over much smaller amounts of land, and the process of current western water-rights negotiations, in which the federal executive branch, the states, and assorted business interests are urging the tribes to abandon theoretical water-rights claims in return for federal delivery of much smaller amounts of water. . . .

The tribes originally removed from the eastern states to Indian Country in the plains west of the Mississippi were assigned huge contiguous territories in which no whites were settled. But in the Southwest, many of the tribes inhabiting areas the United States had acquired after the Mexican War in 1848 (the present-day states of Arizona, California, Colorado, Nevada, New Mexico, and Utah) were living on islands of reserved lands surrounded by Spanish (and later, Mexican) settlements. Seeing that this pattern of concentrated distribution freed much more land for development, the federal government quickly negotiated treaties with Indians in the thinly populated western territories. The tribes relinquished dominion over most of their land (which they hadn't the martial force to control anyway) in return for a much smaller reserved area, which the United States promised to keep free of white incursion and where Indian rule would be exclusive. From 1853 to 1856, fifty-two such treaties were negotiated, involving federal acquisition of about 174 million acres of land from the western tribes.

But for those tribes which did not acquiesce in the new reservation policy after the Civil War, a tragically familiar sequence of events occurred. The completion of the first transcontinental railroad in 1869 stimulated some unauthorized white settling and ranching on tribal territories. This provoked retaliatory Indian attacks, usually countered by the U.S. Cavalry. A peace treaty would ensue; and the tribes would give up most of their lands in return for a smaller reserved area, rations and other supplies as needed, and implements for conversion to farming, animal husbandry, and other "arts of civilization." The fighting was particularly vicious in the Southwest. While the sedentary agrarian tribes (e.g., the Hopi, Papago, Pima, and Pueblo) had been more or less peacefully coexisting with the Spanish and Mexicans for two centuries by the time of the Civil War, the more warlike hunting and gathering tribes had not. In much of Arizona and New Mexico, the Apache and the Navajo constituted the dominant military presence until the latter half of the nineteenth century. Early efforts by the U.S. government to treat with the Apache and the Navajo failed, and continuous guerilla warfare persisted for nearly a decade. In the late 1860s and early 1870s hostilities escalated into reciprocal massacres, with entire villages of friendly Indians or white farming and ranching communities destroyed and all inhabitants slain or enslaved.

It was in this climate of extreme hostility that Congress began to adopt openly retributive Indian policies, which also had the effect of freeing more land for non-Indian resource development. First and foremost, in 1871 it took the constitutionally questionable action of declaring that thereafter no Indian tribe would be recognized by Congress as a nation capable of making treaties. Existing treaties were unaffected. . . .

In the century immediately following constitutional ratification, the United States government unilaterally adjusted the legal status of the Indian tribes down from the sovereign nations (of Revolutionary days) to "domestic dependent nations" in 1823 . . . to nonnational entities in 1871. Concomitant with the loss in status had been the loss of land, first through the Jacksonian removal policy and later through reservation-creating treaty negotiations and guerilla warfare. Congressional policy makers now took what they assumed to be the final step in assimilating the Indians into white society and freeing their remaining lands for maximal resource development: passage of the General Allotment Act (also known as the "Dawes Act") of 1887. The purpose of the act was to facilitate the dissolution of Indian tribes by authorizing the president to allot communally held tribal lands in 160-acre parcels to individual tribal members. After all members had received individual allotments, the secretary of the Interior was to negotiate with the tribes for the sale of the remaining lands to non-Indians.

The act proved to be a disastrous failure for the Indians. It fell even further short of its stated goals than the Homestead Act (on which it was nominally patterned) and for similar reasons: non-Indian interests managed by various means quickly to accumulate title from the individual allottees, who were naive about legal matters. Of the 155.6 million acres held by Indian tribes in 1881, title to roughly 90 million acres (more than half of preallotment holdings) had fallen into non-Indian hands by the time the allotment policy was repudiated fifty years later. Further, about 20 million acres of the reservation lands not allotted were unirrigated desert, considered essentially valueless by most whites. Whether intended or not, the allotment policy's most effective means of encouraging the tribes to meld into white society was simply to relieve them of much of their well-watered, arable land. Throughout the periods of removal, reservation, and allotment, the size of the Indian population in the United States steadily declined. From an estimated one million indigenous people at the outset of continuous European presence, by 1900 the total Indian population had fallen to 237,196—a decline of more than seventy-five percent. . . .

Water Rights and Indian Policy in the Twentieth Century

The humid eastern states had early on inherited the English common law of riparian water rights, a doctrine that included the following features: (1) title to land abutting a stream carries the right to withdraw for "reasonable use" waters from the stream; (2) the rights of all riparians on a watercourse are correlative, in that no user may alter water flow or quality to the degree that a neighboring riparian's use is harmed or precluded; (3) the amount of water withdrawn is not quantified, "reasonable use" and harm to neighboring riparians being the only limitations on withdrawal; and (4) a riparian right is not lost through nonuse, since the right inheres in title to riparian land. . . .

However, Montana and other relatively dry western states had rejected riparian doctrine, primarily because the equal sharing of waters from sparse streams with wide seasonal fluctuations in flow would not assure any one user a water supply sufficient for most agricultural or industrial uses. What therefore evolved was the doctrine of prior appropriation, in which (1) a strict hierarchy of rights is based on the chronological order in which users first began to appropriate waters from a given source (ownership of riparian land not being a prerequisite to such withdrawals); (2) the right is limited to a specific amount of water dedicated to an approved "beneficial use"; (3) nonuse of an appropriative right can result in its forfeiture to other appropriators; and (4) in times of shortage the rights of users are honored in the order of their original appropriation of the waters, with the result that senior appropriators can receive their full share while junior appropriators may get little or nothing.

[In its 1908 *Winters* decision], the Supreme Court [ruled] (1) that in keeping with the policies of western states' water rights, the date a reservation was established was to be considered as the date the waters were reserved (thus making Indians the senior appropriators on many western streams since most reservations were founded from the 1850s through the 1880s); but (2) that unlike state prior-appropriation doctrine, the reserved right was not liable to extinction through nonuse; and (3) that the right need not be quantified if the appropriated waters are used to fulfill the reservation's purpose. . . .

The Interior Department, which through its Bureau of Reclamation (BuRec) was encouraging the rapid appropriation and development of water resources by non-Indian users under state law, was also responsible through its Bureau of Indian Affairs (BIA) for protection of the Indians' reserved water rights in the federal courts. Sadly but predictably, Interior was far more active and successful in discharging its former responsibility than its latter one. . . .

Federalism and Indian Sovereignty: The New Deal, the Eisenhower Years, and the Civil Rights Era.   The willingness of Franklin D. Roosevelt and his congressional supporters to alter existing policies significantly in the interest of economic stabilization and the public welfare had just as substantial an impact on Indian policy as on any other realm of federal endeavor. In 1928 a pretigious privately funded study had revealed the disastrous social and economic effects the allotment policy was wreaking on the Indian tribes; six years later, Washington was ready to follow the report's recommendations and offer the Indians their own new deal.

The offer took the form of the Indian Reorganization Act of 1934. Most important, the act halted the practice of allotting tribal lands to individual Indians and their subsequent sale to non-Indian interests. The sale of remaining unallotted tribal lands to non-Indians was also prohibited, as was the subjection of allotted trust lands to state intestacy laws. Although all matters regarding the use or disposition of natural resources by reservation Indians remained subject to the Interior secretary's approval, the act did empower the tribes to retain their own legal counsel (again, subject to Interior approval). . . .

Just as the New Deal's Reorganization Act abruptly halted the loss of Indian lands through allotment, a practice similar to allotment was just as abruptly resumed by the Congress which came to power with Dwight Eisenhower. With Republican champions of states' rights creating a majority in both houses, the Eighty-third Congress undertook a legislative program which transferred billions of dollars worth of federally controlled natural resources to state and private ownership and dealt a heavy blow to the concept of Indian sovereignty as well. . . .

The postwar, prodevelopment vigor of the American economy combined with states'-rights majorities in both houses of Congress set the stage for another assault on tribal resource rights. Having freed offshore petroleum and natural gas reserves for private development, the Eighty-third Congress now turned its attention to Indian lands. Two major pieces of legislation, both enacted fairly early in the first session, formed the core of a new Indian policy.

The first was a resolution establishing procedures for the future legislative "termination" of Indian reservations: that is, the cessation of all federal trust responsibility for and supervision of reservation lands. Under this new program, the tribes in terminated reservations (1) became subject to state criminal and civil jurisdiction and to state property taxes; (2) were cut off from all federal health, education, welfare, and employment assistance; and (3) in cases where all their lands were sold to non-Indians, experienced a total loss of sovereignty as a governmental entity. Some of the termination acts passed under the Resolution 108 guidelines arranged for entire reservations to be appraised and sold to the highest bidder, with the proceeds distributed to the tribe. A total of 109 bands and tribes were "terminated" during the life of this program, involving a loss of about 1.4 million acres of tribal land. . . .

In 1963, the U.S. government . . . defended the rights of five lower-basin tribes living along the main stem of the Colorado between Hoover Dam and the Mexican border. . . . Justice [Hugo] Black's majority opinion awarded the tribes (which collectively numbered fewer than thirty-five hundred persons) more than ten percent of the entire annual lower-basin share of the Colorado River (about three times the amount granted to Nevada). Further, the Indians' portion of the annual flow was to be subtracted from the allotments to the states in which the various reservations were located. The Court also chose to quantify the *Winters* rights in this case, reserving enough water to service all "practicably irrigable acreage" on the reservations. In a resounding reaffirmation of the doctrine it had articulated half a century earlier, the Supreme Court again let it be known that the creation of Indian reservations also created substantial and (in most cases) superior Indian rights to appurtenant water resources.

As it turned out, this supportive stance of the Warren Court presaged another change of heart in Congress over Indian policy. Just as Congress had begun to follow the Court's lead in the early 1960s on matters affecting the status of other traditionally disenfranchised groups, it once again overhauled federal relations with the tribes. Its first actions in changing Indian policy were actually inactions, by failing to pass any reservation termination bills after 1962. Yet the most striking restatement of policy came in 1968, when the Ninety-first Congress produced the Indian Civil Rights Act. Although this legislation may be seen in one light as a continued limitation on Indian sovereignty (since it imposed Fourteen Amendment restraints on tribal governments), it also effectively halted broader implementation of Public Law 280, by denying states not already having done so the authority to extend their civil and criminal jurisdiction over Indian lands without tribal consent. By the late 1960s, then, the accretion of state control over Indian lands had ended, and the flow of power was once again toward Washington. By the early 1970s, some tribes had actually convinced Congress to repeal the statutes terminating their reservations and to resume federal trust responsibility for their remaining lands.

Even in light of the argument that "Indian policy" has often been a convenient rubric for attaining other governmental ends, three generalizations about the legal history of American Indian water resources still hold true. First, from the 1908 *Winters* decision up through the 1960s, the federal courts for the most part have tended steadfastly to uphold Indian water rights as preemptive federal obligations, while Congress and the executive — because of the Indians' relative lack of political clout — have tended either to ignore the Indian right or to subvert it directly (by facilitating non-Indian water appropriation under state laws). Infrequently, the executive branch has defended their right, in keeping with its court-assigned role as trustee of Indian resources and also when it coincided with other policy objectives. Second, at times when Congress has been most deferential to the states and private developers regarding access to federally protected natural resources, diminution of the Indian resource base has been the greatest (as in the Removal Act, the Allotment Act, the termination acts, and Public Law 280). And third, a strong parallel exists between negotiations over the creation of Indian reservations in the nineteenth century and current negotiations over the development of Indian water resources. In both instances, the tribes have been urged to relinquish resource rights, for which the federal judiciary had afforded strong constitutional protections, in return for congressional and executive promises of assistance in the economic development of a much smaller resource base, which grew even smaller once the original right had been bargained away.

As the governmental institution ostensibly least susceptible to shifting political currents and most sensitive to the honoring of governmental obligations, the federal judiciary has emerged over the course of this century as the primary definer and defender of the Indian water right. Congress has been called upon repeatedly to declare a general policy on these rights, but it has resolutely avoided action on any of the dozens of proposals it has considered; federal executives market water to non-Indians under state law on Monday, defend the Indian right in court on Tuesday, and spend the rest of the week hoping the problem will just go away. Since the federal courts stand at the vortex in this swirl of ambivalence and uncertainty, any perceptible shift in their support for the Indian right will affect the future of that entitlement profoundly. Thus the courts' views on federal-state relations and on the nature and extent of the U.S. obligation to the tribes are of special relevance.

❦ *F U R T H E R   R E A D I N G*

Lloyd Burton, *American Indian Water Rights and the Limits of the Law* (1991)
Rachel Carson, *Silent Spring* (1962)
Marion Clawson, *The Bureau of Land Management* (1971)
Paul J. Culhane, *Public Lands Politics: Interest Group Influence on the Forest Service and Bureau of Land Management* (1981)
Samuel Trask Dana and Sally K. Fairfax, *Forest and Range Policy: Its Development in the United States* (1980)
Bernard DeVoto, *The Easy Chair* (1955)
Thomas R. Dunlap, *Saving America's Wildlife* (1988)
Paul Erlich, *The Population Bomb* (1968)
William C. Everhart, *The National Park Service* (1972)
James M. Glover, "Romance, Recreation, and Wilderness: Influences on the Life and Work of Bob Marshall," *Environmental History Review* 14, no. 4 (Winter 1990), 23–39
Samuel P. Hays, *Beauty, Health, and Permanence: Environmental Politics in the United States, 1955–1985* (1987)
Douglas Helms and Susan L. Flader, eds., *The History of Soil and Water Conservation* (1985)
Harold Ickes, *The Secret Diaries of Harold Ickes*, 3 vols. (1953, 1955)
David E. Lilienthal, *TVA: Democracy on the March* (1944)
Thomas A. Lund, *American Wildlife Law* (1980)
Arthur F. McEvoy, *The Fisherman's Problem: Ecology and Law in the California Fisheries, 1850–1980* (1986)
Robert Marshall, *The People's Forests* (1933)
Donella H. Meadows et al., *The Limits to Growth* (1972)
Robert J. Morgan, *Government Soil Conservation: Thirty Years of the New Decentralization* (1965)
Roderick Nash, *The Rights of Nature: A History of Environmental Ethics* (1989)
―――――, ed., *American Environmentalism* (1990)
Edgar B. Nixon, ed., *Franklin D. Roosevelt and Conservation, 1911–1945*, 2 vols. (1957)
E. Louise Peffer, *The Closing of the Public Domain: Disposal and Reservation Policies, 1900–50* (1951)
Marc Reisner, *Cadillac Desert: The American West and Its Disappearing Water* (1986)
Elmo R. Richardson, *Dams, Parks, and Politics: Resource Development and Preservation in the Truman-Eisenhower Era* (1973)
Roy Robbins, *Our Landed Heritage* (1950)
William G. Robbins, *Lumberjacks and Legislators: Political Economy of the U.S. Lumber Industry, 1890–1941* (1982)
William D. Rowley, *U.S. Forest Service Grazing and Rangelands: A History* (1988)
Stewart Udall, *The Quiet Crisis* (1963)
T. H. Watkins, *Righteous Pilgrim: The Life and Times of Harold Ickes, 1874–1952* (1990)
James Whorton, *Before Silent Spring: Pesticides and Public Health in Pre-DDT America* (1975)
Donald Worster, *Rivers of Empire: Water, Aridity, and the Growth of the American West* (1985)

C H A P T E R

15

The Contemporary Environmental Movement

❦

From the 1970s to the present, the contemporary environmental movement has been a major force in United States history. During the 1970s new legislation more tightly regulated effluents and pollution, increased protection of wilderness and wildlife, and imposed greater controls on uses and disposal of pesticides, toxics, and hazardous wastes. Under the Reagan presidency of the 1980s, however, these successes were undermined by a relaxation of standards, decreasing budgets for federal environmental agencies, and the appointment of probusiness administrators as agency heads. Americans responded by joining environmental organizations in ever greater numbers, and the "big ten" environmental groups redoubled their efforts in Washington. In turn, grassroots groups sprang up across the nation to deal with myriad local issues, among them hazardous-waste sites, toxic chemicals in water and air, garbage dumps and landfills, land development, endangered species, and industrial pollution. The connections between U.S. and global environmental problems became more apparent as ozone depletion spiraled, carbon dioxide built up in the air, more and more species became endangered, forests vanished, and the world population soared. Radical groups such as Greenpeace, Earth First! and the Rainforest Action Network took to direct action to protect whales and dolphins, wolves and grizzly bears, tropical and temperate rainforests, and watersheds. Philosophical challenges to the Western world view and its liberal politics were made by deep ecologists, ecofeminists, bioregionalists, social ecologists, and environmental ethicists. The environmental movement became more diverse, divided, and self-critical. This chapter examines recent assessments of the environmental crisis by mainstream environmentalists, activists, and philosophers.

❦ D O C U M E N T S

The documents focus on developments during the 1980s and early 1990s. The first selection is excerpted from a 1983 speech by William Ruckelshaus, former director of the Environmental Protection Agency, discussing problems of scientific risk assessment — and of drafting legislation that would provide adequate protection from chemical hazards and pollutants. The second document is from the 1987 introduction to Earth First!'s *Ecodefense* manual by Dave Foreman and Bill Haywood, in which the two environmentalists set out the historical rationale for, and underlying assumptions of, the organization's direct-action strategy.

The third document presents the industrialist's point of view. G. M. Keller, chairman of the board and chief executive officer of Chevron Corporation, discusses industrial efforts to mitigate environmental problems. In the fourth document, William Reilly, former head of the Conservation Foundation and subsequently head of the Environmental Protection Agency, assesses the state of the U.S. environment in 1987 and proposes an agenda for the 1990s. A second such assessment, by biologist Peter Raven, director of the Missouri Botanical Garden in St. Louis, also written in 1987 and excerpted in the fifth document, primarily spotlights the state of the global environment.

The next three documents offer perspectives of blacks, Indians, and women. In the sixth document, Carl Anthony, an African-American architect and urban planner in Oakland, California, explains what is at stake for inner-city blacks, and urges them to become environmentalists. Winona LaDuke, an Algonquin from northern Minnesota and a founder of Women of All Red Nations, in the seventh document considers Indian relationships with nature and discusses some current red-white environmental controversies. In the closing document, Irene Diamond and Gloria Orenstein, coauthors of a 1990 collection of articles on ecofeminism, delineate issues that connect women to the environment.

A Federal Director Discusses Environmental Risk, 1983

The Environmental Protection Agency [EPA] is an instrument of public policy, whose mission is to protect the public health and the environment in the manner laid down by its statutes. That manner is to set standards and enforce them, and our enforcement powers are strong and pervasive. But the standards we set, whether technology- or health-related, must have a sound scientific base.

Science and the law are thus partners at EPA, but uneasy partners. The main reason for the uneasiness lies, I think, in the conflict between the way science really works and the public's thirst for certitude that is written into EPA's laws. Science thrives on uncertainty. The best young scientists flock into fields where great questions have been asked but nothing is known. The greatest triumph of a scientist is the crucial experiment that shatters the certainties of the past and opens up rich new pastures of ignorance.

But EPA's laws often assume, indeed demand, a certainty of protection greater than science can provide with the current state of knowledge. The laws do no more than reflect what the public believes and what it often hears from people with scientific credentials on the 6 o'clock news. The public thinks we

Excerpts from William D. Ruckelshaus, "Science, Risk, and Public Policy," *Science*, 221 (September 9, 1983), pp. 1026–8. Copyright 1983 by the American Association for the Advancement of Science.

know what all the bad pollutants are, precisely what adverse health or environmental effects they cause, how to measure them exactly and control them absolutely. Of course, the public and sometimes the law are wrong, but not all wrong. We do know a great deal about some pollutants and we have controlled them effectively by using the tools of the Clean Air Act and the Clean Water Act. These are the pollutants for which the scientific community can set safe levels and margins of safety for sensitive populations. If this were the case for all pollutants, we could breathe more easily (in both senses of the phrase); but it is not so.

More than 10 years ago, EPA had the Clean Air Act, the Clean Water Act, a solid waste law, a pesticide law, and laws to control radiation and noise. Yet to come were the myriad of laws to control toxic substances from their manufacture to their disposal — but that they would be passed was obvious even then.

When I departed EPA a decade ago, the struggle over whether the federal government was to have a major role in protecting our health, safety, and environment was ended. The American people had spoken. The laws had been passed; the regulations were being written. The only remaining question was whether the statutory framework we had created made sense or whether, over time, we would adjust it.

Ten years ago I thought I knew the answer to that question as well. I believed it would become apparent to all that we could virtually eliminate the risks we call pollution if we wanted to spend enough money. When it also became apparent that enough money for all the pollutants was a lot of money, I came to believe that we would begin examining the risks very carefully and structure a system that would force us to balance our desire to eliminate pollution against the costs of its control. This would entail some adjustment of the laws, but not all that much, and it would happen by about 1976. I was wrong.

This time around as administrator of EPA, I am determined to improve our country's ability to cope with the risk of pollutants over where I left it 10 years ago. It will not be easy, because we must now deal with a class of pollutants for which it is difficult, if not impossible, to establish a safe level. These pollutants interfere with genetic processes and are associated with the diseases we fear most: cancer and reproductive disorders, including birth defects. The scientific consensus is that any exposure, however small, to a genetically active substance embodies some risk of an effect. Since these substances are widespread in the environment, and since we can detect them down to very low levels, we must assume that life now takes place in a minefield of risks from hundreds, perhaps thousands, of substances. We can no longer tell the public that they have an adequate margin of safety. . . .

We . . . need to strengthen our risk assessment capabilities. We need more research on the health effects of the substances we regulate. I intend to do everything in my power to make clear the importance of this scientific analysis at EPA. Given the necessity of acting in the face of enormous scientific uncertainties, it is more important than ever that our scientific analysis be rigorous and the quality of our data be high. We must take great pains not to mislead people about the risks to their health. We can help to avoid confusion by ensuring both the quality of our science and the clarity of our language in explaining hazards. . . .

In the future, this being an imperfect world, the rigor and thoroughness of our risk analyses will undoubtedly be affected by many factors, including the toxicity of the substances examined, the populations exposed, the pressure of the regulatory timetable, and the resources available. Despite these often conflicting pressures, risk assessment at EPA must be based only on scientific evidence and scientific consensus. Nothing will erode public confidence faster than the suspicion that policy considerations have been allowed to influence the assessment of risk.

Although there is an objective way to assess risk, there is, of course, no purely objective way to manage it, nor can we ignore the subjective perception of risk in the ultimate management of a particular substance. To do so would be to place too much credence in our objective data and ignore the possibility that occasionally one's intuition is right. No amount of data is a substitute for judgment. . . .

To effectively manage the risk, we must seek new ways to involve the public in the decision-making process. Whether we believe in participatory democracy or not, it is a part of our social regulatory fabric. Rather than praise or lament it, we should seek more imaginative ways to involve the various segments of the public affected by the substance at issue. They need to become involved early, and they need to be informed if their participation is to be meaningful. We will be searching for ways to make our participatory process work better.

For this to happen, scientists must be willing to take a larger role in explaining the risks to the public — including the uncertainties inherent in any risk assessment. Shouldering this burden is the responsibility of all scientists, not just those with a particular policy end in mind. In fact, all scientists should make clear when they are speaking as scientists, ex cathedra, and when they are recommending policy they believe should flow from scientific information. What we need to hear more of from scientists is science. I am going to try to provide avenues at EPA for scientists to become more involved in the public dialog in which scientific problems are described. . . .

In sum, my goal is a government-wide process for assessing and managing environmental risks. Achieving this will take cooperation and goodwill within EPA, among Executive Branch agencies, and between Congress and the Administration, a state of affairs that may partake of the miraculous. Still, it is worth trying, and the effort is worth the wholehearted support of the scientific community. I believe such an effort touches on the maintenance of our current society, in which a democratic polity is grounded in a high-technology industrial civilization. Without a much more successful way of handling the risks associated with the creations of science, I fear we will have set up for ourselves a grim and unnecessary choice between the fruits of advanced technology and the blessings of democracy.

Earth First! Advocates Ecotage, 1987

In early summer of 1977, the United States Forest Service began an 18 month-long inventory and evaluation of the remaining roadless and undeveloped areas on the National Forests and Grasslands of the United States. During this second Roadless Area Review and Evaluation (RARE II), the Forest Service identified 2,686 roadless areas of 5,000 acres or more totaling 66 million acres out of the 187 million acres of National Forest lands. Approximately 15 million acres of roadless areas were not included in RARE II because of sloppy inventory procedures or because they had already gone through land use planning after the first RARE program in the early '70s. All in all, there were some 80 million acres on the National Forests in 1977 retaining a significant degree of natural diversity and wildness (a total area equivalent in size to the state of New Mexico or a square 350 × 350 miles).

About the same time as the Forest Service began RARE II, the Bureau of Land Management (BLM) initiated a wilderness inventory as required by the Federal Land Planning and Management Act of 1976 (FLPMA) on the 189 million acres of federal land that they manage in the lower 48 states. In their initial inventory, BLM identified 60 million acres of roadless areas of 5,000 acres or more (a total area approximately the size of Oregon or a square 300 × 300 miles).

Along with the National Parks & Monuments, National Wildlife Refuges, existing Wilderness Areas and some state lands, these Forest Service and BLM roadless areas represent the remaining natural wealth of the United States. They are the remnant of natural diversity after the industrial conquest of the most beautiful, diverse and productive of all the continents of the Earth: North America. Turtle Island.

Only one hundred and fifty years ago, the Great Plains were a vast, waving sea of grass stretching from the Chihuahuan Desert of Mexico to the boreal forest of Canada, from the oak-hickory forests of the Ozarks to the Rocky Mountains. Bison blanketed the plains — it has been estimated that 60 million of the huge, shaggy beasts moved across the grass. Great herds of pronghorn and elk also filled this Pleistocene landscape. Packs of wolves and numerous grizzly bears followed the immense herds.

One hundred and fifty years ago, John James Audubon estimated that there were several *billion* birds in a flock of passenger pigeons that flew past him for several days on the Ohio River. It has been said that a squirrel could travel from the Atlantic seaboard to the Mississippi River without touching the ground, so dense was the deciduous forest of the East.

At the time of the Lewis and Clark Expedition, an estimated 100,000 grizzlies roamed the western half of what is now the United States. The howl of the wolf was ubiquitous. The condor dominated the sky from the Pacific Coast to the Great Plains. Salmon and sturgeon filled the rivers. Ocelots, jaguars,

---

Excerpts from Dave Foreman and Bill Haywood, *Ecodefense*, Tuscon: Ned Ludd Books, 1987, pp. 10–15. Reprinted by permission of Ned Ludd Books.

margay cats and jaguarundis roamed the Texas brush and Southwestern deserts and mesas. Bighorn sheep in great numbers ranged the mountains of the Rockies, Great Basin, Southwest and Pacific Coast. Ivory-billed woodpeckers and Carolina parakeets filled the steamy forests of the Deep South. The land was alive.

East of the Mississippi, giant tulip poplars, chestnuts, oaks, hickories and other trees formed the most diverse temperate deciduous forest in the world. On the Pacific Coast, redwood, hemlock, Douglas fir, spruce, cedar, fir and pine formed the grandest forest on Earth.

In the space of a few generations we have laid waste to paradise. The tall grass prairie has been transformed into a corn factory where wildlife means the exotic pheasant. The short grass prairie is a grid of carefully fenced cow pastures and wheat fields. The passenger pigeon is no more. The last died in the Cincinnati Zoo in 1914. The endless forests of the East are tame woodlots. The only virgin deciduous forest there is in tiny museum pieces of hundreds of acres. Six hundred grizzlies remain and they are going fast. There are only three condors left in the wild and they are scheduled for capture and imprisonment in the Los Angeles Zoo. Except in northern Minnesota and Isle Royale, wolves are known merely as scattered individuals drifting across the Canadian and Mexican borders (a pack has recently formed in Glacier National Park). Four percent of the peerless Redwood Forest remains and the monumental old growth forest cathedrals of Oregon are all but gone. The tropical cats have been shot and poisoned from our southwestern borderlands. The subtropical Eden of Florida has been transformed into hotels and citrus orchards. Domestic cattle have grazed bare and radically altered the composition of the grassland communities of the West, displacing elk, moose, bighorn sheep and pronghorn and leading to the virtual extermination of grizzly, wolf, cougar, bobcat and other "varmints." Dams choke the rivers and streams of the land.

Nonetheless, wildness and natural diversity remain. There are a few scattered grasslands ungrazed, stretches of free-flowing river undammed and undiverted, thousand-year-old forests, Eastern woodlands growing back to forest and reclaiming past roads, grizzlies and wolves and lions and wolverines and bighorn and moose roaming the backcountry; hundreds of square miles that have never known the imprint of a tire, the bite of a drill, the rip of a 'dozer, the cut of a saw, the smell of gasoline.

These are the places that hold North America together, that contain the genetic information of life, that represent sanity in a whirlwind of madness.

In January of 1979, the Forest Service announced the results of RARE II: of the 80 million acres of undeveloped lands on the National Forests, only 15 million acres were recommended for protection against logging, road building and other "developments." In the big tree state of Oregon, for example, only 370,000 acres were proposed for Wilderness protection out of 4.5 million acres of roadless, uncut forest lands. Of the areas nationally slated for protection, most were too high, too dry, too cold, too steep to offer much in the way of "resources" to the loggers, miners and graziers. Those roadless areas with critical old growth forest values were allocated for the sawmill. Important grizzly habitat in the Northern Rockies was tossed to the oil industry and the loggers. Off-road-vehicle fanatics and the landed gentry of the livestock industry won out in the Southwest and Great Basin.

During the early 1980s, the Forest Service developed its DARN (Development Activities in Roadless Non-selected) list outlining specific projects in specific roadless areas. The implication of DARN is staggering. It is evidence that the leadership of the United States Forest Service consciously and deliberately sat down and asked themselves, "How can we keep from being plagued by conservationists and their damned wilderness proposals? How can we insure that we'll never have to do another RARE?" Their solution was simple and brilliant: get rid of the roadless areas. DARN outlines *nine thousand* miles of road, one and a half million acres of timber cuts, seven million acres of oil and gas leases in National Forest RARE II areas by 1987. In most cases, the damaged acreage will be far greater than the acreage stated because roads are designed to split areas in half and timber sales are engineered to take place in the center of roadless areas, thereby devastating the biological integrity of the entire area. The great roadless areas so critical to the maintenance of natural diversity will soon be gone. Species dependent upon old growth and large wild areas will be shoved to the brink of extinction.

But the situation on the National Forests is even worse than DARN indicated. After a careful review of Forest Service documents, Howie Wolke reported in the June 21, 1985, issue of *Earth First!* that more than 75,000 miles of road are proposed for construction in currently roadless areas on the National Forests over the next fifteen years. This immense road network (enough to encircle the planet three times) will cost the American taxpayer over 3 billion dollars to provide large timber corporations access to a mere 500 million dollars worth of timber.

The BLM wilderness review has been a similar process of attrition. It is unlikely that more than 9 million acres will be recommended for Wilderness out of the 60 million with which the review began. Again, it is the more spectacular but biologically less rich areas that will be proposed for protection.

During 1984, Congress passed legislation designating minimal National Forest Wilderness acreages for most states (generally only slightly larger than the pitiful RARE II recommendations and concentrating on "rocks and ice" instead of crucial forested lands). In the next few years, similar picayune legislation for National Forest Wilderness in the remaining states and for BLM Wilderness will probably be enacted. The other roadless areas will be eliminated from consideration. National Forest Management Plans emphasizing industrial logging, grazing, mineral and energy development, road building, and motorized recreation will be implemented. Conventional means of protecting these millions of acres of wild country will largely dissipate. Judicial and administrative appeals for their protection will be closed off. Congress will turn a deaf ear to requests for additional Wilderness so soon after disposing of the thorny issue. The effectiveness of conventional political lobbying by conservation groups to protect endangered wild lands will evaporate. And in half a decade, the saw, 'dozer and drill will devastate most of what is unprotected. The battle for wilderness will be over. Perhaps 3% of the United States will be more or less protected and it will be open season on the rest. Unless. . . .

Many of the projects that will destroy roadless areas are economically marginal. It is costly for the Forest Service, BLM, timber companies, oil companies, mining companies and others to scratch out the "resources" in these last wild areas. It is expensive to maintain the necessary infrastructure of roads for the exploitation of wild lands. The cost of repairs, the hassle, the delay, the down-time may just be too much for the bureaucrats and exploiters to accept if there is a widely-dispersed, unorganized, *strategic* movement of resistance across the land.

It is time for women and men, individually and in small groups, to act heroically and admittedly illegally in defense of the wild, to put a monkey-wrench into the gears of the machine destroying natural diversity. This strategic monkeywrenching can be safe, it can be easy, it can be fun, and — most importantly — it can be effective in stopping timber cutting, road building, overgrazing, oil & gas exploration, mining, dam building, powerline construction, off-road-vehicle use, trapping, ski area development and other forms of destruction of the wilderness, as well as cancerous suburban sprawl.

But it must be strategic, it must be thoughtful, it must be deliberate in order to succeed. Such a campaign of resistance would follow these principles:

• MONKEYWRENCHING IS NON-VIOLENT

Monkeywrenching is non-violent resistance to the destruction of natural diversity and wilderness. It is not directed toward harming human beings or other forms of life. It is aimed at inanimate machines and tools. Care is always taken to minimize any possible threat to other people (and to the monkey-wrenchers themselves).

• MONKEYWRENCHING IS NOT ORGANIZED

There can be no central direction or organization to monkeywrenching. Any type of network would invite infiltration, *agents provocateurs* and repression. It is truly individual action. Because of this, communication among monkeywrenchers is difficult and dangerous. Anonymous discussion . . . through the Dear Ned Ludd section of the *Earth First! Journal* seems to be the safest avenue of communication to refine techniques, security procedures and strategy.

• MONKEYWRENCHING IS INDIVIDUAL

Monkeywrenching is done by individuals or very small groups of people who have known each other for years. There is trust and a good working relationship in such groups. The more people involved, the greater are the dangers of infiltration or a loose mouth. Earth defenders avoid working with people they haven't known for a long time, those who can't keep their mouths closed, and those with grandiose or violent ideas (they may be police agents or dangerous crackpots).

• MONKEYWRENCHING IS TARGETED

Ecodefenders pick their targets. Mindless, erratic vandalism is counter-productive. Monkeywrenchers know that they do not stop a specific logging sale by destroying any piece of logging equipment which they come across. They make sure it belongs to the proper culprit. They ask themselves what is the most vulnerable point of a wilderness-destroying project and strike there. Senseless vandalism leads to loss of popular sympathy.

• MONKEYWRENCHING IS TIMELY

There is a proper time and place for monkeywrenching. There are also times when monkeywrenching may be counterproductive. Monkeywrenchers generally should not act when there is a non-violent civil disobedience action (a blockade, etc.) taking place against the opposed project. Monkeywrenching may cloud the issue of direct action and the blockaders could be blamed for the ecotage and be put in danger from the work crew or police. Blockades and monkeywrenching usually do not mix. Monkeywrenching may also not be appropriate when delicate political negotiations are taking place for the protection of a certain area. There are, of course, exceptions to this rule. The Earth warrior always thinks: Will monkeywrenching help or hinder the protection of this place?

A Business Leader on Industry's Environmental Responsibilities, 1987

[Let us] take an objective look at the history of environmental issues . . . and take stock of our situation today.

Look back 20 years, and I think it can be stated as a fact that our society *needed* environmental regulation. I don't think the roof will fall in if we acknowledge that.

Increased pollution of all types was a direct by-product of the population boom and the great surge in U.S. industrial activity that followed World War II.

Communities and ecosystems need protection from that pollution . . . and it's unlikely that industry would have cleaned up without some legal imperative to do so.

That's no slur on the ethics of industry. The company that makes such expenditures unilaterally is courting financial disaster. When controls are mandatory, all players have more or less the same handicap.

The point is that industry must accept responsibility for the problems that can be legitimately laid at our doorstep . . . past or present . . . and we must acknowledge that, in a general sense, regulation to protect the environment has been necessary.

By the same token, industry deserves . . . and seldom receives . . . a large share of the credit for developing the technology to reduce wastes and control pollution.

As a nation, we have made tremendous progress in cleaning up the environment . . . and that, too, should be acknowledged. Pollution of all types has been significantly reduced . . . even as industrial activity has greatly increased.

There's an excellent example. . . . We read a lot about the problems of the San Francisco Bay; but the fact is that despite tremendous growth in

Excerpts from G. M. Keller, "Industry and the Environment," *Vital Speeches of the Day*, No. 9, December 15, 1987, pp. 78–80. Reprinted by permission of City News Inc.

population . . . as well as . . . the potential sources of pollution . . . the Bay today is far cleaner than it was in the 1960s.

Industry's record is particularly impressive. The Bay Area Regional Water Quality Control Board, in testimony before Congress, compared industrial discharges of 1960 to those of 1985. They found that the total volume of industrial wastes had been cut by about 75 percent in that period . . . and major types of conventional pollution reduced by more than 90 percent.

We need to get this kind of information across to the public . . . not as a way of saying "We've done enough" . . . "Everything is solved." But just as a way of illustrating that the situation is *not* out of hand . . . we *are* making progress . . . and we will *continue* to find solutions.

We also need to make the point that our search for solutions represents a true commitment . . . not merely an obligation. Our personal values are not really different from those of the general public. As individuals, we too want a safe and wholesome environment. . . .

Administrators of the Environmental Protection Agency have been trying to sell the notion of scientific risk assessment for the last four or five years now. Unfortunately, it's been a very tough sell.

The basic problem seems to be that a significant part of the general public seems to feel that all chemicals are risky . . . and no risks are acceptable.

It's certainly true that our ability to detect infinitesimal quantities of many substances has run far ahead of our knowledge of what those measurements really *mean*.

The popular assumption . . . and too often one played up for political purposes . . . is that *any* detectable impurities have to be harmful . . . that if we can measure it, we ought to get rid of it.

Ironically, one of the truths about our environment . . . emerging from the work of scientists like Dr. Bruce Ames at [The University of California] . . . is that all sorts of fearsome substances occur in nature. We human beings have been living with them throughout our evolution. In large quantities, they can hurt us . . . but in smaller concentrations, they are a part of nature itself . . . and we tolerate many of them without apparent harm.

The point is not that we can afford to be complacent . . . or ignore toxics in our environment. It's simply that we should base our environmental policies on *facts*.

Is compound x at exposure level y for duration z harmful or not? That's a scientific question. Let science try to answer it . . . and let our elected officials *listen* to the answer.

In essence, that's all that risk assessment means. We in industry have to help our neighbors understand that this is the best way . . . maybe the only way . . . of finding out what problems we need to address.

As a step in that direction, I'd like to announce today that Chevron is pledging $1 million over the next several years to support environmental risk assessment research at top universities around the nation.

Our objective is to help stimulate programs that will draw talented people into this field, support them in developing and improving the methodologies for this emerging discipline and . . . ultimately . . . to build a base of scientific knowledge that will help *all* of us better understand the true risks involved in toxics.

We want our contribution to have a direct and *practical* benefit for the public. We hope that the information base will be used by industry, environmental groups and government officials alike in choosing the best route to environmental protection.

A Conservationist Summarizes the State of the Environment, 1987

As the United States approaches the 1990s, two factors above all characterize the state of affairs in environmental policy:

• First, the country faces an array of environmental problems even more daunting than pollution crises of the past generation.

• Second, current policies and institutions, having addressed the easiest matters, seem increasingly unable to deal with these emerging problems. . . .

To be sure, the United States does not now face an environmental crisis. Progress continues in abating some kinds of pollution problems in some places, and in the short haul no impending disasters can be predicted from a failure to address any of the lengthy list of environmental issues. Looming ahead, however, is a set of complex, diffuse, long-term environmental problems portending immense consequences for the economic well-being and security of nations throughout the world, including our own. These problems challenge our country's leadership to establish a new course for U.S. environmental policy at home and abroad. . . .

The Conservation Foundation's . . . *State of the Environment* reports . . . [document] continuing progress over nearly two decades in improving some aspects of environmental quality. Levels of particulates, sulfur dioxide, nitrogen dioxide, and other air pollutants, for example, are trending downward in comparison with levels that were prevalent a decade or more ago. While ozone levels also seem to be dropping, this pollutant remains especially difficult to control; it is anticipated that many communities will not achieve compliance with federal health-based standards for exposure to ozone by the end of 1987, as the law requires. Millions of Americans are affected.

In water quality, too, there are some signs of improvement. Monitoring indicates that levels of fecal coliform and dissolved oxygen are decreasing in some bodies of water. People are swimming and fishing in rivers that once presented hazards to health. Some signs of improved quality are appearing in the Great Lakes — especially Lake Erie, once virtually written off as a dying body of water.

Toxic wastes released into the air or water or disposed of on land still present health and environmental risks, but at least some consideration is now being given to the effects of *new* chemicals *before* they enter commerce. In the

Excerpts reprinted with permission from *State of the Environment: A View Toward the Nineties*, by the Conservation Foundation (now World Wildlife Fund), Washington, DC 1987), pp. xxxix–xlvii.

natural resource area, substantial amounts of land have been protected in parks, wilderness areas, and wildlife refuges. For some endangered wildlife — the whooping crane and the peregrine falcon, for example — the threat of extinction has diminished.

In other words, determined actions to improve environmental quality during the 17 years since Earth Day have yielded positive results. . . .

Also encouraging is the fact that many of the worst effects of the minimalist federal environmental policies prevalent in the early 1980s have been reversed. Integrity and good management have been restored at the U.S. Environmental Protection Agency (EPA). The rhetoric of confrontation, so prevalent during the early Reagan years, has softened somewhat. The State Department's Agency for International Development has taken an active role in U.S. efforts to protect the environment of developing countries. Under U.S. government pressure and new leadership, the World Bank, too, has taken major steps to improve its environmental performance in the developing world. . . . Notwithstanding evident progress, the need for environmental action is at least as great as it has ever been.

The following examples suggest the range of problems and the difficulties in fashioning and implementing responses.

• *Although current air quality programs have helped clean the air in the vicinity of emission sources, many pollutants escape and are carried much longer distances in the upper atmosphere than previously thought, before they fall to earth.* Acid rain is the most publicized example. Another instance is the large amount of toxic chemicals, like PCBs in the Great Lakes, that come from pollution settling out of the air. . . .

• *Indoor air pollution is another serious problem current programs do not address.* Most people spend most of their time indoors, and pollutants inside are found in much higher concentrations than levels outside. One source, smoking, is notoriously difficult to curb. Other sources of indoor pollutants, such as materials or building systems widely used in new construction throughout the country, may not have ready substitutes. . . .

• *Growing conflicts surround the allocation of fresh water supplies.* Especially in the West, state water allocation systems established in the last century have allocated all the available water, and then some, to uses such as irrigation, ranching, and mining. Today, as values are changing, Indian tribes, urban populations, and others are asserting new claims on fresh water for recreation, industrial expansion, and preservation of aquatic environments. . . .

• *Groundwater is becoming increasingly contaminated.* About half the population depends on unseen groundwater resources for drinking water. Hundreds of thousands of Americans at one time or another have had to switch to bottled water. Experience has demonstrated that it is usually far less costly and far less complicated to protect groundwater from contamination than to clean up polluted supplies later. . . .

• *The review and reregistration of approximately 600 basic pesticide ingredients in use in this country are far behind where they should be.* Although this process was mandated in legislation in 1972, EPA estimates that it may take well into the next century to complete the job. In the meantime, environmental experts cite potential threats from pesticides as among the most important risks to public health and the environment.

• *After eight years and $1.5 billion, the Superfund program to clean up toxic waste dumps has yielded disappointing results.* Distressingly little is known about how many toxic waste sites there are and how serious a risk each poses. No one has yet satisfactorily determined the standards to which sites should be cleaned, and the prospects of having agreement on these standards in any reasonable time are dim. . . .

• *Degradation of wildlife refuges and national parklands continues.* More and more, the country's wildlife refuges and national parklands are threatened by energy, commercial, and other developments outside their borders. These developments not only diminish the visual and recreational amenities that parks and refuges provide to many millions of visitors each year, but also threaten the very survival of wildlife and undermine other natural and cultural resources these parks and refuges were established, at least in part, to protect. . . .

• *Soil erosion continues at rates that are unacceptably high in the long term if the nation's farmlands are to continue supporting high levels of agricultural production.* An estimated 106 million acres (or 25 percent of U.S. cropland) exceed the average tolerable erosion levels each year. One especially costly dimension of this problem is the variety of problems caused by eroding soils when they leave the farm: for example, waterways polluted by pesticides and fertilizers carried off by erosion; reservoirs and harbors that silt up faster than predicted; recreational opportunities and wildlife habitat that are lost. . . .

• *Long after their values for flood control and fish and wildlife enhancement have been established, wetlands continue to be lost at a rapid rate.* With 50 percent of the nation's original endowment of wetlands now gone, draining, flooding, filling, cultivation, and development continue to destroy an estimated 300,000 to 500,000 acres per year. Some 80 percent of these losses have been attributable to agriculture. . . .

• *After decades of environmental action by federal, state, and local governments and by citizen groups across the country, degradation of the American landscape is proceeding unchecked.* A steady, perceptible degradation of the countryside from urban sprawl and haphazard development continues to erode the distinctive qualities that differentiate one place from another. No national plan, no federal agency, can orchestrate protection of what Americans value about their communities. . . . These examples hardly exhaust the list of problems. Carbon dioxide buildup in the atmosphere and the projected, accompanying climate change; depletion of the protective ozone shield; the loss of biological diversity; waste of energy; disposal of nuclear wastes; pollution at public facilities; loss of historic structures; threats to continuing productivity of national forests and rangeland; controversy surrounding the use of Alaska's abundant natural resources and the designation of wilderness areas there and in the continental United States; industrial and chemical accidents — these are but a few of the dozens of issues that require urgent attention. . . .

Many of today's environmental problems defy traditional categorization. Acid rain, global climate change, groundwater pollution, toxic substances, hazardous waste—none of these problems fits into the way pollution control programs have been conceived in the past. . . . Setting priorities, however, requires consideration not only of environmental effects but also of factors such as feasibility and costs of curbing problems, and this could generate substantial conflict as various interests in Congress, EPA, and the public argue over what should be the priorities.

Regardless of the controversy, however, public consideration of a new approach to environmental protection is essential. Merely patching up current policies and institutions, helpful as it might be in the short term, simply will not be adequate for the country in the long term. Fundamental changes in concepts, in laws, and in the organizational structure of legislative and executive branch activities are essential if further progress is to be made on long-standing environmental issues and newly recognized ones alike.

A Biologist Warns of a Global Ecological Crisis, 1987

The world that provides our evolutionary and ecological context is in trouble—trouble serious enough to demand our urgent attention. The large-scale problems of overpopulation and overdevelopment are eradicating the lands and organisms that sustain life on this planet. If we can solve these problems, we can lay the foundation for peace and prosperity in the future. By ignoring these issues, drifting passively while attending to what seem more urgent, personal priorities, we are courting disaster.

We live in a world where far more people are well fed, clothed, and housed than ever before. We also live in a world in which up to 100,000 people starve to death every day, in which we consume well over a third of total terrestrial photosynthetic productivity, and in which human activity threatens to eliminate nearly a quarter of those organisms we do not consume, yet upon which our civilization is almost completely dependent for survival. Their permanent loss limits the options available to our children and grandchildren. . . .

The earth's population, which passed the 5 billion mark for the first time this year, is growing at an estimated annual rate of 1.7 percent. This is an ecological force without precedent. Our numbers have doubled since 1950. If present trends continue, the population will double again in approximately 40 years.

There are several profound indicators of the danger this trend presents to the global ecosystem: We consume, co-opt or forego about 40 percent of the total terrestrial photosynthetic productivity. At the same time, regional climatic problems are becoming increasingly apparent. How will we respond to these threats? And why should they concern people living in the relative comfort of the United States?

Excerpts from Peter Raven, "The Global Ecosystem in Crisis," A MacArthur Foundation Occasional Paper, Chicago, Ill: The John D. and Catherine T. MacArthur Foundation, December 1987. Reprinted by permission of the MacArthur Foundation.

The Tropics: Center of Ecological Loss

Many of our most serious problems are centered in the tropics, where biological diversity is concentrated and where whole ecosystems are being permanently disrupted. Three factors influence this destruction: (1) the explosive growth of human populations; (2) widespread and extreme poverty; and (3) ignorance of modern methods of agriculture and forestry.

Population Growth.   As recently as 1950, about 45 percent of the world's 2.5 billion people lived in countries that lie wholly or partly in the tropics. Today, that figure has grown to 55 percent of a global population of more than 5 billion. If present trends continue, nearly two-thirds of the people in the world will be living in these countries (excluding China) by the year 2020. The 1.1 billion people who inhabited the tropics and semi-tropics 36 years ago will grow to about 5 billion people in another 34 years — a quadrupling of the total in just 70 years.

Conversely, the proportion of the population living in developed, industrial nations is falling drastically. For each of us living in countries similar to the United States in 1950, there were approximately two other people living elsewhere; by 2020, that ratio will grow to 5:1.

Widespread Poverty.   The rapidly growing populations of tropical countries include large numbers of poor people. In 1986, for example, the per capita gross national product in the United States was estimated at $14,080; in neighboring Mexico, it was $2,180; in Honduras, $670. Overall, the industrial nations, with less than one quarter of the global population, control about 80 percent of the world's wealth. The largely tropical developing countries, with 54 percent of the population, control about 15 percent of the wealth.

In Africa and Latin America, per capita income continues to decline steadily. Within tropical countries, about one billion of an estimated 2.7 billion people live in absolute poverty. They are unable to count on adequate food, shelter and clothing from one day to the next. Between 300 and 400 million of these people consume a daily diet that provides less than 80 percent of the minimum standards recommended by the United Nations, a diet that can stunt growth and lead to serious health risks. . . .

Ignorance of Productive Farming and Forestry Methods.   In addition to large populations and extensive poverty, tropical countries suffer both from a lack of knowledge of modern farming and forestry procedures and from an unwillingness to apply those methods that are known. Consequently, the natural vegetation in these areas is often consumed as if it were a renewable resource.

Many tropical soils are relatively poor and require careful handling. In the natural ecosystems that develop on such soils, most of the nutrients, except for phosphorus and nitrogen, are held primarily in the vegetation. Cutting and burning the trees release these nutrients to the soil, fertilizing the soil and allowing the temporary cultivation of crops. These excess soil nutrients usually are exhausted within a few years, and the land must be given time to recover.

Some traditional cultivation systems for relatively infertile soils combine trees, which are usually more productive than herbaceous crops, with other plants. Agro-forestry systems of this sort will be increasingly important in meeting the needs of the tropics. Relatively fertile soils must be cultivated intensively by the best methods available, with the most suitable crops. Farmers should be encouraged to implement more productive farming methods through loans for fertilizers, credit for seeds, market information, and the like.

Decline of Tropical Forests

Based on 1981 estimates by the Food and Agriculture Organization of the United Nations (FAO), approximately 2.3 million square miles of tropical evergreen forest now exist. This forest is roughly three-quarters the size of the United States exclusive of Alaska—about half the size of the original forest area. In the late 1970s, at least 40,000 square miles of such forest were being cut each year. If that rate of clear-cutting continues, the world's tropical forests will last about 60 years—assuming no population growth or other pressures.

The decline in tropical forests is due, in part, to consumer demand in industrialized countries. For example, the United States obtains much of its timber from tropical forests. Each year, logging removes about 20,000 square miles of these forests—an area nearly the size of West Virginia. Meanwhile, reforestation is proceeding very slowly in the tropics. Ten trees are cut for each one planted; in Africa, 29 are cut for each one planted. The developed world's consumption of tropical hardwoods has risen 15 times since 1950; consumption in tropical countries has increased only three times. . . .

Impact: On the Global Economy

The destruction of natural resources in the tropics and subtropics is intimately related to the global economy, which is rapidly driving up the export of cash crops from many tropical regions. Often, the result is the displacement of poor farmers, who are forced to farm less suitable lands and destroy the forests located on those lands. This trend has been evident in the Sahel, for example, which exports massive amounts of peanuts and cotton to Europe, and in Thailand, which exports huge quantities of cassava.

But perhaps the most significant economic factor is the international debt, which has had a major impact on relationships among developing and industrial countries in the 1980s. In 1970, the external debt of Third World countries was about $72 billion. Today, it is approximately $1 trillion. A debt of this magnitude clearly encourages many Third World countries to overexploit their natural resources, without creating stable, productive alternatives. Logging restrictions are eased, more forest is destroyed, poor farmers are displaced to regions that will not support them over the long term, and the production of foods for an already malnourished population is decreased in favor of the production of export crops. Austerity measures associated with these economic trends can throw large numbers of people out of work, thus compounding the poverty. . . .

Impact: On the World Climate

Another major problem is the effect of tropical deforestation on the global climate. Deforestation clearly contributes substantially to the amount of carbon dioxide in the atmosphere, an issue of increasing concern. Widespread deforestation also impairs the capacity of some tropical systems to recycle inland rainfall, as has been demonstrated in the Amazon. The same phenomenon also may be related to the past 20 years of drought in Africa. Erosion and soil deterioration that accompany deforestation exacerbate the problems.

Recent findings suggest that the climatic consequences of widespread deforestation may be even more devastating than originally predicted. At the American Geophysical Union's 1986 annual meeting, it was reported that cutting South American evergreen forests would precipitate a regional temperature rise of three to five degrees Centigrade. This would extend the dry season, speed the deterioration of the remaining forests, including reserves, and greatly disrupt agriculture. One can only hazard a guess at the impact such major changes will have on areas beyond the regions directly affected.

Impact: On the African Continent

To date, the effects of forest destruction and climatic change have been most severe in sub-Saharan Africa. Per capita food production in this area has dropped 20 percent since 1960. The FAO [Food and Agricultural Organization of the United Nations] projects that food production will drop another 30 percent over the next 25 years, with population growth greatly exceeding growth in food production. Right now, the majority of people living in the area have too little to eat. Their collective international debt, roughly $200 billion, equals 44 percent of gross domestic product, or 190 percent of export earnings. . . .

Prognosis for the Future

A new kind of global thinking is necessary to manage the world ecosystem properly for the enormous human populations of the future. We now use directly, forego or convert about 40 percent of global terrestrial photosynthetic productivity. This is projected to double in the next 41 years. Ecological stability everywhere is in the interests of all. Yet we are doing relatively little to promote it.

Sustainable agriculture and forestry systems must be developed in every country. When nations are stable and self-sufficient, they can import and export products, repay debts, provide a decent standard of living for their people, improve their governments, and preserve their biological diversity. When they are unstable and dependent, they cannot afford imports, can organize exports only with difficulty, will default on debts, cannot provide for their people (who then may emigrate in large numbers), will tend to have unsuitable and unstable governments, and will squander their biological diversity for limited short-term gain.

The international debt presents a real obstacle to achieving ecological and political stability. In 1985, the $22 billion paid by poor, developing countries to rich, industrial countries contributed substantially to global instability. Payments on this debt should be mitigated or suspended when necessary, or managed in such a way as to add to, rather than to detract from, world stability. . . .

Awareness as a Solution

In more general terms, the key to an orderly management of the ecosystems that support us all lies in an awareness of and compassion for all life—in an appreciation of the fact that we are all part of a living world that is capable, in its full development, of capturing energy from the sun and making it available for the life processes of living organisms.

We cannot avoid profoundly modifying the global biosphere, and in fact have already done so. Nevertheless, we should not respond only when the crises we have caused are so extensive that they threaten our very lives. To do so is to be thoroughly immoral in the fullest meaning of that term.

Carl Anthony Explains Why African-Americans Should Be Environmentalists, 1990

When Martin Luther King Jr. decided to raise his voice in opposition to the war in Vietnam, many of his friends, as well as his critics, told him he ought to stick to domestic issues. He should concentrate on securing civil rights of African Americans in the South and leave foreign policy to the professionals who knew best. But King decided to oppose the war because he knew it was morally wrong and because he understood the link between the brutal exploitation and destruction of the Vietnamese people and the struggle of African Americans and others for justice and freedom in our own land.

Today, African American leadership and the African American community face a similar situation. Every day the newspapers carry stories about the changing atmosphere and climate, threats to the world's water supply, threats to the biodiversity of the rainforest, and the population crisis in poor nations that are growing too fast to be supported by the carrying capacity of their lands. Can we afford to view the social and economic problems of African American communities in isolation from these global trends?

Excerpts from Carl Anthony, "Why African-Americans Should Be Environmentalists," *Earth Island Journal* (Winter 1990), pp. 43–4. Reprinted with permission of the author.

African Americans could benefit from expanding their vision to include greater environmental awareness. For example, a recent study of the deteriorating conditions within the African American community termed young African American males in America "an endangered species." "This description applies, in a metaphorical sense, to the current status of young African American males in contemporary society," writes Jewelle Taylor Gibbs. Her study . . . present[s] a comprehensive interdisciplinary perspective of the social and economic problems of these young people, providing valuable statistics on high school dropout rates, work skills and attitudes, unemployment, robbery, rape, homicide and aggravated assault, drug addiction as well as teenage parenthood. But Gibbs makes no mention of the utter alienation of these young people from the natural environment, which is, after all, the source of Earth's abundance and well-being. The loss of this contact with living and growing things, even rudimentary knowledge of where food and water comes from, must present serious consequences that we, as yet, have no way of measuring.

The study said nothing of the difficult days ahead as American society seeks to make the transition from its current levels of consumption of resources to the more sustainable patterns of the future. Developing an environmental perspective within the African American community could help smooth this transition in several ways:

• by promoting greater understanding of the productive assets of society, including land, water and natural resources,

• by strengthening collaboration with groups seeking to redirect public investment and economic development away from wasteful exploitation of nature toward urban restoration and meeting basic human needs,

• by gaining access to information and resources which enhance the potential of community survival,

• by developing new knowledge and skills to be shared by groups of people who live in the city,

• by strengthening social and political organization and creating new opportunities for leadership within the community.

Environmental organizations in the United States should also modify recruitment efforts in order to expand their constituency to include African Americans and members of other minority groups as participants in shaping and building public support for environmental policies. With the exception of limited collaboration between environmentalists and Native American groups, as well as anti-toxics campaigns, there has been little communication between environmentalists and non-European minority groups in the US. Critical issues — such as population control, limiting human intervention in the ecosystem, or rebuilding our cities in balance with nature — have been discussed almost entirely from a European and often elitist perspective. . . .

The principle of social justice, however, must be at the heart of any effort aimed at bringing African Americans into the mainstream of environmental organizations in the United States. Such a vision must offer a real alternative to a view of the tropical rainforest as an inviolate preserve or a private laboratory for multinational pharmaceutical companies, ignoring the needs of indigenous populations. While recognizing limits to growth, it must avoid misuse of environmental information as a way of rationalizing the economic status quo. It must not misuse concern for endangered species as a way of diluting our responsibility to meet basic needs for human health care, food and shelter. It cannot manipulate terms so that the legitimate need for population control becomes a code word for preserving racial dominance and purity.

Environmental protection must be understood as intimately connected to efforts to eradicate injustice. Solutions must offer a practical guide for goals which can be accomplished in the short run as we seek a path toward a more sustainable future. Environmental organizations can no longer afford to take the view that they are unconcerned about who benefits and who loses from restrictions on economic growth. Shifting resources away from projects which are damaging to the ecosystem toward programs and projects which meet basic human needs must become the highest priority for the environmental movement. In the United States, organizations such as the National Association for the Advancement of Colored People and the Urban League have a real stake in these outcomes. They should be part of the environmental dialogue. New organizations dealing explicitly with urban habitat are needed. . . .

The American inner-city was once a wilderness. Today, islands, estuaries, forests, and riparian habitats that once existed in these locations have been replaced by asphalt, concrete, barbed wire fences, boarded-up stores, crack houses, abandoned factories, landfills and pollution. After generations of isolation and manipulation, the people who live in these places rarely remember what it once was—or speculate on what it might become.

Isolation of African Americans from stewardship of the environment has deep historic roots. It is hard to keep the faith. The African American population migrated to the cities to escape the four centuries of exploitation on the plantations, crop farms and in the coal mines of the South. Displacement from rural countryside is parallel to similar experiences in the Third World. Understanding of these experiences, however painful, is an important resource as we seek a path towards sustainable development. . . .

In order to meet responsibilities for citizenship, African Americans must have opportunities and learn to play a greater role in formulating environmental policies which affect all members of the community. We must find new ways to bridge the gap between environmental advocates and African American communities.

Some of the means to achieve this goal might include:

• Presentations to groups with sustainable memberships by existing environmental organizations and individual resource persons.

• Outreach programs by environmental organizations to promote active learning and exposure to the wilderness experience by minority youth.

• Networks among minority-based organizations, environmental groups, public schools, community colleges and institutions of higher learning in order to expand educational opportunities for minorities in environmental science and related fields.

• Working specifically with inner-city organizations fighting drug abuse to develop environmentally-related projects and therapeutic settings such as tree planting, restoration, urban farming, horticulture therapy, international exchanges, etc.

• Strengthening neighborhood-initiated efforts at law enforcement, prevention and treatment of drug abuse.

• Legislative initiatives linking inner-city needs and environmental projects.

There are some hopeful signs. Environmental concerns of minority groups are already an integral part of the planning [processes in several cities].

Winona LaDuke on Indians' Place in the Ecosystem, 1990

I want to talk about something from our own culture which is the Anishinabe culture, the Algonquin culture. We have an economic system, a whole value system, and part of that value system — part of our whole way of living — is a concept called *reciprocity*.

When I go out and I harvest wild rice up on our lakes in Northern Minnesota, on our reservation, I bring tobacco, *saymah*, and I put the tobacco out. I make an offering when I go out to harvest, and then I collect different things from the land. We do the same thing when we go out hunting — when we go out hunting, whether it's for *wapsh* or *atuk*, rabbit or deer, all the different parts of the creation, we give something in order to get something back from the creation. We have a reciprocal agreement, and this confirms our relationship to the creation — we're a part, an integral part of the creation. We're an integral part of the ecosystem in our areas. Reciprocity is an essential part of our value system, which is very contrary to the industrial value system and the industrial society in the United States. . . .

The tendency in the environmental movement (and the tendency generally) is not to look in a holistic manner at the future, and we need to get away from that. We need to look at things like cultural diversity and not just biological diversity. We don't just need places in the Amazon where the toucan and the jaguar can live. We need places where the Yanomama can live. Where the Kayapo can live, where the Ache can live. All of those indigenous people are integral parts of their ecosystem.

We also need places where the Inishinabe can live, where the Yurok can live, where the Dakota and the Dene can live. *We* are an integral part of the ecosystem just as anything else. Since 1900, a tenth of the forest in the Amazon has disappeared, but *one indigenous nation per year has disappeared* in the Brazilian Amazon. One-third of all groups — 90 out of 270 — have entirely disappeared from the Brazilian Amazon. Corporations cannot get to the forest unless they get rid of the people.

We need to look at a broader context of issues and we need to relearn how to think. Industrial society teaches people to compartmentalize, and many of us

Excerpts from "The Struggle for Cultural Diversity," by Winona LaDuke, in *Race, Poverty, and the Environment* 1, no. 2 (July 1990), 1, 12–13.

are beginning to resist that and look at things in a holistic manner. All of the issues are of course totally related. . . .

We have to look at the bigger picture. It is cultural diversity as well as biological diversity. . . . We need to look at things like industrial law versus natural law. In our experience, natural law looks more to the long term. And when we look to the new society, and the new way of living here, we have to look toward natural law as something that makes sense for all of us. We all have to change how people think in this society. We all have access to power at different levels and in different places — the people who read this have access to power. We need to use it. We need to use it to struggle, and we need to use it to change how people think.

We need to use it to make structural change in society. We are rich in North America because other people are poor. That is how society functions, how society works, and that is what we must change. The concept of reciprocity is critical in our culture, and we are asking you as people of conscience to embrace it. I don't associate the industrial society with a color, I associate it with a value system.

People who have lighter skin pigmentation tend to have more power and access to ways to struggle in this society. And what may be surprising to you is that although Indian people in a lot of communities may be poor, almost every day Indian people pray for white people. In our language we have to pray for everything, and I guess that's how we give back what we can in our reciprocal agreement. Because we can't necessarily do the same things in Congress that you can do, but we can pray. *Megwitch.*

Two Feminists Discuss the Emergence of Ecofeminism, 1990

Today, more than twenty-five years after Rachel Carson's *Silent Spring* first raised a passionate voice of conscience in protest against the pollution and degradation of nature, an ecofeminist movement is emerging globally as a major catalyst of ethical, political, social, and creative change. Although Carson was not an avowed feminist, many would argue that it was not coincidental that a woman was the first to respond both emotionally and scientifically to the wanton human domination of the natural world. Carson's 1962 text prefigured a powerful environmental movement that culminated in the nationwide Earth Day of 1970, but the notion that the collective voices of women should be central to the greening of the Earth did not blossom until the mid to late 1970s.

Ecofeminism is a term that some use to describe both the diverse range of women's efforts to save the Earth and the transformations of feminism in the West that have resulted from the new view of women and nature. With the birth

Excerpts from Irene Diamond and Gloria Orenstein, eds., *Reweaving the World: The Emergence of Ecofeminism*, Sierra Club Books, 1990, pp. ix–xii. Reprinted with permission of Sierra Club Books.

of the Women's Movement in the late 1960s, feminists dismantled the iron grip of biological determinism that had been used historically to justify men's control over women. Feminists argued that social arrangements deemed to be timeless and natural had actually been constructed to validate male superiority and privilege. They asserted that women had the right to be full and equal participants in the making of culture. In this process writers and scholars documented the historical association between women and nature, insisting that women would not be free until the connections between women and the natural world were severed.

But as the decade advanced and as women began to revalue women's cultures and practices, especially in the face of the twin threats of nuclear annihilation and ecocide, many women began to understand how the larger culture's devaluation of natural processes was a product of masculine consciousness. Writers as diverse as Mary Daly, Elizabeth Dodson Gray, Susan Griffin, Carolyn Merchant, Maria Mies, Vandana Shiva, Luisah Teish, and Alice Walker demonstrated that this masculine consciousness denigrated and manipulated everything defined as "other" whether nature, women, or Third World cultures. In the industrialized world, women were impelled to act, to speak out against the mindless spraying of chemicals, the careless disposal of toxic wastes, the unacknowledged radiation seepage from nuclear power plants and weapons testing, and the ultimate catastrophe—the extinction of all life on Earth. In the Third World, women had still more immediate concerns. For women who had to walk miles to collect the water, fuel, and fodder they needed for their households, the devastation wrought by patriarchal fantasies of technological development (for example, the Green revolution, commercial forest management, and mammoth dam projects) was already a daily reality.

In many ways, women's struggle in the rural Third World is of necessity also an ecological struggle. Because so many women's lives are intimately involved in trying to sustain and conserve water, land, and forests, they understand in an immediate way the costs of technologies that pillage the Earth's natural riches. By contrast, in the industrialized world, the connections between women's concerns and ecological concerns were not immediately apparent to many feminists. Community activists such as Rachel E. Bagby, Lois Gibbs, and Carol Von Strom, who were struggling to protect the health of their families and neighborhoods, were among the first to make the connections. Women who are responsible for their children's well-being are often more mindful of the long-term costs of quick-fix solutions. Through the social experience of caretaking and nurturing, women become attentive to the signs of distress in their communities that might threaten their households. When environmental "accidents" occur, it is these women who are typically the first to detect a problem. Moreover, because of women's unique role in the biological regeneration of the species, our bodies are important markers, the sites upon which local, regional, or even planetary stress is often played out. Miscarriage is frequently an early sign of the presence of lethal toxins in the biosphere.

Feminists who had been exploring alternatives to the traditional "woman is to nature as man is to culture" formulation, who were seeking a more fundamental shift in consciousness than the acceptance of women's participation in the marketplace of the public world, began to question the nature versus culture dichotomy itself. These activists, theorists, and artists sought to consciously create new cultures that would embrace and honor the values of caretaking and nurturing — cultures that would not perpetuate the dichotomy by raising nature over culture or by raising women over men. Rather, they affirmed and celebrated the embeddedness of all the Earth's peoples in the multiple webs and cycles of life.

In their hope for the creation of new cultures that would live *with* the Earth, many women in the West were inspired by the myths and symbols of ancient Goddess cultures in which creation was imaged as female and the Earth was revered as sacred. Others were inspired by the symbols and practices of Native-American cultures that consider the effects on future generations before making any community decision. The sources of inspiration were many and varied and led to a diverse array of innovative practices — from tree-planting communities, alternative healing communities, organic food coops, performance art happenings, Witchcraft covens, and the retelling of ancient myths and tales to new forms of political resistance such as the *Chipko* (hugging) tree actions and women's peace camps. Through poetry, rituals, and social activism that connected the devastation of the Earth with the exploitation of women, these activists reinvigorated both feminism and social change movements more generally. The languages they created reached across and beyond the boundaries of previously defined categories. These languages recognized the *lived* connections between reason and emotion, thought and experience. They embraced not only women and men of different races, but all forms of life — other animals, plants, and the living Earth itself. The diverse strands of this retelling and reframing led to a new, more complicated experiential ethic of ecological interconnectedness.

❦ E S S A Y S

The essays view the contemporary environmental movement from legislative, economic, and philosophical vantage points. The first selection, by Theodore Goldfarb, a chemist at the State University of New York at Stony Brook, reviews the major legislative gains of the recent environmental movement. In the second essay, Daniel Faber, a sociologist at Northeastern University, and James O'Connor, a professor of economics at the University of California, Santa Cruz, interpret the environmental movement as a conflict between United States' capitalism and the environmental, labor, and health movements of the twentieth century. In the final essay, Peter Borelli, editor of *Amicus*, the journal of the Natural Resources Defense Council, describes recent environmental critiques of mainstream society and alternative philosophical proposals.

Environmental Legislation

THEODORE GOLDFARB

The current interest in environmentalism has historical roots in the conservation movement of the late 19th and early 20th centuries. This earlier, more limited, recognition of the need for environmental preservation was a response to the wanton destruction wrought by uncontrolled industrial exploitation of natural resources in the post–Civil War period. The clearcutting of forests, in addition to producing large devastated areas, resulted in secondary disasters. Bark and branches left in the cutover areas caused several major midwestern forest fires which leveled villages, killing thousands of people. Severe floods — like the one in Johnstown, Pennsylvania, in 1889 — were caused by the loss of trees which previously had helped to reduce surface water runoff. The Sierra Club and the Audubon Society, the two oldest environmental organizations today, were founded around the turn of the century and helped to organize public opposition to the destructive practice of exploiting resources. Theodore Roosevelt is the most famous of the politicians who championed the cause of conservation. Mining, grazing, and lumbering were brought under government control by such landmark legislation as the Forest Reserve Act of 1891 and the Forest Management Act of 1897. Schools of forestry were established in several of the land grant colleges to help in the effort to develop the scientific expertise needed for the wise management of forest resources.

Compared to this earlier period of concern about the misuse of natural resources, which developed gradually over several decades, the present environmental movement had a nearly explosive beginning. When Rachel Carson's book *Silent Spring* appeared in 1962, its emotional warning about the dangers inherent in the excessive use of pesticides ignited the imagination of an enormous audience of disparate individuals such as wildlife lovers, healthcare professionals, hunters, and farmers, who had become uneasy about the proliferation of new synthetic chemicals in agriculture and industry. Fear of the effects of radiation produced by the atmospheric testing of nuclear weapons had caused widespread public concern. City dwellers were just beginning to recognize the connection between the increasing prevalence of smoky, irritating air and the daily ritual of urban commuter traffic jams. The responses to Carson's book included not only a multitude of scientific and popular debates about the particular issues she had raised but a groundswell of public support for increased environmental controls over all forms of pollution. The rapid change in public perception on environmental issues is graphically demonstrated by the results of public opinion polls. Gallup polls taken in 1965 and 1970 showed an increase from 17 percent to 53 percent in the number of people who rated "reducing pollution of air and water" as one of the three problems they would like the government to devote more attention to. Although other indicators suggest that public concern about the environment may have peaked around 1970, more recent polls indicate continued support by a large majority of the electorate for a strong governmental role in environmental regulation. For example, pollster Louis Harris reported to Congress in 1984 that 69 percent of the public favored making the Clean Air Act more strict.

The rise in environmental consciousness in the United States swelled the ranks of the older voluntary organizations such as the National Wildlife Federation, the Sierra Club, the Isaac Walton League, and the Audubon Society, and led to the establishment of more than 200 new national and regional associations, and as many as 3,000 that operate at the local level. These new organizations vary in their specific purposes and degrees of militancy, but they have been able to unite in support of several major common goals. Such national groups as the Environmental Defense Fund, Friends of the Earth, the Natural Resources Defense Council, Environmental Action, the League of Conservation Voters, and Zero Population Growth have developed considerable expertise in lobbying for legislation, influencing elections, or litigating in the courts. Critics of the environmental movement have frequently pointed out that the membership of these organizations comes from the upper socioeconomic classes. While acknowledging this is true, environmentalists deny that the causes they champion are elitist and cite evidence that most of their goals are supported by majority sentiment among people from all walks of life. . . .

The environmental movement of the 1960s and 1970s produced a profound, and controversial, change in the political climate concerning regulatory legislation. Concerns such as the proliferation of new synthetic chemicals in industry and agriculture, the increased use of hundreds of inadequately tested additives in foods, and the effects of automotive emissions were pressed on Congress by the increasingly influential environmental organizations. Beginning with the Food Additives Amendment of 1958, which required FDA [Food and Drug Administration] approval of all new chemicals used in the processing and marketing of foods, a series of federal and state legislative and administrative actions resulted in the creation of numerous regulations and standards aimed at reducing and reversing environmental degradation.

Congress demonstrated its responsiveness to the environmental movement with the National Environmental Policy Act of 1969. While not specifically prescribing any standards or controls, this act pronounced a national policy requiring an ecological impact assessment for any major federal action. The legislation required the establishment of a three-member Council on Environmental Quality responsible to the president to initiate studies, make recommendations, and prepare an annual Environmental Quality Report. It also requires all agencies of the federal government to prepare a detailed environmental impact statement (EIS) for any major project or proposed legislation in which they are involved. Despite some initial attempts to evade this requirement, court suits by environmental groups have forced compliance, and now new facilities like electrical power plants, interstate highways, dams, harbors, and interstate pipelines can only proceed after preparation and review of an EIS.

Another major step in increasing federal anti-pollution efforts was the establishment in 1970 of the Environmental Protection Agency (EPA). Many programs previously under multipurpose agencies such as the Departments of the Interior, Agriculture, and Health, Education, and Welfare were transferred to this new, central, independent agency. Organized into ten different offices, the EPA was granted authority to do research, propose new legislation, and implement and enforce existing laws concerning air pollution, water pollution, pesticide use, radiation exposure, toxic substances control, solid waste management, and noise abatement.

The year 1970 also marked the establishment of the Occupational Safety and Health Administration (OSHA), the result of a long struggle by organized labor and independent occupational health organizations to focus attention on the special problems of the workplace. A major responsibility of OSHA is the enforcement of legislation regulating the workplace environment. The thousands of synthetic chemicals used in modern industrial activity — most of which have not been tested for effects of chronic exposure — make this task extremely difficult. Estimates of how much industrial chemical exposure contributes to the cancer rate among workers range from 5 to 30 percent. In order to reduce this hazard, priorities have been established for testing and regulation based on numbers of workers exposed as well as inexpensive screening techniques to select the carcinogens that pose the greatest potential risk.

The first major legislation to propose the establishment of national standards for pollution control was the Air Quality Act of 1967. The Clean Air Act of 1970 specified that ambient air quality standards were to be achieved by July 1, 1975 (a goal that was not met, and remains elusive) and that automotive hydrocarbon, carbon monoxide and nitrogen oxide emissions were to be reduced by 90 percent within five years — a deadline that has been repeatedly extended. Specific standards to limit the pollution content of wastewater effluents were prescribed in the Water Pollution Control Act of 1970. The Safe Drinking Water Act of 1974 authorized the EPA to establish federal drinking water standards, applicable to all public water supplies. The Occupational Safety and Health Act of 1970 allowed OSHA to establish strict standards for exposure to harmful substances in the workplace. The Environmental Pesticide Control Act of 1972 gave the EPA authority to regulate pesticide use and to control the sale of pesticides in interstate commerce. In 1976 the EPA was authorized to establish specific standards for the disposal of hazardous industrial wastes under the Resource, Conservation and Recovery Act — but it wasn't until 1980 that the procedures for implementing this legislative mandate were announced. Finally, in 1976, the Toxic Substance Control Act became law, providing the basis for the regulation of public exposure to toxic materials not covered by any other legislation.

All of this environmental legislation in such a short timespan produced a predictable reaction from industrial spokespeople and free market economists. By the late 1970s, attacks on what critics referred to as overregulation appeared with increasing frequency in the media. Antipollution legislation was villainized as a principal contributor to inflation and a serious impediment to continued industrial development.

The actions of the Occupational Safety and Health Administration were singled out as the target of the most vociferous attacks. The inclusion of many ill-advised, poorly written workplace regulations among its codes made this agency vulnerable to ridicule. Demands for OSHA's demise were coupled with accusations that the agency had not achieved a significant reduction in work-related injuries or disease. Defenders of the agency point out the enormity of the task that the poorly-funded agency was supposed to have accomplished in only a few short years of existence. The successful regulation of asbestos and vinyl chloride, two proven causes of cancer and other diseases among thousands of workers, was cited as sufficient evidence of OSHA's effectiveness.

Industry-sponsored studies were publicized to alert the public to the high cost of environmental regulation. Regulatory agencies and environmental organizations responded with their own studies which invariably concluded that the costs were much lower than the industry estimates and were outweighed by much greater social benefits. The actual effect of the standards and regulations on inflation was much debated, with the two sides again producing widely divergent estimates. One truth that the environmentalists could cite with confidence was that industrial estimates of the cost and other negative effects of any proposed regulation generally exceeded the actual costs of putting the regulation into effect.

The Reagan administration interpreted its election mandate as an approval of its promise to get the regulators off the backs of industrial entrepreneurs. This task was given to the various individuals appointed to head and staff the executive departments and regulatory agencies within the federal bureaucracy. Two of the key appointees who responded to this mandate with obvious enthusiasm were former Interior Secretary James Watt and former EPA Administrator Ann Gorsuch (who married and became Ann Burford shortly before resigning). They both drastically reduced the size of their agency's staff and operating budget. The magnitude of these reductions stimulated a counterattack by environmental organizations, bolstered by record numbers of new members, who charged that 20 years of environmental progress was being seriously jeopardized. Mounting public criticism of the neglect of environmental concerns by Reagan's appointees was compounded by allegations of serious misconduct and possible criminal activities attributed to EPA administrators. The resignation of Ms. Burford and many of her subordinates was followed by the recall of William Ruckelshaus, the first EPA Administrator, to again head the agency. Ruckelshaus managed to reverse some of the most blatantly irresponsible policies of his immediate predecessor but his ability to regain public confidence in the EPA was stymied by his own support for the Reagan administration's budget and personnel cuts which do not permit the agency to vigorously pursue its congressional mandate. Environmentalists continue to give the EPA poor grades for its efforts to combat such serious problems as acid rain and toxic waste. . . .

The prevention of nuclear war obviously requires an unprecedented degree of international agreement and cooperation. Many environmental problems such as acid rain, ozone destruction, and climate modification can also result in devastating worldwide effects unless the people of the world can convince their leaders to set aside their usual nationalistic perspectives when facing these problems. The connection between the threats to civilization posed by modern war and ecological disaster have inspired many of the individuals and organizations active in the environmental movement to become participants and leaders in the growing international movement for nuclear disarmament as well. In Western Europe, new "Green" political parties, which were organized around ecological concerns, are vigorously involved in the ban-the-bomb crusade. These parties have attracted substantial public support in Scandinavia, the Netherlands, Austria, and Italy and have won representation in the West German parliament.

It is tempting to take the pessimistic position that any attempt to resolve worldwide conflict is a hopeless cause. It is obviously potentially more productive to adopt the optimistic hope that the prospect of environmental catastrophe will help stimulate the new political forces and perspectives needed to prevent the ultimate holocaust.

Environmental Politics

DANIEL FABER and JAMES O'CONNOR

The Environmental Movement in the United States

Modern environmentalism in the United States partly grew out of the "preservationist" and "conservationist" movements of the late 19th and early 20th centuries. These movements sought to protect threatened species and natural wonders from commodification and capitalization at the hands of rapacious corporations, and to prevent the monopolization of natural resources by a handful of robber barons.

After the Civil War, conservationism developed in response to environmental abuses stemming from rapid capitalist industrial and agricultural expansion. Gifford Pinchot, father of the U.S. Forest Service, explained his goal as one of managing land and resources on a sustainable basis, or maintaining nature as a productive resource as well as amenity by rational state planning. Pinchot and his fellow elite conservationists saw the environment as both public domain and private dominion. By contrast, the preservation movement, embodied by the legendary John Muir, founder of the Sierra Club, aimed to establish national parks as a means to preserve and protect unique natural areas for both present and future generations. While Pinchot once called forests "a manufacturing plant for the production of wood," Muir accorded them a "mystical significance."

Both the conservation and preservation movements had the initial effect of protecting nature for the privileged, not the working classes in the industrial centers. Organizations such as Theodore Roosevelt's Boone and Crockett Club, Sierra Club, and Audubon Society successfully lobbied for the establishment of

Excerpts from Daniel Faber and James O'Connor, "The Struggle for Nature: Environmental Crises and the Crisis of Environmentalism in the United States," *Capitalism, Nature, Socialism*, No. 2 (Summer 1989), pp. 12–21, 28–9, 31–3, 37. Reprinted by permission of Guilford Publications, Inc.

national parks, forest preserves, government mineral leasing, and conservation programs. Reflecting their class positions as factory owners, bankers, and professionals, activists in these organizations paid little or no attention to the work environment and community health and safety.

From the last decades of the 19th century to the Second World War, a different kind of "environmentalism" evolved in the cities, and during the Great Depression, the New Deal organized a massive effort of regional environmental reconstruction. The former, led by middle-class women's groups, public health officials, and physicians sought to solve seemingly intractable problems of public health, pollution, and sanitation. By the 1880s, most cities had built sewerages; the garbage problem was attacked in the 1890s; and sewage and water systems were improved in the early 20th century. Spurred by epidemics and miserable urban health conditions, Congress passed in succession the Pure Food and Drug Act, Meat Inspection Act, and Antiquities Act.

Two decades later, the Great Depression revived conservationism, led by FDR, Harold Ickes, Henry Wallace, and the "father of soil conservation," Hugh Bennet. The dust bowl in the Plains states was the most visible and dramatic problem. But decades of neglect of public lands, wildlife, water quality and flood control, and forests, much of which had been degraded or destroyed as a result of uncontrolled capitalist accumulation, led the Roosevelt government to organize a vast program of ecological reconstruction, particularly in the South, under the auspices of the new Soil Conservation Service, Civilian Conservation Corps, the Tennessee Valley Authority, Pitman-Robinson Federal Aid in Wildlife Restoration Act of 1937, and the Taylor Grazing Act. Thus were both the urban and rural environments, victims of Robber Baron capitalism, in part or whole renewed. Together with the older conservation and preservation movements, the urban public health movement and New Deal Reconstruction programs set decisive precedents for the kinds of environmentalism which emerged during the past forty years.

After World War II, the environmental movement became more broadly based. Middle and working class groups organized to preserve nature throughout the country. Traditional conservation/preservation groups expanded and worked successfully in Congress to achieve the 1964 Wilderness Act, 1974 Forest and Rangeland Renewable Resources Planning Act, and the 1976 Federal Lands Policy and Management Act. Today, 109 million acres are included in the National Forest system, and are regulated on a "multiple use" (read "multiple profit") basis; 77 million acres in the National Park system are closed to mining, timbering, and grazing; and the National Wilderness Preservation system includes over 79 million acres. Thus, the conservation/preservation movement led to the regulation of the capitalization of nature and the restriction of many abuses brought about by appropriation of natural resources for profit, especially in the West.

Conservation organizations were also partially "sublated" into a more broadly based environmentalism which challenged not only the exploitation of natural resources but also of workers in the workplace and community. Modern environmentalism is grounded materially in the growing ecological degradation of town and countryside since the end of World War II. An environmentally conscious salaried class and working class now demand protection against the hazards of petrochemical production, nuclear energy, and other industries. The trade unions are more involved. New dangers to community health and safety led to environmental health struggles. The growth of the new middle class, with its attention to life style and the perceived need to escape the city and its pollution, crowding, and racial tensions, developed new interests in preservation as well as ideas for new commodities for backpacking and other outdoor pursuits. Earth Day in 1970 symbolized the fusing of traditional conservationism and preservationism with middle class, student, and urban environmental concerns into the modern environmental movement.

The 19th and early 20th century preservationists fought to prevent mountains, valleys, and other valued lands from becoming capitalist private property. The modern environmental movement broadened and democratized these struggles to include nature protection for the middle class in the form of residential zoning and local green belts and other public lands. The efforts of the urban and suburban middle classes, and also of the new urban movements of the 1960s and 1970s, expanded both the quantity and quality of nature available for private and social consumption. More and better wilderness and park areas, more and better "environmental quality" demanded as a result of congestion, decentralized industrial siting, pollution, and other threats to the community — these were the issues associated with the new version of the American dream. Struggles to Save Our Land, Save Our Valley, Save Our Mountains, Save Our Streams, Save Our Farmland, Save Our Forests, Save Our Wildlife abounded. In these efforts by communities to protect themselves from the worst excesses of capitalist development, a "no growth" politics emerged, along with demands for local democratic control and regulation of land and natural resources.

From the late 1960s on, environmental issues were propounded in terms of consumerist property rights in a manner potentially contradictory to capitalist accumulation. Political demands for a consumptionist nature presupposed an exclusionary logic against the capitalist exploitation of nature. "Expansion is the condition of exclusion just as exclusion is the condition of expansion. But the fact remains that when it comes to land use, exclusion and expansion are also the conditions of intractable conflict." The results of exclusionary environmental politics contributed to slower economic growth, new barriers to urban renewal and more efficient transportation in some cities, which, in turn, raised housing costs, threatened to stifle the building market, and created demands for higher wages. In short, environmentalism created a layer of inflexibility for self-expanding capital.

The contemporary environmental movement, however, is also organized around issues of environmental quality and human health. Increasingly aware of the connection between the many faces of pollution and community physical and mental well-being, and the links between the structures of urban space and public health, some organizations began to move beyond the politics of conservation and exclusion into the spheres of production and consumption, urban planning and zoning, and other areas which had been neglected since the economic and social reform movements of the Progressive era. In Marxist terminology, environmentalists began to ask hard questions about what was going on *within* the circuits of capital, not only outside of them.

The most important moment for radical organizers and activists was the reemergence of worker health and safety struggles in the workplace and community. Often led by health and safety organizations, these battles sometimes linked the larger labor and environmental movements into ad hoc coalitions around specific legislative initiatives. Occupational health and safety became primarily a worker rather than union issue, but was sometimes generalized and folded into greater demands by consumer and environmental organizations for protection against "negative externalities" or social costs of production. By the late 1960s, and especially in the 1970s, worker health and safety became a powerful political issue for many politicians in coal, uranium, and other mining states, as well as in textile producing regions.

There were attempts to forge organizational links between the largely middle class preservationist-environmental amenities movement and the worker health and safety organizations, but these two wings tended to develop independently of one another in the 1960s. By the end of the decade, the former had forced passage of the National Environmental Policy Act (1969); the Environmental Quality Improvement Act (1970); the Clean Air Act (1970); and the Federal Water Pollution Control Act (1972). For its part, worker militancy combined with a lobbying coalition of more than 100 labor, consumer, religious, and environmental organizations managed to put the Coal Mine Health and Safety Act (1969) and Occupational Health and Safety Act (1970) in place.

In this limited and often ad hoc way, middle class and working class concerns coincided over issues of environmental quality and the exploitation of nature generally. Issues over the degradation of the environment arose around industrial, mining, and construction sites. The labor movement's fight against the exploitation of workers' health and safety intensified in the workplace and spilled over into surrounding communities. Lobbyists for the Steelworkers, Machinists, Auto Workers, and other industrial unions helped shape and pass the 1970 Clean Air Act and the 1972 Clean Water Act amendments. Organizers for the Sierra Club supported the 1973 strike over health and safety issues against Shell Oil by the Oil, Chemical, and Atomic Workers. Yet the "jobs versus environment" dispute soon sabotaged the possibility for more permanent and broad-based alliances between the two movements, especially in the face of growing economic problems in the mid-and-late 1970s.

A crucial aspect of the political strategy of both movements was to reform the Federal government in ways which would make it more democratic and responsive to their perceived needs and demands. The establishment of the Environmental Protection Agency (EPA), the Occupational Health and Safety Administration (OSHA), and the Council on Environmental Quality (CEQ) attempted to bypass traditional natural resource and other agencies captured by corporate interests, and to introduce a modicum of democracy within the state bureaucracy itself.

The creation of EPA, OSHA, and CEQ, the defeat of U.S. imperialism in Southeast Asia and a sense of economic prosperity, together with the Watergate scandal and CIA investigations, produced an optimism throughout liberal and environmental circles about possibilities for more regulation of environmental, urban, and workplace conditions. Relatively strong economic growth and the temporary crisis of national security politics created the space for political negotiation and compromise between the leadership of labor and environmental organizations and traditional liberal-moderate politicians around the passage and funding of legislation. This was reinforced by alliances built around new concerns about toxic pollution and hazardous waste. The National Wildlife Federation and the Sierra Club organized coalitions with consumer organizations, labor unions, and other groups concerned with the health dangers posed by pesticide use and other toxics. New environmental organizations also sprang up in the 1970s, including the Environmental Defense Fund, Environmental Policy Institute, Greenpeace, the National Resources Defense Council, Friends of the Earth, and Environmental Action, whose organizers agitated around new, dangerous technologies and hazardous industries. A modicum of unity between labor and environmental groups around issues of community health was established. From the mid-1970s through the 1980s, old and new local coalitions composed of hundreds of grass-roots groups such as Public Citizen, the Citizens Clearinghouse on Hazardous Waste, and the National Campaign Against Toxic Hazards continued to grow in the context of the crises posed by toxic waste production and disposal.

Environmentalists also joined consumer organizations concerned with the proliferation of dangerous consumer products, an effort originally inspired by Ralph Nader, and, together with health and safety groups, forced passage of the Consumer Product Safety Act of 1972. Environmentalists moved naturally into the area of food additives, dubious baby formulae, and unsafe automobiles while fighting to control hazardous technologies and pollution. Their efforts led to more regulation of food processing, toy manufacturing, drugs, household chemicals, and other consumer goods, although the government stopped short of tracing harmful consumer products back to dangerous production processes and undemocratic economic and regulatory structures.

By the mid-1970s, thousands of groups fighting for conservation and preservation of natural resources, local amenities, worker and community health and safety, safe energy sources, and consumer product safety formed a broad-based but very loosely organized social movement. In 1975, 5.5 million people contributed financially to nineteen leading national organizations, and perhaps another 20 million to over 40,000 local groups. By the end of the decade, Congress had passed twenty major laws regulating consumer products, the environment, and workplace conditions. The legal framework for environmental protection was transformed from a property and tort system to a specialized branch of federal statutory and administrative law. The new federal agencies, in effect, became weapons of the environmental movement.

The effects of these anti-toxic activities, however, proved toxic to capital and profits. Stripped of control of policy in crucial areas, burdened by government regulations and forced inflexibilities, reeling under the weight of high energy prices, economic stagflation and declining labor productivity, and costly environmental, consumer, and worker protection (among other problems), U.S. capital sought ways to avoid, escape, and displace the costs of environmental and labor regulations. Hyper-inflation and peak interest rates at the turn of the decade were sure signs that industrial, mining and other corporations could no longer afford current levels of protection of workers and the environment. U.S. companies faced intense competition on the world market, making it difficult or impossible to pass on higher costs to consumers. The neo-liberalism of the last Carter years and the new Reagan government was not at all supportive of attempts to make the government pick up the environmental protection and clean-up bill. The new ideologies of deregulation and privatization were part of a new and unfavorable political terrain facing both environmentalism and the labor movement.

Environmentalism as a Social Barrier to Capitalist Accumulation

Liberal environmentalists often ignore or downplay the possible effects of the successes of the environmental movement on capitalist profitability. In fact, a good case can be made that environmental struggles and regulations resulted in negative, if unintentional, effects on the conditions of capitalist accumulation. Environmental regulations added to the costs of capital but not to revenues. Unlike new machinery which increases labor productivity and indirectly lowers the unit costs of wage goods (which increases relative surplus value, in Marxist terminology), pollution-abatement devices and clean-up technologies usually increase costs, hence, everything else being the same, reduce profits, or increase prices. This is not true of all pollution control technology. Many U.S. companies employ techniques which help to utilize fuels and raw materials more efficiently, capture and recommodify waste products before they leave the factory, and facilitate greater control over workers and higher labor productivity. However, in the U.S., most pollution control devices are simply added on to existing plant and equipment, and fail to make industry more cost efficient. In the copper industry, for example, the costs of compliance with the Clean Air Act, Water Pollution Control Act, solid waste disposal regulations, and worker health and safety regulations amounted to over 40 percent of total capital expenditures in the industry between 1973 and 1977, making much of the industry uncompetitive in the world market.

It is important to stress that when environmental regulation raises the costs of capital in raw materials (such as copper) and capital goods industries (i.e., industries producing inputs for other industries), higher costs are generalized throughout the economy for all industries. The same regulations applied to consumer goods industries affect the cost of only one or a handful of commodities. In the 1970s, nearly one-half of all capital investment was made in polluting industries — e.g., oil, petrochemicals, electrical power, strip mining, metalworking — supplying inputs to other industries. These were hardest hit by environmental regulations, which, therefore, increased the costs of capital throughout the economy as a whole. A good example was construction costs of the 116 coal-fired electric plants built between 1971–1978, which increased 68 percent in real terms, with 90 percent of this attributable to anti-pollution improvements required by the EPA. Forty-six nuclear plants were built in the same period; real construction costs rose 142 percent, in large part to install devices to minimize accidents.

Business soon began calculating the costs of environmental regulations and their effects on profits. The Business Roundtable's *Cost of Government Regulation* study estimated the incremental costs to 48 member companies of six regulatory agencies (including OSHA and EPA) at $2.6 billion for 1977, about 10 percent of their total capital expenditures, which did not include delays in construction of new plants and equipment and associated financial inflexibilities and uncertainties. Government agencies echoed business's lament when the Council on Environmental Quality conservatively estimated in 1980 that the U.S. spent about $271 billion on pollution abatement between 1972 and 1979 (an additional $518 billion was expected to be needed between 1979 and 1988). According to the Council, the cost of compliance with the Clean Air Act alone was $22 billion in 1979, outlays which were predicted to increase by 38 percent between that year and 1988. Further, the Council of Wage and Price Stability estimated that meeting standards for all 2415 known or suspected carcinogens could entail $526 billion in capital and recurring costs. And the EPA stated that it would cost $44 billion just to clean up the most dangerous hazardous waste dumps in the country. And the costs of cleaning up acid rain, ocean pollution, preventing ozone depletion, and slowing down and/or compensating for the "greenhouse effect" are truly astronomical. . . .

By not designing a comprehensive political and economic strategy, the environmental and labor movements unwittingly helped to provoke the environmental and health crises of the 1980s. The absence of ecological and labor internationalism in opposition to capitalist exploitation has proven disastrous in the Third World, where labor and environmental protection is weak. Ecological racism has caused damage to black and oppressed minority communities at home, even more so under conditions of cost-cutting and economic crisis. Environmentalism's single issue, legislative approach has led capital to displace costs in different forms from one site to another. The movement's weak analysis of capitalism has helped lead to unintended, adverse effects on the well-being of people and their environments. While environmentalists respond to ecological dangers, capital responds to its own iron laws. Regional and local movements and coalitions by and large have not looked beyond their own areas to assess the effects elsewhere of their own local or regional successes in environmental protection. In effect, the environmental movement's legislative victories of the 1960s and 1970s have become one source of its failures in the 1980s.

Hence, environmental quality in the U.S. is worse in 1989 than it was in the 1960s, with some notable exceptions. Since 1982, air pollution such as dust particles, sulfur dioxides (acid rain), and carbon monoxide (respiratory disease) have all increased. There are currently some 30,000–50,000 toxic waste disposal sites (of which only 200 are licensed) with hundreds more being discovered each year. While more than $100 billion has been spent as a result of Clean Water Act regulations, water quality has not improved in most U.S. rivers. More water tables are poisoned; more soil is eroded or rendered unproductive because of salinization and other problems. The occurrence of nitrate, arsenic, and cadmium, all serious pollutants, has increased considerably. Ocean and beach pollution has become a national scandal, as is the threat to coastlines and wildlife sanctuaries. While the environmental movement has consolidated some important victories (e.g., habitat restoration, wilderness preservation, unleaded gasoline), as a general matter, the movement has failed to halt the overall process of environmental destruction in the U.S.; indeed, it has also inadvertently accelerated it. The result is that environmentalists, labor, and community groups today find themselves fighting new forms of environmental degradation as well as the reappearance of older destructive practices. . . .

The reaction at the base was a new grass roots politics, including direct action against timber companies, polluters, and others, as well as hostility toward mainstream environmental politics. The environmental movement's conflicts in the late 1980s are between new direct action groups who want to dramatize examples of environmental destruction and stop them at their source and the politics of institutional consensus, compromise, and professionalization. The problem is that those organizations and labor groups that ignore the global and local connections between the political crisis of interest group politics, and the combined and interrelated force of economic and ecological crises feed divisions within the movement. Not only environmental, worker, and community health is at stake; also at issue is the viability of the traditional political strategies, tactics, and vehicles utilized by environmentalists and other social movements in the 1960s and 1970s. Environmentalists are reluctant to abandon pluralist politics, and the regulatory reform process that ensues from it. Instead of turning to a more holistic grasp of the current economic and ecological crisis, the terms of debate within the movement still reflect the dominant tendency to formulate key assumptions and perspectives with a pluralist — if not eclectic — paradigm. In environmentalism's dominant world view, the crisis of environmentalism is *primarily* seen as a crisis of social values, i.e., competition, privatization, deregulation, and the mastery and domination of nature, as opposed to a harmonious, non-exploitative relationship with nature. . . .

The grass-roots reaction is partly based on new or revitalized ideologies and political strategies. One is the preservationist tradition reborn as "deep ecology," "limits to growth," and "bioregionalism," which constitute the ideological backbone of organizations such as Earth First! and the Rainforest Action Network. Neo-Romantic nature ideologies are also influenced by, and fused into, new eco-feminist ideas and values. These are participatory in the sense that they call for drastic changes in individual lifestyles which reject wasteful forms of consumption and embrace appropriate technology and communitarian visions.

By contrast, most urban forms of grass-root action are more broadly-based, particularly those oriented to issues of hazardous waste and nuclear power. Based on struggles by thousands of locally and regionally based organizations, sometimes acting in coalition with local labor and community groups, struggles for the "right to know" and "source reduction" around toxic wastes have gained strength during the 1980s. . . . This represents a potential blow against the huge California petrochemical, electronics, and farm industries. . . .

For their part, most leaders of mainstream environmentalism as well as government agency heads feel free to criticize grass-roots movements, especially direct action groups, on the grounds of environmental extremism or Utopian bias. This interpretation of the crisis of environmentalism is grounded in the tradition of the old conservation movement. It aims to propose solutions which reconcile the contradictory logics of expansionary versus exclusionary politics, a resolution which the current economic problems of the U.S. appear to make difficult if not impossible. In the context of the shrinkage of political and economic space for environmentalism, which causes mainstream environmental groups to become more conciliatory and compromise-minded, the old "dualism" between traditional preservationism and conservationism is recycled, Muir is now embodied by David Brower and Dave Foreman, Pinchot by William K. Reilly and Jay D. Hair, the latter Executive Vice-President of the National Wildlife Federation, who recently said that "our arguments must translate into profits, earnings, productivity, and economic incentives for industry." William Reilly, the new head of EPA under the Bush administration, has also said that, "we must usher in a new era in the history of environmental policy, an era marked by reconciliation of interests, by imaginative solutions arrived at through cooperation and consensus, by the resolve to listen and work out differences." As President of the Conservation Foundation and U.S. World Wildlife Fund, two organizations with considerable industry backing which merged in 1985, Reilly often helped to make environmental regulations more flexible for corporate interests. . . .

The kind of analysis, hypotheses, judgements, and speculations offered above, however, should not be interpreted as a general negative assessment of the environmental movement. The numerous legislative victories of environmentalism; the increase in ecological consciousness as a result of literally thousands of local struggles and mass education; the specific gains which have not been rolled back; and the rich political experience gained by tens of thousands of activists and organizers constitute a valuable legacy. The environmental movement, taken as a whole, has played a progressive, empowering role in the United States.

Environmental Philosophy

PETER BORELLI

In 1948, the noted astronomer Fred Hoyle anticipated the current situation when he wrote, "Once a photograph of the Earth, taken from the outside is available . . . a new idea as powerful as any other in history will be let loose." That photograph is now available, and with it the understanding that the world we live in is both finite and interconnected.

More recently, Alvin Toffler described the eighties as the dawn of a new era of crisis and opportunity regarding the ultimate survival of the planet.

From Peter Borelli, "The Ecophilosophers," *The Amicus Journal* (Spring 1988), 10, No. 2, pp. 30–39. Reprinted with permission of The Amicus Journal.

"Humanity," he wrote in his best-seller *The Third Wave* (1980), "faces a quantum leap forward. It faces the deepest social upheaval and creative restructuring of all time. Without clearly recognizing it, we are engaged in building a remarkable new civilization from the ground up." . . .

Deep ecology is the most influential new way of interpreting the environmental crisis. Its principles, enunciated in 1972 by Norwegian philosopher Arne Naess, are defined principally in opposition to the established movement, which it terms "shallow" ecology: anthropocentric and utilitarian. In this view, shallows encourage the destructiveness and wastefulness of industrial society even as they seek to reform it. For example, deep ecologists argue that environmental regulations based on emissions standards and tolerances represent licenses to pollute. Thus, NRDC [Natural Resources Defense Council], National Audubon, the National Wildlife Federation, and other such groups are considered shallow by most deeps.

Naess's ideas have been developed in the United States by sociologist Bill Devall and philosopher George Sessions. (Both are Californians and active in the Sierra Club, despite its "shallowness.")

Deep ecology extends the ecological principle of interrelatedness to virtually every aspect of our daily lives. Human and nonhuman species are viewed as having inherent and equal value, from which it follows that humans have no right to reduce the natural diversity of the earth, either directly or indirectly. Direct actions include such things as agriculture, mining, forestry, and technology. Indirect actions include economic and social policies that impinge on other human or nonhuman life forms, as well as population growth, which is viewed as an impediment to "the flourishing of human life and cultures."

Deep ecologists do not specify what the optimal human population of the world should be, but Naess has suggested an unimaginable figure of 1 billion, roughly equal to the total world population in 1800. In 1986, Naess wrote with all seriousness in the journal *Philosophical Inquiry*: "It is recognized that there must be a long range, humane reduction through mild but tenacious political and economic measures. This will make possible, as a result of increased habitat, population growth for thousands of species which are now constrained by human pressures."

John Muir, who may have been this country's first deep ecologist, summed up the biocentric (some might say misanthropic) perspective in these words:

> Pollution, defilement, squalor are words that never would have been created had man lived conformably to Nature. Birds, insects, bears die as cleanly and are disposed of as beautifully. . . . The woods are full of dead and dying trees, yet needed for their beauty to complete the beauty of the living. . . . How beautiful is all Death!

According to Sessions and Devall, the goal of deep ecology is to achieve universal ecological consciousness "in sharp contrast with the dominant world view of technocratic-industrial societies which regards humans as isolated and fundamentally separate from the rest of nature, as superior to, and in charge of, the rest of creation." [former Sierra Club Executive Director Michael] McCloskey's response: "While many of the aims of deep ecologists are appealing as ideals, it is not clear how far or fast they want to go in pursuit of their ideals, nor whether they really want to engage in the process of real-world change."

Indeed, deep ecology is less a movement than a bundle of ideas held to a greater or less degree by a heterogeneous grouping of organizations and individuals. The most visible and best organized are the monkeywrenchers, Earth First!, who take direct action in a variety of wilderness and forestry controversies in the West by arguably nonviolent means. (Naess, incidently, is the author of two studies on Gandhi and reportedly engaged in nonviolent resistance against the Nazis.) Deeps also are found on campuses and in local grass-roots organizations, where their effectiveness is hard to measure.

McCloskey acknowledges that an attitudinal survey of five major environmental groups (Environmental Action, Environmental Defense Fund, National Wildlife Federation, Sierra Club, and the Wilderness Society), conducted by Resources for the Future in 1978, suggests that about 19 percent of their members hold views "that might be associated with the deep ecology movement."

Bioregionalism resembles deep ecology in adopting a radically different world view but is more catholic and tied to a different social base. It is an outgrowth and resurgence of the sixties back-to-the-land movement, and in the spirit of E. F. Schumacher's *Small is Beautiful*, looks for inspiration to cultures and life styles of indigenous peoples and dwellers in the land such as the Amish. Currently, there are more than 100 bioregional groups from Oregon to Maine, which informally exchange information and ideas. Since 1984, there have been two North American Bioregional Congresses attended by representatives from thirty or more states, several Canadian provinces, and Native American tribes.

The term bioregionalism was coined in 1976 by Peter Berg, who, with his wife Judy Goldhaft, runs a bioregional clearinghouse in San Francisco's Mission District called the Planet Drum Foundation. (The drum figures in shamanic ritual.) During the sixties, Berg and Goldhaft were among the founders of the Diggers, an organization that offered refuge to thousands of young people descending on Haight-Ashbury. It was also during this period that they made a cross-country tour of back-to-the-land communes.

The underlying premise of bioregionalism is that the environmental crisis begins at home and revolves around individuals' perceptions of their place in the world. Being a bio requires bearing witness. "All the planetwide pollution problems originate in some bioregion," says Berg. "It's the responsibility of the people who live there to eliminate the source of them. If you strike a five-finger chord—by promoting more community gardens, more renewable energy, accessible public transportation, sustainable agriculture—and you are serious about it, rain forests will stop getting chopped down in direct proportion."

Poet Gary Snyder, whose Pulitzer Prize–winning *Turtle Island* captures the spirit of bioregionalism, told the *Amicus Journal* recently that he saw himself "living on Planet Earth, on Turtle Island, in Shasta Nation. I think in terms of where the plant communities shift, and know where the rivers reach better than

I know the highways now. It's a wonderful way to see the world, and it'll outlast anyone's local political boundary."

Snyder has a bioregional quiz for guests. "Where does the water you drink come from? What is the soil series where you live? Name five edible plants in your region and their seasons. Where does your garbage go?"

Unlike the back-to-the-landers who tended to isolate themselves in self-supporting communes, bioregionalists for the most part live within existing communities where they carve out simplified life styles and become involved in regional land-use issues. While some try to live off the land as farmers, most are wage earners in a variety of trades and professions. In many respects, they are the opposites of yuppies. Young, well-educated, and potentially upwardly mobile, they have chosen to make their living where they want to live rather than the other way around.

In the Sierra Nevada foothills where Snyder lives, he and others have joined long-time residents in electing new planning commissioners concerned about controlling growth. They also are involved in the U.S. Forest Service's management plan for the Tahoe National Forest.

In Northern California's Mattole River area, friends of the Bergs are involved with a watershed bioregional council that has been working with local residents to restore the native king salmon population, destroyed by logging operations that had silted the river.

When drinking-water contamination got out of hand along the Missouri-Arkansas border, a group of people got together to form the Ozark Area Community Congress (OACC), which promotes the use of compost toilets. In 1980, OACC called the first large gathering of the "ecological nation," modeled after tribal consensus as practiced by the Iroquois Federation.

OACC's activities soon attracted attention in Kansas, where it inspired formation of the KAW Council based in Lawrence. Among its founders is thirty-year-old Kelly Kindscher. In 1983, he took a 690-mile "walk" from Kansas City to the foothills of the Colorado Rockies "in the tradition of the Indian vision quest" to get to know his prairie bioregion. KAW now has about 350 members, publishes a newsletter, and is involved in agricultural issues.

A strictly grass-roots movement, the idealism of bioregionalists is balanced against their pragmatism and willingness to work for change within the communities where they live. Many belong to established environmental organizations and are trying to get the Church more involved in environmental issues.

Despite their willingness to work incrementally toward change, most bioregionalists believe the trend toward ecological destruction will not be reversed until there is a spiritual awakening. Father Thomas Berry, director of the Riverdale Center for Religious Research in New York and active with the Hudson Bioregional Council, states, "If we do not alter our attitude and our activities, our children and grandchildren will live not only amid the ruins of the industrial world, but also amid the ruins of the natural world." What is needed, he says, is a "treaty" or spiritual bond between ourselves and the natural world similar to God's covenant with creation after the Flood (*I set my rainbow in the cloud, and it shall be a sign of the covenant between me and the earth.* — Genesis 9:13). Such a treaty would be based on the principle of mutual enhancement. "The [Hudson] river and its valley," he writes, "are neither our enemy to be conquered, nor our servant to be controlled, nor our mistress to be seduced. The river is a pervasive presence beyond all these. It is the ultimate psychic as well as the physical context out of which we emerge into being and by which we are nourished, guided, healed, and fulfilled."

Berry's writings have attracted considerable attention among clerics, scientists, and environmentalists who feel that the Church has turned its back on the biological sciences and belittles "nature worship." Brian Swimme, a California physicist who works with the Institute for Cultural and Creation Spirituality, credits Berry with having developed a "functional cosmology" that goes beyond both science and theology. By combining a contemporary biological view of life with a sense of mystery about the universe, Berry has given new meaning to spiritual devotion and religious responsibility.

Though not actually a movement, the Gaia hypothesis complements the thinking of many of today's environmentalists. First proposed in 1972 by British chemist James Lovelock, who had worked with the NASA [National Aeronautics and Space Administration] team investigating the possibility of life on Mars, it holds that "the evolution of the species of living organisms is so closely coupled with the evolution of their physical and chemical environment that together they constitute a single and indivisible evolutionary process." The idea was drawn from Lovelock's observation that despite being composed of an unstable mixture of reactive gases (such as oxygen and methane), the atmosphere for the entire 3,500 million years since life began has remained remarkably stable. From this he hypothesized that "living matter, the air, the oceans, the land surface, were parts of a giant system which seemed to exhibit the behavior of a living creature." Hence, Gaia, Greek goddess of the earth.

The idea is not new. It surfaced during the nineteenth century when the German geographer Carl Ritter postulated a galvanic force in nature by means of which its separate parts communicated. More recently, the hypothesis has been extended by the controversial work of Boston University biologist Lynn Margulis, who argues that symbiosis and cooperation among all organisms always have been integral to successful existence.

Whether metaphor or reality, Gaia is in serious trouble. The dynamic balance of the biosphere is being radically disrupted by human activities such as the destruction of tropical forests, fossil-fuel consumption, and the release of chlorofluorocarbons.

While there is a widespread belief these days that caring for the earth requires fundamental and even radical change, it is not at all clear that this must extend to electoral politics. In the United States, the environment has been a bipartisan issue with vast public support. As former Senator Gaylord Nelson observed in part one of this series, when he went to Washington in 1963, "There were not more than five broad-gauged environmentalists in the Senate." When he introduced a ban on DDT during his freshman year, he could find only a single sponsor for a companion bill in the House. Were such a bill introduced today, however, the list of sponsors would fill the title page. The environment is now called America's issue, which at the very least means that there is some kind of consensus about the importance of environmental issues, if not their solution.

In the democratic coalition governments of Europe, where representation in parliament is based on the percentage of the national vote won by each party, it has been another story. There, young activists and elements of the middle class have coalesced around the ideas of deep ecology and the goal of achieving *Ökopax* (eco-peace), campaigning for a nuclear-free Europe and against environmental abuses. In 1979, the West Germans formed a coalition: *die Grünen*, or the Greens. By 1983, the Green Party had won 5 percent of the national vote (the minimum share of the vote required to win seats in the Bundestag), and twenty-seven seats in the Bundestag.

The Greens' astonishing entrance onto the political stage was immediately followed by infighting among ecologists, counterculturalists, moralists, feminists, antinuclear activists, and Marxists—each insisting that his or her prescription for the world's ills was most effective. While demonstrating the party's broad base of support, the infighting, nevertheless, has diverted its energy. Less than a year after their entry into parliamentary politics, one of the most articulate of the Greens, a former general in the West German army named Gert Bastion, quit his seat in the Bundestag in disgust. A few months later, Petra Kelly, a founding member, was thrown out of the Bundestag by her own party for ignoring her Bavarian constituents.

Still, by not trivializing their agenda and constantly seeking political compromise, the Greens have survived. Buoyed by protests against a proposed nuclear reprocessing station in Wackersdorf, public reaction to Chernobyl, and progress toward nuclear arms reductions, the Greens won 8.3 percent of the popular vote and forty-two seats in last year's [1987] national election.

The Greens are also active in Italy, where they hold fifteen seats in Parliament; Belgium, where they have formed a coalition with the Social Democrats; and in the United Kingdom, where they fielded 133 candidates in last year's general election and won 1.36 percent of the vote. At last count, there were Greens in seventeen countries, including the United States.

Soon after the West German Greens' first electoral victory, Charlene Spretnak, a Berkeley activist and lecturer on spirituality and feminism, and Fritjof Capra, author of *The Tao of Physics* and founder of an ecological think tank called the Elmwood Institute, teamed up to write *Green Politics*. It called for a U.S. Green movement based not on the German model but on the spiritual insights of deep ecology. The idea was that ecological problems of America were not the direct fault of capitalism but of consumerism caused by an emptiness of spirit.

Though deep ecology disavows central control, Spretnak initiated a loose-knit grass-roots network called the Committees of Correspondence (as during the American Revolution), organized at a meeting of activists in St. Paul, Minnesota, in August 1984. They adopted a platform consisting of "ten key values": ecological wisdom, grass-roots democracy, personal and social responsibility, nonviolence, decentralization, community-based economics, postpatriarchal values (feminism), respect for diversity, global responsibility, and concern for the future. Since then, about seventy-five Green groups have been formed.

. . . [In 1987], about 1,500 Greens gathered in Amherst, Massachusetts, for their first national conference. The stage was set for the Greening of America, but by lunchtime of the first day, the meeting had dissolved into an unhappening, as shouting matches broke out among deep ecologists, feminists, animal liberationists, anarchists, antimilitarists, monkeywrenchers, and graying SDSers. There was little talk of national organization or coalition building.

The Greens face numerous problems in the United States, not the least of which is the entrenchment of a two-party political system. While there is room for new, even radical environmental thinking that challenges the underlying assumptions of modern technology and industrial societies, the Greens must cope with the reality of environmentalism already having been absorbed by American politics. The likelihood of the Greens becoming a third national party is extremely remote, but the possibility of their stimulating effective local coalitions of minorities, women, workers, neighborhood groups, and environmentalists involved in every-day challenges such as toxic exposure and community planning and development, is very real.

In New England, the Greens' first political success came in 1985 in New Haven, Connecticut, where they received 10 percent of the vote, edging out the Republicans as the city's number two party. A local school teacher running for mayor on the Green ticket was defeated, but not without adding interest to the election. Their platform included support for inner-city victory gardens, a program to remove asbestos in homes, public ownership of the local electric utility, and conversion to renewable energy sources. Five black Democrats have since announced their intent to run for aldermen as Greens.

Elsewhere, Greens were instrumental in pressuring the Philadelphia City Council to pass the country's first law mandating trash recycling, and in defeating a luxury condo project in Burlington, Vermont. In Kansas City, the Greens are involved in direct food marketing, buying from area farmers and donating the produce to distribution centers for the homeless. The Lone Star and Longhorn Greens of Austin, Texas, halted construction of a power line through an environmentally sensitive area and successfully ran a candidate for city council. The San Francisco Greens have begun an educational campaign on toxic substances in the home, while their neighbors in the East Bay Green Alliance are restoring a salt marsh.

An important faction among the Greens is social ecology, which holds that environmental problems are rooted in social conditions. The leading spokesman, Murray Bookchin, is a veteran of the old and new lefts and director emeritus of the Institute for Social Ecology in Plainfield, Vermont. Bookchin takes sharp issue with those who "deify" nature.

> Deep ecology has parachuted into our midst quite recently from the Sunbelt's bizarre mix of Hollywood and Disneyland, spiced with homilies from Taoism, Buddhism, spiritualism, reborn Christianity, and, in some cases, ecofascism, while social ecology draws its inspiration from such outstanding radical decentralist thinkers like Peter Kropotkin, William Morris, and Paul Good-

man . . . who have advanced a serious challenge to the present society with its vast hierarchical, sexist, class-ruled, statist apparatus and militaristic history.

"We must achieve not just the reenchantment of nature but the reenchantment of humanity," Bookchin told the Amherst conference. He argued that the deep ecologists view humanity as "an ugly 'anthropocentric' thing — presumably, a malignant product of natural evolution — that is 'overpopulating' the planet, 'devouring' its resources, destroying its wildlife and the biosphere.

"Our wholesale condemnation of technology," he continued, "is a condemnation of some of the best achievements of mankind. The problem begins with our hierarchical society, a monstrous society in which growth and wealth measure progress and culture does not."

Bookchin has likened monkeywrenchers like Earth First! to Nazi thugs, calling its founder, Dave Foreman, a "macho mountain man." He believes that the deep ecologists' preoccupation with world population smacks of elitism and racism. He argues, for example, that Thomas Malthus (1766–1834), the English economist and clergyman who warned that "human population growth would exponentially outstrip food production," was not a prophet but "an apologist for the misery that the Industrial Revolution was inflicting on the English peasantry and working classes."

Dan Chodoroff, also of the Institute for Social Ecology, echoed Bookchin's remarks. "We need not a mindless unity with the rest of nature, but an increased mindfulness . . . a humanistic tradition which looks at the vast fecundity and tremendous diversity of relationships in nature, which need to be developed and applied by human beings."

We began by observing that environmentalism is at a crossroads. This is not necessarily a gloomy state of affairs, but one that requires reflection and regrouping. The biosphere is under greater stress than at any other time in human history, and both our physical and psychic survival require that we act on that knowledge.

Ecology is not only a science, but an ethical confirmation of the wisdom of the great religions. Wes Jackson, a brilliant thinker in the field of sustainable agriculture, reminds us in *Altars of Unhewn Stone* of God's words to Moses after he had delivered the Ten Commandments: *If you make me an altar of stone, you shall not build it of hewn stone; for if you use your tool on it, you have profaned it.* — Exodus 20:25. "The scripture must mean," writes Jackson, "that we are to be more mindful of the creation, more mindful of the original materials of the universe than of the artist."

This same, nonutilitarian world view is reflected in a letter written by Chief Seattle of the Duwamish tribe of Washington State to President Franklin Pierce in 1854:

> Whatever befalls the earth befalls the sons of earth. The white man, too, shall pass — perhaps sooner than other tribes. Continue to contaminate your bed, and you will one night suffocate in your own waste. When the buffalo are all slaughtered, the wild horses all tamed, the secret corners of the forest heavy

with the scent of many men, and the view of ripe hills blotted by talking wires, where is the thicket? Where is the eagle? Gone. And what is it to say goodbye to the swift pony and the hunt? It is the end of living and the beginning of survival.

As we approach the end of this century — and the beginning of the next — it is appropriate to consider if we have made the best use of our atomic- and space-age knowledge. Environmentalists, in particular, should be asking if they have sufficiently advanced their cause. There are many who believe we have not, either because our vision is too dim or our actions too timid.

The danger is not that the cause will suffer for having more than one philosophical or political idea, but that it will fail to have any. It has been noted by many pollsters, for example, that public support for environmental issues has grown over the past twenty years and is now in excess of 80 percent. However, when the same pollsters attempt to measure the salience or prominence of environmental issues in the public mind, they come up with startlingly different results. Virtually nobody (less than 1 percent) considers the environment the number one problem facing the nation, and seldom is it a key factor in national political campaigns. Although this discrepancy says something about the limitations of opinion polls and shallowness of the political process, it also gives some cause for alarm. Either the seriousness of the present situation has not sunk in, or else it has, and it's every man, woman, and child for himself in a mad dash toward yuppie heaven.

The English writer J. A. Walter, in *The Human Home* asks:

> How are Americans to restore the environment to its proper position as an essentially political issue, over which reasonable people will disagree . . .? How can we regain the attitude of those earlier ages which saw the natural world as pointing to the divine without itself being divine? How can we cherish our environment without making a fetish of it?

The answer to such questions lies in recognizing that pollution, plunder, consumption, and waste for the most part are the consequences of political and economic conditions that also account for much of the human misery and strife in the world. This will require a broader, more comprehensive vision on the part of national environmental groups and a pragmatic, more constructive strategy on the part of groups seeking radical change. More important, it will require greater commitment and courage on the part of all environmentalists to challenge the present direction of economic policy and politics. Our choice, as Chief Seattle warned, is between living and surviving.

✸ FURTHER READING

Murray Bookchin, *The Ecology of Freedom* (1982)
Michael Brown, *Laying Waste: The Poisoning of America by Toxic Chemicals* (1979)
Barry Commoner, *The Closing Circle* (1971)
Council on Environmental Quality, *The Global 2000 Report to the President: Entering the Twenty-first Century* (1981)
Thomas R. Dunlap, *DDT: Scientists, Citizens, and Public Policy* (1981)

Theodore Goldfarb, ed., *Taking Sides: Clashing Views on Controversial Environmental Issues*, 3d ed. (1989)

Samuel P. Hays, *Beauty, Health, and Permanence: Environmental Politics in the United States, 1955–1985* (1987)

H. Patricia Hynes, *The Recurring Silent Spring* (1989)

Frances Moore Lappé and Joseph Collins, *Food First* (1977)

John McCormick, *Reclaiming Paradise: The Global Environmental Movement* (1989)

Christopher Manes, *Green Rage* (1990)

G. Tyler Miller, Jr., *Living in the Environment: Concepts, Problems, and Alternatives*, 3d ed. (1991)

Robert Paehlke, *Environmentalism and the Future of Progressive Politics* (1989)

David Pepper, *The Roots of Modern Environmentalism* (1985)

John H. Perkins, *Insects, Experts, and the Insecticide Crisis* (1982)

Philip Reno, *Mother Earth, Father Sky, and Economic Development: Navajo Resources and Their Use* (1981)

Dick Russell, "Environmental Racism: Minority Communities and Their Battle Against Toxics," *The Amicus Journal* 11 (Spring 1989), 22–32

C. Brandt Short, *Ronald Reagan and the Public Lands: America's Conservation Debate, 1979–1984* (1989)

Hawley Truax et al., "Beyond White Environmentalism: Minorities and the Environment," *Environmental Action* (January–February 1990), 19–30

Robert van den Bosch, *The Pesticide Conspiracy* (1980)

World Commission on Environment and Development, *Our Common Future* (1987)

Worldwatch Institute, *State of the World 1990* (1990)

Environmental Legislation

Alaska National Interests Land Act A federal act passed in 1980 preserving certain Alaskan lands and waters with scenic, historic, and wilderness values and providing rural residents the right to continue a subsistence way of life.

Alaskan Native Claims Settlement Act A federal act passed in 1971 giving Alaskan Eskimos, Aleuts, and Native Americans $462.5 million in federal grants, $500 million in federal and state mineral revenues, and 22 million acres of land in exchange for the right to build the Trans-Alaska pipeline that developed North Slope oil reserves.

Broad Arrow Policy Part of the 1691 renewal of the charter of the Province of Massachusetts Bay, reserving for the British crown all trees, on nonprivate lands, measuring 24 inches or more in diameter at a point 12 inches from the ground. The policy was extended to New Hampshire in 1708; to all of New England, New York, and New Jersey in 1711; and to Nova Scotia in 1721.

Clean Air Act A federal act passed in 1955 and amended in 1970, requiring the Environmental Protection Agency to set national air-quality standards for air pollutants that would endanger public health.

Clean Water Act A federal act passed in 1977, changing the name of the federal Water Pollution Control Act of 1972 and requiring that waters be "fishable and swimmable" by 1983.

Dawes Act The General Allotment Act of 1887 authorizing the president to allot communally held Indian tribal lands in 160-acre parcels to tribal members.

Desert Lands Act Passed in 1877, an act providing for the sale of 640 acres of land unfit for cultivation in the western states to any settler who irrigated the land within three years of filing (at $.25 per acre and $1.00 per acre at final proof).

Endangered Species Act A federal act passed in 1973, establishing procedures for identifying and protecting endangered plants and animals in critical habitats, and prohibiting taking, harvesting, hunting, and harming of listed species.

Environmental Impact Statement (EIS) Mandated by the passage of the National Environmental Policy Act of 1969, a requirement that every federal agency prepare and circulate statements "on proposals for legislation and other major federal actions significantly affecting the quality of the human environment."

Environmental Pesticide Control Act A federal act passed in 1972 authorizing the Environmental Protection Agency to regulate pesticide use and to control the sale of pesticides in interstate commerce.

Free Timber Act A federal act passed in 1878, giving residents of nine western states the privilege of cutting timber on public mineral lands for building, agriculture, mining, or other domestic purposes.

General Ordinance of 1785 Passed by the Continental Congress, an ordinance establishing the rectangular land-survey system of townships, 6 miles square divided into 36 sections of 640 acres each, that could be sold at auction for not less than $1 per acre. Section 16 of each township was reserved for schools, and four sections were set aside for government disposal. The ordinance fostered both widespread land speculation and squatter's rights and formed the basis of the Homestead Act's provision of 160 acres (one-quarter section) for individual land claims.

Hatch Act A federal act passed in 1887 to provide financial assistance to states in the establishment of agricultural experiment stations.

Homestead Act A federal act passed in 1862, authorizing any person who was the head of a family or over twenty-one years of age, and who was a citizen of the United States or had declared an intention to become one, to enter upon no more than 160 acres (one-quarter section) of unappropriated land subject to preemption and sale at a minimum price of $1.25 per acre, or not more than 80 acres subject to sale at a minimum price of $2.50 per acre.

Indian Civil Rights Act A federal act passed in 1968, denying states the authority to extend their civil and criminal jurisdiction over Native American lands without tribal consent and imposing certain restraints on tribal governments.

Morrill Act A federal act passed in 1862, granting each state 30,000 acres of public land for sale for the purpose of creating a fund to establish colleges of agriculture and the mechanic arts.

National Environmental Policy Act (NEPA) A federal act passed in 1969, requiring every federal agency to prepare and circulate Environmental Impact Statements (EIS) on proposed legislation and actions affecting the quality of the human environment and creating the Council on Environmental Quality (CEQ) in the Executive Office of the President.

National Parks Act An act of Congress passed in 1916, creating the National Park Service to administer the thirteen national parks, formerly managed by the United States Cavalry, and to administer future national parks and monuments set aside for unusual natural or scenic importance.

Occupational Safety and Health Act (OSHA) A federal act passed in 1970 authorizing the establishment of strict standards for exposure to harmful substances in the workplace.

Railroad Land Grants Made between 1850 and 1871, the federal government's grants to railroads of even-numbered sections (640 acres) of land on either side of a right-of-way on which to build and provide rail service for carrying mail and military troops and for encouraging settlement of western lands.

Reclamation Act A federal act passed in 1902 appropriating funds from the sale of public lands in the arid and semiarid western United States for the purpose of constructing dams and other irrigation works.

Resource Conservation and Recovery Act A federal act passed in 1976 establishing specific standards for disposal of hazardous industrial wastes.

Roadless Areas Review and Evaluation I and II (RARE I and RARE II) Two studies undertaken in 1971 and 1977 respectively by the U.S. Forest Service, with massive public involvement, to identify wilderness areas for protection and open nonwilderness roadless areas to multiple-use management.

Safe Drinking Water Act A federal act passed in 1974, authorizing the Environmental Protection Agency to set federal drinking water standards.

Timber and Stone Act A federal act passed in 1878, providing for the sale in Washington State, Oregon, California, and Nevada of 160 acres of land valuable for timber and stone but unfit for cultivation, for not less than $2.50 per acre.

Timber Culture Act A federal act passed in 1873, donating 160 acres of public land to any person who would plant 40 acres with trees and keep them healthy for a period of ten years.

Toxic Substances Control Act (TOSCA) A federal act passed in 1976 regulating public exposure to toxic materials.

Wilderness Act A federal act passed in 1964, designating certain federal lands as wilderness areas, preventing their development, and defining wilderness as an area "where the earth and its community of life are untrammeled by man, where man himself is a visitor who does not remain."

Environmental Agencies and Organizations

American Indian Movement (AIM) Intertribal Native American movement established in 1968 to promote Indian self-determination and to reclaim older treaty rights to land, water, fish, and wildlife resources.

Appalachian Mountain Club (AMC) A hiking and conservation club in the eastern United States, founded in 1876.

Bureau of Indian Affairs (BIA) An agency in the Department of the Interior responsible for the administration of Native American lands and affairs.

Bureau of Land Management (BLM) An agency in the Department of the Interior created in 1946 out of a merger with the General Land Office and the Grazing Service; responsible for the administration and management primarily of rangelands, deserts, and mineral resources.

Bureau of Reclamation (BuRec) An agency established by the passage of the Reclamation Act (1902) to administer dams and reclamation projects in the western states.

Civilian Conservation Corps (CCC) An agency established in 1937 and extended through 1944 to replace the Office of Emergency Conservation Work of 1933, for the relief of unemployment, the promotion of the natural-resource conservation, and the administration of educational and vocational training.

Council on Environmental Quality (CEQ) An agency created by the National Environmental Policy Act of 1969 (NEPA) in the Executive Office of the President to advise the president on matters of environmental quality and to review agency compliance with NEPA.

Environmental Defense Fund (EDF) Founded in 1967, a citizens' litigating organization, linking science, economics, and law in an effort to create cost-effective solutions to environmental problems.

Environmental Protection Agency (EPA) A federal agency, created by executive reorganization in 1970, with authority to regulate air and water quality, radiation and pesticide hazards, and solid-waste disposal.

Fish and Wildlife Service (FWS) An agency in the Department of the Interior created in 1940 by merging the Bureau of Fisheries in the Department of Commerce and the Bureau of Biological Survey in the Department of Agriculture.

Friends of the Earth (FOE) An environmental organization, founded in 1969, dedicated to protecting the planet from environmental disaster and to preserving biological, cultural, and ethnic diversity.

General Land Office (GLO) An agency established in 1812 to conduct land surveys and to process and record sales, entries, withdrawals, reservations, and leases on public lands. The GLO had primary jurisdiction over the entire public domain until 1946, when it was merged with the Grazing Service into the Bureau of Land Management.

National Audubon Society Initially organized in 1886 and reestablished in 1898, the Audubon Society, named after ornithologist John James Audubon (1875–1951), promotes the study and protection of bird life and publishes *Audubon Magazine* (formerly entitled *Bird Lore*).

National Wildlife Federation (NWF) Founded in 1936, an environmental organization dedicated to the conservation of fish, wildlife, and other natural resources and to the protection of the environment.

Natural Resources Defense Council (NRDC) Founded in 1970, a citizen's litigating organization on behalf of the environment, and the publisher of the journal *Amicus*.

Nature Conservancy A citizen's environmental organization, founded in 1951, to preserve plants, animals, and natural communities that represent the diversity of life on earth, by protecting the lands and water they need to survive.

Sierra Club Founded in 1892 under the leadership of John Muir (1838–1914), an organization to promote enjoyment and protection of the environment.

Soil Conservation Service (SCS) An agency in the Department of Agriculture established in 1935 by passage of the Soil Conservation Act, to provide for the control and prevention of soil erosion.

Tennessee Valley Authority (TVA) An agency created in 1933 for the unified development of the resources of the Tennessee River Valley to achieve flood control, navigation, electric-power generation, reforestation, and the economic well-being of the people of the valley.

United States Department of Agriculture (USDA) An agency in the executive branch of the federal government, given cabinet rank in 1889.

United States Forest Service (USFS) A federal agency in the Department of Agriculture (created in 1886 as the Division of Forestry, transferred from the Department of Interior in 1905, and changed to the Forest Service) responsible for the administration of the nation's forest reserves.

United States Geological Survey (USGS) A federal agency in the Department of the Interior, created in 1879, responsible for land and mineral surveying and mapping.

Wilderness Society An environmental organization, founded in 1935, dedicated to the creation and protection of wilderness areas and to the preservation and management of the nation's public lands, including national parks, national seashores, national forests, national wildlife refuges, and national reservation lands administered by the Bureau of Land Management.

Works Progress Administration (WPA) An agency founded by the Roosevelt administration during the Great Depression to create employment in areas such as conservation, the arts, writing, and theater production.

Glossary

animism The idea found in Native American and pagan philosophies that everything in nature (including what is now considered inanimate) is alive and has an inner spirit, soul, or organizing power.

anthropocentric The idea that the human species is the center of the natural world and that all other parts of that world exist for the sake of humankind.

balance of nature The idea that the earth and its ecosystems tend toward self-regulation and return to states of equilibrium when disturbed.

biocentric The idea that all plants and animals are centers of life and as such have inherent worth and are worthy of moral consideration.

biogeochemical cycles The transfer and flow of elements such as oxygen, carbon, nitrogen, and phosphorus through the air, water, and soil.

biological determinism The priority of biological factors over cultural factors in deciding the outcome of events or the development of personalities.

biomass The total weight of all living matter in a particular area.

biome A complex of animal and plant communities maintained under particular climatic conditions in a given area.

bioregionalism The idea that people and other living and nonliving things in a particular region, usually a watershed, are interdependent and that they should live as much as possible within the resources and ecological constraints of that place.

biota All living animals and plants.

biotic community The complex of interdependent living organisms in a specific area.

capitalism The economic system of private ownership of production operated to gain a profit. **Laissez-faire capitalism** is an early form of United States capitalism in which competition and the free market, rather than the government, regulated production and distribution. **Corporate capitalism** is a later form characterized by increased concentration of wealth and increased government regulation.

chaos theory The mathematical theory that a small effect can lead to a large effect that cannot be predicted by linear (first-power) differential equations (those dealing with infinitesimal differences between variable quantities), and that such complex events may better be described by nonlinear equations.

commodity An article bought or sold. Nature, labor, and even the human body are sometimes regarded as commodities.

consciousness The totality of an individual's thoughts, feelings, impressions, and volitions, or a collective awareness of these by a group of individuals.

conservation The wise and frugal use of natural resources for the benefit of present and future generations.

culture The concepts, habits, and institutions of a particular people in a specific period.

declensionist Relating to a narrative structure, or plot, that portrays environmental history as a downward spiral.

deep ecology The idea, first proposed by Norwegian philosopher Arne Naess, that environmental problems cannot be resolved merely by legislation and regulation but instead require a deeper shift in basic philosophical assumptions about human relationships with the nonhuman world.

diversity-stability hypothesis The theory that complex biological and physical systems result in the long-term maintenance of an ecosystem.

ecocentric The idea that the natural world is an integrated ecological whole and as such is worthy of moral consideration.

ecofeminism The idea that a historical and cultural association exists between women and nature, that both have been dominated in Western culture, and that women can liberate themselves and nature through environmental activism.

ecological imperialism The idea, proposed by environmental historian Alfred Crosby, that biota both advertently and inadvertently are a part of colonization.

ecological revolution A concept developed by environmental historian Carolyn Merchant to characterize major transformations in relationships between humans and nonhuman nature.

ecological succession The replacement of one community of organisms in a particular environment by another community over a period of time.

ecology A branch of science, named by Ernst Haeckel in 1873, that deals with the relationships between and among organisms and their abiotic surroundings, or environment.

ecosystem A self-regulating, self-sustaining community of organisms in relationship with each other and their environment.

ecotage The idea, promoted by the environmental group Earth First! during the 1980s, that nature can be saved by sabotaging the machines and equipment (but not the people) that destroy it.

environment The surroundings, or aggregate of external conditions, that influence the lives of individuals, populations, communities, and societies.

environmental ethics That branch of philosophy that addresses questions of what one *ought* to do to save the environment.

environmentalism Beliefs and actions taken to preserve the environment, encompassing a range of impulses from preservationism, or the intention to save undisturbed nature for its own sake, to conservation, or the maintenance of nature for human use by present and future generations.

equilibrium The tendency for a system to be restored to a particular condition.

exploit (1) To make use of; (2) to use for one's own advantage, profit, or selfish gain.

food web Interlocking systems of organisms and food chains in which energy in the form of food is transferred from one trophic level to another.

homeostatic Maintenance of a constant value or steady state within a narrow range, such as the human body temperature.

homocentric The idea that humans are the center of all existence and deserve moral consideration above all other parts of the natural world.

Hudson River school A group of nineteenth-century American landscape painters who first concentrated on the Hudson River region but also depicted parts of New England, upper New York State, New Jersey, and Pennsylvania, eventually extending to Europe, the American West, and South America.

human ecology The study of human communities and their changes over time with respect to their interactions with other communities, species, and the natural environment.

imperialism The view that the role of human beings and governments is to establish power over nature and over as great an area and as many peoples as possible.

land ethic A term used by twentieth-century ecologist Aldo Leopold to refer to the extension of the ethics of the human community to include "soils, waters, plants, and animals, or collectively: the land."

mechanism A philosophy that arose during the scientific revolution of the seventeenth century that likens the world to a vast machine made up of inert parts that obey the laws of physics and chemistry.

monoculture The raising of only one crop in a field or on a particular piece of land.

nature The physical universe, including all its physical features, processes, organisms, and their interactions. Although nature technically includes human beings, the word often is used to refer to the world as distinct from human beings and their social and cultural institutions.

New Ecology A school of ecology prominent in the 1930s through the 1960s that emphasized the quantitative study of energy, energy exchanges, and ecological efficiency. Major figures included Arthur Tansley, Raymond Lindeman, and Eugene Odum.

organicism A philosophy that the world is like a living organism, such as the human body. Each part of nature, including animals, plants, and minerals, is part of a larger whole and participates in it.

plant associations Groups of plants usually found together in areas having similar ecological conditions.

polyculture The raising of several crops together in one field or on a single piece of land.

portmanteau biota The term used by environmental historian Alfred Crosby to characterize the associated animals, plants, weeds, pests, and pathogens that accompanied people on ships en route to the New World.

positivism The philosophical theory that only mathematical statements and empirically verifiable statements are true and lead to positive knowledge of the external world.

possibilism The philosophical theory that allows for a multitude of choices, influences, or explanations of an event or outcome.

preservation The belief that natural areas should be left in a state undisturbed by human beings.

resource Money, property, or natural entities that can be used to the advantage of an individual or a country.

social ecology The study of human social and economic institutions and communities with respect to their interactions with other humans, species, and the natural environment.

stability Relative constancy over time of the numbers of individuals in a species or of different species in a particular area.

staple (1) A chief or leading crop or commodity regularly grown or sold in a particular place, such as sugar, wheat, or cotton; (2) the fiber of cotton, wool, or flax, with reference to its length and fineness.

steady-state A dynamic balance between the inputs and outputs of a system such as an organism or an ecosystem.

subsistence The means of providing sustenance, support, or livelihood enabling a person to continue to exist.

transcendentalism The idealist, Platonist philosophy held by a group of individuals in the nineteenth-century United States, of which Ralph Waldo Emerson is the most well-known representative. For the transcendentalists, reality was ideal and the material world only a constantly changing appearance. Symbols and emblems in the material world provided clues to ideal truths through visionary insight and spiritual intuition, enabling the human soul to transcend physical limitations and to gain insight into the Oversoul, or divine One.

trophic Relating to food and nutritional processes entailing the transfer of energy from one organism to another.

DOCUMENT SOURCES

Chapter 2 Native American Ecology and European Contact

A Spanish Explorer Views the Pueblos, 1580 From "[Hernán Lamero] Gallegos' Relation of the Chamuscado–Rodríguez Expedition," trans. and ed. George P. Hammond and Agapito Rey. *The Rediscovery of New Mexico, 1580–1594*. Albuquerque, N.M.: The University of New Mexico Press, 1966 [1927], vol. 3, pp. 83–86.

Spanish Explorers Observe Pueblo Irrigation, 1582 From "Report of Antonio Espejo," in George P. Hammond and Agapito Rey, *The Rediscovery of New Mexico, 1580–1594*. Albuquerque, N. M.: The University of New Mexico Press, 1966 [1927], vol. 3, pp. 224–225.

A Spaniard Testifies on the Effects of Pueblo Colonization, 1601 From Gimés de Herra Horta, in George P. Hammond and Agapito Rey. *Don Juan de Oñate, Colonizer of New Mexico, 1595–1628*. Albuquerque, N.M.: University of New Mexico Press, 1953, pp. 643–656.

Nicholas Denys on the Micmac Fur Trade, 1672 From Nicolas Denys, *Description Geographical and Historical of the Coasts of North America, With the Natural History of the Country*. Trans. and ed. William Ganong. Toronto: The Champlain Society, 1910, originally published, Paris, 1672, pp. 399–452; map, frontispiece.

A Jesuit Missionary Recalls Micmac Hunting Rituals, 1691 From Father Chrestien Le Clercq, *New Relation of Gaspesia With the Customs and Religion of the Gaspesian Indians*, trans. and ed. William F. Ganong. Toronto: The Champlain Society, 1910, pp. 276–80, 227–8.

Chapter 3 The New England Forest in the Seventeenth Century

William Bradford Faces a "Hideous and Desolate Wilderness," 1620–35 From *Of Plimoth Plantation*. Boston: Wright and Potter, 1901, pp. 93, 94–96, 111, 114–116, 121, 127–130, 387–389.

John Winthrop Quotes Genesis on Subduing the Earth, 1629 From "Conclusions for the Plantation in New England," in *Old South Leaflets*, no. 50 (1629). Boston: Directors of the Old South Work, 1897, pp. 4–5.

Thomas Morton Praises the New English Canaan, 1632 From Thomas Morton, *New English Canaan*, in Peter Force, ed., *Tracts and Other Papers . . .* Washington, D. C., 1838, vol. II, pp. 10, 36–37, 41–42.

William Wood on Indian Women's Housing and Horticulture, 1634 From *New England's Prospect*. London: Thomas Cotes, 1634, p. 99–100.

Roger Williams on Indian Uses of the Forest, 1643 From *A Key into the Language of America*, London, 1643; reprint Providence, R.I.: Publications of the Narragansett Club, 1866, pp. 87, 98, 123, 157–158, 188–189.

A Timber Merchant's Estate, 1682 From Estate of Major Nicholas Shapleigh of Kittery, Maine, in *York Deeds*, ed. William M. Sargent. Portland, Me.: Brown Thurston and Co., 1889, Part I, Fol. 15–16.

A Governor Enforces the King's Forest Policy, 1730 From Jonathan Belcher, "A Proclamation to Prevent the Destruction or Spoil of His Majesties Woods," in State of New Hampshire, *Miscellaneous Provincial and State Papers, 1725–1890*, compiled and ed. Isaac W. Hammond. Manchester, N.H.: John B. Clark, 1890, vol. 18, pp. 32–35.

Chapter 4 Soil Exhaustion in the Early Tobacco South

John White Depicts Indian Planting and Fishing in Virginia, 1590 From *A Brief and True Report of the New Found Land of Virginia* (1590). With engravings by Theodor de Bry after the drawings of John White. New York: Dover, 1972, pp. 55–56, 68–69.

Virginia Settlers Discover Tobacco, 1614–1617 "Raphe Hamor Extols the Valuable Commodity Tobacco, 1614" from Raphe Hamor the yonger, *A True Discourse of the Present Estate of Virginia*. London: John Beale for W. Welby, 1615, pp. 24–25, 34–35. "John Rolfe on the Ease of Growing Tobacco, 1616–1617" from *A True Relation of the State of Virginia*. New Haven: Yale University Press, 1951, pp. 35–37, 39–40.

A Virginia Planter Describes His Holdings, 1686 From Richard Beale Davis, ed., *William Fitzhugh and His Chesapeake World, 1676–1701*. Chapel Hill: University of North Carolina Press, 1963, pp. 175–176.

Robert Beverley on Indians and Nature in Virginia, 1705 "The Indians of Virginia Are Almost Wasted" and "Have You Pleasure in a Garden?" from *The History and Present State of Virginia*. London: R. Parker, 1705, pp. 232–233, 296–299.

A Traveler Describes Tobacco Cultivation, 1775 From Anonymous, *American Husbandry*. 2 vols. London: J. Bew, 1775, vol. 1, pp. 222–233, 242, 246–248.

Thomas Jefferson on the "Nature" of Blacks and Worn-Out Tobacco Lands, 1787 "Deep-Rooted Prejudices" and "Tobacco Culture Is Fast Declining" from *Notes on the State of Virginia*. London: J. Stockdale, 1787, query XIV, pp. 229–234, 237–240, query XX, pp. 278–279.

Olaudah Equiano Describes His Enslavement, 1791 From *The Interesting Narrative of the Life of Olaudah Equiano*. London: Printed for and sold by the author, 1790, pp. 46–57.

Benjamin Banneker Responds to Thomas Jefferson, 1792 From Benjamin Banneker, "Letter to the Secretary of State [Thomas Jefferson]," in Milton Meltzer, ed., *In Their Own Words: A History of the American Negro, 1619–1865*. New York: Thomas Crowell, 1964, pp. 11–16.

Chapter 5 Farm Ecology in the Early Republic

A Traveler Views the Mistakes of New England Farmers, 1775 From Anonymous, *American Husbandry*. 2 vols. London: J. Bew, 1775, vol. 1, pp. 74–85.

J. Hector St. John de Crèvecoeur Asks, "What Is an American?" 1782 From *Letters From an American Farmer*. New York: E. P. Dutton, 1957; originally published London, 1782, pp. 35–37, 39–43, 61.

Thomas Jefferson on the Agrarian Ideal, 1787 From *Notes on the State of Virginia*. London: J. Stockdale, 1787, query XIX, pp. 276–277.

Benjamin Rush Praises the Market Farmers of Pennsylvania, 1789 From Theodore E. Schmauk, ed., *An Account of the Manners of the German Inhabitants of Pennsylvania*. Lancaster, Pa., 1910, pp. 54–73.

Edward Slader's Account Book, 1807–1812 From Old Sturbridge Village manuscript collection, OSV 451.1/1978.

Anna Howell's Farm Diary, 1820 From manuscript from American Antiquarian Society, Worcester, Mass. Also available on microfilm. Transcribed by C. Merchant. Illustration from May 1820.

John James Audubon Depicts the Squatters of the Mississippi, 1808–1834 From *Delineations of American Scenery and Character* (written 1808–1834). New York: G. A. Baker & Co., 1926, pp. 137–142.

Calvin Colton on Self-Made Men, 1844 From *The Junius Tracts*. New York: Greeley & McElrath, 1844, No. VII, "Labor and Capital," sec. 36, p. 111.

Chapter 8 Mining California's Earth in the Nineteenth Century

Chapter 9 Great Plains Grasslands Exploited

Chapter 15 The Contemporary Environmental Movement